READINGS IN ECONOMETRIC THEORY

Edited by

J. MALCOLM DOWLING
Assistant Professor of Economics

FRED R. GLAHE
Associate Professor of Economics

UNIVERSITY OF COLORADO

COLORADO ASSOCIATED UNIVERSITY PRESS
BOULDER, COLORADO

Colorado Associated University Press
1424 Fifteenth Street
Boulder, Colorado 80302

Library of Congress Catalog Card Number 79-128867
ISBN 87081-004-9

CONTENTS

SIMULTANEOUS EQUATIONS

SMALL SAMPLE PROPERTIES

INTRODUCTION

The first Nobel Prize in economics was awarded to two econometricians, Professors Ragnar Frisch and Jan Tinbergen—a fact that illustrates the importance of econometrics to economic science. Econometrics is relatively young, (as a field of study)edating from the work of Haavelmo (1943, 1944), Frisch (1933, 1934), Tinbergen (1939), Schultz (1938) and others. Earlier thinking on individual problems certainly extends at least back to Elmer Working (1927).

The introduction of econometrics into the graduate programs of most universities has been even more recent. The first textbooks in econometrics were published by Tinbergen (1951) and Tintner (1952). With the exception of Klein's *Textbook* (1953), few new text materials were available until the middle 1960's. Books by Johnston (1963), Goldberger (1964), Christ (1966), Malinvaud (1966), and Dhrymes (1970) then appeared. Twenty years ago few graduate students were trained in econometrics, today virtually all new Ph.D's have had some training; many university departments require one year of econometric studies for all graduate students.

This volume attempts to gather together several important contributions to econometric theory. Read in conjunction with any of the standard econometrics textbooks, these readings should provide the student with a thorough grounding in the theoretical foundations of econometrics. At the same time, this collection of articles when read alone could stand as a complete unit. Each of the readings is sufficiently well-known to speak for itself, so that an introduction might seem unnecessary. One of the objectives of this volume, however, is to make these readings readily available to the beginning econometrician. We think that it would be useful therefore to review in brief how these articles fit into the overall field of econometrics. In addition, this introduction will provide bibliography for further readings in each of the areas discussed. Those readings which appear in this book are labeled with an asterisk.

Economists have continually searched for appropriate statistical tools to provide meaningful inferences about the structure of the economic system. In many cases this could not be achieved by the rote application of statistical techniques developed in other disciplines, such as astronomy and biology. Ronald A. Fisher's development of statistical techniques in the 1920's which allowed inferences to be made from small samples greatly enhanced capabilities in the field. However, the nonreproducible nature of economic observations, the simultaneity of the structural relations making up the economic system, and the dynamic characteristics of the economic process required a new method of approach.[1]

[1]Two good methodological discussions are given by Koopmans (1945), and Marschak (1950*).

In attempting to verify theoretical models, economists most often employed the classical method of least squares (CLS). In using this technique, the set of variables involved in a linear model is normalized so that one variable is dependent (endogenous) and the others independent (predetermined). Then the statistical model specifies that the dependent variable is a function of the independent variables (whose observations are fixed in repeated samples) plus a disturbance. The disturbances are random variables which are independent and identically distributed with zero mean and finite constant variance.

The assumptions of classical least squares (CLS) can be formalized as follows:

1. $\underline{Y} = X \underline{\beta} + \underline{e}$
2. $E(e) = \underline{O}$
3. $E(ee') = \sigma^2 I$
4. X is a T by K matrix.
5. Rank of $X = K \leq T$ where $\underline{Y}$ is a vector of T observations, $\underline{\beta}$ is a vector of K regression coefficients and $\underline{e}$ is a vector of T disturbances.

While least squares yields sample estimates with desirable statistical properties (the Gauss-Markov theorem insures that the estimates of the structural parameters of a model having these properties are best linear unbiased), its appropriateness for analyzing economic problems was soon questioned by economists. One problem which received considerable discussion was the normalization process by which the dependent variable was chosen. Some investigators simply assumed that the direction of causation flowed from the independent variables to the dependent variable and their work was subject to criticism. For example, it may be difficult to ascertain whether price or output is the dependent variable in a simple model of product market equilibrium; errors of measurement in the variables may confound the investigator about the direction in which to minimize the sum of squared deviations. Consequently, numerous researchers abandoned classical least squares in favor of symmetrical methods of fit which stressed invariance with respect to transformations in the data, and neglected specification of the disturbance distribution. Unfortunately, neither of these approaches dealt satisfactorily with the adaptation of statistical methods to the simultaneous nature of many economic phenomena.

Another important problem was the proper specification of the variables in the regression model and the correct assumptions about the disturbance term. Other important problems dealt with the proper specification and estimation of a single equation regression model. For example, the consequences of various misspecifications of the variance-covariance matrix of disturbances were considered, and modifications to CLS were suggested. Measurement errors were introduced as a possible source of estimation bias, and the kinds of information needed for creating remedies were suggested. The recognition of these problems raised questions about the appropriateness of CLS and led to the development of other estimation techniques.

These two major catagories—appropriate specification and estimation of single equation models, and the simultaneous nature of the economic system—have been the subject of much of the literature of theoretical econometrics. They also serve as a useful organization device. The two topics form a base in this introduction for discussing a number of contributions to econometric theory.

SINGLE EQUATION INVESTIGATIONS

Much of the work on single equation specification has centered around the least squares assumption of zero correlation between the independent variables and the disturbance. Other topics of interest include autocorrelation, aggregation, use of a priori information, multicollinearity, and errors in the variables.

Autocorrelation and Distributed Lags

It is quite possible that CLS assumption number 3 might be inappropriate for numerous economic applications. The dynamic nature of many economic models suggests that successive disturbances in time series data may not be statistically independent, while increased use and availability of cross-section data has introduced the possibility of a non-homogenous disturbance variance. CLS does not have desirable statistical properties if used in cases where residuals are autocorrelated. In particular, if there is a positive autocorrelation of the residuals, coefficient standard errors will be biased downward, and in any case will not be minimal. Aitken (1934) has derived an alternative to CLS called generalized least squares, GLS. In his model, assumption number 3 is modified to read $E\ (e'e) = \Omega$, where Ω is a positive definite matrix. This allows for both a heterogeneous disturbance variance and non-zero disturbance covariance. Aitken shows that GLS has all the desirable statistical properties possessed by CLS.

The liklihood of positive autocorrelation is reasonably high for economic time series data. For this reason, application of CLS without knowledge of the residual structure may easily lead to incorrect statistical inference. Several tests for autocorrelation of residuals have been developed, the most widely used being that of Hart and von Neumann (1942) and Durbin and Watson (1950*, 1951*). Theil and Nagar (1961*) have recently suggested an approximation to remove the "no decision" area of the Durbin-Watson test as an alternative for cases where variations in the independent variables are small relative to the series themselves. While neither of these tests specify the exact functional form of the disturbance covariance, they have proved useful for detecting first order autoregressive systems where the predetermined variables are all exogenous. Regrettably, they are biased for higher order autoregressive processes, and in cases where lagged endogenous variables are present among the predetermined variables.

Distributed lag models are a common reason for the presence of lagged endogenous variables in regression equations. Griliches (1967*) provides a thorough review of these models. He summarizes a variety of lag structures developed in recent years and indicates the difficulties in interpreting the results of the various formulations. His discussion of "identifying" the proper lag model from the data is particularly useful.

Once it is concluded that the population residuals are autocorrelated, an assignment of values for the off-diagonal elements in Ω is made and the regression coefficients are estimated via GLS. For additional elaboration on this process, see Goldberger (1964). The simplest and most often abused assumption is that the residuals follow a first order autoregressive process.

Aggregation

The topic of aggregation has received much attention in the literature. It is only briefly covered, however, in most of the standard econometric tests. The first important econometric work in this area was done by Theil (1954). He showed that weighting procedures can be derived so that aggregation does not cause any loss of information critical to the solution of the problem being considered. For example, suppose we are attempting to measure the marginal propensity to consume, using aggregate data. If all individuals over which the aggregation takes place prove to have identical marginal propensities to consume, then identical answers will be yielded by aggregate and disaggregate estimates of the marginal propensity to consume.

Much of the work on aggregation has been concerned with the general conditions for this consistent (or perfect) aggregation. Additional work has been done on the nature of aggregation bias, that is, when aggregation does not yield estimates which are consistent with the underlying micro relationships. H. A. J. Green (1964) presents a good review of the current research in aggregation. Griliches and Grunfeld (1960*) take a slightly different position than most researchers in this field. They argue that models of microeconomic behavior may contain specification errors which do not exist for the macroeconomic relationships. For instance, in the consumption function example cited above, individual consumption may depend upon aggregate as well as individual income. They argue that if this additional variable is neglected, the resulting micro relationships will be inferior to the aggregate because of specification error. Additional references on aggregation are Boot and deWitt (1960), Malinvaud (1956) and W. D. Fisher (1958).

The Use of Extraneous or A Priori Information

Extraneous or a priori information refers to information the researcher may have about the specification of the form of the regression model, and his knowledge of the values or ranges of the regression parameters. For example, in setting up a simple linear consumption function we could use such a priori knowledge: specifically, that the marginal propensity to consume lies between zero and one in estimating the MPC. When used judiciously a priori restrictions on the regression parameters lead to estimates with smaller variances than can be obtained without restrictions. Use of incorrect a priori specification and restrictions can result in estimates which are badly biased. Such use is certainly not to be recommended.

Efficient methods of estimation have been developed in a variety of cases where extraneous information on the range or value of the parameters is available. Durbin (1953) has developed an efficient estimating technique for the case where unbiased estimates of some regression coefficients are available from auxiliary regressions. His method utilizes information about the coefficient from both the main and auxiliary regressions. In this respect it is superior to the usual method of substituting the coefficient in the main regression. Zellner (1961) and Judge and Takayama (1966) have used a model where the regression coefficients are subject to extraneously determined inequality constraints. In this model a quadratic programming technique was developed to solve for the coefficient estimates. Zellner (1962*) has also developed a tecnhique for estimating all the coefficients of a system of equations each having the same number of observations. He incorporates a priori restrictions on the independent variables which appear in each equation. The estimates thus developed are more efficient than they would be if each equation were estimated separately. Tiao and Zellner (1964), Jeffreys (1961) and others have utilized Bayesian methods in estimating the coefficients of the regression model: they included prior distributions of the parameters in conjunction with sample information. Judge and Yancey (1970) provide a systematic exposition of the above methods. They also review some additional techniques for utilizing extraneous information in regression analysis.

Multicollinearity

In formulating and testing models of economic behavior, it is possible that some of the independent variables are highly intercorrelated. This may be due to chance, to structural relationships outside the model in question, or to lack of data with which to delineate each of the variables sufficiently. In the second case, the model should be modified to include the external functional relationship causing the multicollinearity. In the other cases, the researcher is more or less stuck, unless he can find additional data. Fortunately, in the absence of specification errors, multicollinearity does not bias the regression coefficient estimates. If specification errors are present, however, it may amplify bias. Multicollinearity does reduce the influence of individual variables as reflected by raising standard errors of the estimators. When estimates of the structural parameters are desired, this creates problems since these structural estimates will have very wide confidence intervals.

The multicollinearity deadlock may be broken by using additional data from other sources to estimate the coefficients for some of the collinear variables. A number of demand studies have followed this practice, estimating the income coefficient for cross-section data and using this estimate in a time series regression. This use of extraneous information has been criticized, however, by Meyer and Kuh (1957*). They argue that the structures from which the external estimates are derived are not necessarily equivalent to the structure being estimated.

Another complication has arisen with the utilization of high speed electronic computers and increased availability of data. It is often difficult to detect the presence of multicollinearity directly. Large models may include a number of independent variables; none of these is highly collinear with any other, but together they create a nearly singular cross products matrix from the observations. Starting with the assumption that multicollinearity is a sample phenomena, Farrar and Glauber (1967*) develop a series of tests for multicollinearity in the structure of independent variables. Knowledge of this structure enables the researcher to obtain data, to drop some variables from the model, or to develop additional structural equations explaining the collinear relationship. A different approach to the multicollinearity problem is provided by Toro-Vizcarrondo and Wallace (1968). They replace the criterion of minimum variance unbiasedness with that of mean square error. A test is developed for the situation where the omission of a variable "probably" reduces the mean square error by reducing the variance.

Errors in Variables

In the section on autocorrelation and distributed lags we reviewed research on the nature of the disturbance term and the relevant assumptions for econometric model building. There we were concerned with the general problem of errors in equations; that is, the characteristics of the disturbances in regression models where the variables are measured without error. Now it is also possible that, for various reasons, the variables we wish to observe can not be measured without error. If this is true, our focus shifts to the problem of errors in variables.

This topic has received systematic treatment as a branch of statistics. Kendall and Stuart (1964) and Johnston (1963) provide a good textbook treatment of the problem and Friedman (1957) applies the errors in variables model to consumption theory. Madansky (1959*) reviews the problem and introduces several alternatives to CLS in the two variable regression case, and outlines how they can be applied. Sargan (1958*) utilized a more general framework for analyzing errors in variables. He considers the possibilities of both errors in variables and errors in equations in a multivariate model.

The existence of errors in the independent variables results in CLS estimates that are both biased and inconsistent. This is due to intercorrelation between the residual and the independent variables. Each of the alternatives to CLS (instrumental variables, grouping of observations, weighted regression) attempts to remove this interdependency by making some assumption in order to reduce the number of unknown variables. In many ways the errors in variable problems provide a link to simultaneous equation topics discussed below. Both problems involve the interdependence of the disturbance and the independent variables. While the causes of this collinearity differ between the two models, in many respects the methods of treating it are similar. In both cases the method of instrumental variables has been used to remove the covariation between the regressors and the disturbance.

Miscellaneous Problems

Before moving on to the discussion of simultaneous equations, a number of miscellaneous topics should be noted in the literature. Applications of classical analysis of variance and covariance have been made by a number of econometricians. These techniques have been particularly useful in the analysis of temporal stability of cross-section relationships over time. The work of Kuh (1959*), Chow (1960*), Suits (1957*) and others is important in this regard. Spectral and cross-spectral analysis of economic time series has become an extremely important area of econometric research in the past few years. Good introductions to this new area can be found in Hannan (1960), Granger (1964), Nerlove (1964), Jenkins and Watts (1969), and Dhyrmes (1970).

The application of principle component and factor analysis to economic problems has become more general in recent years. Kloek and Mennes (1960) have used principle components to reduce the number of exogenous variables in the model. Researchers have encountered a number of methodological difficulties in interpreting the results of factor analysis. It appears to be useful, if not of convincing value, in areas where a strong theoretical framework has not been developed. A concise theoretical treatment of the factor model is presented by Lawley and Maxwell, (1963) while several economic applications have been reported by Adelman and Morris (1967).

SIMULTANEOUS EQUATION INVESTIGATION

We turn now to the problem of the simultaneous nature of economic life. It was noted above that symmetrical methods of fit, which ignored the problem of how the dependent variable was specified, did not deal satisfactorily with the problem of simultaneity. The breakthrough in this area was made by Haavelmo (1943, 1944, 1947*). Haavelmo postulated that economic activity could be analyzed as a simultaneous system of stochastic equations. Instead of determining a single dependent variable in a single equation, Haavelmo obtained a joint distribution of dependent variables from the simultaneous structure. The implications for classical least squares were many. If more than one jointly dependent variable appeared in a particular equation, least squares estimation yielded biased and inconsistent estimates of the population parameters. This resulted from intercorrelation between the jointly dependent variables and the residual. In the classical model this was precluded by the assumed fixed nature of all the independent variables. When the simultaneous nature of economic life is admitted, on the other hand, this assumption becomes untenable.

The Identification Problem

Once the framework of the model is expanded to include more than one structural relationship, the problem of identification emerges. In developing a model, more than one structure or point in the parameter space may be consistent with the available data. In econometrics this characteristic is called underidentification. For example, our structural model might imply that we have linear supply and demand functions, both of which involve only quantity and price. In this case, no set of observations, however, large, on price and quantity can isolate the parameters of the demand curve or the supply curve. In other words, neither function is identifiable. Suppose, however, our specification of the model includes a sufficient number of restrictions on the parameter space, including the variance-covariance matrix of the disturbances. Then, a series of observations on the (perhaps enlarged) set of variables will permit the identification of both demand and supply curves.

The structural model must have a priori identification properties which are determined independently of the parameters. Analysis of the identification properties of the model can help in selecting an appropriate estimating technique. Fortunately, economic theory usually leads to the identification of most structural relations. Often several independent variables are excluded from each structural relation so that overidentification is usually quite common.

A number of writers have made important contributions on the subject of identification. The first systematic work was done by Koopmans (1949). Later important references include Koopmans and Hood (1953), Koopmans, Rubin and Leipnik (1950) and Basmann (1960*). Fisher (1959*, 1966) provides a generalized treatment of the conditions for identifiability.[2]

Estimating Methods

In order to obtain better estimates, several alternatives to CLS have been suggested. Shortly after the appearance of the Haavelmo articles, Koopmans, Rubin and Leipnik (1950) developed a general procedure utilizing the method of maximum likelihood. In their model, the likelihood function of the jointly dependent variables, conditional upon the independent variables, is a function of the matrix of coefficients of both the independent and dependent variables for all structural equations in the system plus the contemporaneous covariance matrix of the disturbances for all equations. This method utilizes all the information in the system of equations and has been named full

[2]The Samuleson theorem used by Fisher in the 1959 article was later shown to be false, and has been replaced by the Gale-Nikaido theorem. For a complete discussion, see Fisher (1966) pp. 157-160.

information maximum likelihood, FIML. Generally the numerical analysis problems encountered in maximizing this likelikhood function are extremely difficult because of several nonlinearities. However, Chernoff and Divinsky (1953) give some computation procedures and Eisenpress (1962) has written an FIML computer program which has been relatively successful.

A special case of FIML where the matrix of jointly dependent variables becomes triangular has been treated by Wold (1959, 1960) and others. These recursive models (as opposed to interdependent or nonrecursive models) establish a stepwise chain of causation from one equation to the next. If in addition to recursiveness, the contemporaneous disturbances in each of the equations are uncorrelated, FIML and CLS yield identical estimates; no further attention then need be given to alternatives to CLS. The Triptych of Strotz and Wold (1960a*, 1960b*, 1960c*) is a useful review of some of the issues involved in the interpretation and measurement of recursive versus interdependent equation systems. Wold and Strotz (1960a*) give a methodological framework for interpreting recursive systems and for determining how they compare with interdependent systems. Strotz (1960b*) examines the implications for maximum likelihood estimation when interdependent models are regarded as approximation to recursive models. Wold (1960c*) investigates the properties of a conditional causal chain model. Recently Fisher (1965) and Dhrymes (1970) have argued that large econometric models may have a so-called block recursive nature; that is, different sectors of the model are recursive, for which CLS is an appropriate estimating technique.

Another maximum likelihood method was developed by Anderson and Rubin (1949*, 1950*). They maximized the likelihood of the sample subject only to the restrictions of the equation to be estimated. This method was appropriately named limited information maximum likelihood (LIML) by later writers. Koopmans and Hood (1953) derived the same estimator using the least variance ratio technique.

Theil (1953) and Basmann (1957), working independently, developed a method now called two stage least squares (TSLS). This method surpasses LIML in calculational simplicity, requiring only the straightforward application of classical least squares twice. Theil (1958) and more recently Nagar (1962*) have developed more general estimators called k-class and double k-class of which CLS, TSLS and LIML are special cases.

Two additional estimating techniques have been developed since 1960. Both use all the information in the model and in this respect are similar to FIML. Zellner and Theil (1962) have developed a method called three stage least squares, THSLS. In simplified terms, the method is an application of generalized least squares developed by Aitken (1934), where all of the parameters of the system are estimated simultaneously. Two stage least squares estimates are used in estimating the covariance matrix of disturbances. Rothenburg and Leeders (1964) have developed a shortcut version of FIML called linearized maximum likelihood (LML); they take only the first iteration of the FIML method, using a step size of one. While more burdensome computationally than THSLS, LML has more desirable asymptotic properties for certain assumptions. In particular, if lagged endogenous variables appear as independent variables, or if the covariance matrix of disturbances is restricted, LML has a smaller asymptotic variance than THSLS.

All of the above estimation techniques have desirable asymptotic properties. Without going into detailed differences between estimators for various model specification, some observations seem warranted. Under fairly general assumptions about the generating model, all of the above techniques provide consistent estimates of the structural parameters of the model. That is, the sample estimate of the parameter converges to the value of the population parameters in probability. In this sense each estimate is superior to CLS, which is generally inconsistent for interdependent models.

Assuming the population disturbances are normally distributed, TSLS, LIML, k-class and ouble k-class become equally efficient estimators as sample size goes to infinity, given the same a priori information. That is, their variance around the true population parameter is as small or smaller than any other consistent and asymptotically normal estimator.

TSLS and FIML are also asymptotically efficient when a priori information for the entire model is considered. Zellner and Theil (1962) have shown that THSLS is more efficient than TSLS under fairly general assumptions about the structure of the model.

SMALL SAMPLE INVESTIGATIONS

While the asymptotic properties of the various estimators are a legitimate area of study, applied econometricians do not frequently make inferences from an infinitely large sample. Consequently, a number of studies of the so-called small sample properties of the various estimation techniques have been made. These studies can be made in two ways, theoretically or using Monte Carlo techniques.

Theoreti cal Analysis

Nagar (1959*, 1962), and Basmann (1961*, 1073*) have pioneered in developing theoretical models of small sample properties. Nagar's work is more general; he works with the approximate distributions of k-class and double k-class estimators. Many of his results are extremely detailed. In general, he concludes that small sample bias for a particular equation will be small if the sample size is large and if the number of independent variables outside the equation just equals the number of jointly dependent variables in the equation. Nagar produces evidence that TSLS provides a smaller sampling variance of the sample parameters than does LIML, especially if the number of predetermined variables outside the equation is small. Basmann, on the other hand, develops the exact sampling distributions of several TSLS estimators. In several special cases he shows that the distribution does not have a finite variance; he uses this fact as argument against the employment of Monte Carlo mean squared errors in comparing the usefulness of various alternative estimating techniques.

Monte Carlo Analysis

Despite Basmann's arguments, a number of researchers have used Monte Carlo techniques in evaluating the small sample properties of different estimating techniques. Although still in its infancy, this branch of econometrics has grown concurrently with the capability of high speed computing machines to permit numerous replications at low cost. Essentially, the Monte Carlo technique allows a large number of samples to be drawn from a known population. Sample statistics can then be calculated in various ways and compared with the true population parameters. The key to the technique is random sampling from some specified disturbance distribution. The disturbance errors, combined with known structural parameters and sets of values for the independent variables, generate the sample values for the jointly dependent variables.

The main conclusions of several Monte Carlo studies can be briefly summarized. Although exceptions and some contradictions can be found, the work of Summers (1965*), Quandt (1965), Christ (1960*) and Neiswanger and Yancy (1959), and others, has the following implications: (1) Estimation techniques which use all the information in the system, such as FIML or THSLS, are more likely to be erroneous when the model is incorrectly specified; they are the best methods to use, however, when there are no specification errors. (2) Of the single equation estimates TSLS and LIML, TSLS is a slightly superior method whether or not the model is properly specified; and (3) CLS is inferior to any of the other techniques when the model is properly specified, but is superior to full information methods when the model is poorly specified.

J.M.D.
F.R.G.
Boulder
Trinity, 1970

REFERENCES

Adelman, I. and C. T. Morris (1967) *Society, Politics and Economic Development: A Quantitative Approach.* Baltimore, the Johns Hopkins Press.

Aitken, A. C. (1934) On Least Squares and Linear Combination of Observations, *Proceedings of the Royal Society of Edinburgh,* Vol. LV, 1934-1935, pp. 42-48.

Anderson, and Rubin (1949) Estimation of the Parameters of a Single Equation in a Complete System of Stochastic Equations, *Annals of Mathematical Statistics,* Vol. 20, No. 1 (March), pp. 46-63.

Anderson, and Rubin (1950) The Asymptotic Properties of Estimates of the Parameters of a Single Equation in a Complete System of Stochastic Equations, *Annals of Mathematical Statistics,* Vol. 21, No. 4 (December), pp. 570-582.

Basmann, R. L. (1957) A Generalized Classical Method of Linear Estimation of Coefficients in a Structural Equation, *Econometrica,* Vol. 25, No. 1 (January), pp. 77-83.

Basmann, R. L. (1960) On Finite Sample Distributions of Generalized Classical Linear Identifiability Test Statistics, *Journal of the American Statistical Association,* Vol. 55, No. 292 (December), pp. 650-659.

Basmann, R. L. (1961) A Note on the Exact Finite Sample Frequency Functions of Generalized Classical Linear Estimators in Two Leading Overidentified Cases, *Journal of the American Statistical Association,* Vol. 56, No. 295 (September) pp. 619-636.

Basmann, R. L. (1963) A Note on the Exact Finite Sample Frequency Functions of Generalized Classical Linear Estimators in a Leading Three Equation Case, *Journal of the Aoerican Statistical Association,* Vol. 58, No. 301 (March), pp. 161-171.

Boot, J. C. G. and G. M. deWit (1960) Investment Demand: An Empirical Contribution to the Aggregation Problem, *International Economic Review,* Vol. 1, No. 1 (January), pp. 3-30.

Chernoff, Herman, and Nathan Divinsky (1953) The Computation of Maximum-Likelihood Estimates of Linear Structural Equations. Chapter X in Hood and Koopmans (1953), pp. 236-302.

Chow, Gregory C. (1960) Tests of Equality Between Sets of Coefficients in Two Linear Regressions, *Econometrica,* Vol. 28, No. 3 (July), pp. 591-605.

Christ, C. (1960) Simultaneous Equation Estimation: Any Verdict Yet? *Econometrica* Vol. 28, No. 4 (October), pp. 835-845.

Christ, C. (1966) *Econometric Models and Methods.* New York, Wiley.

Dhrymes, Phoebus J. (1970) *Econometrics, Statistical Foundations and Applications.* New York, Harper and Row.

Durbin, J. (1953) A Note On Regression Where There is Extraneous Information About One of the Coefficients, *Journal of the American Statistical Association,* Vol. 48, (December), pp. 799-808.

Durbin, J., and G. S. Watson (1950) Testing for Serial Correlation in Least Squares Regression I. *Biometrika* 37 (December), pp. 409-428.

Durbin, J., and G. S. Watson (1951) Testing for Serial Correlation in Least Squares Regression. II.*Biometrikak 38* (June), pp. 159-178.

Eisenpress, H. (1962) Note on the Computation of Full-Information Maximum Likelihood Estimates of Coefficients of a Simultaneous System, *Econometrica*, Vol. 30, No. 2 (April), pp. 343-348.

Farrar, D. and R. Glauber (1967) Multicollinearity in Regression Analysis: The Problem Revisited, *Review of Economics and Statistics*, Vol. 49, (February), pp. 92-107.

Fisher, Franklin M. (1959) Generalization of the Rank and Order Conditions for Identifiability, *Econometrica*, Vol. 27, No. 3 (July), pp. 431-447.

Fisher, F. M. (1965) Dynamic Structure and Estimation in Economy-Wilde Econometric Models, Chapter 15 in J. S. Duesenberry, G. Fromm, L. R. Klein and E. Kuh eds., *The Brookings Quarterly Econometric Model of the United States*, Chicago and Amsterdam, Rand McNally and North-Holland.

Fisher, F. M. (1966) *The Indentification Problem in Econometrics*, New York, McGraw-Hill.

Fisher, W. D. (1958) Criteria for Aggregation and Input-Output Analysis, *Review of Economics and Statistics*, Vol. 40, (August), pp. 250-260.

Friedman, M. (1957) *A Theory of the Consumption Function*, Princeton, Princeton University Press.

Frisch, R. (1933) *Pitfalls in the Statistical Construction of Demand and Supply Curves.* Veroffentlichungen der Frankfurter Gesellschaft fur Konjuncturforschung, Neue Folge, Heft 5. Leipzig, Hans Buske Verlag.

Frisch, R. (1934) *Statistical Confluence Analysis by Means of Complete Regression Systems.* Oslo, Universitetets Okonomiske Institutt.

Goldberger, A. S. (1964) *Econometric Theory*, New York, Wiley.

Granger, C. W. J. in association with M. Hatanaka (1964) *Spectral Analysis of Economic Time Series.* Princeton, Princeton University Press.

Green, H. A. J. (1964) *Aggregation in Economic Analysis: An Introductory Survey.* Princeton, Princeton University Press.

Griliches, Z. (1967) Distributed Lags: A Survey, *Econometrica*, Vol. 35, No. 1 (January), pp. 16-49.

Grunfeld, Y. and Z. Griliches (1960) Is Aggregation Necessarily Bad? *Review of Economics and Statistics*, Vol. 42, No. 1 (February), pp. 1-15.

Haavelmo, Trygve (1943) The Statistical Implications of a System of Simultaneous Equations, *Econometrica*, Vol. 11, No. 1 (January), pp. 1-12.

Haavelmo, Trygve (1944) The Probability Approach in Econometrics, *Econometrica*, Vol. 12, Supplement (July), 118 pp.

Haavelmo, Trygve (1947) Methods of Measuring the Marginal Propensity to Consume, Chapter IV in Hood and Koopmans (1953), pp. 75-91. Also in *Journal of the American Statistical Association*, Vol. 42, No. 237 (March, 1947), pp. 105-122.

Hannan, E. J. (1960) *Time Series Analysis*, London and New York, Methuen and Wiley.

Hart, B. I., and John von Neumann (1942) Tabulation of the Probabilities for the Ratio of the Mean Square Successive Differences to the Variance. *Annals of Mathematical Statistics*, Vol. 13, pp. 207-214.

Hood, W. C. and T. C. Koopmans (editors) (1953) *Studies in Econometric Method*, Cowles Commission Monograph 14, New York, Wiley.

Johnston, J. (1963) *Econometric Methods*, New York, McGraw-Hill.

Jenkins, Gwilym M. and Donald G. Watts (1969) *Spectral Analysis and its Applications*, San Francisco, Holden-Day.

Judge, G. G. and T. Takayama (1966) Inequality Restrictions in Regression Analysis. *Journal of the American Statistical Association,* Vol. 61, pp. 166-181.

Judge, G. G. and T. A. Yancey (1970) The Use of Prior Information in Estimating the Parameters of Economic Relationships, *Metroeconomica*, Forthcoming.

Kendall, M. G., and A. Stuart (1958) and (1961) *The Advanced Theory of Statistics,* Vols. I and II, New York, Hafner.

Kloek, T. and L. B. M. Mennes (1960) Simultaneous Equations Estimation Based on Principal Components of Predetermined Variables. *Econometrica,* Vol. 28, pp. 45-61.

Koopmans, T. C. (1945) Statistical Estimation of Simultaneous Economic Relations, *Journal of the American Statistical Association,* Vol. 40, No. 232, Pt. 1 (December), pp. 448-466).

Koopmans, T. C. (1946) Identification Problems in Economic Model Construction. Chapter II in Hood and Koopmans (1953), pp. 27-48. Also in *Econometrica,* Vol. 17, No. 2 (April, 1949), pp. 125-144.

Koopmans, T. C. (editor) (1950) *Statistical Inference in Dynamic Economic Models.* Cowles Commission Monograph 10, New York, Wiley.

Koopmans, T. C. and W. C. Hood (1953) The Estimation of Simultaneous Linear Economics Relationships. Chapter VI in Hood and Koopmans (1953), pp. 112-199.

Koopmans, T. C., H. Rubin, and R. B. Leipnik (1950) Measuring the Equation Systems of Dynamic Economics. Chapter II in Koopmans (1950), pp. 53-237.

Klein, L. A. (1953) *A Textbook of Econometrics*, Evanston, Illinois, Row Peterson.

Kuh, E. (1959) The Validity of Cross-Sectionally Estimated Behavior Equations in Time Series Applications, *Econometrica*, Vol. 27 (April), pp. 197-214.

Lawley, D. N. and A. E. Maxwell (1963) *Factor Analysis as a Statistical Method.* London Butterworths.

Madansky, Albert (1959) The Fitting of Straight Lines When Both Variables are Subject to Error, *Journal of the American Statistical Association*, Vol. 54, No. 285 (March), pp. 173-205.

Malinvaud, E. (1956) L'agregation dans les Modeles Economiques, *Cahiers du Seminaire d'Econometrie*, No. 4, Paris, pp. 69-146.

Malinvaud, E. (1966) *Statistical Methods of Econometrics,* Chicago, Rand McNally, and Amsterdam, North-Holland Publishing Co.

Marschak, Jacob (1950) Statistical Inference in Economics: An Introduction. Chapter I in Koopmans (1950), pp. 1-50.

Meyer, J. and E. Kuh (1957) How Extraneous are Extraneous Estimators? *Review of Economics and Statistics*, Vol. 39 (November), pp. 380-393.

Nagar, A. L. (1959) The Bias and Moment Matrix of the General k-Class Estimators of the Parameters in Simultaneous Equations, *Econometrica*, Vol. 27, No. 4 (Oct.) pp. 575-595.

Nagar, A. L. (1962) Double k-Class Estimators of Parameters in Simultaneous Equations and Their Small Sample Properties, *International Economic Review,* Vol. 3, No. 2 (May), pp. 168-188.

Neiswanger, W. A., and T. A. Yancey (1959) Parameter Estimates and Autonomous Growth, *Journal of the American Statistical Association,* Vol. 54, No. 286 (June), pp. 389-402.

Nerlove, M. (1964) Spectral Analysis of Seasonal Adjustment Procedures, *Econometrica,* Vol. 32, No. 3 (July), pp. 241-286.

Quandt, E. (1965) On Certain Small Sample Properties of k-Class Estimators, *International Economic Review*, Vol. 6, No. 1 (January), pp. 92-104.

Rothenberg, J., and C. T. Leenders (1964) Efficient Estimation of Simultaneous Equation Systems, *Econometrica*, Vol. 32, Nos. 1-2 (January-April), pp. 57-76.

Sargan, J. D. (1958) The Estimation of Economic Relationships Using Instrumental Variables, *Econometrica*, Vol. 26, No. 3 (July), pp. 393-415.

Schultz, Henry (1938) *The Theory and Measurement of Demand.* Chicago, University of Chicago Press.

Strotz, R. H. (1960) Interdependence as a Specification Error, *Econometrica*, Vol. 28, No. 2 (April), pp. 428-441.

Strotz, R. H. and H. O. A. Wold (1960) Recursive vs. Nonrecursive Systems: An Attempt at Synthesis, *Econometrica,* Vol. 28, No. 2 (April), pp. 417-427.

Suits, D. B. (1957) Use of Dummy Variables in Regression Equations, *Journal of the American Statistical Association*, Vol. 52. (December) pp. 548-551.

Summers, R. (1965) A Capital Intensive Approach to the Small Sample Properties of Various Simultaneous Equation Estimators, *Econometrica*, Vol, 33, No. 1 (Jan.) pp. 1-41.

Theil, H. (1953) Estimation and Simultaneous Correlation in Complete Equations Systems. The Hague, Central Plan Bureau, mimeographed memorandum.

Theil, H. (1954) *Linear Aggregation of Economic Relations.* Amsterdam, North-Holland.

Theil, H. (1958) and (1961) *Economic Forecasts and Policy.* (Contributions to economic Analysis No. 15.) Amsterdam, North-Holland Publishing Co., First edition, 1958; second edition, 1961.

Theil, H. and A. L. Nagar (1961) Testing the Independence of Regression Disturbances, *Journal of the American Statistical Association,* Vol. 56, No. 296 (December), pp. 793-806.

Tiao, G. C. and Zellner (1964) Bayes' Theorem and the Use of Prior Knowledge in Regression Analysis. *Biometrica*, Vol. 41, pp. 219-230.

Tinbergen, Jan (1938) Statistical Evidence on the Acceleration Principle, *Economica,* N. S. Vol. 5 (May), pp. 164-176. Reprinted in Tinbergen (1951), pp. 215-229.

Tinbergen, Jan (1939) *Statistical Testing of Business Cycle Theories*, Vol. II: Business Cycles in the U.S.A. 1919-1932. Geneva, League of Nations.

Tinbergen, Jan (1951) *Econometrics* Philadelphia, Blakiston.

Tintner, Gerhard (1952) *Econometrics.* New York, Wiley.

Toro-Vizcarrondo, C. and T. D. Wallace (1968) A Test of the Mean Square Error Criterion for Restrictions in Linear Regression. *Journal of the American Statistical Association*, Vol. 63, pp. 558-572.

Wold, H. O. A. (1959) Ends and Means in Econometric Model Building, pp. 355-434 *Probability and Statistics,* U. Grenander, editor, New York, Wiley.

Wold, H. O. A. (1960) A Generalization of Causal Chain Models, *Econometrica*, Vol. 28, No. 2 (April), pp. 443-463.

Working, E. J. (1927) What do Statistical Demand Curves Show? *Quarterly Journal of Economics*, Vol. 41, (February), pp. 212-235.

Zellner, A. (1961) Linear Regression With Inequality Constraints on the Coefficients: An Application of Quandratic Programming and Linear Decision Rules, International Center for Management Science, Report 6l09 (MS No. 9).

Zellner, A. (1962) An Efficient Method of Estimating Seemingly Unrelated Regressions and Tests for Aggregation Bias, *Journal of the American Statistical Association*, Vol. 57, No. 298 (June), pp. 348-368.

Zellner, A. and H. Theil (1962) Three-Stage Least Squares: Simultaneous Estimation of Simultaneous Equations, *Econometrica*, Vol. 30, No. 1 (January), pp. 54-78.

But we have fallen on bad times. Which means we are data oriented. If the data doesn't all fall into neat rows and add up to preconceived sums, we must reject it. True wisdom would tell us otherwise but, fools that we are, we keep on crying out that only Facts are true, only Data counts. No dreams allowed. Not a hair of intuition, please. No romance. No fun.

Ray Bradbury
From the Introduction to *The Collected Works of Buck Rogers in the 25th Century,* Chelsea House Publishers, 1969.

METHODOLOGY

STATISTICAL INFERENCE IN ECONOMICS: AN INTRODUCTION

BY J. MARSCHAK

0. PURPOSE OF THE VOLUME

0.1. The Problem

Quantitative economic study has a threefold basis: it is necessary to formulate economic hypotheses, to collect appropriate data, and to confront hypotheses with data. The latter task, statistical inference in economics, was discussed at a Cowles Commission conference held at the University of Chicago from January 27 to February 1, 1945. Staff members of the Cowles Commission prepared, and circulated in advance, some of the papers; others were delivered by the Commission's guests.[1]

In its *Annual Report* for 1944 and for subsequent years, the Commission stressed the importance of adapting statistical methods to the peculiarities of the data and the objectives of economic research. The economist's objectives are similar to those of an engineer but his data are like those of a meteorologist. The economist is often required to estimate the effects of a given (intended or expected) change in the "economic structure," i.e., in the very mechanism that produces his data. None of these changes can he produce beforehand, as in a laboratory experiment; and since some of the changes envisaged have never happened before, the economist often has to estimate the results of changes that he has never observed.

The economist can do this if his past observations suffice to estimate the relevant structural constants prevailing before the change. Having estimated the past structure the economist can estimate the effects of varying it. He can thus help to choose those variations of structure that would produce – from a given point of view – the most desirable results. That is, he can advise on policies (of a government or a firm).

Thus, practical considerations bring about the economist's concern with economic structure. Hypotheses about economic structure are also known as economic theories. They try to state relations that describe the behavior and environment of men and determine the values taken at any time by economic variables such as prices, output, and consumption of various goods and services, and the prices and amounts of various assets. As there are several variables the economic structure must involve several simultaneous relations to determine them. In this, economic theory is analogous to theories used in experimental science.

Also, economic variables as well as those of experimental science are, in principle, random (stochastic) variables: that is, their properties are described by probability distributions. In particular, the stochastic character of the observed data can often be ascribed to their dependence on stochastic nonobservable variables: such nonobservable variables are random "errors" in the observation of single variables or random "shocks" suffered by the relations connecting

---

[1] The guests included R. L. Anderson, T. Haavelmo, H. Hotelling, W. G. Madow, H. B. Mann, G. Tintner, and A. Wald. Staff members who participated in the conference were L. Hurwicz, L. R. Klein, T. C. Koopmans, R. Leipnik, J. Marschak, and H. Rubin. T. W. Anderson and T. Haavelmo joined the staff at a later date.

them. However, an experimenter could replace the natural conditions by laboratory conditions. To study one of the several relations, the experimenter observes the random values taken by one variable when the other observables that determine it are made reasonably free of the influence of errors and shocks. The economist cannot thus control variables and isolate relations. His data are produced by the existing economic structure, as described by a system of simultaneous relations between these random variables: the observables themselves, the errors, and the shocks. To use such data for the estimation of the system – "structural estimation" – is a new statistical problem.

This new statistical problem is thus forced upon the economist by the occurrence or consideration of structural changes (including policy changes on which his advice is sought), and by his inability to make experiments of either of two kinds: experiments producing in advance the considered change in structure (e.g., wind-tunnel experiments on airplanes), and experiments in which some of the random variables of nature are given fixed values (e.g., experiments to test fundamental laws of physics). See [J.Marschak, 1947B].

The role of simultaneous equations is familiar to economic theorists. But it has often been forgotten by economic statisticians who tried to estimate a single stochastic relation as if no other such relations had taken part in determining the observed values of the variables. On the other hand, economic theorists are apt to forget that the observed economic variables are, in general, stochastic. To be susceptible of empirical tests an economic hypothesis must be formulated as a statistical one, i.e., be specified in terms of probability distributions.

The statistical problem of the economist is complicated by the fact that many an economic relationship connects current and past values of the same or other variables involved. The economic structure determines, accordingly, not a set of constant values, one for each variable, but a set of probable paths, one for each variable, provided certain initial values are given. This dynamic character of economic structure creates, in the absence of experiments, further statistical difficulties: many economic data have the form of time series in which successive items are not independent. Statistical inference from time series of this kind involves further new problems.

Thus, economic data are generated by systems of relations that are, in general, stochastic, dynamic, and simultaneous. Occurring jointly, these three properties give rise to unsolved problems of statistical inference from the observed data to the relations.

Yet these very relations constitute economic theory and knowledge of them is needed for economic practice.

0.2. *The Discussion*

All these difficulties, under names like "pitfalls in demand and supply analysis" (Ragnar Frisch), "lack of independence in economic time series," etc., have caused uneasiness for a long time. Of the many attempts to grapple with the problem, Ragnar Frisch's contributions [1929, 1931, 1933, 1934, 1938] were probably the most stimulating ones. However, he did not take full account of the random disturbances (shocks) in the economic relations, nor of the simultaneous character of these relations. Moreover, Frisch's hypotheses on random disturbances (errors) in variables were not specified in probability terms. The latter, but not the former, defect was corrected in the early work of Koopmans [1937] and Wald [1940]. A new milestone was reached in 1943 when two articles were published in *Econometrica* by Haavelmo [1943], and by Mann and Wald [1943]. Haavelmo formulated the economist's simultaneous-equations model as a statistical hypothesis by assuming a random disturbance (shock) in each equation, in addition to random errors in each observable variable, and by specifying the distribution of these (unobservable) random quantities [Haavelmo, 1944, esp. Chapter III]. Mann and Wald outlined a solution of the estimation problem arising from the new formulation, though only for the case of large samples, and omitting the observation errors. For a set of short time series of interrelated variables, the contemporary (and incomplete) work on time series in a single variable has to be utilized as a start; and important suggestions can also be expected from the study of continuous random processes that is being developed currently in the service of other sciences. As to combining shocks and errors in one equation system, recent investigations of T. W. Anderson and L. Hurwicz [1947] were stimulated by discussions with G. Tintner.

For its quantitative studies of economic behavior, the Cowles Commission had to expect much from the criticism of statisticians who had contributed to the estimation of simultaneous equations and to the theory of time series. Such was the object of the conference. Earlier drafts of articles II, V, VI, XI, XII, XIV, XV, XVI, XVII, XVIII, XIX, were prepared for the conference. Articles III, VIII, X, XIII, are discussions that were contributed in the conference and written up shortly afterwards.

Articles or parts of articles added or substantially expanded later are I, II-*2.3*, II-*3.3*, II-*4*, IV, VI, VII, IX, XI-*10.2*, XIV, XV. The revision was helped by discussions with persons not present at the conference: especially on the problem of computations [II-*4*] with A. Adrian Albert and John von Neumann. An alternative method of structural estimation, that of "limited information," suggested by M. A. Girshick and worked out by T. W. Anderson and H. Rubin [1949], is briefly presented in this volume by T. W. Anderson [IX]. Other conference contributions, by L. R. Klein [1946 A] and by W. G. Madow [1945], have been published elsewhere. Madow's subject was explored further by R. B. Leipnik [1947].

The manuscript of the present volume was completed early in 1947, but publication has been delayed by typographical and other printing difficulties.

In the next two sections of the present introductory paper, the author has drawn freely on the results attained in the papers that follow and on suggestions made in the daily work and discussion within the Cowles Commission. His debt to Leonid Hurwicz and Tjalling C. Koopmans is particularly heavy.

We have tried to achieve conformity in terminology and, to some extent, in notation. However, since the several contributions differ in purpose as well as in emphasis, rigorous uniformity is neither possible nor desirable.

Most of the contributions to this volume presuppose on the part of the reader a general knowledge of mathematical principles of statistics; to explain these principles to a more general reader would take more space than is available. The present introduction, in summarizing the purpose and the main results of the studies collected in this volume, is addressed to the mathematically-minded economist rather than to the statistician. Hence - the use made of nonstochastic models (section *1*) and the attention paid, in the stochastic case, to the properties of populations (section *2.5.1*) as distinct from samples. This summary, too, has to be terse. For a less compressed treatment and further economic illustrations and applications the reader is referred to the following publications of Cowles Commission staff members: [Girshick and Haavelmo, 1947], [Haavelmo, 1943, 1944, 1947 A, 1947 B], [Hurwicz, 1947], [Klein, 1946 B, 1947, 1950], [Koopmans, 1945, 1949], [Marschak and Andrews, 1944], [Marschak, 1947 A, 1947 B]. The group continues to work on statistical inference in economics, both in general and with respect to specific economic models.[1] It is hoped that the present volume

---

[1]See the *Annual Report* of the Cowles Commission, in particular the *Five-Year Report* for 1942-46.

will stimulate further cooperation of mathematical statisticians and economists in solving the many problems that have been indicated but not solved in this volume. Plans are under way for a parallel monograph (No. 12) of a more expository character, in which emphasis is placed on a discussion of the main ideas and techniques developed in this volume with the help of simple illustrative models, rather than on formal mathematical proof.

1. NONSTOCHASTIC MODELS

Economic relations are, in general, stochastic. They involve variables whose properties are described with the aid of probability distributions. Moreover, the estimates of parameters of these relations, obtained by statistical methods from a limited number of observations, are also random variables.

However, important distinct properties of empirical economics can be brought out even if, for simplicity, we assume the data to be measured exactly and to satisfy exactly the relations of theory. The equations or inequalities serving to determine the parameters of such relations from observations are free from random variables. The problem of estimation degenerates into that of determination. This simplifies the study of certain "prestatistical" problems facing the economic statistician – in particular that of identification (section *1.3*), and also helps to see why, as indicated in section *0.1*, these problems originate in the need for policy decisions in the absence of experiments.

In the present section we shall deal with this special, or degenerate, case to meet in particular the habits of readers with economic rather than statistical background.

1.1. The Model

1.1.0. Denote the observable variables (or observables) by a vector $x \equiv (x_1, \ldots, x_N)$. The first, second, ..., Tth observations on x, succeeding each other in time, or arranged in space or in any other way, form a matrix:

$$X^o \equiv [\ x_n(t)\ ], \qquad n = 1, \ldots, N, \quad t = 1, \ldots, T;$$

or

$$X^o \equiv \begin{bmatrix} x(1) \\ \cdots \\ x(T) \end{bmatrix}.$$

We call *a priori information* all statements (either true or false) arrived at independently of any knowledge of X^0. We call *model* $\mathfrak{S}$ the a priori information on a system of mutually consistent and independent equations

$$\varphi_g(x, \alpha_{(g)}) = 0, \qquad g = 1, \ldots, G, \tag{1.1}$$

where $\alpha_{(g)}$ is a vector of P_g parameters. We shall denote the vector of all parameters of the system by $\alpha \equiv (\alpha_{(1)}, \ldots, \alpha_{(G)})$, and write $\sum_g P_g = P$; we shall also write[1] $\bar{\varphi} \equiv (\varphi_1, \ldots, \varphi_G)$.

1.1.1. We shall assume throughout that $\mathfrak{S}$ defines a) the form of $\bar{\varphi}$, and b) the "a priori restrictions," i.e., equations or inequalities in parameters α.

1.1.2. To provide this information we must make full use of our independent knowledge of existing production conditions (technology, legal statutes, etc.) and of plausible, if not necessarily rational, individual behavior. The equations of the model must refer to individual agents in specified markets (as consumers or manufacturers of certain goods, or as workers, bankers, landlords, etc.).

1.1.3. However, to reduce the model to a manageable size, variables referring to single individuals in finely subdivided markets must be grouped into aggregates. Suppose the value of some variable relevant to a practical decision (see below, section *1.2.3*) is calculated on the basis of such an aggregative model. This value will contain an error inasmuch as it will deviate from the corresponding value calculated on the basis of a true, detailed model, with separate equations for each commodity and individual. Optimum aggregation should combine highest manageability (e.g., shortest computations) with smallest error. This aggregation problem (which includes that of index numbers) has not been solved or even formulated in detail, nor will it be studied in this volume.

1.1.4. The model $\mathfrak{S}$ is called *self-contained* if $G = N$; *sectional* if $G < N$.

We call a model *complete* if it is either self-contained or has the following property: a subset of x containing $K = N - G$ elements – call this subset $z \equiv (z_1, \ldots, z_K)$ – is determined by K

---

[1] Subscripts indicate the elements of a vector which are scalars or functions: x_n, φ_g. In the present article, subvectors formed from the elements of a vector are indicated by subscripts in parentheses: $\alpha_{(g)}$. In addition, it will here prove convenient to use a barred letter for a vector whose elements are functions: $\bar{\varphi}$.

possibly unknown "subsidiary" equations

(1.2) $$\varphi_{G+k}(z) = 0, \quad k = 1, \ldots, K,$$

which are independent of the equation (1.1); the equations (1.2) do not contain any elements of x that are not in z. Denote the latter elements by vector $y \equiv (y_1, \ldots, y_G)$. Then, assuming differentiability,

(1.3) $$\frac{\partial \varphi_{G+k}}{\partial y_g} = 0, \quad g = 1, \ldots, G, \quad k = 1, \ldots, K.$$

A model that is not complete is called incomplete (or partial).

The observables z are called *exogenous* and the observables y *endogenous*, with respect to the model $\mathfrak{S}$.

Equation (1.1) can be rewritten as

(1.4) $$\varphi_g(y, z; \alpha_{(g)}) = 0, \quad g = 1, \ldots, G.$$

1.2. *Structural Changes and Policies*

1.2.1. Structure and reduced form.

1.2.1.1. We call *structure* S all properties of the equations (1.4), including the properties not known a priori. Any model $\mathfrak{S}$ is a class of structures. Each structure is defined by the functional forms of the equations and the values of the parameters occurring in them. We can write[1]

(1.5) $$S \equiv (\overline{\varphi}, \alpha).$$

When the equations (1.4) are thus fully specified we call them *structural equations*. We call α the structural parameters. Concepts defined in section *1.1.4* with reference to the model ("complete," "sectional" model; variables exogenous to a model; etc.) will also be applied to a structure without causing ambiguity.

1.2.1.2. Given the structure S, equations (1.4) can be solved for y in terms of z, involving new parameters which we shall denote

[1] In what follows quantities depending on S will be introduced. They are, properly speaking, "functionals" with respect to the argument $\overline{\varphi}$ and "functions" with respect to the argument α, although we shall denote and refer to them as "functions" of S.

by vector π:

$$y = \bar{\eta}(z;\ \pi), \tag{1.6}$$

say, where $\bar{\eta}$ is a vector whose elements are functions. Equation system (1.6) is called *reduced form*.[1] $\bar{\eta}$ depends on $\bar{\varphi}$; π is obtained by applying a transformation to the parameters α in (1.4). This transformation itself depends on the functions $\bar{\varphi}$. If we call this transformation $\bar{\pi}_{\varphi}$, we can write, accordingly,

$$\pi = \bar{\pi}_{\varphi}(\alpha) = \bar{\pi}(S), \tag{1.7}$$

say; furthermore, we can also write $\bar{\eta}_{\varphi}$ instead of $\bar{\eta}$ to emphasize the dependence of the functions $\bar{\eta}$ on the functions $\bar{\varphi}$. Thus

$$y = \bar{\eta}_{\varphi}[z;\ \bar{\pi}_{\varphi}(\alpha)]. \tag{1.8}$$

1.2.1.3. If the structural functions φ are linear, the functions $\bar{\eta}$ and $\bar{\pi}_{\varphi}$ will also be linear, and the set of parameters $\pi = \bar{\pi}_{\varphi}(\alpha)$ of the reduced form corresponding to a given structure S will be unique. If the functions φ are nonlinear, several sets of parameters α may be compatible with the structure S. We shall neglect here this complication although it does occur in economic theory, as in the case of "multiple equilibrium" [Marshall, app. H].

1.2.1.4. Apart from very special cases, the reduced forms (each one characterized by a function set $\bar{\eta}$ and a parameter set π) compatible with a given structure S will be finite in number, or at least denumerable; in a linear model the reduced form is unique.

On the other hand the number of structures compatible with a given reduced form $(\bar{\eta},\ \pi)$ may or may not be (nondenumerably) infinite. Even if the model is linear, the structure may or may not be uniquely determined by the reduced form. (See also below, section *1.3.*)

1.2.2. Use of observations.

1.2.2.1. Suppose the period (or, say, the geographical area) of observations consists of elements 1, ..., T, and is so chosen that the structure maintains throughout it the value

$$S^o \equiv (\bar{\varphi}^o,\ \alpha^o).$$

Then the following equations are satisfied by the observations X^o:

[1] See [IX] where $\bar{\varphi}$ and consequently $\bar{\eta}$ are linear functions.

$$\varphi_g^o[x(t); \alpha_{(g)}^o] = 0, \quad g = 1, \ldots, G, \quad t = 1, \ldots, T. \tag{1.9}$$

The structure S^o is called *observational structure.* We can similarly consider the equations

$$y(t) = \bar{\eta}^o[z(t), \pi^o], \qquad t = 1, \ldots, T, \tag{1.10}$$

where

$$\bar{\eta}^o \equiv \bar{\eta}^o_{\varphi^o} \tag{1.11}$$

and

$$\pi^o \equiv \bar{\pi}_{\varphi^o}(\alpha^o) \equiv \bar{\pi}(S^o); \tag{1.12}$$

the "observational reduced form" is given by $\bar{\eta}^o; \pi^o$. It follows from definitions that (1.10) is satisfied by observations X^o.

1.2.2.2. The form of the functions $\bar{\eta}_{\varphi^o}$ and $\bar{\pi}_{\varphi^o}$ is determined by the functions $\bar{\varphi}^o$ of the model. If the latter are linear so are the former. The model also provides restrictions on α^o, and these restrictions can be transformed, by (1.12), into equations or inequalities in π^o. If the model is linear, a unique set of parameters π^o will correspond to the set of structural parameters α^o. Furthermore, if T, the number of observations, is sufficiently large, the equations (1.9) together with the restrictions, determine the parameters π^o of the observational reduced form, given the observations X^o. We shall denote this operation by $\mathbb{P}_1$, so that

$$\mathbb{P}_1 X^o = \pi^o. \tag{1.13}$$

1.2.2.3. As stated in section *1.2.1.4*, a given reduced form may or may not determine the structure uniquely. Therefore, although, as just stated, the observational reduced form can be determined from the model, given the observations X^o (if their number T is sufficiently large), it may be impossible to determine a unique observational structure from the model and the observations *however large their number T.* It may sometimes be possible, in other words, to replace a given structure by any one of an infinite number of other structures without contradicting the observations. There exists thus a problem of *identifying a structure* (treated below in section *1.3*) but no problem of identifying a reduced form.

1.2.3. Structural changes and policies.

1.2.3.1. The observational structure S^o may be different from some structure S valid for a different period (or geographical area, etc.). Suppose we know the "structural changes" $\mathfrak{J}$, a transformation that carries S^o into S: $S = \mathfrak{J}S^o$. If, in addition, we know S^o from observations, we can obtain $S \equiv (\varphi, \alpha)$ and hence also the functions $\bar{\eta}_\varphi$ and $\bar{\pi}_\varphi$ and therefore the parameters π of the reduced form. It is then possible to evaluate[1] y for a given z.

1.2.3.2. We shall distinguish between two kinds of structural changes: the *controllable* ones, $\mathfrak{J}_c$; and the *uncontrollable* ones, $\mathfrak{J}_u$. The former ones are also called "structural policy;" the introduction, or abolition, of price control is an example. We can distinguish similarly between two sets of exogenous variables: the controllable ones, z_c; and the uncontrollable ones, z_u. The fixing of z_c is called "nonstructural" (or "routine") policy: for example the annual revision of tax rates [Marschak, 1947 A].

1.2.3.3. The policy-maker (on behalf of a government, of an individual firm, etc.) tries to maximize the "gain," or "welfare," ω, a certain function of the observables which, in principle, must be supposed to be known to him:

$$(1.14) \qquad \omega = \omega(y, z) = \omega\{\bar{\eta}_\varphi[z;\bar{\pi}_\varphi(\alpha)], z\}$$
$$= \omega_\varphi[z;\bar{\pi}_\varphi(\alpha)],$$

say. Thus the gain (welfare) function ω and the functions φ of the model combine to determine the function ω_φ of exogenous variables which is to be maximized, given the structure $(\bar{\varphi}, \alpha)$.

1.2.3.4. Suppose structural changes are neither intended nor expected for the period (or area) to which policy is to be applied, compared with the period (or area) of observation. (The policy consists, in this case, in fixing the value of z_c only: it is "nonstructural.") In this case, $\mathfrak{J}_c$ as well as $\mathfrak{J}_u$ is the identical transformation and we have $\varphi = \varphi^o$, $\alpha = \alpha^o$, and

$$(1.15) \qquad \pi = \pi_{\varphi^o} \quad \text{(a set of constants).}$$

Thus the gain

$$(1.16) \qquad \omega = \omega_{\varphi^o}(z;\pi) = \omega_{\varphi^o}(z_c, z_u;\pi)$$

---

[1] But see section *1.2.1.3* for a qualification.

can be affected only by variations in z_c. Best policy is the value $\hat{z}_c$ of z_c that gives ω its maximum value $\hat{\omega}$:

$$(1.17) \qquad \hat{\omega} = \max_{z_c} \omega_{\varphi^o}(z_c, z_u; \pi^o) = \omega_{\varphi^o}(\hat{z}_c, z_u; \pi^o).$$

By comparing the values of ω for varying z_c at fixed z_u, the best policy $\hat{z}_c$ can be determined for any given value of the uncontrollable variables z_u, provided the parameters π^o of the (observational) reduced form are known. But π^o can indeed be found from the observations X^o (section 1.2.2.2). The operation (1.13),

$$\mathfrak{P}_1 X^o = \pi^o,$$

depends on the model only and is called "predictive determination when structure is unchanged."[1] Operation $\mathfrak{P}_1$ provides, then, the parameters π^o, to be used for the choice of policy under unchanged structure.

1.2.3.5. As a rule, however, some structural changes will be intended or expected, or both. That is, neither $\mathfrak{J}_c$ nor $\mathfrak{J}_u$ will, in general, be the identical transformation. We have $S = \mathfrak{J} S^o$, where $\mathfrak{J} = \mathfrak{J}_c \mathfrak{J}_u$ (neglecting the question of the order in which the transformations are applied). Further, by (1.14) and (1.15), we have

$$(1.18) \qquad \omega = \omega_{\varphi}[z; \pi_{\varphi}(\alpha)] = \omega^*(z; S),$$

say, where the form of the function ω^* depends on the form of the gain function ω only. Further,

$$(1.19) \qquad \omega^*(z, S) = \omega^*(z_c, z_u; \mathfrak{J} S^o)$$

$$= \omega^{**}(z_c, z_u; \mathfrak{J}_c, \mathfrak{J}_u; \varphi^o, \alpha^o).$$

Best policy is defined by values $\hat{z}_c$, $\hat{\mathfrak{J}}_c$ that jointly maximize the gain. Let the maximum gain be

$$(1.20) \qquad \hat{\omega} = \omega^{**}(\hat{z}_c, z_u; \hat{\mathfrak{J}}_c, \mathfrak{J}_u; \varphi^o, \alpha^o).$$

---

[1]See [VI].

By comparing the values of ω for varying z_c, $\mathfrak{J}_c$, given the values of the uncontrollable exogenous variables and given the uncontrollable changes in structure, one can determine the best policies $(\hat{z}_c, \hat{\mathfrak{J}}_c)$, provided the observational structure S^o is known. The practical procedure is, in principle, as follows: from S^o and any given $\mathfrak{J} = \mathfrak{J}_c \mathfrak{J}_u$ derive the new structure $S = \mathfrak{J} S^o$ for the period of policy application; from S derive the parameters $\pi = \pi(S)$; and compute the variables y and the gain ω as in (1.14).

1.2.3.6. An operation $\mathfrak{s} X^o = S^o$ determining S^o from the observations X^o will be called *structural determination;* the question of its existence will be discussed in section *1.3.* If structural determination is possible, it is possible to derive the parameters π by applying in succession the operations $\mathfrak{s}$ and $\mathfrak{J}$:

$$\pi = \bar{\pi}(S) = \bar{\pi}(\mathfrak{J}\, \mathfrak{s}\; X^o) = \mathfrak{P}_{\mathfrak{J}}\, X^o, \tag{1.21}$$

say. The operation $\mathfrak{P}_{\mathfrak{J}}$ thus defined is called *predictive determination when structure undergoes a given change* $\mathfrak{J}$.

1.2.3.7. Structural determination provides a master key for predictive determination, and for the calculation of alternative gains, for *any* of the various possible structural changes. The structural changes to be considered are seldom known long in advance. Therefore, although formally $\pi = \bar{\pi}(\mathfrak{J}\mathfrak{s}\, X^o)$ can be computed without a stop, it is preferable and often essential to pause at the step $\mathfrak{s} X^o = S^o$. The knowledge of observational structure means greater flexibility with regard to various alternative policies. This is one reason why people are interested in any kind of theory!

1.2.3.8. However, the considered transformations $\mathfrak{J}$ (structural policies and uncontrollable structural changes) and the subset of variables relevant to the evaluation of the gain, may happen to be such as to make the knowledge of all parameters α^o of the structure S^o unnecessary. A partial knowledge of S^o – some elements of α^o, or perhaps some functions of them – may be all that is needed.

1.2.3.9. It was required in section *1.1.2* that the equations of the model describe plausible behavior of specified economic agents, thus making full use of our a priori knowledge of behavior (rational or otherwise). We now see a further practical reason for shunning relations that do not refer to specified economic agents. We call such relations "anonymous." Consider changes in human behavior, institutions, technology. The gain (personal or social) due to any such intended or expected change cannot be evaluated unless behavior, institutions, and technology are explicitly stated; such statements must be provided by the form, and by the values of parameters, of the equations of the model; that is, by the structure.

1.2.3.10. As an example, consider the following – admittedly oversimplified – model:

(1) demand for a commodity depends on its price and on national income;

(2) supply depends on price;

(3) demand equals supply;

and it is assumed that

(4) we can treat national income as exogenous.

Suppose we want to evaluate the effect of replacing free demand of the public by a fixed demand determined by the government; that is, relation (1) is replaced by

(1′) demand = a constant.

If we know the form and parameters of (2) we can evaluate, with the help of (1′) and (3), the price the suppliers will ask and the government will have to pay. Suppose, however, that instead of (1), (2), (3), we had at our disposal the following relation obtained by elimination of demand from (1), using (3), (2):

(5) price depends on income.

This "anonymous" relation (which, in this case, is a reduced form) can be computed from observations (section *1.2.2.2*) but cannot help to evaluate the effect of structural policy, i.e., the effect of replacing (1) by (1′). For another example, see [Marschak, 1947B].

1.3. Identification

1.3.1. It was remarked in section *1.2.2.3* that a given set of observations, however numerous, or a given reduced form, will not, in general, determine a unique structure. For a rigorous introduction to this *problem of identification* in the case of stochastic models we refer to [I–2] and [IV]. For the purposes of the present paper, it is convenient to approach the problem by using the concept of reduced form and studying it first in the nonstochastic case.

Consider equations (1.8) and the structure $S^o \equiv (\varphi^o, \alpha^o)$. Denote by $\mathfrak{S}^o_*$ the class of all structures $S^o_* \equiv (\varphi^o_*, \alpha^o_*)$ that are compatible with the model $\mathfrak{S}$ and yield the same reduced form as the structure S^o. The latter condition means that the following equations are satisfied identically in z:

$$(1.22) \qquad y = \bar{\eta}_{\varphi^o}[z\,;\, \bar{\pi}_{\varphi^o}(\alpha^o)] = \bar{\eta}_{\varphi^o_*}[z\,;\, \bar{\pi}_{\varphi^o_*}(\alpha^o_*)].$$

S^o is said to be *uniquely identifiable* by the model $\mathfrak{S}$ if S^o is the only element of $\mathfrak{S}^o_*$, i.e., if every $S^o_* = S^o$. Furthermore, S^o is said to be *incompletely identifiable* by the model $\mathfrak{S}$ if the class $\mathfrak{S}^o_*$ contains a nondenumerably infinite number of elements. Only in the former case is it possible to determine α^o uniquely from the parameters of the reduced form, $\pi^o = \bar{\pi}_{\varphi^o}(\alpha^o)$, provided the functions φ^o and the a priori restrictions on α^o are given.

1.3.2. The concept of identifiability can be easily extended to any subset of α^o, say $\alpha^o_{(i)}$ (*partial identification*): for example, all or some of the parameters of some of the equations (1.4) may be uniquely determinable from the parameters of the reduced form.

1.3.3. If a subset of α^o is nonidentifiable it is impossible to determine it from X^o *however large the number of observations* T. If α^o is completely and uniquely identifiable, it can be obtained from X^o using equations (1.9) jointly with the a priori restrictions, provided T is sufficiently large: this is structural determination, denoted in section *1.2.3.6* by $\mathfrak{D}$. A similar statement applies to any subset $\alpha^o_{(i)}$.

1.3.4. As an example, let $x = (y_1, y_2, z_1)$ be the coordinates of a point and let $\varphi_g(x) = 0$, $g = 1, 2$, be a pair of equations of two distinct planes. The observations on x will yield a set of collinear points which will determine a straight line – corresponding to (1.6) – permitting the prediction of y_1 or y_2 for a given z_1. But it will be impossible to reconstruct any particular pair of planes. A (partial) identification is, however, possible if, for example, it is known a priori that one of the planes is vertical; in which case this plane (but not the other one) is identifiable.

1.3.5. This corresponds to the economic example of section *1.2.3.10* with y_1 = demand (=supply), y_2 = price, z_1 = income. The parameters of (2) but not those of (1) are identifiable. If

(2) were modified into

(2′) supply depends on price and wage rate,

with wage rate assumed exogenous [Koopmans, 1945 p.451] all parameters of the structure would become identifiable.

1.3.6. The conditions of identifiability in a linear stochastic model are studied in [II-2]; their application to a nonstochastic model is easily derived. The most important criteria are supplied by the presence or absence of variables in each of the equations of the system (1.4). In particular, the occurrence of different exogenous variables in different equations contributes to identifiability.

1.3.7. Let the number of endogenous variables, $G = 1$; assume φ_1 is linear, and normalize the parameters α by choosing the coefficient of y_1 to be equal to 1:

(1.23) $$y_1 - \sum \alpha_k z_k = 0.$$

The *linear uniequational structure* (1.23) *is always identifiable*, and $\alpha = \pi$, provided there exist no linear relations between the z's. The proposition can be easily extended to nonlinear uniequational structures, apart from trivial modifications.

1.3.8. Predictive determination when structure is unchanged, i.e., the operation $\mathfrak{P}_1 X^o$ in (1.13) is possible, regardless of whether or not the observational structure S^o is identifiable.

1.3.9. Predictive determination when structure undergoes a known change $\mathfrak{J}$, i.e., the operation $\pi = \mathfrak{P}_{\mathfrak{J}} X^o$ in (1.21) is possible when all parameters α^o are identifiable, and impossible when none of them are identifiable.

1.3.10. However, the structural change $\mathfrak{J}$ and the gain function ω may be such as to require the knowledge of some but not all elements of α^o (section *1.2.3.8*); in this case partial identifiability (section *1.3.2*) is all that is needed. Also, $\mathfrak{J}$ and ω may be such as to require the knowledge, not of the parameters α^o themselves, but of some functions of them; in which case unique identifiability of every single parameter separately is not necessary for the choice of best policy.

1.3.11. An incomplete model has more endogenous variables than it has equations (section *1.1.4*). For example a uniequational model involving two or more endogenous variables is incomplete. The parameters of such a model form a subset of the parameters of some complete model. The parameters of the incomplete model may or may not be determinable from observations since the structure may or may not be partially identifiable (section *1.3.2*), by the complete model, with respect to the particular subset of its parameters.

1.4. Use of Experiments

1.4.0. We shall now distinguish between: *original* structure S^{oo}, *future* structure $S = \mathfrak{J} S^{oo}$, and *observational* structure $S^{o} = \mathbb{Q} S^{oo}$. In the preceding section observations were supposed to be made on the original structure, so that $\mathbb{Q}$ was the identical transformation. This is indeed the situation in nonexperimental science. Experiments, on the other hand, consist in applying certain transformations that change the original structure and in getting observations from the new structure $S^{o} = \mathbb{Q} S^{oo}$ that is thus obtained. The transformations $\mathbb{Q}$ are chosen in such a way as to permit predictive determination under future structure S without determining either S or the (possibly nonidentifiable) original structure S^{oo}. According to the nature of the transformation $\mathbb{Q}$, there are various types of experiments. Two particular types of experiments deserve our attention [Marschak, 1947 B].

1.4.1. Experiments of type I: imitation of future structure (example: wind tunnels for testing airplanes). Here $\mathbb{Q} = \mathfrak{J}$, hence $S^{o} = S$ and $\pi^{o} = \pi$. The structural change occurs between S^{oo} and S. To evaluate y for a given z under the future structure S, and thus to evaluate the gain ω, it suffices to determine π^{o} by the operation $\mathbb{P}_1 X^{o} = \pi$ (section *1.2.2.2*). This does not require identifiability of either S^{oo} or S.

1.4.2. Experiments of type II: creation of uniequational complete structure (example: controlled experiments in the physical laboratory). Let the original structure S^{oo} correspond to a model

$$(1.24) \qquad \varphi_g^{oo}(y, z; \alpha_{(g)}^{oo}) = 0, \qquad g = 1, \ldots, G.$$

Let $\mathbb{Q}_1$ be the operation of replacing all equations (1.24) but the first by the equations

$$(1.25) \qquad y_g = z_{K+g}, \qquad g = 2, \ldots, G,$$

where the quantities $(z_{K+1}, \ldots, z_{K+G}) \equiv$ vector z_* are fixed by the experimenter at various values $z_*(1), \ldots, z_*(T)$, these values being mutually independent. Denote the resulting observations by matrix X_1^o; they can be regarded as produced by an uni-equational complete structure involving a vector of parameters $\alpha_{(1)}^o$, as follows:

$$\mathbb{O}_1 S^{oo} = S_1^o = (\varphi_1^o, \alpha_{(1)}^o);$$

that is,

$$\varphi_1^o(y_1, z, z_*; \alpha_{(1)}^o) = 0, \tag{1.26}$$

where $\varphi_1^o = \varphi_1^{oo}$, and $\alpha_{(1)}^o = \alpha_{(1)}^{oo}$. The vector $\alpha_{(1)}^o$ of structural parameters is related by trivial transformations (e.g., dividing by a constant if φ_1^o is linear) to the vector of parameters $\pi_{(1)}^o$ ($= \alpha_{(1)}^{oo}$) of the reduced form

$$y_1 = \eta_{\varphi^o}(z, z_*; \pi_{(1)}^o). \tag{1.27}$$

Hence the subset $\alpha_{(1)}^{oo}$ ($= \alpha_{(1)}^o$) can be determined (section *1.3.7*) even though the set α^{oo} may be nonidentifiable.

If it is desired to determine the whole set α^{oo}, experiments $\mathbb{O}_1, \mathbb{O}_2, \ldots, \mathbb{O}_G$ can be applied in succession.

2. STOCHASTIC MODELS

2.1. *Random Disturbances*

2.1.1. The stochastic character of economic relations will be recognized even by an out-and-out determinist. His world is, in principle, ruled by a set of very many equations in very many variables (both economic and other). But to make his theory verifiable by observation he will have to shorten the set considerably. The numerous causes that determine the error incurred in measuring a variable are not listed separately; instead, their joint effect is represented by the probability distribution of the error, a random variable. Also, the numerous causes that determine, say, the velocity of a gas particle are conveniently represented by the probability distribution of this velocity, a random variable. The economist acts similarly. He allows for random errors of observation; and he represents the vagaries of, say, changing fashion by random "disturbances" or "shocks" that obey certain probability distributions; he thus cuts short the complicated causal explanation of why tastes fluctuate in the way they do.

The nondeterminist, on the other hand, will find it unnecessary to give any justification for the presence of random elements in economic models except by appealing directly to the "erratic," "unpredictable" character of certain types of events including human behavior; though he, too, will have to assume those events to be bound by certain probability distributions: even if actions are unpredictable, certain actions remain more probable than others.

2.1.2. Denote by $w \equiv (w_1, \ldots, w_J)$ the vector of nonobservable random disturbances affecting economic observations, and by $x \equiv (x_1, \ldots, x_N)$ the vector of observable variables. We shall call a stochastic model $\mathfrak{S}$ the a priori information on a system of equations

$$(2.1) \qquad \varphi_g(x, w;\ \alpha_{(g)}) = 0, \qquad g = 1, \ldots, G,$$

and on the joint distribution density

$$(2.2) \qquad f(w;\ \varepsilon),$$

where ε as well as $\alpha_{(g)}$ denote parameter vectors. As in section *1.1.0* we shall write $\alpha \equiv (\alpha_{(1)}, \ldots, \alpha_{(G)})$. We shall assume, in particular, that a priori information exists a) on the forms of the functions $\bar{\varphi} \equiv (\varphi_1, \ldots, \varphi_G)$ and f; and b) on some equations or inequalities in the parameters of these functions. We shall call ***structure*** all properties of the equations (2.1) and of the distribution (2.2) including the properties not known a priori.

If $w = 0$, we have the nonstochastic case treated in section *1* of this article.

2.1.3. If it is possible to substitute for w from (2.1), the distribution density function f of the disturbances can be transformed into the distribution density function of the observable vector x:

$$(2.3) \qquad g_x(x),$$

say. Given the form of the functions φ and f and given their parameters α, ε, the distribution function g_x and its parameters are determined. Certain parts of the present volume [II-2 and IV] deal with the converse problem: given the distribution (2.3) of the observables, determine the properties of the equations (2.1) and the properties of the distribution (2.2) of the disturbances. Well-known methods permit estimation of the distribution of the observables (2.3) from the observations. But to use the knowledge of that distribution to determine the properties of (2.1) and (2.2) raises a new problem in inference, that of identification. The relation between the stochastic model and the distribution of the observables will show certain analogies with the relation, already studied, between the nonstochastic model and the reduced form.

2.1.4. The random disturbances w may include as a subset a vector of additive *disturbances in variables* (additive errors of observations, or briefly, *errors*) $v = (v_1, \ldots, v_N)$. Thus the model (2.1), (2.2) can be rewritten, slightly changing notation,

$$\begin{aligned} &\varphi_g(x - v,\ w') = 0 \\ (2.4) \qquad & \\ &f(v,\ w'), \qquad\qquad g = 1, \ldots, G, \end{aligned}$$

where the vector w' is complementary to v in w, i.e., $w \equiv (v, w')$.

2.1.5. There are also random *disturbances in relations*, especially of the additive kind, which we call for brevity *shocks*, $(u_1, \ldots, u_G) \equiv u$, a subset of w'. If we denote by vector w'' the complement of u in w' so that $w \equiv (u,\ v,\ w'')$, we can rewrite the model (again slightly changing the meaning of φ):

$$\begin{aligned} &\varphi_g(x - v,\ w'') = u_g, \\ (2.5) \qquad & \\ &f(u,\ v,\ w''), \qquad\qquad g = 1, \ldots, G. \end{aligned}$$

2.1.6. If w'' is empty the model may be called "simple shock-and-error model" [T. W. Anderson and Hurwicz, 1947]. In the present volume the contributions of the Cowles Commission staff are confined to the more special case where w'' and v are empty: the "simple shock model." Other studies, [Frisch and Mudgett, 1931], [Koopmans, 1937], [Wald, 1940], [Tintner, 1946], [Reiersøl, 1945], and [Geary, 1942], may be said to deal with another special case: the "simple error model," in which both w'' and u are empty.

2.1.7. Although even the simpler stochastic models present considerable difficulties, economists will probably be right in calling the statisticians' attention to more complicated models, i.e., those in which w'' is not empty, and this for three reasons:

(1) there may be nonadditive errors of observation;

(2) there may be nonadditive shocks, since an economic relation can be disturbed in a variety of ways (for example, a linear relation, say a demand curve, can fluctuate owing to random changes in its constant term as well as in any of the coefficients, see [XVIII], [XIX]);

(3) there occur "prospective"[1] variables, such as prospective profits, prices, etc., that affect people's behavior and must enter the equations of the model.

As a rule the economist cannot observe these (except by difficult questioning of a sample of people). But he may have hypotheses describing the determination of each of these variables in the minds of people: such "forecast equations" [Hurwicz, 1946, p.130 ff.] would relate the "prospective" variables to certain "actual" variables (such as the current or lagged national income, etc.) or to the observations on the "actual" variables. These additional structural equations will be themselves subject to psychological fluctuations, expressed as random disturbances, additive or nonadditive. By use of the forecast equations, the prospective variables can be eliminated. The model thus derived can be used in predicting effects of structural changes occurring in equations other than the forecast equations. The derived model will involve functions of the random disturbances that occurred in the forecast equations. Even if they occurred additively in the forecast equations, these disturbances will enter the model, generally, in a nonadditive fashion, i.e., as elements of w'' in (2.5).

However, the remaining parts of this article and the bulk of the monograph itself will deal with simple shock models only, though some of the statements might be generalized to apply to the general model (2.5).

2.2. *Shock Model and Structure*

2.2.1. The introduction of shocks, i.e., additive random

[1]The word "anticipated" variables is sometimes suggested. But this would seem to exclude expectations that do not come true. The term "expected" might be confused with the statistical term, expected (= mean) values.

disturbances in relations (excluding other random disturbances), can be considered as weakening the nonstochastic hypothesis (1.1): the observable variables $x \equiv (x_1, \ldots, x_N)$ are related by a system of equations

(2.6) $$\varphi_g(x, \alpha_{(g)}) = u_g, \qquad g = 1, \ldots, G,$$

the distribution function (probability density) of the random vector $u \equiv (u_1, \ldots, u_G)$ being denoted by

(2.7) $$f(u; \varepsilon)$$

where $\alpha_{(g)}$ and ε are parameter vectors. Thus each equation (other than definitional equations that can be properly eliminated from the system) is subject to a disturbance.

A priori information on the functions and parameters in (2.6), (2.7) constitutes a shock *model*, $\mathfrak{S}$. A shock *structure*, S, consists of all properties of those functions and parameters:

$$S \equiv (\varphi, f, \alpha, \varepsilon),$$

where vector $\alpha \equiv (\alpha_{(1)}, \ldots, \alpha_{(G)})$. If, as will be assumed, the model supplies the forms of the functions (in addition to some a priori restrictions on the parameters), it is permissible also to write, more briefly, $S \equiv (\alpha, \varepsilon)$, provided φ, f do not change. The structural properties to be estimated from the observations will then be the numerical values of α, ε; or, more generally, some relations, not known a priori, between the parameters.

2.2.2. We can apply the earlier definition (section *1.1.4*) of a self-contained model ($G=N$) and a sectional model ($G<N$). But the definition of a complete model and of exogenous vs. endogenous variables must be supplemented. The "subsidiary" system of equations will, in general, involve random shocks of its own, so that (1.2) becomes

(2.8) $$\varphi_{G+k}(z) = u_k^{(k)}, \qquad k = 1, \ldots, K = N - G.$$

Rewriting the earlier condition (1.3) as

(2.9) $$\frac{\partial \varphi_{G+k}}{\partial y_g} = 0, \qquad g = 1, \ldots, G, \qquad k = 1, \ldots, K,$$

we see that this condition is not sufficient to make the variables z determinable outside of the system (2.6). To make them thus determinable, and the considered model complete, we must add the condition that the shocks u of the considered model and the shocks $u^{(z)} \equiv (u_1^{(z)}, \ldots, u_K^{(z)})$ of the subsidiary model be distributed independently:

$$f_x(u, u^{(z)}) = f(u) \cdot f_z(u^{(z)}), \tag{2.10}$$

where f_x, f, f_z are density functions. If both conditions (2.9) and (2.10) are fulfilled, the model

$$\begin{aligned} &\varphi_g(y, z; \alpha_{(g)}) = u_g, \\ &f(u; \varepsilon), \qquad\qquad g = 1, \ldots, G, \end{aligned} \tag{2.11}$$

is said to be complete, with y as the endogenous and z the exogenous set of observables.

2.2.3. The distribution (2.3), $g_x(x)$, of the observable vector can always be represented as a product of a conditional and a marginal distribution

$$g_x(x', x'') \equiv g(x' \mid x'') \cdot g_{x''}(x''), \tag{2.12}$$

where x', x'' is any pair of mutually complementary subsets of x. Suppose now that the model is complete; put $x' = y$, $x'' = z$, and denote by vector λ the parameters of the conditional distribution $g(y \mid z)$:

$$g_x(y, z) \equiv g(y \mid z; \lambda) \cdot g_z(z), \tag{2.13}$$

say. We observe that, by section 2.2.2, z is determined by the subsidiary model and is independent of u, the random disturbances of the considered model. The parameters of the ("subsidiary") marginal distribution $g_z(z)$ are not related to the parameters λ of the other factor in (2.13), the conditional distribution of the endogenous variables

$$g(y \mid z; \lambda). \tag{2.14}$$

This distribution is determined by the structure S, as is seen by solving the structural equations in (2.11) for y. The *reduced form*,

$$y = \bar{\eta}_{\varphi}[z, u; \bar{\pi}_{\varphi}(\alpha)], \tag{2.15}$$

differs from that of the nonstochastic case (1.8) inasmuch as it involves the random vector u. Given z, the value taken by $u \equiv (u_1, \ldots, u_G)$ determines the value taken by $y \equiv (y_1, \ldots, y_G)$. The distribution of y depends on the elements of the structure $S \equiv (f, \varphi, \alpha, \varepsilon)$; this can be expressed thus:

$$g(y \mid z; \lambda) = g_{f,\varphi}(y \mid z; \lambda), \tag{2.16}$$

$$\lambda = \bar{\lambda}(\alpha, \varepsilon) = \bar{\lambda}_{f,\varphi}(\alpha, \varepsilon) = \bar{\lambda}(S). \tag{2.17}$$

Thus the structure S determines the form and the parameters of the conditional distribution $g(y \mid z; \lambda)$.

On the other hand, S does not determine the distribution $g_z(z)$, the other factor in the product in (2.13). For the purpose of estimating S from observations, we have to consider not the joint distribution $g_x(y,z)$ but merely the conditional distribution $g(y|z)$: that is, we can disregard the possibly random character of z, and treat z as if it were fixed in repeated samples of y.

2.2.4. The reduced form (2.15) is a system of stochastic equations. In the nonstochastic case, the prediction of y from z involved knowledge of π, the parameters of the reduced form. In the stochastic case, the prediction of y consists in estimating the parameters (mean, variance, etc.) of the conditional distribution of y, given z. That is, λ, the parameters of the conditional distribution $g(y|z; \lambda)$ are to be estimated. Now consider (2.17), and let

$$\lambda^o = \bar{\lambda}(S^o) = \bar{\lambda}(\alpha^o, \varepsilon^o) \tag{2.18}$$

be the parameters of the conditional distribution during the observation period, that is, of the distribution

$$g^o[y(t) \mid z(t); \lambda^o], \qquad t = 1, \ldots, T. \tag{2.19}$$

It is possible to compute from observations an estimate l^o of the vector λ^o by an operation

$$\mathfrak{P}_1 X^o = l^o ; \tag{2.20}$$

operation $\mathfrak{P}_1$ is called *predictive estimation when structure is unchanged.* The notation is analogous to but not identical with that of (1.13) of the nonstochastic case. There we dealt with predictive determination of the reduced form, here with predictive estimation of the distribution of observables.

2.2.5. If changes of structure are intended or expected, the operation $\mathfrak{P}_1$ will, in general, not suffice for the prediction of y from z.

Suppose it is possible to compute estimates (a^o, e^o) of the parameter vectors $(\alpha^o, \varepsilon^o)$ of the observational structure S^o. Call this operation $\mathfrak{S}$:

$$\text{est } S^o \equiv (a^o, e^o) = \mathfrak{S} X^o . \tag{2.21}$$

$\mathfrak{S}$ thus denotes *structural estimation* (analogous to the structural determination of section *1.2.3.6*). Now let the observational structure undergo a change $\mathfrak{I}$: i.e., $\mathfrak{I} S^o = S$. The estimates l of the parameters λ of the new distribution of observables are obtained by the operation

$$\begin{aligned} l &= \bar{\lambda}(a, e) = \bar{l}[\mathfrak{I}(a^o, e^o)] \\ &= \bar{\lambda}(\mathfrak{I}\, \mathfrak{S} X^o) = \mathfrak{P}_{\mathfrak{I}} X^o, \end{aligned} \tag{2.22}$$

say; the operation $\mathfrak{P}_{\mathfrak{I}}$ is called *predictive estimation when structure undergoes a given change* $\mathfrak{I}$.

Whether optimal properties of the estimates a^o, e^o are preserved under subsequent transformations $\mathfrak{I}$, $\bar{\lambda}$, depends on the estimating methods; in particular, the function ψ of a maximum-likelihood estimate of a parameter θ is the maximum-likelihood estimate of the function $\psi(\theta)$.

2.2.6. One can interpret the operations (2.20) and (2.22) more generally. l^o and l may be used to denote, not the point estimates of the parameters λ^o and λ, but the estimates of the parameters of the joint distribution of those estimates or the estimates of their confidence regions. However, this interpretation need not be applied in the present article.

2.2.7. Structural estimation is needed, in particular, when

structural changes are intended, i.e., when *structural policies* are being undertaken. This was shown in section *1.2.3.5* with regard to structural determination when the model was nonstochastic. Section *2.5.1.3* illustrates the stochastic case.

We have to modify the earlier treatment since y and consequently the gain (welfare) ω as previously defined are random variables. For example, the real income (of a firm or of a nation, as the case may be) is the quotient of money income over price level, i.e., a function of endogenous variables y. Real income therefore depends on the value of exogenous variables z and on the distribution $g(y \mid z\,;\,\lambda)$, and is a random variable. We must, accordingly, redefine the gain (welfare) ω, i.e., the quantity which the policy-maker tries to maximize. The policy-maker will prefer a high mean value of real income to a low mean value; he may possibly at the same time prefer a small variance of income to a large variance. In short, he will prefer certain probability distributions of income to others. He will maximize a quantity ω that is a functional of the probability distribution function of income.[1] But the probability distribution of income depends on the value of the exogenous variables z and on the distribution $g(y \mid z\,;\,\lambda)$. Since the form of g is fixed a priori (depending on the function forms φ, f of the model), the gain ω is a known function of the distribution parameters λ and of z only. By (2.17) the parameters λ depend on the structure S in a way uniquely determined by the model. The structure S is, in turn, (analogously to section *1.2*) the result of controlled or uncontrolled changes applied to the observational structure. Thus

$$\lambda = \bar{\lambda}(S) = \bar{\lambda}(\mathfrak{J}_c \mathfrak{J}_u S^o). \tag{2.23}$$

Furthermore, the exogenous variables can be either controlled (z_c) or uncontrolled (z_u) by the policy-maker. His aim is thus to get

$$\hat{\omega} = \omega(\hat{z}_c, z_u, \hat{\mathfrak{J}}_c \mathfrak{J}_u S^o), \tag{2.24}$$

where ω is a known gain function, and $\hat{z}_c$, $\hat{\mathfrak{J}}_c$ are, respectively, the optimal values of controllable exogenous variables and of

[1] Compare [Hurwicz, 1946, p.132], [Tintner, 1942]. This statement can be shown to be implied in the statement that the mean value of utility of real income is maximized.

controllable structural changes. That is, $\hat{\omega}$ is a maximum of ω with respect to policies $(z_c, \mathfrak{Z}_c)$.

To estimate the best policy $(\hat{z}_c, \hat{\mathfrak{Z}}_c)$, for a given set $(z_u, \mathfrak{Z}_u)$, of uncontrolled exogenous variables and uncontrolled structural changes, one has to have an estimate of the observational structure S^o, i.e., to have the estimates (a^o, e^o) of the observational structural parameters $(\alpha^o, \varepsilon^o)$.

In practice, the maximization of ω with respect to policies consists in estimating for each considered policy $(z_c, \mathfrak{Z}_c)$, the parameters λ of the conditional distribution of y given z, and the consequent probability distribution of (say) real income. The policy which gives the probability distribution that is preferable to all others is then chosen.

2.2.8. *Relation between regression, reduced form, and structural equations.* Sometimes the series of alternative policies considered will be such as to make it unnecessary to know the joint conditional G-variate distribution (2.14) of all endogenous variables after the change in structure. It may suffice to know the distribution of some particular subset, say $y_{(d)}$ of y, that is, the distribution

(2.25) $$g_{(d)}(y_{(d)}, z; \lambda_{(d)}).$$

Such conditional distribution is easily derived from the general conditional distribution (2.14).[1] The set $y_{(d)}$ is called the *predictand;* the *predictor* is, in this case, the whole exogenous set z. Practical importance may be attached in particular to the simplest case, viz., the univariate conditional distributions

(2.26) $$g_1(y_1 \mid z; \lambda_1), \quad . \ . \ . \ . \ , \quad g_G(y_G \mid z; \lambda_G).$$

In particular, one may be interested in the first moments of such distributions, e.g., in the expectation

(2.27) $$\mathcal{E}(y_1 \mid z) = R(z; \chi_{(1)}).$$

R is the regression function of y_1 on z. Its parameters, denoted here by the vector $\chi_{(1)}$, are called regression coefficients if R happens to be linear, so that, writing $\chi_{(1)} \equiv (\chi_{10}, \chi_{11}, \ldots, \chi_{1K})$,

[1] See [VI].

(2.28) $$\mathcal{E}(y_1 \mid z) = \sum_1^K \chi_{1k} z_k + \chi_{10}.$$

A sufficient condition for the function R in (2.27) to be linear is that the functions φ, f of the model be linear and normal, respectively. We can then conveniently split the structural coefficients α into two subsets $\beta \equiv \{\beta_{gh}\}$ and $\gamma \equiv \{\gamma_{gk}\}$, $(g,h = 1, \ldots, G;\ k = 0, \ldots, K)$, denoting respectively the coefficients of endogenous and of exogenous variables; further we can choose the constant terms γ_{g0} so as to make $\mathcal{E}u = 0$. The model (2.11) becomes:

(2.29) $$\sum_{h=1}^{G} \beta_{gh} y_h + \sum_{k=1}^{K} \gamma_{gk} z_k + \gamma_{g0} = u_g, \quad g = 1, \ldots, G,$$

$$f(u),$$

where $f(u)$ is normal. In this case the reduced form (2.15) will also be linear; for example the first equation of the reduced form will be

(2.30) $$y_1 = \sum_1^K \pi_{1k} z_k + \pi_{10} + \text{a linear function of } u.$$

Taking the expectation of y_1 given z, we find that the regression coefficients $\chi_{(1)}$ and the coefficients $\pi_{(1)}$ of the reduced form coincide: see (2.28).

Furthermore, suppose our complete model consists of one equation only ($G = 1$); if we choose the units of the z's so as to make $\beta_{11} = 1$, we can write the unique structural equation as

(2.31) $$y_1 - \sum_{k=0}^{K} \gamma_{1k} z_k - \gamma_{10} = u_1.$$

In this particular case the coefficients π_1 of the reduced form will coincide not only with the regression coefficients $\chi_{(1)}$ but also with the structural coefficients $\gamma_{(1)}$. [This applies, of course, also to the case where a complete model involving $G > 1$ variables can be split into G uniequational complete models such as (2.31); in each of which, one endogenous variable depends on exogenous variables only.] In general, however, there will be no such coincidence. An example will be given in section 2.5.1.2.

2.2.9. *Predicting exogenous variables.* If the conditional distribution (2.19) estimated from past observations is known to remain valid for $t > T$, this distribution, or any of its practically relevant conditional distributions (2.25) can be used, respectively, as the future distribution of y, or of a subset $y_{(d)}$, for given future values of z.

However, it may also be desirable to make predictions about exogenous variables, in particular the uncontrolled ones, z_u. It is seen from section 2.2.7 that the choice of best policy presupposes the knowledge of uncontrolled factors: z_u as well as $\mathfrak{Z}_u$. It is possible to estimate future values of the variables z_u if they are related to observable variables that do not enter the model considered. For example, suppose prediction is done on behalf of a firm to help it in the choice of its policies. The firm's sales is an endogenous variable in the model describing the demand and production conditions for the firm's product. This model contains national income as an exogenous variable which the firm cannot control. The national income itself is an endogenous variable of another model; this may also include exogenous variables such as foreign crops (which affect the demand for this country's exports of manufactured goods, and hence affect this country's income). Thus the firm will be interested in predicting national income, using distributions such as (2.26), where y_1 would denote national income, and z will include foreign crops z_1. However, another variable endogenous to the national economy model – e.g., the imports y_2 – can be usefully included in the predictor set, if, in the future, information on national income becomes available later than information on imports. The prediction of y_1 for a given z and a specified value of y_2 is more accurate than the prediction of y_1 from z with the value of y_2 unspecified. Thus, it may be useful to derive from the observational distribution $g^o(y \mid z)$ a distribution

$$g^o_{(d,r)}(y_{(d)} \mid y_{(r)}, z), \tag{2.32}$$

say; this distribution is more general than (2.25) in that its predictor set (y_r, z) includes endogenous variables, $y_{(r)}$. In particular, we may derive a regression equation to estimate

$$\mathcal{E}(y_1 \mid y_2, z). \tag{2.33}$$

We may also want to estimate a variable exogenous not only to the relevant model (e.g., the model of the firm) but also to the model (e.g., of the national economy) from the variables of which it has to be estimated. For example, foreign crops z_1 may be of direct interest to the firm and also may influence national imports y_2; but observations on factors determining foreign crops may be unavailable. If data on y_2 become known earlier than those on z_1, z_1 can be estimated from y_2. This case differs from the preceding one inasmuch as z_1 may be a nonstochastic variable. However, it may be possible to use the past distribution $g^o(y \mid z ; \lambda^o)$ of the observables to derive a confidence region for z_1 (looked upon as a parameter): values of z_1 such as would give rise to the known values of y_2 only with a small probability (lower than a preassigned significance level) will lie outside the confidence limits for z_1.

2.2.9.1. These remarks are of some importance in view of many attempts to use endogenous variables as predictors; e.g., to predict national income from contemporaneous imports, or retail sales, etc. It may be possible to determine such a relation from past observations. But its usefulness is limited to the cases just mentioned. To choose between various national policies, it cannot be useful to be able to predict national income from imports, since the latter are themselves affected by any policy chosen. For purposes of private policies, on the other hand, such prediction can be useful. But such prediction is possible only inasmuch as information on imports is available earlier than that on national income; and only if, in addition, the relevant aspects of the national economic structure can be assumed unchanged between the period of observation and the time when the private policy is going to be applied. The same considerations are valid for the case when, because of a lag in the available data, variables endogenous to the national economy are used to estimate exogenous ones.

2.3. *Identification*

2.3.1. In section *1.3* it was shown for nonstochastic models that structure can be determined to the extent that the a priori conditions (i.e., the model) suffice to make the structure uniquely identifiable. In this case, only one structure will correspond to a given reduced form. Or, in terms of parameters: if only one set α^o corresponds to a given set π^o, then, since π^o can always be determined from (sufficiently numerous) observations, the set α^o can also be so determined.

In the stochastic case, a structure is said to be uniquely identifiable by the model if only one structure compatible with the model corresponds to a given conditional distribution of the observations. Or, in terms of parameters: if only one set α^o, ε^o, corresponds to a given set λ^o, then, since λ^o can be estimated from the observations, the structural parameters α^o, ε^o can also be so estimated.

2.3.2. The structural transformations $\mathfrak{J}_c$, $\mathfrak{J}_u$ and the gain functional ω may be such as to make identifiability of all parameters α^o, ε^o unnecessary for the choice of best policy. Section *1.3.10* on partial identifiability applies accordingly.

2.3.3. If the structure, or a part of it, is not identifiable its estimation is not possible, however numerous the observations on the variables treated as observables in the model. However, observations on other variables may provide additional information (which is a priori with respect to the structure considered; see section *1.1.0*) such as to make the structure, or its relevant part, identifiable. The failure of a model to identify the structure is not a ground for rejecting the model; rather, it calls for additional information, to be provided by a new type of observations. Suppose, for example, that the relation describing the investment behavior of the aggregate of American firms is not identifiable within a model that involves, in addition to this relation, relations describing the behavior of consumers, lenders, etc. This would make it necessary to add a new type of information, based, e.g., on records of single firms, or on interviews with businessmen.

2.3.4. The a priori information provided by the model may involve the parameters α of the structural equations as well as the parameters ε of the shock distribution. If no a priori information on the parameters ε of the shock distribution exists, and if a nonstochastic structure

$$\varphi_g(y, z; \alpha_{(g)}) = 0, \qquad g = 1, \ldots, G, \tag{2.34}$$

is not completely identifiable, then the parameters α of the stochastic structure

$$\text{(2.35)} \qquad \begin{aligned} &\varphi_g(y,\ z;\ \alpha_{(g)}) = u_g\,, \\ &f(u\,;\,\varepsilon), \qquad\qquad g = 1,\ \ldots,\ G, \end{aligned}$$

will also not be completely identifiable; but information on the distribution $f(u;\varepsilon)$, if available, may make (2.35) completely identifiable. Thus the example in section *1.3.5* may or may not hold for the stochastic case if information on the shock distribution is available: such as the knowledge that the shocks on the demand side are not correlated with those on the supply side; or knowledge of the ratio between the variances, etc.: [Frisch, 1933], [Mann and Wald, esp. p.219], [Marschak and Andrews, §§ 18 – 22], and sections *2.5.1.1, 2.5.1.4* below.

2.3.5. In particular, a uniequational complete model is completely identifiable, apart from trivial transformations (section *1.3.7*). Hence the remarks in section *1.4.2*, on the role of experiments (of type II) in making the observational structure identifiable, will apply. If, in addition (section *2.2.8*), the uniequational complete model generated by an experiment is linear with shocks distributed normally, the structural coefficients will not only be identifiable but will coincide with the regression coefficients. The model can then also be regarded as one in which one (the "dependent") variable is subject to measurement errors while all others are free from such errors: a familiar case in the history of the application of statistics to experiments. It arises in nonexperimental science only if the mechanism producing the observations can be adequately represented by a model involving only one nonlagged endogenous variable.

2.4. *Dynamic Models*

2.4.1. A model is called dynamic if it has at least one of the following two properties: 1) at least one observable variable occurs in the structural equations with values taken at various points of time (this includes the case of time derivatives, differences, and integrals over time); 2) at least one equation contains functions of time (trend, seasonal fluctuations, etc.). If the first property is present the model is called *multitemporal*; if both properties are absent, it is called *unitemporal*.

2.4.2. We obtain a *discrete multitemporal* shock model if the equations in (2.11) are replaced by

$$\varphi_g[y'(t), \ldots, y'(t-\tau_{y'}), z'(t), \ldots, z'(t-\tau_{z'}); \alpha_{(g)}] = u_g(t), \tag{2.36}$$

and the distribution of shocks in (2.11) by

$$f[u(t), \ldots, u(t-\tau_{y'}); \varepsilon]. \tag{2.37}$$

The time interval between two successive observations is chosen as a time unit; time lags smaller than 1 are not admitted by the model; $\tau_{y'}$ and $\tau_{z'}$ denote the largest time lag with which the corresponding variables occur; and t takes all integral values through the time interval during which the model is supposed to be valid.

2.4.3. A case of great practical importance arises when successive shocks are mutually independent; that is,

$$\begin{aligned} &f[u(t), u(t-1), \ldots, u(t-\tau_{y'})] \\ &= f[u(t)]\cdot f[u(t-1)] \cdot \cdot \cdot f[u(t-\tau_y)], \end{aligned} \tag{2.38}$$

say. If this condition is fulfilled then, as shown in [I-*1*] and [XVII], lagged variables can be treated as additional variables in judging the identifiability of a structure. Lagged endogenous variables can then be treated as if they were fixed in repeated samples (i.e., like exogenous variables). The following model can then be regarded as a complete one:

$$\varphi_g[y(t), z(t); \alpha_{(g)}] = u_g(t), \quad g = 1, \ldots, G, \tag{2.39}$$

$$f[u(t); \varepsilon], \tag{2.40}$$

where the notation in (2.36) has been changed as follows:

$$\begin{aligned} y'(t) &\equiv y(t) \equiv \text{“jointly dependent variables,”} \\ [y'(t-1), \ldots, y'(t-\tau_{y'}), z'(t), \ldots, z'(t-\tau_{z'})] &\equiv z(t) \\ &\equiv \text{“predetermined variables,”} \end{aligned} \tag{2.41}$$

following Koopmans' terminology [XVII].

2.4.4. It is plausible to assume, as in (2.38), the statistical independence of successive shocks if the time interval between two successive observations is not too short. It would be more realistic to study models in which at least some of the observables $y(t)$, $z(t)$, and also some of the shocks $u(t)$ are functions of a continuous time variable. Some properties of such continuous stochastic models are outlined in [XVI]. However, the remainder of this volume deals with discrete models and most of the time assumes condition (2.38) to be valid.

2.4.5. The reduced form defined in (2.15) applies to the multitemporal model with variables $y(t)$ and $z(t)$ defined by (2.41). The variables on the right-hand side of the reduced form (the predictor set) occur with lags no higher than those in the structural equations. However, other kinds of predictor sets can be considered. In the *separated form* each nonlagged variable is expressed as depending only on its own lagged values and on the exogenous variables with or without lags; this is possible because, by "shifting time back," one can obtain enough structural equations to eliminate the lagged values of other endogenous variables. One can go further and eliminate the lagged values of all endogenous variables, leaving only the exogenous variables (with and without lags) as the predictor set: the *resolved form*.

As shown by Tinbergen, the separated form (his "final equation") can be used to build up, year by year, the path of a single endogenous variable beginning with given initial values and giving effect every year to changes in exogenous variables; that is, the solution of each equation of the reduced form (looked upon as a difference equation) expresses the predictand variable as a function of time ("cyclical fluctuations") and of exogenous variables.

Corresponding to the reduced, the separated, and the resolved forms in which a multitemporal model can be written, there are three kinds of distributions with which predictive estimation under unchanged structure can be concerned, and which can be estimated (in principle) regardless of whether the structure is or is not identifiable. However, as will be shown below (section 2.5.3), only in the case of reduced form, but not in the case of separated and of resolved form, is the estimation amenable to known methods.

2.5. *Estimation*

2.5.0. Before we summarize the results obtained in this

volume with regard to the estimation of relevant parameters from finite samples, we shall restate and illustrate certain population properties. We shall then discuss the estimation of regression equations, and of complete and incomplete structures, and add a few remarks on the choice of models.

2.5.1. Population properties. Important differences between, on the one hand, the structural parameters α, and, on the other, the parameters π of the reduced form and the regression parameters χ, will be briefly restated. (It is understood that the parameters to be treated here are generated by the observational structure S^o; but the superscript ^{o} is omitted from the symbols where no ambiguity arises.) To fix the ideas we shall assume the model to be linear with normally distributed shocks and shall give examples when certain elements of χ or π are or are not equal to some elements of α.

While χ and π can always be estimated from observations, the same is not true of the structural parameters α unless they are identifiable. Furthermore (section 2.2.8) the coefficients $\pi_{(1)}$, of that equation of the reduced form which determines the endogenous variable y_1, are equal to the coefficients $\chi_{(1)}$ of the corresponding regression equation. If there exists a structural equation relating y_1 to the exogenous subset z and containing no endogenous variables, its coefficients $\alpha_{(1)}$ will also be equal to $\chi_{(1)}$; provided this structural equation, if stated together with the distribution – $f_1(u_1)$, say – of its shock-variable, constitutes a complete model. The latter condition implies (section 2.2.2) that u_1 is distributed independently of the shock variables $u_2, \ldots, u_G$ entering the remaining structural equations. If the structural equation considered contains lagged endogenous variables, and if successive shocks are independent, the statements just made can be extended so as to include in z not only the exogenous but also the lagged endogenous variables (section 2.4.3).

For example, structural and regression coefficients will coincide in each of the following complete models (each is assumed to be linear, with successive shocks independent and normally distributed; the choice of the "dependent" variable in the regression will be indicated in each case by the phrase describing the model). Of these four models, the first three are uniequational, while the last one can be partitioned into two uniequational complete models.[1]

[1] A more complicated model partitionable into four uniequational models is given in [Bentzel and Wold, p.104].

(1) Current yield per acre depends on current temperature and current rainfall.

(2) Current yield per acre depends on current temperature and rainfall, and also on the amount of fertilizers fixed by the experimenter.

(3) Current yield per acre depends on current and past temperature and rainfall, and on the decision farmers made in the previous year regarding the amount of fertilizers.

(4) Market price of a nonstorable good depends on supply (demand equation); supply depends on previous year's price (supply equation); the behavior of buyers and that of sellers undergo mutually independent shocks.

2.5.1.1. In the following example[1] on the other hand, each structural equation contains more than one endogenous variable, and cannot therefore (taken together with the distribution of its shock variable) be regarded as a complete model in itself; but the two equations together constitute a complete model. We shall show that the structural coefficients will not be equal to any of the regression coefficients. Let y_1 (national product, identical with national income, or the supply of all goods) and y_2 (demand for all goods) obey the following equations for any time t:

$$y_2(t) - \beta_1 y_1(t) - \beta_0 = u_1(t) \quad \text{(behavior of buyers)},$$

$$y_2(t) - \quad y_1(t) \qquad = u_2(t) \quad \text{(behavior of producers)}.$$

The model does not contain predetermined variables. Its random shocks are $u_1(t)$ ("shift of demand") and $u_2(t)$ ("failure to adjust production to demand"). Each pair of values $u_1(t), u_2(t)$ determines

$$y_1(t) = [u_1(t) - u_2(t) + \beta_0] \; / \; (1 - \beta_1),$$

$$y_2(t) = [u_1(t) - \beta_1 u_2(t) + \beta_0] \; / \; (1 - \beta_1).$$

Suppose successive shocks are independent and the joint distribution $f[u_1(t), u_2(t)]$ of the shocks is normal and independent of time.

[1] For more fully developed examples from the same branch of economics see [Haavelmo, 1947 A].

Let its moments be

(2.42) $\mathcal{E}\, u_1(t)\, u_2(t) = 0; \qquad \mathcal{E}\, u_1^2(t) = \sigma_{11}; \qquad \mathcal{E}\, u_2^2(t) = \sigma_{22}.$

Then the distribution $g(y_1, y_2)$ of the observables is normal and has moments

(2.43)
$$\mathcal{E} y_1 \equiv \mathcal{E} y_2 = \beta_0 / (1-\beta_1); \qquad \sigma_{y_1 y_2} = (\sigma_{11} + \beta_1 \sigma_{22}) / (1-\beta_1)^2;$$
$$\sigma_{y_1 y_1} = (\sigma_{11} + \sigma_{22}) / (1-\beta_1)^2; \qquad \sigma_{y_2 y_2} = (\sigma_{11} + \beta_1^2 \sigma_{22}) / (1-\beta_1)^2.$$

These are four mutually independent equations (not counting the identity $\mathcal{E} y_1 \equiv \mathcal{E} y_2$) to determine the four unknown structural parameters $S = (\beta_1, \beta_0, \sigma_{11}, \sigma_{22})$ from the parameters of the distribution $g(y_1, y_2)$ of the observables. The structural parameters are completely identifiable.

2.5.1.2. Consider now the regression of y_2 on y_1:

$$\mathcal{E}(y_2 \mid y_1) = \chi_1 y_1 + \chi_0,$$

say, and

(2.44) $\chi_1 = \sigma_{y_1 y_2} / \sigma_{y_1 y_1} = (\sigma_{11} + \beta_1 \sigma_{22}) / (\sigma_{11} + \sigma_{22}),$

which approaches β_1 or 1 as $\sigma_{11} / \sigma_{22} \to 0$ or $\to \infty$, respectively. Thus β_1, the "marginal propensity to spend," is distinct from the regression coefficient χ_1 of spending (y_2) on income (y_1), except in a limiting case when the behavior of buyers is not subject to random shocks (while the behavior of producers is).

2.5.1.3. This example also illustrates the different practical purposes of estimating β_1, β_0 or χ_1, χ_0. Suppose a firm expects a given change in the economic structure; for example, a rise in the "marginal propensity to spend" whereby β_1 will be replaced by $k\beta_1$; suppose the other three structural parameters are known to stay unchanged. If the firm wants to use old observations on y_1, y_2 to predict the distribution of these variables under the new circumstances, it will have first to obtain β_1, β_0, σ_{11}, σ_{22} from observations, and then insert the new set of structural parameters

$(k\beta_1, \beta_0, \sigma_{11}, \sigma_{22})$ into (2.43). Furthermore, if the firm wants to estimate national spending from national income (because the latter is published earlier than the former; section *2.2.9.1*), it will have to use, not the old regression coefficient (2.44), but a new regression coefficient, $(\sigma_{11} + k\beta_1\sigma_{22})/(\sigma_{11} + \sigma_{22})$. This cannot be obtained from χ_1, but can be obtained from the old structural parameters $(\beta_1, \beta_0, \sigma_{11}, \sigma_{22})$ since k is known. Only if the structure is known to remain unchanged can χ_1 be used.

2.5.*1*.*4*. If the structure were not identifiable, there would be no way to predict effects of known structural changes. This would be the case, for example, if the a priori assumption – in (2.42) – of noncorrelated shocks could not be admitted. We should then have five structural parameters to determine; the four equations (2.43) would therefore not suffice. On the other hand, the structure would be identifiable, even with the noncorrelation assumption dropped, if a different predetermined variable had been introduced into each of the two equations of the model.

2.5.2. *Estimation of regression coefficients.* When structure is known to remain unchanged, estimates of regression coefficients χ, together with other parameters of the distribution of observables, help to estimate the future distribution of predictand variables for given values of others, and hence to estimate future positions of maximum gain. When, on the other hand, structure is known to undergo a given change, the estimation of future values of variables requires knowledge of the structural parameters (α, ε). We have seen (section 2.2.*8*) that in the special case of certain uniequational complete models (and of models that can be decomposed into such uniequational complete models), $\alpha = \chi$. In this case, if $q = q(X^o)$ is a function of observations X^o that is an unbiased estimate of the parameters χ, then $\mathcal{E}q = \chi = \alpha$; that is, q can serve as an unbiased estimate of structural parameters. In general, however, there is no equality between α and χ. Therefore a function of observations that is an unbiased estimate of χ cannot be an unbiased estimate of α, even for infinitely large samples. If such a function is used as an estimate of α for predictive estimation under a structure subjected to given changes, the future endogenous variables, and hence the future gains, will be estimated with a bias; consequently, other than optimal policies will be chosen.

This does not make the estimation of regression coefficients useless: uniequational complete models of the appropriate type may exist; and structures do not always change. Hence our interest in reconsidering the properties of regression coefficients.

In a general multitemporal model, the variables are connected by a set of equations

$$\varphi_g[y_1(t), \ldots, y_1(t-\tau_1), y_2(t), \ldots, y_G(t-\tau_G), z] = u_g,$$

$$g = 1, \ldots, G,$$

where z denotes exogenous variables (lagged as well as nonlagged). The regression equation for y_1 - denoting by $(y_{(r)}, z)$ the whole predictor set - is

$$\mathcal{E}[y_1(t) \mid y_{(r)}, z] = R(y_{(r)}, z),$$

which has not been studied in general. The simplest case is that of the linear regression equation with $y_{(r)}$ empty:

$$\text{(2.45)} \qquad \mathcal{E}[y_1(t) \mid z] = \sum_1^K \chi_{1k} z_k + \chi_{10};$$

it is satisfied when $y_1(t)$ and z are connected by an uniequational unitemporal model, cf. (2.31):

$$\text{(2.46)} \qquad y_1(t) - \sum_1^K \gamma_{1k} z_k - \gamma_{10} = u_1(t),$$

provided successive shocks $u_1(t)$, $u_1(t+1)$, ..., are normally and independently distributed. Certain optimal properties of the least-squares estimate of χ $(=\gamma)$ are well established for this case. The case has to be generalized in two important directions (possibly, but not necessarily, preserving the assumptions of linearity and normality of the structure): 1) the complete model may be made multiequational; 2) the complete model may be made multitemporal.

In the case of multiequational (but unitemporal) model, the properties of the least-squares estimate and the maximum-likelihood estimate of the regression coefficients, and in particular the conditions of equivalence of these two estimates, have been studied in [VI] and [VII] by Hurwicz and Koopmans for large as well as small samples.

For the case of a uniequational multitemporal model with only one lag,

$$y_1(t) = \alpha y_1(t-1) + u_1(t), \tag{2.47}$$

where $u_1(t)$ is distributed normally with a constant variance and with zero covariances $\mathcal{E} u_1(t) u_1(t')$, $t \neq t'$, Hurwicz [XV] shows that the least-squares estimate of the regression (and structural) coefficient α has a bias. For $T = 20$ (a length of time series common to economic studies based on annual data of the interwar period), the bias approaches 9 per cent as $\alpha \to 0$. The bias seems to disappear as the sample increases or as $\alpha \to 1$.

2.5.3. This bias in the regression estimates from short time series will in general exist in every multitemporal model. If the model is multiequational, there arises, in addition, the question of the *choice of predictors*. Each predictand variable can be expressed as a function of the predictor variables and of the shock variables as in (2.15) and (2.30). Only contemporary shock variables will be involved provided the predictor variables occur with the same lags as those of the structural equations. Such is the case with the reduced form (see section 2.4.5). The predictand will then be related to the predictor by an equation such as (2.30), where the z's would stand for exogenous as well as lagged endogenous variables; and where the successive random terms will be independent. In this case, least-squares large-sample estimates of the coefficients of the variables will have the usual optimal properties. But it is different in the case of the "resolved" and the "separated" forms (section 2.4.5). In these cases, structural shocks relating to various points of time will be contained in the same equation, as the result of eliminating certain endogenous variables after replacing t by $t-1$, $t-2$, ..., or "shifting the time back." Therefore successive random terms of a "resolved" or a "separated" form are not independent; and the least-squares estimates of corresponding regression equations will, in general, be biased.[1]

2.5.4. As stated in section 2.3.2, expected or intended structural changes may be of such a nature that the estimation of all the parameters of a complete model is not necessary for purposes of

[1] Pointed out by Haavelmo. See [Klein, 1946 B, p.303 ff.].

prediction and policy: hence the practical importance of *partial structural estimation,* i.e., the estimation of a selected set of parameters. Such estimation is possible if the set of parameters in question is identifiable, even though some or all of the remaining parameters may not be identifiable. In particular, the estimation of the parameters of a few selected structural equations, or even of a single structural equation (e.g., demand equation) has an obvious practical interest.

On the other hand, the expected or intended changes of structure may not be known long beforehand. It is therefore often desirable to have estimated the structure completely.

2.5.5. The method of *complete structural estimation* most fully discussed in the volume is that of maximum likelihood. The joint probability density of all the observed values of the variables is regarded as a function (the likelihood function) of the structural parameters. Those values of the parameters for which this function attains its highest value are called maximum-likelihood estimates. In important classes of cases these estimates are "consistent" (they converge with probability 1 to the true values in the limit for infinitely large samples) and "efficient" (they have, in large samples, variances that never exceed those of any other normally distributed estimate). In [Mann and Wald] are discussed the maximum-likelihood estimates obtained when all available a priori information is used and when the model is as follows: a completely identifiable complete system of linear difference equations with no exogenous variables; shocks mutually independent; the model generates a stationary process, i.e., the observable variables would converge in time to constant values if shocks were absent. These authors proved the consistency (but not the efficiency) of the estimates under these conditions; they also showed that, in the absence of a priori restrictions, the structure is not identifiable. In [II-*3*] Koopmans and Rubin estimate the parameters of a complete linear model that is more general owing to the introduction of exogenous variables. Their discussion also covers the estimation of the parameters of some identifiable structural equations if other equations of the complete system are not identifiable. They give a proof of the consistency of the estimates which takes account of these two generalizing assumptions. In [XIV] Rubin extends the proof to a simple case of a nonstationary ("explosive") process.

There is an alternative maximum-likelihood method for obtaining consistent estimates of structural parameters: each equation of the structure is estimated separately via the reduced form as described in section *2.5.6*. For each equation this procedure has to use at least as much a priori information as is necessary to make that equation identifiable; but it leaves unused a (possibly large) part of the remaining a priori information. This method will therefore lead, in general, to less efficient estimates (i.e., larger sampling variances of the estimates) than the maximum-likelihood method using all information described above, although both kinds of estimates have the consistency property. For brevity, we call the two estimation methods "information-preserving maximum-likelihood estimation" and "limited-information maximum-likelihood estimation," respectively. The latter method is also known as the "method of reduced forms."

The practical usefulness of the consistency property of estimates diminishes if the sample becomes small. Small sample properties of structural estimates have not been studied, except [XV] for the uniequational multitemporal model, equation (2.47) of the present article. The bias found in the estimate in this case suggests that in general both proposed methods of estimating multitemporal structures are biased if applied to short time series.

2.5.6. Incomplete (partial) structural estimation. A complete model (and structure) was defined above, in sections *1.1.4, 1.2.1.1,* and 2.2.2. Obviously the limited-information maximum-likelihood method just described can be used to estimate complete as well as incomplete structures. At the time when this introduction is being written this method appears to be best developed. But other suggestions for estimating incomplete structures will also be discussed below (section *2.5.6.1*) after adding a few more remarks on the reduced forms method.

The coefficients π of a linear reduced form (2.30) are regression coefficients of a nonlagged endogenous variables on exogenous and lagged endogenous variables. Their least-squares estimates have the consistency property. At the same time, they are functions of the structural parameters. This suggests that consistent estimates of structural coefficients can be obtained by applying appropriate transformations to the least-squares estimates of the coefficients of the reduced form. Similarly, parameters (e.g., the variance) of the estimated distribution of the random terms of the reduced form can be transformed into the parameters of the distribution of the shocks in the structural equations. The suggestion has been familiar for some time[1] but has been applied rigorously for the first

[1] See, for example, [Mann and Wald, p.219], [Haavelmo, 1944, pp. 103 - 104].

time by T. W. Anderson, M. A. Girshick, and H. Rubin; their joint work is summarized in [IX]. Since an equation of the reduced form has as many unknown coefficients as there are predetermined variables in the system, it will, in general, have more parameters than the structural equations (or equation) to be estimated. Hence equations connecting the unknown estimates of structural parameters with estimates of parameters of the reduced form may be more numerous than the number of these unknowns. To avoid this overdeterminacy, part of the available information has to be dropped. In particular, the method of reduced forms, which has been applied so far only to one equation at a time - in [Girshick and Haavelmo], [Haavelmo, 1947 A], [Klein, 1947, 1950] - does not use the observations on jointly dependent variables outside of this equation, though it does use the observations on predetermined variables of the system. The only a priori information this method uses are the linear restrictions on the parameters of the equation in question (including the prescription as to which variables enter this equation).

2.5.6.1. Other procedures of incomplete structural estimation were suggested by Koopmans [1945] and by Wald [VIII]. To estimate the parameters of F $(< G)$ structural equations, Koopmans proposed the following approximation method. The $G-F$ "complementary" equations of the model are "sketched in," e.g., by using admittedly biased single-equation least-squares estimates or some a priori guesses. Then proceed with the estimation of the parameters of the F equations to be estimated. The estimates of the remaining parameters of the complete model will then be improved compared with what they would be if the complementary part of the model were entirely neglected.

Wald's suggestion, [VIII], is different: even if we do not know anything about the complementary part of the model, our a priori knowledge about the F equations that interest the investigator may be sufficient to exclude hosts of originally admissible hypotheses about these equations, and thus to construct confidence regions for parameter estimates. For example, if we know that successive shocks are independent, then a set of values of the structural parameters must be rejected whenever the estimate of shocks computed from observations (the "residuals") fails to have approximately the characteristics of a random series. The elaboration of the method will consist of showing how to use a priori knowledge concerning an incomplete model to construct shortest confidence regions. Essentially, the difference between Koopmans' and Wald's suggestions on the estimation of incomplete models consists in attaching different weight to our knowledge of the complementary part of the entire model.

The method of reduced forms makes use of the maximum-likelihood principle, since least-squares estimates of regression coefficients are maximum-likelihood estimates (under normally distributed shocks); however, it leaves unused certain types of available a priori knowledge. In Wald's approach to incomplete systems, still fewer known restrictions are used.

For a given number F $(\leq G)$ of equations that are to be estimated, the choice of method will depend on two considerations: the mathematical and computational simplicity on the one hand, and the degree of use of available information on the other. For $F = 1$, the reduced forms method is less laborious than the approach via the estimation of the complete system (Wald's method has not yet been studied in this respect). But the complete estimation has one advantage over the other methods: it utilizes in full the a priori information on the model as well as the observations on all variables of the system.

2.6. *The Choice of Model*

There are many competing sets of a priori restrictions that can be imposed upon the structural parameters without contradicting what we know of human behavior and environment; and there is a wide variety of functional forms to specify the relations and distributions involved. It is often asserted that the choice is much wider in economics than in other empirical sciences. The usual testing considers only one hypothesis (and its negation) at a time. This is an inadequate procedure when a number of hypotheses classifiable according to a large number of attributes are in competition. In this volume no attempt is made to approach this problem.[1] In fact, the present volume is little concerned with the testing of hypotheses. Yet, the following remarks implied in the basic ideas of this volume seem appropriate.

A completely identifiable structure is said to be "just identifiable" by the model if the omission of one of the a priori restrictions of the model makes the structure incompletely identifiable; a completely identifiable structure that is not just identifiable is called overidentifiable. If several alternative overidentifying models are acceptable on a priori grounds, each

---

[1] See [Wald, 1942, pp. 8 - 9], [Brookner]. This is the problem of "multiple (as distinguished from dual) decisions."

of them (and its negation) can be tested against data by the existing methods; this is, in fact, attempted in [IX-6]. However, new methods are needed to test the whole set of such models simultaneously.

Regarding the great variety of functions equally appropriate, on a priori grounds, to describe structural economic relations, one may expect some help from the statisticians' recent attempts at nonparametric estimation of distribution functions [Wald and Wolfowitz]. Certain weak a priori restrictions on the structural relations, such as the sign of certain partial derivatives, the independence of successive shocks, etc., the economist can assert with better conscience than the restrictions upon, say, the degree of polynomials chosen to describe the structural relations. If confidence limits for joint probability densities of the variables could be estimated on the basis of such weak restrictions, predictive estimation under properly defined structural changes might become possible without introducing stronger but less justifiable hypotheses.

REFERENCES

ANDERSON, R. L., "Use of Variance Components in the Analysis of Hog Prices in Two Markets," *Journal of the American Statistical Association,* Vol. 42, December, 1947, pp. 612-634.

ANDERSON, T. W., and LEONID HURWICZ, "Errors and Shocks in Economic Relationships," Paper presented at the meeting of The Econometric Society, September 6-18, 1947, in Washington, D.C.; abstract in *Econometrica,* Vol. 16, January, 1948, pp. 36-37.

ANDERSON, T. W., and HERMAN RUBIN, "Estimation of the Parameters of a Single Stochastic Difference Equation in a Complete System," *Annals of Mathematical Statistics,* Vol. 20, March, 1949, pp. 46-63 (and to be included in *Cowles Commission Paper, New Series, No. 36*).

________, "Asymptotic Properties of Estimates of the Parameters of a Single Equation in a Complete System of Stochastic Equations," to be published (and to be included in *Cowles Commission Paper, New Series, No. 36*).

ANDREWS, WILLIAM H., JR., *see* JACOB MARSCHAK and WILLIAM H. ANDREWS, JR.

BENTZEL, H., and H. WOLD, "On Statistical Demand Analysis from the Viewpoint of Simultaneous Equations," *Skandinavisk Aktuarietidskrift,* Vol. 29, Nos. 1-2, 1946, pp. 95-114.

BIRKHOFF, GARRETT, and SAUNDERS MACLANE, *A Survey of Modern Algebra,* New York: The Macmillan Co., 1941, 450 pp.

BROOKNER, RALPH J., "Choice of One Among Several Statistical Hypotheses," *Annals of Mathematical Statistics,* Vol. 16, September, 1945, pp. 221-242.

CHERNOFF, HERMAN, "Gradient Methods of Maximization in Estimating Economic Parameters," Paper presented at the Madison meeting of The Econometric Society, September 7-10, 1948; abstract in *Econometrica,* Vol. 17, January, 1949, pp. 75-76.

CRAMÉR, HARALD, *Random Variables and Probability Distributions,* London: Cambridge, England: The University Press, 1937, 120 pp.

DAVID, F. N., and J. NEYMAN, "Extension of the Markoff Theorem on Least Squares," *Statistical Research Memoirs,* Vol. II, London: Department of Statistics, University of London, University College, 1938, pp. 105-116.

DIXON, WILFRID J., "Further Contributions to the Problem of Serial Correlation," *Annals of Mathematical Statistics,* Vol. 15, June, 1944, pp. 119-144.

DOOB, J. L., "The Elementary Gaussian Processes," *Annals of Mathematical Statistics,* Vol. 15, September, 1944, pp. 229-282.

FRISCH, RAGNAR, 1929, "Correlation and Scatter in Statistical Variables," *Nordic Statistical Journal,* Vol. 1, 1929, pp. 36-102.

________, 1933, *Pitfalls in the Construction of Statistical Demand Curves,* Veröffentlichungen der Frankfurter Gesellschaft für Konjunkturforschung, Neue Folge, Heft 5, Leipzig: Hans Buske Verlag, 1933, 39 pp.

________, 1934, *Statistical Confluence Analysis by Means of Complete Regression Systems,* Oslo: Universitetets Økonomiske Institutt, 1934, 192 pp.

________, 1938, "Statistical Versus Theoretical Relations in Economic Macrodynamics," Memorandum prepared for a conference in Cambridge, England, July 18-20, 1938, to discuss drafts of Tinbergen's League of Nations Publications; mimeographed.

FRISCH, RAGNAR, and BRUCE D. MUDGETT, "Statistical Correlation and the Theory of Cluster Types," *Journal of the American Statistical Association,* Vol. 26, December, 1931, pp. 375-392.

GEARY, R. C., 1942, "Inherent Relations between Random Variables," *Proceedings of the Royal Irish Academy,* Vol. 47, Section A, March, 1942, pp. 63-196.

________, 1943, "Relations between Statistics: The General and the Sampling Problem when the Samples Are Large," *Proceedings of the Royal Irish Academy,* Vol. 49, Section A, December, 1943, pp. 177-196.

GIRSHICK, M. A., and TRYGVE HAAVELMO, "Statistical Analysis of the Demand for Food: Examples of Simultaneous Estimation of Structural Equations," *Econometrica,* Vol. 15, April, 1947, pp. 79-110 (and reprinted as *Cowles Commission Paper, New Series, No. 24*).

HAAVELMO, TRYGVE, 1943, "The Statistical Implications of a System of Simultaneous Equations," *Econometrica,* Vol. 11, January, 1943, pp. 1-12.

________, 1944, "The Probability Approach in Econometrics," *Econometrica,* Vol. 12, Supplement, July, 1944, 118 pp. (and reprinted as *Cowles Commission Paper, New Series, No. 4*).

________, 1947-A, "Methods of Measuring the Marginal Propensity to Consume," *Journal of the American Statistical Association,* Vol. 42, March, 1947, pp. 105-122 (and reprinted as *Cowles Commission Paper, New Series, No. 22*).

________, 1947-B, "Quantitative Research in Agricultural Economics: The Interdependence Between Agriculture and the National Economy," *Journal of Farm Economics,* Vol. 24, 1947, pp. 910-924 (and included in *Cowles Commission Paper, New Series, No. 27*).

________, *see also* M. A. GIRSHICK and TRYGVE HAAVELMO.

HARDY, G. H., J. E. LITTLEWOOD, and G. PÓLYA, *Inequalities,* Cambridge, England: The University Press, 1934, 314 pp.

HOTELLING, HAROLD, 1933, "Analysis of a Complex of Statistical Variables in Principal Components," *Journal of Educational Psychology,* Vol. 24, September and October, 1933, pp. 417-444 and 498-520.

________, 1936-A, "Simplified Calculation of Principal Components," *Psychometrika,* Vol. 1, March, 1936, pp. 27-35.

________, 1936-B, "Relations Between Two Sets of Variables," *Biometrica,* Vol. 28, December, 1936, pp. 321-377.

________, 1940, "The Selection of Variates for Use in Prediction with Some Comments on the Problem of Nuisance Parameters," *Annals of Mathematical Statistics,* Vol. 11, September, 1940, pp. 271-283.

________, 1943-A, "Some New Methods in Matrix Calculation," *Annals of Mathematical Statistics*, Vol. 14, March, 1943, pp. 1-34.

________, 1943-B, "Further Points on Matrix Calculation and Simultaneous Equations," *Annals of Mathematical Statistics*, Vol. 14, December, 1943, pp. 440-441.

________, 1949, "Practical Problems of Matrix Calculation," *Proceedings of the Berkeley Symposium on Probability and Statistics*, Jerzy Neyman, ed., Berkeley and Los Angeles: University of California Press, 1949, pp. 275-293.

HURWICZ, LEONID, 1944, "Stochastic Models of Economic Fluctuations," *Econometrica*, Vol. 12, April, 1944, pp. 114-124 (and reprinted as *Cowles Commission Paper, New Series, No. 3*).

________, 1946, "Theory of the Firm and of Investment," *Econometrica*, Vol. 14, April, 1946, pp. 109-136 (and reprinted as *Cowles Commission Paper, New Series, No. 16*).

________, 1947, "Some Problems Arising in Estimating Economic Relations," *Econometrica*, Vol. 15, July, 1947, pp. 236-240.

________, *see also* T. W. ANDERSON and LEONID HURWICZ.

________, *see also* JACOB MARSCHAK; LEONID HURWICZ; *et al.*

JOHNSON, EVAN, JR., "Estimates of Parameters by Means of Least Squares," *Annals of Mathematical Statistics*, Vol. 11, December, 1940, pp. 453-456.

KENDALL, M. G., "A New Measure of Bank Correlation," *Biometrika*, Vol. 30, June, 1938, pp. 81-93.

KLEIN, LAWRENCE R., 1946-A, "Macroeconomics and the Theory of Rational Behavior," *Econometrica*, Vol. 14, April, 1946, pp. 93-108 (and reprinted as *Cowles Commission Paper, New Series, No. 14*).

________, 1946-B, "A Post-Mortem on Transition Predictions of National Product," *Journal of Political Economy*, Vol. 54, August, 1946, pp. 289-308 (and reprinted as *Cowles Commission Paper, New Series, No. 18*).

________, 1947, "The Use of Econometric Models as a Guide to Economic Policy," *Econometrica*, Vol. 15, April, 1947, pp. 111-151 (and reprinted as *Cowles Commission Paper, New Series, No. 23*).

________, 1950, *Economic Fluctuations in the United States, 1921-1941*, Cowles Commission Monograph No. 11, New York: John Wiley & Sons, 1950, about 170 pp.

KOOPMANS, TJALLING C., 1937, *Linear Regression Analysis of Economic Time Series*, Haarlem: De Erven F. Bohn N. V., 1937, 150 pp.

________, 1942, "Serial Correlation and Quadratic Forms in Normal Variables," *Annals of Mathematical Statistics*, Vol. 13, March, 1942, pp. 14-33.

________, 1945, "Statistical Estimation of Simultaneous Economic Relations," *Journal of the American Statistical Association*, Vol. 40, December, 1945, pp. 448-466 (and reprinted as *Cowles Commission Paper, New Series, No. 11*).

________, 1949, "Identification Problems in Economic Model Construction," *Econometrica*, Vol. 17, April, 1949, pp. 125-144 (and reprinted as *Cowles Commission Paper, New Series, No. 31*).

________, *see also* JACOB MARSCHAK; LEONID HURWICZ; *et al.*

LEIPNIK, ROY B., "Distribution of the Serial Correlation Coefficient in a Circularly Correlated Universe," *Annals of Mathematical Statistics*, Vol. 18, March, 1947, pp. 80-87 (and included in *Cowles Commission Paper, New Series, No. 21*).

________, *see also* JACOB MARSCHAK; LEONID HURWICZ; *et al.*

LITTLEWOOD, J. E., *see* G. H. HARDY, J. E. LITTLEWOOD, and G. PÓLYA.

MACDUFFEE, CYRUS COLTON, *Vectors and Matrices*, Menasha, Wisconsin: Mathematical Association of America, 1943, 192 pp.

MACLANE, SAUNDERS, *see* GARRETT BIRKHOFF and SAUNDERS MACLANE.

MADOW, WILLIAM G., "Note on the Distribution of the Serial Correlation Coefficient," *Annals of Mathematical Statistics*, Vol. 16, September, 1945, pp. 308-310.

MANN, HENRY B., "Nonparametric Tests against Trend," *Econometrica*, Vol. 13, July, 1945, pp. 245-259.

MANN, H. B., and A. WALD, "On the Statistical Treatment of Linear Stochastic Difference Equations," *Econometrica*, Vol. 11, July-October, 1943, pp. 173-220.

MARSCHAK, JACOB, 1947-A, "Economic Structure, Path, Policy, and Prediction," *American Economic Review, Papers and Proceedings of the 59th Annual Meeting of the American Economic Association*, Vol. 37, May, 1947, pp. 81-84.

________, 1947-B, "Statistical Inference from Nonexperimental Observations: An Economic Example," Paper presented at the meeting of the International Statistical Institute and The Econometric Society, September 6-18, 1947, in Washington, D.C.; to be published in 1950 in *Proceedings of the International Statistical Conference* (and to be reprinted as *Cowles Commission Paper, New Series, No. 32*); abstract in *Econometrica*, Vol. 16, January, 1948, pp. 53-55.

MARSCHAK, JACOB, and WILLIAM H. ANDREWS, JR., "Random Simultaneous Equations and the Theory of Production," *Econometrica*, Vol. 12, July-October, 1944, pp. 143-205 (and reprinted as *Cowles Commission Paper, New Series, No. 5*).

MARSCHAK, JACOB; LEONID HURWICZ; TJALLING C. KOOPMANS and ROY B. LEIPNIK; "Estimating Relations from Nonexperimental Observations," Papers presented at the Cleveland meeting of The Econometric Society, January 24-27, 1946; abstracts in *Econometrica*, Vol. 14, April, 1946, pp. 165-172 (and included in *Cowles Commission Paper, New Series, No. 17*)

MARSHALL, ALFRED, *Principles of Economics*, Eighth Edition, London: Macmillan & Co., 1920, 754 pp.

MUDGETT, BRUCE D., *see* RAGNAR FRISCH and BRUCE D. MUDGETT.

NEYMAN, J., "Outline of a Theory of Statistical Estimation Based on the Classical Theory of Probability," *Philosophical Transactions of the Royal Society of London, Series A*, Vol. 236, August 30, 1937, pp. 330-380.

________, *see also* F. N. DAVID and J. NEYMAN.

PIERCE, B. O., *A Short Table of Integrals*, New York: Ginn and Co., 1929, 156 pp.

PÓLYA, G., *see* G. H. HARDY, J. E. LITTLEWOOD, and G. PÓLYA.

REIERSØL, OLAV, "Residual Variables in Regression and Confluence Analysis,"

Skandinavisk Aktuarietidskrift, Vol. 28, Nos. 3-4, 1945, pp. 201-217.

RUBIN, HERMAN, 1945, "On the Distribution of the Serial Correlation Coefficient," *Annals of Mathematical Statistics,* Vol. 16, June, 1945, pp. 211-215 (and reprinted as *Cowles Commission Paper, New Series, No. 10*).

________, 1946, "Asymptotic Distribution of Moments from a System of Linear Stochastic Difference Equations," Abstract No. 332 in *Bulletin of the American Mathematical Society,* Vol. 52, September, 1946, pp. 827-828.

________, 1948, "Some Results on the Asymptotic Distribution of Maximum- and Quasi-Maximum-Likelihood Estimates," Abstract No. 529 in *Bulletin of the American Mathematical Society,* Vol. 54, November, 1948, p. 1080, and in *Annals of Mathematical Statistics,* Vol. 19, December, 1948, p. 598.

________, 1949, "Properties of Maximum- and Quasi-Maximum-Likelihood Estimates of Parameters of a System of Linear Stochastic Difference Equations with Serially Correlated Disturbances," abstract in *Annals of Mathematical Statistics,* Vol. 20, March, 1949, p. 137.

________, *see also* T. W. ANDERSON and HERMAN RUBIN.

SNEDECOR, GEORGE W., *Calculation and Interpretation of Analysis of Variance and Covariance,* Ames, Iowa: Collegiate Press, Inc., 1934, 96 pp.

TINBERGEN, J., *Statistical Testing of Business-Cycle Theories:* Vol. I, *A Method and Its Application to Investment Activity;* Vol. II, *Business Cycles in the United States of America, 1919-1932;* Geneva: League of Nations, 1939, 164 and 244 pp.

TINTNER, GERHARD, 1942, "A Contribution to the Nonstatic Theory of Production," in *Studies in Mathematical Economics and Econometrics, in Memory of Henry Schultz,* O. Lange, F. McIntyre, T. O. Yntema, eds., Chicago: The University of Chicago Press, 1942, pp. 92-109.

________, 1946, "Multiple Regression for Systems of Equations," *Econometrica,* Vol. 14, January, 1946, pp. 5-36.

ULLMAN, JOSEPH, "The Probability of Convergence of an Iterative Process of Inverting a Matrix," *Annals of Mathematical Statistics,* Vol. 15, June, 1944, pp. 205-213.

WALD, ABRAHAM, 1940, "The Fitting of Straight Lines If Both Variables Are Subject to Error," *Annals of Mathematical Statistics,* Vol. 11, September, 1940, pp. 284-300.

________, 1942, *On the Principles of Statistical Inference,* Notre Dame Mathematical Lectures, No. 1, South Bend, Indiana: University of Notre Dame, 1942, 47 pp.

________, 1944, "Note on a Lemma," *Annals of Mathematical Statistics,* Vol. 15, September, 1944, pp. 330-333.

________, *see also* H. B. MANN and A. WALD.

WALD, A., and J. WOLFOWITZ, "Confidence Limits for Continuous Distribution Functions," *Annals of Mathematical Statistics,* Vol. 10, June, 1939, pp. 105-118.

WATSON, G. N., *see* E. T. WHITTAKER and G. N. WATSON.

WAUGH, F. V., "A Note Concerning Hotelling's Method of Inverting a Partitioned Matrix," *Annals of Mathematical Statistics,* Vol. 16, June, 1945, pp. 216-217.

WHITTAKER, E. T., and G. N. WATSON, *A Course of Modern Analysis*, American Edition, Cambridge, England: The University Press; New York: The Macmillan Co., 1945, 608 pp.

WILKS, S. S., *Mathematical Statistics*, Princeton: Princeton University Press, 1943, 284 pp.

WILLIAMS, J. D., "Moments of the Ratio of the Mean Square Successive Differences to the Mean Square Difference in Samples from a Normal Universe," *Annals of Mathematical Statistics*, Vol. 12, June, 1941, pp. 239-241.

WINTNER, A., *Lectures by Aurel Wintner on Asymptotic Distributions and Infinite Convolutions*, Ann Arbor, Michigan: Edwards Brothers, 1938, 54 pp.

WOLD, HERMAN, *A Study in the Analysis of Stationary Time Series*, Uppsala: Almqvist & Wiksells, 1938, 214 pp.

________, *see also* H. BENTZEL and H. WOLD.

WOLFOWITZ, J., *see* A. WALD and J. WOLFOWITZ.

References from STATISTICAL INFERENCE IN DYNAMIC ECONOMIC MODELS
Cited by Jacob Marschak in the Preceding Reading

II. Measuring the Equation Systems of Dynamic Economics, by T.C. Koopmans, H. Rubin, and R.B. Leipnik

III. Note on the Identification of Economic Relations, By A. Wald

IV. Generalization of the Concept of Identification, By L. Hurwicz

V. Remarks on Frisch's Confluence Analysis and Its Use in Econometrics, by T. Haavelmo

VI. Prediction and Least Squares, By L. Hurwicz

VII. The Equivalence of Macimum-Likelihood and Least-Squares Estimates of Regression Coefficients, By T.C. Koopmans

VIII. Remarks on the Estimation of Unknown Parameters in Incomplete Systems of Equations, By A. Wald

IX. Estimation of the Parameters of a Single Equation by the Limited-Information Maximum-Likelihood Method, By T.W. Anderson, Jr.

X. Some Computational Devices, By H. Hotelling

XI. Variable Parameters in Stochastic Processes: Trend and Seasonality, By L. Hurwicz

XII. Nonparametric Tests against Trend, By H.B. Mann

XIII. Tests of Significance in Time-Series Analysis, By R.L. Anderson

XIV. Consistency of Maximum-Likelihood Estimates in the Explosive Case, By H. Rubin

XV. Least-Squares Bias in Time Series, By L. Hurwicz

XVI. Models Involving a Continuous Time Variable, By T.C. Koopmans

XVII. When Is an Equation System Complete for Statistical Purposes?, By T.C. Koopmans

XVIII. Systems with Nonadditive Disturbances, By L. Hurwicz

XIX. Note on Random Coefficients, By H. Rubin

SINGLE EQUATIONS

TESTING FOR SERIAL CORRELATION IN LEAST SQUARES REGRESSION. I

By J. DURBIN and G. S. WATSON

A great deal of use has undoubtedly been made of least squares regression methods in circumstances in which they are known to be inapplicable. In particular, they have often been employed for the analysis of time series and similar data in which successive observations are serially correlated. The resulting complications are well known and have recently been studied from the standpoint of the econometrician by Cochrane & Orcutt (1949). A basic assumption underlying the application of the least squares method is that the error terms in the regression model are independent. When this assumption—among others—is satisfied the procedure is valid whether or not the observations themselves are serially correlated. The problem of testing the errors for independence forms the subject of this paper and its successor. The present paper deals mainly with the theory on which the test is based, while the second paper describes the test procedures in detail and gives tables of bounds to the significance points of the test criterion adopted. We shall not be concerned in either paper with the question of what should be done if the test gives an unfavourable result.

Since the errors in any practical case will be unknown the test must be based on the residuals from the calculated regression. Consequently the ordinary tests of independence cannot be used as they stand, since the residuals are necessarily correlated whether the errors are dependent or not. The mean and variance of an appropriate test statistic have been calculated by Moran (1950) for the case of regression on a single independent variable. The problem of constructing an exact test has been completely solved only in one special case. R. L. & T. W. Anderson (1950) have shown that for the case of regression on a short Fourier series the distribution of the circular serial correlation coefficient obtained by R. L. Anderson (1942) can be used to obtain exact significance points for the test criterion concerned. This is due to the coincidence of the regression vectors with the latent vectors of the circular serial covariance matrix. Perversely enough, this is the very case in which the test is least needed, since the least squares regression coefficients are best unbiased estimates even in the non-null case, and in addition estimates of their variance can be obtained which are at least asymptotically unbiased.

The latent vector case is in fact the only one for which an elegant solution can be obtained. It does not seem possible to find exact significance points for any other case. Nevertheless, bounds to the significance points can be obtained, and in the second paper such bounds will be tabulated. The bounds we shall give are 'best' in two senses: first they can be attained (with regression vectors of a type that will be discussed later), and secondly, when they are attained the test criterion adopted is uniformly most powerful against suitable alternative hypotheses. It is hoped that these bounds will settle the question of significance one way or the other in many cases arising in practice. For doubtful cases there does not seem to be any completely satisfactory procedure. We shall, however, indicate some approximate methods which may be useful in certain circumstances.

The bounds are applicable to all cases in which the independent variables in the regression model can be regarded as 'fixed'. They do not therefore apply to autoregressive schemes and similar .models in which lagged values of the dependent variable occur as independent variables.

A further slight limitation of the tables in the form in which we shall present them is that they apply directly only to regressions in which a constant term or mean has been fitted. They cannot therefore be used as they stand for testing the residuals from a regression through the origin. In order to carry out the test in such a case it will be necessary to calculate a regression which includes a fitted mean. Once the test has been carried out the mean can be eliminated by the usual methods for eliminating an independent variable from a regression equation (e.g. Fisher, 1946).

Introduction to theoretical treatment

Any single-equation regression model can be written in the form

$$y = \beta_1 x_1 + \beta_2 x_2 + \ldots + \beta_k x_k + \epsilon$$

in which y, the dependent variable, and x, the independent variable, are observed, the errors ϵ being unobserved. We usually require to estimate $\beta_1, \beta_2, \ldots, \beta_k$ and to make confidence statements about the estimates given only the sample

$$\begin{matrix} y_1 & x_{11} & x_{21} & \cdots & x_{k1} \\ y_2 & x_{12} & x_{22} & \cdots & x_{k2} \\ \vdots & \vdots & \vdots & & \vdots \\ y_n & x_{1n} & x_{2n} & \cdots & x_{kn} \end{matrix}$$

Estimates can be made by assuming the errors $\epsilon_1, \epsilon_2, \ldots, \epsilon_n$ associated with the sample to be random variables distributed with zero expectations independently of the x's. If the estimates we make are maximum likelihood estimates, and if our confidence statements are based on likelihood ratios, we can regard the x's as fixed in repeated sampling, that is, they can be treated as known constants even if they are in fact random variables. If in addition $\epsilon_1, \epsilon_2, \ldots, \epsilon_n$ can be taken to be distributed independently of each other with constant variance, then by Markoff's theorem the least squares estimates of $\beta_1, \beta_2, \ldots, \beta_k$ are best linear unbiased estimates whatever the form of distribution of the ϵ's. Unbiased estimates of the variances of the estimates can also be obtained without difficulty. These estimates of variance can then be used to make confidence statements by assuming the errors to be normally distributed.

Thus the assumptions on which the validity of the least squares method is based are as follows:

(*a*) The error is distributed independently of the independent variables with zero mean and constant variance;

(*b*) Successive errors are distributed independently of one another.

In what follows autoregressive schemes and stochastic difference equations will be excluded from further consideration, since assumption (*a*) does not hold in such cases. We shall be concerned only with assumption (*b*), that is, we shall assume that the x's can be regarded as 'fixed variables'. When (*b*) is violated the least squares procedure breaks down at three points:

(i) The estimates of the regression coefficients, though unbiased, need not have least variance.

(ii) The usual formula for the variance of an estimate is no longer applicable and is liable to give a serious underestimate of the true variance.

(iii) The t and F distributions, used for making confidence statements, lose their validity.

In stating these consequences of the violation of assumption (b) we do not overlook the fact, pointed out by Wold (1949), that the variances of the resulting estimates depend as much on the serial correlations of the independent variables as on the serial correlation of the errors. In fact, as Wold showed, when all the sample serial correlations of the x's are zero the estimates of variance given by the least squares method are strictly unbiased whether the errors are serially correlated or not. It seems to us doubtful, however, whether this result finds much application in practice. It will only rarely be the case that the independent variables are serially uncorrelated while the errors are serially correlated. Consequently, we feel that there can be little doubt of the desirability of testing the errors for independence whenever the least squares method is applied to serially correlated observations.

To find a suitable test criterion we refer to some results obtained by T. W. Anderson (1948). Anderson showed that in certain cases in which the regression vectors are latent vectors of matrices $\mathbf{\Psi}$ and $\mathbf{\Theta}$ occurring in the error distribution, the statistic $\dfrac{\mathbf{z}'\mathbf{\Theta}\mathbf{z}}{\mathbf{z}'\mathbf{\Psi}\mathbf{z}}$, where $\mathbf{z}$ is the column vector of residuals from regression, provides a test that is uniformly most powerful against certain alternative hypotheses. The error distributions implied by these alternative hypotheses are given by Anderson and are such that in the cases that are likely to be useful in practice $\mathbf{\Psi} = \mathbf{I}$, the unit matrix. These results suggest that we should examine the distribution of the statistic $r = \dfrac{\mathbf{z}'\mathbf{A}\mathbf{z}}{\mathbf{z}'\mathbf{z}}$ (changing the notation slightly) for regression on any set of fixed variables, $\mathbf{A}$ being any real symmetric matrix.

In the next section we shall consider certain formal properties of r defined in this way, and in §3 its distribution in the null case will be examined. Expressions for its moments will be derived, and it will be shown that its distribution function lies between two distribution functions which could be determined. In §4 we return to discuss the question of the choice of an appropriate test criterion with rather more rigour and a specific choice is made. In the final section certain special properties of this test criterion are given.

2. Transformation of r

We consider the linear regression of y on k independent variables $x_1, x_2, \ldots, x_k$. The model for a sample of n observations is

$$\begin{pmatrix} y_1 \\ y_2 \\ \vdots \\ y_n \end{pmatrix} = \begin{pmatrix} x_{11} & x_{21} & \cdots & x_{k1} \\ x_{12} & x_{22} & \cdots & x_{k2} \\ \vdots & \vdots & & \vdots \\ x_{1n} & x_{2n} & \cdots & x_{kn} \end{pmatrix} \begin{pmatrix} \beta_1 \\ \beta_2 \\ \vdots \\ \beta_k \end{pmatrix} + \begin{pmatrix} \epsilon_1 \\ \epsilon_2 \\ \vdots \\ \epsilon_n \end{pmatrix},$$

or in an evident matrix notation, $\mathbf{y} = \mathbf{X}\boldsymbol{\beta} + \boldsymbol{\epsilon}$.

The least squares estimate of $\boldsymbol{\beta}$ is $\mathbf{b} = \{b_1, b_2, \ldots, b_k\}$ given by $\mathbf{b} = (\mathbf{X}'\mathbf{X})^{-1}\mathbf{X}'\mathbf{y}$.

The vector $\mathbf{z} = \{z_1, z_2, \ldots, z_n\}$ of residuals from regression is defined by

$$\begin{aligned} \mathbf{z} &= \mathbf{y} - \mathbf{X}\mathbf{b} \\ &= \{\mathbf{I}_n - \mathbf{X}(\mathbf{X}'\mathbf{X})^{-1}\mathbf{X}'\}\mathbf{y}, \end{aligned}$$

where $\mathbf{I}_n$ is the unit matrix of order n.

Thus
$$\mathbf{z} = \{\mathbf{I}_n - \mathbf{X}(\mathbf{X}'\mathbf{X})^{-1}\mathbf{X}'\}(\mathbf{X}\boldsymbol{\beta}+\boldsymbol{\epsilon})$$
$$= \{\mathbf{I}_n - \mathbf{X}(\mathbf{X}'\mathbf{X})^{-1}\mathbf{X}'\}\boldsymbol{\epsilon}$$
$$= \mathbf{M}\boldsymbol{\epsilon} \text{ say.}$$

It may be verified that $\mathbf{M} = \mathbf{M}' = \mathbf{M}^2$; that is, $\mathbf{M}$ is idempotent.*

We now examine the ratio of quadratic forms $r = \dfrac{\mathbf{z}'\mathbf{A}\mathbf{z}}{\mathbf{z}'\mathbf{z}}$, where $\mathbf{A}$ is a real symmetric matrix. Transforming to the errors we have

$$r = \frac{\boldsymbol{\epsilon}'\mathbf{M}'\mathbf{A}\mathbf{M}\boldsymbol{\epsilon}}{\boldsymbol{\epsilon}'\mathbf{M}'\mathbf{M}\boldsymbol{\epsilon}} = \frac{\boldsymbol{\epsilon}'\mathbf{M}\mathbf{A}\mathbf{M}\boldsymbol{\epsilon}}{\boldsymbol{\epsilon}'\mathbf{M}\boldsymbol{\epsilon}}.$$

We shall show that there exists an orthogonal transformation which simultaneously reduces the numerator and denominator of r to their canonical forms; that is, there is an orthogonal transformation $\boldsymbol{\epsilon} = \mathbf{H}\boldsymbol{\zeta}$ such that

$$r = \frac{\sum_{i=1}^{n-k} \nu_i \zeta_i^2}{\sum_{i=1}^{n-k} \zeta_i^2}.$$

It is well known that there is an orthogonal matrix $\mathbf{L}$ such that

$$\mathbf{L}'\mathbf{M}\mathbf{L} = \begin{pmatrix} \mathbf{I}_{n-k} & \mathbf{O} \\ \mathbf{O} & \mathbf{O} \end{pmatrix},$$

where $\mathbf{I}_{n-k}$ is the unit matrix of order $n-k$, and $\mathbf{O}$ stands for a zero matrix with appropriate numbers of rows and columns. This corresponds to the result that $\sum_{i=1}^{n} z_i^2$ is distributed as χ^2 with $n-k$ degrees of freedom. Thus

$$\mathbf{L}'\mathbf{M}\mathbf{A}\mathbf{M}\mathbf{L} = \mathbf{L}'\mathbf{M}\mathbf{L}.\mathbf{L}'\mathbf{A}\mathbf{L}.\mathbf{L}'\mathbf{M}\mathbf{L}$$
$$= \begin{pmatrix} \mathbf{I}_{n-k} & \mathbf{O} \\ \mathbf{O} & \mathbf{O} \end{pmatrix} \begin{pmatrix} \mathbf{B}_1 & \mathbf{B}_3 \\ \mathbf{B}_2 & \mathbf{B}_4 \end{pmatrix} \begin{pmatrix} \mathbf{I}_{n-k} & \mathbf{O} \\ \mathbf{O} & \mathbf{O} \end{pmatrix}$$
$$= \begin{pmatrix} \mathbf{B}_1 & \mathbf{O} \\ \mathbf{O} & \mathbf{O} \end{pmatrix},$$

where $\begin{pmatrix} \mathbf{B}_1 & \mathbf{B}_3 \\ \mathbf{B}_2 & \mathbf{B}_4 \end{pmatrix}$ is the appropriate partition of the real symmetric matrix $\mathbf{L}'\mathbf{A}\mathbf{L}$.

Let $\mathbf{N}_1$ be the orthogonal matrix diagonalizing $\mathbf{B}_1$, i.e.

$$\mathbf{N}_1'\mathbf{B}_1\mathbf{N}_1 = \begin{pmatrix} \nu_1 & & & \\ & \nu_2 & & \\ & & \ddots & \\ & & & \nu_{n-k} \end{pmatrix}$$

the blank spaces representing zeros. Then $\mathbf{N} = \begin{pmatrix} \mathbf{N}_1 & \mathbf{O} \\ \mathbf{O} & \mathbf{I}_k \end{pmatrix}$ is orthogonal, so that $\mathbf{H} = \mathbf{L}\mathbf{N}$ is orthogonal.

* This matrix treatment of the residuals is due to Aitken (1935).

Consequently
$$\mathbf{H'MH} = \mathbf{N'L'MLN}$$
$$= \mathbf{N'}\begin{pmatrix} \mathbf{I}_{n-k} & \mathbf{O} \\ \mathbf{O} & \mathbf{O} \end{pmatrix}\mathbf{N}$$
$$= \begin{pmatrix} \mathbf{I}_{n-k} & \mathbf{O} \\ \mathbf{O} & \mathbf{O} \end{pmatrix},$$

so that
$$\mathbf{H'MAMH} = \mathbf{H'MH}.\mathbf{H'AH}.\mathbf{H'MH}$$
$$= \begin{pmatrix} \nu_1 & & & & \\ & \nu_2 & & & \mathbf{O} \\ & & \ddots & & \\ & & & \nu_{n-k} & \\ & & \mathbf{O} & & \mathbf{O} \end{pmatrix}.$$

Putting $\boldsymbol{\epsilon} = \mathbf{H}\boldsymbol{\zeta}$, we have
$$r = \frac{\sum_{i=1}^{n-k} \nu_i \zeta_i^2}{\sum_{i=1}^{n-k} \zeta_i^2}.$$

This result can be seen geometrically by observing that $\boldsymbol{\epsilon}'\mathbf{MAM}\boldsymbol{\epsilon} =$ constant and $\boldsymbol{\epsilon}'\mathbf{M}\boldsymbol{\epsilon} =$ constant are hypercylinders with parallel generators, the cross-section of $\boldsymbol{\epsilon}'\mathbf{M}\boldsymbol{\epsilon}$ constant being an $[n-k]$ hypersphere.

Determination of $\nu_1, \nu_2, \ldots, \nu_{n-k}$

By standard matrix theory $\nu_1, \nu_2, \ldots, \nu_{n-k}$ are the latent roots of $\mathbf{MAM}$ other than k zeros; that is, they are the latent roots of $\mathbf{M}^2\mathbf{A}$, since the roots of the product of two matrices are independent of the order of multiplication.* But $\mathbf{M}^2\mathbf{A} = \mathbf{MA}$ since $\mathbf{M}^2 = \mathbf{M}$. Consequently $\nu_1, \nu_2, \ldots, \nu_{n-k}$ are the latent roots of $\mathbf{MA}$ other than k zeros.

Suppose now that we make the real non-singular transformation of the x's, $\mathbf{P} = \mathbf{XG}$. Then $\mathbf{M} = \mathbf{I}_n - \mathbf{P}(\mathbf{P'P})^{-1}\mathbf{P'}$; that is, $\mathbf{M}$ is invariant under such transformations. We choose $\mathbf{G}$ so that the column vectors $\mathbf{p}_1, \mathbf{p}_2, \ldots, \mathbf{p}_k$ of $\mathbf{P}$ are orthogonal and are each of unit length, i.e.
$$\mathbf{p}_i'\mathbf{p}_j = \begin{cases} 1 (i = j) \\ 0 (i \neq j) \end{cases}$$
so that
$$\mathbf{P'P} = \mathbf{I}_n.$$

This amounts to saying that we can replace the original independent variables by a normalized orthogonal set without affecting the residuals.

We have, therefore,
$$\mathbf{M} = \mathbf{I}_n - (\mathbf{p}_1\mathbf{p}_1' + \mathbf{p}_2\mathbf{p}_2' + \ldots + \mathbf{p}_k\mathbf{p}_k')$$
$$= (\mathbf{I}_n - \mathbf{p}_1\mathbf{p}_1')(\mathbf{I}_n - \mathbf{p}_2\mathbf{p}_2')\ldots(\mathbf{I}_n - \mathbf{p}_k\mathbf{p}_k')$$
$$= \mathbf{M}_1\mathbf{M}_2\ldots\mathbf{M}_k, \quad \text{say.}$$

Each factor $\mathbf{M}_i$ has the same form as $\mathbf{M}$, the matrix $\mathbf{P}$ being replaced by the vector $\mathbf{p}_i$; it is idempotent of rank $n-1$ as can be easily verified. From the derivation it is evident that the $\mathbf{M}_i$'s commute. This is an expression in algebraic terms of the fact that we can fit regressions on orthogonal variables separately and in any order without affecting the final result.

* See, for instance, C. C. Macduffee, *The Theory of Matrices* (Chelsea Publishing Company, 1946), Theorem 16·2.

Returning to the main argument we have the result that $\nu_1, \nu_2, \ldots, \nu_{n-k}$ are the roots of $\mathbf{M}_k \ldots \mathbf{M}_2 \mathbf{M}_1 \mathbf{A}$ other than k zeros. From the form of the products we see that any result we establish about the roots of $\mathbf{M}_1 \mathbf{A}$ in terms of those of $\mathbf{A}$ will be true of the roots of $\mathbf{M}_2 \mathbf{M}_1 \mathbf{A}$ in terms of those of $\mathbf{M}_1 \mathbf{A}$. This observation suggests a method of building up a knowledge of the roots of $\mathbf{M}_k \ldots \mathbf{M}_2 \mathbf{M}_1 \mathbf{A}$ in stages starting from the roots of $\mathbf{A}$ which we assume known.

We therefore investigate the latent roots of $\mathbf{M}_1 \mathbf{A}$, say $\theta_1, \theta_2, \ldots, \theta_{n-1}, 0$. These are the roots of the determinantal equation

$$|\mathbf{I}_n \theta - \mathbf{M}_1 \mathbf{A}| = 0,$$

i.e.

$$|\mathbf{I}_n \theta - (\mathbf{I}_n - \mathbf{p}_1 \mathbf{p}_1') \mathbf{A}| = 0. \tag{1}$$

Let $\mathbf{T}$ be the orthogonal matrix diagonalizing $\mathbf{A}$, i.e.

$$\mathbf{T}'\mathbf{A}\mathbf{T} = \mathbf{\Lambda} = \begin{pmatrix} \lambda_1 & & & \\ & \lambda_2 & & \\ & & \ddots & \\ & & & \lambda_n \end{pmatrix},$$

where $\lambda_1, \lambda_2, \ldots, \lambda_n$ are the latent roots of $\mathbf{A}$. Pre- and post-multiplying (1) by $\mathbf{T}'$ and $\mathbf{T}$, we have

$$|\mathbf{I}_n - (\mathbf{I}_n - \mathbf{l}_1 \mathbf{l}_1') \mathbf{\Lambda}| = 0,$$

where $\mathbf{l}_1 = \{l_{11}, l_{12}, \ldots, l_{1n}\}$ is the vector of direction cosines of $\mathbf{p}_1$ referred to the latent vectors of $\mathbf{A}$ as axes. (Complications arising from multiplicities in the roots of $\mathbf{A}$ are easily overcome in the present context.) Dropping the suffix from $\mathbf{l}_1$ for the moment, we have

$$|\mathbf{I}_n \theta - (\mathbf{I}_n - \mathbf{l}\mathbf{l}') \mathbf{\Lambda}| = 0.$$

Writing out the determinant in full,

$$\begin{vmatrix} \theta - \lambda_1 + l_1^2 \lambda_1, & l_1 l_2 \lambda_2 & \ldots & l_1 l_n \lambda_n \\ l_2 l_1 \lambda_1 & \theta - \lambda_2 + l_2^2 \lambda_2 & \ldots & \vdots \\ \vdots & \vdots & \ldots & \vdots \\ l_n l_1 \lambda_1 & \ldots & \ldots & \theta - \lambda_n + l_n^2 \lambda_n \end{vmatrix} = 0.$$

Subtracting l_2/l_1 times the first row from the second row, l_3/l_1 times the first from the third, and so on, we can expand the determinant to give the equation

$$\prod_{j=1}^{n} (\theta - \lambda_j) + \sum_{i=1}^{n} l_i^2 \lambda_i \sum_{j \neq i}^{n} (\theta - \lambda_j) = 0.$$

Reducing and taking out a factor θ corresponding to the known zero root of $\mathbf{M}_1 \mathbf{A}$ gives

$$\sum_{i=1}^{n} l_i^2 \prod_{j \neq i}^{n} (\theta - \lambda_j) = 0. \tag{2}$$

$\theta_1, \theta_2, \ldots, \theta_{n-1}$ are the roots of this equation.

We notice that when $l_r = 0$, $\theta - \lambda_r$ is a factor of (2) so that $\theta = \lambda_r$ is a solution. Thus when $\mathbf{p}_1$ coincides with a latent vector of $\mathbf{A}$, $\theta_1, \theta_2, \ldots, \theta_{n-1}$ are equal to the latent roots associated with the remaining $n-1$ latent vectors of $\mathbf{A}$. In the same way if $\mathbf{p}_2$ also coincides with a latent vector of $\mathbf{A}$, the roots of $\mathbf{M}_2 \mathbf{M}_1 \mathbf{A}$ other than two zeros are equal to the latent roots associated with the remaining $n-2$ latent vectors of $\mathbf{A}$. Thus, in general, if the k regression vectors coincide with k of the latent vectors of $\mathbf{A}$, $\nu_1, \nu_2, \ldots, \nu_{n-k}$ are equal to the roots associated with the remaining $n-k$ latent vectors of $\mathbf{A}$. This result remains true if the regression vectors are (linearly independent) linear combinations of k of the latent vectors of $\mathbf{A}$.

For other cases it would be possible to write down an equation similar to (2) giving the roots of $\mathbf{M}_2\mathbf{M}_1\mathbf{A}$ in terms of $\theta_1, \theta_2, \ldots, \theta_{n-1}$, and so on. In this way it would be theoretically possible to determine $\nu_1, \nu_2, \ldots, \nu_{n-k}$. The resulting equations would, however, be quite unmanageable except in the latent vector case just mentioned.

Inequalities on $\nu_1, \nu_2, \ldots, \nu_{n-k}$

We therefore seek inequalities on $\nu_1, \nu_2, \ldots, \nu_{n-k}$. For the sake of generality we suppose that certain of the regression vectors, say $n-k-s$ of them, coincide with latent vectors of $\mathbf{A}$ (or are linear combinations of them). We are left with s of the ν's for which we require inequalities in terms of the remaining $s+k$ λ's. We renumber them so that

$$\nu_1 \leqslant \nu_2 \leqslant \ldots \leqslant \nu_s,$$
$$\lambda_1 \leqslant \lambda_2 \leqslant \ldots \leqslant \lambda_{s+k}.$$

We proceed to show that $$\lambda_i \leqslant \nu_i \leqslant \lambda_{i+k} \quad (i = 1, 2, \ldots, s). \tag{3}$$

It is convenient to establish first an analogous result for the full sets of ν's and λ's. We therefore arrange the suffixes so that

$$\nu_1 \leqslant \nu_2 \leqslant \ldots \leqslant \nu_{n-k},$$
$$\lambda_1 \leqslant \lambda_2 \leqslant \ldots \leqslant \lambda_n.$$

We also arrange the θ's so that $$\theta_1 \leqslant \theta_2 \leqslant \ldots \leqslant \theta_{n-1}.$$

It was noted above that if $l_r = 0$, λ_r is a root of (2). Also if any two of the λ's, say λ_r and λ_{r+1}, are equal, then $\lambda_r = \lambda_{r+1}$ is a root of (2). These are the only two cases in which any of the λ's is a root of (2).

For the remaining roots let $$f(\theta) = \sum_{i=1}^{n} l_i^2 \prod_{j \neq i}^{n} (\theta - \lambda_i).$$

Then $$f(\lambda_r) = l_r^2 \prod_{j \neq r}^{n} (\lambda_r - \lambda_j),$$

so that if $f(\lambda_r) > 0$ then $f(\lambda_{r+1}) \leqslant 0$, and if $f(\lambda_r) < 0$ then $f(\lambda_{r+1}) \geqslant 0$. Since $f(\theta)$ is continuous there must therefore be a root in every interval $\lambda_r \leqslant \theta \leqslant \lambda_{r+1}$. Thus

$$\lambda_i \leqslant \theta_i \leqslant \lambda_{i+1} \quad (i = 1, 2, \ldots, n-1). \tag{4}$$

To extend this result we recall that $\mathbf{M}_1\mathbf{A}$ has one zero root in addition to $\theta_1, \theta_2, \ldots, \theta_{n-1}$. Suppose $\theta_l \leqslant 0 \leqslant \theta_{l+1}$; then the roots of $\mathbf{M}_1\mathbf{A}$ can be arranged in the order

$$\theta_1 \leqslant \theta_2 \leqslant \ldots \leqslant \theta_l \leqslant 0 \leqslant \theta_{l+1} \leqslant \ldots \leqslant \theta_{n-1}.$$

Let the roots of $\mathbf{M}_2(\mathbf{M}_1\mathbf{A})$ be $\phi_1, \phi_2, \ldots, \phi_{n-1}$ together with one zero root. Then by (4)

$$\theta_1 \leqslant \phi_1 \leqslant \theta_2 \leqslant \phi_2 \leqslant \ldots \leqslant \theta_l \leqslant \phi_l \leqslant 0 \leqslant \phi_{l+1} \leqslant \ldots.$$

But $\mathbf{M}_2\mathbf{M}_1\mathbf{A}$ certainly has two zero roots, since $\mathbf{M}_2\mathbf{M}_1\mathbf{A}$ has rank at most $n-2$. Thus either ϕ_l or ϕ_{l+1} must be zero. Rejecting one of them and renumbering we have

$$\lambda_i \leqslant \phi_i \leqslant \lambda_{i+2} \quad (i = 1, 2, \ldots, n-2).$$

Applying the same argument successively we have

$$\lambda_i \leqslant \nu_i \leqslant \lambda_{i+k} \quad (i = 1, 2, \ldots, n-k).$$

Deleting cases of equality due to regression vectors coinciding with latent vectors of $\mathbf{A}$ we have (3).

The results of this section will be gathered into a lemma.

LEMMA. If $\mathbf{z}$ and $\boldsymbol{\epsilon}$ are $n \times 1$ vectors such that $\mathbf{z} = \mathbf{M}\boldsymbol{\epsilon}$, where $\mathbf{M} = \mathbf{I}_n - \mathbf{X}(\mathbf{X}'\mathbf{X})^{-1}\mathbf{X}'$, and if $r = \dfrac{\mathbf{z}'\mathbf{A}\mathbf{z}}{\mathbf{z}'\mathbf{z}}$, where $\mathbf{A}$ is a real symmetric matrix, then

(a) There is an orthogonal transformation $\boldsymbol{\epsilon} = \mathbf{H}\boldsymbol{\zeta}$, such that

$$r = \frac{\sum_{i=1}^{n-k} \nu_i \zeta_i^2}{\sum_{i=1}^{n-k} \zeta_i^2},$$

where $\nu_1, \nu_2, \ldots, \nu_{n-k}$ are the latent roots of $\mathbf{MA}$ other than k zeros;

(b) If $n-k-s$ of the columns of $\mathbf{X}$ are linear combinations of $n-k-s$ of the latent vectors of $\mathbf{A}$, then $n-k-s$ of the ν's are equal to the latent roots corresponding to these latent vectors; renumbering the remaining roots such that

$$\nu_1 \leqslant \nu_2 \leqslant \ldots \leqslant \nu_s,$$

$$\lambda_1 \leqslant \lambda_2 \leqslant \ldots \leqslant \lambda_{s+k},$$

then

$$\lambda_i \leqslant \nu_i \leqslant \lambda_{i+k} \quad (i = 1, 2, \ldots, s).$$

We deduce the following corollary:

COROLLARY

$$r_L \leqslant r \leqslant r_U,$$

where

$$r_L = \frac{\sum_{i=1}^{s} \lambda_i \zeta_i^2 + \sum_{i=s+1}^{n-k} \lambda_{i+k} \zeta_i^2}{\sum_{i=1}^{n-k} \zeta_i^2}$$

and

$$r_U = \frac{\sum_{i=1}^{n-k} \lambda_{i+k} \zeta_i^2}{\sum_{i=1}^{n-k} \zeta_i^2}.$$

This follows immediately by appropriate numbering of suffixes, taking $\lambda_{s+k+1} \ldots \lambda_n$ as the latent roots corresponding to the latent regression vectors and arranging the remainder so that $\lambda_i \leqslant \lambda_{i+1}$. The importance of this result is that it sets bounds upon r which do not depend upon the particular set of regression vectors. r_L and r_U are the best such bounds in that they can be attained, this being the case when the regression vectors coincide with certain of the latent vectors of $\mathbf{A}$.

3. DISTRIBUTION OF r

It has been pointed out that when the errors are distributed independently of the independent variables the latter can be regarded as fixed. There is one special case, however, in which it is more convenient to regard the x's as varying. We shall discuss this first before going on to consider the more general problem of regression on 'fixed variables'.

The case we shall consider is that of a multivariate normal system. In such a system the regressions are linear and the errors are distributed independently of the independent variables. It will be shown that if $y, x_1, \ldots, x_k$ are distributed jointly normally such that the regression of y on the x's passes through the origin, and if successive observations are independent, then r is distributed as if the residuals $z_1, \ldots, z_n$ were independent normal variables. That is, the regression effect disappears from the problem. Similarly, when the regression does not pass through the origin r is distributed as if the z's were residuals from the sample mean of n normal independent observations.

This is perhaps not a very important case in practice, since it will rarely happen that we shall wish to test the hypothesis of serial correlation in the errors when it is known that successive observations of the x's are independent. Nevertheless, it is convenient to deal with it first before going on to discuss the more important case of regression on 'fixed variables'.

To establish the result we consider the geometrical representation of the sample and observe that the sample value of r depends only on the direction in space of the residual vector z. If the x's are kept fixed and the errors are normal and independent, $\mathbf{z}$ is randomly directed in the $[n-k]$ space orthogonal to the space spanned by the x vectors. If the x's are allowed to vary $\mathbf{z}$ will be randomly directed in the $[n]$ space if and only if the x's are jointly normal and successive observations are independent (Bartlett, 1934). In this case the direction of $\mathbf{z}$ is distributed as if $z_1, z_2, \ldots, z_n$ were normal and independent with the same variance. Thus when $y, x_1, \ldots, x_k$ are multivariate normal such that the regression of y on x passes through the origin, r is distributed as if the residuals from the fitted regression through the origin were normal and independent variables.

In the same way it can be shown that if we fit a regression including a constant term, r is distributed as if the z's were residuals from a sample mean of normal independent variables whether the population regression passes through the origin or not.

Regression on 'fixed variables'

To examine the distribution of r on the null hypothesis in the 'fixed variable' case we assume that the errors $\epsilon_1, \epsilon_2, \ldots, \epsilon_n$ are independent normal variables with constant variance, i.e. they are independent $N(0, \sigma^2)$ variables. Transforming as in §2 we have

$$r = \frac{\sum_{i=1}^{n-k} \nu_i \zeta_i^2}{\sum_{i=1}^{n-k} \zeta_i^2}.$$

Since the transformation is orthogonal, $\zeta_1, \zeta_2, \ldots, \zeta_{n-k}$ are independent $N(0, \sigma^2)$ variables. It is evident that the variation of r is limited to the range (ν_1, ν_{n-k}).

Assuming the ν's known, the exact distribution of r has been given by R. L. Anderson (1942) for two special cases: first for $n-k$ even, the ν's being equal in pairs, and second for $n-k$ odd, the ν's being equal in pairs with one value greater or less than all the others. Anderson's expressions for the distribution function are as follows:

$$P(r > r') = \sum_{i=1}^{m} \frac{(\tau_i - r')^{\frac{1}{2}(n-k)-1}}{\alpha_i} \quad (\tau_{m+1} \leqslant r' \leqslant \tau_m),$$

where

$n-k$ *even*: the ν_i's form $\frac{1}{2}(n-k)$ distinct pairs denoted by $\tau_1 > \tau_2 > \ldots > \tau_{\frac{1}{2}(n-k)}$ and

$$\alpha_i = \prod_{j \neq i}^{\frac{1}{2}(n-k)} (\tau_i - \tau_j),$$

$n-k$ *odd*: the ν_i's form $\frac{1}{2}(n-k-1)$ distinct pairs as above together with one isolated root τ less than all the others and $\alpha_i = \lambda \prod_{j \neq i}^{\frac{1}{2}(n-k-1)} (\tau_i - \tau_j) \sqrt{(\tau_i - \tau)}$.

The expression for $n-k$ odd, $\tau > \tau_1$ is obtained by writing $-r$ for r.

Formulae for the density function are also given by Anderson.

For the case in which the ν's are all different and $n-k$ is even the $[\frac{1}{2}(n-k)-1]$th derivative of the density function has been given by von Neumann (1941), but up to the present no elementary expression for the density function itself has been put forward. Von Neumann's expression for the derivative is as follows:

$$\frac{d^{\frac{1}{2}(n-k)-1}}{dr^{\frac{1}{2}(n-k)-1}}f(r) = 0, \quad m \text{ even}$$

$$= \frac{(-1)^{\frac{1}{2}(n-k-m-1)}\left(\frac{n-k}{2}-1\right)!}{\pi\sqrt{\left(-\prod_{j=1}^{n-k}(r-\nu_i)\right)}}, \quad m \text{ odd}$$

for $\nu_m < r < \nu_{m+1}$, $m = 1, 2, \ldots, n-k-1$.

To use these results in any particular case the ν's would need to be known quantities, which means in practice that the regression vectors must be latent vectors of **A**. In addition, the roots associated with remaining $n-k$ latent vectors of **A** must satisfy R. L. Anderson's or von Neumann's conditions.

The results can also be applied to the distributions of r_L and r_U, the lower and upper bounds of r, provided the appropriate λ's satisfy the conditions. Using the relations

$$F_L(r) \geqslant F(r) \geqslant F_U(r), \tag{5}$$

where F_L and F_U are the distribution functions of r_L and r_U we would then have limits to the distribution function of r. The truth of the relations (5) can be seen by noting that r_L and r are in (1, 1) correspondence and $r_L \leqslant r$ always.

Approximations

R. L. Anderson's distribution becomes unwieldy to work with when $n-k$ is moderately large, and von Neumann's results can only be used to give an exact distribution when $n-k$ is very small. For practical applications, therefore, approximate methods are required.

We first mention the result, pointed out by T. W. Anderson (1948), that as $n-k$ becomes large r is asymptotically normally distributed with the mean and variance given later in this paper. For moderate values of $n-k$, however, it appears that the distributions of certain statistics of the type r are better approximated by a β-distribution, even when symmetric.* One would expect the advantage of the β over the normal approximation to be even greater when the ν's are such that the distribution of r is skew. For better approximations various expansions in terms of β-functions can be used. One such expansion was used for most of the tabulation of the distribution of von Neumann's statistic (Hart 1942). Another method is to use a series expansion in terms of Jacobi polynomials using a β-distribution expression as weight function. (See, for instance, Courant & Hilbert,† 1931, p. 76.) The first four terms of such a series will be used for calculating some of the bounds to the significance points of r tabulated in our second paper.

Moments of r

To use the above approximations we require the moments of r. First we note that since r is independent of the scale of the ζ's we can take σ^2 equal to unity. We therefore require the moments of $r = u/v$, where $u = \sum_{i=1}^{n-k} \nu_i \zeta_i^2$ and $v = \sum_{i=1}^{n-k} \zeta_i^2$, $\zeta_1, \zeta_2, \ldots, \zeta_{n-k}$ being independent $N(0, 1)$ variables.

* See, for instance, Rubin (1945), Dixon (1944), R. L. Anderson and T. W. Anderson (1950).

† Note, however, the misprint: $x^q(1-x)^{p-q}$ should read $x^{q-1}(1-x)^{p-q}$.

It is well known (Pitman, 1937; von Neumann, 1941) that r and v are distributed independently. Consequently

$$E(u^s) = E(r^s v^s) = E(r^s)\,E(v^s),$$

so that

$$E(r^s) = \frac{E(u^s)}{E(v^s)},$$

that is, the moments of the ratio are the ratios of the moments.

The moments of u are most simply obtained by noting that u is the sum of independent variables $\nu_i \zeta_i^2$, where ζ_i^2 is a χ^2 variable with one degree of freedom. Hence the sth cumulant of u is the sum of sth cumulants, that is

$$\kappa_s(u) = 2^{s-1}(s-1)!\sum_{i=1}^{n-k} \nu_i^s,$$

since

$$\kappa_s(\nu_i \zeta_i^2) = 2^{s-1}(s-1)!\,\nu_i^s.$$

In particular

$$\kappa_1(u) = \Sigma\nu_i, \quad \kappa_2(u) = 2\Sigma\nu_i^2.$$

The moments of u can then be obtained from the cumulants.

The moments of v are simply those of χ^2 with $n-k$ degrees of freedom, i.e.

$$E(v) = n-k,$$

$$E(v^2) = (n-k)(n-k+2), \text{ etc.}$$

Hence

$$E(r) = \mu_1' = \frac{1}{n-k}\sum_{i=1}^{n-k} \nu_i = \bar{\nu} \quad \text{say.} \tag{6}$$

To obtain the moments of r about the mean we have

$$r - \mu_1' = \frac{\Sigma(\nu_i - \bar{\nu})\,\zeta_i^2}{\Sigma\zeta_i^2} = \frac{u'}{v} \quad \text{say.}$$

As before the moments of $r-\mu_1'$ are the moments of u' divided by the moments of v. The moments of u' are obtained from the cumulants

$$\kappa_s(u') = 2^{s-1}(s-1)!\sum_{i=1}^{n-k} (\nu_i - \bar{\nu})^s.$$

In this way we find

$$\left.\begin{aligned} \operatorname{var} r = \mu_2 &= \frac{2\Sigma(\nu_i-\bar{\nu})^2}{(n-k)(n-k+2)}, \\ \mu_3 &= \frac{8\Sigma(\nu_i-\bar{\nu})^3,}{(n-k)(n-k+2)(n-k+4)}, \\ \mu_4 &= \frac{48\Sigma(\nu_i-\bar{\nu})^4 + 12\{\Sigma(\nu_i-\bar{\nu})^2\}^2}{(n-k)(n-k+2)(n-k+4)(n-k+6)}. \end{aligned}\right\} \tag{7}$$

It must be emphasized at this point that the moments just given refer to regression through the origin on k independent variables. If the regression model includes a constant term, that is, if the calculated regression includes a fitted mean, and if, as is usual, we wish to distinguish the remaining independent variables from the constant term, then k must be taken equal to $k'+1$ in the above expressions, k' being the number of independent variables in addition to the constant. We emphasize this point, since it is k' that is usually referred to as the number of independent variables in such a model.

The expressions given will enable the moments of r to be calculated when the ν's are known. In most cases that will arise in practice, however, the ν's will be unknown and it will be impracticable to calculate them. We therefore require means of expressing the power sums $\Sigma \nu_i^2$ in terms of known quantities, namely the matrix **A** and the independent variables.

To do this we make use of the concept of the trace of a matrix, that is, the sum of its leading diagonal elements. This is denoted for a matrix **S** by tr **S**, **S** being of course square. It is easy to show that the operation of taking a trace satisfies the following simple rules:

(*a*) $\operatorname{tr}(\mathbf{S}+\mathbf{T}) = \operatorname{tr}\mathbf{S}+\operatorname{tr}\mathbf{T}$,

(*b*) $\operatorname{tr}\mathbf{ST} = \operatorname{tr}\mathbf{TS}$ whether **S** and **T** are square or rectangular.

From these rules we deduce a third:

(*c*) $\operatorname{tr}(\mathbf{S}+\mathbf{T})^q = \operatorname{tr}\mathbf{S}^q + \binom{q}{1}\operatorname{tr}\mathbf{S}^{q-1}\mathbf{T} + \binom{q}{2}\operatorname{tr}\mathbf{S}^{q-2}\mathbf{T}^2 + \ldots + \operatorname{tr}\mathbf{T}^q$,

when **S** and **T** are square. In addition, we note that $\operatorname{tr}\mathbf{S} = \sum_{i=1}^{m} \sigma_i$, where $\sigma_1, \sigma_2, \ldots, \sigma_m$ are the latent roots of **S**, and in general that $\operatorname{tr}\mathbf{S}^q = \sum_{i=1}^{m} \sigma_i^q$.

Thus we have immediately $$\sum_{i=1}^{n-k} \nu_i^q = \operatorname{tr}(\mathbf{MA})^q,$$

since $\nu_1, \nu_2, \ldots, \nu_{n-k}$ together with k zeros are the latent roots of **MA**.

In cases in which the independent variables are known constants it is sometimes possible to construct the matrix **MA** directly and hence to obtain the mean and variance of r in a fairly straightforward way.

For models of other types in which the independent variables can take arbitrary values further reduction is needed. For the mean we require

$$\begin{aligned}\Sigma \nu_i &= \operatorname{tr}\mathbf{MA} = \operatorname{tr}\{\mathbf{I}_n - \mathbf{X}(\mathbf{X}'\mathbf{X})^{-1}\mathbf{X}\}\mathbf{A} \\ &= \operatorname{tr}\mathbf{A} - \operatorname{tr}\mathbf{X}(\mathbf{X}'\mathbf{X})^{-1}\mathbf{X}'\mathbf{A} \quad \text{by rule } (a) \\ &= \operatorname{tr}\mathbf{A} - \operatorname{tr}\mathbf{X}'\mathbf{AX}(\mathbf{X}'\mathbf{X})^{-1} \quad \text{by rule } (b). \end{aligned} \tag{8}$$

The calculation of this expression is not as formidable an undertaking as might at first sight appear, since $(\mathbf{X}'\mathbf{X})^{-1}$ will effectively have to be calculated in any case for the estimation of the regression coefficients. It is interesting to note incidentally that the matrix $\mathbf{X}'\mathbf{AX}(\mathbf{X}'\mathbf{X})^{-1}$ in the expression is a direct multivariate generalization of the statistic r.

For the variance we require

$$\begin{aligned}\Sigma \nu_i^2 &= \operatorname{tr}(\mathbf{MA})^2 = \operatorname{tr}\{\mathbf{A} - \mathbf{X}(\mathbf{X}'\mathbf{X})^{-1}\mathbf{X}'\mathbf{A}\}^2 \\ &= \operatorname{tr}\mathbf{A}^2 - 2\operatorname{tr}\mathbf{X}'\mathbf{A}^2\mathbf{X}(\mathbf{X}'\mathbf{X})^{-1} + \operatorname{tr}\{\mathbf{X}'\mathbf{AX}(\mathbf{X}'\mathbf{X})^{-1}\}^2,\end{aligned} \tag{9}$$

by rules (*b*) and (*c*).

Similarly

$$\begin{aligned}\Sigma \nu_i^3 = \operatorname{tr}\mathbf{A}^3 &- 3\operatorname{tr}\mathbf{X}'\mathbf{A}^3\mathbf{X}(\mathbf{X}'\mathbf{X})^{-1} \\ &+ 3\operatorname{tr}\{\mathbf{X}'\mathbf{A}^2\mathbf{X}(\mathbf{X}'\mathbf{X})^{-1}\mathbf{X}'\mathbf{AX}(\mathbf{X}'\mathbf{X})^{-1}\} + \operatorname{tr}\{\mathbf{X}'\mathbf{AX}(\mathbf{X}'\mathbf{X})^{-1}\}^3,\end{aligned} \tag{10}$$

$$\begin{aligned}\Sigma \nu_i^4 = \operatorname{tr}\mathbf{A}^4 &- 4\operatorname{tr}\mathbf{X}'\mathbf{A}^4\mathbf{X}(\mathbf{X}'\mathbf{X})^{-1} + 6\operatorname{tr}\{\mathbf{X}'\mathbf{A}^3\mathbf{X}(\mathbf{X}'\mathbf{X})^{-1}\mathbf{X}'\mathbf{AX}(\mathbf{X}'\mathbf{X})^{-1}\} \\ &- 4\operatorname{tr}[\mathbf{X}'\mathbf{A}^2\mathbf{X}(\mathbf{X}'\mathbf{X})^{-1}\{\mathbf{X}'\mathbf{AX}(\mathbf{X}'\mathbf{X})^{-1}\}^2] + \operatorname{tr}\{\mathbf{X}'\mathbf{AX}(\mathbf{X}'\mathbf{X})^{-1}\}^4,\end{aligned} \tag{11}$$

and so on.

When the independent variables are orthogonal these expressions can be simplified somewhat since $\mathbf{X}'\mathbf{X}$ is then a diagonal matrix. Thus

$$\operatorname{tr}\mathbf{X}'\mathbf{AX}(\mathbf{X}'\mathbf{X})^{-1} = \sum_{i=1}^{k} \frac{\mathbf{x}_i'\mathbf{A}\mathbf{x}_i}{\mathbf{x}_i'\mathbf{x}_i},$$

$\mathbf{x}_i$ standing for the vector of sample values of the ith independent variable. Each term in the summation has the form r in terms of one of the independent variables. Similarly for $\operatorname{tr}\mathbf{X}'\mathbf{A}^2\mathbf{X}(\mathbf{X}'\mathbf{X})^{-1}$, $\operatorname{tr}\mathbf{X}'\mathbf{A}^3\mathbf{X}(\mathbf{X}'\mathbf{X})^{-1}$, etc. We have also

$$\operatorname{tr}\{\mathbf{X}'\mathbf{A}\mathbf{X}(\mathbf{X}'\mathbf{X})^{-1}\}^2 = \sum_{i=1}^{k}\left(\frac{\mathbf{x}_i'\mathbf{A}\mathbf{x}_i}{\mathbf{x}_i'\mathbf{x}_i}\right)^2 + 2\sum_{i\neq j}^{k}\frac{(\mathbf{x}_i'\mathbf{A}\mathbf{x}_j)^2}{\mathbf{x}_i'\mathbf{x}_i\,\mathbf{x}_j'\mathbf{x}_j}.$$

Thus when the regression vectors are orthogonal the following formulae enable us to calculate the mean and variance of r:

$$\left.\begin{aligned}\Sigma\nu_i &= \operatorname{tr}\mathbf{A} - \sum_{i=1}^{k}\frac{\mathbf{x}_i'\mathbf{A}\mathbf{x}_i}{\mathbf{x}_i'\mathbf{x}_i},\\ \Sigma\nu_i^2 &= \operatorname{tr}\mathbf{A}^2 - 2\sum_{i=1}^{k}\frac{\mathbf{x}_i'\mathbf{A}^2\mathbf{x}_i}{\mathbf{x}_i'\mathbf{x}_i} + \sum_{i=1}^{k}\left(\frac{\mathbf{x}_i'\mathbf{A}\mathbf{x}_i}{\mathbf{x}_i'\mathbf{x}_i}\right)^2 + 2\sum_{i<j}^{k}\frac{(\mathbf{x}_i'\mathbf{A}\mathbf{x}_j)^2}{\mathbf{x}_i'\mathbf{x}_i\mathbf{x}_j'\mathbf{x}_j}.\end{aligned}\right\}\quad(12)$$

The mean and variance are obtained by substituting these values in (6) and (7).

Similar results apply when $\mathbf{X}$ is partitioned into two or more orthogonal sets of variables. For instance, when $\mathbf{X}$ consists of the constant vector $\{c, c, \dots, c\}$ together with the matrix $\dot{\mathbf{X}}$ of deviations from the means of the remaining $k-1$ variables, i.e.

$$\dot{\mathbf{x}}_{ij} = \mathbf{x}_{ij} - \overline{\mathbf{x}}_i (i = 2, 3, \dots, k;\ j = 1, 2, \dots, n),$$

then $$\operatorname{tr}\mathbf{X}'\mathbf{A}\mathbf{X}(\mathbf{X}'\mathbf{X})^{-1} = \frac{\mathbf{i}'\mathbf{A}\mathbf{i}}{n} + \operatorname{tr}\dot{\mathbf{X}}'\mathbf{A}\dot{\mathbf{X}}(\dot{\mathbf{X}}'\dot{\mathbf{X}})^{-1},$$

$$\operatorname{tr}\{\mathbf{X}'\mathbf{A}\mathbf{X}(\mathbf{X}'\mathbf{X})^{-1}\}^2 = \left(\frac{\mathbf{i}'\mathbf{A}\mathbf{i}}{n}\right)^2 + \frac{2\mathbf{i}'\mathbf{A}\dot{\mathbf{X}}(\dot{\mathbf{X}}'\dot{\mathbf{X}})^{-1}\dot{\mathbf{X}}'\mathbf{A}\mathbf{i}}{n} + \operatorname{tr}\{\dot{\mathbf{X}}'\mathbf{A}\dot{\mathbf{X}}(\dot{\mathbf{X}}'\dot{\mathbf{X}})^{-1}\}^2,$$

where $\mathbf{i}$ is the equiangular vector $\{1, 1, \dots, 1\}$. When this is a latent vector of $\mathbf{A}$ corresponding to a latent root of zero, $\mathbf{i}'\mathbf{A} = \mathbf{O}$. We then have the important result that (8)–(11) apply without change except that the original variables $\mathbf{X}$ are replaced by the deviations from their means $\dot{\mathbf{X}}$. This result holds whenever $\mathbf{x}'\mathbf{A}\mathbf{x}$ is invariant under a change of origin of $\mathbf{x}$.

Before closing this treatment of moments we should mention one difficulty in using them for obtaining approximations in terms of β-distributions and associated expansions. In constructing such approximations one usually knows the range within which the variable is distributed. In the present problem, however, the range is (ν_1, ν_{n-k}), which will often be unknown and impracticable to determine. In such cases it will accordingly be necessary to use approximations to ν_1 and ν_{n-k} before the distributions can be fitted.

Characteristic function of u and v

An alternative method of obtaining the moments of u and v is to use their joint characteristic function. This is given by

$$\begin{aligned}\phi(t_1, t_2) &= \frac{1}{(2\pi)^{\frac{1}{2}(n-k)}}\int\dots\int\exp(it_1\Sigma\nu_i\zeta_i^2 + it_2\Sigma\zeta_i^2 - \tfrac{1}{2}\Sigma\zeta_i^2)\,d\zeta_1\dots d\zeta_{n-k}\\ &= \prod_{j=1}^{n-k}(1-2\nu_j it_1 - 2it_2)^{-\frac{1}{2}}\\ &= (1-2it_2)^{\frac{1}{2}k}\prod_{j=1}^{n-k}(1-2it_2-2\nu_j it_1)^{-\frac{1}{2}}(1-2it_2)^{-\frac{1}{2}k}\\ &= (1-2it_2)^{\frac{1}{2}k}\,|\,\mathbf{I}_n(1-2it_2) - 2it_1\mathbf{MA}\,|^{-\frac{1}{2}},\end{aligned}$$

since $\nu_1 \dots \nu_{n-k}$ together with k zeros are the roots of the equation $|\,\mathbf{I}_n\nu - \mathbf{MA}\,| = 0$.

A more manageable expression can be obtained by considering first the case of a single independent variable. The characteristic function $\phi_1(t_1 t_2)$ is then given by

$$\frac{1}{\phi_1^2} = \prod_{j=1}^{n-1} (1-2\theta_j it_1 - 2it_2), \tag{13}$$

where $\theta_1, \theta_2, \ldots, \theta_{n-1}$ are the roots of the equation

$$\sum_{i=1}^{n} l_i^2 \prod_{j \neq i}^{n} (\theta - \lambda_j) = 0. \tag{2 bis}$$

Consequently

$$\prod_{j=1}^{n-1} (\theta - \theta_j) = \sum_{i=1}^{n} l_i^2 \prod_{j \neq i}^{n} (\theta - \lambda_j)$$

$$= \prod_{j=1}^{n} (\theta - \lambda_j) \sum_{j=1}^{n} \frac{l_j^2}{\theta - \lambda_j}$$

for all values of θ except $\lambda_1, \lambda_2, \ldots, \lambda_n$. From (13)

$$\frac{1}{\phi_1^2} = (2it_1)^{n-1} \prod_{j=1}^{n-1} \left(\frac{1-2it_2}{2it_1} - \theta_j\right)$$

$$= (2it_1)^{n-1} \prod_{j=1}^{n} \left(\frac{1-2it_2}{2it_1} - \theta_j\right) \sum_{j=1}^{n} \frac{l_j^2}{\dfrac{1-2it_2}{2it_1} - \lambda_j}$$

$$= \prod_{j=1}^{n} (1-2\lambda_j it_1 - 2it_2) \sum_{j=1}^{n} \frac{l_j^2}{(1-2\lambda_j it_1 - 2it_2)}. \tag{14}$$

The left-hand factor of this expression is the characteristic function of u and v that would be obtained if the z's were independent normal variables, the right-hand factor giving the modification due to the fitting of a regression on a single independent variable.

To reduce the expression further we note that $\dfrac{1}{1-2\lambda_j it_1 - 2it_2}$ $(j = 1, 2, \ldots, n)$ are the latent roots of the matrix

$$\{(1-2it_2)\mathbf{I}_n - 2it_1 \mathbf{A}\}^{-1} = \mathbf{B}^{-1} \text{ say.}$$

Moreover, the latent vectors of $\mathbf{B}^{-1}$ are the same as those of $\mathbf{A}$ so that $l_1, l_2, \ldots, l_n$ are the direction cosines of the vector $\mathbf{x}$ relative to these latent vectors. Consequently

$$\sum_{j=1}^{n} \frac{l_i^2}{1-2\lambda_j it_1 - 2it_2} = \frac{\mathbf{x}'\mathbf{B}^{-1}\mathbf{x}}{\mathbf{x}'\mathbf{x}},$$

where $\mathbf{x}$ is the independent variable concerned. Also

$$\prod_{j=1}^{n} (1-2\lambda_j it_1 - 2it_2) = |\mathbf{B}|.$$

Thus

$$\frac{1}{\phi_1^2} = |\mathbf{B}| \frac{\mathbf{x}'\mathbf{B}^{-1}\mathbf{x}}{\mathbf{x}'\mathbf{x}}. \tag{15}$$

It is interesting to note that the second factor takes the general form r.

By a direct extension of this argument it can be shown that for regression on k independent variables the characteristic function is given by

$$\frac{1}{\phi^2} = |\mathbf{B}_1| \prod_{s=1}^{k} \frac{\mathbf{x}_s'\mathbf{B}_s^{-1}\mathbf{x}_s}{\mathbf{x}_s'\mathbf{x}_s},$$

where

$$\mathbf{B}_s = (1-2it_2)\mathbf{I}_n - 2it_1 \mathbf{M}_{s-1} \ldots \mathbf{M}_2 \mathbf{M}_1 \mathbf{A},$$

the $\mathbf{M}_i$'s being defined as in §2. This result could also be written down directly given (15) in virtue of the reproductive property of the products ... $\mathbf{M}_2\mathbf{M}_1\mathbf{A}$ mentioned in §2.

Putting $t_2 = 0$ we obtain the characteristic function of u. The cumulants and hence the moments can then be obtained by the expansion of $\log \phi$.

4. Choice of test criterion*

To decide upon a suitable test criterion an important consideration is the set of alternative hypotheses against which it is desired to discriminate. The kind of alternative we have in mind in this paper is such that the correlogram of the errors diminishes approximately exponentially with increasing separation of the observations. A convenient model for such hypotheses is the stationary Markoff process

$$\epsilon_i = \rho\epsilon_{i-1} + u_i \quad (i = \ldots -1, 0, 1, \ldots), \tag{16}$$

where $|\rho| < 1$ and u_i is normal with mean zero and variance σ^2 and is independent of $\epsilon_{i-1}, \epsilon_{i-2}, \ldots$ and $u_{i-1}, u_{i-2}, \ldots$. The null hypothesis is then the hypothesis that $\rho = 0$ in (16).

It has been shown by T. W. Anderson (1948) that no test of this hypothesis exists which is uniformly most powerful against alternatives (16). Anderson also showed, however, that for certain regression systems with error distributions close to that given by (16) tests can be obtained which are uniformly most powerful against one-sided alternatives (16) and which give type B_1 regions for two-sided alternatives (16).

These regression systems include cases in which the regression vectors are constant vectors coinciding with latent vectors of a matrix $\mathbf{\Theta}$ (or with linear combinations of k of them) and in which the error distributions have density functions of the form

$$K \exp\left[-\frac{1}{2\sigma^2}\{(1+\rho^2)\boldsymbol{\epsilon}'\boldsymbol{\epsilon} - 2\rho\boldsymbol{\epsilon}'\mathbf{\Theta}\boldsymbol{\epsilon}\}\right]. \tag{17}$$

For such cases the uniformly most powerful test of the hypothesis $\rho = 0$ against alternatives $\rho > 0$ is given by $r > r_0$, where $r = \dfrac{\mathbf{z}'\mathbf{\Theta}\mathbf{z}}{\mathbf{z}'\mathbf{z}}$, $\mathbf{z}$ being the vector of residuals from least squares regression, and r_0 being determined to give a critical region of appropriate size. For two-sided alternatives to $\rho = 0$ the type B_1 test is given by $r < r_2$, $r > r_3$, where r_2 and r_3 are determined so as to give a critical region of appropriate size and to satisfy the relation

$$\int_{r_2}^{r_3} rp(r)\,dr = E(r)\int_{r_2}^{r_3} p(r)\,dr,$$

$p(r)$ being the density function of r in the null case.

We recall that whatever the regression vectors,

$$r_L \leqslant r \leqslant r_U, \tag{18}$$

where r_L and r_U are defined in the Corollary, §2. Now r_L and r_U have distributions in the null case identical with distributions of r obtained from residuals from regressions on certain latent vectors of the matrix $\mathbf{A}$. Thus if we put $\mathbf{\Theta} = \mathbf{A}$ in (17) we can say that when the lower bound r_L in (18) is attained (or the upper bound), the statistic $r = \dfrac{\mathbf{z}'\mathbf{A}\mathbf{z}}{\mathbf{z}'\mathbf{z}}$ gives a test which is uniformly most powerful against one-sided alternatives (16) and which is of type B_1 against two-sided alternatives.

The error distribution for the stationary Markoff process (16) has the density function

$$K \exp\left[-\frac{1}{2\sigma^2}\left\{(1+\rho^2)\sum_{i=1}^{n}\epsilon_i^2 - \rho^2(\epsilon_1^2+\epsilon_n^2) - 2\rho\sum_{i=2}^{n}\epsilon_i\epsilon_{i-1}\right\}\right]. \tag{19}$$

* This section is based on the treatment given by T. W. Anderson (1948).

Taking $\boldsymbol{\epsilon}'\boldsymbol{\Theta}\boldsymbol{\epsilon} = \sum_{i=2}^{n} \epsilon_i \epsilon_{i-1}$ in (17) gives a density function

$$K \exp\left[-\frac{1}{2\sigma^2}\left\{(1+\rho^2)\sum_{i=1}^{n}\epsilon_i^2 - 2\rho\sum_{i=2}^{n}\epsilon_i\epsilon_{i-1}\right\}\right], \tag{20}$$

while taking $\boldsymbol{\epsilon}'\boldsymbol{\Theta}\boldsymbol{\epsilon} = \sum_{i=1}^{n} \epsilon_i^2 - \frac{1}{2}\sum_{i=2}^{n}(\epsilon_i - \epsilon_{i-1})^2$ in (17) gives a density function

$$K \exp\left[-\frac{1}{2\sigma^2}\left\{(1+\rho^2)\sum_{i=1}^{n}\epsilon_i^2 - \rho(\epsilon_1^2+\epsilon_n^2) - 2\rho\sum_{i=2}^{n}\epsilon_i\epsilon_{i-1}\right\}\right]. \tag{21}$$

These are both close to (19). Thus following Anderson we conjecture that either value of $\boldsymbol{\Theta}$ would give a good statistic r for testing against alternatives (16). Between the two statistics there is not much to choose. We ourselves have adopted a slight modification of the second, partly for reasons of computational convenience and partly because of similarity to von Neumann's statistic δ^2/s^2 (1941) already well known to research workers.

The statistic we have adopted is defined by

$$d = \frac{\sum_{i=2}^{n}(z_i - z_{i-1})^2}{\sum_{i=1}^{n} z_i^2},$$

which is related to $\frac{\delta^2}{s^2}$ by $\frac{\delta^2}{s^2} = \frac{nd}{n-1}$. This is a special case of the general statistic $r = \frac{\mathbf{z}'\mathbf{A}\mathbf{z}}{\mathbf{z}'\mathbf{z}}$ discussed in § 2 and § 3, in which

$$\mathbf{A} = \mathbf{A}_d = \tfrac{1}{2}\begin{pmatrix} 1 & -1 & 0 & 0 & \ldots & \ldots & 0 \\ -1 & 2 & -1 & 0 & \ldots & \ldots & \ldots \\ 0 & -1 & 2 & -1 & \ldots & \ldots & \ldots \\ 0 & 0 & -1 & 2 & \ldots & \ldots & \ldots \\ \ldots & \ldots & \ldots & \ldots & \ldots & \ldots & \ldots \\ \ldots & \ldots & \ldots & \ldots & \ldots & 2 & -1 \\ 0 & \ldots & \ldots & \ldots & 0 & -1 & 1 \end{pmatrix}.$$

In the notation of the previous paragraph we would take $\boldsymbol{\Theta} = \mathbf{I} - \frac{1}{2}\mathbf{A}_d$ to give the density (21). Now the latent vectors of the matrices $\mathbf{A}_d$ and $\boldsymbol{\Theta}$ in this equation are the same. Thus when the regression vectors are latent vectors of $\mathbf{A}_d$ the statistic d provides a uniformly most powerful test against one-sided alternatives (21). In particular the test given by d when the bounds r_L and r_U are attained is uniformly most powerful.

The main alternative to using d or a related statistic as a test criterion would be to use one of the circular statistics such as

$$r_c = \frac{\sum_{i=1}^{n} z_i z_{i-1}}{\sum_{i=1}^{n} z_i^2}$$

or

$$d_c = \frac{\sum_{i=1}^{n}(z_i - z_{i-1})^2}{\sum_{i=1}^{n} z_i^2},$$

where we define $z_0 \equiv z_n$ in each case. T. W. Anderson (1948) has shown that r_c and d_c give uniformly most powerful tests against one-sided alternatives in the circular population having a density function

$$K \exp\left[-\frac{1}{2\sigma^2}\left\{(1+\rho^2)\sum_{i=1}^{n} \epsilon_i^2 - 2\rho \sum_{i=1}^{n} \epsilon_i \epsilon_{i-1}\right\}\right], \tag{22}$$

where $\epsilon_0 \equiv \epsilon_n$. r_c was the statistic adopted by R. L. Anderson & T. W. Anderson (1950) for testing the residuals from regression on a Fourier series.

The disadvantage of r_c and d_c is that (22) is not so close to (19) as (20) or (21). The advantage is that since the latent roots of the associated values of **A** are equal in pairs, the results of R. L. Anderson (1942) can sometimes be used to obtain exact distributions in the null case. The roots of $\mathbf{A}_d$, on the other hand, are all distinct. We conclude that d or a related non-circular statistic would seem to be preferable whenever an approximation to the distribution is sufficient, but that a circular statistic would seem to be preferable if exact results are required at the expense of some loss of power. We mention that the computations involved in using Anderson's exact distribution become very tedious as the number of degrees of freedom increases.

The next question that arises is how good these statistics are as test criteria in cases in which the regression vectors are not latent vectors. Such cases are of course by far the more frequent in practice. It is evident that we can expect the power of the test to diminish as the regression vectors depart from the latent vectors, since the least squares regression coefficients are not then maximum likelihood estimates in the non-null case. Thus any test based on least squares residuals cannot even be a likelihood ratio test. Against this three points can be made. The first is that we still have a valid test, though possibly of reduced power. Secondly, it is desirable on grounds of convenience to have a test based on least squares residuals even though it is not an optimal test. Thirdly, the statistic r necessarily lies between the bounds r_L and r_U and when these bounds are attained the test is optimal. We note also that it is only for the latent vector case that the distribution problems have been approached with any success.

5. Some special results

To obtain the moments of d we need the powers of $\mathbf{A}_d$. Because of the symmetry of these matrices they are completely specified by the top left-hand triangle. Thus we can write

$$\mathbf{A}_d \doteq \begin{array}{ccc} 1 & -1 & 0 \\ & 2 & -1 \\ & & 2 \end{array}$$

We find

$$\mathbf{A}_d^2 \doteq \begin{array}{cccc} 2 & -3 & 1 & 0 \\ & 6 & -4 & 1 \\ & & 6 & -4 \\ & & & 6 \end{array}$$

$$\mathbf{A}_d^3 \doteq \begin{array}{cccccc} 5 & -9 & 5 & -1 & 0 & 0 \\ & 19 & -15 & 6 & -1 & 0 \\ & & 20 & -15 & 6 & -1 \\ & & & 20 & -15 & 6 \end{array}$$

$$\mathbf{A}_d^4 \doteq \begin{array}{ccccccc} 14 & -28 & 20 & -7 & 1 & 0 & 0 \\ & 62 & -55 & 28 & -8 & 1 & 0 \\ & & 70 & -56 & 28 & -8 & 1 \\ & & & 70 & -56 & 28 & 1 \end{array}$$

Rather than use these matrices as they stand, however, it will probably be more convenient to proceed by finding the sums of squares of the successive differences of the z's. Denoting the sth differences by $\Delta^s z$ we have

$$\left.\begin{aligned}
z'\mathbf{A}_d z &= \sum_{i=1}^{n-1} (\Delta z_i)^2,\\
z'\mathbf{A}_d^2 z &= \Sigma(\Delta^2 z_i)^2 + (z_1 - z_2)^2 + (z_{n-1} - z_n)^2,\\
z'\mathbf{A}_d^3 z &= \Sigma(\Delta^3 z_i)^2 + 4z_1^2 + 9z_2^2 + z_3^2 - 12z_1z_2 - 6z_2z_3 + 4z_1z_3 + \text{a similar expression in } z_n, z_{n-1}, z_{n-2},\\
z'\mathbf{A}_d^4 z &= \Sigma(\Delta^4 z_i)^2 + 13z_1^2 + 45z_2^2 + 17z_3^2 + z_4^2 - 48z_1z_2 - 54z_2z_3 - 8z_3z_4 + 28z_1z_3 + 12z_2z_4\\
&\quad - 6z_1z_4 + \text{a similar expression in } z_n, z_{n-1}, z_{n-2}, z_{n-3}.
\end{aligned}\right\} \tag{23}$$

For the circular definition of d, i.e.

$$d_c = \frac{\sum_{i=1}^{n} (z_i - z_{i-1})^2}{\sum_{i=1}^{n} z_i^2} = \frac{\mathbf{z}'\mathbf{A}_{dc}\mathbf{z}}{\mathbf{z}'\mathbf{z}} \quad \text{with } z_0 \equiv z_n,$$

the correction terms disappear, giving

$$z'\mathbf{A}_{dc}^s z = \sum_{i=1}^{n} (\Delta^s z_i)^2, \quad \text{where} \quad z_{-i} \equiv z_{n-i}.$$

The latent roots of $\mathbf{A}_d$ are given by

$$\lambda_j = 2\left\{1 - \cos\frac{\pi(j-1)}{n}\right\} \quad (j = 1, 2, \ldots, n) \tag{24}$$

(von Neumann 1941). The first four power sums are:

$$\left.\begin{aligned}
\sum_{j=1}^{n} \lambda_j &= 2(n-1),\\
\Sigma\lambda_j^2 &= 2(3n-4),\\
\Sigma\lambda_j^3 &= 4(5n-8),\\
\Sigma\lambda_j^4 &= 2(35n-64).
\end{aligned}\right\} \tag{25}$$

The latent vector corresponding to the zero root λ_1 is $\{1, 1, \ldots, 1\}$, which is the regression vector corresponding to a constant term in the regression model. For regressions with a fitted mean, therefore, we need only consider the remaining $n-1$ λ's which we renumber accordingly so that

$$\lambda_j = 2\left(1 - \cos\frac{\pi j}{n}\right) \quad (j = 1, 2, \ldots, n-1).$$

With these λ's we have from the Corollary, §2,

$$d_L \leqslant d \leqslant d_U, \tag{26}$$

where

$$d_L = \frac{\sum_{i=1}^{n-k'-1} \lambda_i \zeta_i^2}{\sum_{i=1}^{n-k'-1} \zeta_i^2}, \tag{27}$$

$$d_U = \frac{\sum_{i=1}^{n-k'-1} \lambda_{i+k'} \zeta_i^2}{\sum_{i=1}^{n-k'-1} \zeta_i^2}, \tag{28}$$

k' being the number of independent variables in the model in addition to the constant term.

With the error distribution assumed in §3 the limits of the mean of d are given by

$$E(d) \leqslant E(d_U) = 2 - \frac{2}{n-k'-1} \sum_{j=k'+1}^{n-1} \cos\frac{\pi j}{n}$$

$$\geqslant E(d_L) = 2 - \frac{2}{n-k'-1} \sum_{j=1}^{n-k'-1} \cos\frac{\pi j}{n}.$$

We state without proof the limits of the variance of d:

$$\operatorname{var}(d) \leqslant \frac{16}{(n-k'-1)(n-k'+1)} \sum_{j=1}^{\frac{1}{2}(n-k'-1)} \cos^2\frac{\pi j}{n} \quad (n-k' \text{ odd}),$$

$$\leqslant \frac{16}{(n-k'-1)(n-k'+1)} \sum_{j=1}^{\frac{1}{2}(n-k')-1} \cos^2\frac{\pi j}{n} + \frac{8(n-k'-2)}{(n-k'-1)^2(n-k'+1)} \cos^2\frac{(n-k')\pi}{2n} \quad (n-k' \text{ even}),$$

$$\geqslant \frac{16}{(n-k'-1)(n-k'+1)} \sum_{i=k'+1}^{\frac{1}{2}(n-1)} \cos^2\frac{\pi j}{n} \quad (n \text{ odd}),$$

$$\geqslant \frac{16}{(n-k'-1)(n-k'+1)} \sum_{i=k'+1}^{\frac{1}{2}(n-2)} \cos^2\frac{\pi j}{n} \quad (n \text{ even}).$$

To give some idea of how the distribution of d can vary for different regression vectors we give a short table of the limiting means and variances.

		$k'=1$		$k'=3$		$k'=5$	
		Mean	Variance	Mean	Variance	Mean	Variance
$n=20$	Lower	1·89	0·157	1·65	0·101	1·38	0·048
	Upper	2·11	0·200	2·35	0·249	2·62	0·313
$n=40$	Lower	1·95	0·090	1·84	0·077	1·72	0·063
	Upper	2·05	0·100	2·16	0·111	2·28	0·124
$n=60$	Lower	1·97	0·062	1·89	0·057	1·82	0·051
	Upper	2·03	0·067	2·11	0·071	2·18	0·077

We wish to record our indebtedness to Prof. R. L. Anderson for suggesting this problem to one of us.

REFERENCES

AITKEN, A. C. (1935). *Proc. Roy. Soc. Edinb.* **55**, 42.
ANDERSON, R. L. (1942). *Ann. Math. Statist.* **13**, 1.
ANDERSON, R. L. & ANDERSON, T. W. (1950). *Ann. Math. Statist.* **21**, 59.
ANDERSON, T. W. (1948). *Skand. AktuarTidskr.* **31**, 88.
BARTLETT, M. S. (1934). *Proc. Camb. Phil. Soc.* **30**, 327.
COCHRANE, D. & ORCUTT, G. H. (1949). *J. Amer. Statist. Soc.* **44**, 32.

COURANT, R. & HILBERT, D. (1931). *Methoden der Mathematischen Physik.* Julius Springer.
DIXON, W. J. (1944). *Ann. Math. Statist.* **15**, 119.
FISHER, R. A. (1946). *Statistical Methods for Research Workers*, 10th ed. Oliver and Boyd.
HART, B. I. (1942). *Ann. Math. Statist.* **13**, 207.
MORAN, P. A. P. (1950). *Biometrika* **37**, 178.
VON NEUMANN, J. (1941). *Ann. Math. Statist.* **12**, 367.
PITMAN, E. J. G. (1937). *Proc. Camb. Phil. Soc.* **33**, 212.
RUBIN, H. (1945). *Ann. Math. Statist.* **16**, 211.
WOLD, H. (1949). 'On least squares regression with auto-correlated variables and residuals.' (Paper read at the 1949 Conference of the International Statistical Institute.)

TESTING FOR SERIAL CORRELATION IN LEAST SQUARES REGRESSION. II

1. Introduction

In an earlier paper (Durbin & Watson, 1950) the authors investigated the problem of testing the error terms of a regression model for serial correlation. Test criteria were put forward, their moments calculated, and bounds to their distribution functions were obtained. In the present paper these bounds are tabulated and their use in practice is described. For cases in which the bounds do not settle the question of significance an approximate method is suggested. Expressions are given for the mean and variance of a test statistic for one- and two-way classifications and polynomial trends, leading to approximate tests for these cases. The procedures described should be capable of application by the practical worker without reference to the earlier paper (hereinafter referred to as Part I).

It should be emphasized that the tests described in this paper apply only to regression models in which the independent variables can be regarded as 'fixed variables'. They do not, therefore, apply to autoregressive schemes and similar models in which lagged values of the dependent variable occur as independent variables.

2. The bounds test

Throughout the paper the procedures suggested will be illustrated by numerical examples. We begin by considering some data from a demand analysis study.

Example 1. *Annual consumption of spirits from* 1870 *to* 1938. The data (given in Table 1) were compiled by A. R. Prest, to whose paper (1949) reference should be made for details of the source material. As is common in econometric work the original observations were transformed by taking logarithms:

y = log consumption of spirits per head;

x_1 = log real income per head;

x_2 = log relative price of spirits (i.e. price of spirits deflated by a cost-of-living index).

We suppose that the observations satisfy the regression model

$$y = \beta_0 + \beta_1 x_1 + \beta_2 x_2 + \epsilon, \tag{1}$$

where β_0 is a constant, β_1 is the income elasticity, β_2 is the price elasticity, and ϵ is a random error with zero mean and constant variance.

To test the errors for serial correlation the following sums of squares and products are required:

$\Sigma(y-\bar{y})^2$	$= 5{\cdot}000123$	$\Sigma(y-\bar{y})(x_2-\bar{x}_2)$	$= -3{\cdot}763579$	$\Sigma(\Delta x_2)^2$	$= 0{\cdot}083559$
$\Sigma(x_1-\bar{x}_1)^2$	$= 0{\cdot}632006$	$\Sigma(x_1-\bar{x}_1)(x_2-\bar{x}_2)$	$= 1{\cdot}014984$	$\Sigma\Delta y\Delta x_1$	$= 0{\cdot}014685$
$\Sigma(x_2-\bar{x}_2)^2$	$= 2{\cdot}966354$	$\Sigma(\Delta y)^2$	$= 0{\cdot}112592$	$\Sigma\Delta y\Delta x_2$	$= -0{\cdot}076399$
$\Sigma(y-\bar{y})(x_1-\bar{x}_1)$	$= -1{\cdot}321973$	$\Sigma(\Delta x_1)^2$	$= 0{\cdot}023539$	$\Sigma\Delta x_1\Delta x_2$	$= 0{\cdot}000527$

$\Sigma(\Delta y)^2$ stands for the sum of squares of the first differences of the y's, and $\Sigma \Delta y \Delta x$ stands for the sum of products of the first differences of the y's times the corresponding first differences of the x's, etc. Thus the first term in $\Sigma(\Delta y)^2$ is $(1{\cdot}9794 - 1{\cdot}9565)^2 = 0{\cdot}00052441$, and the first term in $\Sigma \Delta y \Delta x_1$ is $(1{\cdot}9794 - 1{\cdot}9565)(1{\cdot}7766 - 1{\cdot}7669) = 0{\cdot}00022213$. Since there are 69 observations there are 69 terms in each of the first six summations, and 68 in each of the second six summations.

Table 1. *Annual consumption of spirits from* 1870 *to* 1938

Year	Consumption y	Income x_1	Price x_2	Year	Consumption y	Income x_1	Price x_2
1870	1·9565	1·7669	1·9176	1905	1·9139	1·9924	1·9952
1871	1·9794	1·7766	1·9059	1906	1·9091	2·0117	1·9905
1872	2·0120	1·7764	1·8798	1907	1·9139	2·0204	1·9813
1873	2·0449	1·7942	1·8727	1908	1·8886	2·0018	1·9905
1874	2·0561	1·8156	1·8984	1909	1·7945	2·0038	1·9859
1875	2·0678	1·8083	1·9137	1910	1·7644	2·0099	2·0518
1876	2·0561	1·8083	1·9176	1911	1·7817	2·0174	2·0474
1877	2·0428	1·8067	1·9176	1912	1·7784	2·0279	2·0341
1878	2·0290	1·8166	1·9420	1913	1·7945	2·0359	2·0255
1879	1·9980	1·8041	1·9547	1914	1·7888	2·0216	2·0341
1880	1·9884	1·8053	1·9379	1915	1·8751	1·9896	1·9445
1881	1·9835	1·8242	1·9462	1916	1·7853	1·9843	1·9939
1882	1·9773	1·8395	1·9504	1917	1·6075	1·9764	2·2082
1883	1·9748	1·8464	1·9504	1918	1·5185	1·9965	2·2700
1884	1·9629	1·8492	1·9723	1919	1·6513	2·0652	2·2430
1885	1·9396	1·8668	2·0000	1920	1·6247	2·0369	2·2567
1886	1·9309	1·8783	2·0097	1921	1·5391	1·9723	2·2988
1887	1·9271	1·8914	2·0146	1922	1·4922	1·9797	2·3723
1888	1·9239	1·9166	2·0146	1923	1·4606	2·0136	2·4105
1889	1·9414	1·9363	2·0097	1924	1·4551	2·0165	2·4081
1890	1·9685	1·9548	2·0097	1925	1·4425	2·0213	2·4081
1891	1·9727	1·9453	2·0097	1926	1·4023	2·0206	2·4367
1892	1·9736	1·9292	2·0048	1927	1·3991	2·0563	2·4284
1893	1·9499	1·9209	2·0097	1928	1·3798	2·0579	2·4310
1894	1·9432	1·9510	2·0296	1929	1·3782	2·0649	2·4363
1895	1·9569	1·9776	2·0399	1930	1·3366	2·0582	2·4552
1896	1·9647	1·9814	2·0399	1931	1·3026	2·0517	2·4838
1897	1·9710	1·9819	2·0296	1932	1·2592	2·0491	2·4958
1898	1·9719	1·9828	2·0146	1933	1·2635	2·0766	2·5048
1899	1·9956	2·0076	2·0245	1934	1·2549	2·0890	2·5017
1900	2·0000	2·0000	2·0000	1935	1·2527	2·1059	2·4958
1901	1·9904	1·9939	2·0048	1936	1·2763	2·1205	2·4838
1902	1·9752	1·9933	2·0048	1937	1·2906	2·1205	2·4636
1903	1·9494	1·9797	2·0000	1938	1·2721	1·1182	2·4580
1904	1·9332	1·9772	1·9952				

The regression coefficients are calculated by inverting the matrix

$$\begin{bmatrix} \Sigma(x_1-\bar{x}_1)^2 & \Sigma(x_1-\bar{x}_1)(x_2-\bar{x}_2) \\ \Sigma(x_1-\bar{x}_1)(x_2-\bar{x}_2) & \Sigma(x_2-\bar{x}_2)^2 \end{bmatrix},$$

giving for the estimates of β_1 and β_2

$$\begin{bmatrix} b_1 \\ b_2 \end{bmatrix} = \begin{bmatrix} 2{\cdot}966354 & -1{\cdot}014984 \\ -1{\cdot}014984 & 0{\cdot}632006 \end{bmatrix} \begin{bmatrix} -1{\cdot}321973 \\ -3{\cdot}763579 \end{bmatrix},$$

i.e.

$$b_1 = -0{\cdot}120142, \quad b_2 = -1{\cdot}227647.$$

Let z denote the residual from regression, i.e.

$$z = y - \bar{y} - b_1(x_1 - \bar{x}_1) - b_2(x_2 - \bar{x}_2).$$

Then
$$\Sigma z^2 = \Sigma(y-\bar{y})^2 - b_1\Sigma(y-\bar{y})(x_1-\bar{x}_1) - b_2\Sigma(y-\bar{y})(x_2-\bar{x}_2)$$
$$= 0{\cdot}22095.$$

The statistic to be used for testing for serial correlation is

$$d = \frac{\Sigma(\Delta z)^2}{\Sigma z^2}. \tag{2}$$

The reasons for choosing this statistic have been given in Part I and need not be discussed here. Now

$$\Delta z = \Delta y - b_1 \Delta x_1 - b_2 \Delta x_2,$$

so that

$$\Sigma(\Delta z)^2 = \Sigma(\Delta y)^2 + b_1^2\Sigma(\Delta x_1)^2 + b_2^2\Sigma(\Delta x_2)^2 - 2b_1\Sigma\Delta y\,\Delta x_1 - 2b_2\Sigma\Delta y\,\Delta x_2 + 2b_1b_2\Sigma\Delta x_1\Delta x_2$$
$$= 0{\cdot}054967.$$

Substituting in (2) we have $d = 0{\cdot}2488$.

We must now decide what departures from the null hypothesis of serial independence of the errors ϵ need be considered. Experience with econometric data such as the present indicates a test against the existence of positive serial correlation. If the errors were positively serially correlated, d would tend to be relatively small, while if the errors were negatively serially correlated d would tend to be large. We therefore require a critical value of d, say d^*, such that if the observed value of d is less than d^* we may infer that positive serial correlation is established at the significance level concerned.

It was shown in Part I that exact critical values of this kind cannot be obtained. However, it is possible to calculate upper and lower bounds to the critical values. These are denoted by d_U and d_L. If the observed d is less than d_L we conclude that the value is significant, while if the observed d is greater than d_U we conclude that the value is not significant at the significance level concerned. If d lies between d_L and d_U the test is inconclusive.

Significance points of d_L and d_U are tabulated for various levels in Tables 4, 5 and 6. In addition, a diagram is given to facilitate the test procedure in the most usual case of a test against positive serial correlation at the 5 % level (Fig. 1). k' is the number of independent variables.

In the present example $n = 69$ and $k' = 2$, so that at the 5 % level $d_L = 1{\cdot}54$ approximately. The observed value $0{\cdot}25$ is less than this and therefore indicates significant positive serial correlation at the 5 % level. In fact, the observed value is also significant at the 1 % level.

The procedure for other values of k' is exactly similar. In all cases the value of d given by (2) is calculated, the z's being the residuals from regression, and the appropriate table is consulted.

Tests against negative serial correlation and two-sided tests

Tests against negative serial correlation may sometimes be required. For instance, it is a common practice in econometric work to analyse the first differences of the observations rather than the observations themselves, on the ground that the serial correlation of the transformed errors is likely to be less than that of the original errors. We may wish to ensure that the transformation has not overcorrected, thus introducing negative serial correlation into the transformed errors. To make a test against negative serial correlation, d is calculated as above and subtracted from 4. The quantity $4-d$ may now be treated as though it were the value of a d-statistic to be tested for positive serial correlation. Thus if $4-d$ is less than d_L, there is significant evidence of negative serial correlation, and if $4-d$ is greater than d_U, there is not significant evidence; otherwise the test is inconclusive.

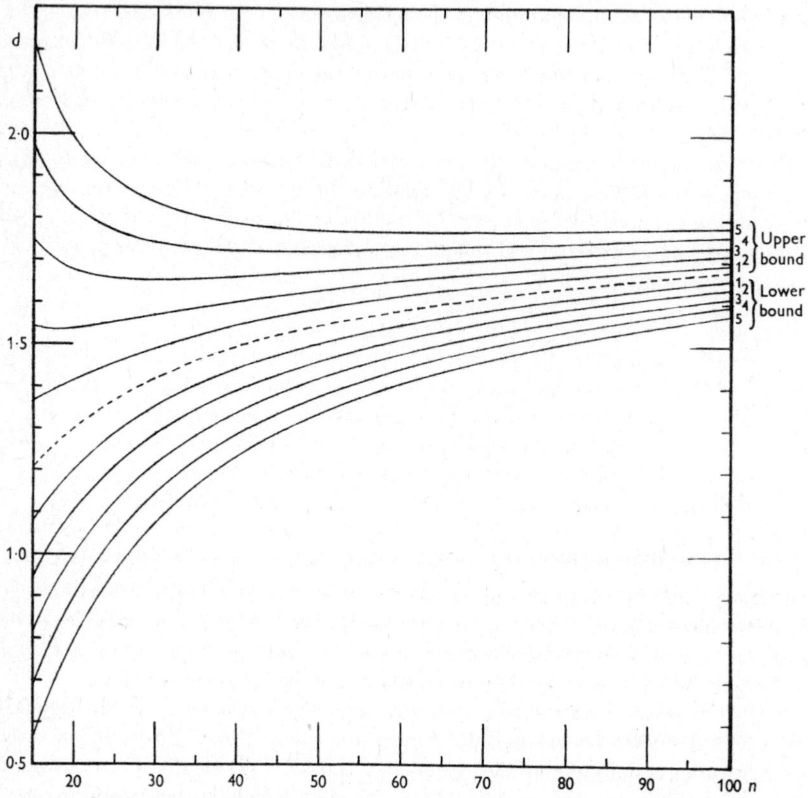

Fig. 1. Graphs of 5% values of d_L and d_U against n for $k'=1, 2, 3, 4, 5$.

When there is no prior knowledge of the sign of the serial correlation, two-sided tests may be made by combining single-tail tests. Using only equal tails, d will be significant at level α if either d is less than d_L or $4-d$ is less than d_L, non-significant if d lies between d_U and $4-d_U$ and inconclusive otherwise; the level α may be 2, 5 and 10 %. Thus, by using the 5 % values of d_L and d_U from Table 4, a two-sided test at the 10 % level is obtained.

3. Regression through the origin

The procedures described so far apply only to cases in which means have been fitted in the regressions, i.e. the fitted regression equations take the form

$$y-\bar{y} = b_1(x_1-\bar{x}_1)+\ldots+b_{k'}(x_{k'}-\bar{x}_{k'}). \qquad (3)$$

These are the most common cases in practice. However, we occasionally require a fitted regression through the origin of the form

$$y = B_1 x_1 + \ldots + B_{k'} x_{k'}. \tag{4}$$

Tables 4, 5 and 6 do not apply directly to the residuals from regressions of this type. To test for serial correlation in such cases an equation of the form (3) must first be fitted. The residuals from the resulting regression may then be tested by the procedures of §§ 2 and 4. This gives a perfectly valid test even though (4) might be the more appropriate regression to fit for other purposes.

In order to avoid inverting more than one matrix the following method, due to Cochran (1938), should be used. First of all, the regression coefficients of equation (4) are determined. In this operation the inverse of the matrix of squares and cross-products of $x_1, \ldots, x_{k'}$ will be calculated; denote this matrix by $\mathbf{C} = \{c_{ij}\}$ and the means of the variables $y, x_1, \ldots, x_{k'}$ by $\bar{y}, \bar{x}_1, \ldots, \bar{x}_{k'}$. Then

$$\begin{bmatrix} b_1 \\ \vdots \\ b_{k'} \end{bmatrix} = \begin{bmatrix} B_1 \\ \vdots \\ B_{k'} \end{bmatrix} - nB_0 \mathbf{C} \begin{bmatrix} \bar{x}_1 \\ \vdots \\ \bar{x}_{k'} \end{bmatrix},$$

where

$$B_0 = \frac{\sum_{i=1}^{k'} B_i \bar{x}_i - \bar{y}}{\sum\sum_{i,j=1}^{k'} c_{ij} \bar{x}_i \bar{x}_j - 1}.$$

4. Approximate procedure when the bounds test is inconclusive

No satisfactory procedure of general application seems to be available for cases in which the bounds test is inconclusive. However, an approximate test can be made, and this should be sufficiently accurate if the number of degrees of freedom is large enough, say greater than 40. For smaller numbers this test can only be regarded as giving a rough indication.

The method used is to transform d so that its range of variation is approximately from 0 to 1 and to fit a Beta distribution with the same mean and variance. The mean and variance of d vary according to the values of the independent variables, so the first step is to calculate them for the particular case concerned. The method of calculation will be illustrated by means of the data of Example 1, although in practice an approximate test would not be required for this case since the bounds test has given a definite answer.

The description of the computing procedure is greatly facilitated by the introduction of matrix notation. Thus the set $\{y_1, y_2, \ldots, y_n\}$ of observations of the independent variable, is denoted by the column vector $\mathbf{y}$. In the same way the set

$$\begin{bmatrix} x_{11} & x_{21} & \cdots & x_{k'1} \\ \vdots & \vdots & & \vdots \\ x_{1n} & x_{2n} & \cdots & x_{k'n} \end{bmatrix}$$

of observations of the independent variables is denoted by the matrix $\mathbf{X}$. We suppose that all these observations are measured from the sample means. The corresponding sets of first differences of the observations are denoted by $\Delta\mathbf{y}$ and $\Delta\mathbf{X}$. The numerator of (2) is the quadratic form

$$(\Delta\mathbf{z})'(\Delta\mathbf{z}) = \mathbf{z}'\mathbf{A}\mathbf{z},$$

where **A** is the real symmetric matrix

$$\begin{bmatrix} 1 & -1 & 0 & \dots & \dots & \dots & 0 \\ -1 & 2 & -1 & \dots & \dots & \dots & \dots \\ 0 & -1 & 2 & \dots & \dots & \dots & \dots \\ \dots & \dots & \dots & \dots & \dots & \dots & \dots \\ \dots & \dots & \dots & \dots & \dots & \dots & 0 \\ \dots & \dots & \dots & \dots & \dots & 2 & -1 \\ 0 & \dots & \dots & \dots & 0 & -1 & 1 \end{bmatrix}.$$

The moments of d are obtained by calculating the traces of certain matrices. The trace of a square matrix is simply the sum of the elements in the leading diagonal. For example, the trace of **A**, denoted by $\mathrm{tr}\,\mathbf{A}$, is $2(n-1)$, where n is the number of rows or columns in **A**.

It was shown in Part I that the mean and variance of d are given by

$$E(d) = \frac{P}{n-k'-1}, \tag{5}$$

$$\mathrm{var}\,(d) = \frac{2}{(n-k'-1)(n-k'+1)}\{Q - PE(d)\}, \tag{6}$$

where
$$P = \mathrm{tr}\,\mathbf{A} - \mathrm{tr}\,\{\mathbf{X'AX(X'X)^{-1}}\}, \tag{7}$$

and
$$Q = \mathrm{tr}\,\mathbf{A}^2 - 2\,\mathrm{tr}\,\{\mathbf{X'A^2X(X'X)^{-1}}\} + \mathrm{tr}\,[\{\mathbf{X'AX(X'X)^{-1}}\}^2]. \tag{8}$$

The elements of $(\mathbf{X'X})^{-1}$ will have been obtained for the calculation of the regression coefficients, and the elements of $\mathbf{X'AX}$ for the calculation of d; for $\mathbf{X'AX} = (\mathbf{\Delta X})'(\mathbf{\Delta X})$, so that the (i, j)th element of $\mathbf{X'AX}$ is simply the sum of products $\Sigma \Delta x_i \Delta x_j$. Thus the only new matrix requiring calculation is $\mathbf{X'A^2X}$. Now $\mathbf{X'A^2X}$ is very nearly equal to $(\mathbf{\Delta^2 X})'(\mathbf{\Delta^2 X})$, where $\mathbf{\Delta^2X}$ represents the matrix of second differences of the independent variables. Thus the (i, j)th element of $\mathbf{X'A^2X}$ will usually be given sufficiently closely by $\Sigma(\Delta^2 x_i)(\Delta^2 x_j)$, where $\Delta^2 x_i$ stands for the second difference of the ith independent variable. (More exactly

$$(\mathbf{X'A^2X})_{ij} = \Sigma(\Delta^2 x_i)(\Delta^2 x_j) + (x_{i1} - x_{i2})(x_{j1} - x_{j2}) + (x_{in-1} - x_{in})(x_{jn-1} - x_{jn}).)$$

The calculations will be exemplified by the data of Example 1. Referring to § 2 we see that

$$\mathbf{X'AX} = \begin{bmatrix} 0{\cdot}023539 & 0{\cdot}000527 \\ 0{\cdot}000527 & 0{\cdot}083559 \end{bmatrix},$$

$$(\mathbf{X'X})^{-1} = \begin{bmatrix} 2{\cdot}966354 & -1{\cdot}014984 \\ -1{\cdot}014984 & 0{\cdot}632006 \end{bmatrix}.$$

Although $\mathrm{tr}\,\mathbf{X'AX(X'X)^{-1}}$ is simply the sum of the two diagonal elements of the product of these two matrices, we shall need the remaining two elements below, so the whole matrix is computed giving

$$\mathbf{X'AX(X'X)^{-1}} = \begin{bmatrix} 0{\cdot}069290 & -0{\cdot}023559 \\ -0{\cdot}083248 & 0{\cdot}052275 \end{bmatrix}.$$

Thus
$$\begin{aligned}\mathrm{tr}\ \mathbf{X'AX(X'X)^{-1}} &= 0{\cdot}069290 + 0{\cdot}052275 \\ &= 0{\cdot}121565.\end{aligned}$$

Substituting in (7) and (5) and remembering that $\operatorname{tr}\mathbf{A} = 2(n-1) = 136$ in the present case, we have

$$E(d) = \frac{135{\cdot}878435}{66} = 2{\cdot}05876.$$

The matrix of sums of squares and products of second differences is found to be

$$\mathbf{X}'\mathbf{A}^2\mathbf{X} = \begin{bmatrix} 0{\cdot}035867 & -0{\cdot}004495 \\ -0{\cdot}004495 & 0{\cdot}116368 \end{bmatrix}.$$

$\operatorname{tr}\mathbf{X}'\mathbf{A}^2\mathbf{X}(\mathbf{X}'\mathbf{X})^{-1}$ is obtained by multiplying the first column of $(\mathbf{X}'\mathbf{X})^{-1}$ into the first row of $\mathbf{X}'\mathbf{A}^2\mathbf{X}$ and adding the product of the second column of $(\mathbf{X}'\mathbf{X})^{-1}$ into the second row of $\mathbf{X}'\mathbf{A}^2\mathbf{X}$ giving $\operatorname{tr}\mathbf{X}'\mathbf{A}^2\mathbf{X}(\mathbf{X}'\mathbf{X})^{-1} = 0{\cdot}189064$. $\operatorname{tr}[\{\mathbf{X}'\mathbf{A}\mathbf{X}(\mathbf{X}'\mathbf{X})^{-1}\}^2]$ is simply the sum of squares of the elements of the matrix $\mathbf{X}'\mathbf{A}\mathbf{X}(\mathbf{X}'\mathbf{X})^{-1}$ i.e. $0{\cdot}0150189$. Also

$$\operatorname{tr}\mathbf{A}^2 = 2(3n-4) = 406.$$

Substituting in (8) and (6) we have

$$\operatorname{var} d = \frac{2}{66 \times 68}(405{\cdot}636891 - 135{\cdot}878435 \times 2{\cdot}05876)$$

$$= 0{\cdot}0561033.$$

We now assume that $\frac{1}{4}d$ is distributed in the Beta distribution with density

$$\frac{1}{B(p,q)}\left(\frac{d}{4}\right)^{p-1}\left(1-\frac{d}{4}\right)^{q-1}.$$

This distribution gives

$$E(d) = \frac{4p}{p+q},$$

$$\operatorname{var} d = \frac{16pq}{(p+q)^2(p+q+1)},$$

from which we find p and q by the equations

$$\left.\begin{aligned} p+q &= \frac{E(d)\{4-E(d)\}}{\operatorname{var} d} - 1, \\ p &= \tfrac{1}{4}(p+q)\,E(d). \end{aligned}\right\} \quad (9)$$

To test against positive serial correlation we require the critical value of $\frac{1}{4}d$ at the lower tail of the distribution. If $2p$ and $2q$ are integers, this can be obtained from Catherine Thompson's tables (1941), or indirectly from tables of the variance ratio or Fisher's z, such as those in the Fisher-Yates tables (1948); if $2p$ and $2q$ are not both integers, a first approximation may be found using the nearest integral values. Thus $F = \frac{p(4-d)}{qd}$ is distributed as the variance ratio and $z = \frac{1}{2}\log_e F$ is Fisher's z, both with $n_1 = 2q$, $n_2 = 2p$ degrees of freedom.

For moderately large numbers of observations a convenient way of finding the significance point when $2p$ and $2q$ are not integral is to use Carter's (1947) approximation to Fisher's z. This states that the critical value of z is approximately

$$\frac{\xi\sqrt{(h+\lambda)}}{h} - \left(\frac{1}{2q}-\frac{1}{2p}\right)\left(\lambda+\frac{5}{6}-\frac{s}{3}\right),$$

where

$$s = \frac{1}{2p}+\frac{1}{2q}, \quad h = \frac{2}{s}, \quad \lambda = \frac{\xi^2-3}{6}.$$

The values of ξ and λ to be used for 5 and 1 % tests against positive serial correlation are as follows:

	5%	1%
ξ	1·6449	2·3263
λ	0·0491	0·4020

Returning to the numerical example we find from (9)

$$p = 36{\cdot}1495, \quad q = 34{\cdot}0860, \qquad \text{whence} \quad F = 15{\cdot}99 \quad \text{and} \quad z = 1{\cdot}3848.$$

Carter's approximation gives a critical 1 % value of z of 0·278, which is less than the observed value, thus indicating significant serial correlation. Here the significance is so marked that it may be seen immediately by referring to a table of significant points of z or F around $n_1 = n_2 = 70$ (e.g. Snedecor, 1937).

For testing against negative serial correlation the same procedure is used except that d is replaced throughout by $4-d$.

5. One- and two-way classifications

In any regression analysis where the independent variables assume the same values in all applications it would be theoretically possible to dispense with the bounds and tabulate the significance points of d once and for all. This could be done, for instance, for analysis of variance models such as one- and two-way classifications and for polynomial regressions with equally spaced variate values. The calculation of tables of this type is rather a formidable task and only one set has so far been published, namely, the significance points of the circular serial correlation coefficient of the least squares residuals from Fourier regressions, tabulated by R. L. & T. W. Anderson (1950). Pending the publication of further tables the bounds test of the present paper may be used, with the approximate procedure described in § 4 for cases in which the bounds do not give a decisive result, or when the n and k' are beyond the range of Tables 4, 5 and 6. In the present section the calculation of d is described for one- and two-way classifications and expressions are given for its mean and variance, while in the next section the same is done for polynomial regressions.

It is convenient to think of the observations as a time series consisting of monthly observations recorded for a number of years, though the results are of course of general application. We may fit constants for years only or for months only or for both months and years. An exact test of serial correlation in the 'months only' case may be made by means of R. L. & T. W. Anderson's tables (1950). For the 'years only' and the 'months and years' case no exact test is at present available. The tests described in this paper may, however, be used in all three cases.

If there are s 'years' each of t 'months', the mean and variance of d for the three models are as follows:

'Years' only:

$$\left.\begin{aligned} E(d) &= 2\left(1+\frac{1}{t}-\frac{1}{st}\right), \\ \operatorname{var} d &= \frac{4}{s(t-1)(st-s+2)}\left\{st-2s-\frac{2s}{t}+\frac{4}{t}+\frac{5s}{t^2}-\frac{8}{t^2}-\frac{2}{st}+\frac{2}{st^2}\right\}. \end{aligned}\right\} \tag{10}$$

'Months' only:

$$\left.\begin{aligned} E(d) &= 2\left(1-\frac{1}{st}\right), \\ \operatorname{var} d &= \frac{4}{t(s-1)(st-t+2)}\left\{st-t-1+\frac{1}{s^2}-\frac{2}{st}+\frac{2}{s^2t}\right\}. \end{aligned}\right\} \tag{11}$$

'Years and months':

$$\left.\begin{aligned} E(d) &= 2\left\{1+\frac{1}{t}-\frac{1}{s(t-1)}\right\}, \\ \operatorname{var} d &= \frac{4}{(s-1)(t-1)^2(st-t-s+3)} \\ &\quad \left\{st^2-t^2-3st+3t+4-\frac{2t}{s}+\frac{7s}{t}-\frac{12}{t}-\frac{5s}{t^2}+\frac{2t}{s^2}+\frac{6}{t^2}\right\}. \end{aligned}\right\} \tag{12}$$

These formulae were found by substituting the appropriate matrices into the general formulae given in Part I. The subsequent reductions were straightforward but extremely tedious.

Example 2. To illustrate the test procedures for models of this kind we shall consider the two-way classification of the data in Table 2 on the receipts of butter (in units of 1,000,000 lb.) at five markets (Boston, Chicago, San Francisco, Milwaukee and St Louis). The same data, for 1935, 1936 and 1937 only, were used by R. L. & T. W. Anderson (1950) for illustrating their procedure for testing serial correlation in the 'months only' case. The figures in parentheses are residuals from the monthly averages.

Table 2. *Receipts of butter (millions of lb. weight) at five U.S.A. markets*

Month	Year					Average
	1933	1934	1935	1936	1937	
Jan.	58·3 (+8·20)	52·6 (+2·50)	48·9 (−1·20)	48·3 (−1·80)	42·4 (−7·70)	50·10
Feb.	51·3 (+5·28)	46·9 (+0·88)	43·4 (−2·62)	47·1 (+1·08)	41·4 (−4·62)	46·02
March	58·1 (+5·86)	57·9 (+5·66)	43·8 (−8·44)	52·4 (+0·16)	49·0 (−3·24)	52·24
April	55·1 (+1·86)	54·2 (+0·96)	50·8 (−2·44)	55·3 (+2·06)	50·8 (−2·44)	53·24
May	74·6 (+5·94)	70·6 (+1·94)	67·6 (−1·06)	64·7 (−3·96)	65·8 (−2·86)	68·66
June	83·9 (+2·64)	73·3 (−7·96)	83·7 (+2·44)	79·5 (−1·76)	85·9 (+4·64)	81·26
July	73·5 (+1·56)	70·3 (−1·64)	82·7 (+10·76)	62·6 (−9·34)	70·6 (−1·34)	71·94
Aug.	73·3 (+11·78)	66·4 (+4·88)	60·8 (−0·72)	51·3 (−10·22)	55·8 (−5·72)	61·52
Sept.	63·0 (+7·96)	56·7 (+1·66)	55·4 (+0·36)	51·0 (−4·04)	49·1 (−5·94)	55·04
Oct.	58·3 (+5·58)	57·2 (+4·48)	48·4 (−4·32)	54·0 (+1·28)	45·7 (−7·02)	52·72
Nov.	55·1 (+9·20)	47·7 (+1·80)	37·7 (−8·20)	45·2 (−0·70)	43·8 (−2·10)	45·90
Dec.	56·5 (+9·70)	44·9 (−1·90)	41·0 (−5·80)	44·9 (−1·90)	46·7 (−0·10)	46·80
Average	63·42	58·22	55·35	54·69	53·92	57·12
Total	761·0	698·7	664·2	656·3	647·0	3427·2

Source: *Agricultural Statistics*, United States Government Printing Office, Washington, D.C., 1939, p. 390.

We require to test for serial correlation in the model

$$y_{ij} = \mu+\alpha_i+\beta_j+\epsilon_{ij} \quad (i=1,2,\ldots,5;\ j=1,2,\ldots,12),$$

where y_{ij} is the observation in the jth month of the ith year, μ, α_i and β_j are constants and ϵ_{ij} is the error term.

The least squares estimates of μ, α_i and β_j are m, $a_i - m$ and $b_j - m$, where m is the sample mean of all the observations and a_i and b_j are the means of observations in the ith year and the jth month respectively. Thus the residuals are given by

$$z_{ij} = y_{ij} - a_i - b_j + m.$$

The test is made as before by calculating

$$d = \frac{\Sigma(\Delta z_{ij})^2}{\Sigma z_{ij}^2},$$

where the Δz_{ij}'s are the first differences of the residuals when arranged as a single time series.

$\Sigma(\Delta z)^2$ may be calculated by working out the individual residuals from the monthly averages and finding their first differences. The difference between the December value of one year and the January value of the succeeding year then needs to be adjusted to take account of the difference between the two yearly averages. For instance, the difference between the 'months only' residuals for December 1933 and January 1934 is

$$2{\cdot}50 - 9{\cdot}70 = -7{\cdot}20.$$

From this must be subtracted the difference between the 1934 and 1933 yearly averages, i.e. $58{\cdot}22 - 63{\cdot}42 = -5{\cdot}20$. The net difference is therefore $-7{\cdot}20 + 5{\cdot}20 = -2{\cdot}00$. The sum of the resulting differences squared is $\Sigma(\Delta z)^2$. For the calculation of Σz^2 the normal method for the residual sum of squares may be used, i.e. find the sum of squares of the original observations and subtract the sums of squares due to the fitted constants. Alternatively, with the above method of calculating $\Sigma(\Delta z)^2$, the sum of squares of the residuals from the monthly averages may be calculated directly, from which it only remains to subtract the sum of squares due to years.

For the data in the table we find $\Sigma(\Delta z)^2 = 1191{\cdot}2454$ and $\Sigma z^2 = 850{\cdot}8890$, giving $d = \dfrac{1191{\cdot}2454}{850{\cdot}8890} = 1{\cdot}4000$. It remains to test the significance of this value of d by the method of § 4. For this purpose the formulae (12) may be evaluated with $s = 5$ and $t = 12$ to give

$$E(d) = 2{\cdot}1303, \quad \operatorname{var} d = 0{\cdot}077964.$$

If $\frac{1}{4}d$ is assumed to have a Beta-distribution with parameters p, q, then values of $E(d)$ and $\operatorname{var} d$ may be substituted in the formulae (9) to give

$$p = 26{\cdot}6758, \quad q = 23{\cdot}4125.$$

The observed value of d is $1{\cdot}4000$, so that

$$F = \frac{p(4-d)}{pd} = 2{\cdot}16,$$

with $n_1 \sim 47$, $n_2 \sim 53$ degrees of freedom. A cursory examination of the significant points of F shows that the 5 % point is certainly less than 1·63, while the 1 % point is less than 2·00. Thus our value of F is significant at the 1 % level, and the hypothesis of serial independence of the errors in the above model may be considered untenable.

6. Polynomial regressions

An important application of the least squares method in time-series analysis is in the fitting of polynomial trend lines. When the values of the time variate (or its equivalent in other applications) are spaced at equal intervals, the fitting is carried out most expeditiously by means of orthogonal polynomials. In what follows we shall assume that the ξ' polynomials tabulated by Fisher & Yates (1948), and in a more extended form by Anderson & Houseman (1942), have been used. The regression model is

$$y = \beta_0 + \beta_1 \xi_1' + \beta_2 \xi_2' + \dots + \beta_{k'} \xi_{k'}' + \epsilon,$$

where ξ_1' is the polynomial of ith degree in x, the independent variable, which we suppose takes the values $1, 2, \dots, n$, $\beta_0, \beta_1, \dots, \beta_{k'}$ are constants and ϵ is the error term. We require to test the error term for serial correlation.

The test procedure is a good deal less laborious in this application than in the ordinary regression case described in § 2. We shall illustrate it by considering the following example. The data were taken by Anderson & Houseman (1942) from Schultz's demand studies (1938) to illustrate the routine procedure of fitting the polynomials. We shall not, therefore, give details of the initial calculations but refer the reader instead to Anderson & Houseman's bulletin.

Table 3. *Price of sugar*, 1875–1936

Year	Price	Year	Price	Year	Price	Year	Price
1875	67	1891	6	1907	6	1923	44
1876	65	1892	3	1908	10	1924	35
1877	73	1893	8	1909	8	1925	15
1878	55	1894	1	1910	10	1926	15
1879	48	1895	2	1911	13	1927	18
1880	56	1896	5	1912	10	1928	15
1881	57	1897	5	1913	3	1929	10
1882	52	1898	10	1914	7	1930	6
1883	45	1899	9	1915	16	1931	4
1884	28	1900	13	1916	29	1932	0
1885	24	1901	10	1917	37	1933	3
1886	21	1902	5	1918	38	1934	1
1887	20	1903	6	1919	50	1935	3
1888	30	1904	8	1920	74	1936	7
1889	36	1905	13	1921	22		
1890	22	1906	5	1922	19		

Example 3. A polynomial time trend is to be fitted to 62 annual sugar prices (1875–1936) given in Table 3. The prices are in terms of mills (tenths of a cent) coded by subtracting 40 mills from each price.

Anderson & Houseman find the following values for the sums of squares and products, giving the regression coefficients shown:

$$\begin{aligned}
&\Sigma y = 1{,}336 && b_0 = 21{\cdot}548 \\
&\Sigma(y-\bar{y})^2 = 25{,}250 && \\
&\Sigma(\xi_1')^2 = 79{,}422 && \Sigma(\xi_2')^2 = 1{,}270{,}752 \\
&\Sigma(\xi_3')^2 = 139{,}238{,}112 && \Sigma(\xi_4')^2 = 103{,}639{,}568{,}032 \\
&\Sigma(y\xi_1') = -20{,}286 && b_1 = -0{\cdot}2554 \\
&\Sigma(y\xi_2') = 72{,}775 && b_2 = 0{\cdot}05727 \\
&\Sigma(y\xi_3') = -1{,}080{,}557 && b_3 = -0{\cdot}0077605 \\
&\Sigma(y\xi_4') = -7{,}599{,}201 && b_4 = -0{\cdot}00007332
\end{aligned}$$

To test for serial correlation we must calculate

$$d = \frac{\Sigma(\Delta z)^2}{\Sigma z^2}.$$

Taking first the case in which terms only as far as ξ_3' are fitted,

$$z = y - b_0 - b_1\xi_1' - b_2\xi_2' - b_3\xi_3'$$

and

$$\Sigma z^2 = 25{,}250 - (-0{\cdot}2554)(-20{,}286) - (0{\cdot}05727)(72{,}775) - (-0{\cdot}0077605)(-1{,}080{,}557)$$
$$= 7515, \tag{13}$$

$$\Sigma(\Delta z)^2 = \Sigma(\Delta y)^2 - 2b_1\Sigma\Delta y\,\Delta\xi_1' - 2b_2\Sigma\Delta y\,\Delta\xi_2' - 2b_3\Sigma\Delta y\,\Delta\xi_3' + \sum_{i=1}^{3}\sum_{j=1}^{3} b_i b_j \Sigma\Delta\xi_i'\Delta\xi_j'. \tag{14}$$

$\Sigma(\Delta y)^2$ is calculated directly as the sum of the squares of the first differences of the series of observations of y; its value here is 2590. For the remaining terms, indirect methods are much quicker. It may be verified that

$$\left.\begin{aligned}
\Sigma\Delta y\,\Delta\xi_1' &= (y_n - y_1)\,\Delta\xi_1'(0),\\
\Sigma\Delta y\,\Delta\xi_2' &= -2\lambda_2\Sigma y - (y_n + y_1)\,\Delta\xi_2'(0),\\
\Sigma\Delta y\,\Delta\xi_3' &= -\frac{6\lambda_3}{\lambda_1}\Sigma y\xi_1' + (y_n - y_1)\,\Delta\xi_3'(0),\\
\Sigma\Delta y\,\Delta\xi_4' &= -\lambda_4\left[\frac{12}{\lambda_2}\Sigma y\xi_2' + \left\{\frac{1}{\lambda_2}(n^2-1) - \frac{3n^2-13}{7}\right\}\Sigma y\right] - (y_n + y_1)\,\Delta\xi_4'(0),\\
\Sigma\Delta y\,\Delta\xi_5' &= \lambda_5\left[\frac{20}{\lambda_3}\Sigma y\xi_3' + \left\{\frac{1}{\lambda_3}(3n^2-7) - \frac{10}{\lambda_1}\frac{n^2-13}{3}\right\}\Sigma y\xi_1'\right] + (y_n - y_1)\,\Delta\xi_5'(0),
\end{aligned}\right\} \tag{15}$$

and that, with $(i \leqslant j)$,

$$\left.\begin{aligned}
\Sigma\Delta\xi_i'\Delta\xi_j' &= -2\xi_j'(1)\,\Delta\xi_i'(0) \quad (i+j \text{ even}),\\
&= 0 \qquad\qquad\qquad\quad (i+j \text{ odd}).
\end{aligned}\right\} \tag{16}$$

In these expressions it is assumed that the original time variate x takes the values $1, 2, \ldots, n$. $\xi_j'(1)$ denotes the value of ξ_j' for $x = 1$. Similarly, $\Delta\xi_j'(0)$ denotes the value of $\Delta\xi_j'$ for $x = 0$, i.e. $\xi_j'(1) - \xi_j'(0)$. y_1 and y_n are the first and last observations in the series of values of the dependent variate. The λ_i is given for each n at the foot of the appropriate column of ξ_i' values in the published tables.

The values of $\Delta\xi_i'(0)$ are obtained by writing down the first few terms of the series $\xi_i'(x)$ for $x = 1, 2, \ldots,$ and preparing a small table of differences. $\Delta\xi_i'(0)$ is then found by simple addition. It should be noted that the values of $\xi_i'(x)$ should be read upwards starting at the bottom of the published table, and that the signs should be reversed for polynomials of odd degree. Example 3, with $n = 62$, gives the following lay-out. The values of $\Delta\xi_i'(0)$ required are printed in italics:

x	ξ_1'	$\Delta\xi_1'$
		2
1	−61	
		2
2	−59	
		2
3	−57	

x	ξ_2'	$\Delta\xi_2'$	$\Delta^2\xi_2'$
		−31	
1	305		1
		−30	
2	275		1
		−29	
3	246		1
		−28	
4	218		

x	ξ_3'	$\Delta\xi_3'$	$\Delta^2\xi_3'$	$\Delta^3\xi_3'$
		769		
1	−3599		−61	
		708		2
2	−2891		−59	
		649		2
3	−2242		−57	
		592		2
4	−1650		−55	
		437		
5	−1113			

Substituting in formulae (15, 16) we have

$$\begin{aligned}
\Sigma\Delta y\Delta\xi_1' &= (7-67)(2) = -120,\\
\Sigma\Delta y\Delta\xi_2' &= (-2)(\tfrac{1}{2})(1336)-(7+67)(-31) = 958,\\
\Sigma\Delta y\Delta\xi_3' &= -\frac{6}{2\cdot 3}(-20{,}286)+(7-67)\,769 = -25{,}854,\\
\Sigma(\Delta\xi_1')^2 &= -2(-61)(2) = 244,\\
\Sigma(\Delta\xi_2')^2 &= -2(305)(-31) = 18{,}910,\\
\Sigma(\Delta\xi_3')^2 &= -2(-3599)(769) = 5{,}535{,}262,\\
\Sigma\Delta\xi_1'\Delta\xi_2' &= \Sigma\Delta\xi_2'\Delta\xi_3' = 0,\\
\Sigma\Delta\xi_1'\Delta\xi_3' &= -2(-3599)(2) = 14{,}396.
\end{aligned}$$

We now have all the quantities necessary for the calculation of $\Sigma(\Delta z)^2$. Substituting in (14) we have

$$\begin{aligned}
\Sigma(\Delta z)^2 = {} & 2590-2(-0{\cdot}2554)(120)-2(0{\cdot}05727)(958)\\
& -2(-0{\cdot}0077605)(-25{,}854)+2(-0{\cdot}2554)(-0{\cdot}0077605)(14{,}396)\\
& +(0{\cdot}2554)^2(244)+(0{\cdot}05727)^2(18{,}910)+(0{\cdot}0077605)^2(5{,}535{,}262)\\
= {} & 2486{\cdot}06.
\end{aligned}$$

Thus
$$d = \frac{2486{\cdot}06}{7515} = 0{\cdot}3308.$$

Reference to Table 6 shows that this value is significant at the 1 % level and therefore provides significant evidence of the existence of positive serial correlation.

When a polynomial of the fourth degree is fitted to the data a value of d of 0·3603 is obtained. This still remains highly significant at the 1 % level.

Mean and variance of d

The quickest way of calculating the mean and variance of d for polynomial regressions is to use the numerical procedure described below. It is, however, possible to obtain explicit formulae, and these have been calculated for polynomials up to the fifth degree. Owing to the complexity of the resulting expressions we shall only give them for $k' = 1, 2, 3$.

Taking first the numerical procedure, let $\boldsymbol{\xi}_1, \ldots, \boldsymbol{\xi}_k$ denote the column vectors of values of the polynomials (the usual prime is omitted in the vector form since we wish to use the same sign for the matrix operation of transposition). The mean and variance of d are given by (5) and (6) with

$$P = 2(n-1)-\sum_{i=1}^{k'}\frac{\boldsymbol{\xi}_i'\mathbf{A}\boldsymbol{\xi}_i}{\boldsymbol{\xi}_i'\boldsymbol{\xi}_i},$$

$$Q = 2(3n-4)-2\sum_{i=1}^{k'}\frac{\boldsymbol{\xi}_i'\mathbf{A}^2\boldsymbol{\xi}_i}{\boldsymbol{\xi}_i'\boldsymbol{\xi}_i}+\sum_{i=1}^{k'}\left(\frac{\boldsymbol{\xi}_i'\mathbf{A}\boldsymbol{\xi}_i}{\boldsymbol{\xi}_i'\boldsymbol{\xi}_i}\right)^2+2\sum_{j=2}^{k'}\sum_{i=1}^{j-1}\frac{(\boldsymbol{\xi}_i'\mathbf{A}\boldsymbol{\xi}_i)^2}{\boldsymbol{\xi}_i'\boldsymbol{\xi}_i\boldsymbol{\xi}_j'\boldsymbol{\xi}_j},$$

as was shown in Part I, $\mathbf{A}$ being the matrix defined in § 4. The quantities $\boldsymbol{\xi}_i'\boldsymbol{\xi}_i$ are the sums of squares of the values of ξ_i', given at the foot of the ξ' tables. The quantities $\boldsymbol{\xi}_i'\mathbf{A}\boldsymbol{\xi}_j$ and $\boldsymbol{\xi}_i'\mathbf{A}^2\boldsymbol{\xi}_i$ may be found from the expressions

$$\boldsymbol{\xi}_i'\mathbf{A}\boldsymbol{\xi}_j = \begin{cases} -2\xi_j'(1)\,\Delta\xi_i'(0) & (i+j \text{ even}),\\ 0 & (i+j \text{ odd}),\end{cases}$$

$$\boldsymbol{\xi}_i'\mathbf{A}^2\boldsymbol{\xi}_i = 2\xi_i'(1)\,\Delta^3\xi_i'(-1)+2\Delta\xi_i'(0)\,\Delta\xi_i'(1).$$

The values of $\xi_i'(x)$ and its differences may easily be found from the published tables.

Applying the method to Example 3 we find

$$P = 122 - \frac{244}{79{,}422} - \frac{18{,}910}{1{,}270{,}752} - \frac{5{,}535{,}262}{139{,}238{,}112}$$

$$= 121{\cdot}9423,$$

$$Q = 368 - 2\left(\frac{8}{79{,}422} + \frac{1860}{1{,}270{,}752} + \frac{1{,}074{,}508}{139{,}238{,}112}\right)$$

$$+\left(\frac{244}{79{,}422}\right)^2 + \left(\frac{18{,}910}{1{,}270{,}752}\right)^2 + \left(\frac{5{,}535{,}262}{139{,}238{,}112}\right)^2$$

$$+2\left(\frac{14{,}396}{79{,}422 \times 139{,}238{,}112}\right)$$

$$= 367{\cdot}9832.$$

The explicit formulae for P and Q are as follows:

$$P = 2\left(n - 1 - \sum_{i=1}^{k'} p_i\right),$$

where $$p_1 = \frac{6}{n(n+1)}, \quad p_2 = \frac{30}{(n+1)(n+2)}, \quad p_3 = \frac{84(n^2+1)}{n(n+1)(n+2)(n+3)},$$

and $$Q = 2\left(3n - 4 + \sum_{i=1}^{k'} q_i\right),$$

where $$q_1 = 2p_1^2 - \frac{24}{n(n^2-1)}, \quad q_2 = 2p_2^2 - \frac{360}{(n^2-1)(n+2)},$$

$$q_3 = 2p_3^2 + \frac{336(n-2)(n-3)}{n^2(n+1)^2(n+2)(n+3)} - \frac{336(3n^2+10n-7)}{n(n^2-1)(n+2)(n+3)}.$$

Appendix on the calculation of the tables

1. *Tables* 4, 5 *and* 6. The exact distributions of d_L and d_U, whose significance points are required for Tables 4, 5 and 6, are not known. When transformed to the range (0, 1), their probability densities may, however, be represented by the series

$$g(x) = \frac{x^{p-1}(1-x)^{q-1}}{B(p,q)}\left\{1 + \sum_{s=1}^{\infty} a_s G_s(x)\right\}, \tag{17}$$

where the G's are the polynomials (Jacobi) which are orthogonal on the range (0, 1) with respect to the weight function $\dfrac{x^{p-1}(1-x)^{q-1}}{B(p,q)}$. These polynomials are defined by (see Courant & Hilbert,* 1931)

$$G_s(x) = 1 - \frac{p+q-1+s}{p}x + \frac{(p+q-1+s)(p+q+s)}{p(p+1)}x^2 - \dots$$

$$+(-1)^s \frac{(p+q-1+s)(p+q+s)\dots(p+q+2-2s)}{p(p+1)\dots(p+s-1)}x^s.$$

The coefficients a_s may be determined by the method of moments; the distribution of d_L and d_U is then a series of Incomplete Beta Functions.

* Note, however, the misprint: $x^q(1-x)^{p-q}$ should read $x^{q-1}(1-x)^{p-q}$.

The weight function was chosen to be the density of the Beta-distribution with the correct mean and variance. (An alternative weight function giving the right order of vanishing of (17) at $x = 0$ and $x = 1$ was also tried but it was found to be less satisfactory.) With this weight function, the coefficients a_1 and a_2 in (17) were zero. Terms as far as $G_4(x)$ were used.

Table 4. *Significance points of d_L and d_U*: 5 %

n	$k'=1$		$k'=2$		$k'=3$		$k'=4$		$k'=5$	
	d_L	d_U	d_L	d_U	d_L	d_U	d_L	d_U	d_L	d_U
15	1·08	1·36	0·95	1·54	0·82	1·75	0·69	1·97	0·56	2·21
16	1·10	1·37	0·98	1·54	0·86	1·73	0·74	1·93	0·62	2·15
17	1·13	1·38	1·02	1·54	0·90	1·71	0·78	1·90	0·67	2·10
18	1·16	1·39	1·05	1·53	0·93	1·69	0·82	1·87	0·71	2·06
19	1·18	1·40	1·08	1·53	0·97	1·68	0·86	1·85	0·75	2·02
20	1·20	1·41	1·10	1·54	1·00	1·68	0·90	1·83	0·79	1·99
21	1·22	1·42	1·13	1·54	1·03	1·67	0·93	1·81	0·83	1·96
22	1·24	1·43	1·15	1·54	1·05	1·66	0·96	1·80	0·86	1·94
23	1·26	1·44	1·17	1·54	1·08	1·66	0·99	1·79	0·90	1·92
24	1·27	1·45	1·19	1·55	1·10	1·66	1·01	1·78	0·93	1·90
25	1·29	1·45	1·21	1·55	1·12	1·66	1·04	1·77	0·95	1·89
26	1·30	1·46	1·22	1·55	1·14	1·65	1·06	1·76	0·98	1·88
27	1·32	1·47	1·24	1·56	1·16	1·65	1·08	1·76	1·01	1·86
28	1·33	1·48	1·26	1·56	1·18	1·65	1·10	1·75	1·03	1·85
29	1·34	1·48	1·27	1·56	1·20	1·65	1·12	1·74	1·05	1·84
30	1·35	1·49	1·28	1·57	1·21	1·65	1·14	1·74	1·07	1·83
31	1·36	1·50	1·30	1·57	1·23	1·65	1·16	1·74	1·09	1·83
32	1·37	1·50	1·31	1·57	1·24	1·65	1·18	1·73	1·11	1·82
33	1·38	1·51	1·32	1·58	1·26	1·65	1·19	1·73	1·13	1·81
34	1·39	1·51	1·33	1·58	1·27	1·65	1·21	1·73	1·15	1·81
35	1·40	1·52	1·34	1·58	1·28	1·65	1·22	1·73	1·16	1·80
36	1·41	1·52	1·35	1·59	1·29	1·65	1·24	1·73	1·18	1·80
37	1·42	1·53	1·36	1·59	1·31	1·66	1·25	1·72	1·19	1·80
38	1·43	1·54	1·37	1·59	1·32	1·66	1·26	1·72	1·21	1·79
39	1·43	1·54	1·38	1·60	1·33	1·66	1·27	1·72	1·22	1·79
40	1·44	1·54	1·39	1·60	1·34	1·66	1·29	1·72	1·23	1·79
45	1·48	1·57	1·43	1·62	1·38	1·67	1·34	1·72	1·29	1·78
50	1·50	1·59	1·46	1·63	1·42	1·67	1·38	1·72	1·34	1·77
55	1·53	1·60	1·49	1·64	1·45	1·68	1·41	1·72	1·38	1·77
60	1·55	1·62	1·51	1·65	1·48	1·69	1·44	1·73	1·41	1·77
65	1·57	1·63	1·54	1·66	1·50	1·70	1·47	1·73	1·44	1·77
70	1·58	1·64	1·55	1·67	1·52	1·70	1·49	1·74	1·46	1·77
75	1·60	1·65	1·57	1·68	1·54	1·71	1·51	1·74	1·49	1·77
80	1·61	1·66	1·59	1·69	1·56	1·72	1·53	1·74	1·51	1·77
85	1·62	1·67	1·60	1·70	1·57	1·72	1·55	1·75	1·52	1·77
90	1·63	1·68	1·61	1·70	1·59	1·73	1·57	1·75	1·54	1·78
95	1·64	1·69	1·62	1·71	1·60	1·73	1·58	1·75	1·56	1·78
100	1·65	1·69	1·63	1·72	1·61	1·74	1·59	1·76	1·57	1·78

A first set of significance points was obtained using the weight function as a first approximation; these values were then adjusted using the higher terms of the series. The first set of values was calculated partly by Wise's* (1950) method and partly by means of Carter's (1947) approximation. The adjustments necessary were found to be small and to vary very slowly with p and q; they could therefore be calculated by the following method which reduces to a minimum interpolation in the *Tables of the Incomplete Beta Function* (1948).

* We are indebted to Mr Wise for some helpful correspondence on his method.

First, p and q may be replaced by the integers nearest them. For these integers an exact significance point may be found by quadratic inverse interpolation. The difference of this exact point and the first approximation to it is the required adjustment. The adjustment required for the fourth moment turned out to be negligible to the order of accuracy aimed at and could have been ignored. The adjustments were so small and regular that it was only

Table 5. *Significance points of d_L and d_U*: 2·5 %

n	$k'=1$		$k'=2$		$k'=3$		$k'=4$		$k'=5$	
	d_L	d_U	d_L	d_U	d_L	d_U	d_L	d_U	d_L	d_U
15	0·95	1·23	0·83	1·40	0·71	1·61	0·59	1·84	0·48	2·09
16	0·98	1·24	0·86	1·40	0·75	1·59	0·64	1·80	0·53	2·03
17	1·01	1·25	0·90	1·40	0·79	1·58	0·68	1·77	0·57	1·98
18	1·03	1·26	0·93	1·40	0·82	1·56	0·72	1·74	0·62	1·93
19	1·06	1·28	0·96	1·41	0·86	1·55	0·76	1·72	0·66	1·90
20	1·08	1·28	0·99	1·41	0·89	1·55	0·79	1·70	0·70	1·87
21	1·10	1·30	1·01	1·41	0·92	1·54	0·83	1·69	0·73	1·84
22	1·12	1·31	1·04	1·42	0·95	1·54	0·86	1·68	0·77	1·82
23	1·14	1·32	1·06	1·42	0·97	1·54	0·89	1·67	0·80	1·80
24	1·16	1·33	1·08	1·43	1·00	1·54	0·91	1·66	0·83	1·79
25	1·18	1·34	1·10	1·43	1·02	1·54	0·94	1·65	0·86	1·77
26	1·19	1·35	1·12	1·44	1·04	1·54	0·96	1·65	0·88	1·76
27	1·21	1·36	1·13	1·44	1·06	1·54	0·99	1·64	0·91	1·75
28	1·22	1·37	1·15	1·45	1·08	1·54	1·01	1·64	0·93	1·74
29	1·24	1·38	1·17	1·45	1·10	1·54	1·03	1·63	0·96	1·73
30	1·25	1·38	1·18	1·46	1·12	1·54	1·05	1·63	0·98	1·73
31	1·26	1·39	1·20	1·47	1·13	1·55	1·07	1·63	1·00	1·72
32	1·27	1·40	1·21	1·47	1·15	1·55	1·08	1·63	1·02	1·71
33	1·28	1·41	1·22	1·48	1·16	1·55	1·10	1·63	1·04	1·71
34	1·29	1·41	1·24	1·48	1·17	1·55	1·12	1·63	1·06	1·70
35	1·30	1·42	1·25	1·48	1·19	1·55	1·13	1·63	1·07	1·70
36	1·31	1·43	1·26	1·49	1·20	1·56	1·15	1·63	1·09	1·70
37	1·32	1·43	1·27	1·49	1·21	1·56	1·16	1·62	1·10	1·70
38	1·33	1·44	1·28	1·50	1·23	1·56	1·17	1·62	1·12	1·70
39	1·34	1·44	1·29	1·50	1·24	1·56	1·19	1·63	1·13	1·69
40	1·35	1·45	1·30	1·51	1·25	1·57	1·20	1·63	1·15	1·69
45	1·39	1·48	1·34	1·53	1·30	1·58	1·25	1·63	1·21	1·69
50	1·42	1·50	1·38	1·54	1·34	1·59	1·30	1·64	1·26	1·69
55	1·45	1·52	1·41	1·56	1·37	1·60	1·33	1·64	1·30	1·69
60	1·47	1·54	1·44	1·57	1·40	1·61	1·37	1·65	1·33	1·69
65	1·49	1·55	1·46	1·59	1·43	1·62	1·40	1·66	1·36	1·69
70	1·51	1·57	1·48	1·60	1·45	1·63	1·42	1·66	1·39	1·70
75	1·53	1·58	1·50	1·61	1·47	1·64	1·45	1·67	1·42	1·70
80	1·54	1·59	1·52	1·62	1·49	1·65	1·47	1·67	1·44	1·70
85	1·56	1·60	1·53	1·63	1·51	1·65	1·49	1·68	1·46	1·71
90	1·57	1·61	1·55	1·64	1·53	1·66	1·50	1·69	1·48	1·71
95	1·58	1·62	1·56	1·65	1·54	1·67	1·52	1·69	1·50	1·71
100	1·59	1·63	1·57	1·65	1·55	1·67	1·53	1·70	1·51	1·72

necessary to calculate them at 39 places in the entire set of tables, the remainder being obtained by linear interpolation. The adjustments were negligible for numbers of observations greater than 40.

As a partial check on the calculating procedure it was applied to the calculation of the significance points for a related distribution for which exact significance points were available. To make the circumstances as unfavourable as possible the case $n = 16$, $k' = 5$ at the

Table 6. *Significance points of d_L and d_U*: 1 %

	$k'=1$		$k'=2$		$k'=3$		$k'=4$		$k'=5$	
n	d_L	d_U	d_L	d_U	d_L	d_U	d_L	d_U	d_L	d_U
15	0·81	1·07	0·70	1·25	0·59	1·46	0·49	1·70	0·39	1·96
16	0·84	1·09	0·74	1·25	0·63	1·44	0·53	1·66	0·44	1·90
17	0·87	1·10	0·77	1·25	0·67	1·43	0·57	1·63	0·48	1·85
18	0·90	1·12	0·80	1·26	0·71	1·42	0·61	1·60	0·52	1·80
19	0·93	1·13	0·83	1·26	0·74	1·41	0·65	1·58	0·56	1·77
20	0·95	1·15	0·86	1·27	0·77	1·41	0·68	1·57	0·60	1·74
21	0·97	1·16	0·89	1·27	0·80	1·41	0·72	1·55	0·63	1·71
22	1·00	1·17	0·91	1·28	0·83	1·40	0·75	1·54	0·66	1·69
23	1·02	1·19	0·94	1·29	0·86	1·40	0·77	1·53	0·70	1·67
24	1·04	1·20	0·96	1·30	0·88	1·41	0·80	1·53	0·72	1·66
25	1·05	1·21	0·98	1·30	0·90	1·41	0·83	1·52	0·75	1·65
26	1·07	1·22	1·00	1·31	0·93	1·41	0·85	1·52	0·78	1·64
27	1·09	1·23	1·02	1·32	0·95	1·41	0·88	1·51	0·81	1·63
28	1·10	1·24	1·04	1·32	0·97	1·41	0·90	1·51	0·83	1·62
29	1·12	1·25	1·05	1·33	0·99	1·42	0·92	1·51	0·85	1·61
30	1·13	1·26	1·07	1·34	1·01	1·42	0·94	1·51	0·88	1·61
31	1·15	1·27	1·08	1·34	1·02	1·42	0·96	1·51	0·90	1·60
32	1·16	1·28	1·10	1·35	1·04	1·43	0·98	1·51	0·92	1·60
33	1·17	1·29	1·11	1·36	1·05	1·43	1·00	1·51	0·94	1·59
34	1·18	1·30	1·13	1·36	1·07	1·43	1·01	1·51	0·95	1·59
35	1·19	1·31	1·14	1·37	1·08	1·44	1·03	1·51	0·97	1·59
36	1·21	1·32	1·15	1·38	1·10	1·44	1·04	1·51	0·99	1·59
37	1·22	1·32	1·16	1·38	1·11	1·45	1·06	1·51	1·00	1·59
38	1·23	1·33	1·18	1·39	1·12	1·45	1·07	1·52	1·02	1·58
39	1·24	1·34	1·19	1·39	1·14	1·45	1·09	1·52	1·03	1·58
40	1·25	1·34	1·20	1·40	1·15	1·46	1·10	1·52	1·05	1·58
45	1·29	1·38	1·24	1·42	1·20	1·48	1·16	1·53	1·11	1·58
50	1·32	1·40	1·28	1·45	1·24	1·49	1·20	1·54	1·16	1·59
55	1·36	1·43	1·32	1·47	1·28	1·51	1·25	1·55	1·21	1·59
60	1·38	1·45	1·35	1·48	1·32	1·52	1·28	1·56	1·25	1·60
65	1·41	1·47	1·38	1·50	1·35	1·53	1·31	1·57	1·28	1·61
70	1·43	1·49	1·40	1·52	1·37	1·55	1·34	1·58	1·31	1·61
75	1·45	1·50	1·42	1·53	1·39	1·56	1·37	1·59	1·34	1·62
80	1·47	1·52	1·44	1·54	1·42	1·57	1·39	1·60	1·36	1·62
85	1·48	1·53	1·46	1·55	1·43	1·58	1·41	1·60	1·39	1·63
90	1·50	1·54	1·47	1·56	1·45	1·59	1·43	1·61	1·41	1·64
95	1·51	1·55	1·49	1·57	1·47	1·60	1·45	1·62	1·42	1·64
100	1·52	1·56	1·50	1·58	1·48	1·60	1·46	1·63	1·44	1·65

extreme of the tabulated values was examined. The distributions of d_L and d_U for these values were modified to give latent roots occurring in equal pairs, i.e. five pairs in all. The new roots were chosen to lie midway between the roots of the original distribution, thus preserving its asymmetry and general character. By pairing the roots in this way the exact significance points could be determined using results given by R. L. Anderson (1942). The significance points obtained by the approximate procedure agreed with these exact significance points to the order of accuracy required here.

7. An exact bounds test

We have given elsewhere (Watson & Durbin, 1951) a general method of constructing exact tests of serial independence which do not require the use of circular definitions of the serial correlation coefficient. The method can be used to obtain the exact distributions of bounding statistics similar to d_L and d_U. The advantage of having exact distributions is obtained at the cost of throwing away a certain amount of relevant information.

For testing the independence of the errors in a regression model a statistic d' is defined which is a slight modification of d. If the number of observations is even, $2m$ say, then

$$d' = \frac{(z_1-z_2)^2+\ldots+(z_{m-1}-z_m)^2+(z_{m+1}-z_{m+2})^2+\ldots+(z_{2m-1}-z_{2m})^2}{\sum_1^{2m} z_i^2},$$

and if it is odd, $2m+1$ say, then

$$d' = \frac{(z_1-z_2)^2+\ldots+(z_{m-1}-z_m)^2+(z_{m+2}-z_{m+3})^2+\ldots+(z_{2m}-z_{2m+1})^2}{\sum_1^{2m+1} z_i^2},$$

where the z's are the least-squares residuals. The only difference from d is that one or two of the squared differences are omitted from the numerator of d'. Thus when m is small a substantial fraction of the relevant information is sacrificed.

The theory developed in Part I can be applied to show that d' lies between two values d'_L and d'_U. In contrast to d, exact significance points can be calculated for d'_L and d'_U using the results of R. L. Anderson (1942), except for the case of an even number of observations and an odd number of independent variables, for which the exact distribution of d'_L has not been found. A short table of such values for odd numbers of observations is given in Table 7. This table may be used for testing the significance of an observed value of d' in exactly the same way as Table 4 is used for testing the significance of an observed value of d.

Table 7. *Significance points of d'_L and d'_U: 5 %*

n	$k'=1$		$k'=2$		$k'=3$		$k'=4$		$k'=5$	
	d'_L	d'_U	d'_L	d'_U	d'_L	d'_U	d'_L	d'_U	d'_L	d'_U
13	0·69	0·97	0·56	1·15	—	—	—	—	—	—
15	0·80	1·04	0·67	1·20	0·55	1·36	—	—	—	—
17	0·89	1·11	0·77	1·24	0·65	1·38	0·54	1·57	0·44	1·74
19	0·96	1·16	0·85	1·27	0·75	1·40	0·64	1·56	0·54	1·71
21	1·02	1·20	0·92	1·30	0·82	1·42	0·72	1·56	0·63	1·69
23	1·07	1·24	0·98	1·33	0·89	1·44	0·80	1·56	0·71	1·68

The calculations required even for such a short table were very heavy, and our chief motive for including it is the satisfaction of demonstrating that the problem has an exact solution. In practice we ourselves would prefer to use Table 4 owing to the greater power and simplicity of the statistic d.

REFERENCES

Anderson, R. L. (1942). *Ann. Math. Statist.* **13**, 1.

Anderson, R. L. & Anderson, T. W. (1950). *Ann. Math. Statist.* **21**, 59.

Anderson, R. L. & Houseman, E. E. (1942). Tables of orthogonal polynomial values extended to $N = 104$. *Res. Bull. Iowa St. Coll.* no. 297.

Carter, A. H. (1947). *Biometrika*, **34**, 352.

Cochran, W. G. (1938). *J.R. Statist. Soc., Suppl.*, **5**, 171.

Courant, R. & Hilbert, D. (1931). *Methoden der Mathematischen Physik.* Berlin: Julius Springer.

Durbin, J. & Watson, G. S. (1950). *Biometrika*, **37**, 409.

Fisher, R. A. & Yates, F. (1948). *Statistical Tables.* Edinburgh: Oliver and Boyd.

Pearson, K. (1948). *Tables of the Incomplete Beta Function.* Cambridge University Press.

Prest, A. R. (1949). *Rev. Econ. Statist.* **31**, 33.

Schultz, Henry (1938). *Theory and Measurement of Demand*, pp. 674–7. University of Chicago Press.

Snedecor, G. W. (1937). *Statistical Methods.* Collegiate Press.

Thompson, Catherine (1941). *Biometrika*, **32**, 151.

Watson, G. S. & Durbin, J. (1951). Exact tests of serial correlation using non-circular statistics. (To be published).

Wise, M. E. (1950). *Biometrika*, **37**, 208.

Corrections to Part I. (Durbin & Watson, 1950)

We are grateful to Prof. T. W. Anderson for pointing out an error in the section headed 'Inequalities on $\nu_1, \nu_2, \ldots, \nu_{n-k}$'. Part (*b*) of the lemma and its corollary have been correctly applied in the remaining parts of the paper, but are incorrectly stated.

The necessary corrections are as follows:

p. 415. The second paragraph beginning 'We therefore seek...' should read:

'We therefore seek inequalities on $\nu_1, \nu_2, \ldots, \nu_{n-k}$. For the sake of generality we suppose that certain of the regression vectors, say s of them, coincide with latent vectors of **A** (or are linear combinations of them). From the results of the previous section it follows that the problem is reduced to the consideration of $k-s$ arbitrary regression vectors, while **A** may be supposed to have s zero roots together with the roots of **A** not associated with the s latent vectors mentioned above. These roots may be renumbered so that

$$\lambda_1 \leqslant \lambda_2 \leqslant \ldots \leqslant \lambda_{n-s}.$$

We proceed to show that

$$\lambda_i \leqslant \nu_i \leqslant \lambda_{i+k-s} \quad (i = 1, 2, \ldots, n-k).\text{'} \qquad (3)$$

p. 415. The next to the last sentence should read:

'Allowing for cases in which regression vectors coincide with latent vectors of **A** we have (3).'

p. 416. Lemma (*b*) should read:

'If s of the columns of **X** are linear combinations of s of the latent vectors of **A**, and if the roots of **A** associated with the remaining $n-s$ latent vectors of **A** are renumbered so that

$$\lambda_1 \leqslant \lambda_2 \leqslant \ldots \leqslant \lambda_{n-s},$$

then

$$\lambda_i \leqslant \nu_i \leqslant \lambda_{i+k-s} \quad (i = 1, 2, \ldots, n-k).\text{'}$$

p. 416. Corollary should read:

$$\text{'}r_L \leqslant r \leqslant r_U,$$

where

$$r_L = \frac{\sum_{i=1}^{n-k} \lambda_i \zeta_i^2}{\sum_{i=1}^{n-k} \zeta_i^2}$$

and

$$r_U = \frac{\sum_{i=1}^{n-k} \lambda_{i+k-s} \zeta_i^2}{\sum_{i=1}^{n-k} \zeta_i^2}.\text{'}$$

p. 416: line 16. 'λ_{s+k+1}' should read 'λ_{n-s+1}'.

The following misprints should also be noted.

p. 414, line 13. The equation should read:

$$'| \mathbf{I}_n \theta - (\mathbf{I}_n - \mathbf{1}_1 \mathbf{1}_1') \mathbf{\Lambda} | = 0.'$$

p. 414, line 22. The equation should read:

$$'\prod_{j=1}^{n} (\theta - \lambda_j) + \sum_{i=1}^{n} l_i^2 \lambda_i \prod_{j \neq i}^{n} (\theta - \lambda_j) = 0.'$$

p. 417, last line but two. The formula should read:

$$'\alpha_i = \prod_{j \neq i}^{\frac{1}{2}(n-k-1)} (\tau_i - \tau_j) \sqrt{(\tau_i - \tau)}.'$$

TESTING THE INDEPENDENCE OF REGRESSION DISTURBANCES

H. THEIL AND A. L. NAGAR

This article deals with the distribution of the Von Neumann ratio of least-squares estimated regression disturbances. This distribution is approximated by a beta distribution under the condition that the behaviour of explanatory variables of the regression over time is sufficiently smooth. Two examples are presented, together with a table containing 1 and 5 per cent significance limits for a number of observations ranging from 15 to 100 and a number of coefficients adjusted ranging from 2 to 6.

1. INTRODUCTION

THE possibility of serial correlation of disturbances presents a serious problem in time series regression analysis. The most well-known contribution to this field is that of Durbin and Watson [1, 2], who formulated a test procedure of the null-hypothesis of residual independence based on the Von Neumann ratio of the least-squares estimated disturbances:[1,2]

$$Q = \frac{\sum \{\hat{u}(t) - \hat{u}(t-1)\}^2}{\sum \hat{u}(t)^2}, \tag{1.1}$$

where $\hat{u}(t)$ is the least-squares estimator of the disturbance $u(t)$ in the regression equation

$$y(t) = \beta_1 x_1(t) + \cdots + \beta_\Lambda x_\Lambda(t) + u(t). \tag{1.2}$$

This contribution is, however, only a partial one, since it does not specify precise significance limits but only upper (Q_U) and lower (Q_L) bounds to these. Hence the inference takes the following form: If $Q<Q_L$, the null-hypothesis is rejected (at the significance level corresponding to Q_L) in favour of the alternative hypothesis of positive serial correlation; if $Q>Q_U$, the null-hypothesis is not rejected; and if $Q_L<Q<Q_U$, no inference is possible.

Obviously, the "region of ignorance," i.e., the interval (Q_L, Q_U), presents a great difficulty, especially if it is large. And it is large when the number of observations is small or moderate (around 20, say) and the number of explanatory variables not very small. This implies an inconvenience for the practical research worker, for he is then confronted with a situation in which he has no guidance; and it implies a danger insofar as the practical worker feels that he can interpret "no inference possible" as equivalent with "no need to reject the null-hypothesis of independence," for this will necessarily lead to bias in the sense that too many cases of positive serial correlation are overlooked.

---

[1] Reference is also made to Hannan [3, 4] and to Hildreth and Lu [5].

[2] The Von Neumann ratio will be interpreted throughout this paper as the sum of squares of the first differences of the least-squares estimated disturbances divided by the sum of squares of the estimated disturbances themselves. This is not identical with the ratio of the mean square successive difference to the variance of the disturbance estimates, the difference being a factor $T/(T-1)$ where T is the number of observations. We follow Durbin and Watson in this respect because it facilitates slightly the computations.

These remarks should in no way be interpreted as a criticism of Durbin's and Watson's pioneering work. As a matter of fact, the present article (which presents unique although approximate significance limits) is based very heavily on their results. This paper, too, is based on the Von Neumann ratio of the estimated disturbances. It is concerned with the derivation of significance limits of this ratio for the case in which the first and second differences of the explanatory variables are small in absolute value compared with the range of the corresponding variable itself.[3] This condition is met satisfactorily for most economic time series, except of course when such a series has already been transformed on first-difference basis prior to the regression computation; in that case our procedure is not recommended. In addition, a convenient though approximate method is indicated for computing a revised regression in the case when the null-hypothesis is rejected.

2. TWO EXAMPLES

We shall deal with regressions of the type

$$y(t) = \beta_1 x_1(t) + \beta_2 x_2(t) + \cdots + u(t), \tag{2.1}$$

where the values taken by the x's are assumed nonstochastic (one of them may be 1 for all t, so that the corresponding β represents then a constant term), while the disturbances (the u's) are supposed to be normally distributed with zero mean and constant variance σ^2. In the null-hypothesis the u's are assumed to be mutually independent. We shall write T for the number of observations, and Λ for the number of coefficients in (2.1)—i.e., the number of explanatory variables plus one for the constant term (if there is a constant term).

The procedure will be illustrated with two numerical examples, one of which deals with the demand for spirits in the United Kingdom from 1870 to 1938, the other with the demand for textiles in the Netherlands from 1923 to 1939.[4] In both cases we have annual data (hence $T=69$ for the spirits example, $T=17$ for the textile example) and in both cases y refers to the logarithm of consumption per head, x_1 to the logarithm of real income per head, and x_2 to the logarithm of the deflated price of the commodity. Hence β_1 stands for the income elasticity and β_2 for the price elasticity of spirits in Britain and of textile in the Netherlands in the periods just-mentioned.

It will prove convenient to follow Durbin's and Watson's example by computing not only the sums of squares and products of the variables themselves but also those of their first (backward) differences, like $\Delta y(t) = y(t) - y(t-1)$. They are shown in Table 1. This procedure has three advantages. First, it leads to an easy computation of the Von Neumann ratio as will become clear at the end of this section. Second, it enables us to judge to what extent the approximations to be applied in Section 3 are acceptable. Third, it is computa-

[3] It is worth-while to add that this condition is in most cases particularly acceptable when the observations are arranged, not in chronological order, but according to increasing values of the explanatory variable (assuming that there is only one such variable). The use of Q in this manner amounts to a test for linearity of the regression. Reference is made to Prais and Houthakker [7, p. 53].

[4] The spirits example was also used by Durbin and Watson for illustrative purposes; it is due to Prest [8]. For the underlying time series we refer to Table 1, p. 160 of reference [2] and call the attention to a printing error in the income column: the last observation should be 2.1182. The time series of the textile example are given in the Appendix of this paper.

TABLE 1. SUMS OF SQUARES AND PRODUCTS

	y	x_1	x_2	1	Δy	Δx_1	Δx_2	1	
				Spirits					
y	221.262 982	238.367 612	255.009 106	122.1562	.112 627	.014 683	−.076 413	−.6844	Δy
x_1		266.286 023	287.819 282	135.3888		.023 539	.000 527	.3513	Δx_1
x_2			312.604 832	146.1679			.083 559	.5404	Δx_2
1				69				68	1
				Textile					
y	76.658 975	72.596 420	67.441 918	36.0763	.024 866	.001 829	−.018 766	.2223	Δy
x_1		68.841 788	64.064 566	34.2078		.002 930	.001 562	.0308	Δx_1
x_2			59.759 499	31.8339			.021 104	−.2169	Δx_2
1				17				16	1

tionally convenient for the procedure which will be proposed in Section 4.2 in case the null-hypothesis of residual independence is rejected.

The elasticities are then estimated by solving the normal equations in the conventional manner, which gives:

$$\text{spirits}\begin{cases} b_1 = -\ 0.120 \\ b_2 = -\ 1.228 \end{cases} \qquad \text{textile}\begin{cases} b_1 = \quad 1.143 \\ b_2 = -\ 0.829. \end{cases} \tag{2.2}$$

Next, we consider the sums of squares of the least-squares estimated disturbances:

$$\text{spirits: } \sum \hat{u}(t)^2 = 0.22096; \qquad \text{textile: } \sum \hat{u}(t)^2 = 0.002567, \tag{2.3}$$

which enable us to compute standard errors of the estimated elasticities under the condition that the null-hypothesis is true. They are obtained in the usual manner, which gives:

$$\text{spirits}\begin{cases} s_b \ = 0.108 \\ s_{b_2} = 0.050 \end{cases} \qquad \text{textile}\begin{cases} s_{b_1} = 0.156 \\ s_{b_2} = 0.036. \end{cases} \tag{2.4}$$

Finally, we consider the first differences of the estimated disturbances, whose sum of squares is

$$\begin{aligned} \sum_t \{\Delta\hat{u}(t)\}^2 = \sum_t \{\Delta y(t)\}^2 - 2 \sum_\lambda b_\lambda \sum_t \Delta x_\lambda(t) \Delta y(t) \\ + \sum_\lambda \sum_{\lambda'} b_\lambda b_{\lambda'} \sum_t \Delta x_\lambda(t) \Delta x_{\lambda'}(t). \end{aligned} \tag{2.5}$$

Using the right-hand part of Table 1, we find

$$\text{spirits: } \sum \{\Delta\hat{u}(t)\}^2 = 0.05497; \quad \text{textile: } \sum \{\Delta\hat{u}(t)\}^2 = 0.004943. \tag{2.6}$$

The Von Neumann ratio of the least-squares estimated disturbances is then

$$\begin{aligned} Q = \frac{\sum \{\Delta\hat{u}(t)\}^2}{\sum \hat{u}(t)^2} &= 0.249 \text{ for spirits;} \\ &= 1.926 \text{ for textile,} \end{aligned} \tag{2.7}$$

which is the statistic which will be used for testing the null-hypothesis of residual independence. The reader who is interested in results only is advised to proceed immediately to Section 4.[5]

3. THE APPROXIMATE DISTRIBUTION OF THE VON NEUMANN RATIO OF LEAST-SQUARES ESTIMATED REGRESSION DISTURBANCES

3.1. INTRODUCTORY

It will prove convenient to arrange the values taken by our variables in vectors and matrices. Thus, we write y for the vector of T values taken by the dependent variable and X for the $T\times\Lambda$ matrix of values taken by the explanatory variables. Further, we write u for the column vector of the T "true" disturbances, and $\hat{u}$ for its least-squares estimator. Then, as is well-known (see e.g. [10, p. 211]):

$$\hat{u} = [I - X(X'X)^{-1}X']u, \tag{3.1}$$

where I is the unit matrix of order T; and

$$Q = \frac{\hat{u}'A\hat{u}}{\hat{u}'\hat{u}}, \tag{3.2}$$

where A is the symmetric $T\times T$ matrix

$$A = \begin{bmatrix} 1 & -1 & 0 & \cdots & 0 & 0 \\ -1 & 2 & -1 & \cdots & 0 & 0 \\ 0 & -1 & 2 & \cdots & 0 & 0 \\ \cdot & \cdot & \cdot & \cdots & \cdot & \cdot \\ 0 & 0 & 0 & \cdots & 2 & -1 \\ 0 & 0 & 0 & \cdots & -1 & 1 \end{bmatrix}. \tag{3.3}$$

It is well-known that Q lies between 0 and 4, but it is less generally realized that these limits cannot always be attained if Q refers to least-squares estimated disturbances. Take e.g. $\Lambda=2$, one of the explanatory variables representing the constant term. Then $Q=0$ would imply that all disturbances are equal (to ϵ, say) and the observed points of the two-dimensional scatter are all located on a straight line parallel to the regression line; which is impossible because the least-squares procedure implies that the regression line is then automatically shifted upward by an amount ϵ. In fact, the attainable limits of Q are determined by the roots of the matrix

$$K = A - AX(X'X)^{-1}X'. \tag{3.4}$$

This matrix is positive semi-definite with Λ zero roots. The minimum of Q is—as stated by Durbin and Watson—the smallest of the $T-\Lambda$ positive roots, the maximum is equal to the largest root. Let us indicate the positive roots by

[5] Except that he is also advised to check whether it is indeed true that the behaviour of the explanatory variables is sufficiently smooth in the sense that their first and second differences are small compared with the range of the corresponding variable itself. This can be done by comparing the second moments of the first differences with the moments about the mean of the corresponding original variables.

$\nu_1, \nu_2, \cdots$; then the following result is available for the expectation of Q under the null-hypothesis stated:[6]

$$\mu(Q) = \frac{1}{T - \Lambda} \sum_i \nu_i = \bar{\nu}, \text{ say}; \tag{3.5}$$

and for the next three moments about the mean:

$$\begin{cases} \mu_2 = \dfrac{2\sum (\nu_i - \bar{\nu})^2}{(T - \Lambda)(T - \Lambda + 2)}; \\ \mu_3 = \dfrac{8\sum (\nu_i - \bar{\nu})^3}{(T - \Lambda)(T - \Lambda + 2)(T - \Lambda + 4)}; \\ \mu_4 = \dfrac{48\sum (\nu_i - \bar{\nu})^4 + 12\{\sum (\nu_i - \bar{\nu})^2\}^2}{(T - \Lambda)(T - \Lambda + 2)(T - \Lambda + 4)(T - \Lambda + 6)}. \end{cases} \tag{3.6}$$

These results are exact and will be used in the next sections (3.2–3.5) to fit a beta distribution to the true distribution of Q under certain approximations.

3.2. THE MEAN

According to (3.5), the expectation of Q is $1/(T-\Lambda)$ times the sum of the roots of K, or what amounts to the same thing, $1/(T-\Lambda)$ times the trace of K (the sum of the diagonal elements of K). Applying some elementary properties of traces of matrices, we find

$$\begin{aligned} tr\, K &= tr\, A - tr\, AX(X'X)^{-1}X' \\ &= (2T - 2) - tr\, (X'X)^{-1}X'AX, \end{aligned} \tag{3.7}$$

see (3.3). Now $X'AX$ is the matrix of sums of squares and products of the first differences of the explanatory variables:

$$X'AX = \left[\sum_t \Delta x_\lambda(t) \Delta x_{\lambda'}(t) \right], \tag{3.8}$$

and these sums of squares and products are usually on the average small compared with the corresponding elements of $X'X$. This leads to the presumption that we might be able to neglect the trace term behind the second equality sign of (3.7) relative to $(2T-2)$. In fact, for our two examples of Section 2 we have

$$\begin{aligned} tr\, K &= (138 - 2) - 0.122 \text{ for spirits;} \\ &= (34 - 2) - 0.518 \text{ for textile,} \end{aligned} \tag{3.9}$$

which shows that the error committed by neglecting the trace term amounts to less than one-tenth of one per cent in the spirits example, and about $1\frac{1}{2}$ per cent in the textile example. Generally, one should expect this feature when the behaviour of the explanatory variables over time is sufficiently smooth. The fact that the error is larger in the latter example is primarily due to the rather

[6] These results are derived by using the fact that under the null-hypothesis Q is stochastically independent of its own denominator [1, pp. 418–9], so that any moment of Q is equal to the ratio of the corresponding moments of numerator and denominator. The latter moments are derived by means of the χ^2-distribution.

small range of variation of per capita income in the Netherlands during the period considered.

An alternative interpretation of the trace term is also instructive. The matrix $(X'X)^{-1}X'AX$ can be interpreted as the matrix of least-squares regression coefficients in a set of regressions in which X represents the values taken by the independent variables in each of the equations, and the successive columns of AX the values taken by the various dependent variables. Now AX is essentially the matrix of second differences of the X-variables, apart from sign and from terminal effects. More precisely:

$$AX = \begin{bmatrix} x_\lambda(1) - x_\lambda(2) \\ -x_\lambda(1) + 2x_\lambda(2) - x_\lambda(3) \\ \vdots \\ -x_\lambda(T-2) + 2x_\lambda(T-1) - x_\lambda(T) \\ -x_\lambda(T-1) + x_\lambda(T) \end{bmatrix} = \begin{bmatrix} -\Delta x_\lambda(2) \\ -\Delta^2 x_\lambda(3) \\ \vdots \\ -\Delta^2 x_\lambda(T) \\ \Delta x_\lambda(T) \end{bmatrix}, \tag{3.10}$$

where $\lambda = 1, \cdots, \Lambda$. Hence $(X'X)^{-1}X'AX$ is minus the coefficient matrix of the regressions of the second differences of the explanatory variables on these variables themselves (apart from terminal effects), so that the trace of that matrix is simply the sum of the "own" coefficients—relating $\Delta^2 x_\lambda$ with x_λ, for $\lambda = 1, \cdots, \Lambda$.

We suggest to neglect the trace term in (3.7), because this simplifies the approach considerably. On combining this with (3.5), we obtain

$$EQ \approx 2 \cdot \frac{T-1}{T-\Lambda}. \tag{3.11}$$

3.3 THE VARIANCE

According to (3.6), the numerator of the variance of Q equals $\sum(\nu_i - \bar{\nu})^2$ apart from a factor 2, which can also be written $\sum \nu_i^2 - (T-\Lambda)\bar{\nu}^2$. On applying (3.5), we therefore have

$$\sum (\nu_i - \bar{\nu})^2 = \sum \nu_i^2 - (T - \Lambda)(EQ)^2, \tag{3.12}$$

see Section 3.2. Considering $\sum \nu_i^2$, we observe that the square of a latent root of a matrix K is also a latent root of K^2, so $\sum \nu_i^2$ is equal to the trace of K^2. For this trace we have

$$\sum \nu_i^2 = tr\, K^2 = tr\, A^2 - tr\, A^2 X(X'X)^{-1}X'$$
$$- tr\, AX(X'X)^{-1}X'A + tr\, AX(X'X)^{-1}X'AX(X'X)^{-1}X',$$

which can also be written in the form:

$$\sum \nu_i^2 = (6T - 8) - 2\, tr(X'X)^{-1}X'A^2X + tr[X'AX(X'X)^{-1}]^2, \tag{3.13}$$

given the fact that $tr\, A^2$, being the sum of squares of all elements of A, is equal to $6T - 8$.

Considering the second term on the right of (3.13), we note that $X'A^2X$

$=(AX)'AX$ is the matrix of the sums of squares and products of the second differences of the explanatory variables apart from terminal effects; see (3.10). We should expect that the elements of this matrix are small compared with the corresponding elements of $X'X$ when the behaviour of our explanatory variables is sufficiently smooth, so that the first trace term on the right of (3.13) is then small. The same thing can be expected to be true under the same condition for the second trace term. For our two examples the decomposition (3.13) is as follows:

$$\begin{aligned}\sum \nu_i^2 &= (414 - 8) - 0.378 + 0.015 \text{ for spirits;}\\ &= (102 - 8) - 1.450 + 0.161 \text{ for textile,}\end{aligned} \tag{3.14}$$

which shows that the error caused by neglecting the last two terms amounts to less than one-tenth of one per cent in the spirits case, and less than $1\frac{1}{2}$ per cent in the textile case. We can go on in this way by combining the approximation for $\sum \nu_i^2$ and $\sum \nu_i$ to find the corresponding approximation error in $\sum(\nu_i - \bar{\nu})^2$; this is still on the small side, viz., about one-tenth of one per cent for the spirits case, but slightly larger for that of textile, viz., 5 per cent.

Our suggestion is to approximate $\sum \nu_i^2$ by the first term on the right of (3.13) when the behaviour of the explanatory variables is smooth, and to combine this with the approximation of Section 3.2 to derive the variance. This gives:

$$\operatorname{var} Q \approx 2 \cdot \frac{6T - 8 - (T - \Lambda)\left(2\dfrac{T-1}{T-\Lambda}\right)^2}{(T-\Lambda)(T-\Lambda+2)} = 4 \cdot \frac{T^2 - 3\Lambda T + 4\Lambda - 2}{(T-\Lambda)^2(T-\Lambda+2)}. \tag{3.15}$$

3.4 SKEWNESS AND KURTOSIS

For the moments of the third and fourth order we can proceed in the same way. By neglecting $tr\ (X'X)^{-1}X'A^3X$, etc., we find for the third moment of Q:

$$\mu_3 \approx -\frac{32(\Lambda - 1)(T^2 - 5\Lambda T + 8\Lambda - 4)}{(T-\Lambda)^3(T-\Lambda+2)(T-\Lambda+4)}; \tag{3.16}$$

and, when dividing this by the cube of the standard deviation, we obtain the Pearsonian skewness coefficient[7]

$$\sqrt{\beta_1} \approx -\frac{4(\Lambda-1)(T^2 - 5\Lambda T + 8\Lambda - 4)(T - \Lambda + 2)^{1/2}}{(T-\Lambda+4)(T^2 - 3\Lambda T + 4\Lambda - 2)^{1(1/2)}} \approx -\frac{4(\Lambda - 1)}{T^{1(1/2)}}, \tag{3.17}$$

where the last ratio retains only the leading term (of order $T^{-1\frac{1}{2}}$). In the same way, by neglecting such terms as $tr\ (X'X)^{-1}X'A^4X$, we obtain an expression for μ_4 involving T and Λ only. After dividing this fourth moment by the square of the variance, we obtain the Pearsonian kurtosis coefficient:

$$\beta_2 \approx 3 - \frac{6}{T}, \tag{3.18}$$

terms of higher order of smallness than $1/T$ being neglected.

---

[7] The Pearsonian coefficients β_1 and β_2 should not be confused with the coefficient vector β of the regression problem. The former coefficients play a role in Sections 3.4 and 3.5 only.

The results (3.17) and (3.18) imply that the skewness coefficient of the Von Neumann ratio of the estimated regression disturbances deviates from zero (the symmetry value) to the order $1/T^{1\frac{1}{2}}$, and that the kurtosis coefficient deviates from 3 (the value of mesokurtosis) to the order $1/T$; at least, when it is true that successive differences in the values taken by the explanatory variables are sufficiently small.

3.5 A BETA APPROXIMATION

The results obtained so far will be used to fit a beta distribution (with range to be determined) to the distribution of Q; that is, we shall determine the parameters of the beta distribution and its range by identifying its moments with those of the Q-distribution to a satisfactory order of approximation. As is well-known, a beta variable in the range (0, 1) has the following density function:

$$\frac{1}{\beta(a, b)} \cdot x^{a-1}(1-x)^{b-1};$$

and its mean and variance are

$$Ex = \frac{a}{a+b}; \qquad \text{var } x = \frac{ab}{(a+b)^2(a+b+1)}, \tag{3.19}$$

respectively, while the skewness and kurtosis coefficients are given by

$$\sqrt{\beta_1} = \frac{2(b-a)(a+b+1)^{1/2}}{(a+b+2)(ab)^{1/2}} \tag{3.20}$$

$$\beta_2 - 3 = \frac{6[(a+b+1)(a-b)^2 - (a+b+2)ab]}{ab(a+b+2)(a+b+3)}. \tag{3.21}$$

The last two coefficients are independent of origin and scale and thus independent of the range that will be adjusted. Hence we should identify the right-hand sides of (3.20) and (3.21) with those of (3.17) and (3.18), respectively, which gives

$$a = \tfrac{1}{2}(T + \Lambda); \qquad b = \tfrac{1}{2}(T - \Lambda + 2), \tag{3.22}$$

terms of higher order of smallness than $T^0 = 1$ being neglected in the right-hand sides of (3.22). On substituting (3.22) into (3.20) and (3.21), we find that the skewness and kurtosis coefficients of the two distributions are identical to order $T^{-1\frac{1}{2}}$ and T^{-1}, respectively.

The range of our beta distribution will be written $(c, 4-d)$, which implies that Q is transformed to a beta variable

$$x = \frac{Q-c}{4-(c+d)} \tag{3.23}$$

in the range (0, 1) The mean is then

$$Ex = \frac{EQ - c}{4-(c+d)} = \frac{a}{a+b} = \frac{T+\Lambda}{2(T+1)} \tag{3.24}$$

in accordance with (3.19) and (3.22). In the same way, the variance is

$$\operatorname{var} x = \frac{\operatorname{var} Q}{\{4-(c+d)\}^2} = \frac{ab}{(a+b)^2(a+b+1)} = \frac{T^2+2T-\Lambda^2+2\Lambda}{4(T+1)^2(T+2)} \cdot \quad (3.25)$$

By substituting EQ as specified in (3.11) and var Q as specified in (3.15), we obtain the following solutions for c and d:

$$c = \frac{4\Lambda^2 - 1}{T^2} \quad \text{and} \quad d = \frac{3}{T^2}, \quad (3.26)$$

terms of higher order of smallness than $1/T^2$ being neglected. By substituting (3.26) into (3.24) and (3.25) we find that the means coincide to the order $1/T^2$ and the variances to the order $1/T^3$.[8]

Summarizing, we have adjusted a beta distribution to the distribution of the Von Neumann ratio of the least-squares estimated regression disturbances under the condition that the first and higher order differences in the explanatory variables are small compared with the range of the corresponding variables themselves. The approximation is such that the means coincide to the second order; that is, whereas the asymptotic mean is 2 and hence $0(T^0)=0(1)$, the means coincide to $0(T^{-2})$.The variances, too, coincide to the second order: the asymptotic sampling variance is $4/T$ and the two variances have identical terms to $0(T^{-3})$. The skewness coefficients are identical to the one-and-a-halfth order: the asymptotic value of $\sqrt{\beta_1}$ is zero, and the two coefficients coincide to $0(T^{-1\frac{1}{2}})$. The kurtosis coefficients, finally, coincide to the first order, since the asymptotic value of β_2 is 3 while the two β_2's coincide to $0(T^{-1})$. Hence the accuracy of the approximation diminishes for higher-order moments; which is as it should be, for the lower-order moments are the more basic determinants of the distribution.

4. THE PROCEDURE RECOMMENDED

4.1. TESTING THE NULL-HYPOTHESIS

Table 2 contains the 1 and 5 per cent significance points of Q for testing the null-hypothesis of residual independence against the alternative hypothesis that successive disturbances are positively correlated.[9] The test is thus of the "one-sided" type. The number of coefficients adjusted (Λ) is 2, 3, $\cdots$, 6 where $\Lambda=2$ refers either to one explanatory variable plus a constant term, or to two explanatory variables in case the regression is fitted through the origin; similarly for higher Λ-values. The number of observations varies from 15 to

[8] A direct approximation of the range of Q consists of approximating the $(\Lambda+1)$st (i.e., the smallest positive) root and the Tth root of K by those of A, see Section 3.1. The roots of A are $(2 \sin j\pi/2T)^2$ where $j=0, \cdots, T-1$; see [9, p. 611]. Hence these roots are $\pi^2\Lambda^2/T^2$ and $4-\pi^2/T^2$, respectively, to order $1/T^2$, which differs slightly from the method developed in the text, the latter method being simpler computationally.

[9] For computing the significance points of Q we use the relation between the beta variate x and Q given in Section 3.5, viz.,

$$Q = \frac{4\Lambda^2 - 1}{T^2} + \left(4 - \frac{4\Lambda^2+2}{T^2}\right)x.$$

Using the tables of Incomplete Beta Function [6] we obtain the values of x corresponding to $P=.05$ and $.01$ by inverse interpolation for even values of $T+\Lambda$; those for odd values were obtained by linear interpolation between adjacent values of T, given Λ. The computations were carried out on the electronic computers of *BULL-Nederland N.V.* at Amsterdam, and we gratefully acknowledge the help given to us by Dr. J. Berghuis.

TABLE 2. SIGNIFICANCE POINTS OF THE VON NEUMANN RATIO OF LEAST-SQUARES ESTIMATED REGRESSION DISTURBANCES

T (Number of observations)	Λ (Number of coefficients adjusted)									
	2		3		4		5		6	
	1%	5%	1%	5%	1%	5%	1%	5%	1%	5%
15	1.07	1.36	1.24	1.53	1.43	1.73	1.65	1.94	1.88	2.16
16	1.08	1.37	1.24	1.53	1.42	1.71	1.62	1.90	1.83	2.11
17	1.10	1.38	1.25	1.53	1.41	1.69	1.59	1.87	1.79	2.06
18	1.12	1.39	1.25	1.53	1.40	1.68	1.57	1.85	1.75	2.02
19	1.13	1.40	1.26	1.53	1.40	1.67	1.56	1.83	1.72	1.99
20	1.15	1.41	1.26	1.53	1.40	1.67	1.54	1.81	1.70	1.96
21	1.16	1.42	1.27	1.53	1.40	1.66	1.53	1.80	1.68	1.94
22	1.17	1.43	1.28	1.54	1.40	1.66	1.53	1.78	1.66	1.92
23	1.19	1.44	1.29	1.54	1.40	1.65	1.52	1.77	1.65	1.90
24	1.20	1.45	1.29	1.54	1.40	1.65	1.51	1.77	1.64	1.89
25	1.21	1.45	1.30	1.55	1.40	1.65	1.51	1.76	1.63	1.87
26	1.22	1.46	1.31	1.55	1.40	1.65	1.51	1.75	1.62	1.86
27	1.23	1.47	1.32	1.55	1.41	1.65	1.51	1.75	1.61	1.85
28	1.24	1.48	1.32	1.56	1.41	1.65	1.51	1.74	1.60	1.84
29	1.25	1.48	1.33	1.56	1.41	1.65	1.50	1.74	1.60	1.83
30	1.26	1.49	1.34	1.57	1.42	1.65	1.50	1.73	1.60	1.82
31	1.27	1.50	1.34	1.57	1.42	1.65	1.50	1.73	1.59	1.82
32	1.28	1.50	1.35	1.57	1.43	1.65	1.50	1.73	1.59	1.81
33	1.29	1.51	1.36	1.58	1.43	1.65	1.51	1.73	1.59	1.81
34	1.30	1.51	1.36	1.58	1.43	1.65	1.51	1.72	1.58	1.80
35	1.31	1.52	1.37	1.58	1.44	1.65	1.51	1.72	1.58	1.80
36	1.31	1.52	1.38	1.59	1.44	1.65	1.51	1.72	1.58	1.79
37	1.32	1.53	1.38	1.59	1.44	1.65	1.51	1.72	1.58	1.79
38	1.33	1.53	1.39	1.59	1.45	1.65	1.51	1.72	1.58	1.79
39	1.34	1.54	1.39	1.60	1.45	1.66	1.51	1.72	1.58	1.79
40	1.34	1.54	1.41	1.61	1.46	1.66	1.52	1.72	1.58	1.78
45	1.37	1.56	1.42	1.61	1.47	1.67	1.53	1.72	1.58	1.78
50	1.40	1.58	1.44	1.63	1.49	1.67	1.54	1.72	1.59	1.77
55	1.43	1.60	1.47	1.64	1.51	1.68	1.55	1.72	1.59	1.77
60	1.45	1.62	1.48	1.65	1.52	1.69	1.56	1.73	1.60	1.77
65	1.47	1.63	1.50	1.66	1.53	1.70	1.57	1.73	1.60	1.77
70	1.49	1.64	1.51	1.67	1.55	1.70	1.58	1.73	1.61	1.77
75	1.50	1.65	1.53	1.68	1.56	1.71	1.59	1.74	1.62	1.77
80	1.52	1.66	1.54	1.69	1.57	1.72	1.60	1.74	1.62	1.77
85	1.53	1.67	1.55	1.70	1.58	1.72	1.60	1.75	1.63	1.77
90	1.54	1.68	1.56	1.70	1.59	1.73	1.61	1.75	1.64	1.78
95	1.55	1.69	1.57	1.71	1.60	1.73	1.62	1.75	1.64	1.78
100	1.56	1.69	1.58	1.72	1.60	1.74	1.63	1.76	1.65	1.78

100, but from 40 onwards they are only specified for intervals of 5. When $T > 100$, a normal approximation is sufficiently close; one can use

$$y = \frac{Q - 2\cdot\dfrac{T-1}{T-\Lambda}}{2/\sqrt{T+2}}, \tag{4.1}$$

which is approximately a normal variate with zero mean and unit variance under the null-hypothesis; it is based on the mean (3.11) and on the variance (3.15) to $0(T^{-2})$. The corresponding significance points are

$$1 \text{ per cent: } Q = 2\left(\frac{T-1}{T-\Lambda} - \frac{2.32635}{\sqrt{T+2}}\right)$$

$$5 \text{ per cent: } Q = 2\left(\frac{T-1}{T-\Lambda} - \frac{1.64485}{\sqrt{T+2}}\right),$$

which differ from the values of Table 2 for $T=90$ only in the third place behind the decimal point. This result shows also that the limit of the significance points is 2, that the convergence to this limit takes place with speed $1/\sqrt{T}$, and that the effect of different numbers of coefficients adjusted is of the order $1/T$.

A comparison of the table for $\Lambda=3$ and $T=70$ and 17 with the numerical values obtained in (2.7) shows that the null-hypothesis should be rejected for the spirits example and not rejected for the textile example, in both cases both at the 1 and the 5 per cent level. A comparison of Table 2 with the tables prepared by Durbin and Watson shows that our results are very close to their upper limits Q_U. This is not surprising, for these limits are attained when the vectors of values taken by the explanatory variables are all characteristic vectors of A as defined in (3.3) corresponding to a zero root; which simply implies that the first differences of these variables should vanish.[10] That their tables are not identical with ours is due to the fact that different approximations were used; we do not wish to claim that our table is more accurate than theirs.

4.2 WHAT TO DO WHEN THE NULL-HYPOTHESIS IS REJECTED

The simplest alternative hypothesis to the null-hypothesis is that of a first-order Markov scheme:

$$u(t) = \rho u(t-1) + \epsilon_t \quad \text{where} \quad 0 < \rho < 1, \tag{4.2}$$

the ϵ_t being mutually independent normal deviates with constant variance. The parameter ρ is the first-order autocorrelation of the disturbances and of course unknown. But if we decide to reject the null-hypothesis and to re-estimate the regression coefficient by taking account of the autocorrelation, we can estimate ρ conveniently by means of Q. For Q can be regarded as an estimator of

---

[10] This could be used as an argument to use the upper limits immediately; but it is of course more satisfactory to indicate precisely the nature of the approximation errors involved.

$$\frac{\operatorname{var}(u - u_{-1})}{\operatorname{var} u} = 2(1 - \rho),$$

hence we could take $\hat{\rho} = 1 - \frac{1}{2}Q$. But we can proceed in a slightly more refined manner by using the limits c and $4-d$ as specified in (3.26), which indicate that Q is confined to a smaller range than (0, 4) even if the null-hypothesis is true. We shall define $\hat{\rho}$ as a decreasing linear function of Q which takes the value 1 when $Q=c$ and the value -1 when $Q=4-d$. This gives

$$\hat{\rho} = \frac{T^2(2 - Q) + 2\Lambda^2 - 2}{2T^2 - 2\Lambda^2 - 1},$$

which is virtually equivalent with

$$\hat{\rho} = \frac{T^2(1 - \frac{1}{2}Q) + \Lambda^2}{T^2 - \Lambda^2}. \tag{4.3}$$

On applying (4.3) to the spirits example [see (2.7)], we obtain $\hat{\rho}=0.879$. Let us then write the regression equation

$$y(t) = \alpha + \beta_1 x_1(t) + \beta_2 x_2(t) + u(t)$$

in the form

$$\begin{aligned} y(t) - \rho y(t-1) &= \alpha(1-\rho) + \beta_1\{x_1(t) - \rho x_1(t-1)\} \\ &\quad + \beta_2\{x_2(t) - \rho x_2(t-1)\} + \{u(t) - \rho u(t-1)\}, \end{aligned} \tag{4.4}$$

which is obtained by subtracting ρ times the regression equation lagged one year. On combining (4.4) with (4.2), we see that the disturbances of (4.4) are the ϵ's of (4.2), so that the autocorrelation difficulty is now removed. We can also write (4.4) in the form:

$$\begin{aligned} (1-\rho)y(t) + \rho\Delta y(t) &= \alpha(1-\rho) + \beta_1\{(1-\rho)x_1(t) + \rho\Delta x_1(t)\} \\ &\quad + \beta_2\{(1-\rho)x_2(t) + \rho\Delta x_2(t)\} + \epsilon_t, \end{aligned}$$

which shows that least-squares estimation requires such sums of squares and products as

$$\begin{aligned} &\sum_t \{(1-\rho)y(t) + \rho\Delta y(t)\}\{(1-\rho)x_1(t) + \rho\Delta x_1(t)\} \\ &\quad = (1-\rho)^2 \sum y(t)x_1(t) + \rho(1-\rho)\sum y(t)\Delta x_1(t) \\ &\quad\quad + \rho(1-\rho)\sum x_1(t)\Delta y(t) + \rho^2 \sum \Delta y(t)\Delta x_1(t). \end{aligned}$$

Given ρ, these sums of squares and products can be computed by using Table 1, which contains the moments of the original variables and of their first differences, and Table 3, which contains such "mixed" moments as $\sum y(t)\Delta x_1(t)$ involving both first differences and the original variables. Using $\hat{\rho}=0.879$ instead of ρ, we find for the estimated income elasticity 0.312 and for the estimated price elasticity -1.123, which are indeed more plausible results than (2.2); the corresponding standard errors are 0.165 and 0.077, respectively.

TABLE 3. ADDITIONAL SUMS OF PRODUCTS FOR THE SPIRITS EXAMPLE

	y	x_1	x_2
Δy	−1.048 513	−1.359 344	−1.554 634
Δx_1	0.611 650	0.694 187	0.761 012
Δx_2	0.853 259	1.057 843	1.224 067

It is to be noted that this procedure involves two different kinds of approximations. The first is the obvious approximation $\rho = \hat{\rho}$, which neglects the sampling variability of $\hat{\rho}$. The second is somewhat less obvious but nonetheless fundamental: we use our data for three purposes, viz., to test the independence of the disturbances, to estimate the dependence in case the hypothesis is rejected, and to re-estimate the regression coefficients in that same case. It is clear that this procedure violates the classical set-up of regression theory and that it is safe to regard the standard errors just-mentioned as understating the unreliability of the point estimates, at least on the average.

APPENDIX

TABLE 4. TIME SERIES FOR THE TEXTILE EXAMPLE

	y	x_1	x_2
1923	1.99651	1.98543	2.00432
24	1.99564	1.99167	2.00043
25	2.00000	2.00000	2.00000
26	2.04766	2.02078	1.95713
27	2.08707	2.02078	1.93702
28	2.07041	2.03941	1.95279
29	2.08314	2.04454	1.95713
30	2.13354	2.05038	1.91803
31	2.18808	2.03862	1.84572
32	2.18639	2.02243	1.81558
33	2.20003	2.00732	1.78746
34	2.14799	1.97955	1.79588
35	2.13418	1.98408	1.80346
36	2.22531	1.98945	1.72099
37	2.18837	2.01030	1.77597
38	2.17319	2.00689	1.77452
39	2.21880	2.01620	1.78746

Source: y = logarithm of per capita consumption of textile, obtained by dividing the money value of textile consumption by family households (*Statistische en econometrische onderzoekingen*, 4, 1949, No. 3, 136–9) by pN;

p = retail price index of clothing for the city of Amsterdam (internal data of the *Bureau van Statistiek der Gemeente Amsterdam*);

N = population of the Netherlands (Central Bureau of Statistics, *Bevolking van Nederland naar leeftijd en geslacht, 1900–1952*, 1953, pp. 12–18);

x_1 = logarithm of real per capita income, obtained by dividing the money value of income of family households (*Statistische en econometrische onderzoekingen*, 4, 1949, No. 3, 102–3) by πN;

π = general retail price index (*Maandschrift van het Centraal Bureau voor de Statistiek*);

x_2 = logarithm of the deflated price index of clothing, i.e., of the ratio p/π.

REFERENCES

[1] Durbin, J. and Watson, G. S., "Testing for Serial Correlation in Least Squares Regression," I. *Biometrika*, 37 (1950), 409–28.

[2] Durbin, J. and Watson, G. S., "Testing for Serial Correlation in Least Squares Regression," II. *Biometrika*, 38 (1951), 159–78.

[3] Hannan, E. J., "Exact Tests for Serial Correlation," *Biometrika*, 42 (1955), 133–42.

[4] Hannan, E. J., "An Exact Test for Serial Correlation in Time Series," *Biometrika*, 42 (1955), 316–26.

[5] Hildreth, C. and Lu, J. Y., *Demand Relations with Autocorrelated Disturbances*. Technical Bulletin No. 276, Agricultural Experiment Station, Michigan State University, 1960.

[6] Pearson, K., *Tables of the Incomplete Beta Function*. Cambridge, 1948.

[7] Prais, S. J. and Houthakker, H. S., *The Analysis of Family Budgets*. Cambridge, 1955.

[8] Prest, A. R., "Some Experiments in Demand Analysis." *The Review of Economics and Statistics*, 31 (1949), 33–49.

[9] Ruben, H., "Probability Content of Regions Under Spherical Normal Distributions," I. *The Annals of Mathematical Statistics*, 31 (1960), 598–618.

[10] Theil, H., *Economic Forecasts and Policy*. Second Edition. Amsterdam, 1961.

DISTRIBUTED LAGS: A SURVEY

BY ZVI GRILICHES[1]

Several recent generalizations of the geometrically declining distributed lag model are reviewed and the associated statistical estimation problems are discussed. Attention is drawn to the practical difficulties of distinguishing between different lag schemes and models on the basis of usual economic data. This leads to a discussion of the more general problem of estimating mixed autoregressive schemes with serially correlated disturbances and a review of the existing theoretical rationale for the various suggested distributed lag models.

"The fault in so many mathematical studies of this type is not so much in sinning as in the lack of realization that one is sinning, or even a lack of acknowledgement of any conceivable type of sin."

R. BELLMAN [8, p. 15]

1. INTRODUCTION

THE HISTORY of distributed lag models dates back to the 1930's and the work of Irving Fisher and Tinbergen.[2] Similar topics were also discussed widely in the business cycles literature under the guise of "dynamic multipliers," "flexible accelerator," and "habit persistence."[3] But the recent popularity of distributed lags as a workable econometric technique is due mostly to the work of Koyck [**36**], Cagan [**12**], and Nerlove [**46, 47**].

Cagan suggested the adaptive expectations model in which expectations (p^*) are revised in proportion to the error associated with the previous level of expectations

$$p^*_{t+1} - p^*_t = \beta(p_t - p^*_t), \qquad 0 < \beta < 1 .$$

This model implies a geometrically declining distributed lag form for expected prices as a function of all past prices:

$$p^*_{t+1} = \sum_{i=0}^{\infty} \beta(1-\beta)^i p_{t-i} .$$

Cagan used such a variable in a more general equation of the form

$$y_t = ap^*_t + u_t ,$$

trying out different β's, constructing the associated $\hat{p}^*$ series, and choosing that β which led to the highest R^2 in the above equation. It can be shown that if the model

[1] The work on this paper was supported, in part, by a grant from the National Science Foundation. I have benefited from discussing this topic with D.V.T. Bear, D. Jorgenson, M. Miller, L. Telser, E. H. Thornber, T. D. Wallace, and A. Zellner.

[2] For a summary of the early history of this subject, see Alt [**3**] and Nerlove [**47**].

[3] See, for example, Hicks [**29**], Solow [**55, 56**], Chenery [**13**], Brown [**11**], and Allen [**1**].

is correct and the search procedure finds that β which maximizes the R^2, the resulting estimates are maximum likelihood estimates. The procedure is quite laborious, though. Somewhat earlier, assuming a geometric lag distribution, Koyck showed that an equation of the form

$$y_t = a\Sigma(1-\lambda)\lambda^i x_{t-i} + u_t$$

could be reduced or solved, by lagging it once, multiplying through by λ and subtracting it from the original equation, to yield

$$y_t - \lambda y_{t-1} = a(1-\lambda)\sum_{i=0}^{\infty}\lambda^i x_{t-i} - a(1-\lambda)\lambda\sum_{i=0}^{\infty}\lambda^i x_{t-i-1} + u_t - \lambda u_{t-1},$$

$$y_t = a(1-\lambda)x_t + \lambda y_{t-1} + u_t - \lambda u_{t-1},$$

which is much simpler to estimate, except for the fact that if the original disturbances u_t were serially independent, this is not true any more of the disturbances in the transformed equation.

Nerlove combined the Cagan adaptive expectations model with Koyck's reduction procedure to provide both an acceptable rationale and a feasible estimation procedure applicable to a wide range of problems. In addition, he suggested an alternative justification for the assumed form of the lag: the partial adjustment model. In this model, current values of the independent variables determine the "desired" value of the dependent variable:

$$y_t^* = ax_t + u_t,$$

but only some (fixed) fraction of the desired adjustment is accomplished within any one particular time period:

$$y_t - y_{t-1} = \gamma(y_t^* - y_{t-1}),$$

$$y_t = a\gamma x_t + (1-\gamma)y_{t-1} + \gamma u_t.$$

This model leads to exactly the same reduced equation as the adaptive expectations model, except that it does not induce additional serial correlation in the disturbances if there was none to start out with.

This type of model has been used widely and successfully in various econometric investigations (see, for example, the studies in Harberger [**28**]). But like any successful scientific advance, it raised as many questions as it answered. Some of these questions are quite fundamental; others represent technical limitations on the usefulness of the procedure.

It is impossible to discuss all the major issues in a field within the scope of one paper. I shall concentrate, therefore, on those topics where substantial progress has been made recently. Some important unsolved problems will receive only very brief attention. The main purpose of this paper is to draw attention to the practical difficulties of distinguishing between different lag schemes and lag models from the data. We may be asking too much of our data. We want them to test our theories, provide us with estimates of important parameters, and disclose to us the exact time form of the interrelationships between the various variables. Progress in this area is likely to be slow until we have a much better theoretical base for imposing a time-lag structure on the data.

The plan of this paper is as follows: First we shall introduce the notion of a lag-generating function, the convenient lag operator notation, and several generalizations of the geometrically declining lag form. Next we shall turn to the statistical difficulties of distinguishing between various lag forms and lag generating models. This will lead us into a discussion of the more general problem of estimating mixed autoregressive schemes with serially correlated disturbances, and we shall close with a review of the existing theoretical rationale (and often lack of it) for the various suggested distributed lag models.

2. LAG GENERATING FUNCTIONS AND LAG OPERATORS[4]

We are interested in defining and estimating equations of the form

$$y_t=\beta_0 x_t+\beta_1 x_{t-1}+\beta_2 x_{t-2}+\ldots+u_t$$

where x_t is an exogenous (or at least predetermined) variable, u_t is a stationary random variable with mean zero and a fixed covariance structure (it may or may not be serially correlated), and the β's have a finite sum ($\Sigma_i \beta_i < \infty$) and are all of the same sign. The last restriction gives us the narrower class of distributed lags, where a given effect of a change in x is distributed, divided up, between differently dated y's.[5] This is a strong restriction and we shall come back to review the rationale for it in the last section of this paper. It allows us to rewrite this equation as

$$y_t=\beta[w_0 x_t+w_1 x_{t-1}+w_2 x_{t-2}+\ldots]+u_t$$

where now the $w_i \geqslant 0$ are all non-negative and sum to unity, $\Sigma_{i=0}^{\infty} w_i=1$. In this equation the current level of y is a function of a number of past values of x, with the w's telling us the relative influence of differently lagged values of the x's on today's y.[6] The sequence of w's describes the form of the lag, the time-shape of an economic reaction.

Since the w's are non-negative and sum to one, they can be identified, formally, with probabilities defined over the set of non-negative integers (0, 1, 2, 3, ... ∞). This is very convenient, since in discussing the form of the lag and various parameters associated with it (such as the average lag and the variance of the lag) we can utilize all the available results about different types of probability distributions

[4] This section draws heavily on Feller [**17**, Ch. 12], Jorgenson [**33**], and Solow [**57**]. See also Allen [**1**, Ch. 6, and Appendix A].

[5] This is a special usage. The concept of a distributed lag has also been applied to any relationship between y and past x's.

[6] $w_j = \beta_j / \Sigma_i \beta_i$

and their moments. In particular, we shall make use of the notion of a generating function for the sequence w_0, w_1, w_2 ....

Using a dummy variable, z, we define a polynomial function

$$A(z)=a_0+a_1z+a_2z^2+a_3z^3+\ldots.$$

If this function converges in some interval $-z_0<z<z_0$, then $A(z)$ is called the generating function of the sequence (a_i). In addition, if all the a_i's are non-negative and $A(1)=1$, i.e., they sum to unity, then $A(z)$ is a probability generating function. The advantages of using the notion of a probability generating function are three-fold: (1) $A(z)$ may reduce itself to a relatively simple algebraic form even though the sequence a_i is quite complicated; (2) one can get the parameters (moments) of the probability distribution directly as functions of the derivatives of the generating function; and (3) it facilitates greatly the derivation of distributions of sums of random variables, or for our purposes, the cascading or convolution of several lag distributions.

For example, consider the geometric probability (lag) distribution with the sequence of w's given by

$$w_i=(1-\lambda)\lambda^i.$$

Then taking $|z|\leqslant 1$, the generating function of this sequence simplifies to

$$W(z) = (1-\lambda)[1+\lambda z+\lambda^2z^2+\lambda^3z^3+\ldots]$$

$$= \frac{(1-\lambda)}{1-\lambda z}.$$

The mean of the non-negative variable distributed with such a probability distribution is given by

$$E(x) = \sum_{i=0}^{\infty} ip_i=P'(1)$$

where $P'(1)$ is the first derivative of the probability generating function evaluated at $z=1$. Thus in our example, the mean lag in the case of a geometric lag distribution can be found from

$$E\Theta = W'(1),$$

$$W'(z) = \frac{d}{dz}\left(\frac{(1-\lambda)}{1-\lambda z}\right)=\lambda(1-\lambda)(1-\lambda z)^{-2},$$

and setting $z=1$, we have

$$E\Theta=W'(1)=\lambda/1-\lambda.$$

Similarly, the variance of the lag distribution is given by

$$\text{Var}(x)=P''(1)+P'(1)-[P'(1)]^2$$

which in the special case of the geometric lag form reduces itself to

$$\text{Var } \Theta = \lambda/(1-\lambda)^2 \,.$$

We may often want to consider the effect of passing a variable (signal) x through a series (cascade) of lag distributions. Thus, for example, in studying the lag between investment in research and improvements in productivity, we can think of it as the result of several lags—the lag between the investment of funds and the time inventions actually begin to appear, the lag between the invention of an idea or device and its development up to a commercially applicable stage, and the lag which is introduced by the process of diffusion: it takes time before all the old machines are replaced by the better new ones. In each of these cases, the lag is not a fixed lag but some distribution. The form of the total lag between R and D investment and the growth in average productivity is given by a convolution of the individual lag distributions.

More formally, let x and y be non-negative independently distributed integral valued random variables with $\text{pr}(x=i)=a_i$ and $\text{pr}(y=j)=b_j$; then the event $(x=i,\ y=j)$ has the probability $a_i b_j$. The sum $S=x+y$ is a new random variable and the event $S=r$ is the union of the events

$$(x=0,\ y=r),\ \ (x=1,\ y=r-1),\ \ (x=2,\ y=r-2)\ldots.$$

These events are mutually exclusive and therefore the distribution $c_r=\text{pr}(S=r)$ is given by

$$c_r = a_0 b_r + a_1 b_{r-1} + a_2 b_{r-2} + \ldots + a_{r-1} b_1 + a_r b_0 \,.$$

The series c_r is a convolution of (a_i) and (b_j), and its generating function is a product of the generating functions $A(z)$ and $B(z)$. That is, if x and y are non-negative integral valued mutally independent random variables with generating functions $A(z)$ and $B(z)$, then their sum $S=x+y$ has the generating function

$$C(z) = A(z)\,B(z)\,.$$

Convolution is an associative and commutative operation.

For example, let investment affect the level of patenting with a lag whose generating function is given by $W_1(z)$, let these new inventions be embodied in new investment with a lag $W_2(z)$ and let new investment affect total factor productivity with a lag $W_3(z)$; then the total lag distribution of productivity behind investment is given by

$$W_T(z) = W_1(z)\,W_2(z)\,W_3(z)\,.$$

If each of these component lags has the same geometric form with the same parameter λ, their convolution will be of the form

$$W_T(z) = \frac{(1-\lambda)^3}{(1-\lambda z)^3} = \frac{1-3\lambda+3\lambda^2-\lambda^3}{1-3\lambda z+3\lambda^2 z^2-\lambda^3 z^3}$$

which is a third-order Pascal distribution. It is likely to be bell-shaped (provided

$$W(L) = \frac{A(L)}{T(L)}$$

and $u_t = T(L)^{-1} e_t$. For the resulting sequence to be an acceptable distributed lag function (non-negative and convergent) it is sufficient for both sequences defined by $A(L)$ and $T(L)^{-1}$ to be convergent and non-negative. A necessary condition for $T(L)^{-1}$ to be convergent and non-negative is that the maximal root of the associated characteristic equation $T(z^{-1})=0$ be positive, and less than one. In addition, if we want well-behaved smooth lag distributions, it is sufficient (for non-negative $A(L)$) that all the roots of $T(z^{-1})=0$ are real and positive (small negative roots or pairs of complex roots would introduce small saw-toothed or smooth oscillations into the form of the lag functions).[10] If, in fact, all the roots of $T(z^{-1})=0$ are positive, then $T(L)^{-1}$ can be written as a convolution of a number of geometrically declining lag distributions, the number convoluted being equal to the number of roots of $T(z^{-1})=0$.

The second order case will serve to illustrate the derivation of the coefficients of $W(L) = A(L)T(L)^{-1}$. Let

$$y_t = a_0 x_t + a_1 x_{t-1} + t_1 y_{t-1} + t_2 y_{t-2} + v_t \,.$$

We are interested in deriving the time path of a transitory shock in x on all future y's. Consider the expected response in y from a unit transitory change in x. That is, we shall assume that

$$y_{t-1} = y_{t-2} = x_{t-1} = 0\,,$$
$$x_t = 1, \text{ and } x_{t+i} = 0,\ i > 0\,.$$

Then

$$\begin{aligned} r_0 &= a_0\,, \\ r_1 &= a_1 + t_1 a_0\,, \\ r_2 &= t_1(a_1 + t_1 a_0) + t_2 a_0\,, \\ r_j &= t_1 r_{j-1} + t_2 r_{j-2}\,. \end{aligned}$$

These are almost what we want, except that they sum to more than unity: To get the w_i's we have to divide through by the sum of the r series. This sum is given by

$$\Sigma r_i = \beta \Sigma w_i = \beta = (a_0 + a_1)/(1 - t_1 - t_2)\,.$$

Therefore, we can write the general expression for w_i as

$$w_j = t_1 w_{j-1} + t_2 w_{j-2}$$

with

$$w_0 = \frac{a_0}{a_0 + a_1}(1 - t_1 - t_2) \text{ and } w_1 = \frac{a_1}{a_0 + a_1}(1 - t_1 - t_2) + t_1 w_0\,.$$

[10] This, of course, imposes severe constraints on the admissible range of the coefficients of $T(L)$. We shall discuss below how stringent these restrictions really are. These restrictions are sufficient but not necessary. More general conditions for the non-negativity of $A(L)T(L)^{-1}$ are discussed in Jorgenson [**33**]. In general they take the form of non-linear inequalities between the coefficients of $A(L)$ and $T(L)$. Some simple cases are discussed below.

In general, the w_i's are given by a kth order difference equation (where k is the order of the $T(L)$ polynomial) with initial conditions given by $A(L)$ and the condition that the w_i's sum to unity, $W(1)=1$. The roots of this difference equation in w_j and of $T(z^{-1})=0$ are, of course, the same. Denoting these roots by $\lambda_1, \lambda_2, \lambda_3, \ldots,$ we can also write (when all these roots are distinct)

$$w_i = A_1 \lambda_1^i + A_2 \lambda_2^i + \ldots$$

where the A's are given by the initial conditions. This last form is not convenient computationally but it may be used to analyze the statistical properties of such derived $\hat{w}_i$'s.

To simplify matters we shall focus our attention mainly on models in which $A(L)$ degenerates to a constant and hence $W(L)$ can be written as $aT(L)^{-1}$.

Note that as we went from

$$T(L)y_t = A(L)x_t + e_t$$

to

$$y_t = A(L)T(L)^{-1}x_t + v_t\,,$$

if the original e_t's were serially uncorrelated the new $v_t = T(L)^{-1}e_t$ will be correlated.

3. GENERALIZING THE FORM OF THE LAG

One of the main advantages of the geometrically declining lag form is the ease with which it can be estimated—everything depends on only one additional parameter. This is done, however, at the cost of forcing a particular form of the lag on the data. This form has a certain plausibility and is consistent with several expectations and partial adjustment models. Nevertheless, it is quite restrictive. In particular, with the growing availability of quarterly and monthly data the assumption that the biggest response occurs immediately at the beginning of the adjustment period seems rather unfortunate.[11]

There are several ways of getting around this problem. One can tinker with the Koyck model, allowing several separate early terms in the w_i sequence before starting the geometric decline. Thus, for the lag-generating function

$$W(L) = w_0 + w_1 L + w_2 L^2 + w_2 \lambda L^3 + w_2 \lambda^2 L^4 + \ldots\,,$$

the peak response could occur at lag 1 or 2 rather than at zero. For this generating function, we have

[11] In the discussion of physical "delay" systems it is usually assumed the $w_0 = 0$, i.e., that it takes some minimal amount of time for a mechanism to respond to an input or signal and therefore the instantaneous response is zero. In economics, however, where the time unit is relatively long, it is not unreasonable to assume that some response occurs during the same *period* though not necessarily at the same instant and hence we admit the possibility of $w_0 > 0$.

$$W(L) = w_0 + w_1 L + w_2 L^2(1 + \lambda L + \lambda^2 L^2 + ...)$$

$$= \frac{w_0 + (w_1 - \lambda w_0)L + (w_2 - \lambda w_1)L^2}{1 - \lambda L} = \frac{A(L)}{T(L)}$$

which can be interpreted as a special case of the class of rational distributed lag functions. Here, we would estimate

$$y_t = a_0 x_t + a_1 x_{t-1} + a_2 x_{t-2} + \lambda y_{t-1} + u_t$$

including both several lagged values of the independent variable and the lagged value of the dependent variable.

Alternatively, one could try some other simple one-parameter scheme on a finite number of w's. The simplest form is given by a moving average with equal weights

$$w_i = \frac{1}{N} \quad \text{for} \quad 0 \leqslant i < N,$$

$$w_i = 0 \quad \text{for} \quad i \geqslant N.$$

To estimate such a scheme, one would construct different length moving averages of x_t and choose the best one (i.e., iterate an N).

A more elaborate alternative, with first rising and then declining weights, is the "inverted V" due to de Leeuw **[15]**, where

$$w_i = i + 1 \quad \text{for} \quad 0 \leqslant i < \frac{N}{2},$$

$$w_i = N - i \qquad i \geqslant \frac{N}{2},$$

$$w_i = 0 \qquad i \geqslant N.$$

While often useful in practice, this type of model is relatively clumsy and inelegant. Finite moving averages do not have, unfortunately, a finite auto-regressive representation. That is, if the sequence of w's in $W(L)$ is finite, $W(L)^{-1}$ will usually be infinite. This makes difficult both the mathematical and statistical treatment of such models, e.g., see **[2]**.

Solow **[57]** suggested the Pascal distribution as a general flexible two-parameter form for lag distributions. The Pascal distribution gives

$$w_i = \binom{r+i-1}{i}(1-\lambda)^r \lambda^i$$

which depend on the two parameters r and λ. We shall consider only positive integer valued r's.[12] Using the lag operator notation, we can write the associated

[12] While non-integer valued r's still define an admissible probability distribution (the negative binomial), $W(L)$ does not have a simple inverse.

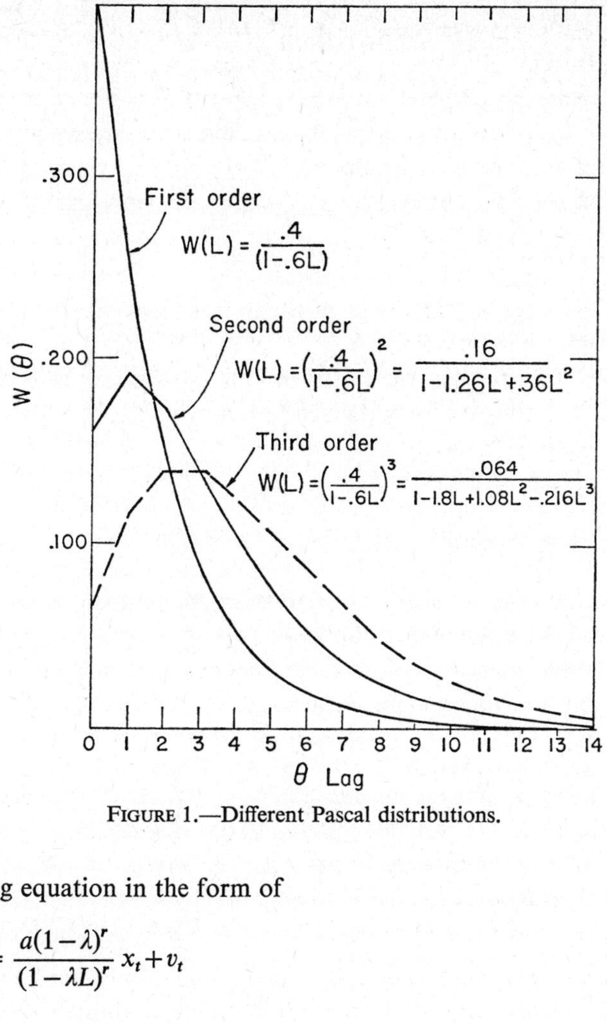

FIGURE 1.—Different Pascal distributions.

distributed lag equation in the form of

$$y_t = \frac{a(1-\lambda)^r}{(1-\lambda L)^r} x_t + v_t$$

or

$$(1-\lambda L)^r y_t = a(1-\lambda)^r x_t + (1-\lambda L)^r v_t \, .$$

Consider the case $r=2$:

$$(1-\lambda L)^2 y_t = (1-2\lambda L+\lambda^2 L^2) y_t = a(1-\lambda)^2 x_t + (1-\lambda L)^2 v_t \, ,$$
$$y_t = a(1-\lambda)^2 x_t + 2\lambda y_{t-1} - \lambda^2 y_{t-2} + v_t - 2\lambda v_{t-1} + \lambda^2 v_{t-2} \, ,$$

which leads to a two parameter second order difference equation.[13] The general Pascal case results in weights which satisfy an rth order difference equation with all roots real, positive, and equal. The simple geometrically declining lag form is given by the special case of $r=1$. Several such distributions are depicted in Figure 1.

[13] The weights in this case are given by $w_t = (1-\lambda)^2 (1+i)\lambda^t$. This is the same form as suggested by Theil and Stern **[59]**.

The difficulty with Solow's proposal is that it leads to an estimation problem with non-linear constraints. We have three independent variables (x_t, y_{t-1}, y_{t-2}), but only two parameters (a and λ) to be estimated. It is feasible but messy to estimate subject to these constraints and the problem is even more complicated if the order of the scheme is not known in advance.

In the Jorgenson [33] rational distributed lag function approach, instead of constraining the lag polynomial

$$(1-\lambda L)^r y_t = a(1-\lambda)^r x_t$$

to have equal roots and thus forcing oneself into a difficult estimation problem, one allows the roots to be unequal. The resulting difference equation may still imply an acceptable distributed lag function. Thus, for example

$$(1-\lambda_1 L)(1-\lambda_2 L)(1-\lambda_3 L)y_t = \alpha x_t$$

can be rewritten as

$$(1-t_1 L - t_2 L^2 - t_3 L^3)y_t = \alpha x_t$$

where $t_1 = \lambda_1 + \lambda_2 + \lambda_3$, $t_2 = -(\lambda_1\lambda_2 + \lambda_1\lambda_3 + \lambda_2\lambda_3)$, and $t_3 = \lambda_1\lambda_2\lambda_3$.

Jorgenson also proved that any arbitrary lag function $W(L)$ can be approximated by a rational form:

$$y_t = \frac{A(L)}{T(L)} x_t \,.$$

In practice one will not be interested in a $T(L)$ polynomial of higher order than two or three. Higher order polynomials imply the estimation of four or five or more coefficients for as many lagged values of y. At this point one may as well go back to the $W(L)$ form directly and approximate it by four or five separate lagged values of x. I shall discuss in some detail only the relatively simple case

$$y_t = \frac{a}{(1-bL-cL^2)} x_t$$

where $A(L)$ is a zero order and $T(L)$ is a second order polynomial in the lag operator. It is the simplest generalization of the Koyck model to a second-order lag function:

$$y_t = ax_t + by_{t-1} + cy_{t-2} \,.$$

For such an equation to imply a non-negative lag distribution for x,

$$y_t = \frac{a}{1-b-c} \Sigma w_i x_{t-i}, \qquad w_i > 0 \,,$$

b and c must satisfy the following restrictions: (1) $0<b<2$, (2) $-1<c<1$, (3) $1-b-c>0$, (4) $b^2 \geqslant -4c$.

Constraints (1) and (3) imply (2). These constraints are illustrated in Figure 2.

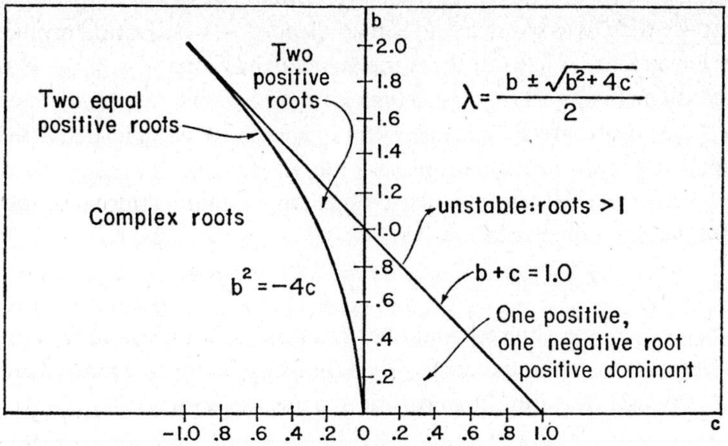

FIGURE 2.—Constraints on the admissible range of coefficients in the equation $y_t = ax_t + by_{t-1} + cy_{t-2}$.

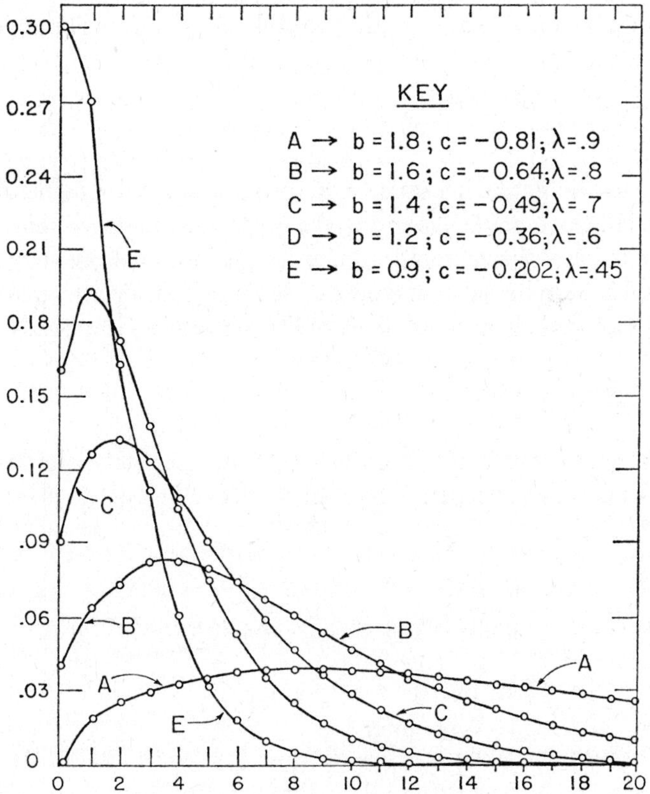

FIGURE 3.—Second order Pascal distributions.

In the area of $1>b>0$, $0<c<1$ one root is negative. For small values of this root, the lag distribution is similar to the simple exponential but is somewhat flattened (skewed to the right). For large values of the negative root, the implied lag distribution becomes quite wiggly and hence unsatisfactory. The small area where $b<1$ and $c<0$ gives rise to lag distributions very similar to those of the simple geometric ($c=0$) but converging to zero somewhat faster. Thus the only new area of interest (besides the line $0<b<1, c=0$) is the thin pie-slice area bounded by $1<b<2, b+c=1$, and $b^2=-4c$. Only within this area do we get distributions that look distinctly (and sensibly) different from the simple geometric. This area is quite small and gets even smaller, relatively, for higher order systems (see Newman [**49**], p. 22).

Some of the strictly Pascal distributions (all along the $b^2=-4c$ line) are shown in Figure 3. In Figure 4 we move off the boundary and into the interior of the admissible coefficients region and find that rather small differences in these coefficients imply very different lag distributions. The source of this difficulty can be perhaps best understood if we remember that $W(L)$ is the reciprocal or inverse of $T(L)$. It is clear that small changes in a set of numbers may imply rather large

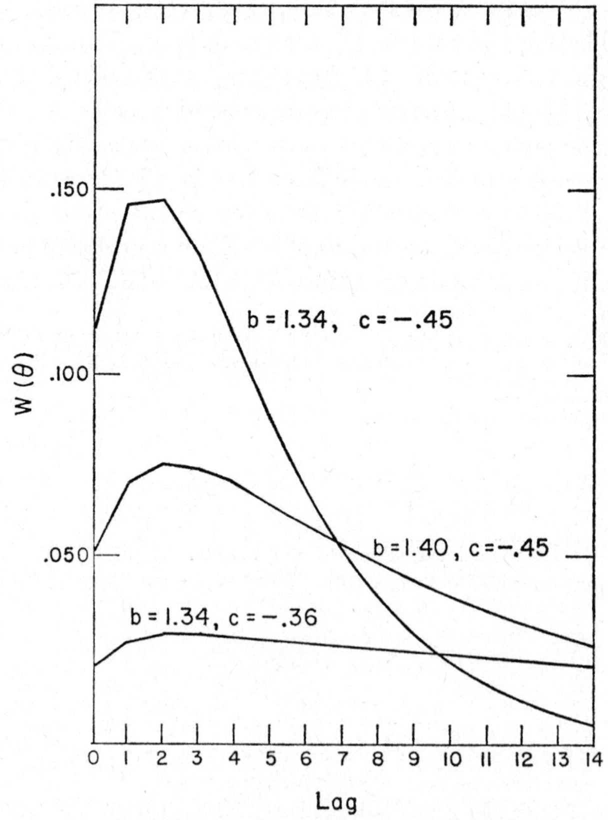

FIGURE 4.—Different second order lag functions.

changes in the reciprocals of their differences. This sensitivity raises the question whether the generalization to more complicated shapes of the lag distribution is worth the trouble if we cannot determine this shape with any degree of accuracy.

The preceding analysis can be illustrated by the results of a recent investment study using quarterly data for U.S. manufacturing 1948–1962 (Griliches and Wallace [**25**]). Among the various equations estimated in that study one of the better fitting was

$$y_t = f(x_1, x_2, x_3) + \underset{(.117)}{1.150}y_{t-1} - \underset{(.110)}{.331}y_{t-2}, \quad N=62,$$

where y_t, x_1, x_2, x_3 are net investment, a stock price index (lagged two quarters), interest rate (industrial bonds, lagged two quarters), and capital stock respectively. On the face of it the estimated coefficients of the lagged dependent variables are quite good by conventional standards: the t ratios are about 10 and 3, and hence they are both highly significant, have the right signs, and satisfy all the *a priori* restrictions.[14] But if one inquires about the potential range of the coefficients consistent with the data by varying each of these coefficients by two standard errors, the possible range covers the explosive case, the complex root case, and an appallingly wide range of possible lag shapes (including some impossible ones).

Actually, things are not all that bad though they are bad enough. It is illegitimate to consider varying both coefficients by two standard errors independently of each other. The correct procedure is to construct a confidence region for both b and c at some predetermined confidence level. Such a 95% confidence ellipse for these coefficients is pictured in Figure 5.[15] Note that we have gained something by considering both coefficients simultaneously—we can reject the explosive case. But the acceptable region for the two coefficients is still quite wide implying a wide

[14] Throughout this section we are assuming that the disturbances e_t in the form $y_t = ax + by_{t-1} + cy_{t-2} + e_t$ are serially uncorrelated. The consequences of serial correlation will be discussed in the next section.

[15] It is computed from the equation

$$[(b - \hat{b})(c - \hat{c})] \begin{bmatrix} \sigma_b^2 & \sigma_{bc} \\ \sigma_{bc} & \sigma_c^2 \end{bmatrix}^{-1} \begin{bmatrix} (b - \hat{b}) \\ (c - \hat{c}) \end{bmatrix} = 2F^2_{n\text{-}h}\ (100 - \alpha)$$

where $F^2_{n\text{-}h}\ (100 - \alpha)$ is the critical value of the F-distribution at the $100 - \alpha$ percent level. This formula is adapted from Goldberger [**20**, p. 178]. To plot the ellipse, the following relationship is useful:

$$d_b = \frac{\sigma_{bc}}{\sigma_c^2}\, d_c \pm \frac{\sqrt{\Delta}}{\sigma_c^2}\, \sqrt{2\sigma_c^2 F(100-\alpha) - d_c^2}$$

where $d_b = b - \hat{b}$, $d_c = c - \hat{c}$, and $\Delta = \sigma_b^2\sigma_c^2 - (\sigma_{bc})^2$. The expression for d_c is symmetrical.

All these formulae are approximate since no explicit allowance is made for the fact that y_{t-1} and y_{t-2} are stochastic variables. Also, they are derived without the use of the *a priori* restrictions on the b and c coefficients. See Zellner [**65**, Section 8] for the derivation of Bayesian confidence ellipses (contours of the posterior distribution) in a similar context.

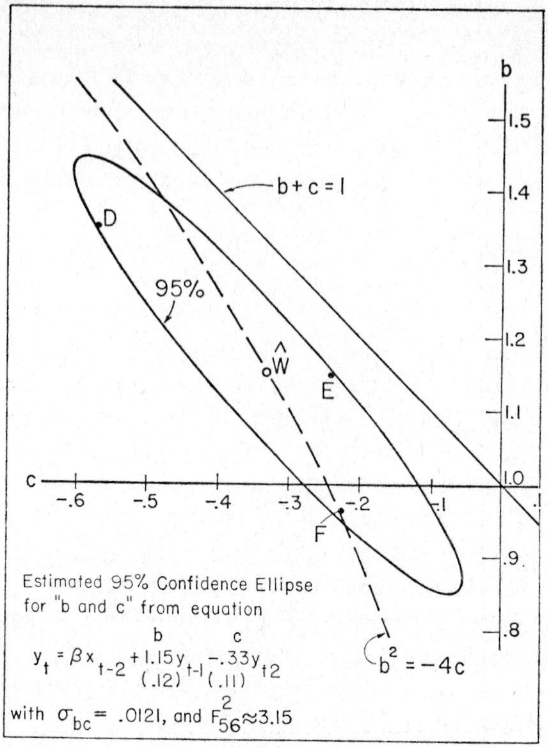

FIGURE 5.

range of possible lag distributions. Several such distributions are illustrated in Figure 6. Even if we reject the *a priori* unacceptable complex root case (e.g., the point F in Figure 5 and the associated distribution F in Figure 6) the range of acceptable alternative lag distributions is still distressingly wide. Our uncertainty about the possible shape of the lag distribution has not been reduced by much. The data are not plentiful or good enough to discriminate between different answers to such a fine question.

Nevertheless, if we are willing to ask somewhat narrower questions we may be able to get better answers. Thus, instead of asking about the general shape of the whole lag distribution we may focus our attention on a particular summary parameter such as the average lag, which may be estimable with more certitude. In the second order case, the average lag Θ is given by

$$\Theta = \sum_{i=0}^{\infty} iw_i / \Sigma w_i = \frac{\lambda_1 + \lambda_2 - 2\lambda_1 \lambda_2}{(1-\lambda_1)(1-\lambda_2)} = \frac{b+2c}{1-b-c}$$

where $b = \lambda_1 + \lambda_2$, $c = -\lambda_1 \lambda_2$, and λ_1 and λ_2 are the respective roots of the auxiliary equation. In our example, the estimated average lag is

$$\hat{\Theta} = (1.1498 - 2 \cdot 0.3310)/(1 - 1.1498 + .3310) = 2.7\,.$$

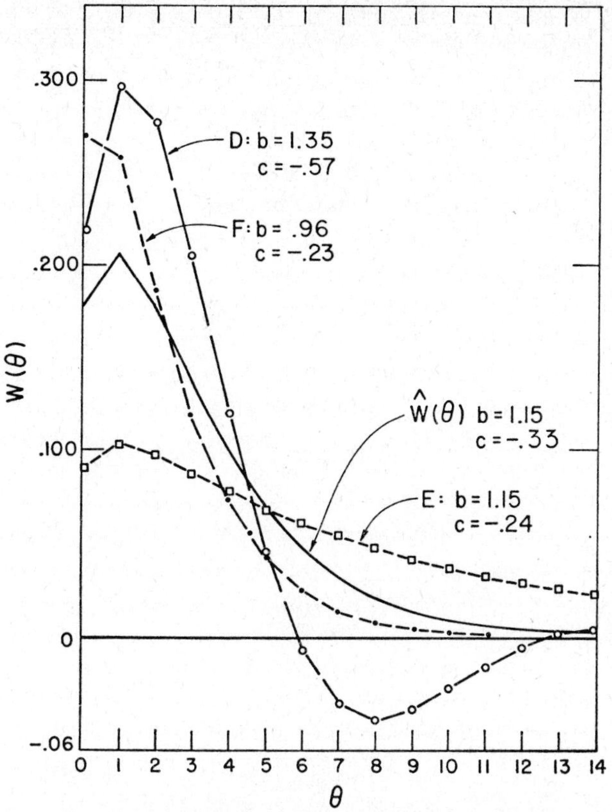

FIGURE 6.—Alternate lag distributions consistent with the estimated $\hat{W}(\Theta)$ at the 95 per cent confidence level.

Since the x variables of interest are as of $t-2$, we have to add 2 to this estimated average lag. Thus, e.g., the average lag of investment behind the rate of interest is estimated at 4.7 quarters or somewhat more than a year.

To get an exact confidence interval for the average lag we shall use an approach due to Fieller.[16] The estimated average lag is a ratio of two *linear* functions of random variables, say $\hat{\Theta}=H/G$, where $H=\hat{b}+2\hat{c}$, and $G=1-\hat{b}-\hat{c}$. Define the transformed variable

$$Z=H-G\Theta .$$

Its expected value is zero, and its variance is equal to Var $Z=$ Var $H+\Theta^2$ Var $G-2\Theta$ Cov HG. Under the standard assumptions of normality, the ratio of Z^2 to the estimated Var Z has the F distribution with 1 and N degrees of freedom. The

[16] See Fuller **[18]** for a convenient exposition of Fieller's approach. It is more exact than the approximate variance approach used in the first draft of this paper. I am indebted to T. D. Wallace for suggesting it to me. In all of this, we are ignoring the special problem raised by the fact that b and c came from equations involving lagged dependent variables.

limits of the exact confidence interval for Θ can be found by solving the following quadratic in Θ:

$$\Theta^2(G^2-t^2 \text{ Var } G)-2\Theta(HG-t^2 \text{ Cov } HG)+H^2-t^2 \text{ Var } H=0$$

where t^2 is the square of the appropriate t statistic given the desired confidence level and the available degrees of freedom.[17]

In our example, we have

$$G=.1813, \quad H=.4878, \text{ and}$$

$$\sigma_b^2=.01384, \quad \sigma_c^2=.01207, \quad \sigma_{bc}=-.01214$$

that imply Var $H=.01354$, Var $G=.00162$, and Cov $HG=-.00154$. The square of the t statistic at the two-tailed .05 significance or .95 confidence level for 56 degrees of freedom is approximately 4. Thus we have

$$.02639\ \Theta^2-.18924\ \Theta+.18379=0\,.$$

The two roots of this equation are $\Theta_1=1.1$ and $\Theta_2=6.0$. The data are thus consistent (at the 95 per cent confidence level) with an overall average lag between 3.1 and 8.0 quarters. This interval is still quite wide, but it could be reduced with better data and more observations.[18]

4. INTERPRETATION, IDENTIFICATION, AND SERIAL CORRELATION

One of the difficulties with the Koyck type distributed lag model and its generalizations is that there are a number of very different reasons why one may wish to introduce lagged values of the dependent variable into the equation. For example, it can be shown (Griliches **[22]**) that if the true equation is not a distributed lag model but just a regular relation between contemporaneous variables

$$y_t=ax_t+u_t$$

with serially correlated residuals[19]

$$u_t=\rho u_{t-1}+e_t$$

and we estimate

$$y_t=ax_t+by_{t-1}+v_t$$

introducing the irrelevant y_{t-1} variable into the estimating equation, we will usually get significant and sensible coefficients and will reduce the serial correlation

17 Note that we need $G=1-b-c$ significantly different from zero for the interval to be closed. In our case $G=.18$ and $\sigma_G=.04$.

18 Note the asymmetry of this interval (1 to 6) around the estimated average of 2.7. This is one of the main advantages of the Fieller approach. The approximate variance approach would have given us a symmetric and less exact interval.

19 This is a special case of a more general specification error of leaving out any serially correlated variable (e.g., trend) from the original equation.

in the estimated residuals.[20] Thus, the partial adjustment model will work even though it is wrong. Actually, however, matters are not as bad as they look. As long as there are some exogenous variables in the model, one can distinguish (albeit with difficulty) between these two hypotheses. If the coefficient of x_{t-1} is negative and significant when added to the partial adjustment model and approximately equal to $-ab$ we may conclude that our original specification was in error.[21]

As an example, consider the following set of estimates of the elasticity of substitution in U.S. manufacturing in 1958, based on the ACMS method (Arrow et al. [5]). The dependent variable is the logarithm of value added per man-hour. The exogenous variable is the logarithm of the wage rate per man-hour. The units of observation are two-digit manufacturing industries within and across states, totalling 417.

A direct estimate of the elasticity of substitution gives

$$\log V/L_{58} = A_1 + \underset{(.047)}{1.198} \log w_{58}\,, \qquad R^2 = .606\,.$$

The possibility of only partial adjustment to a change in wage rates leads us to estimate

$$\log V/L_{58} = A_2 + \underset{(.037)}{.233} \log w_{58} + \underset{(.024)}{.827} \log V/L_{57}\,, \qquad R^2 = .890\,.$$

Here the coefficient of the lagged dependent variable is highly significant, and the fit of the equation is very much improved (the estimated σ is still above unity, $\hat{\sigma} = .233/(1-.827) = 1.35$). It implies, though, a distressingly low rate of adjustment of about 17 per cent per year. We are led, therefore, to consider the alternative hypothesis that these results are due not to the adjustment model but to serial correlation in the true disturbances (due to left-out variables or other possible misspecifications of the original model). We estimate then

$$\log V/L_{58} = A_3 + \underset{(.089)}{1.056} \log W_{58} + \underset{(.022)}{.855} \log V/L_{57} - \underset{(.022)}{.900} \log w_{57}\,, \quad R^2 = .918\,.$$

If the serial correlation model is right, the third coefficient should equal minus the product of the first two, which it does approximately ($.900 \approx 1.056 \times .855 = .903$). Since we do not have any alternative explanation for a significant negative coefficient of the lagged wage rate variable, we reject the partial adjustment model and accept the serial correlation one.[22]

20 The true equation can be written in this case as

$$y_t = ax_t + \varrho y_{t-1} - a\varrho x_{t-1} + e_t\,.$$

21 If it is positive it can be interpreted as coming from the slightly generalized Koyck model:

$$y_t = a_0 x_t + a_1 x_{t-1} + b y_{t-1} + u_t\,.$$

22 The matter should not rest here. Serial correlation does not explain anything. The next step is to find out what is the misspecification that is causing it. For additional discussion of these data and other related results, see Griliches [25].

This dichotomy between the partial adjustment and serial correlation models may be a bit too sharp. The same results are consistent with a rational distributed lag form

$$\frac{a_0+a_1 L}{1-\lambda L}.$$

A negative a_1 coefficient is admissible here, but it essentially undoes the work of the simple geometric lag form. Ours is a degenerate case

$$\frac{1.056-.900\,L}{1-.855\,L}=\frac{1.056(1-.852\,L)}{(1-.855\,L)}\simeq 1.056$$

and the partial adjustment model with its implied average lag of five years is a misspecified version of the more general rational form. When the correct form is estimated, including x_{t-1}, the implied average lag is essentially zero.

In general, we cannot distinguish between $T(L)y_t=u_t$ and $y_t=G(L)u_t$. In the presence of an exogenous x variable, however, the hypothesis $T(L)\,y_t=ax_t+u_t$ and $u_t=G(L)e_t$ implies

$$G(L)^{-1}T(L)y_t=aG(L)^{-1}x_t+e_t\,.$$

Here, $G(L)^{-1}$ can be estimated from the coefficients of x_{t-h}, and then $T(L)$ can be derived from the coefficients of y_{t-h}.

For example, consider the equation

$$y_t=a_0 x_t+a_1 x_{t-1}+b_0 z_t+b_1 z_{t-1}+c_1 y_{t-1}+c_2 y_{t-2}+u_t$$

where we have two exogenous variables (x and z). Such an equation could arise from a bona fide distributed lag model of the form

$$y_t=\frac{1}{1-c_1 L-c_2 L^2}\left[(a_0+a_1 L)x_t+(b_0+b_1 L)z_t\right]+v_t$$

in which case a_1 and b_1 can be either positive or negative (within limits). Alternatively, we could have had a first order lag scheme and a second order serial correlation scheme in the disturbances:

$$y_t=\frac{1}{1-\gamma L}(\alpha x_t+\beta z_t)+\frac{v_t}{(1-\rho L)(1-\gamma L)}$$

which can be rewritten as

$$(1-\gamma L)(1-\rho L)y_t=(1-\rho L)(\alpha x_t+\beta z_t)+v_t\,.$$

This model implies that a_1 and b_1 are both negative, and moreover

$$\frac{a_1}{a_0}=\frac{b_1}{b_0}=-\rho$$

where ρ is one of the roots of the second order difference equation in y_t.

Another assumption that leads to a similar equation is that y_t is a function of x_t

and z_t with different first order geometric lag schemes

$$y_t = \frac{\alpha x_t}{1-\lambda_1 L} + \frac{\beta z_t}{1-\lambda_2 L} + u_t$$

and hence

$$(1-\lambda_1 L)(1-\lambda_2 L)y_t = \alpha(1-\lambda_2 L)x_t + \beta(1-\lambda_1 L)z_t + v_t\,.$$

Again, both a_1 and b_1 should be negative, but now

$$\frac{a_1}{a_0} = -\lambda_1 \quad \text{and} \quad \frac{b_1}{b_0} = -\lambda_2$$

where λ_1 and λ_2 are the two separate roots of the second order difference equation implied by coefficients of y_{t-1} and y_{t-2}. The difference between the first model and the other two is in the existence of additional restrictions on the signs of the a_1 and b_1 coefficients and their relationships to the other coefficients in the equation. The difference between the last two is in whether the $a_0 a_1$ and $b_0 b_1$ pairs of coefficients are or are not in the same ratio to each other. With enough observations and good data one may be able to distinguish between these various alternatives though the prospects for that are not very good in the average econometric study.

Serial correlation in the disturbances is much more of a threat in distributed lag models than in the classical regression case. There it may result in somewhat inefficient estimates. Here it is likely to lead to inconsistent ones. Moreover, in the likely case of positive serial correlation, the estimated adjustment coefficients are biased downward and the estimated average lags are biased upward. This may explain the preponderance of relatively low reaction, expectation, or adjustment coefficients in recent estimates of distributed lag models. Nor can one guard against serial correlation in this case by observing the Durbin–Watson statistic. It is also biased and for the same reasons. The same source of the upward bias in the coefficients of lagged dependent variables will lead to a downward bias in the serial correlation of the estimated residuals.

For the first order model

$$y_t = \alpha x_t + \beta y_{t-1} + u_t$$

with serially correlated disturbances

$$u_t = \rho u_{t-1} + e_t$$

the large sample bias of the simple least squares coefficient of y_{t-1} is given by[23]

$$\text{plim}\, b - \beta = \frac{\rho(1-\beta^2)}{1+\beta\rho} \cdot \frac{1}{1 + \dfrac{\alpha^2 \sigma^2_{z-1\cdot x}}{\sigma^2_w}}$$

[23] See Griliches **[22]** and Malinvaud **[41**, Ch. 14] for the derivation of this and related formulae.

where z and w are the β-weighted geometrically declining moving averages of x and u respectively in the solved version of this equation

$$y_t = \alpha z_t + w_t,$$

where

$$z_t = \sum_i \beta^i x_{t-1}, \quad w_t = \sum_i \beta^i u_{t-1},$$

and $\sigma^2_{z-1 \cdot x}$ is that part of the variance of z which is uncorrelated with x_{t+1}. If we were to assume, in addition, that x_t is also a first order Markov process with the parameter r, the last part of the bias formula can be simplified to

$$\text{plim } b - \beta = \frac{\rho(1-\beta^2)}{1+\beta\rho} \cdot \frac{1}{1 + \dfrac{\alpha^2 \sigma_x^2}{\sigma_u^2} \cdot \dfrac{(1-r^2)(1-\beta\rho)}{(1-\beta r)^2(1+\beta\rho)}}.$$

It is clear that as long as $\rho > 0$, b will overestimate β. Since the estimate of the average lag is given by $b/1-b$, it will also be overestimated.

A special case of the above problem is worth considering in greater detail. Let the true model be a second order lag scheme,

$$y_t = \alpha x_t + \beta y_{t-1} + \gamma y_{t-2} + e_t,$$

but a first order model is estimated instead:

$$y_t = a x_t + b y_{t-1} + v_t.$$

In this case

$$\text{plim } b = \beta + \gamma \text{ plim } b_{y_{t-2} y_{t-1} \cdot x_t}.$$

Let x_t be a stationary and serially uncorrelated process,[24] then

$$\sigma^2_{y_{t-1}} = \sigma^2_y$$

and

$$\text{plim } b_{y_{t-2} y_{t-1} \cdot x_t} = \text{plim } b_{y_{t-2} y_{t-1}} = \text{plim } b_{y_{t-1} y_{t-2}} = \text{plim } b.$$

Hence

$$\text{plim } b = \beta + \gamma \text{ plim } b$$

$$= \frac{\beta}{1-\gamma}.$$

24 This assumption simplifies the algebra greatly, since we can now lump x_t with e_t, and consider just the case of fitting a first order auto-regressive scheme when a second order one is appropriate. Allowing x_t to be positively serially correlated changes the magnitudes but not the direction of the results derived below.

In the usual case of two positive roots, $\gamma<0$ and b will underestimate β.[25] Nevertheless, we will still overestimate the average lag. In the second order model, the average lag is given by

$$\bar{\Theta} = \frac{\beta+2\gamma}{1-\beta-\gamma}$$

while the estimated average lag from the misspecified first order model would tend to

$$\text{plim } \hat{\bar{\Theta}} = \text{plim } \frac{b}{1-b} = \frac{\frac{\beta}{1-\gamma}}{1-\frac{\beta}{1-\gamma}} = \frac{\beta}{1-\beta-\gamma}.$$

Even though we underestimate the true coefficient of y_{t-1}, we will still overestimate the mean lag as long as $\gamma<0$. For example, consider the second order Pascal case with two equal roots of .7 each. Then $\beta=1.4$, $\gamma=-.49$, the true $\bar{\Theta} = \frac{1.4-.98}{1-1.4+.49} = \frac{.42}{.09} = 4.7$, while the estimated average lag from the first order equation tends to

$$\hat{\bar{\Theta}} \rightarrow \frac{1.4}{.09} = 15.6,$$

which is three times as large as the true one.

There are several possible sources of serial correlation in such models. Even if the original disturbances are not serially correlated, the reduction procedure may induce it. If the e_t's in

$$y_t = aT(L)^{-1}x_t + e_t$$

are serially uncorrelated, the v_t's in

$$T(L)y_t = ax_t + v_t$$

will be serially correlated, since $v_t = T(L)e_t$. Alternatively, if the v_t's are assumed to be uncorrelated, then the e_t's must be correlated. As far as I can see, there is no strong economic argument for making the uncorrelation assumption at one end of the procedure rather than at the other. Note, though, that if we have estimated

$$y_t = ax_t + \lambda y_{t-1} + e_t$$

and the model is correct, the e_t's are serially uncorrelated, and we use the estimated $\hat{\lambda}$ to construct an expected x_t^* series by defining

$$x_t^* = (1-\hat{\lambda})\Sigma\hat{\lambda}^i x_{t-i}$$

and then fit

$$y_t = \beta x_t^* + v_t,$$

[25] These conclusions are reversed in the less likely case of $\gamma>0$. This is a case, for relatively large γ's, of a saw-toothed distributed lag function.

we may get much poorer results. The second form may perform much worse even though it is implied by the first. But this should not necessarily be interpreted as a contradiction of the original model, since the poorer performance of the alternative version is actually predicted by it. If the first model is correct

$$v_t = \Sigma \lambda^i e_{t-i}$$

and

$$\sigma_v^2 = \frac{\sigma_e^2}{1-\lambda^2},$$

i.e., the residual variance in the second form should be larger by a factor of $1/1-\lambda^2$, which for $\lambda = .8$ is about 4. Thus only if the increase in the residual variance is significantly larger than is predicted by $1/1-\lambda^2$ or if the estimated β is very much inconsistent with that implied by $a = \beta(1-\lambda)$, does the poor performance of the second form cast a real doubt on the correctness of the first.

For the case where the only serial correlation is that due to the reduction process, the estimation problem was solved by Koyck [**36**] and Klein [**34**] by noting that the model

$$y_t = a\gamma x_t + (1-\gamma)y_{t-1} + u_t - (1-\gamma)u_{t-1}$$

can be rewritten in the form of

$$(y_t - u_t) - (1-\gamma)(y_{t-1} - u_{t-1}) - a\gamma x_t = 0$$

which can be interpreted as an errors in the variables model. Usually, the errors in the variables model is very difficult to handle since very little is known about the relative variances of these errors, but in this case the variance–covariance matrix of the error is known (up to a constant). It is equal to

$$\Omega = \begin{bmatrix} 1 & 0 & 0 \\ 0 & 1 & 0 \\ 0 & 0 & 0 \end{bmatrix}$$

and the estimation procedure is relatively straightforward. But this solution to the problem is not a very useful one, since it depends crucially on the original disturbances being uncorrelated.[26] If we are going to assume serially uncorrelated disturbances somewhere, we might as well assume them to be uncorrelated in the transformed form, as is done in the partial adjustment model. On the other hand, if the u_t's are correlated, the proposed procedure is neither consistent nor efficient.

No matter at which form of the system one looks, one should expect, because of the likelihood of specification error, serial correlation in the true disturbances. Ignoring it will result in biased estimates of the cofficients even in the adjustment model (Griliches [**22**] Malinvaud [**40**]) and an identification problem: Do people adjust slowly, or do left out variables change slowly?

To guard against it we need an estimation procedure that takes it into account or

[26] Even in that case it is not fully efficient. See Amemiya and Fuller [**4**].

is consistent in its presence. This brings us to the general problem of estimating an equation of the form

$$y_t = \alpha x_t + \gamma y_{t-1} + u_t$$

where we could have a number of x's including lagged terms and a number of lagged y's, and where u_t is serially correlated. We assume u_t to be a stationary random process with a constant covariance function. It is assumed to be independent of x_t, but not necessarily independent of y_{t-1}. In fact, it will usually not be independent of y_{t-1}, since y_{t-1} is itself a weighted average of past u's.

There are two possible approaches to the problem raised by serial correlation in this model: (1) assume a particular form for this dependence and estimate its parameters jointly with the others; (2) use instrumental variables.

If we assume that the time dependence of the u's can be adequately represented by a first order Markov process (this is, in fact, a very specific and sometimes restrictive assumption),[27] we write

$$u_t = \rho u_{t-1} + e_t \,.$$

Combining both equations and substituting for $u_{t-1} = y_{t-1} - ax_{t-1} - \gamma y_{t-2}$, we have

$$y_t = ax_t - a\rho x_{t-1} + (\rho + \gamma) y_{t-1} - \gamma\rho y_{t-2} + e_t \,.$$

This can be estimated directly, since e_t is uncorrelated. A direct estimate is not efficient, however, since it requires the estimation of four parameters while the original problem only calls for three. This is more obvious if we rewrite the above equation as

$$y_t - \rho y_{t-1} = \alpha(x_t - \rho x_{t-1}) + \gamma(y_{t-1} - \rho y_{t-2}) + e_t \,.$$

One can estimate the first equation subject to the non-linear constraints on the coefficients using available non-linear regression programs. Or one can iterate on ρ in the second form of this equation.

More generally, if

$$T(L) y_t = a x_t + u_t \,,$$
$$u_t = G(L) e_t \,,$$

then

$$G(L)^{-1} T(L) y_t = a G(L)^{-1} x_t + e_t \,.$$

Provided that $G(L)^{-1}$ and $T(L)$ can be represented by low order lag polynomials, the equation is estimable and the separate components may be identified. Given the capacity of modern electronic computers, this approach is entirely feasible.[28]

[27] If this is the reduced form of an adaptive expectations model, this assumption implies that the original disturbance u_t in $y_t = bx_t^* + u_t$ was generated by a second order scheme:

$$u_t = (\gamma + \varrho) u_{t-1} - \gamma\varrho u_{t-2} + e_t \,.$$

[28] See Fuller and Martin **[19]**, Sargan **[54]**, and Zellner et al. **[66]** for more details. The "three pass" method suggested by Taylor and Wilson **[58]** does not in general result in consistent estimators and hence is not recommended, particularly since feasible consistent methods are available.

It requires, however, very specific assumptions about the exact form of dependence of the true disturbances. For operational purposes we have to assume that the dependence is of the form of a first order or at the most second or third order autoregressive process. A still open question is the robustness of this procedure against higher order or moving average process alternatives.

An alternative approach arises from noting the formal similarity of this problem, the problem of the possible correlation of the true disturbance with one or more of the variables that are treated as independent, and the simultaneous equation problem.

In the equation

$$y_t = \alpha x_t + \gamma y_{t-1} + u_t$$

y_{t-1} is really endogenous and hence may be correlated with u_t. This similarity suggests immediately solutions of the form (a) use instrumental variables, or more formally, (b) use a two-stage procedure substituting for y_{t-1}, $\hat{y}_{t-1}$ predicted by a finite term approximation to the true reduced form equation of this system:

$$y_t = \alpha \Sigma \gamma^i x_{t-i} + \Sigma \gamma^i u_{t-i} .$$

That is, first estimate the unconstrained form

$$y_t = b_0 x_t + b_1 x_{t-1} + b_2 x_{t-2} + b_3 x_{t-3} + \ldots + v_t$$

including additional lagged x_t terms as long as they add to the explanation of y_t and the available degrees of freedom permit it. Substitute $\hat{y}_{t-1}$ predicted by this estimated equation into

$$y_t = \alpha x_t + \gamma \hat{y}_{t-1} + u_t + \gamma v_{t-1}$$

and re-estimate. Since $\hat{y}_{t-1}$ is made up only out of the x's it is uncorrelated with the disturbance (by assumption and by construction). This two-stage procedure should yield a consistent estimator of γ.[29]

The general instrumental variable approach is discussed by Sargan **[53]**. Liviatan **[37]** suggested the use of x_{t-1} as an instrumental variable in the specific context of this model. He also suggested the use of more than one lagged value of x to gain efficiency. Some relatively discouraging Monte Carlo investigations of the single instrumental variable procedure are reported in Malinvaud **[40]**. Liviatan's approach is investigated by Hannan **[27]**, who suggests a modification and extension of it using spectral analysis techniques.[30] A recent application of this type of procedure can be found in Sargan **[54]**. Clearly, the consistency of the instrumental variables or two-stage approaches does not depend on particular assumptions

[29] Note that we have almost come full circle. This procedure is very close to the original Cagan suggestion of estimating $y_t = \beta x_t^* + w_t$, using that weighted average of past x's which maximized the R^2 in this equation.

[30] Hannan's spectral analysis technique is discussed further in Amemiya and Fuller **[4]** and applied by Wallis **[62]**.

about the structure of the disturbances. This is their main virtue. They do assume, however, that the x's are truly exogenous, or at least not part of the same structure of feedback relationships as the y's.

There remains the additional possibility of gaining efficiency from the yet unutilized constraints that parameters like γ must lie in the interval $0 < \gamma < 1$, that the $T(L)^{-1}$ sequence is non-negative, and that parameters like ρ must lie in the interval $-1 < \rho < +1$. Such restrictions lead to non-linear inequality constraints and are very difficult to handle by classical procedures.[31] Here progress is most likely to come along Bayesian lines. For an example, see Zellner and Tiao **[68]** and Thornber **[60]**.

5. THEORETICAL AD-HOCKERY

While widely and variously used, most distributed lag models have almost no or only a very weak theoretical underpinning. Usually the form of the lag is assumed *a priori* rather than derived as an implication of a particular behavioral hypothesis. Exceptions to this statement are the adaptive expectations and partial adjustment models, which in part explains their recent popularity.[32] But even here, the theoretical rationalizations offered are often only skin deep

The adaptive expectations model has the best and most extensive theoretical background and literature since it ties in rather well with the statistical theory of optimal prediction. Muth **[45]**, Nerlove and Wage **[48]**, Whittle **[63]**, and others have shown that moving averages with exponentially declining weights are optimal (linear) predictors (in a mean-square-error sense) for certain types of non-stationary random-walk cases. Cox **[14]** showed that if the process to be predicted is stationary, models of this sort may be still quite efficient even if not optimal. While not many economic series fit strictly into the random-walk of first (or second) differences hypothesis, such forecasting procedures have been advocated as a

[31] If the unconstrained estimates of the second order equation result in an inadmissible set of estimates (such as D in Figure 5) and an implied pair of complex roots, one is justified in assuming that the constrained maximum likelihood estimators will be on the lower boundary of the admissible set and hence reestimating the equation subject to the exact (Pascal) non-linear constraint $b^2 = -4c$.

[32] While the simple adaptive expectations and partial adjustment models lead to similar estimating equations, they are not, as is sometimes asserted, operationally equivalent. If we are willing to assume that the underlying disturbances are serially uncorrelated, the two models will differ in their estimation implications. They also differ in the presence of non-expectational variables. But the most important difference is conceptual. The adaptive expectations model attributes the lags to uncertainty and the discounting of current information. The partial adjustment model attributes the same lags to technological and psychological inertia and to the rising cost of rapid change. Circumstances (or experiments) are conceivable in which one could discriminate between these two hypotheses. For example, a government guaranteed price for next year's crop should dispose of most of the information uncertainty. If lags still persist, they must be due to other slow adjustment reasons.

management science technique to be followed by enlightened businessmen in forecasting their own sales and related series (e.g., see Holt et al. **[31]**).

The partial adjustment model has not fared as well. Its basic premise is the existence of some kind of costs of adjustment which in turn justify the observed inertia in the responsiveness of entrepreneurs and consumers to economic stimuli. But neither the exact meaning or the consequences of these costs of adjustments are very clear. The problem is discussed in general terms in Eisner and Strotz **[16]** and solved explicity for a particular (very much simplified) capital accumulation problem. They show that if the revenue and cost of adjustment functions are quadratic, the optimal rate of net investment will decline exponentially as the new equilibrium level is approached. The basic rationale of such a model can be illustrated by the following non-rigorous and highly simplified example. Assume that the firm incurs two types of cost: (1) a cost of being out of equilibrium (e.g. foregone profits), and (2) a cost of change. If both cost functions can be approximated by quadratic terms, we can write the firm's overall loss function as

$$L=\alpha(S_t-S_t^*)^2+\beta(S_t-S_{t-1})^2$$

where S_t^* is the desired equilibrium level of S_t, S_{t-1} is the current (given) level of this variable, and the problem is to choose S_t (given S_{t-1} and S_t^*) so as to minimize L. Differentiating L with respect to S_t, setting this derivative equal to zero and solving, we have

$$\frac{dL}{dS_t} = 2\alpha(S_t-S_t^*)+2\beta(S_t-S_{t-1})=0\,,$$

$$S_t = \frac{\alpha}{\alpha+\beta}S_t^* + \frac{\beta}{\alpha+\beta}S_{t-1}\,,$$

$$S_t-S_{t-1} = \frac{\alpha}{\alpha+\beta}(S_t^*-S_{t-1})\,.$$

Thus, the adjustment coefficient depends on the relative importance of (marginal) out-of-equilibrium costs to the (marginal) adjustment costs. Not surprisingly, the higher the adjustment costs, the slower the rate of adjustment.

The work of Eisner and Strotz has been recently extended and generalized in a number of still unpublished papers.[33] If the problem can be put into a form in which the optimal path is determined by a set of linear differential equations (e.g. if one starts with quadratic revenue and cost functions) or if the system of non-linear differential equations can be adequately approximated by a linear set around the equilibrium path, the optimal (or approximately optimal) adjustment path to a once and for all change in the equilibrium level is of the same form as implied by the partial adjustment or flexible accelerator models. The adjustment coefficient,

[33] See Lucas **[38]** and **[39]**, Gould **[21]** and Treadway **[61]**.

however, is not a constant but depends on the rate of interest and the relative curvatures of the revenue and cost of adjustment functions. Little is known, however, about optimal adjustment paths to continuously changing equilibria levels. Presumably some of the work on inventory theory and production scheduling should be relevant here (e.g., see Holt and Modigliani [**30**]). Moreover, there is a growing literature on regulation (Whittle [**63**]), optimal control (Pontryagin et al. [**51**]), and adaptive control under uncertainty (Bellman [**8**]), all of which should have something to contribute to the solution of the problem of the optimal form of the adjustment path towards an uncertain equilibrium level. An important and encouraging illustration of the possibilities of such an approach is given in two papers by Box and Jenkins [**9**, **10**] in which they combine the optimal control problem (with quadratic revenue and adjustment cost functions) with the problem of responding to an uncertain stimulus variable which has to be predicted on the basis of past data. A superficial glance at this literature tells one that many of the restrictions imposed on the standard expectations or adjustment models in economics cannot be in general derived from the properties of optimal solutions to such problems.

For example, we usually assume that if

$$w_i = (1-\lambda)\lambda^i, \quad \text{then } 0<\lambda<1 \;;$$

or more generally, $w_i > 0$. The expected variable is a proper average of its past values with all weights positive. But why? Because we assume that we are distributing a given (long-run) effect of a change in x on y over a number of periods. But why should the distribution be always positive? Actually, neither optimal prediction theory nor optimal control (adjustment) theory imply that all the weights should be non-negative. Nerlove and Wage [**48**] show that for a particular second difference random walk the optimal forecast weights can in fact change sign. The optimal weights, as shown by Bailey [**7**] can be also functions of complex numbers, and hence on occasion negative. In optimal control theory it may pay to over-adjust (if costs are not symmetric) and to oscillate.[34]

It is not obvious, theoretically, that all long-run responses should be larger than short-run. This is clearly wrong for inventory models and other speculative situations. The standard theory of the firm case has been investigated by Mundlak [**44**] using the Le Chaterlier principle, identifying the long run with the unconstrained

[34] Even if the true model is assumed to have only positive weights we may wish to allow the estimated approximate weight sequence to have complex roots and some negative terms. For example, if we are trying to approximate a finite term distributed lag scheme, such as the inverted V, by a convolution of several geometric distributions, the latter will always have a non-negligible positive right tail (it will be skewed to the right) and hence will approximate only poorly any abrupt approach to zero. In such a situation, a lag function with complex roots will cross the axis and may represent a much better approximation (in the mean-square error sense) to the true form, even if it does involve a series of small oscillating but rapidly converging negative and positive values in the far past.

case, while the short run is subject to some constraint. He shows that $\partial x_i/\partial p_i$ is larger in the unconstrained case for own effects, $i=j$, but this is not necessarily true for cross-effects ($\partial x_i/\partial p_j$.) Thus, it may be reasonable to assume in the supply equation,

$$q_t = a_1 W(L) p_t + a_2 G(L) w_t + u_t \,,$$

that $W(L)$ is non-negative (where $W(L)$ is the lag distribution of the response to the change in the price of the product), but there is no theoretical argument for making the same assumption for $G(L)$, the lag distribution of the response to a change in the wage rate.[35]

As of the moment, we do not have a useful rigorous theory of optimal adjustment paths. The subject is very important and appears still to be wide open.

6. CONCLUSIONS

There are several important issues that have not been treated in this paper; we have alluded briefly to the problem presented by the assumption of different lag distributions for different variables. In principle one can handle it, but for more than two variables it quickly becomes very messy. Let

$$y_t = \frac{a_1}{1-\lambda_1 L} x_{1t} + \frac{a_2}{1-\lambda_2 L} x_{2t} + u_t \,;$$

then we have

$$(1-\lambda_1 L)(1-\lambda_2 L) y_t = a_1(1-\lambda_2 L) x_{1t} + a_2(1-\lambda_1 L) x_2 + (1-\lambda_1 L)(1-\lambda_2 L) u_t$$

or

$$\begin{aligned} y_t - (\lambda_1+\lambda_2) y_{t-1} + \lambda_1 \lambda_2 y_{t-2} = {} & a_1 x_{1t} - \lambda_2 a_1 x_{1t-1} + a_2 x_{2t} - \lambda_1 a_2 x_{2t-2} \\ & + u_t - (\lambda_1+\lambda_2) u_{t-1} + \lambda_1 \lambda_2 u_{t-2} \end{aligned}$$

which, with some difficulty, is still estimable. More complicated or higher order schemes lead to even more trouble.

Very little work has been done on the simultaneous equations problem. Clearly, if

$$\begin{aligned} d &= a W(L) p_t + e_t \,, \\ s &= b G(L) p_t + v_t \,, \end{aligned}$$

and p_t is such that $d_t = s_t$, there will be problems. Even if the system is recursive it is not enough to assume that the contemporaneous disturbances e_t and v_t are uncorrelated (Wise **[64]**). Some work on the necessary conditions for identification in such systems has been done by Phillips **[50]**.

Also, very little has been done on the effects of aggregation in such models. Mundlak **[43]** showed that aggregation over time (e.g., from quarterly to annual

[35] This is related to the recent discussion of the inability of qualitative economics to sign, unambiguously, cross-derivatives of behavioral response relations.

data) will in general result in a misspecification of the model. It will also induce a positive dependence between the aggregated true disturbances and the lagged values of the aggregate dependent variable and cause us to overestimate the implied average lags. It is not surprising then that estimates based on annual data often imply longer lags than similar estimates based on quarterly data (e.g., compare the quarterly and annual dynamic consumption function estimates in Griliches et al. [**24**] and Klein and Goldberger [**35**], respectively). There is also some scattered evidence for a similar effect of aggregation over individuals, with much shorter lags estimated at the micro level.

What have we then to suggest to the econometrician who still wants to fit such models (and most of us, including myself, will continue doing it)? Here are a few commandments for virtuous living:

First, if one is working with strongly trending data one should investigate whether the independent variables (the x's) provide an adequate explanation for these trends. Do not throw the problem into the residual category without doing something about trend removal. The standard statistical theory applies only to the case of stationary disturbances. In practice, with estimated roots close to unity, it is difficult to discover whether these high estimates are due to a slowly growing component of the series or to long lags in adjustment. Second, test for the possibility of misspecification of the model by including additional lagged terms of the independent variables. Third, if non-linear regression routines are available, use them to test simultaneously for the presence of serial correlation. If not, have some written.[36] Fourth, forget about the Durbin–Watson statistic in this context as a test for serial correlation in the original disturbances. It is very badly biased. Fifth, do not expect the data to give a clear-cut answer about the exact form of the lag. The world is not that benevolent. One should try to get more implications from theory about the correct form of the lag and impose it on the data. Sixth, interpret the coefficients of a distributed lag model with great care, since the same reduced form can arise from very different structures. Moreover, different reduced forms may not differ much in the fit that they provide to the data, but have widely different implications as to the underlying structure that generated the data. Finally, not all is hopeless, but to get better answers to such complicated questions we shall need better data and much larger samples.

REFERENCES

[1] Allen, R. G. D.: *Mathematical Economics*. London: Macmillan, 1956.

[2] Almon, S.: "The Distributed Lag between Capital Appropriations and Expenditures," *Econometrica*, 33 (1), (1965).

[36] See Martin [**42**] for a write-up of such a program.

[3] ALT, F. L.: "Distributed Lags," *Econometrica*, 10 (2), (1942).

[4] AMEMIYA, T., AND W. FULLER: "A Comparative Study of Alternative Estimators in a Distributed-Lag Model," *Econometrica*, forthcoming.

[5] ARROW, K. J., M. B. CHENERY, B. S. MINHAS AND R. M. SOLOW: "Capital-Labor Substitution and Economic Efficiency," *Review of Economics and Statistics*, 43 (3), (1961).

[6] BAILEY, M. J.: *National Income and the Price Level.* New York: McGraw-Hill, 1962, pp. 223–268.

[7] ———: "Prediction of an Autoregressive Variable Subject both to Disturbances and to Errors of Observation," *Journal of the American Statistical Association*, 60, (1962), p. 309.

[8] BELLMAN, R.: *Adaptive Control Processes: A Guided Tour.* Santa Monica: RAND Corporation, 1961.

[9] BOX, G. P. E., AND G. M. JENKINS: "Some Statistical Aspects of Adaptive Optimization and Control," *Journal of the Royal Statistical Society*, Series B, 24 (2), (1962).

[10] ———: "Further Contributions to Adaptive Quality Control: Simultaneous Estimation of Dynamics: Non-Zero Costs," *Bulletin of the International Statistical Institute*, 34th Session, Ottawa, (1963).

[11] BROWN, T. M.: "Habit Persistence and Lags in Consumer Behavior," *Econometrica*, 22 (3), (1952).

[12] CAGAN, P.: "The Monetary Dynamics of Hyper Inflations," in Friedman, Ed., *Studies in the Quantity Theory of Money*. Chicago: University of Chicago Press, 1956.

[13] CHENERY, H.: "Over Capacity and the Acceleration Principle," *Econometrica*, 20 (1), (1952).

[14] COX, D. R.: "Prediction by Exponentially Weighted Moving Averages and Related Methods," *Journal of the Royal Statistical Society*, Series B, 23 (2), (1961).

[15] DE LEEUW, F.: "The Demand for Capital Goods by Manufacturers: A Study of Quarterly Time Series," *Econometrica*, 20 (3), (1962).

[16] EISNER, R., AND R. STROTZ: "Determinants of Business Investment," in CMC, *Impacts of Monetary Policy*. Englewood Cliffs, N.J.: Prentice-Hall Inc., 1963.

[17] FELLER, W.: *An Introduction to Probability Theory and Its Applications*, Vol. 1. New York: John Wiley and Sons, 1950.

[18] FULLER, W. A.: "Estimating the Reliability of Quantities Derived from Empirical Production Functions," *Journal of Farm Economics*, 44 (1), (1962).

[19] FULLER, W. A., AND J. E. MARTIN: "The Effects of Autocorrelated Errors on the Statistical Estimation of Distributed Lag Models," *Journal of Farm Economics*, 43 (1), (1961).

[20] GOLDBERGER, A. S.: *Econometric Theory*. New York: John Wiley and Sons, 1964.

[21] GOULD, J. P.: "A Microeconomic Approach to the Demand for Physical Capital," unpublished paper presented at the New York Meeting of the Econometric Society, 1965.

[22] GRILICHES, Z.: "A Note on the Serial Correlation Bias in Estimates of Distributed Lags," *Econometrica*, 29 (1), (1961).

[23] ———: "Production Functions in Manufacturing: Some Preliminary Results," in NBER, *The Theory and Empirical Analysis of Production*, Studies in Income and Wealth, Vol. 31, 1967.

[24] GRILICHES, Z., G. S. MADDALA, R. LUCAS, AND N. WALLACE: "Notes on Estimated Aggregate Quarterly Consumption Functions," *Econometrica*, 30 (3), (1962).

[25] GRILICHES, Z., AND N. WALLACE: "The Determinants of Investment Revisited," *International Economic Review*, 6 (3), (1965).

[26] HANNAN, E. J.: *Time Series Analysis*. London: Methuen, 1960.

[27] ———: "The Estimation of Relationships Involving Distributed Lags," *Econometrica*, 33 (1), (1965).

[28] HARBERGER, A. C., Ed.: *The Demand for Durable Goods*. Chicago: University of Chicago Press, 1960.

[29] HICKS, J. R.: *A Contribution to the Theory of the Trade Cycle.* Oxford: Oxford University Press, 1950.

[30] HOLT, C. C., AND F. MODIGLIANI: "Firm Cost Structures and the Dynamic Responses of Inventories, Production, Work Force and Orders to Sales Fluctuations," in Joint Economic Committee, *Inventory Fluctuations and Economic Stabilization*, Part II (1962), 87th Congress.

[31] HOLT, C. C., F. MODIGLIANI, J. F. MUTH, AND H. SIMON: *Planning Production, Inventories, and Work Force.* Englewood Cliffs, N. J.: Prentice-Hall, 1960.

[32] JORGENSON, D. W.: "Capital Theory and Investment Behavior," *American Economic Review*, 53 (2), (1963).

[33] ———: "Rational Distributed Lag Functions," *Econometrica*, 34 (1), (1966).

[34] KLEIN, L. R.: "The Estimation of Distributed Lags," *Econometrica*, 26 (4), (1958).

[35] KLEIN, L. R., AND A. S. GOLDBERGER: *An Econometric Model of the U.S., 1929–1952.* Amsterdam: North-Holland Publishing Co., 1955.

[36] KOYCK, L. M.: *Distributed Lags and Investment Analysis.* Amsterdam: North-Holland Publishing Co., 1954.

[37] LIVIATAN, N.: "Consistent Estimation of Distributed Lags," *International Economic Review*, 4 (1), (1963).

[38] LUCAS, R. E. JR.: "Distributed Lags and Optimal Investment Policy," unpublished dittoed paper, 1965.

[39] ———: "Optimal Investment Policy and the Flexible Accelerator," *International Economic Review*, 8 (1), 1967.

[40] MALINVAUD, E.: "Estimation and prévision dans les modèles économiques autoregressifs," *Review of the International Statistical Institute*, 29 (2), (1961).

[41] ———: *Méthodes statistiques de l'économétrie.* Paris: Dunod, 1964.

[42] MARTIN, J. E.: "Computer Programs for Estimating Certain Classes of Non-linear Distributed Lag Models," Maryland Agricultural Experiment Station, Misc. Publication No. 546, 1965.

[43] MUNDLAK, Y.: "Aggregation Over Time in Distributed Lag Models," *International Economic Review*, 2 (2), (1961).

[44] ———: "On the Microeconomic Theory of Distributed Lags," *Review of Economics and Statistics*, 48 (1), 1966.

[45] MUTH, J. F.: "Optimal Properties of Exponentially Weighted Forecasts," *Journal of the American Statistical Association*, 55, (1960).

[46] NERLOVE, M.: "Estimates of the Elasticities of Supply of Selected Agricultural Commodities," *Journal of Farm Economics*, 38 (2), (1956).

[47] ———: *Distributed Lags and Demand Analysis*, USDA, Agriculture Handbook No. 141, Washington, 1958.

[48] NERLOVE, M., AND S. WAGE: "On the Optimality of Adaptative Forecasting," *Management Science*, 10 (2), (1964).

[49] NEWMAN, P.: "Approaches to Stability Analysis," *Economica*, 34, (1961).

[50] PHILLIPS, A. W.: "Some Notes on the Estimation of Time-Forms of Reactions in Interdependent Dynamic Systems," *Economica*, 29, (1956).

[51] PONTRYAGIN, L. S., et al.: *The Mathematical Theory of Optimal Processes.* New York: John Wiley and Sons, 1962.

[52] QUENOUILLE, M. H.: *The Analysis of Multiple Time Series.* London: Griffin, 1957.

[53] SARGAN, J. D.: "The Estimation of Economics Relationships Using Instrumental Variables," *Econometrica*, 26 (3), (1958).

[54] ———: "Wages and Prices in the United Kingdom: A Study in Econometric Methodology," *Colston Papers*, Vol. 16. London: Butterworths Scientific Publishers, 1964.

[55] SOLOW, R. M.: "A Note on Dynamic Multipliers," *Econometrica*, 19 (3), (1951).

[56] ———: "On the Structure of Linear Models," *Econometrica*, 20 (1), (1952).

[57] ———: "On a Family of Lag Distributions," *Econometrica*, 28 (2), (1960).

[58] TAYLOR, L. D., AND T. A. WILSON: "Three-pass Least Squares: A Method for Estimating Models with a Lagged Dependent Variable," *Review of Economics and Statistics*, 46 (4), (1964).

[59] THEIL, H., AND R. M. STERN: "A Simple Unimodal Lag Distribution," *Metroeconomica*, 12 (II-III), (1960).

[60] THORNBER, H.: "An Autoregressive Model: Bayesian Versus Sampling Theory Analyses," Report 6504 of the Center for Mathematical Studies in Business and Economics, University of Chicago, 1965. Presented at the First World Congress of the Econometric Society, Rome.

[61] TREADWAY, A.: "Optimal Investment Dynamics and Distributed Lag Models," unpublished, University of Chicago, 1966.

[62] WALLIS, K. F.: "Distributed Lag Relationships between Retail Sales and Inventories," unpublished Technical Report No. 14, Institute for Mathematical Studies in the Social Sciences, Stanford University, 1965.

[63] WHITTLE, P.: *Prediction and Regulation by Linear Least Squares Methods*. London, 1963.

[64] WISE, J.: "Regression Analysis of Relationships between Autocorrelated Time Series," *Journal of the Royal Statistical Society*, Series B, 18 (2), (1956).

[65] ZELLNER, A.: "Bayesian Inference and Simultaneous Equation Econometric Models," unpublished paper presented at the First World Congress of the Econometric Society, Rome, 1965.

[66] ZELLNER, A., D. S. HUANG, AND L. C. CHEN: "Further Analysis of the Short-Run Consumption Function with Emphasis on the Role of Liquid Assets," *Econometrica*, 33 (3), (1965).

[67] ZELLNER, A., AND C. J. PARK: "Bayesian Analysis of a Class of Distributed Lag Models," The Econometric Annual of the *Indian Economic Journal*, 13 (3), (1965).

[68] ZELLNER, A., AND G. C. TIAO: "Bayesian Analysis of the Regression Model with Autocorrelated Errors," *Journal of the American Statistical Association*, 59, (1964).

IS AGGREGATION NECESSARILY BAD?

Yehuda Grunfeld and Zvi Griliches *

PREVIOUS treatments of the aggregation problem have been almost entirely theoretical.[1] The purpose of the present paper is to shed some further light on this topic by presenting and analyzing two sets of empirical results. These results were obtained in two econometric studies dealing with quite different subjects, the common element being that in both cases similar explanatory equations were fitted to both "micro" and "macro" data.

Theil's work provides both the theoretical framework and the point of departure for our work. It is worthwhile, however, to stress at the outset the difference between our approach and that of Theil. While Theil starts with the fundamental assumption of perfectly specified micro equations and proceeds to show the errors that result from aggregation, we ask ourselves the question: What are the proper assumptions to be made about the micro equations? Our main argument will be that *in practice* we do not know enough about micro behavior to be able to specify micro equations perfectly. Hence, empirically estimated micro relations, whether those of individual consumers or of individual producers, should not be assumed to be perfectly specified either in an economic sense or in a statistical sense. Aggregation of economic variables can, and in fact frequently does, reduce these specification errors. Hence, aggregation does not only produce an aggregation error, but may also produce an aggregation gain.

Another difference between our approach and that of Theil and most other students of the aggregation problem is that we are concerned mainly with the power and degree of "explanation" obtained rather than with errors in estimating the economic coefficients. The measure that we will use to indicate the "degree of explanation" obtained will be the multiple correlation coefficient and the residual variance of the macro equation, but our results can be generalized to other measures of closeness of fit.

Section I describes the relevant results of a study of investment behavior of single firms. Section II presents the results of regional and national analyses of the demand for fertilizer. Section III analyzes the relationship between micro and macro correlation coefficients. Section IV explores the conditions under which an aggregate equation may explain aggregate behavior better than the explanation derived by aggregating the predictions of micro equations. Finally, Section V lists some of the limitations of this study, summarizes the results, and draws some more general conclusions pertinent to econometric research in general.

I. Investment Behavior of Single Firms

The main results of this study are summarized elsewhere.[2] Here, it will suffice to present

* This is a joint paper. The order of authorship was decided by the toss of a coin. The only parts of the paper for which separate responsibility can be established are the original bodies of data and their analysis. This will be indicated below.

The authors are indebted to H. Theil for stimulating their interest in this problem, and to Dorothy Brady, Carl Christ, Leo A. Goodman, and Trygve Haavelmo for valuable comments. The authors, however, retain the responsibility for both the inferences and the remaining errors. This work has been supported by funds from the Ford Foundation, National Science Foundation, and the Public Finance Workshop at the University of Chicago.

[1] The major work in this area is H. Theil, *Linear Aggregation of Economic Relations* (Amsterdam, 1954). For additional references, see the literature cited there. Partial summaries of Theil's book, plus some additional applications, are available in R. G. D. Allen, *Mathematical Economics* (London, 1956), chapter 20; Z. Griliches, "Specification Bias in Estimates of Production Functions," *Journal of Farm Economics*, XXXIX (1957), 8–20; and H. Theil, "Specification Errors and the Estimation of Economic Relationships," *Review of the International Statistical Institute*, XXV (1957), 41–51.

[2] Y. Grunfeld, "The Determinants of Corporate Invest-

a brief outline of the economic model and the data. The study investigated the expenditures on plant and equipment and maintenance and repairs by eight large firms from 1935 to 1954. The amount spent by each firm on plant and equipment plus maintenance and repairs was found to be a function of the stock of plant and equipment at the beginning of the year and the market value of the firms at the beginning of the year. All variables were measured in 1947 dollars. The market value of the firm was found by adding the market value of all shares to the book value of all debts outstanding at the beginning of each year. A least-squares regression was computed relating the dependent variable to the two independent variables. The multiple coefficients of determination obtained for each firm are presented in Table 1. In addition, the

TABLE 1.—INVESTMENT STUDY

Corporation	R^2
General Motors	.919
General Electric	.705
United States Steel	.471
Atlantic Refining	.680
Union Oil	.764
Diamond Match	.643
Goodyear Tire and Rubber	.666
American Steel Foundries	.142
Aggregate of eight corporations	.926
Composite for eight corporations	.906

SOURCE: Y. Grunfeld, op. cit., 90, 116.

variables were aggregated over all eight firms and a multiple regression was computed relating aggregate annual investment plus maintenance and repairs to the aggregated (lagged) stock of plant and equipment and the (lagged) value of all eight firms. The multiple coefficient of determination of this regression denoted "aggregate of eight corporations" is presented in the next to the last row of Table 1. It will immediately be observed that the multiple coefficient of determination of the aggregate regression *is larger than any one* of the multiple coefficients of determination of the single firm regressions.

A more relevant measure of the explanatory power of the eight regressions is found by asking: How well do the predictions from all the eight micro regressions taken together explain aggregate investment? We can define a "composite R^2" as the percentage of the total variance of aggregate investment explained by the variation in the sum of "predicted" investment from each of the individual micro regressions. This is equivalent to getting the residuals in all eight individual regressions, adding them each year over all the eight corporations, computing the variance of this sum, dividing it by the variance of the aggregate, and subtracting from one. If we denote the variance of the *sum* of the residuals from all the micro regressions by S_c^2 and the variance of the aggregate dependent variable by S_y^2; we can define the "composite coefficient of multiple determination" in the following way:

$$R_c^2 = 1 - \frac{S_c^2}{S_y^2}.$$

If we denote the variance of the residuals in the aggregate regression by S_a^2 and the coefficient of multiple determination of the regression on the aggregates by R_a^2, then the relation between the composite multiple coefficient of determination and the coefficient of determination of the aggregate regression can be expressed as follows:

$$R_c^2 = 1 - \frac{S_c^2}{S_a^2}(1 - R_a^2).$$

Hence, the relation between the two measures of fit depends on the relation between the variance of the *sum* of the residuals in the separate regressions to the variance of the residuals of the regression computed from the sums of the variables.

The composite coefficient of determination measures the percentage of the variation in the aggregate dependent variable that can be explained by all the regression lines computed for the single corporations. A comparison of the composite R^2 to the aggregate R^2 answers, therefore, the question whether by computing regressions for the single corporations we obtain more information about the *aggregate* dependent variable than by simply taking a regression of the aggregate dependent variable on the aggregates of the independent variables.

ment" (Unpublished Ph.D. thesis, University of Chicago, 1958). See also the further analysis of these same data along somewhat different lines by J. C. G. Boot and G. M. de Wit, "Investment Demand: An Empirical Contribution to the Aggregation Problem," *International Economic Review* (in press).

The composite coefficient of multiple determination computed for the eight regressions is presented in the last row of Table 1. It will be observed that this coefficient is *lower* than the coefficient of multiple determination of the aggregate regression. This result implies that if we want to explain the *aggregate* investment behavior of the eight corporations, we are better off if we first aggregate all the variables and then compute one regression, than if we compute separate regressions for each firm and then "aggregate their explanations." If our aim were only to explain aggregate investment, we would have gained nothing from disaggregation.

II. Regional Demand Functions for Fertilizer

This study is also treated at length elsewhere, and only a brief description of it will be given here.[3] The annual consumption of fertilizer (weighted primary plant nutrients) in each of the nine Census regions during 1931–56 is assumed to be a function of the "real" price of fertilizer, that is, the price paid per plant nutrient unit divided by an index of prices received for crops, and of lagged fertilizer consumption. The assumed and estimated demand function is linear in the logarithms of the variables.[4]

The coefficients of multiple determination in each of the nine regional regressions are presented in Table 2. In addition, Table 2 also reports on two aggregate United States regressions and two "composite" aggregate coefficients of multiple determination. Because of the non-linearity of the micro equations, there are at least two possible aggregation procedures. The first, labelled U.S., is to aggregate linearly and then take the logarithms of the sums. In this procedure, we commit not only an aggregation error but also a "form of equation error."

TABLE 2. — DEMAND FOR FERTILIZER: REGIONAL, AGGREGATE, AND "COMPOSITE" COEFFICIENTS OF MULTIPLE DETERMINATION

Region and Aggregate	R^2
New England	.949
Middle Atlantic	.982
East North Central	.985
West North Central	.989
South Atlantic	.966
East South Central	.963
West South Central	.969
Mountain	.970
Pacific	.985
U.S. (log Σ)	.983
U.S.* (Σ log)	.986
Composite: U.S.	.982
U.S.*	.987

Alternatively, one can add the logarithms of all the variables, and use their sums as macro variables. The latter leads to the aggregate regression labelled U.S.*. Since we have two different aggregates, we have also computed two comparable composite R^2's. The U.S.* composite is simply the variance of the sum of the actual regional residuals divided by the variance of the U.S.* aggregate fertilizer consumption and subtracted from one. For the U.S. composite we first take the antilogarithms of the residuals, sum them, take the logarithm of the sum, compute its variance, and compare that to the variance of the U.S. aggregate.

As is apparent from Table 2, in contrast to the investment study, the macro fertilizer function performs neither better nor worse than the micro functions. The R^2's for the two U.S. aggregates are not higher than all the regional R^2's but are close to the upper limit of the range of the regional R^2's. The composite R^2's are practically the same as the R^2's of the aggregate regressions, indicating that if our main interest were to explain aggregate U.S. fertilizer consumption, we would not gain anything from a disaggregation to the regional level (holding the number of variables and the form of the equation constant).

It is worthwhile to point out the following differences between the fertilizer and investment studies: In the investment study the micro units are firms; in the fertilizer study they are regions, and regions are already aggregates of considerable size. Also, the fit of the micro equations is much higher in the fertilizer study,

[3] See Zvi Griliches, "Distributed Lags, Disaggregation, and Regional Demand Functions for Fertilizer," *Journal of Farm Economics* (February 1959). For the general framework of this study, see Zvi Griliches, "The Demand for Fertilizer: An Economic Interpretation of a Technical Change," *Journal of Farm Economics* (August 1958).

[4] Actually, the model used is somewhat more complicated. It assumes that "long-run" or "desired" fertilizer use is a function of the "real" price of fertilizer but that actual fertilizer use changes in any one year only by some proportion of the difference between the "desired" and the actual level of fertilizer use. The long-run demand function and the adjustment relation taken together lead to the estimation of an equation relating current fertilizer use to the current real price of fertilizer and lagged fertilizer use.

due largely to the introduction of lagged fertilizer consumption as an independent variable, leaving much less room for the aggregation procedure to result in an improvement over the micro results.

To sum up the main results of the two studies, we have seen that the R^2 of the aggregate relation *can* be higher than any one of the R^2's of the micro relations and also higher than the composite R^2 of all the micro relations. We are thus led to ask the following two questions: (1) What factors determine the magnitude of the aggregate R^2 relative to the magnitudes of the R^2's of the micro relations, and (2) what factors determine the size of the aggregate R^2 relative to the size of the composite R^2.

III. Size of Correlation Coefficients: Micro vs. Macro[5]

It is useful to disprove two misconceptions about the aggregate correlation coefficient. The first is that the aggregate correlation coefficient is some weighted average of the micro correlation coefficients. That this is wrong is an obvious implication of the investment study results, in which the multiple correlation coefficient of the aggregate equation was outside the range of multiple correlation coefficients of the separate micro equations. The second, and more subtle, misconception is that the higher aggregate correlation coefficients are necessarily a consequence of the Law of Large Numbers or the Central Limit Theorem.[6] Since in the case of the aggregate R^2 we are dealing essentially with the ratio of two variances, it is not clear how the Law of Large Numbers could be relevant. Nor are the implications of the Central Limit Theorem apparent. The Central Limit Theorem says that the distribution of a linear combination of random variables will under some general conditions tend to normality, but it does not imply that the variance of a *sum* of random variables will be smaller than the sum of the variances. The argument that we will present does not depend on either of these "laws."[7]

The fact that the aggregate R^2 is usually higher than the micro R^2's is due mainly to what may be best called a "grouping" or "synchronization" effect. It is the result of the empirical fact that most of the groupings that are likely to be used are such that aggregation will increase the variance of the denominator of R^2 relative to its numerator. The synchronization effect can be expressed as follows: The higher the correlation between the independent variables of different individuals or behavior units, ceteris paribus, the higher the R^2 of the aggregate equation relative to the R^2's of the micro equations.

The easiest way of establishing this result is to consider a very simple case of aggregation. Let $y_{it} = bx_{it} + u_{it}$ for all i, $i = 1 \ldots K$ and $t = 1 \ldots T$ (e.g., assume that y_{it} is consumption of an individual, x_{it} his income, and u_{it} a random disturbance, where both y_{it} and x_{it} are measured from their respective means). Assume that all individuals have the same b, that the variance of x_{it} over t, S^2_{xi}, is the same for all i, and that the variance of u_{it}, S^2_{ui}, is also the same for all i. Further, assume that the intercorrelation as among individuals of the independent variable is the same for all pairs of individuals and is equal to ρ_x and also that the intercorrelation of the disturbances is the same for all pairs of individuals and is equal to ρ_u.[8] Under these as-

[5] As applied to cross-sectional data and different levels of aggregation, this problem has been discussed by sociologists under the name of "ecological correlation." See Leo A. Goodman, "Some Alternatives to Ecological Correlation," *American Journal of Sociology*, LXIV (May 1959), 610–25, and the literature cited there. Also, G. U. Yule and M. G. Kendall touch briefly on this problem in their discussion of "the modifiable unit" and "the attenuation effect." See their *An Introduction to the Theory of Statistics*, 14th ed. (London, 1950), 310–15.

[6] Yule and Kendall attribute the higher R^2 in the aggregate to a "sampling effect," but they do not state explicitly what they mean. See Yule and Kendall, op. cit., 314. Theil attributes the relative improvement in explanation with aggregation to the operation of the Central Limit Theorem. "If the conditions of the Central Limit Theorem are fulfilled . . . , the variances of the macro disturbances tend to be smaller in a relative sense as the number of individuals (or commodities, etc.) increases, so that the 'predictive power' of macro equations may seem to be greater than that of micro equations." Theil, op. cit., 114–15. Actually, this has very little to do with the Central Limit Theorem, as we shall see below.

[7] Aggregation will lead to higher R^2's if *two* assumptions are fulfilled: (a) the disturbances are truly random, i.e., there is no correlation between the micro disturbances of different individuals; (b) aggregation is *not* random with respect to the independent variables. Both the Law of Large Numbers and the Central Limit Theorem usually assume (a), and to that extent they are relevant. But assumption (a) is not sufficient by itself and the conclusions of these theorems are not relevant for our purposes.

[8] These restrictive assumptions will be relaxed below.

sumptions we can write the ratio between the aggregate r^2 and the micro r^2 as follows:[9]

$$\frac{r_A^2}{r_i^2} = \frac{b^2 S_{xi}^2 + S_{ui}^2}{b^2 S_{x_i}^2 + S_{u_i}^2 \dfrac{1+(K-1)\rho_u}{1+(K-1)\rho_x}}. \qquad (1.0)$$

From equation (1.0), we see that the relation between the aggregate r^2 and the micro r^2's depends on the relative size of ρ_u, the intercorrelation among the disturbances, and ρ_x, the intercorrelation among the independent variables.

The intercorrelation among the independent variables is a phenomenon that is determined by the kind of data that we usually employ in econometric time series studies. Since the data are not a result of an experiment controlled by the econometrician, our independent variables will possess some uncontrolled properties, and in particular they will in most cases be positively intercorrelated. For example, prices paid by different individuals for the same commodity will usually be positively correlated over time, and the incomes of different individuals may also be positively correlated. In contrast, the properties of the disturbances will depend not only on the properties of the data but also on the properties of the economic model used. If our economic model is a complete one, in the sense that it contains all the variables that are assumed to influence the dependent variable in a systematic manner, then one would expect that the disturbances would be "truly" random — that is, they would not be related systematically to any conceivable explanatory variable, and, hence, they would also be uncorrelated with the disturbances in the other micro equations. In this "ideal" situation $\rho_u = 0$ and the r^2 of the aggregate equation will always be larger than the r^2's of the micro equation as long as there exists a positive synchronization among the independent variables. The higher this positive synchronization, the larger will be the r^2 of the aggregate equation in relation to the r^2 of the micro equations. Actually, it does not have to be very large to result in a substantial increase in the aggregate coefficient of determination. If $b = 1$, $S_x^2 = 10$, $S_u^2 = 5$, $\rho_x = .1$, and $K = 101$, then $r_i^2 = .67$, and $r_A^2 = .96$; if $S_{xi}^2 = 5$ instead of 10, then $r_i^2 = .5$ and $r_A^2 = .75$; and if $S_{xi}^2 = 5$ and $K = 1001$ instead of 101, then $r_i^2 = .5$ and $r_A^2 = .95$.

In general, we cannot really hope to have a "complete" model in the sense discussed above. The degree of synchronization in the disturbances of the micro equations will, thus, depend on the type of incompleteness of our model. In some econometric studies there may be a presumption that ρ_u is negative. Most economic variables, particularly quantities of goods, are subject to some constraints, at least in the short run. For example, total consumption of food during a particular year could not exceed a predetermined supply, and total quantity of investment goods that can be purchased in one year is also limited (especially if we assume a constant price for these goods). Thus, as one firm tries to expand, due to some unexpected factors, it is likely to impose a burden, or perhaps some contraction, on other firms. The existence of such external diseconomies is not usually introduced explicitly into the micro equations. But if we ignore them, then they are likely to lead to a negative ρ_u.

A negative intercorrelation of the disturbances is not required, however, for the macro correlation coefficient to exceed the micro correlation coefficient. All that is necessary is that ρ_u be smaller than ρ_x, i.e., the intercorrelation of the u's be smaller than the intercorrelation of the x's. These results are based on a set of rather restrictive assumptions. Most of these assumptions can be relaxed without affecting the substance of our conclusions but only at the cost of much more algebra. If we did not assume equal variances and covariances we could still restate our results in terms of *average* intercorrelation or synchronization coefficients. To apply the same results in a cross-sectional context it turns out to be more convenient, however, to use the "intra-class correlation coefficient" as our measure of synchronization.[10] We can also abandon the assumption of equal micro coefficients, the b's, and in addition generalize from ordinary to multiple correlations. The formulas become more complicated as many more things can happen in a more complex world, but the substance

[9] See Appendix A for the derivation of (1.0).

[10] For a definition of an intra-class correlation coefficient see Yule and Kendall, op. cit., 272–77, 512–13; and Appendix B below.

of our arguments remains unimpaired. The relaxation of some of these assumptions with the concomitant proliferation of algebra is relegated to Appendixes B through E.

We get higher correlation coefficients when we aggregate because the grouping of data into years, states, income classes, and other economic groupings is not random with respect to the independent variables. This happens not only in time-series studies but also in cross-sectional studies, and it happens because within each group the individuals are likely to be more alike with respect to independent variables than with respect to disturbances. But these higher correlation coefficients do not really imply that the macro equations have a higher explanatory power than micro equations, since they do not prove that we have less unexplained variation on the macro level, only that we compare the unexplained variation to a larger base. Thus the "gain" may be only apparent. A higher correlation coefficient in the aggregate does not by itself imply that aggregation is necessarily good, only that we are using a different yardstick.

IV. All Micro Regressions vs. Aggregate Regression

The comparison of the composite explanatory power of all the micro regressions to that of the macro regression is quite a different problem from that discussed in the previous section. Synchronization of the independent variables cannot explain why an aggregate R^2 should be higher than the composite R^2. It will affect both measures in the same way. This is easily seen if we recall that in the previous section we compared two "relative" measures of fit, with two different denominators. In this case, however, the denominators are the same, and we are really comparing two "absolute" measures of fit, measured in the same units.

It is a curious fact that one aggregate regression can offer a better explanation of the variability of the aggregate dependent variable than the combined results of a large number of micro regressions. At first glance, it looks as if the micro equations contain all the information contained in the macro equation and more — how then can the macro equation give a "better" explanation? Since the multiple R^2 of the aggregate equation and the composite R^2 have the same denominator, namely the variance of the dependent variable, we are essentially asking ourselves under what conditions will the variance of the residuals of the macro equation be smaller than the variance of the sum of the residuals of the micro equations. To investigate the relationship between these two variances, we shall make use of a relationship derived by Theil:[11]

$$E\{u(t)^2\} = \text{var}\{\sum_i u_i(t) + \sum_{k,i} V_{ki}(t)\, b_{ki}\} \quad (6.0)$$

where $u(t)$ is the calculated disturbance in the macro equation, $u_i(t)$ is the micro disturbance in the ith micro equation, b_{ki} is the kth micro parameter in the ith micro equation, and $V_{ki}(t)$ is the residual in the "auxiliary regression" of the kth variable in the ith micro equation on all the macro variables.

The residual of the auxiliary regression deserves special attention. It is the residual obtained by correlating the kth independent variable in the ith equation or x_{ki} to all the macro independent variables X_k, $k = 1 \ldots K$. Thus,

$$V_{ki}(t) = x_{ki}(t) - \sum_k P_{ki}\, X_k(t) \quad (6.1)$$

where the P_k's are the regression coefficients of the auxiliary equations.

Theil has this to say about expression (6.0)[12]

> This expression is always larger than the variance of the sum of the micro disturbances, unless the non-stochastic part of the right hand side of (6) vanishes. . . . In general the second moment about zero of a macro disturbance is larger than the variance of the sum of the corresponding micro disturbances. Exceptions to this rule (such that "larger than" must be replaced by "equal to") can, of course, always be obtained by fixed-weights and constant terms aggregation of the types considered above.

In other words, the residual variance of the macro equation must be larger than the variance of the sum of residuals from the micro equations. The empirical evidence presented in sections I and II seems, however, to contradict this rule!

The contradiction is, of course, only apparent. Theil's conclusion is correct within the framework of his assumptions. But our examples, and perhaps most of the cases which we face in actual empirical work, will not fulfill his as-

[11] Theil, *Linear Aggregation*, 115.
[12] Idem.

sumptions. His two major assumptions are: (1) the x's, and, hence, the second term of the right-hand part of (6.0) are non-stochastic; and (2) the micro equations are perfectly specified. The violation of either asumption could lead to our result. If you grant Theil's assumptions, then (6.0) simplifies to

$$E\{u(t)^2\} = \text{var}\{\sum_i u_i(t)\} + \{\sum_{k,i} V_{ki}(t)\, b_{ki}\}^2 \qquad (6.2)$$

and it is easily seen that $Eu(t)^2$ must be larger than var $\{\sum_i u_i(t)\}$. If, however, the x's are not non-stochastic, then (6.0) does not simplify to (6.2). It is our contention that a negative covariance between $b_{ki}V_{ki}(t)$ and $u_i(t)$ is quite likely. If this is true, then the variance of the macro disturbances *could* be smaller than variance of the sum of micro disturbances.

Theil, in line with most discussions of regression analysis, assumes that the x's, the independent variables, are fixed, predetermined, or chosen by the experimenter. In practice, however, the economist is faced with data generated without his supervision, for a different purpose, and by a rather obscure mechanism. Hence, the particular distribution of x's is neither random nor chosen by the econometrician according to some optimal design. For example, the theory of consumption is formulated in terms of "expected" or "permanent" income or prices, but we often identify these abstract concepts with the actual ex post observations on income and prices. If an individual's income in one year is abnormally high relative to the income of others, this may mean that it is higher than his expected or normal income, and he may "under-react" to his present income in his consumption expenditure. This will tend to yield a negative residual for that year in his calculated consumption function. But at the same time, because his income is abnormally high in relation to aggregate income for that year there will tend to be a positive residual in the auxiliary equation since the auxiliary equation will in this case relate the income of the individual to aggregate income.

It is more useful, however, to reinterpret this example in terms of the violation of the perfect specification assumption. Actually, instead of having just disposable income as one variable, we should have had additional variables, e.g., an individual's consumption may depend not only on his own but also on other people's income, perhaps also on aggregate national income. While it is useful, for analytical purposes, to assume that we have specified the micro equations correctly, that our model is "complete" and "right," it is clearly impossible to expect this to be always true in practice. Most of our models do not pretend to completeness. But if our micro equations are not correctly specified, their residuals will now contain an additional term, which we shall call the "specification error" (at the *micro level*), and they will be larger than the "true" micro disturbances. The relationship of the variance of the residuals from the aggregate equation to the variance of the sum of residuals from the (underspecified) micro equations will, then, depend on the size of the aggregation error relative to the size of the specification error.[13]

To illustrate, consider a very simple model of micro behavior which includes the assumption that the aggregate variable contains some information relevant to the individual decision maker. Let

$$y_i = b_{y1i2}\, x_{1i} + b_{y21i} x_2 + u_i \qquad (7.0)$$

where $x_2 = \sum_i x_{1i}$. However, instead of estimating these micro equations, we estimate (7.1) $y_i = b_{y1i}\, x_{1i} + w_i$, ignoring the contribution of the aggregate variable.[13a] At the same time, we also estimate the aggregate equation

$$\sum_i y_{1i} = b_2\, x_{2t} + u_t\,. \qquad (7.2)$$

What we want to know is whether $\sum_t u_t^2$, the residual variance of the macro equation, will be larger or smaller than $\sum_t(\sum_i w_{it})^2$; the variance of the sum of the residuals from the incorrectly specified micro equations. Is the aggregation error worse than the specification error?

[13] While it will be useful to contrast the "specification error" with the "aggregation error," these labels may be somewhat misleading. Actually, in many contexts it is useful to think of specification error as the general term and aggregation error as a special case of specification error. Cf. Theil, op. cit. What we are contrasting are the results of leaving one macro variable out of K micro equations with the results of leaving out K micro variables from the macro equation. Our labels, though slightly misleading, are useful as shorthand.

[13a] Note that for purposes of simplicity we have dropped the subscript t from all the variables.

The sum of micro residuals, $\sum_i w_{it}$, and the macro residual u_t can be expressed as follows:[14]

$$\sum_i w_{it} = \sum_i (u_{it} + b_{y2,1i} V_{21i}) \tag{7.3}$$

$$u_t = \sum_i (u_{it} + b_{y1i,2} V_{1i2}) \tag{7.4}$$

where V_{21i} is the residual in the auxiliary regression of x_2 on x_{1i}, and V_{1i2} is the residual in the "other" regression, the regression of x_{1i} on x_2.

Assuming that the "true" u_i's are uncorrelated with all the x's, the variances of (7.3) and (7.4) can be each expressed as a sum of three parts: the variance of the sum of the true disturbances, a weighted sum of variances of V's (the second term in 7.3 and 7.4), and a term involving the covariances of the respective V_i's and V_j's. After some additional manipulation, these terms can be written as follows:[15]

$$S^2_{\Sigma w_i} = S^2_{\Sigma u_i} + \sum_i S^2_{y_i} (1 - r^2_{2i}) \beta^2_{y2.i} \tag{7.5}$$
$$+ \sum_{i,j}^{k,k-1} S_{yi} S_{yj} \{1 - r^2_{2i} - r^2_{2j} + r_{2i} r_{2j} r_{ij}\} \beta_{y2.i} \beta_{y2.j}$$

$$S^2_u = S^2_{\Sigma u_i} + \sum_i S^2_{yi} (1 - r^2_{2i}) \beta^2_{yi.2}$$
$$+ \sum_{i,j}^{k,k-1} S_{yi} S_{yj} \{r_{ij} - r_{2i} r_{2j}\} \beta_{yi.2} \beta_{yj.2} \tag{7.6}$$

where S^2_{yi} is the variance of the ith micro dependent variable, r_{2i} is the correlation coefficient between x_2 and x_{1i}, r_{ij} is the correlation coefficient of x_{1i} with x_{1j}, and the β's are the beta coefficients of the micro equations.[16] The correlation of the micro independent variables with the aggregate independent variable (x_2) is measured by r_{2i}, and the intercorrelation between any pair of micro independent variables or their synchronization is measured by r_{ij}. The beta coefficients measure the impact of a change in x on y in units of standard deviations of both variables, and are thus approximate measures of the relative importance of the respective independent variables in accounting for the variation in the dependent variable. Henry Schultz called them "coefficients of direct determination."[17]

Note that the first term in both (7.5) and (7.6) is the same and that we need only worry about the relative size of the last two terms in each of these expressions. Several interesting statements can be made about these expressions:

(a) If there is perfect synchronization of the independent variables, i.e., $r_{ij} = 1$ for all i and j, and therefore, $r^2_{2i} = 1$, then both "errors" are zero and there will be no difference between them. Also, the higher the synchronization the smaller will be the absolute magnitude of each of these errors, and hence also the less the difference between them.[18] This is in striking contrast to the conclusions of the previous section where high synchronization implied high macro R^2's relative to the micro R^2's.

(b) It is easily seen that the variance terms are symmetric in $\beta^2_{y2.1}$ and $\beta^2_{y1.2}$. Hence, as far as the variance terms are concerned, it would suffice for $\beta^2_{y2.1}$ to exceed $\beta^2_{y1.2}$, for the specification error to exceed the aggregation error. All that is necessary is that the macro independent variable x_2 be "more important" than the micro independent variable x_{1i} in explaining the variability of the micro dependent variable y_i.

(c) It is also true, but less apparent, that if K is not very small and there is synchronization, i.e., $r_{ij} > 0$, the covariance terms of the specification error will be positive but the covariance terms of the aggregation error will be negative. Hence, $\beta^2_{y2.1}$ (the proportion of total micro variability attributable directly to the macro variable) will not have to be as high as $\beta^2_{y1.2}$ to result in the aggregate R^2 exceeding the composite R^2.

To prove this last statement, note that the sign of the covariances is essentially determined by the sign of the last term in the bracket. For the specification error covariances this is $(1 - r^2_{2i} - r^2_{2j} + r_{2i} r_{2j} r_{ij})$. If neither of these r's is very large, or if r_{ij} is positive and smaller than r^2_{2i}, then this term will be positive. In fact, if we assume that there is positive synchronization, $r_{ij} > 0$, then it can be shown that in general

[14] See Appendix F for the proof of this and subsequent formulas in this section.

[15] For proof see Appendix F.

[16] Note that for simplicity we have dropped the subscript 1. Whenever i or j appears by itself, it means $1i$ or $1j$.

[17] H. Schultz, *The Theory and Measurement of Demand* (Chicago, 1938), 218–19 and 740–43.

[18] This last statement is strictly true only at the limit. Since both errors are of the same order of magnitude, as each of them goes to zero, the difference between them will eventually also go to zero. With some additional simplifying assumptions it can be shown that the difference will actually go *monotonically* to zero as synchronization increases provided that K is not "too small," but this is not necessarily true in general.

$r_{2i}^2 > r_{ij}$. In particular, if r_{ij} is the same for all i and j, $i \neq j$, then

$$r_{2i}^2 = r_{2j}^2 = \frac{1+(K-1)\,r_{ij}}{K} \tag{7.7}$$

and the bracket in the last term of 7.5 becomes

$$1 - r_{2i}^2(2 - r_{ij})$$
$$= \frac{K - \{1 + (K-1)\,r_{ij}\}\,(2 - r_{ij})}{K} \tag{7.8}$$

which is always negative for $K = 2$, but is positive for large K and not too high r_{ij}.

Similarly, given these same assumptions, we can simplify the bracket terms of the aggregation error covariances to

$$r_{ij} - r_{2i}\,r_{2j} = \frac{r_{ij} - 1}{K} \tag{7.9}$$

which is always negative.

Two more statements can be made about the relative size of these two errors without making additional assumptions:

(d) If the micro equations have the same regression coefficients, the aggregation error will vanish, but the specification error will not. A corollary to this statement is that the wider is the dispersion of the micro b's (or the micro $\beta_{y1.2}$ and $\beta_{y2.1}$), the larger will be the aggregation error relative to the specification error.

(e) The aggregation error will be reduced and the specification error will be increased if there is a positive correlation between r_{2i}^2 and $\beta_{y1.2i}^2$ and a negative correlation between r_{21i}^2 and $\beta_{y2.1i}^2$. This would mean that "unsynchronized people," those with low r_{21i}^2, do not respond much to their own variables, discounting them because of their unsychronization, and rely more on the aggregate variables in determining their behavior, whereas "well-synchronized people" give more weight to their own variables and less to the aggregate variable.

The key factors that will increase the aggregate R^2 in relation to the composite R^2 are thus the relative importance of the macro and micro independent variables in the *micro equation* and the number of micro relations over which the aggregation is performed. If the aggregate variable is more important in determining the magnitude of the micro dependent variable than the micro variable, then the specification error will be larger than the aggregation error. This means that in the process of aggregation, we obtain a net gain in explanation. This, however, is not a necessary condition for a gain, only a sufficient one. As the number of individuals over which we aggregate increases, the less "important" have the left-out macro variables to be relative to the left-in variables and still lead to an aggregation gain.

Contrary to the case in the previous section, however, the more synchronization there is among the micro independent variables, the less difference there is likely to be between these two measures. On the other hand, if the individuals are alike with respect to their micro parameters, this will eliminate the aggregation error, but will only increase the specification error. In a sense, these two errors are independent of each other and the elimination of one does not imply the elimination of the other. As long as our micro relations are not perfect, there can be a gross gain from aggregation, due to the elimination of the specification error, and a gross loss due to the aggregation of differing micro relations. Whether there is a net gain is uncertain, but not improbable.

The corollary of this whole discussion is that if we suspect that macro variables are important, we should include them in our micro analysis. This consideration led us to go back and include the *aggregate* market value of all the firms in each of the micro equations explaining the investment of a particular firm. When the micro regressions are recomputed, including this additional variable, and a new composite R^2 computed, it is now equal to .930, as against .906 previously, which is higher, though not significantly, than the R^2 of .926 of the macro equation.[19]

V. Limitations and Conclusions

We have emerged, out of the sea of algebra, with two major conclusions: (1) It is quite likely that a macro equation will have a higher R^2 than a micro equation, but this is not very relevant in judging the performance of either equation; (2) considering the more relevant comparison, the aggregate equation may explain

[19] And this happens in spite of the partial correlation coefficient of the aggregate value of the firms not significantly differing from zero in six of the eight equations.

the aggregate data better than all micro equations combined if our micro equations are not "perfect." Since perfection is unlikely, aggregation may result in a "net gain."

It is worthwhile to emphasize some of the limitations of the foregoing analysis. We have limited ourselves to relatively simple examples. Some of our conclusions can be easily generalized to more complicated cases, others are not so easily generalized. We have not tried to investigate the problem in all of its possible generality, the algebra even at this stage being rather formidable. Hence, while we surmise that our conclusions will remain valid for more complicated cases, we have not proved it. Also, we have not investigated, except by implication, the results of aggregation procedures in the presence of measurement errors in the independent variables. In particular, the poor quality of micro data may be another source of aggregation gain.

It should be reiterated, however, that we do not claim that a perfectly specified micro system would not out-perform a macro equation, only that we do not live in a world of perfect micro systems. In particular, most of our economic theory, though couched in micro language, has really been derived with aggregates in mind. It is a theory that explains "average" behavior, never claiming to be able to explain the behavior of a particular individual. Marshall's "representative firm" was an attempt to bridge this micro and macro gap by formalizing micro behavior using only a small number of variables which were believed to be central in explaining aggregate behavior. To give an "adequate" explanation of individual behavior would require a much more detailed theory; such a theory, among other things, would have to account for the interdependence in the behavior of individuals. Most of the theoretical work has concentrated, however, on improving and making more rigorous the existing theory, a theory essentially designed for the explanation of aggregates.

It is undoubtedly true that disaggregation has certain advantages. In particular, it may suggest to us how to improve our theory. It may be futile, however, to expect that disaggregation will result in a better explanation of the aggregates without an appropriate change in the model. Different levels of aggregation require theories with different levels of abstraction.

In the light of this discussion, an econometrician could reach two alternative conclusions. One would be to try to improve our theory so that it would be more applicable to micro data. Alternatively, one could concentrate on improving the macro theories and estimation techniques. The authors are somewhat prejudiced in favor of the second direction, as they doubt that economists have a comparative advantage in deriving theories that would explain adequately individual behavior. But surely both directions are worth pursuing. It is worth remembering, however, that aggregation is not necessarily bad if one is interested in the aggregates.

APPENDIX A: RELATIONSHIP BETWEEN MICRO AND MACRO r²'s: THE SIMPLEST CASE

Consider the following relations:

$$r_i^2 = \frac{b_i^2 S_{xi}^2}{b_i^2 S_{xi}^2 + S_{ui}^2} \quad (1.1) \quad \text{and} \quad r_A^2 = \frac{b_A^2 S_X^2}{b_A^2 S_X^2 + S_U^2} \quad (1.2)$$

where r_i^2 is the r^2 of a micro equation, r_A^2 is the r^2 of the aggregate equation, $X_t = \sum_i x_{it}$, and S_U^2 is the calculated residual variance of the aggregate equation. The ratio of r_A^2 to r_i^2 is given by

$$\frac{r_A^2}{r_i^2} = \frac{b_A^2 S_X^2}{b_i^2 S_{xi}^2} \cdot \frac{b_i^2 S_{xi}^2 + S_{ui}^2}{b_A^2 S_X^2 + S_U^2}. \quad (1.3)$$

Assuming that $b_i = b_j = b_A = b$, this simplifies to

$$\frac{r_A^2}{r_i^2} = \frac{b^2 + S_{ui}^2 / S_{xi}^2}{b^2 + S_U^2 / S_X^2} \quad (1.4)$$

We can write

$$S_X^2 = \sum_i S_{xi}^2 + \sum_{i,j} S_{x_i x_j}. \quad (1.5)$$

Also, from the assumption that all the b's are equal it follows that we can write

$$S_u^2 = \sum_i S_{u_i}^2 + \sum_{i,j\,(i \neq j)} S_{u_i u_j}. \quad (1.6)$$

If we now assume that $S_{xi}^2 = S_{xj}^2$ for all i and j, $S_{xi\,xj} = S_{x_h x_l}$ for all i, j, h, and l, $i \neq j$ and $h \neq l$, and make similar assumptions about S_{ui}^2 and S_{uiuj}, we can rewrite (1.5) and (1.6) as

$$S_X^2 = K S_{x_i}^2 \{1 + (K-1)\,\rho_x\} \quad (1.7)$$

$$S_U^2 = K S_{u_i}^2 \{1 + (K-1)\,\rho_u\} \quad (1.8)$$

where $\rho_x = \dfrac{S_{x_i x_j}}{S_{x_i} S_{x_j}}$ and $\rho_u = \dfrac{S_{u_i u_j}}{S_{u_i} S_{u_j}}$ for all i and j, $i \neq j$.

Using this we rewrite (1.4) as

$$\frac{r^2_A}{r^2_i} = \frac{b^2 + \dfrac{S^2_{u_i}}{S^2_{x_i}}}{b^2 + \dfrac{S^2_{u_i}\{1+(K-1)\rho_u\}}{S^2_{x_i}\{1+(K-1)\rho_x\}}} . \qquad (1.9)$$

Finally, multiplying by S^2_{xi}, we get (1.0) in the text.

APPENDIX B: UNEQUAL VARIANCES AND COVARIANCES

The variance of a particular aggregate can be expressed as follows:

$$S^2_X = K S^2_{x_{it}} \{1 + r_X (K-1)\} \qquad (2.0)$$

where S^2_{xit} is the over-all variance of x_{it} over all i and t, r_x is the intra-class correlation coefficient, and K is the number of units or individuals within each group or year.[20] The intra-class correlation coefficient measures the alikeness of the members of each class. If within each group or year all the individual x's are the same, $r_X = 1$. If the variability of x's within each group is essentially the same as in the population at large, $r_x = 0$. It differs from the average inter-correlation coefficient in measuring the inter-correlation not from the individual means but from the over-all mean. The over-all population variance differs from an average of the individual variances used in Appendix A in including also the variability of the individual averages. Thus

$$S^2_{x_{it}} = \overline{S^2_{x_i}} + S^2_{\bar{x}_i} . \qquad (2.1)$$

Similar formulas apply for the u's. Substituting these in (1.4), we get

$$\frac{r^2_A}{r^2_i} = \frac{b^2 + S^2_{u_i}/S^2_{x_i}}{b^2 + \dfrac{(\overline{S^2_{u_i}} + S^2_{\bar{u}_i})\{1+r_u(K-1)\}}{(\overline{S^2_{x_i}} + S^2_{\bar{x}_i})\{1+r_x(K-1)\}}} . \qquad (2.2)$$

The same conclusions follow except for the additional proviso that $S^2_{\bar{u}_i} < S^2_{\bar{x}_i}$.

APPENDIX C: THE RELATIONSHIP BETWEEN THE COEFFICIENTS IN CROSS-SECTIONS

The comparison here is not between an individual regression and an aggregate one, but between a regression using all the $T \times K$ observations, and a regression using only T observations on aggregates summed over K. That is, the micro regression here would be one which would use the observations for all the individuals in the population or sample. The aggregate uses the sum of certain groups instead. The micro r^2 is given by

$$r^2_m = \frac{b^2 S^2_{x_{it}}}{b^2 S^2_{x_{it}} + S^2_{u_{it}}} . \qquad (3.0)$$

Using all the previous results, we have

$$\frac{r^2_A}{r^2_m} = \frac{b^2 + \dfrac{S^2_{u_{it}}}{S^2_{x_{it}}}}{b^2 + \dfrac{S^2_{u_{it}}\{1+r_u(K-1)\}}{S^2_{x_{it}}\{1+r_x(K-1)\}}} . \qquad (3.1)$$

The intra-class correlation coefficient is useful here because it does not depend on the pairing of particular i's and j's in different groups. One does not have to have the same individual in different states, while it was natural to think of the same individual being observed in different years.

APPENDIX D: UNEQUAL SLOPES

The major complication here is that the macro disturbance is no longer a simple function of the micro disturbances. It can be shown (see Theil, op. cit., page 115), that

$$u_t = \sum_i u_{it} + \sum_i b_i V_{it} \qquad (4.0)$$

where the V_{it}'s are the residuals in the auxiliary regressions of the micro x's on the macro X. The more closely the micro x's are correlated with each other, the closer will they be correlated with the aggregate X, and hence the smaller the V_i's. The variance of the macro disturbance is now

$$S^2_U = K(\overline{S^2_{u_i}} + S^2_{\bar{u}_i})\{1+r_u(K-1)\} + \sum_{i,j} b_i b_j S_{V_i V_j} . \qquad (4.1)$$

Also, we have now to distinguish between the aggregate b_A and the individual b_i. All this leads then to

$$\frac{r^2_A}{r^2_i} = \frac{b^2_A}{b^2_i} \cdot \frac{b^2_i + S^2_{u_i}/S^2_{x_i}}{b^2_A + \dfrac{(\overline{S^2_{u_i}} + S^2_{\bar{u}_i})\{1+r_u(K-1)\} + \sum_{i,j} b_i b_j S_{V_i V_j}}{(\overline{S^2_{x_i}} + S^2_{\bar{x}_i})\{1+r_x(K-1)\}}} . \qquad (4.2)$$

All the previous conclusions follow provided that the particular b_i is not too different from the aggregate b_A and the synchronization of the x's is relatively high. The last proviso insures that the new term, $\sum_{i,j} b_i b_j S_{V_i V_j}$

[20] For further details on the intra-class correlation coefficient see Yule and Kendall, op. cit., 272–77.

will be relatively small. Under the special assumptions of Appendix A, equal variances and covariances, it can be shown that $\sum_{i,j} b_i b_j S_{V_i V_j}$ reduces itself to $S^2_{x_i}(1-\rho_x)S^2_{b_i}$, where $S^2_{b_i}$ is the variance of the micro slopes among individuals and ρ_x is the synchronization coefficient; and $b_A = \overline{b_i}$.

APPENDIX E: THE CASE OF MULTIPLE CORRELATION

The multiple coefficient of determination can be expressed in matrix notation as follows:

$$R^2 = \frac{b' X' X b}{b' X' X b + u' u} \qquad (5.0)$$

where X is the matrix of the independent variables, b a vector of the coefficients, and u the vector of disturbances. If aggregation does not bias b downwards, then the relationship of macro R^2 to micro R^2 will depend on what happens to $X'X$ relative to $u'u$ as we aggregate; $X'X$ is the matrix of variances and covariances of the independent variables. If there is sychronization, then the diagonal terms, the macro variances, will be on the order of $K\{1+r_x(K-1)\}$ and, hence, larger than K times the micro variances. If the disturbances are unsynchronized, this synchronization of the independent variables will result in an aggregate R^2 larger than the micro R^2's. This is a counterpart of the case discussed for one independent variable. In the case of more than one independent variable, however, another kind of synchronization comes into play, namely, that between one independent variable of individual i with a different independent variable of individual j. If this synchronization is also positive, the macro covariances of the independent variables will be larger than K times the covariances of the micro variables.[21] This will make our conclusion hold *a fortiori* as long as the synchronization of the disturbances does not exceed the synchronization of the independent variables.

APPENDIX F: VARIANCE OF MACRO RESIDUAL VS. VARIANCE OF SUM OF MICRO RESIDUALS

For the simplified model used in section IV, we know that

$$w_{it} = b_{y1i.2}\, x_{1it} + b_{y2.1i}\, x_{2t} + u_{it} - b_{y1i}\, x_{1it}. \qquad (8.0)$$

But it can be shown that (see Yule and Kendall, op. cit., 300 and Theil, "Specification Errors. . . ," op. cit.) that

$$b_{y1} = b_{y1.2} + b_{21}\, b_{y2.1}. \qquad (8.1)$$

Hence

$$w_{it} = u_{it} + b_{y2.1i}\{x_{2t} - b_{21i}x_{1it}\} = u_{it} + b_{y2.1i}V_{21i} \qquad (8.2)$$

and

$$S^2(\sum_i w_{it}) = S^2_{\Sigma u_i} + \sum_i b^2_{y2.1i} S^2_{V_{2i}} + \sum_{i,j}^{K,K-1} b_{y2.1i}\, b_{y2.1j}\, S_{V2i\,V2j}. \qquad (8.3)$$

But, it is known that

$$S^2_{V_{2i}} = S^2_{x_2}(1 - r^2_{2i}) \qquad (8.4)$$

and

$$\beta^2_{y2.1i} = b^2_{y2.1i}\{S^2_{x_2}/S^2_{y_i}\}. \qquad (8.5)$$

Hence we can rewrite

$$\sum_i b^2_{y2.1i} S^2_{V_{2i}} = \sum_i S^2_{y_i}(1 - r^2_{2i})\,\beta^2_{y2.1i}. \qquad (8.6)$$

Consider now $S_{V_{2i}V_{2j}}$ which is defined as

$$S_{V_{21i}V_{21j}} = S_{(x_2 - b_{21i}x_{1i})(x_2 - b_{21j}x_{1i})} \qquad (8.7)$$
$$= S^2_2 - \frac{S_{2i}}{S^2_i} S_{2i} - \frac{S_{2j}}{S^2_j} S_{2j} + \frac{S_{2i}S_{2j}}{S_i S_j} S_{ij}$$
$$= S^2_{x_2}\{1 - r^2_{2i} - r^2_{2j} + r_{2i}\, r_{2j}\, r_{ij}\}.$$

Substituting (8.6) and (8.7) in (8.3) and redefining the b's as β's, leads to

$$S^2_{\Sigma w_i} = S^2_{\Sigma u_i} + \sum_i S^2_{y_i}(1 - r^2_{2_i})\beta^2_{y2.i} \qquad (8.8)$$
$$+ \sum_{i,j}^{K,K-1} S_{yi} S_{yj}\{1 - r^2_{2i} - r^2_{2j} + r_{2i} r_{2j} r_{ij}\}\,\beta_{y2.i}\,\beta_{y2.j}.$$

Similarly we know that

$$\sum_i y_i = \sum_i b_{yi.2}\, x_i + \sum_i b_{y2.i}\, x_2 + \sum u_i \qquad (9.0)$$

but we estimate

$$\sum_i y_i = b_2\, x_2 + u. \qquad (9.1)$$

Therefore,

$$u = \sum_i b_{yi.2}\, x_i + x_2 \sum_i b_{y2.i} + \sum_i u_i - b_2\, x_2. \qquad (9.2)$$

Again it can be shown that

$$b_2 = \sum_i b_{y2.i} + \sum_i b_{i2}\, b_{yi.2}. \qquad (9.3)$$

Substituting (9.3) into (9.2) leads to

$$u = \sum_i u_i + \sum_i b_{yi.2}\{x_i - b_{i2}\, x_2\} \qquad (9.4)$$
$$= \sum u_i + \sum b_{yi.2}\, V_{i2}.$$

And hence

$$S^2_u = S^2_{\Sigma ui} + \sum_i b^2_{yi.2} S^2_{Vi2} + \sum_{i,j}^{K,K-1} b_{yi.2}\, b_{yj.2}\, S_{V_{i2}V_{j2}}. \qquad (9.5)$$

The only "new" term here is

$$S_{V_{i2}V_{j2}}.$$

But it can be broken down into

$$S_{V_{i2}V_{j2}} = S_{ij} - \frac{S_{2i}}{S^2_2} S_{2j} - \frac{S_{2j}}{S^2_2} S_{2i} + \frac{S_{2i}S_{2j}}{S^2_2 S^2_2} S^2_2 = \qquad (9.6)$$

[21] This assumes that all the b's have the same sign. But if we allow them to differ in sign, then for these conclusions to hold, the correlation between x_{hi} and x_{kj} should have the same sign as the product $b_h . b_k$.

$$= S_{ij} - \frac{S_{2i}S_{2j}}{S_2^2} = S_i S_j \{ r_{ij} - r_{2i} r_{2j} \} .$$

Substituting (9.6) and formulas similar to (8.4) and (8.5) into (9.5) lead to

$$S_u^2 = S_{\Sigma u_i}^2 + \sum_i S_{yi}^2 (1 - r_{2i}^2)\, \beta_{y1i.2}^2$$
$$+ \sum_i S_{yi} S_{yj} \{ r_{ij} - r_{2i} r_{2j} \}\, \beta_{y1i.2}\, \beta_{y1j.2}. \qquad (9.7)$$

Under the assumptions that $S_{1i}^2 = S_{1j}^2$ and $S_{ij} = S_{hk}$ for $i \neq j$ and $h \neq k$, it can be shown that

$$r_{21i}^2 = \frac{(S_{21i})^2}{S_2^2 S_{1i}^2} = \frac{\{S_{1i}^2 + (K-1) S_{ij}\}^2}{K S_i^2 \{1 + (K-1)\rho_{ij}\} S_i^2}$$

$$= \frac{\{S_i^2 \{1 + (K-1)\rho_{ij}\}^2}{S_i^4 K \{1 + (K-1)\rho_{ij}\}} = \frac{1 + (K-1)\rho_{ij}}{K} . \qquad (9.8)$$

SPECIFICATION ERRORS AND THE ESTIMATION OF ECONOMIC RELATIONSHIPS

by

H. Theil

1. INTRODUCTION

The usual first step in the estimation and testing procedures of economic relationships is the formulation of a "maintained hypothesis". As is well-known,[1] this amounts to a specification of the general framework within which the estimation or testing is carried out. Most of the results in this field have been derived under the assumption that the "maintained hypothesis" is correct. This is indeed in accordance with its name: the hypothesis is not subject to test, but "maintained".

In practice, no investigator can hope for more than that such a hypothesis is approximately correct. In that case the conclusions of testing or estimation, based on this hypothesis, are also subject to an error of approximation. It is true that it is not at all inconceivable that the correctness of the "maintained" hypothesis is tested; for instance, one can test the overidentifying restrictions on a structural equation which is part of a system of equations.[2] However, if the question whether the hypothesis is really maintained or rejected is made dependent on the outcome of such a test, this is not without consequences for the remaining part of the estimation or testing procedure.

The present paper is devoted to an analysis of the consequences of erroneously specified "maintained hypotheses". The approach can be briefly described as follows. Suppose that a certain hypothesis H is correct, whereas the investigator assumes incorrectly that another hypothesis $\bar{H}$ is correct. Suppose further that the investigator proceeds to estimate on the basis of $\bar{H}$. The question is: what can be said about the resulting estimator in the light of the correct hypothesis? We shall confine ourselves to the expectation of the estimator just mentioned.

This approach is the same as the one followed by the author in his monograph on aggregation problems [5]; in fact, the present paper is to be regarded as a generalisation. Section 2 is devoted to specification errors in linear regression analysis. It is shown in Section 3 under what conditions the criterion of minimum residual variance (= maximum multiple correlation) is satisfactory for deciding which of a number of alternative hypotheses is correct. Linear aggregation of linear microrelations to linear macrorelations is a special case of the result of Section 2; this is proved in Section 4. Substitution elasticities, quadratic and logarithmically linear relations are considered in the Sections 5, 6 and 7, respectively; these, too, are special cases.[3]

2. SPECIFICATION ERRORS IN REGRESSION ANALYSIS

Suppose that we are interested in some variable of which T observations are available, $y(1), \ldots, y(t), \ldots, y(T)$; in vector form, y. We shall interpret y as a stochastic

---

[1] See e.g. [3], p. 178—179.

[2] Ibidem, p. 178—185.

[3] For an interesting application in the field of agricultural production functions, cf. [1].

vector. We shall further assume that this variable is linearly dependent on certain other variables $x_1, \ldots, x_\Lambda$ with values $x_\lambda(t)$ for the t-th observation. This leads to the equation

$$y = X\beta + u, \tag{2.1}$$

where X is the matrix $[x_\lambda(t)]$, β a vector of parameters and u a vector of disturbances. More specifically, we introduce the following hypothesis, which is supposed to be "true":

Hypothesis H. *y is a column vector of T stochastic real elements, and it is determined by equation* (2.1) *with the following specifications*:

(i) *X is a matrix of order $T \times \Lambda$ and rank $\Lambda \geqq 1$; its elements are real and nonstochastic;*

(ii) *β is a column vector of Λ nonstochastic real elements;*

(iii) *u is a column vector of T stochastic real elements; the joint distribution of these elements is arbitrary, except that each has zero expectation:*

$$Eu = 0. \tag{2.2}$$

Given this hypothesis, and given the observed matrices X, y, it is possible to derive an estimator of β. As is well-known, the least-squares estimator

$$b = (X'X)^{-1}X'y \tag{2.3}$$

is then unbiased [though it does not have the optimal Markov properties, unless it is further specified that $E(uu') = \sigma^2 I$ for some positive scalar σ^2].

Suppose, however, that the investigator does not use X as the matrix of values taken by the explanatory variables, but some other matrix $\bar{X}$ of order $T \times \bar{\Lambda}$ with rank $\bar{\Lambda}$. This may be due to several alternative causes. For example, the investigator may not know Hypothesis H; and he may think that an alternative Hypothesis $\bar{H}$ amounting to a replacement of (2.1) by

$$y = \bar{X}\bar{\beta} + \bar{u}, \tag{2.4}$$

etc. (all symbols of Hypothesis H being replaced by corresponding symbols with bars, except y and T), is correct. Needless to say, the two hypotheses H and $\bar{H}$ cannot in general be correct both at the same time. By subtracting (2.4) from (2.1), we find for the expectation of $\bar{u}$ under Hypothesis H

$$E\bar{u} = X\beta - \bar{X}\bar{\beta}, \tag{2.5}$$

provided $\bar{X}$ is nonstochastic; and this implies $E\bar{u} \neq 0$ in general, for whatever $\bar{\beta}$.[4] Another possibility leading to the choice of $\bar{X}$ instead of X occurs if the correctness of Hypothesis H is known to the investigator, and if he has no empirical data about some of the columns of X. If the corresponding variables are deleted, this amounts to the acceptance of a Hypothesis $\bar{H}$ with $\bar{\Lambda} < \Lambda$. We have still another possibility if the variables for which no information is available are replaced by substitutes; and so on.

Let us then assume that the investigator derives the following statistic:

$$\bar{b} = (\bar{X}'\bar{X})^{-1}\bar{X}'y. \tag{2.6}$$

[4] If the columns of X and those of $\bar{X}$ are linearly dependent, then we have $E\bar{u} = 0$ for some suitable $\bar{\beta}$; this is a special case of the theorem which follows.

This is simply the least-squares expression which is obtained if we take y as the dependent vector and $\bar{X}$ as the explanatory matrix. Needless to say, $\bar{b}$ is in general of limited value when we want to use it as an estimator of β, especially if $\bar{\Lambda} \neq \Lambda$. But it is at least interesting to know how $\bar{b}$ and β are related. For, if this relation is known, it must be possible to draw inferences about the consequences of the erroneous specification. The following simple result is then of interest:

Theorem 1. *Suppose that Hypothesis H is true; furthermore that $\bar{X}$ is some matrix of order $T \times \bar{\Lambda}$ and rank $\bar{\Lambda} \geq 1$, its elements being real and nonstochastic. Then the statistic $\bar{b}$ of* (2.6) *is an unbiased estimator of*

$$P\beta (= E\bar{b}), \tag{2.7}$$

where P is the coefficient matrix of the least-squares regressions of X (the correct explanatory variables) on $\bar{X}$ (the incorrect ones):

$$P = (\bar{X}'\bar{X})^{-1}\bar{X}'X. \tag{2.8}$$

The proof is very simple:

$$E\bar{b} = (\bar{X}'\bar{X})^{-1}\bar{X}'Ey = (\bar{X}'\bar{X})^{-1}\bar{X}'X\beta = P\beta.$$

A few additional remarks are in order. First, this result can be easily generalized for other methods of linear unbiased estimation, like Aitken's method of generalized least-squares; the only thing one has to do is to replace the P of least-squares by the corresponding matrix according to the statistical method considered.[5] Secondly, Theorem 1 is of course mainly interesting insofar as it enables the investigator to draw inferences about β, given $E\bar{b}$; or about $E\bar{b}$, given β. This is possible only if he knows something about P. According to the definition, P is implicitly given by the regressions

$$X = \bar{X}P + \text{matrix of residuals}, \tag{2.9}$$

which will be called the *auxiliary regression equations.*[6] Knowledge of P implies, therefore, knowledge of the variation and the covariation of the correct and the incorrect explanatory variables. As will be explained below, such knowledge is sometimes available. Here, we shall take one very simple example.

Suppose that the specification of $\bar{X}$ as the matrix of explanatory variables is correct except for one column; say, all variables $x_1, \ldots, x_{\Lambda-1}$ are correctly specified and used in the regression procedure, but x_Λ is replaced by some substitute x'_Λ. Clearly, the estimators b and $\bar{b}$ [cf. (2.3) and (2.6)] have then an equal number of components ($\Lambda = \bar{\Lambda}$); and all corresponding components except the last have an identical economic meaning. Still, it can be shown that, in general, all components of $E\bar{b}$ are different from the corresponding components of $\beta = Eb$. For the matrix P, which is square in this case, will now be the unit matrix except for its last column; and this last column will generally consist of nonzero elements only. Comparing this with (2.7), we must conclude that each component of $E\bar{b}$ does not only depend on the corresponding component of β, but also on the β-component of the incorrectly specified variable x_Λ. In formulae:

$$E\bar{b}_\lambda = \beta_\lambda + p_{\lambda\Lambda}\beta_\Lambda \qquad (\lambda = 1, \ldots, \Lambda),$$

---

[5] See e.g. [5], p. 116—125.

[6] The special case mentioned in footnote 4 occurs if the residuals of all these regressions vanish.

the p's being the coefficients of the regression

$$x_\Lambda(t) = \sum_{\lambda=1}^{\Lambda-1} p_{\lambda\Lambda}\, x_\lambda(t) + p_{\Lambda\Lambda}\, x'_\Lambda(t) + \text{residual}.$$

It seems reasonable to define, in this case, the difference $E\bar{b}_\lambda - \beta_\lambda = p_{\lambda\Lambda}\,\beta_\Lambda$ as the *specification bias* of the estimator $\bar{b}_\lambda$. As is easy to see, the estimators $\bar{b}_1, \ldots, \bar{b}_{\Lambda-1}$ have no specification bias if their variables are all uncorrelated with the incorrectly specified variable x_Λ.

3. THE CRITERION OF MINIMUM RESIDUAL VARIANCE

Since it is in general not known with certainty whether a particular hypothesis is correct, there is the problem of choice among several alternative hypotheses. A frequently applied criterion is that of the highest multiple correlation. The usual justification of this procedure is not satisfactory. The investigator feels that the work he has performed is of better quality if he can point out that the proportion of the variance which he has been unable to "explain" is negligible; however, there is no law in economics which states that such proportions are small or even "as small as possible". Nevertheless, there is a better justification, which we shall now consider.

Let us denote by $v = y - Xb$ and $\bar{v} = y - \overline{Xb}$ the least-squares residuals of the correct and the incorrect specifications, respectively. The sum of squares of the residuals v is

$$v'v = u'\,[I - X(X'X)^{-1}X']'\,[I - X(X'X)^{-1}X']\,u = u'\,[I - X(X'X)^{-1}X']\,u,$$

which can be written as

$$v'v = u'Mu \quad \text{with } M = I - X(X'X)^{-1}X'. \tag{3.1}$$

Similarly:

$$\bar{v}'\bar{v} = (X\beta + u)'\,\bar{M}(X\beta + u) \quad \text{with } \bar{M} = I - \bar{X}(\bar{X}'\bar{X})^{-1}\bar{X}'. \tag{3.2}$$

As is well-known, unbiased estimation requires that a correction for loss of degrees of freedom is made by multiplying $v'v$ by $T/(T-\Lambda)$. In the same way, we shall multiply $\bar{v}'\bar{v}$ by $T/(T-\bar{\Lambda})$. Consider then

Theorem 2. *Suppose that the assumptions of Theorem 1 are satisfied; subject, however, to the further specification that $E(uu') = \sigma^2 I$, where σ^2 is a positive real number and I the unit matrix of order T. Then the sum of squares of the components of the residual vector $v = y - \overline{Xb}$, when corrected for loss of degrees of freedom,*

$$\frac{T}{T-\bar{\Lambda}}\,\bar{v}'\bar{v},$$

has an expectation which exceeds or equals T times σ^2.

The interpretation is this: If the specification is incorrect, i.e., if $\bar{X} \neq X$, then the sum of squares of the residuals (corrected for loss of degrees of freedom) is on the average larger than the sum of squares of the residuals implied by the use of the correct specification; in other words, the residual variance shows then an *upward* (at least not downward) *specification bias.* On the average, therefore, the criterion of minimum residual variance leads to the correct choice of the specification; and the same is of course true for the equivalent criterion of maximum multiple correlation ($\bar{R}^2$).[7]

The proof is as follows. When taking the expectation of (3.2), we find

$$(3.3) \qquad E(\bar{v}'\bar{v}) = (X\beta)'\bar{M}X\beta + E(u'\bar{M}u) \geqq E(u'\bar{M}u) = \sigma^2 \operatorname{tr} \bar{M} = \sigma^2 (T-\bar{\Lambda}),$$

where tr $\bar{M}$ stands for the sum of the diagonal elements of $\bar{M}$, and where use is made of the positive semi-definiteness of $\bar{M}$.[8] This leads immediately to Theorem 2.

It should be added that the assumption of a nonstochastic $\bar{X}$ is essential. If it is not satisfied, the matrix $\bar{M}$ is also stochastic, so that the derivation (3.3) is no longer applicable. In particular, terms of the type $(X\beta)'E(\bar{M}u)$ will play a rôle in the right-hand side of (3.3), and these may be positive or negative. If $\bar{X}$ is distributed independently of u, no problem arises, for then we may confine ourselves to conditional probability distributions, the condition being that $\bar{X}$ is as observed. Otherwise, however, the criterion of minimum residual variance may be good or bad on the average.[9]

4. LINEAR AGGREGATION

An application of the analysis of Section 2, where it is indeed possible to say something more about the matrix P, is that of linear aggregation. Let us assume that the correct specification according to economic theory is in terms of microvariables, whereas the specification adopted is in terms of macrovariables. Then it can be shown that the interrelations between macrovariables and corresponding microvariables imply certain restrictions on P. We shall go briefly into this matter here, since it has been analysed extensively elsewhere [5].

Suppose that, for individual i ($i = 1, \ldots, I$), the microvariable y_i is a linear function of certain other microvariables $x_{\lambda h}$ ($\lambda = 1, \ldots, \Lambda$; $h = 1, \ldots, H_\lambda$):

$$(4.1) \qquad y_i(t) = \sum_{\lambda=1}^{\Lambda} \sum_{h=1}^{H_\lambda} \beta_{\lambda h,i}\, x_{\lambda h}(t) + u_i(t),$$

$u_i(t)$ being a random disturbance. For example, y_i. is the consumption of sugar by family i, x_{1h} ($h = 1, \ldots, H_1$) the price of sugar charged by retailer h, etc. We proceed to construct the following sum aggregates:

$$(4.2) \qquad y(t) = \sum_i y_i(t); \quad x_\lambda(t) = \sum_h x_{\lambda h}(t).$$

---

[7] Note, however, that if one of the specifications is characterised by a lag such that its testing requires the first observation to be dropped (which frequently happens), the two criteria are not exactly equivalent. An adjustment is then necessary.

[8] Proof: for any vector x of appropriate order, $x'\bar{M}x = x'\bar{M}'\bar{M}x = (\bar{M}x)'\bar{M}x \geqq 0$. That $\bar{M}$ is positive semi-definite rather than positive-definite follows from the fact that, if $x = \bar{X}z$ for some vector z of appropriate order, $x'\bar{M}x = 0$. This corresponds with the special case of footnote 4.

[9] The problem of maximum correlation has been considered earlier of Hotelling [2], who went even farther by analysing the significance of the difference between two correlation coefficients. Hotelling's approach is, however, quite different. His null-hypothesis amounts to equal parent correlations for the two competing specifications, so that a combination of all explanatory variables of the two specifications combined gives then in general a higher multiple correlation. Here, we assume that the correct specification (2.1) contains all relevant variables. Or in other words, Hotelling accepts the criterion of maximum correlation as given, whereas we try to justify it.

We can also take arbitrary linear combinations of the microvariables (with fixed coefficients), rather than simple sums; but this involves no real increase in generality.

It follows from (4.1) that the correct specification, based on microtheory, for the macrovariable y is

$$y(t) = \sum_{\lambda, h} \beta_{\lambda h}\, x_{\lambda h}(t) + \sum_{i} u_i(t)\,, \tag{4.3}$$

where $\beta_{\lambda h}$ is a "derived microparameter":

$$\beta_{\lambda h} = \sum_{i} \beta_{\lambda h, i} \tag{4.4}$$

On the other hand, if we follow the usual approach of a regression in the aggregates, this implies the specification

$$y(t) = \sum_{\lambda} \beta_{\lambda}\, x_{\lambda}(t) + u(t) \tag{4.5}$$

for some β_{λ}, $u(t)$. Clearly, the zero-expectation hypothesis for all macrodisturbances $u(t)$ individually is not tenable in general, for whatever β_{λ}, even when all microdisturbances $u_i(t)$ have zero expectation. This situation is hence identical with that of Section 2; and so we may ask how the expectations of the macrocoefficients of the regression of y on $x_1, \ldots, x_{\Lambda}$ are related to the microparameters. To do so, let us assume that Hypothesis H is satiesfied with respect to the specification (4.3); and let us write $\psi = \sum_{\lambda} H_{\lambda}$, X_{ψ} for the $T \times \psi$ matrix of microvalues $x_{\lambda h}(t)$, β_{ψ} for the column vector of the ψ derived microparameters, u for the column vector of the T disturbance sums $\Sigma u_i(t)$, X_{Λ} for the $T \times \Lambda$ matrix of macrovalues $x_{\lambda}(t)$, y for the column vector of values $y(t)$, and b_{Λ} for the least-squares estimator in the regression of y on X_{Λ}. (4.3) can then be written in the form

$$y = X_{\psi}\beta_{\psi} + u, \tag{4.6}$$

and b_{Λ} is defined as

$$b_{\Lambda} = (X'_{\Lambda} X_{\Lambda})^{-1} X'_{\Lambda} y. \tag{4.7}$$

Applying Theorem 1 we find

$$Eb_{\Lambda} = P\beta_{\psi}, \tag{4.8}$$

where P is the $\Lambda \times \psi$ matrix $[B_{\lambda, \lambda' h}]$ of the least-squares coefficients in the auxiliary regressions

$$x_{\lambda' h}(t) = \sum_{\lambda} B_{\lambda, \lambda' h}\, x_{\lambda}(t) + \text{residual}. \tag{4.9}$$

It follows that each component of Eb_{Λ}, say the λ-th, is a homogeneous linear combination of all microparameters, including the "noncorresponding" microparameters $\beta_{\lambda' h}$ with $\lambda' \neq \lambda$. Summation over h of (4.9) shows, however, that the sum of weights is unity for corresponding microparameters $\beta_{\lambda h}$, and zero for the noncorresponding ones, $\beta_{\lambda' h}$ with $\lambda' \neq \lambda$:

$$\sum_{h} B_{\lambda, \lambda' h} = \delta_{\lambda \lambda'} \tag{4.10}$$

$\delta_{\lambda \lambda'}$ being the Kronecker delta ($=0$ if $\lambda \neq \lambda'$, 1 if $\lambda = \lambda'$). To take the example with which we started in the beginning of this section, the macroestimate of the slope with respect to the average sugar price depends not only on the "corresponding" microparameters which describe the influence of the individual sugar prices on individual consumption; but it depends also on the "noncorresponding" microparameters, like those which describe the influence of prices of competing products on individual sugar consumption. Indeed, the expectation of the macroestimator is a homogeneous linear combination of the corresponding (derived) microparameters, viz. the individual sugar price coefficients, plus a linear combination of all other microparameters, viz. the noncorresponding ones; but, whereas the weights of the former combination have sum unity, the sum of the weights of the latter vanishes.

5. ON THE USE OF ELASTICITIES OF SUBSTITUTION

In the analysis of the consumption of two competing commodities, a rather frequent use is made of the specification

$$\frac{X_1}{X_2} = A \left[\frac{P_1}{P_2}\right]^{\varepsilon} e^{u}, \tag{5.1}$$

where the X's are the quantities consumed, the P's the prices, A and ε parameters, and u a disturbance. The problem is then to estimate ε (the elasticity of substitution) from a given sample of observations.

In general, however, equation (5.1) is not regarded as a fundamental behaviour equation. Instead, it is usually considered as being derived from two separate demand equations. When specifying the latter equations with constant elasticities, we can write them in the form

$$X_i = A_i M^{\eta_i} \prod_{j=1}^{n} P_j^{\varepsilon_{ij}} e^{u_i} \qquad (i = 1, 2), \tag{5.2}$$

where M represents the total income of the buyers and n the total number of commodities. Writing lower-case letters for logarithms, it is easily seen that (5.1) implies

$$x_1 - x_2 = a + \varepsilon(p_1 - p_2) + u, \tag{5.3}$$

whereas (5.2) implies

$$x_1 - x_2 = (a_1 - a_2) + (\eta_1 - \eta_2)m + \sum_{j=1}^{n} (\varepsilon_{1j} - \varepsilon_{2j})p_j + (u_1 - u_2). \tag{5.4}$$

Suppose then that we consider (5.4) as the correct specification. It is possible, of course, to go back further and to analyse the underlying microequations; but it is much simpler to carry out the analysis in two separate steps, one dealing with the aggregation and the other with the problem considered here. So Hypothesis H is supposed to be applicable to (5.4); and hence (5.3) is an incorrect specification, except for the possibility

$$\begin{aligned} \eta_1 &= \eta_2 \\ \varepsilon_{11} + \varepsilon_{12} &= \varepsilon_{21} + \varepsilon_{22} \\ \varepsilon_{1j} &= \varepsilon_{2j} \qquad \text{for } j \geqq 3, \end{aligned} \tag{5.5}$$

in which case the two specifications are equivalent. This special case implies that changes in income and in the prices of other commodities have the same proportionate effect of the consumption of the two commodities, and that a proportional change of the prices P_1 and P_2 has the same proportionate effect on X_1 and X_2.

These conditions are rather drastic, and so it is of some interest to analyse the implications of the more general case in which (5.5) is not fulfilled. Denoting the least-squares estimator of ε by e and applying Theorem 1, we find for the expectation of e:

$$Ee = r_0(\eta_1 - \eta_2) + \sum_{j=1}^{n} r_j(\varepsilon_{1j} - \varepsilon_{2j}), \tag{5.6}$$

where the r's are the multiplicative coefficients of the auxiliary least-squares regressions

$$\begin{aligned} m &= q_0 + r_0(p_1 - p_2) + \text{residual} \\ p_j &= q_j + r_j(p_1 - p_2) + \text{residual} \end{aligned} \tag{5.7}$$

There are no restrictions on the r's, except that $r_1 - r_2 = 1$. It follows that income elasticities (η_1 and η_2) and elasticities with respect to prices of other commodities (ε_{1j} and ε_{2j} for $j \geqq 3$) play a disturbing rôle in the incorrect specification. For the income elasticities, this can be illustrated with the following simple example. Suppose that commodity 1 has a more pronounced luxury character than commodity 2; i.e., $\eta_1 > \eta_2$. Suppose further that its price P_1 rises relative to P_2 in booms, and *vica versa* in depressions. Then, if the period of analysis covers some complete trade cycles, we have $r_0 > 0$ and hence $r_0(\eta_1 - \eta_2) > 0$. The elasticity of substitution is then characterised by an upward specification bias as far as the income variable is concerned.

6. LINEAR VERSUS QUADRATIC RELATIONS

One of the problems with which the econometrician is frequently faced is that of the choice of linear or curvilinear relationships. It is usually difficult to decide on the basis of limited material whether a curvilinear specification should be used. At many occasions, the linear approach is then adopted, first because of the investigator's justifiable desire for simplicity, second because it is frequently believed that, even if the curvilinear specification is correct, the coefficients of the linear specification are at least adequate for the estimation of slopes in the centre of gravity of the observed point set. The present and the final section will be devoted in particular to the latter aspect.

First, we shall assume that the correct specification is quadratic:

$$y = \alpha_0 + \alpha_1 x + \alpha_2 x^2 + u, \tag{6.1}$$

whereas the specification used is linear. So we shall be interested in the slope of the regression of y on x (b, say). Applying Theorem 1, we find that the only auxiliary regression which is not trivial is

$$x^2 = q + rx + \text{residual}, \tag{6.2}$$

after which the expectation of b becomes $Eb = \alpha_1 + \alpha_2 r$. The coefficient r can be conveniently expressed in terms of moments of the independent variable. Writing $\bar{x}$ for the mean of its T values and μ_k for its k-th moment about the mean, we have

$$r = \frac{\mu_3}{\mu_2} + 2\,\bar{x} = \bar{x}(2 + \gamma_1 v),$$

where γ_1 is the Pearsonian measure of skewness, $\mu_3/\mu_2^{3/2}$, and v the coefficient of variation $\mu_2^{1/2}/\bar{x}$. Hence

$$Eb = \alpha_1 + \alpha_2\bar{x}\,(2+\gamma_1 v)\,. \tag{6.3}$$

But the slope in the centre of gravity according to the correct specification, (6.1), is $\alpha_1 + 2\,\alpha_2\bar{x}$. Our conclusion is, therefore, that the regression coefficient of the linear specification is an unbiased estimator of the slope in the centre of gravity if, and only if, the distribution of the independent variable is symmetric. When this condition is not met, there is a specification bias of b with respect to the slope in the centre of gravity. If α_2 and γ_1 have the same sign, this bias is upward; otherwise, downward.

7. LINEAR VERSUS LOGARITHMICALLY LINEAR RELATIONS

Our final application, viz. that of a correct specification which is linear in the logarithms and an incorrect specification which is linear in the variables themselves, is interesting because, contrary to the preceding examples, Theorem 1 is not immediately applicable. Let us write for the correct specification:

$$\log y = \alpha + \beta \log x + u, \tag{7.1}$$

and suppose that the least-squares regression adopted is that of y on x (which leads to a multiplicative coefficient b', say). The difficulty is that the left-hand dependent variables of the two competing specifications ($\log y$ and y) are not the same. So the assumptions of Theorem 1 are not satisfied. However, we can re-formulate our problem such that the difficulty is avoided. Let us write (7.1) in the form

$$y = A\, x^{\beta} e^{u}, \tag{7.2}$$

where $A = e^{\alpha}$. Consider then the following Taylor expansion:[1]

$$ye^{-u} = Ax^{\beta} = A\left[x_0^{\beta} + \beta x_0^{\beta-1}(x-x_0) + \frac{\beta(\beta-1)}{2!}x_0^{\beta-2}(x-x_0)^2 + \dots\right]$$

$$= y_0\left[1 + \beta\frac{x-x_0}{x_0} + \frac{\beta(\beta-1)}{2!}\left\{\frac{x-x_0}{x_0}\right\}^2 + \dots\right],$$

where x_0 is an arbitrary positive number and $y_0 = Ax_0^{\beta}$. So we have

$$y = y_0\left[1 + \beta\frac{x-x_0}{x_0} + \frac{\beta(\beta-1)}{2!}\left\{\frac{x-x_0}{x_0}\right\}^2 + \dots\right]\sum_0^{\infty}\frac{u^r}{r!}\,. \tag{7.3}$$

---

[1] We assume that appropriate convergence conditions are met. For the present analysis this means (cf. the choice $x_0 = \bar{x}$ in a later part of this section) that the highest x-value should be smaller than twice the average $\bar{x}$. If this condition is not satisfied, the observations with the highest x-values should be deleted such that it is satisfied.

Furthermore, we write

$$Y_0 = y_0 \sum_0^\infty \frac{u^r}{r\,!}$$

$$Y_1 = y_0\, \beta \frac{x - x_0}{x_0} \sum_0^\infty \frac{u^r}{r\,!}$$

$$\ldots\ldots\ldots,$$

so that

$$y = \sum_0^\infty Y_k\,. \tag{7.4}$$

We shall consider each of the Y's separately as linear functions of $(x - x_0)/x_0$ – and hence of x –, after we shall obtain y by adding in accordance with (7.4). The result can be simplified considerably if we suppose, in addition to the assumptions of Theorem 1, that the disturbances of (7.1) are normally and independently distributed with common variance σ^2. In that case we have

$$E \sum_0^\infty \frac{u^r}{r\,!} = 1 + \sum_{r=1}^\infty \frac{Eu^{2r}}{(2r)!} = \tag{7.5}$$

$$= 1 + \sum_{r=1}^\infty \frac{1}{(2r)!} \frac{(2r)\,!\,(Eu^2)^r}{r\,!\,2^r} = e^{\frac{1}{2}\sigma^2}\,,$$

where use is made of a well-known identity of the moments of normal distributions.[11]

We proceed to consider the regressions of the Y's on $(x - x_0)/x_0$:

$$Y_k = A_k + B_k \frac{x - x_0}{x_0} + \text{residual} \qquad (k = 0, 1, \ldots). \tag{7.6}$$

The numerical values of the A's and B's depend, of course, on the value of x_0 which is chosen. The further expressions will be simplified if we take $x_0 = \bar{x}$, the mean of the T x-values. We shall do so; and we shall also introduce the moments μ_k of $(x - \bar{x})/\bar{x}$ (not of x). For the expectations of the least-squares B's we then find

$$EB_k = \bar{y} \frac{\beta^{[k]}}{k\,!} \frac{\mu_{k+1}}{\mu_2} e^{\frac{1}{2}\sigma^2} \tag{7.7}$$

where $\bar{y} = A\bar{x}^\beta$, $\mu_1 = 0$ and

$$\beta^{[k]} = \beta(\beta - 1) \ldots (\beta - k + 1)\,.$$

So, after summation in accordance with (7.4), we obtain for the expectation of the estimator b' in the least-squares regression of y on x:

$$Eb' = \frac{\bar{y}}{\bar{x}} e^{\frac{1}{2}\sigma^2} \sum_0^\infty \frac{\beta^{[k]}}{k\,!} \frac{\mu_{k+1}}{\mu_2}\,;$$

and hence the expectation of the elasticity in the centre of gravity is

---

[11] See e.g. [4], p. 39.

$$(7.8)\qquad Ee' = \frac{x}{\bar{y}}\,Eb' = e^{\frac{1}{2}\sigma^2} \sum_{0}^{\infty} \frac{\beta^{[k]}}{k!} \frac{\mu_{k+1}}{\mu_2} =$$

$$= \beta \left\{ 1 + \tfrac{1}{2}(\beta - 1)\frac{\mu_3}{\mu_2} + \tfrac{1}{2}(\beta - 1)(\beta - 2)\frac{\mu_4}{\mu_2} + \ldots \right\} e^{\frac{1}{2}\sigma^2} =$$

$$= \beta \left\{ 1 + \tfrac{1}{2}(\beta - 1)\,\gamma_1 v + \ldots \right\} e^{\frac{1}{2}\sigma^2},$$

where γ_1 and v are the coefficients of skewness and of variation, respectively, of the independent variable x [not of $(x - \bar{x})/\bar{x}$], just as in Section 6. The result (7.8) illustrates the two kinds of specification errors that have been made. The first is concerned with the nonlinearity and is comparable with the specification error of the preceding section; it is measured by the term between curled brackets. Clearly, if $\beta = 1$, there is no specification bias resulting from this source, simply because the relation between y and x is then linear. The second source of error is concerned with the treatment of the disturbances. According to the correct specification, $\log y$ contains a component which is normally distributed with zero mean and constant variance. The specification adopted deals with y, not with $\log y$; and this leads to the factor $e^{\frac{1}{2}\sigma^2}$, which is always > 1, so that it implies, *ceteris paribus*, a bias of e' away from zero.

REFERENCES

[1] Griliches, Z. Specification bias in estimates of production functions. "Journal of farm economics", 39 : 1, p. 8–20, 1957.

[2] Hotelling, H. The selection of variates for use in prediction with some comments on the general problem of nuisance parameters. "Annals of mathem. stat.", 11, p. 271—283, 1940.

[3] Koopmans, T. C., and W. C. Hood. The estimation of simultaneous linear economic relationships. In: "Studies in econometric method", ed. by W. C. Hood and T. C. Koopmans, New York, J. Wiley and Sons, 1953, p. 112—199.

[4] Rao, C. R. *Advanced statistical methods in biometric research.* New York, J. Wiley and Sons, 1952.

[5] Theil, H. *Linear aggregation of economic relations.* Amsterdam, North Holland Publ. Co., 1954.

AN EFFICIENT METHOD OF ESTIMATING SEEMINGLY UNRELATED REGRESSIONS AND TESTS FOR AGGREGATION BIAS*

ARNOLD ZELLNER

In this paper a method of estimating the parameters of a set of regression equations is reported which involves application of Aitken's generalized least-squares [1] to the whole system of equations. Under conditions generally encountered in practice, it is found that the regression coefficient estimators so obtained are at least asymptotically more efficient than those obtained by an equation-by-equation application of least squares. This gain in efficiency can be quite large if "independent" variables in different equations are not highly correlated and if disturbance terms in different equations are highly correlated. Further, tests of the hypothesis that all regression equation coefficient vectors are equal, based on "micro" and "macro" data, are described. If this hypothesis is accepted, there will be no aggregation bias. Finally, the estimation procedure and the "micro-test" for aggregation bias are applied in the analysis of annual investment data, 1935–1954, for two firms.

1. INTRODUCTION

GIVEN a set of regression equations, we consider the problem of estimating regression coefficients efficiently. It is only under special conditions, stated explicitly below, that classical least-squares applied equation-by-equation yields efficient coefficient estimators. For conditions generally encountered, we propose an estimation procedure which yields coefficient estimators at least asymptotically more efficient than single-equation least-squares estimators. In this procedure regression coefficients in all equations are estimated simultaneously by applying Aitken's generalized least-squares [1] to the whole system of equations. To construct such Aitken estimators, we employ estimates

* This paper was written when the author was visiting Fulbright Professor at the Netherlands School of Economics and Associate Professor on leave, University of Wisconsin. It is with much pleasure that he acknowledges the benefit derived from discussions (and cigars) with Professor H. Theil and Mr. P. J. M. van den Bogaard. Thanks are also due to Miss E. van der Hoeven for assistance with the calculations and expert typing.

of the disturbance terms' variances and covariances based on the residuals derived from an equation-by-equation application of least-squares.[1] While we apply this estimation procedure in the analysis of temporal cross-section data, annual micro-investment data, 1935–1954, we recognize that the procedure is more generally applicable. For example, it can be applied in the analysis of data provided by a single cross-section budget study when regressions for several commodities are to be estimated. Another application would be in time-series regression analyses of the demands for a variety of consumption (or investment) goods. A fourth application is to regression equations in which each equation refers to a particular classification category and the observations refer to different points in space, as in Barten and Koerts' analysis of voters' transitions from party to party within various voting districts [2].

Further, within the estimation framework a test of the equality of regression coefficient vectors, and thus of the absence of one important type of aggregation bias, is described and applied in the analysis of micro-investment relations. Like the estimation procedure, this testing procedure is more generally applicable. Finally, a procedure for testing for aggregation bias which utilizes just macro-data is developed.

The plan of the paper is as follows. In Section 2 we describe the system and the proposed estimation procedure. Section 3 is devoted to establishing the properties of estimators constructed in Section 2 and to providing an explicit statement of the gain in efficiency over single-equation least-squares estimation. We then turn to some aspects of the aggregation problem in Section 4, in particular to consideration of two tests for aggregation bias, one employing micro-data, the other macro-data. Then the estimation and one testing procedure are applied in Section 5. Lastly, we present some concluding remarks in Section 6.

2. EFFICIENT ESTIMATION OF SEEMINGLY UNRELATED REGRESSION EQUATIONS

Let

$$y_\mu = X_\mu \beta_\mu + u_\mu \tag{2.1}$$

be the μ'th equation of an M equation regression system with y_μ a $T\times 1$ vector of observations on the μ'th "dependent" variable, X_μ a $T\times l_\mu$ matrix with rank l_μ, of observations on l_μ "independent" nonstochastic variables, β_μ a $l_\mu\times 1$ vector of regression coefficients and u_μ, a $T\times 1$ vector of random error terms, each with mean zero. The system of which (2.1) is an equation may be written as:

$$\begin{bmatrix} y_1 \\ y_2 \\ \vdots \\ y_M \end{bmatrix} = \begin{bmatrix} X_1 & 0 & \cdots & 0 \\ 0 & X_2 & \cdots & 0 \\ \vdots & \vdots & & \vdots \\ 0 & 0 & \cdots & X_M \end{bmatrix} \begin{bmatrix} \beta_1 \\ \beta_2 \\ \vdots \\ \beta_M \end{bmatrix} + \begin{bmatrix} u_1 \\ u_2 \\ \vdots \\ u_M \end{bmatrix} \tag{2.2}$$

$$y = X\beta + u \tag{2.3}$$

[1] This procedure, modified in certain respects, has been applied to estimate the parameters of "simultaneous equation" econometric models in reference [13].

where $y \equiv [y_1' y_2' \cdots y_M']'$, $\beta \equiv [\beta_1' \beta_2' \cdots \beta_M']'$, $u \equiv [u_1' u_2' \cdots u_M']'$ and X represents the block-diagonal matrix on the r.h.s. of (2.2). The $MT \times 1$ disturbance vector in (2.2) and (2.3) is assumed to have the following variance-covariance matrix:

$$\Sigma = V(u) = \begin{bmatrix} \sigma_{11}I & \sigma_{12}I & \cdots & \sigma_{1M}I \\ \sigma_{21}I & \sigma_{22}I & \cdots & \sigma_{2M}I \\ \vdots & \vdots & & \vdots \\ \sigma_{M1}I & \sigma_{M2}I & \cdots & \sigma_{MM}I \end{bmatrix} = \begin{bmatrix} \sigma_{11} & \sigma_{12} & \cdots & \sigma_{1M} \\ \sigma_{21} & \sigma_{22} & \cdots & \sigma_{2M} \\ \vdots & \vdots & & \vdots \\ \sigma_{M1} & \sigma_{M2} & \cdots & \sigma_{MM} \end{bmatrix} \otimes I \qquad (2.4)$$

$$= \Sigma_c \otimes I,$$

where I is a unit matrix of order $T \times T$ and $\sigma_{\mu\mu'} = E(u_{\mu t} u_{\mu' t})$ for $t = 1, 2, \cdots, T$ and $\mu, \mu' = 1, 2, \cdots, M$.

In temporal cross-section regressions, t represents time and (2.3) implies constant variances and covariances from period to period as well as the absence of any auto or serial correlation of the disturbance terms. The $\sigma_{\mu\mu'}$ with $\mu = \mu'$ are then the variances and with $\mu \neq \mu'$ the covariances of the micro-units' disturbance terms (or dependent variables) for any time period. In a single cross-section budget study where t represents the t'th household and each equation "explains" expenditure on a particular commodity, $\sigma_{\mu\mu'}$ is the covariance between the disturbance term in the equation for commodity μ (or expenditure on commodity μ) and that in the equation for commodity μ' (or expenditure on μ') while $\sigma_{\mu\mu}$ is the variance of the disturbance term in the equation for expenditure on commodity μ (or alternatively, the variance of expenditure on commodity μ). The form of (2.4) implies that the $\sigma_{\mu\mu'}$ are the same for all households and that there is no correlation between different households' disturbances (or expenditures). Lastly, in application to geographic problems, t stands for the t'th geographic region and the form of (2.3) is such that there are correlations between disturbances or dependent variables relating to a particular region but not to different regions. Also disturbance variances and covariances are assumed to be constant from region to region.

In a formal sense we now regard (2.2) or (2.3) as a single-equation regression model and apply Aitken's generalized least-squares [1]. That is, we pre-multipy both sides of (2.3) by a matrix H which is such that $E(Huu'H') = H\Sigma H' = I$. In terms of transformed variables, the original variables pre-multiplied by H, the system now satisfies the usual assumptions of the least-squares model. Thus application of least-squares[2] will yield, as is well-known, a best linear unbiased estimator, which is

$$b^* = (X'H'HX)^{-1}X'H'Hy = (X'\Sigma^{-1}X)^{-1}X'\Sigma^{-1}y. \qquad (2.5)$$

In constructing this estimator, we need the inverse of Σ which is given by:

---

[2] The quadratic form to be minimized in the Aitken approach is not the sum of squares of the original disturbance terms but, as is well-known, that of the transformed disturbances, namely $u'H'Hu$, or $u'\Sigma^{-1}u$. As will be pointed out below, there are good common-sense reasons for applying least squares to the transformed variables, reasons which make clear why it is that the Aitken estimator is more efficient than the classical least-squares estimator based on the original variables.

$$\Sigma^{-1} = V^{-1}(u) = \begin{bmatrix} \sigma^{11}I & \cdots & \sigma^{1M}I \\ \vdots & & \vdots \\ \sigma^{M1}I & \cdots & \sigma^{MM}I \end{bmatrix} = \Sigma_c^{-1} \otimes I. \tag{2.6}$$

Then the Aitken estimator of the coefficient vector, given in (2.5), is

$$b^* = \begin{bmatrix} b_1^* \\ b_2^* \\ \vdots \\ b_M^* \end{bmatrix} = \begin{bmatrix} \sigma^{11}X_1'X_1 & \sigma^{12}X_1'X_2 & \cdots & \sigma^{1M}X_1'X_M \\ \sigma^{21}X_2'X_1 & \sigma^{22}X_2'X_2 & \cdots & \sigma^{2M}X_2'X_M \\ \vdots & \vdots & & \vdots \\ \sigma^{M1}X_M'X_1 & \sigma^{M2}X_M'X_2 & \cdots & \sigma^{MM}X_M'X_M \end{bmatrix}^{-1} \times \begin{bmatrix} \sum_{\mu=1}^{M} \sigma^{1\mu}X_1'y_\mu \\ \vdots \\ \sum_{\mu=1}^{M} \sigma^{M\mu}X_M'y_\mu \end{bmatrix} \tag{2.7}$$

and the variance-covariance matrix of the estimator b^* is easily shown to be $(X'\Sigma^{-1}X)^{-1}$ or

$$V(b^*) = \begin{bmatrix} \sigma^{11}X_1'X_1 & \sigma^{12}X_1'X_2 & \cdots & \sigma^{1M}X_1'X_M \\ \sigma^{21}X_2'X_1 & \sigma^{22}X_2'X_2 & \cdots & \sigma^{2M}X_2'X_M \\ \vdots & \vdots & & \vdots \\ \sigma^{M1}X_M'X_1 & \sigma^{M2}X_M'X_2 & \cdots & \sigma^{MM}X_M'X_M \end{bmatrix}. \tag{2.8}$$

The estimator in (2.7) possesses all of the usual optimal properties of Aitken estimators; that is, it is a best linear unbiased estimator.[3] Further, with an added normality assumption, it is also a maximum-likelihood estimator. It is to be noted that (2.6) is identical with estimators provided by single-equation least-squares if the disturbance terms have a diagonal variance-covariance matrix, i.e., if $\sigma_{\mu\mu'} = \sigma_{\mu'\mu} = 0$ for $\mu' \neq \mu$. Also, if $X_1 = X_2 = \cdots = X_M$, (2.6) "collapses" to yield single-equation least-squares estimators even if disturbance terms in different equations are correlated ($\sigma_{\mu'\mu} \neq 0$), and these are, as is well-known, the same as maximum-likelihood estimators. However, when the X_μ are not all the same and when the disturbance terms in different equations are correlated, the estimator in (2.6) will differ from the single-equation least-squares estimators.

If Σ is unknown, as it usually is, it is impossible to use (2.6) and (2.7) in practice. What we propose to do is to employ an estimate of $\{\sigma^{\mu\mu'}\}$ in constructing the Aitken estimator. This estimate is,[4]

---

[3] The single-equation least-squares estimator of the coefficient vector in (2.2) is a member of the linear class of estimators to which the Aitken estimator belongs.

[4] Here, for simplicity, we assume that there are . "independent" variables in each regression. Then the variance estimators in (2.9) will be unbiased. However, the covariance estimators will only be asymptotically unbiased. When the independent variables in different equations are highly correlated, as is the case in many applications, the small-sample bias in the covariance estimators in (2.9) will be small. In reference [14, p. 14] an unbiased covariance estimator is presented.

$$(T-l)\Sigma_e = (T-l)\{s_{\mu\mu'}\} = \{\hat{u}_\mu' \hat{u}_{\mu'}\} = \{(y_\mu - X_\mu\hat{\beta}_\mu)'(y_{\mu'} - X_{\mu'}\hat{\beta}_{\mu'})\} \quad (2.9)$$

where $\hat{\beta}_\mu$ is the usual single-equation least-squares estimator, $(X_{\mu'}X_\mu)^{-1}X_{\mu'}y_\mu$. Thus (2.9) is an estimate of the disturbance variance-covariance matrix formed from the single-equation least-squares residuals. Given that we have the estimate $\{s_{\mu\mu'}\}$, we can obtain by inversion the matrix $\{s^{\mu\mu'}\}$ the elements of which are employed to form the estimator:

$$b = \begin{bmatrix} b_1 \\ b_2 \\ \vdots \\ b_M \end{bmatrix} = \begin{bmatrix} s^{11}X_1'X_1 & s^{12}X_1'X_2 & \cdots & s^{1M}X_1'X_M \\ s^{21}X_2'X_1 & s^{22}X_2'X_2 & \cdots & s^{2M}X_2'X_M \\ \vdots & \vdots & & \vdots \\ s^{M1}X_M'X_1 & s^{M2}X_M'X_2 & \cdots & s^{MM}X_M'X_M \end{bmatrix}^{-1} \begin{bmatrix} \sum_{\mu=1}^{M} s^{1\mu}X_1'y_\mu \\ \vdots \\ \sum_{\mu=1}^{M} s^{M\mu}X_M'y_\mu \end{bmatrix}. \quad (2.10)$$

It will be shown that $b = b^* + 0(T^{-1})$, that $T^{1/2}(b-\beta)$ and $T^{1/2}(b^*-\beta)$ have the same asymptotic normal distribution, and that the moment matrix of b is:

$$V(b) = \begin{bmatrix} s^{11}X_1'X_1 & s^{12}X_1'X_2 & \cdots & s^{1M}X_1'X_M \\ s^{21}X_2'X_1 & s^{22}X_2'X_2 & \cdots & s^{2M}X_2'X_M \\ \vdots & \vdots & & \vdots \\ s^{M1}X_M'X_1 & s^{M2}X_M'X_2 & \cdots & s^{MM}X_M'X_M \end{bmatrix}^{-1} + o(T^{-1}), \quad (2.11)$$

where $0(T^{-1})$ denotes a quantity which is of the order T^{-1} in probability and $o(T^{-1})$ denotes terms of higher order of smallness than T^{-1}.

3. PROPERTIES OF THE TWO-STAGE AITKEN ESTIMATOR

3.1. Moment Matrix and Asymptotic Distribution

We now turn to providing proofs of the statements made at the end of Section 2 regarding the properties of the estimator in (2.9).

Let $\Sigma_e = (\Sigma_c + \Delta_1) \otimes I$ be the estimated disturbance covariance matrix where $\Sigma_c \otimes I$ is given by (2.3) and Δ_1 is a matrix whose elements are the sampling errors of the single-equation least-squares estimators of the elements of Σ_c and these sampling errors are known to be $0(T^{-1/2})$ in probability ($\equiv$i.p.). Thus,

$$\begin{aligned} \Sigma_e^{-1} &= (\Sigma_c + \Delta_1)^{-1} \otimes I = [\Sigma_c^{-1} - \Sigma_c^{-1}\Delta_1\Sigma_c^{-1} + \cdots] \otimes I \\ &= \Sigma^{-1} - \Delta_2 \cdots \end{aligned} \quad (3.1)$$

and

$$\Delta_2 = \left\{ \sum_{i=1}^{M} \sum_{j=1}^{M} \sigma^{\mu i} \delta_{ij}^{(1)} \sigma^{j\mu'} \right\} \otimes I = \{\delta_{\mu\mu'}^{(2)}\} \otimes I$$

where $\delta_{\mu\mu'}^{(2)}$ is $0(T^{-1/2})$ i.p. and terms of higher order of smallness have been neglected. Now the two-stage Aitken estimator is

$$b = (X'\Sigma_e^{-1}X)^{-1}X'\Sigma_e^{-1}y$$

or

$$b - \beta = (X'\Sigma_e^{-1}X)^{-1}X'\Sigma_e^{-1}u$$

where $y \equiv (y_1', y_2', \cdots, y_M')'$, $u \equiv (u_1', u_2', \cdots, u_M')'$, $b \equiv (b_1', b_2', \cdots, b_M')'$, $\beta \equiv (\beta_1', \beta_2', \cdots, \beta_M')'$ and X denotes the block-diagonal matrix on the r.h.s. of (2.2). Then utilizing (3.1), we have

$$\begin{aligned} b - \beta &= [X'(\Sigma^{-1} - \Delta_2)X]^{-1}X'(\Sigma^{-1} - \Delta_2)u \\ &= \{[X'\Sigma^{-1}X][I - (X'\Sigma^{-1}X)^{-1}X'\Delta_2X]\}^{-1}X'(\Sigma^{-1} - \Delta_2)u \qquad (3.2) \\ &= [(X'\Sigma^{-1}X)^{-1} + (X'\Sigma^{-1}X)^{-1}(X'\Delta_2X)(X'\Sigma^{-1}X)^{-1} + \cdots]X'(\Sigma^{-1} - \Delta_2)u \end{aligned}$$

where terms of higher order of smallness than $0(T^{-1\frac{1}{2}})$ have been deleted in the square brackets. Rearranging terms, we find

$$b - \beta = b^* - \beta + \Delta_3, \qquad (3.3)$$

where b^* is the "pure" Aitken estimator and

$$\Delta_3 = -(X'\Sigma^{-1}X)^{-1}X'\Delta_2u + (X'\Sigma^{-1}X)^{-1}X'\Delta_2X(X'\Sigma^{-1}X)^{-1}X'\Sigma^{-1}u, \qquad (3.4)$$

terms of higher order of smallness being again neglected. Considering the second term on the r.h.s. of (3.3) we observe that $X'\Sigma^{-1}u$ is $0(T^{1/2})$ i.p., which means that the term as a whole is $0(T^{-1})$ i.p. The same applies to the first term, for the order of $X'\Delta_2u$ is that of Δ_2 multiplied by that of $X'u$, that is, $0(1)$.

If we then take the expectation of both sides of (3.2), we find that the bias of b is at most of $0(T^{-1})$. Furthermore, since $b^* - \beta$ is $0(T^{-1/2})$ i.p. and Δ_3 is $0(T^{-1})$ i.p., the asymptotic covariance matrix of $b - \beta$ is the same as that of $b^* - \beta$. Finally, since it is known that under general conditions the asymptotic distribution of $T^{1/2}(b^* - \beta)$ is normal, the asymptotic distribution of $T^{1/2}(b - \beta)$ is the same as that of $T^{1/2}(b^* - \beta)$, because the difference of these two quantities, $T^{1/2}\Delta_3$, has zero probability limit; see the convergence theorem in reference [5, p. 254].

3.2. The Gain in Efficiency

Since the Aitken estimator of $\{\beta_2', \beta_2', \cdots, \beta_M'\}'$ in (2.2) differs from that derived by application of least-squares equation-by-equation, it must be the case that the Aitken estimator is more efficient. Essentially, this gain in efficiency occurs because in estimating the coefficients of a single equation, the Aitken procedure takes account of zero restrictions on coefficients occurring in other equations. These zero restrictions can be seen clearly if the system in (2.2) is rewritten as:

$$(y_1 y_2 \cdots y_M) = (X_1 X_2 \cdots X_M)\begin{bmatrix} \beta_1 & 0 & \cdots & 0 \\ 0 & \beta_2 & \cdots & 0 \\ \vdots & \vdots & & \vdots \\ 0 & 0 & \cdots & \beta_M \end{bmatrix} + (u_1 u_2 \cdots u_M). \qquad (3.5)$$

It is instructive to consider a system[5] with a disturbance covariance matrix such that $\sigma_{\mu\mu}=\sigma^2$ and $\sigma_{\mu\mu'}=\sigma^2\rho$ for $\mu\neq\mu'$, or $\Sigma_c=\sigma^2\,[(1-\rho)I+\rho ee']$ where I is a unit matrix of size $M\times M$ and $e'=[1, 1, \cdots, 1]$, a $1\times M$ vector. Then $\Sigma_c^{-1}=\alpha I-\gamma ee'$ with $\alpha^{-1}=\sigma^2(1-\rho)$ and $\gamma=\alpha\rho/[1+(M-1)\rho]$. Then for the covariance matrix of the estimator b^*, we have

$$V(b^*) = [X'(\Sigma_c^{-1}\otimes I)X]^{-1}$$

$$= \begin{bmatrix} (\alpha-\gamma)X_1'X_1 & -\gamma X_1'X_2 & \cdots & -\gamma X_1'X_M \\ -\gamma X_2'X_1 & (\alpha-\gamma)X_2'X_2 & \cdots & -\gamma X_2'X_M \\ \vdots & \vdots & & \vdots \\ -\gamma X_M'X_1 & -\gamma X_M'X_2 & \cdots & (\alpha-\gamma)X_M'X_M \end{bmatrix}^{-1}. \tag{3.6}$$

For the two dimensional case ($M=2$) the covariance matrix of the first equation's coefficient vector estimator is:

$$V(b_1^*) = [(\alpha-\gamma)X_1'X_1 - \frac{\gamma^2}{\alpha-\gamma}X_1'X_2(X_2'X_2)^{-1}X_2'X_1]^{-1} \tag{3.7}$$

and it can be shown that [cf. 14]

$$|V(b_1^*)| = \frac{(1-\rho^2)^{l_1}}{\prod_{\mu=1}^{l_1}(1-\rho^2r_\mu^2)}\,|\sigma^2(X_1'X_1)^{-1}| \tag{3.8}$$

where l_1 is the number of independent variables in the first equation ($l_1\leq l_2$) and r_μ is the μ'th canonical correlation coefficient associated with the sets of variables in X_1 and X_2. Since $0\leq r_\mu^2\leq 1$, it is clear that the generalized variance of b_1^* will be smaller than or equal to $|\sigma^2(X_1'X_1)^{-1}|$, the generalized variance of the "single-equation" least squares estimator of the first equation's coefficient vector. If $r_\mu=0$ for all μ, as would be the case if $X_1'X_2=0$, the expression in (3.6) reduces to $(1-\rho^2)^{l_1}|\sigma^2(X_1'X_1)^{-1}|$ which represents the minimal generalized variance for given ρ and σ^2.

Further from (3.6), with $X_\mu'X_{\mu'}=0$ for $\mu\neq\mu'$, we obtain

$$V(b_1^*) = \left[\frac{1-\rho}{1-\dfrac{\rho}{1+\rho(M-1)}}\right]\sigma^2(X_1'X_1)^{-1} \tag{3.9}$$

and thus as the number of equations, M, approaches infinity with $X_\mu'X_{\mu'}=0$ for $\mu, \mu'=1, 2, \cdots, M$ and $\mu\neq\mu'$, then $V(b_1^*)$ approaches $(1-\rho)\sigma^2(X_1'X_1)^{-1}$.

4. TESTING FOR AGGREGATION BIAS

4.1. Testing with Micro-Data

It is, of course, possible to develop tests of a variety of hypotheses about the

---

[5] This case was suggested to the author by one of the *Journal's* editors (cf. [14] for additional results). Since we have illustrative purposes in mind, we neglect the fact that elements of the disturbance covariance matrix must be estimated.

coefficient vector in (2.2). One particularly important hypothesis in the case that $X_1, X_2, \cdots, X_M$ are all of the same size and represent matrices of observations on particular variables relating to different micro-units is the following one:

$$H_0: \beta_1 = \beta_2 = \cdots = \beta_M. \tag{4.1}$$

The hypothesis in (4.1) states that micro-units are homogeneous insofar as their regression coefficient vectors are concerned. Further if (4.1) is valid, there will be no aggregation bias involved in simple linear aggregation [7, 11]. That is, with simple linear aggregation, we form[6]

$$\bar{y} = \sum_\mu y_\mu, \qquad \bar{X} = \sum_\mu X_\mu$$

and estimate $\bar{\beta}$ in:

$$\bar{y} = \bar{X}\bar{\beta} + \bar{u} \tag{4.2}$$

where

$$\bar{u} = \sum_\mu u_\mu.$$

The expectation of the least-squares estimator of $\bar{\beta}$ is given by:

$$E\bar{b} = \sum_\mu B_\mu \beta_\mu \tag{4.3}$$

where $B_\mu = (\bar{X}'\bar{X})^{-1}\bar{X}'X_\mu$. Clearly

$$\sum_\mu B_\mu = I \quad \text{since} \quad \sum_\mu X_\mu \equiv \bar{X}.$$

Thus if hypothesis (4.1) is true, the expectation of the macro-estimator $\bar{b}$ will be equal to the micro-parameter vector.

In testing (4.1), it is necessary to use a test statistic which takes account of the fact that the disturbances in the micro-regressions are correlated. Fortunately such a test has been described in the literature [10, p. 82]. The test statistic, employed for testing such restrictions on regression systems, is given by:

$$F_{q,n-m} = \frac{n-m}{q} \times \frac{y'\Sigma^{-1}X(X'\Sigma^{-1}X)^{-1}C'[C(X'\Sigma^{-1}X)^{-1}C']^{-1}C(X'\Sigma^{-1}X)^{-1}X'\Sigma^{-1}y}{y'\Sigma^{-1}y - y'\Sigma^{-1}X(X'\Sigma^{-1}X)^{-1}X'\Sigma^{-1}y} \tag{4.4}$$

where n is the number of observations on y, m the number of independent variables, q the number of restrictions on the system, and C the matrix of the restrictions, $C\beta=0$. In terms of the system in (2.2), $n=MT$, $m=Ml$ and $q=(M-1)l$. The restrictions given by the hypothesis (4.1) can be expressed as follows:

---

[6] This convenient matrix representation of this aspect of the aggregation problem is presented by Kloek [7].

$$C\beta = \begin{bmatrix} I & -I & 0\cdots 0 & 0 & 0 \\ 0 & I & -I\cdots 0 & 0 & 0 \\ \cdot & \cdot & \cdot & \cdot & \cdot \\ \cdot & \cdot & \cdot & \cdot & \cdot \\ \cdot & \cdot & \cdot & \cdot & \cdot \\ 0 & 0 & 0\cdots I & -I & 0 \\ 0 & 0 & 0\cdots 0 & I & -I \end{bmatrix} \begin{bmatrix} \beta_1 \\ \beta_2 \\ \cdot \\ \cdot \\ \cdot \\ \cdot \\ \beta_M \end{bmatrix} = \begin{bmatrix} 0 \\ 0 \\ 0 \\ \cdot \\ \cdot \\ \cdot \\ 0 \end{bmatrix}. \tag{4.5}$$

The unit and zero matrices in (4.5) are of order $l \times l$. Thus there are $q=(M-1)l$ restrictions, as stated above. Roy's [10, p. 82] very elegant derivation of this test does not involve the likelihood-ratio approach. However, as shown in a straight-forward manner in Appendix A, the likelihood-ratio approach leads to the same test statistic. If the disturbance covariance matrix were known (4.4) would give an exact test of the hypothesis in (4.1). When an estimate of this matrix is employed in constructing the test statistic, we show in Appendix B that the resulting statistic, say $\tilde{F}$, is equal to the statistic in (4.4) plus an error which is $0(n^{-1/2})$ in probability. Then by a theorem in [5, p. 254], $\tilde{F}$ will have the same asymptotic distribution as $F_{q,n-m}$. But, as shown in Appendix A, $-2 \log \lambda = qF_{q,n-m} + 0(n^{-1})$ where λ is the likelihood ratio for testing the hypothesis in (4.1). It is known [8, p. 259 and 12, p. 151] that $-2 \log \lambda$, and thus $qF_{q,n-m}$ (and $q\tilde{F}$), is asymptotically distributed as $\chi_q^2 = \chi_{(M-1)l}^2$, where $l(M-1)$ is the number of restrictions involved in (4.1).

For small samples there is some question about how to proceed. We can compute $q\tilde{F}$ and use $q\tilde{F}$'s asymptotic distribution, χ_q^2, assuming that the asymptotic results apply. Another alternative, which may be better, would be to assume that $\tilde{F}$'s distribution is closely approximated by that of $F_{q,n-m}$.[7]

4.2. Testing for Aggregation Bias with Macro-Data

When just macro-data are available, it is customary to estimate a macro-relation, for example that in (4.2), and then to proceed as if no aggregation bias were present. Obviously it would be desirable to have a test of the hypothesis of no aggregation bias, particularly one which employs just macro-data. A test of this sort is developed below. Initially, we restrict ourselves to consideration of a simple system involving two micro-regressions, each with one independent variable:

$$\begin{cases} y_1(t) = \beta_{11}x_{11}(t) + \beta_{10} + u_1(t) \\ y_2(t) = \beta_{21}x_{21}(t) + \beta_{20} + u_2(t). \end{cases} \tag{4.6}$$

The corresponding macro-relation, obtained by adding these two micro-equations, is:

$$\bar{y}(t) = \left[\frac{\beta_{11}x_{11}(t) + \beta_{21}x_{21}(t)}{x_{11}(t) + x_{21}(t)}\right]\bar{x}(t) + \beta_0 + \bar{u}(t) \tag{4.7}$$

where, as before, a bar over a variable denotes a sum of micro-variables. Now it is seen that the coefficient of $\bar{x}(t)$ in (4.9) is a weighted average of β_{11} and

[7] A similar problem arises in connection with the small-sample properties of identifiability test statistics in reference [3].

β_{21} with weights $w_1(t) = x_{11}(t)/[x_{11}(t)+x_{21}(t)]$ and $1-w_1(t)$. Introducing these weights explicitly, (4.7) becomes:

$$\bar{y}(t) = \beta_{21}\bar{x}(t) + (\beta_{11} - \beta_{21})w_1(t)\bar{x}(t) + \beta_0 + \bar{u}(t). \tag{4.8}$$

If data are available giving $w_1(t)$, $t=1, 2, \cdots, T$, it is possible to form the variable $w_1(t)\bar{x}(t)$, run the regression in (4.8), and test the hypothesis that the coefficient of $w_1(t)\bar{x}(t)$ is equal to zero. This is a test of the hypothesis $\beta_{11}=\beta_{21}$ and if accepted as true means that no aggregation bias is present. In a practical case, $w_1(t)$ might be a firm's proportion of industry sales in year t. Data on market shares might be available while micro-data on certain "dependent" variables might not be available.

If data on $w_1(t)$ are not available, it may be that an investigator is willing to stipulate on *a priori* theoretical grounds or on some other basis that $w_1(t)$ is a function of a variable for which data are available. To be specific suppose $w_1(t) = \alpha_0 + \alpha_1 Z(t)$.[8] On substituting in (4.8) we obtain:

$$\bar{y}(t) = [\beta_{21} + \alpha_0(\beta_{11} - \beta_{21})]\bar{x}(t) + (\beta_{11} - \beta_{21})\alpha_1 Z(t)\bar{x}(t) + \beta_0 + \bar{u}(t). \tag{4.9}$$

Now, regressing[9] $\bar{y}(t)$ on $\bar{x}(t)$ and $Z(t)\bar{x}(t)$ and testing the hypothesis that the coefficient of the second variable is zero constitutes a test of the hypothesis of equality of micro-parameters and thus of no aggregation bias.

This testing procedure can easily be extended to cover more complicated specifications. For example, if there are M micro-regressions in (4.6) rather than two, (4.7) becomes:

$$\bar{y}(t) = \beta_{M1}\bar{x}(t) + \sum_{i=1}^{M-1} (\beta_{i1} - \beta_{M1})w_i(t)\bar{x}(t) + \beta_0 + \bar{u}(t) \tag{4.10}$$

where $w_i(t) = x_{i1}(t)/\bar{x}(t)$. If we now have $w_i(t) = \alpha_{0i} + \alpha_i Z(t)$, this last expression becomes

$$\begin{aligned}\bar{y}(t) = &\left[\beta_{M1} + \sum_{i=1}^{M-1} (\beta_{i1} - \beta_{M1})\alpha_{0i}\right]\bar{x}(t) \\ &+ \left[\sum_{i=1}^{M-1} (\beta_{i1} - \beta_{M1})\alpha_i\right] Z(t)\bar{x}(t) + \beta_0 + \bar{u}(t).\end{aligned} \tag{4.11}$$

Again a simple regression of $\bar{y}(t)$ on $\bar{x}(t)$ and $Z(t)\bar{x}(t)$ is all that is needed to test the hypothesis of micro-parameter equality. Further, the procedure can be extended to apply to systems with more than one independent variable in each regression. In all cases, however, the application of the test is conditional upon there being meaningful relations between the weights, the w_i, and some variable or variables for which data are available.

5. APPLICATION OF METHODS TO INVESTMENT DEMAND

To illustrate the methods described above, we utilize the investment equation developed by Grunfeld [6] and described in Boot and de Witt [4]. Grunfeld's

[8] If this relation is stochastic, say, $w_1(t) = \alpha_0 + \alpha_1 Z(t) + v(t)$, where $v(t)$ is a stochastic disturbance term, the approach shown below leads to a regression model in which one (or some) of the independent variables have "measurement error." Problems of estimation and testing associated with such models are not considered in this paper.

[9] It is assumed that $Z(t)$ is an exogenous variable. Or alternatively, $Z(t)$ can be a polynomial in exogenous variables.

investment function involves a firm's current gross investment, $I(t)$, being dependent on the firm's beginning-of-year capital stock, $C(t-1)$ and the value of its outstanding shares at the beginning of the year, $F(t-1)$. That is, the micro-investment function is:

$$I(t) = \alpha_0 + \alpha_1 C(t-1) + \alpha_2 F(t-1) + u(t), \qquad t = 1, 2, \cdots, T. \quad (5.1)$$

Herein we present estimates of (5.1) for two firms, General Electric and Westinghouse, by the method described above and by single-equation least-squares. The annual data, 1935–1954, are taken from reference [4].

For convenience we relabel the variables as follows:

Firm	$I(t)$	$C(t-1)$	$F(t-1)$	1
General Electric	$y_1(t)$	$x_{11}(t)$	$x_{12}(t)$	$x_{13}(t)$
Westinghouse	$y_2(t)$	$x_{21}(t)$	$x_{22}(t)$	$x_{23}(t)$

The equation system to be estimated is then:

$$\begin{bmatrix} y_1 \\ y_2 \end{bmatrix} = \begin{bmatrix} X_1 & 0 \\ 0 & X_2 \end{bmatrix} \begin{bmatrix} \beta_1 \\ \beta_2 \end{bmatrix} + \begin{bmatrix} u_1 \\ u_2 \end{bmatrix},$$

where $X_1(t) = [x_{11}(t) x_{12}(t) x_{13}(t)]$, $x_2(t) = [x_{21}(t) x_{22}(t) x_{23}(t)]$, $\beta_1' = [\beta_{11}\beta_{12}\beta_{10}]$ and $\beta_2' = [\beta_{21}\beta_{22}\beta_{20}]$. Let $Z_1 = [y_1 X_1]$ and $Z_2 = [y_2 X_2]$ and $Z = [Z_1 Z_2]$. In our case we have for the submatrices[10] of $Z'Z$:

$$\left[\begin{array}{c|c} y_1'y_1 & y_1'X_1 \\ \hline X_1'y_1 & X_1'X_1 \end{array}\right] = \left[\begin{array}{c|ccc} 254113.50 & 1005863.46 & 4093308.29 & 2045.8 \\ \hline & 4395946.84 & 15769824.07 & 8003.2 \\ & & 78628914.21 & 38826.5 \\ & & & 20 \end{array}\right]$$

$$\left[\begin{array}{c|c} y_1'y_2 & y_1'X_2 \\ \hline X_1'y_2 & X_1'X_2 \end{array}\right] = \left[\begin{array}{c|ccc} 103869.607 & 221467.99 & 1531586.94 & 2045.8 \\ \hline 413156.104 & 974281.31 & 6153588.29 & 8003.2 \\ 1719503.680 & 3369944.27 & 27247303.72 & 38826.5 \\ 857.83 & 1712.8 & 13418.2 & 20 \end{array}\right]$$

$$\left[\begin{array}{c|c} y_2'y_2 & y_2'X_2 \\ \hline X_2'y_2 & X_2'X_2 \end{array}\right] = \left[\begin{array}{c|ccc} 43732.4023 & 90592.412 & 643262.570 & 857.83 \\ \hline & 220345.72 & 1344261.18 & 1712.8 \\ & & 9942109.78 & 13418.2 \\ & & & 20 \end{array}\right]$$

and the remaining one is just the transpose of one already shown above.

---

[10] Just the upper parts of symmetric matrices are shown. It should be noted that the elements of y_2 are given to two decimal places in the original data whereas all other data are given accurate to one decimal place.

We first compute the single-equation least-squares estimates in the usual way to obtain:

$$\hat{\beta}_1 = \begin{bmatrix} \hat{\beta}_{11} \\ \hat{\beta}_{12} \\ \hat{\beta}_{10} \end{bmatrix} = \begin{bmatrix} 0.151693870 \\ 0.026551189 \\ -9.956306513 \end{bmatrix} \text{ and } \hat{\beta}_2 = \begin{bmatrix} \hat{\beta}_{21} \\ \hat{\beta}_{22} \\ \hat{\beta}_{20} \end{bmatrix} = \begin{bmatrix} 0.092406491 \\ 0.052894127 \\ -0.509390038 \end{bmatrix}.$$

To get the estimated disturbance covariance matrix conveniently, we write

$$[y_1 \; y_2] = [X_1 \; X_2] \begin{bmatrix} \hat{\beta}_1 & 0 \\ 0 & \hat{\beta}_2 \end{bmatrix} + [\hat{u}_1 \; \hat{u}_2]$$

or

$$Y = XB + \hat{U}.$$

Then,

$$\begin{aligned} \hat{U}'\hat{U} &= (Y - XB)'(Y - XB) = Y'Y - B'X'XB \\ &= \begin{bmatrix} y_1'y_1 & y_1'y_2 \\ y_2'y_1 & y_2'y_2 \end{bmatrix} - \begin{bmatrix} \hat{\beta}_1'X_1'X_1\hat{\beta}_1 & \hat{\beta}_1'X_1'X_2\hat{\beta}_2 \\ \hat{\beta}_2'X_2'X_1\hat{\beta}_1 & \hat{\beta}_2'X_2'X_2\hat{\beta}_2 \end{bmatrix} \\ &= \begin{bmatrix} 13216.5899 & 3988.0118 \\ & 1821.2808 \end{bmatrix}, \end{aligned}$$

which is equal to $(T-3)\{s_{\mu\mu'}\}$ where $T=20$, the number of observations on each variable. We now invert this last matrix to obtain $(T-3)^{-1}\{s^{\mu\mu'}\}$:

$$(T-3)^{-1}\{s^{\mu\mu'}\} = \begin{bmatrix} .000223009584 & -.0004883319216 \\ & .00161832608 \end{bmatrix}.$$

We can now obtain the estimate of the moment matrix of the two-stage Aitken estimators by forming and inverting the following matrix:

$$\begin{bmatrix} s^{11}X_1'X_1 & s^{12}X_1'X_2 \\ s^{21}X_2'X_1 & s^{22}X_2'X_2 \end{bmatrix}.$$

The inverse of this last matrix is shown below. Elements on the diagonal are estimated coefficient estimator variances while off-diagonal elements are estimated covariances.

$$\left[\begin{array}{ccc:ccc} .0006006 & -.0000360 & -.1704 & .0007562 & -.0000197 & -.0515761 \\ & .0001885 & -.3516 & -.0003914 & .0001447 & -.0635894 \\ & & 789.6028 & .4573140 & -.2731373 & 155.8156 \\ \hdashline & & & .0026914 & -.0005191 & .1177480 \\ & & & & .0001972 & -.0878539 \\ & & & & & 54.2149 \end{array}\right]$$

To obtain two-stage Aitken coefficient estimates, we multiply the last matrix into the following vector:

$$\begin{bmatrix} s^{11}X_1'y_1 + s^{12}X_1'y_2 \\ s^{21}X_2'y_1 + s^{22}X_2'y_2 \end{bmatrix} = (T-3)\begin{bmatrix} 22.565127 \\ 73.180290 \\ 0.037338 \\ \cdot\;\cdot\;\cdot\;\cdot\;\cdot \\ 38.460988 \\ 293.105260 \\ 0.389245 \end{bmatrix}.$$

The point estimates so obtained along with their estimated variances are shown in Table 1. Also shown are the single-equation least-squares estimates and their estimated variances.

TABLE 1. RESULTS OF TWO-STAGE AITKEN AND SINGLE-EQUATION LEAST-SQUARES ESTIMATION OF MICRO-INVESTMENT FUNCTIONS

Micro-unit	Coefficient of	Two-Stage Aitken Method		Single-Equation Least-Squares	
		Coefficient estimate	Variance of coefficient estimator	Coefficient estimate	Variance of coefficient estimator
General Electric	C-1	.1326	.0006006	.1517	.0006605
	F-1	.0421	.0001885	.0266	.0002423
	1	−32.4807	789.6	−9.9563	984.1
Westinghouse	C-1	.0459	.002691	.0924	.003147
	F-1	.0611	.0001972	.0529	.0002468
	1	−2.0113	54.21	−.5094	64.24

It is seen from the results in Table 1 that application of the estimation procedure described above has resulted in a significant reduction (about 20 per cent) in the estimated coefficient estimator variances as compared with those of single-equation least-squares. The estimated correlation between the disturbances in the two equations is 0.81. Thus from what has been said in Section 3.2, the maximum gain to be expected is approximately $1-(0.81)^2=034$ times the single-equation estimated variances. That the maximum gain was not realized is due to the fact that $X_1'X_2\neq 0$.

We note also in Table 1 that the point estimates yielded by the two methods differ. This is to be expected since different quadratic forms are minimized in the two approaches and also, obviously, if one method is more efficient than another, the estimates yielded by the two methods cannot always, or even usually, be identical. What it is important to realize is that it makes good sense to use the Aitken quadratic form. In this form we have weighted deviations;

that is, the data in the sample are not all given the same weight but are weighted by elements of the covariance matrix's inverse. In a single-equation case with heteroscedasticity present, this means weighting the square of each deviation by the reciprocal of its variance, an extremely sensible procedure. With the use of direct least-squares, all squared deviations are given the same weight, a rather unsatisfactory weighting of the evidence in the sample. Similar considerations apply to use of Aitken's quadratic form in connection with equation systems.

We now turn to an application of the test for micro-parameter equality, described in Section 4.1. In the present application, the numerator of the test statistic is from (4.4):

$$M(T-l)\left[\sum_{\mu=1}^{2} y_\mu' s^{\mu 1} X_1 \quad \sum_{\mu=1}^{2} y_\mu' s^{\mu 2} X_2\right]\begin{bmatrix} X_1'X_1 s^{11} & X_1'X_2 s^{12} \\ X_2'X_1 s^{21} & X_2'X_2 s^{22}\end{bmatrix}^{-1}\begin{bmatrix} I \\ -I\end{bmatrix} \tag{5.2}$$

$$\times\left\{[I \quad -I]\begin{bmatrix} X_1'X_1 s^{11} & X_1'X_2 s^{12} \\ X_2'X_1 s^{21} & X_2'X_2 s^{22}\end{bmatrix}^{-1}\begin{bmatrix} I \\ -I\end{bmatrix}\right\}^{-1}$$

$$\times [I \quad -I]\begin{bmatrix} X_1'X_1 s^{11} & X_1'X_2 s^{12} \\ X_2'X_1 s^{21} & X_2'X_2 s^{22}\end{bmatrix}^{-1}\begin{bmatrix} \sum_{\mu=1}^{2} X_1' s^{1\mu} y_\mu \\ \sum_{\mu=1}^{2} X_2' s^{2\mu} y_\mu\end{bmatrix}$$

where $s^{\mu\mu'}$ has been substituted for $\sigma^{\mu\mu'}$; $M=2$, $l=3$, $T-l=17$ and the unit matrices are of size 3×3. Most of the expressions appearing have already been computed in the estimation of the system. However, the second inverse appearing in the expression must be computed. We have

$$A = [I \quad -I]\begin{bmatrix} X_1'X_1 s^{11} & X_1'X_2 s^{12} \\ X_2'X_1 s^{21} & X_2'X_2 s^{22}\end{bmatrix}^{-1}\begin{bmatrix} I \\ -I\end{bmatrix} = [I \quad -I]\begin{bmatrix} B_{11} & B_{12} \\ B_{21} & B_{22}\end{bmatrix}\begin{bmatrix} I \\ -I\end{bmatrix}$$
$$= [(B_{11} - B_{21}) - (B_{12} - B_{22})],$$

where the definition of B_{ij} is obvious and the inverse of A is:[11]

$$(T-3)^{-1}A^{-1} = \begin{bmatrix} 86.805843 & 264.059312 & .125732 \\ & 1573.005191 & .531040 \\ & & .000321 \end{bmatrix}.$$

Then we form

$$\begin{bmatrix} B_{11} & B_{12} \\ B_{21} & B_{22}\end{bmatrix}\begin{bmatrix} I \\ -I\end{bmatrix} A^{-1}[I \quad -I]\begin{bmatrix} B_{11} & B_{12} \\ B_{21} & B_{22}\end{bmatrix}$$
$$= \begin{bmatrix} (B_{11} - B_{12})A^{-1}(B_{11} - B_{21}) & (B_{11} - B_{12})A^{-1}(B_{12} - B_{22}) \\ (B_{21} - B_{22})A^{-1}(B_{11} - B_{21}) & (B_{21} - B_{22})A^{-1}(B_{12} - B_{22}) \end{bmatrix},$$

a symmetric matrix which we calculated as, $(T-3)^{-1}$ times

[11] The factor $(T-3)^{-1}$ comes in since we have used $(T-3)^{-1}\{s^{\mu\mu'}\}$ rather than $\{s^{\mu\mu'}\}$.

$$\begin{bmatrix} .004370 & .000520 & -3.278245 & .007015 & .000798 & -1.258503 \\ & .002809 & -5.853262 & -.005526 & .002064 & -.957263 \\ & & 13326.484 & 7.392666 & -4.519575 & 2552.105 \\ & & & .039913 & -.007692 & 1.620036 \\ & & & & .002956 & -1.369759 \\ & & & & & 824.893611 \end{bmatrix}.$$

The last step in calculation of the numerator is to pre- and postmultiply this last matrix by the vectors shown in (5.2) which are given above. The result is 0.582278 which must be multiplied by $M(T-1)=2(17)=34$ to yield $19.797(T-3)$ which is the value of the numerator of the test statistic.

The denominator of the test statistic in (4.4) is, with $s^{\mu\mu'}$ replacing $\sigma^{\mu\mu'}$:

$$(M-1)l\left\{\left[\sum_{\mu=1}^{2} y_\mu' s^{\mu 1} y_1 + \sum_{\mu=1}^{2} y_\mu' s^{\mu 2} y_2\right] - \left[\sum_{\mu=1}^{2} y_\mu' s^{\mu 1} X_1 \quad \sum_{\mu=1}^{2} y_\mu' s^{\mu 2} X_2\right]\right. \tag{5.3}$$

$$\times \begin{bmatrix} X_1' X_1 s^{11} & X_1' X_2 s^{12} \\ X_2' X_1 s^{21} & X_2' X_2 s^{22} \end{bmatrix}^{-1} \begin{bmatrix} \sum_{\mu=1}^{2} X_1' s^{1\mu} y_\mu \\ \sum_{\mu=1}^{2} X_2' s^{2\mu} y_\mu \end{bmatrix}.$$

Everything in this last expression has been computed with the exception of:

$$(T-3)^{-1}\left[\sum_{\mu=1}^{2} y_\mu' s^{\mu 1} y_1 + \sum_{\mu=1}^{2} y_\mu' s^{\mu 2} y_2\right] = 26.000130.$$

Then by direct operations, (5.3) is calculated to be equal to

$$(M-1)l(1.911752)(T-3) = 3(1.911752)(T-3) = 5.735(T-3).$$

We now have:

$$\tilde{F} = \frac{19.797}{5.735} = 3.452.$$

As mentioned above, there are at least two alternative procedures, each with its own approximations, which are candidates for testing the hypothesis in (4.1): (a) we can utilize the fact that $q\tilde{F}$ is, as shown in Appendix B, asymptotically distributed as χ_q^2 with $q=(M-1)1=3$; or (b) we can assume that since $\tilde{F}$ and $F_{q,n-m}$ differ by an amount which is $0(T^{-1/2})$ i.p. the distribution of $\tilde{F}$ will be closely approximated by that of $F_{q,n-m}$. The relevant 95 per cent critical values for (a) and (b) are: $\chi_3^2(.95)=2.605$ and $F_{3,34}(.95)=2.88$. Thus, in this case, both procedures lead to rejection, at the 95 per cent level, of the hypothesis of regression-coefficient vector equality and, therefore, in simple aggregation bias will probably be present.[12]

[12] The macro-test for aggregation is not applied since in this instance no meaningful relations for the weights (see above) are available.

6. CONCLUDING REMARKS

We have presented a method of estimating coefficients in *generally encountered* sets of regression equations which is more efficient than an equation-by-equation application of least-squares. Application of this method to estimate micro-investment functions[13] has led to estimates of coefficient estimator variances about 20 per cent smaller than those of equation-by-equation least-squares. Such a substantial reduction in these variances is indeed a satisfying feature of the application shown above, a feature which will characterize those applications to systems in which the disturbances of different equations are highly correlated and the independent variables of different equations are not highly correlated. Further, while we have applied (and also discussed) the procedure for only the situation involving one regression per micro-unit, it is also possible to extend the method to situations in which these are several regressions per micro-unit.

Lastly, we have described two tests for aggregation bias, one a "micro-test," the other a "macro-test." The micro-test which takes account of the fact that an estimated disturbance covariance matrix is employed in the test statistic involves test of an important hypothesis, namely that, in our application, different micro-units are characterized by the same regression coefficients. Clearly this is important knowledge and the test which provides it should be applied. Finally, the macro-test for aggregation bias, described above, requires knowledge that certain auxiliary relations are true. This is, at present, a weakness of this test. How one proceeds when one is uncertain about the validity of these auxiliary relations is an open question. Then, too, when the auxiliary relations are stochastic, other problems arise, as noted above. These are issues which will receive attention in future work.

APPENDIX

A. LIKELIHOOD-RATIO TEST FOR MICRO-REGRESSION COEFFICIENT VECTOR EQUALITY

Under the hypothesis (4.1), $\beta_1 = \beta_2 = \cdots = \beta_M$, the system in (2.2) can be written as

$$\begin{bmatrix} y_1 \\ \vdots \\ y_M \end{bmatrix} = \begin{bmatrix} X_1 \\ \vdots \\ X_M \end{bmatrix} \beta_1 + \begin{bmatrix} u_1 \\ \vdots \\ u_M \end{bmatrix},$$

or

$$y = Z\beta_1 + u.$$

Now transform variables by premultiplication by H where H is such that $E(Huu'H') = \sigma_\omega^2 I$. Let $Hy = \dot{y}$, $HZ = \dot{Z}$ and $Hu = \dot{u}$. Then we have for the likelihood function under the hypothesis, $L(\omega)$,

[13] It is possible to employ the coefficient estimates to obtain a new estimate of the disturbance covariance matrix and then a new set of coefficient estimates, and so on. The small-sample properties of this iterative procedure have not as yet been established.

$$L(\omega) = (2\pi)^{-\frac{1}{2}MT}(\sigma_\omega^2)^{\frac{1}{2}MT} \exp\left[-\tfrac{1}{2}\dot{u}'\dot{u}/\sigma_\omega^2\right]. \tag{A.1}$$

When maximum-likelihood estimators are substituted in (A.1), we obtain

$$L(\hat{\omega}) = (2\pi)^{-\frac{1}{2}MT}(\hat{\sigma}_\omega^2)^{-\frac{1}{2}MT} \exp\left[-\tfrac{1}{2}MT\right]$$

where $\hat{\sigma}_\omega^2 = (1/MT)\hat{u}'\hat{u} = (1/MT)(\dot{y} - \dot{Z}b_1)'(\dot{y} - \dot{Z}b_1)$ and $b_1 = (\dot{Z}'\dot{Z})^{-1}\dot{Z}'\dot{y}$.

Under the hypothesis Ω involving no restrictions on the coefficients, we have the system in (2.3). Again we transform the variables by premultiplication by H to obtain:

$$\dot{y} = \dot{X}\beta + \dot{u},$$

where $\dot{y} = Hy$, $\dot{X} = HX$ and $\dot{u} = Hu$. The likelihood function now is:

$$L(\Omega) = (2\pi)^{-\frac{1}{2}MT}(\sigma_\Omega^2)^{-\frac{1}{2}MT} \exp\left[-\tfrac{1}{2}\dot{u}'\dot{u}/\sigma_\Omega^2\right]$$

which upon substitution of maximum-likelihood estimates becomes:

$$L(\hat{\Omega}) = (2\pi)^{-\frac{1}{2}MT}(\hat{\sigma}_\Omega^2)^{-\frac{1}{2}MT} \exp\left[-\tfrac{1}{2}MT\right]$$

where $\hat{\sigma}_n^2 = (1/MT)\dot{u}'\dot{u} = (1/MT)(\dot{y} - \dot{X}b)'(\dot{y} - \dot{X}b)$ and $b = (\dot{X}'\dot{X})^{-1}\dot{X}'\dot{y}$.

The estimated likelihood ratio, λ, is then

$$\lambda = \frac{L(\hat{\omega})}{L(\hat{\Omega})} = \frac{(\hat{\sigma}_\omega^2)^{-\frac{1}{2}MT}}{(\hat{\sigma}_\Omega^2)^{-\frac{1}{2}MT}}$$

and

$$-2\log\lambda = MT\log\left(\frac{\hat{\sigma}_\omega^2}{\hat{\sigma}_\Omega^2}\right),$$

which is asymptotically distributed as $\chi^2_{(M-1)l}$ [cf. 8, p. 259 and 12, p. 151.].

We must now show that

$$\frac{\hat{\sigma}_\omega^2}{\hat{\sigma}_\Omega^2} = 1 + \frac{q}{n-m} F_{q,n-m} \tag{A.2}$$

where $F_{q,n-m}$ is given by (4.4) and $q = (M-1)l$ and $n - m = M(T - l)$. If (A.2) holds, we can write [cf. 8, p. 262]

$$\begin{aligned} n\log\frac{\hat{\sigma}_\omega^2}{\hat{\sigma}_\Omega^2} &= n\log\left[1 + \frac{q}{n-m}F_{q,n-m}\right] \\ &= \frac{nq}{n-m}F_{q,n-m} - n\left(\frac{q}{n-m}\right)^2 F_{q,n-m}^2 + \cdots \\ &= qF_{q,n-m} + 0(n^{-1}) \end{aligned}$$

and then by the convergence theorem in Cramer [5, p. 254], $n \log \hat{\sigma}_\omega^2/\hat{\sigma}_\Omega^2 = MT \log \hat{\sigma}_\omega^2/\hat{\sigma}_\Omega^2$ and $qF_{q,n-m} = (M-1)lF_{(M-1)l,M(T-l)}$ have the same asymptotic distribution, namely χ_q^2.

To show that (A.2) is valid, we write:

$$\frac{q}{n-m} F_{q,n-m} = \frac{\hat{\sigma}_\omega^2 - \hat{\sigma}_\Omega^2}{\hat{\sigma}_\Omega^2}$$

$$= \frac{(\dot{y} - Zb_1)'(\dot{y} - Zb_1) - (\dot{y} - Xb)'(\dot{y} - Xb)}{(\dot{y} - \dot{X}b)'(\dot{y} - \dot{X}b)} \tag{A.3}$$

$$= \frac{b'X'Xb - b_1'Z'Zb_1}{\dot{y}'\dot{y} - b'\dot{X}'\dot{X}b} = \frac{\dot{y}'X(X'X)^{-1}X'\dot{y} - \dot{y}'\dot{Z}(Z'Z)^{-1}Z'\dot{y}}{\dot{y}'\dot{y} - \dot{y}'\dot{X}(\dot{X}'\dot{X})^{-1}\dot{X}'\dot{y}}.$$

Now the denominator of this last expression is $y'\Sigma^{-1}y - y'\Sigma^{-1}X(X'\Sigma^{-1}X)^{-1} \times X'\Sigma^{-1}y$ in terms of the original variables and this is the denominator of $[q/(n-m)]F_{q,n-m}$; see (4.4). The numerator of (A.3) is

$$y'\Sigma^{-1}[X(X'\Sigma^{-1}X)^{-1}X' - Z(Z'\Sigma^{-1}Z)^{-1}Z']\Sigma^{-1}y. \tag{A.4}$$

Now

$$Z = \begin{bmatrix} X_1 \\ X_2 \\ \vdots \\ X_M \end{bmatrix} = \begin{bmatrix} X_1 & 0 & \cdots & 0 \\ 0 & X_2 & \cdots & 0 \\ \vdots & \vdots & & \vdots \\ 0 & 0 & \cdots & X_M \end{bmatrix} \begin{bmatrix} I \\ I \\ \vdots \\ I \end{bmatrix} = XJ$$

where J is a column of unit matrices. Then (A.4) becomes:

$$y'\Sigma^{-1}X[(X'\Sigma^{-1}X)^{-1} - J(J'X'\Sigma^{-1}XJ)^{-1}J']X'\Sigma^{-1}y$$

or

$$y'\Sigma^{-1}X(X'\Sigma^{-1}X)^{-1}[X'\Sigma^{-1}X - X'\Sigma^{-1}XJ(J'X'\Sigma^{-1}XJ)^{-1}J'X'\Sigma^{-1}X] \cdot (X'\Sigma^{-1}X)^{-1}X'\Sigma^{-1}y. \tag{A.5}$$

For (A.5) to be equal to the numerator of $\{q/(n-m)\}F_{q,n-m}$, we must have

$$X'\Sigma^{-1}X - X'\Sigma^{-1}XJ(J'X'\Sigma^{-1}XJ)^{-1}J'X'\Sigma^{-1}X = C'[C(X'\Sigma^{-1}X)^{-1}C']^{-1}C.$$

That this last equality is true is established by premultiplying both sides by $C(X'\Sigma^{-1}X)^{-1}$ to obtain:

$$C[I - J(J'X'\Sigma^{-1}XJ)^{-1}J'X'\Sigma^{-1}X] = C.$$

Then post-multiplying both sides by J to obtain:

$$C[IJ - J] = CJ.$$

From the definition of C and J, it is seen that both sides of the last equation are just zero matrices. Thus the validity of (A.2) is established.

B. DERIVATION OF THE ASYMPTOTIC DISTRIBUTION OF THE TEST STATISTIC EMPLOYED FOR TESTING MICRO-REGRESSION COEFFICIENT VECTOR EQUALITY

In this part we establish that when a consistent estimate Σ_e of Σ is employed in (4.4), the resultant test statistic, say $\tilde{F}$, is equal to $F_{q,n-m}$ plus an error which is of order $n^{-1/2}$ i.p. and thus that they have the same asymptotic distribution. For the denominator of $\tilde{F}$ aside from a multiplicative factor, we have

$$y'\Sigma_e^{-1}y - y'\Sigma_e^{-1}X(X'\Sigma_e^{-1}X)^{-1}X'\Sigma_e^{-1}y \tag{B.1}$$

or, with $\Sigma_e = \Sigma + \Delta_1$,

$$y'(\Sigma + \Delta_1)^{-1}y - y'(\Sigma + \Delta_1)^{-1}X[X'(\Sigma + \Delta_1)^{-1}X]^{-1}X'(\Sigma + \Delta_1)^{-1}y,$$

where Δ_1 is $0(n^{-1/2})$ i.p. We now make the following expansions:

$$(\Sigma + \Delta_1)^{-1} = \Sigma^{-1} - \Sigma^{-1}\Delta_1\Sigma^{-1} + \cdots = \Sigma^{-1} + \Delta_2 \tag{B.2}$$

and

$$\begin{aligned}[X'(\Sigma + \Delta_1)^{-1}X]^{-1} &= [X'(\Sigma^{-1} + \Delta_2)X]^{-1} \\ &= (X'\Sigma^{-1}X)^{-1} - (X'\Sigma^{-1}X)^{-1}X'\Delta_2X(X'\Sigma^{-1}X)^{-1} + \cdots \\ &= (X'\Sigma^{-1}X)^{-1} + \Delta_3,\end{aligned} \tag{B.3}$$

where, i.p., Δ_2 is $0(n^{-1/2})$ and Δ_3 is $0(n^{-1\ 1/2})$. Utilizing these results, (B.1) becomes:

$$y'(\Sigma^{-1} + \Delta_2)y - y'(\Sigma^{-1} + \Delta_2)X[(X'\Sigma^{-1}X)^{-1} + \Delta_3]X'(\Sigma^{-1} + \Delta_2)y$$

or

$$y'\Sigma^{-1}y - y'\Sigma^{-1}X(X'\Sigma^{-1}X)^{-1}X'\Sigma^{-1}y + \Delta_4$$

where Δ_4 is $0(n^{1/2})$ i.p. Thus the expression in (B.1) is equal to the quantity appearing in the denominator of (4.4) plus Δ_4, or $\chi^2_{m-n} + \Delta_4$.

For the numerator of $\tilde{F}$, again aside from a multiplicative factor, we have

$$\begin{aligned}&y'\Sigma_e^{-1}X(X'\Sigma_e^{-1}X)^{-1}C'[C(X'\Sigma_e^{-1}X)^{-1}C']^{-1}C'(X'\Sigma_e^{-1}X)^{-1}X'\Sigma_e^{-1}y \\ &\quad = y'(\Sigma^{-1} + \Delta_2)X(X'\Sigma^{-1}X + X'\Delta_2X)^{-1}C'\{C[(X'\Sigma^{-1}X)^{-1} + \Delta_3]C'\}^{-1} \\ &\quad \times C'(X'\Sigma^{-1}X + X'\Delta_2X)^{-1}X'(\Sigma^{-1} + \Delta_2)y\end{aligned} \tag{B.4}$$

where (B.2) and (B.3) have been employed. Now the following expansions are required:

$$\begin{aligned}(X'\Sigma^{-1}X + X'\Delta_2X)^{-1} &= [I + (X'\Sigma^{-1}X)^{-1}X'\Delta_2X]^{-1}(X'\Sigma^{-1}X)^{-1} \\ &= [I - (X'\Sigma^{-1}X)^{-1}X'\Delta_2X + \cdots](X'\Sigma^{-1}X)^{-1} \\ &= (X'\Sigma^{-1}X)^{-1} + \Delta_5,\end{aligned} \tag{B.5}$$

where Δ_5 is $0(n^{-1\ 1/2})$ i.p., and

$$
\begin{aligned}
\{C[(X'\Sigma^{-1}X)^{-1} + \Delta_3]C'\}^{-1} &= \{C(X'\Sigma^{-1}X)^{-1}C' + C\Delta_3 C'\}^{-1} \\
&= \{I + [C(X'\Sigma^{-1}X)^{-1}C']^{-1}C\Delta_3 C'\}^{-1}[C(X'\Sigma^{-1}X)^{-1}C']^{-1} \\
&= \{I - [C(X'\Sigma^{-1}X)^{-1}C']^{-1}C\Delta_3 C' + \cdots\}[C(X'\Sigma^{-1}X)^{-1}C']^{-1} \\
&= [C(X'\Sigma^{-1}X)^{-1}C']^{-1} + \Delta_6,
\end{aligned} \tag{B.6}
$$

where Δ_6 is $0(n^{1/2})$ i.p. Substituting (B.5) and (B.6) in (B.4), we obtain:

$$
\begin{aligned}
&y'(\Sigma^{-1} + \Delta_2)X[(X'\Sigma^{-1}X)^{-1} + \Delta_5]C'\{[C(X'\Sigma^{-1}X)^{-1}C']^{-1} + \Delta_6\}C' \\
&\qquad\qquad \times [(X'\Sigma^{-1}X)^{-1} + \Delta_5]X'(\Sigma^{-1} + \Delta_2)y
\end{aligned}
$$

which upon expansion becomes

$$
y'\Sigma^{-1}X(X'\Sigma^{-1}X)^{-1}C'[C(X'\Sigma^{-1}X)^{-1}C']^{-1}C'(X'\Sigma^{-1}X)^{-1}X'\Sigma^{-1}y + \Delta_7,
$$

or just the quantity in the numerator of (4.4) plus Δ_7 which is $0(n^{1/2})$ i.p., or $\chi_q^2 + \Delta_7$.

Then we obtain from the above results,

$$
\begin{aligned}
\tilde{F} &= \frac{n-m}{q}\cdot\frac{\chi_q^2 + \Delta_7}{\chi_{n-m}^2 + \Delta_4} = \frac{n-m}{q}\cdot\frac{\chi_q^2}{\chi_{n-m}^2}\left(1 + \frac{\Delta_7}{\chi_q^2}\right)\left(1 + \frac{\Delta_4}{\chi_{n-m}^2}\right)^{-1} \\
&= \frac{n-m}{q}\cdot\frac{\chi_q^2}{\chi_{n-m}^2} + 0(n^{-\frac{1}{2}})
\end{aligned}
$$

since $(1+\Delta_4/\chi_{n-m}^2)^{-1} = 1 - \Delta_4/\chi_{n-m}^2 + \cdots$ and both Δ_7/χ_q^2 and Δ_4/χ_{n-m}^2 are $0(n^{-1/2})$ i.p.

$$
\tilde{F} = F_{q,n-m} + 0(n^{-\frac{1}{2}}). \tag{B.7}
$$

The result in (B.7) gives us some confidence in employing $\tilde{F}$ for our test statistic; however, it must be recognized that there is still some question about the degrees of freedom associated with $\tilde{F}$ in small samples since in our procedure Σ_e is not an independent estimate of Σ. The small-sample properties of $\tilde{F}$ deserve further investigation. Finally, it is to be noted that since the probability limit of the error in (B.7) is zero, $q\tilde{F}$ will have the same asymptotic distribution as $qF_{q,n-m}$, namely, a χ_q^2 as indicated in part A of the Appendix.

REFERENCES

[1] Aitken, A. C., "On Least-Squares and Linear Combination of Observations," *Proceedings of the Royal Society of Edinburgh*, 55 (1934–35), 42–8.

[2] Barten, A. P., and Koerts, J. "Transition Frequencies in Voting Behaviour." Forthcoming Report of the Econometric Institute.

[3] Basmann, R. L., "On Finite Sample Distributions of Generalized Classical Linear Identifiability Test Statistics," *Journal of the American Statistical Association*, 55 (1960), 650–9.

[4] Boot, J. C. G., and de Witt, G. M. "Investment Demand: An Empirical Contribution to the Aggregation Problem," *International Economic Review*, 1 (1960), 3–30.

[5] Cramér, H., *Mathematical Methods of Statistics*. Princeton: Princeton University Press, 1946.

[6] Grunfeld, Y., *The Determinants of Corporate Investment.* Unpublished Ph.D. thesis (University of Chicago, 1958).

[7] Kloek, T., "Note on Convenient Matrix Notations in Multivariate Statistical Analysis and in the Theory of Linear Aggregation." Report 6017 of the Econometric Institute of the Netherlands School of Economics (1960).

[8] Mood, A. M., *Introduction to the Theory of Statistics.* New York: McGraw-Hill Book Company, 1950.

[9] Rao, C. R., *Advanced Statistical Methods in Biometric Research.* New York: John Wiley and Sons, 1952.

[10] Roy, S. N., *Some Aspects of Multivariate Analysis.* New York: John Wiley and Sons, 1957.

[11] Theil, H., *Linear Aggregation of Economic Relations.* Amsterdam: North-Holland Publishing Company, 1954.

[12] Wilks, S. S., *Mathematical Statistics.* Princeton: Princeton University Press, 1943.

[13] Zellner, A., and Theil, H. "Three-Stage Least-Squares: Simultaneous Estimation of Simultaneous Equations." *Econometrica,* 30 (1962), 54-78.

[14] Zellner, A. and Huang, D. S. "Further Properties of Efficient Estimators for Seemingly Unrelated Regression Equations." Systems Formulation and Methodology Workshop Paper 6101, Social Systems Research Institute, University of Wisconsin, 1961, to appear in the *International Economic Review.*

HOW EXTRANEOUS ARE EXTRANEOUS ESTIMATES?

Edwin Kuh and John R. Meyer*

IN order to overcome the harmful effects on regression and correlation estimates of using highly collinear time series observations, and in order to obtain "structurally" more accurate estimates of income elasticities of demand, economic statisticians have turned increasingly to the device of "extraneous estimators." This technique has been most commonly employed in demand studies but also could be used in other applications. In the case of demand functions the procedure has been to obtain the income coefficient from cross-section budget data for which the price variables are presumably constant. Thus an estimate of the partial regression of quantity on income, with price given, is obtained. This cross-section estimate of the income regression-coefficient is then multiplied by the time-series aggregate of income, and the product is in turn subtracted from the annual time series of quantity demanded, to form a new dependent variable. This new dependent variable, as a possibly unintended consequence, usually has a larger variance than the original dependent series, which often displays little variation beyond the simplest trend component. Having been thus "corrected," the dependent series is then regressed against the time series of the price variables to obtain an estimate of the price elasticity of demand.[1]

It should be fairly clear that when the purpose is to make short-run forecasts, the described techniques often may be unnecessary and in many instances could actually prove harmful.[2] Specifically, someone making forecasts need not be especially worried about multicollinearity. If some of the explanatory variables are multicollinear, the prediction interval obtained from such a set of observations will be quite large. By eliminating a number of the collinear variables it will usually be possible to substantially reduce the prediction interval for given values of included independent variables. Of course, while the elimination of collinear explanatory variables will tend to reduce the prediction interval, the actual prediction, *by hypothesis*, will change very little. Hence the pragmatic forecaster might be indifferent to the extent of collinearity, while the more sophisticated forecaster will not be indifferent; both will make similar forecasts and the actual errors of the forecast will be approximately the same.

The combined use of cross-section and time-series data is therefore intended to overcome multicollinearity (which entails the arbitrary "splitting up" of the influence of the explanatory variables) in order to obtain structurally more accurate estimates of the various coefficients. The question, however, can legitimately be asked: Exactly what structure does the statistician seek to estimate? Insofar as demand studies are concerned, it is quite possible, as will shortly be argued at length, that the kind of behavior measured from cross-section

* For helpful comments and discussions on an earlier draft of this paper, we are indebted to John S. Chipman, Gregory Chow, James S. Duesenberry, John Lintner, Guy H. Orcutt, Robert Solow, and Charles Zwick. The authors were aided in preparing this paper by research grants from the School of Industrial Management, Massachusetts Institute of Technology, and Division of Research, Harvard Business School (under a Rockefeller Foundation grant for a Study of Profits and the Functioning of the Economy).

[1] While the techniques used differ in some important respects, the rationale is fully explained in each of the following sources: Richard Stone, *The Measurement of Consumers' Expenditure and Behavior in the United Kingdom 1920–1938* (Cambridge, England, 1954); and particularly J. Durbin, "A Note on Regression When There is Extraneous Information About One of the Coefficients," *Journal of the American Statistical Association*, XLVIII (December 1953), 799–808; Herman Wold and Lars Juréen, *Demand Analysis* (New York, 1953). This method has also been used by J. Tobin, "A Statistical Demand Function for Food in the U.S.A.," *Journal of the Royal Statistical Society*, Series A, CXIII (Part II 1950), 113–41. A comprehensive review article, William C. Hood, "Empirical Studies of Demand," *Canadian Journal of Economics and Political Science*, XXI (August 1955), 309–27, provides a worthwhile reference on the subject. The distinction between long- and short-run estimates is to be found in the useful paper by Richard J. Foote, *Price Elasticity of Demand for Nondurable Goods with Emphasis on Food*, Agricultural Marketing Service Bulletin 96, USDA (Washington, D.C., 1956).

[2] Although none of the people who have used the combined techniques has had short-run forecasting as his immediate goal, it seems useful to indicate how such prediction fits into the scheme of possible objectives.

data is commonly long-run in nature, while that which one observes with annual time-series data is more often of a short-run character. If this proposition is right, it is simply not permissible to combine promiscuously an estimate which reflects one type of structural behavior with data which explicitly reflect a different sort of behavior. It is, of course, conceivable that if the cross-section and time-series models can be fully and accurately specified and, in addition, if the time-series data are transformed (e.g., through averaging or otherwise observing only trend movements), both the cross-section and time-series analyses will yield essentially long-run estimates. The possibilities of achieving such commensurability in practice, however, are severely circumscribed by the immutable presence of technological irreversibilities and other dynamic influences whose measurement and elimination have thus far proved intractable in time-series analyses. The obverse possibility, that of obtaining data on short-run adjustments from a properly designed budget study (e.g., one that included observations only on families that had recently experienced a substantial income change), is somewhat more feasible but of less intrinsic interest.[3] In sum, it is correct to seek information which is not collinear in order to obtain statistically efficient estimates, but it is improper to combine different structures in the effort to overcome this particular obstacle. Ideally, one would wish to find a time-series "experiment" which reflected the desired behavior in a non-collinear manner. Short of such an experiment, the unpleasant characteristics of much time-series information cannot be overcome through the combination of what are fundamentally long-run estimates with those of a short-run character.

It is the purpose of this paper to reconsider the economic and statistical interpretation of the results obtained when these precepts have not been fully observed in existing work, particularly in studies on the demand for food.

[3] Wold alone of those using the technique has clearly recognized the validity of these propositions. He therefore used absolute price series and did not remove any trend effects (Wold and Juréen, 240–42). However, in periods of relative stability (i.e., minor trend movements), like those of the 1920's and 1930's to which these studies pertain, a time series will still reflect mainly short-run variations.

The principal conclusions can be summarized as follows: Cross-section estimates of income elasticities have usually been much larger than those obtainable by straightforward time-series analysis for the same commodities; as a consequence, the result of removing "income effects" from the consumption series is usually to increase the conditional variance to be explained in the dependent series. In turn, this has commonly led to a larger estimate of the price elasticity of demand than would otherwise be obtained. The basic reasons for these discrepancies are: (1) cross-section data tend to measure long-run and other effects that are not observable, for a number of reasons, in short period (particularly *first difference*) time-series variations; and (2) the paucity and character of cross-section data usually make it possible to estimate only outlay rather than quantity elasticities from these sources.

Various Interpretations of Combined Cross-Section and Time-Series Estimates

There are several available alternatives for evaluating the errors of estimation and multiple correlations obtained from combined cross-section, time-series studies. A comparison of the properties of these different measures is a matter not only of technical statistical interest but is also a source of further information about the empirical relationships between cross-section and time-series estimates of income elasticities.

In the first place, two very different measures have been proposed for the error variance of the final regression function. One suggested alternative is simply to use the variance of the observed residuals defined to be the discrepancies between the estimates yielded by the final equation and the original values of the dependent variable. The second possibility is to adjust this error variance by a correction factor that eliminates the new sources of observation error introduced by the use of cross-section estimates. These statements can be specified more formally by employing the following notation, which closely follows that of Stone and Durbin. Let:

y be the original time-series values of the dependent variable;

- x_1 be the time-series values of the independent variable whose partial regression coefficient has been estimated on data other than time series;
- $x_2, x_3, \cdots, x_k$ be the remaining independent variables, whose parameters are to be estimated simultaneously on time series;
- $\hat{b}_1$ be the extraneously estimated partial regression coefficient;
- z be the "corrected" dependent variable, i.e., $z = y - \hat{b}_1 x_1$;
- b'_1 be the simple regression coefficient of y on x_1, i.e., $b' = \dfrac{\Sigma x_1 y}{\Sigma x_1^2}$;
- b_1 be the partial regression coefficient of y regressed on x_1, the values of $x_2, x_3, \cdots, x_k$ held constant;
- $b^*_2; b^*_3, \cdots, b^*_k$ be time-series estimates of partial regression coefficients with z, the adjusted time series as the dependent variable;
- $\hat{s}_1^2$ be the estimated error variance of the extraneously estimated regression coefficient.

Assume for simplicity of exposition that the regression equation is linear in logarithms, so that regression coefficients are at the same time constant elasticities. Also, there are n periods in the observed time series, and all variables are measured as deviations from their sample means. Then, the simple error variance, that is, the first of the two alternatives, can be expressed as:

$$S_e^2 = \frac{\sum_1^n (y - \hat{b}_1 x_1 - b^*_2 x_2 - \cdots - b^*_k x_k)^2}{n - k}. \quad (1)$$

This is the measure of error variance employed by Wold. The "corrected error variance" (employed by Stone and Durbin), reduces to

$$S^{*2}_e = \frac{\left\{(n - k)S_e^2 - (1 - R_{12})\hat{s}_1^2 \sum^n x_1^2\right\}}{n - k}, \quad (2)$$

where R_{12} is the multiple correlation of x_1 with the remaining $(k - 1)$ explanatory variables. As pointed out previously, introduction of the second term on the right side of the numerator in (2) corrects for the fact that the error sum of squares in (1) is an overestimate of the true error sum of squares, since some of the unexplained variation is attributable to variance in the estimate of the regression coefficient of variable x_1. It is obvious that $S_e^2 \geqq S^{*2}_e$ since the second term of (2)'s numerator involves only the product of non-negative numbers.

There are also two possible interpretations of the dependent variable with two corresponding variances. First, there is the sample variance based on the simple sum of squares of the original dependent variable; that is:

$$S_y^2 = \frac{\sum^n y^2}{n - 1}. \quad (3)$$

In terms of ultimate objectives, this is the variance that the investigator is usually attempting to explain. However, consideration might be given to a second alternative based on the "reduced" dependent variable, $y - \hat{b}_1 x_1$, obtained by eliminating the effects of variable x_1 through use of the cross-section parameter estimate. Designating this new variable by z, it has a sample variance defined by

$$S_z^2 = \sum^n \frac{z^2}{n-1} = \sum^n \frac{(y - \hat{b}_1 x_1)^2}{n-1} \quad (4)$$

Stone employs both these measures of dependent variable variances. Wold uses only the simple variance, S_y^2.

It is useful to consider the interrelationships between (3) and (4). The economic interrelationships in cases of demand studies are straightforward. The income variable, x_1, was introduced into the regression equation on the assumption that it would have a pronounced effect upon the quantity demanded, y. Thus, the income coefficient, $\hat{b}_1$, should be such that, when multiplied by the income time series, x_1, the "conditional sum of squares," $\Sigma(y - \hat{b}_1 x_1)^2$, will be the variation in y which has not been explained by income and remains to be explained by prices.

Conditions that must rule for $S_y^2 \leqq S_z^2$, that is for the conditional variance to be larger than the original variance, can be quickly stated:

$$\begin{aligned} \Sigma y^2 &\leqq \Sigma(y - \hat{b}_1 x_1)^2 \\ \Sigma y^2 &\leqq \Sigma y^2 - 2\hat{b}_1 \Sigma x_1 y + \hat{b}_1^2 \Sigma x_1^2 \\ 0 &\leqq -2\hat{b}_1 b'_1 \Sigma x_1^2 + \hat{b}_1^2 \Sigma x_1^2 \\ 2\hat{b}_1 b'_1 &\leqq \hat{b}_1^2 \\ 2b' &\leqq \hat{b}_1. \end{aligned} \quad (5)$$

In words, only when the cross-section regression coefficient estimate $(\hat{b_1})$ is more than twice as large as the *simple* time-series regression coefficient (b'_1) of y on x_1, will be conditional variance (S^2_z) be greater than the unconditional variance (S^2_y). This in turn raises the question: Under what circumstances would a time-series analysis alone yield partial coefficients twice the size of the simple coefficients? That is, when will $b'_1 > 2\, b$?

TABLE 1. — ILLUSTRATIVE LIMITING VALUES OF CORRELATIONS BETWEEN INCOME AND PRICE REQUIRED FOR THE INCOME PARTIAL REGRESSION COEFFICIENT TO EQUAL OR EXCEED TWICE THE SIMPLE INCOME REGRESSION COEFFICIENT

Income-Price Correlation Must be:		Given that the
Greater than or equal to — (1)	Less than or equal to — (2)	ratio $\pm \frac{r_{y1}}{r_{y2}}$ equals: [a] (3)
Inadmissible	.0000	0.0
Inadmissible	−.366	0.5
1.000	−.500	1.0
.843	−.593	2.0
.795	−.629	3.0
.772	−.647	4.0
.707	−.707	∞

[a] When the ratio r_{y1}/r_{y2} is negative, the above table still holds if the following two modifications are made: (a) the headings on columns (1) and (2) must be reversed; and (b) column (1) values must be negative and column (2) values must be positive.

NOTE: The values listed above satisfy the inequality $2\frac{r_{y1}}{r_{y2}} r^2_{12} - r_{12}\frac{r_{y1}}{r_{y2}} > 0$ in which r_{y1}/r_{y2} is treated as a parameter. This relation has been obtained after some rearrangement from the inequality $b_{y1.2} > 2b_{y1}$ or $\frac{b_{y1} - b_{y2}\, b_{21}}{1 - b_{12}b_{21}} > 2\, b_{y1}$. In addition, the correlation r_{y1} cannot exceed the larger root of the quadratic, shown in the first column, obtained when the above inequality is equated to zero, nor be less than the smaller root, shown in the second column. This is a consequence of restricting r_{y1} and r_{y2} to values that are consistent with a partial correlation less than or equal to one in absolute value, for given values of r_{12}. That is, if $r_{y1} = a\, r_{y2}$, then $\pm r_{y2} \leqslant \pm \sqrt{\frac{1 - r^2_{12}}{1 + a^2 - 2a\, r_{12}}}$ for partial correlations that involve these three simple correlations to be less than one absolutely.

Partials will substantially exceed simple regression coefficients only if the intercorrelations between independent variables are reasonably large. As shown in Table 1 and its appended note, the partial regression coefficient will be twice or more the size of the simple coefficient in a three variable case only when the intercorrelation in absolute terms is at least equal to or greater than either of the simple correlations between the independent variables and the dependent. Furthermore, as long as the simple time-series correlation between the dependent variable and the variable whose parameter is extraneously estimated is equal to or larger in absolute terms than that between the dependent and the other variable (i.e., $|r_{y1}| \geqq |r_{y2}|$), the intercorrelation must always be equal to or larger than .5 in absolute terms. Since the income parameter is the extraneously estimated coefficient in demand studies, and the income with quantity time series correlation is nearly always absolutely greater than the price with quantity simple correlation, the condition that $r_{12} \geqq |.5|$ must almost invariably be met if $b_1 \geqq 2b'_1$. As r_{y1} becomes larger than r_{y2}, moreover, the more r_{12} must exceed $|.5|$ for the necessary "doubling conditions" to hold. Finally, in many instances in which the correlations between the dependent and independent variables are reasonably substantial, there is no permissible value of the intercorrelation which will yield partial coefficients twice the size of the simple regression parameter.

It is therefore interesting that most demand studies have used *relative* rather than *simple* price and *real* rather than *monetary* income as independent variables, so that irrelevant covariation arising from changes in the absolute price level has been largely eliminated. Under such circumstances, there is really no *a priori* reason, as there is when nominal money values are employed, for believing that the two independent variables should be especially positively or negatively correlated (with the possible exception of new commodities). Consequently, one of the basic reasons underlying the use of combined cross-section, time-series methods becomes less justifiable when relative price and real income are the independent variables, and it is doubtful whether the partial regression coefficient will differ markedly from the simple when the variables are defined in this fashion.

Furthermore, there are certain additional characteristics of the United Kingdom's and Sweden's food economy which suggest that a high correlation between the two major explanatory variables, relative price and real income, is unlikely. The United Kingdom and, to a lesser extent, Sweden import most of their food; therefore the elasticity of food supply *to* these countries will be very high for reasonably wide variations in quantity. One cannot suppose it to be infinite since the United Kingdom has been an important world importer. Nevertheless, *systematic* covariance, arising because high United Kingdom or Swedish income would be associated with high (domestic) supply price, should be substantially less than it would be in a closed economy. In addition, few if any students of international business cycles argue that incomes in the world's trading countries have been so synchronized since the end of World War I that correlation between United Kingdom and Swedish incomes and world food prices would be indirectly created.[4] Hence, on economic grounds one would expect small correlation between relative food prices and real income in the two countries during the interwar period, so that b_1 and b'_1 should be approximately equal. In actual fact, for Stone's data, the correlation between the relative price of all food and real income is .38, a figure which is not significant at the 5 per cent level. Furthermore, the same point is indirectly borne out by two additional pieces of empirical information: (1) the close similarity between Wold's simple and partial income coefficients obtained solely from time series; and (2) the almost even split in negative and positive time-series correlations between relative price and real income in those few cases for which Stone reports such results (pages 388–405).

With two different measures of the error variance and of the dependent variable's variation used in combined cross-section, time-series studies, four combinations of these values are possible and therefore four different measures of multiple correlation can be constructed for the same cross-section, time-series least-squares function. Furthermore, knowledge of the relative magnitudes of the different measures of the constituent variances enables us to infer the relative magnitudes of the different measures of multiple correlation, and vice versa.

Specifically, the ratio of the error variance to the original variance of the dependent variable, the coefficient of non-determination, is equal to one less the square of the multiple correlation. The previously defined alternative measures of the error and dependent variable variance thus define the following coefficients of non-determination and multiple correlation:

$$\frac{S^2_e}{S^2_y}, \qquad R'^2 = 1 - \frac{S^2_e}{S^2_y} \tag{6}$$

$$\frac{S^2_e}{S^2_z}, \qquad R^2 = 1 - \frac{S^2_e}{S^2_z} \tag{7}$$

$$\frac{S^{*2}_e}{S^2_y}, \qquad R^{*2} = 1 - \frac{S^{*2}_e}{S^2_y} \tag{8}$$

$$\frac{S^{*2}_e}{S^2_z}, \qquad R''^2 = 1 - \frac{S^{*2}_e}{S^2_z} \tag{9}$$

All of these variance ratios have been used to measure the goodness of fit of combined cross-section, time-series demand functions except the last, which has no readily intelligible interpretation. Of the remaining three, Wold always uses (6), while Stone uses both (7) and (8). The multiple correlation coefficient R' used by Wold seems distinctly the most straightforward. This multiple correlation squared is approximately the proportion of the total variance of the dependent variable explained by all the explanatory variables collectively. While the true error sum of squares is overstated as Durbin has shown (and indeed may be so much so that the multiple correlation is negative), the combined sources of variation are given to the statistician. Formally, the R^* coefficient has a certain amount to recommend it, but it would appear to be an unnecessary refinement to take account of cross-section sampling error in this fashion, for if the arguments of this paper are correct, sampling error is likely to be small compared with the "specification" error introduced by the incompatibility of the cross-section and time-series models presently employed. Furthermore, R^* also can assume negative values.

The multiple correlation coefficient defined in (7), R, would appear to be definitely inferior to the previous two. If the objective is to find out how well one has explained variations in the quantity demanded, a change in the definition of the dependent variable, as has been made in (7), leads to a new statistical measure whose economic significance is not particularly clear.

If we consider only the three multiple cor-

[4] The United Kingdom and Sweden are, moreover, two notable exceptions to the interwar cyclical pattern in that both experienced their most severe postwar depression troughs in the 1920's and were relatively less affected than most other countries by the depression of the early 1930's.

relations that have actually been used, it is relatively easy to define their normal quantitative relationship to one another according to the relative sizes of the different variances. Explicitly, because $S_e^2 \geq S_e^{*2}$ *and assuming* $S_y^2 \geq S_z^2$:

$$\frac{S_e^2}{S_z^2} \geq \frac{S_e^2}{S_y^2} \geq \frac{S_e^{*2}}{S_y^2} \qquad (10)$$

so that $$R^2 \leq R'^2 \leq R^{*2}.$$

In words, the multiple correlation between the residual consumption series (derived by eliminating income effects on the basis of a cross-section estimate of the income elasticity) and the price series should be the smallest of the three multiple correlations.[5] On the other hand, the multiple correlation based on an error variance revised to take account of errors of estimation in the cross-section parameter should normally be the largest of the three. As pointed out previously, these relationships will hold as long as the cross-section estimate of the income elasticity is not more than twice the size of the income elasticity that would have been obtained from the simple regression on a straightforward time-series basis. Consequently, the relative magnitudes of the multiple correlations might tell us if the cross-section estimate has resulted in $S_z^2 \geq S_y^2$. If the estimate has this consequence, so that the cross-section estimate is incompatible with the time-series data according to the reasoning above, the inequality $R^2 \leq R^{*2}$ will be reversed. Therefore, questionably large cross-section estimates can be discovered by comparing these correlations; however, even if $R^2 \leq R^{*2}$ the cross-section estimate might not have been an appropriate one, and the variation to be explained by the remaining variables could still be larger than it was prior to the "elimination" of the income effects on quantity demanded.

Consequently, if both R^2 and R^{*2} are reported, it is possible to make a rough determination of the relative magnitudes of cross-section and time-series estimates of income elasticities. Stone, as pointed out previously, does report both R^2 and R^{*2} for virtually all of his functions, listing the results of approximately 200 regressions relating to the demand for just under 50 different commodity groups. In roughly nine out of ten cases, $R^2 \geq R^{*2}$ which means that in the same proportion of instances the cross-section estimate of the income elasticity must be *at least* twice the size of the gross estimate that would be obtained from a time-series analysis. While Tobin and Wold report only the multiple correlation R', they present direct evidence on the relative magnitude of income elasticities obtained from cross-section and time-series analyses. Tobin, who analyzes only the aggregate demand for food in the United States, obtains a total income elasticity of .56 from the cross-section as compared with .27 (on a partial regression basis) for the time-series data. Only Wold's results (shown in Table 1) obtained from an analysis of Swedish markets and budgets, do not lead to a definite conclusion that the cross-section income elasticity estimates will greatly exceed those obtained from time series.[6]

Comparison of Cross-Section and Time-Series Estimates of Income Elasticities

Outlay vs. quantity elasticities. There are many reasons why cross-section estimates of income elasticities might be expected to exceed those derived from time series. In studies done to date, the most important is that cross-section elasticities almost invariably have been, because of the nature of available data, "outlay" instead of quantity elasticities. In other words, within broadly defined commodity groups, increased outlays by higher income groups reflect increased prices paid for higher quality as well as increased quantity. Consequently, we shall use the term "outlay elasticity" to describe an elasticity whose *dependent* variable is outlay or

[5] Conceptually, one less parameter is to be estimated from the sample observations for (7) in contrast with (6) and (8), so that its error sum of squares should actually be divided through by $(n - k + 1)$ instead of $(n - k)$ to obtain an unbiased estimate of the error variance. Therefore, the inequalities do not hold strictly; the actual error in the conclusions from this source is so negligible that it can be ignored.

[6] Actually, Wold's evidence is very mixed. In the first place, Wold computes both quantity and expenditure elasticities from the cross-section data; the quantity elasticities are lower than the time-series estimates in a slight majority of instances; the expenditure elasticities, on the other hand, are more often larger than smaller than the time-series estimates.

price per physical unit or an index number based on a reference year is used.

Thus there are four possible combinations even if we limit ourselves to considering simple Paasche or Laspeyres series in indexed and average value form. Specifically, for an aggregate sales figure, $\Sigma P_{ti}Q_{ti}$ (where t designates the current year, o the base year, and i the m qualities), we would obtain the following four results from using these four price series as deflators:

(a) $$\frac{\Sigma P_{ti}Q_{ti}}{\frac{\Sigma P_{ti}Q_{ti}}{\Sigma Q_{ti}}} = \Sigma Q_{ti}$$ [Average value moving weight (Paasche type) price deflation.]

(b) $$\frac{\Sigma P_{ti}Q_{ti}}{\frac{\Sigma P_{ti}Q_{ti}}{\Sigma P_{0i}Q_{ti}}} = \Sigma P_{0i}Q_{ti}$$ [Paasche price index deflation.]

(c) $$\frac{\Sigma P_{ti}Q_{ti}}{\frac{\Sigma P_{ti}Q_{0i}}{\Sigma Q_{0i}}} = \frac{\Sigma P_{ti}Q_{ti}}{\Sigma P_{ti}Q_{0i}} \Sigma Q_{0i}$$ [Average value constant weight (Laspeyres type) price deflation, which equals a Paasche quantity index times the quantity sold in the base period.]

(d) $$\frac{\Sigma P_{ti}Q_{ti}}{\frac{\Sigma P_{ti}Q_{0i}}{\Sigma P_{0i}Q_{0i}}} = \frac{\Sigma P_{ti}Q_{ti}}{\Sigma P_{ti}Q_{0i}} \Sigma P_{0i}Q_{0i}$$ [Laspeyres price index deflation, which equals a Paasche quantity index times the *value* of the base-year sales.]

It is reasonably obvious that quality changes will be reflected in all but the first of these "quantity" series, since in every case but this the quantities of the different qualities are weighted by price.[11] Consequently, a time-series elasticity obtained by relating income to one of these last three variables will likely reflect both quality and quantity effects. In actual practice, Wold with few exceptions has used price series of type (a) or has obtained physical quantity data directly, which would yield the same result. Stone, on the other hand, has employed both direct estimates of quantity obtained by simple aggregation using physical weights and has also used price-weighted quantity aggregates; in the same fashion, Stone uses both simple price indexes based on prices for a selected few qualities which are aggregated on the basis of fixed weights and the relatively more complex price indexes of the Fisher "ideal" type that employ moving weights. This means that some of Stone's quantity and price series will reflect quality changes while others will not.

The question therefore arises of the relative extent to which quality differences will be observed under such conditions in Stone's time series and cross-sections. This is an extremely difficult question to answer categorically because of inadequate empirical evidence. Furthermore, conflicting *a priori* tendencies are discernible. For instance, many, if not most, improvements in the quality of goods consumed over time will be due to technological advances that permit greater consumption of higher quality goods. If quantity series are used that reflect this quality improvement, that is, series such as those obtained by deflation of types (b), (c), and (d), the result will be an apparent increase in the consumption of the technologically improved good. If this technological advance is more rapid than that experienced in other sections and is reflected in a relative price reduction and, in addition, if the good in question enters into the consumer price index's "basket of goods," the technologically induced quality increase will be reflected in both the price and income elasticities. Such a result is, of course, not in conflict with the tenets of established consumer behavior theory.[12] But the process of technological development that results in quality improvements over time is clearly very different from the process which causes differences in the qualities of goods consumed by different income groups at a given point of time when technology is constant.

In addition many quality improvements may not be reflected in either price or income. This would be the case of a good whose price per unit as determined for price index purposes remains constant but whose quality continually improves. If a good under analysis is subject to such unmeasured or implicit price decreases, and consumers actually respond to these

[11] All the above discussion has been couched in terms of the dependent variable being obtained by deflating an aggregate sales figure with a price series or index. If the procedure were reversed, i.e., a physical quantity series is blown up into value terms in order to obtain a dependent variable recorded in money units so as to be commensurable with a cross-section regression estimate, the same remarks would apply.

[12] It again makes a difference, however, how prices are measured; specifically, if an average value moving weight series of the Paasche type is used, relative price reductions brought on by technological improvements will not be recorded automatically.

changes, the effect will be to obtain lower price and income elasticities than would have been obtained had recorded prices increased, thereby reflecting improved quality.[13] Again, there is no particular reason to believe that observations on a cross-section, pertaining to a limited period in which the technological factor is relatively constant, will accurately reflect these influences.

Quality effects and the "timing" of the cross-section. The quality differential in time-series and cross-section elasticities will depend in part on the time period to which the cross-section pertains. If we assume, for example, that new goods appear as a trend function of time and that a large number of new goods will always appear outside the categories of consumption being analyzed, the bill of available consumer goods competing for income will be constantly enlarging. Under such conditions, we could expect that the quantity/income slope of the established or older categories of consumption, such as food, will tend to decline over time.[14] This would mean that income elasticities obtained from cross-section data pertaining to a year near the end of the time series will be lower (and vice versa) than those obtained by a cross-section analysis of a year at the start of the period.[15]

In addition, if we assume as before that some non-linearity in the degree of "quantity saturation" of consumers in different income categories is likely, any income redistribution in favor of low income groups will reduce the quality effects observable on a cross-section. These differences would not be germane if the weights for aggregating the income elasticities obtained from cross-sections were shifted to take account of the changing importance of the different income classes over time. Instead, though, the usual procedure is to fix the weights as they existed in the cross-section year, and it will therefore again make a difference whether the cross-section year is at the beginning or end of the time-series period.[16]

Rigidities in consumer behavior. Another circumstance that will tend to differentiate the quality aspects observable in time series and cross-sections is the possibility of sociological rigidities in people's tastes and consumption habits. Any assumption of rigidities in food tastes rests, at bottom, on the premise that a desire for a certain quality of food is something that often, although certainly not always, is developed over time. In other words, whether one likes French vintage wine or ale with one's dinner is likely to be heavily dependent on one's early training, income, and education and not immediately sensitive to current changes in income position. To the extent that people in high income brackets come from high income backgrounds, the cross-section will reveal quality differentials associated with income strata that are the result of a cumulative training and development that may have extended over a number of years or even generations. Differentials in taste that take time to cultivate will therefore be more

[13] Except when explicit and different reasons are given, overestimates will arise when the ratio of the dependent variable's variance to that of the independent variable under discussion is less than it would have been had the index number overcome the defect in question.

[14] Wold reports the results obtained from three cross-sections widely separated in time (1913, 1923, and 1933), and these do, in fact, indicate that the food consumption/income slope has apparently been declining over time (pages 265, 271, 274).

[15] These usually ignored new good influences often occur as trends. Hence, least squares bias can be the consequence when relative price, as it so often does, displays a trend too; more generally, such a result suggests the need of including a further variable that measures the effects due to an expanding bill of consumer goods. Furthermore, if an estimate (assumed for the moment to be correct) of quantity/income slope is derived from a cross-section near the end of the time-series period and if the cross-section slopes display trend behavior, the result will be a downward trend in the error term of the conditional regression of quantity on price (unless real income has a sufficient upward trend to offset this development); thus if price is negatively correlated with time this will mean an overestimate of the price elasticity and, conversely, if price is positively correlated with time, an underestimate of the price elasticity will result. The same arguments hold, moreover, with suitable sign adjustments, if the income elasticity is derived from a year at the start of the time-series period. The relative prices of most foods declined from 1920 to 1940, but only slightly, so that the result, if the income estimate were otherwise suitable, would have been a small tendency toward overestimation of the price elasticity.

[16] Specifically, if the weights pertain to a year near the end of the period and income has not greatly increased but has only been redistributed in favor of lower income groups over time, the cross-section would (because it places greater emphasis on the groups with the higher quantity adjustments) reflect less quality influence than the time-series estimate. Of course, if the total level of income increased at the same time the redistribution took place, this effect would be partially offset because of the relatively reduced importance of the very lowest income groups.

observable on the cross-section than in short-period time-series movements.[17]

Essentially, this observation amounts to a slight elaboration of the well-known Duesenberry-Modigliani ratchet effect, in which the central feature is the observable tendency toward the short-run persistency of consumption habits. If the persistency effect is a correct description of consumer behavior, we might expect a short-run consistency in both consumer tastes and quantity preferences that would result in the cross-section estimate of the income elasticity exceeding that of the time series. While the cross section would basically measure long-run effects, on the assumption that the majority of the observed families have enjoyed their present relative real income for some time, the same would not be true of income changes observed over time. Specifically, income changes over time would represent temporary shifts, and it would be expected that the recipients or losers from income changes would not adjust immediately to the consumption habits of their new income group. Of course, if the income of society moved from one plateau to another after the fashion of comparative statics, this effect might be expected to wash out if the time periods observed were sufficiently long.

Trend, "transient income," and the measurement of consumer responses. The extent of the discrepancies between time-series and cross-section estimates will also depend on the length of the time series and the kind of analytical techniques used with the time-series data. For example, time-series regression equations that include a trend term or have been first differenced (thus effectively removing a trend) will reflect primarily short-run rather than long-run effects. Furthermore, the variation in time series pertaining to periods of little noticeable trend movement will embody primarily short- rather than long-run influences. The interwar years, 1920 to 1940, which have provided data for most of the time-series demand studies, generally display such stability. It would therefore seem that most of the existing time-series studies of demand reflect short- rather than long-run behavior. The possibility cannot be denied, however, that if sufficiently long time series were obtained for periods of reasonably rapid growth, time-series investigations could uncover long-run relationships. Many of these same considerations apply, moreover, when assessing the results obtained from cross sections. For example, cross-section studies taken at a point of time corresponding to rapid growth in the economy or violent cyclical change could very well reflect short-run, transitory influences. The cross-section data used by Wold and Stone, however, should be free from major short-run influences because they pertain to years in the 1930's (or occasionally the 1920's) when economic conditions were roughly stable. In addition, it could be argued that in relatively rigid social structures, like those of England and Sweden, the chances of short-run variation obscuring long-run variation on the cross-section are clearly less than they are in more fluid social structures.

While the evidence is not entirely one-sided, the preceding arguments, based on empirical observations and *a priori* reasoning, strongly suggest that income elasticities estimated from cross-section data have been, as a rule, substantially in excess of those that would have been obtained from a time-series analysis. This view might appear to contradict recent literature on the consumption function, according to which budget study estimates of the income coefficient will tend to be too low on the average.[18] The most elaborate statement of this argument,

[17] A behavioral hypothesis that superficially runs counter to the relative income theory of consumption on the subject of non-competing groups might usefully be borrowed from factor market discussions in international trade theory. More generally, emulative and relative income effects on consumption are most likely to predominate among closely adjacent income groups, and non-competing consumption patterns are most likely to prevail between more distantly separated income classes, although numerous interconnections will, of course, exist among all groups. This possibility is strongly supported when, as in the United Kingdom in the interwar period, income bracket separation has been reinforced with social class distinctions and corresponding cultural differentiation.

[18] Milton Friedman, *A Theory of the Consumption Function* (Princeton, 1957); Franco Modigliani and Richard Brumberg, "Utility Analysis and the Consumption Function: An Interpretation of Cross-Section Data," in Kenneth K. Kurihara, ed., *Post Keynesian Economics* (New Brunswick, 1954), 388–436; Dorothy S. Brady, "Family Saving, 1888 to 1950," in Raymond W. Goldsmith, Dorothy S. Brady, and Horst Mendershausen, *A Study of Saving in the United States*, III, Special Studies (Princeton, 1956); and Margaret Reid, "Savings by Family Units in Consecutive Periods," in Walter W. Heller et al., ed., *Savings in the Modern Economy* (Minneapolis, 1953).

given by Professor Friedman, asserts that actual consumption depends upon expected or permanent income, while actual annual income includes a transient component. Hence, consumption will be less responsive to changes in actual income than it will be to changes in permanent income. The coefficient for permanent income, Professor Friedman believes, would most adequately reflect long-run secular behavior.[19] Even if this argument is correct, the "true" income coefficient (defined in Professor Friedman's terms to measure consumption responses to changes in permanent income) could be higher than that actually obtained on a cross-section and still might be inappropriately high for combined use with time-series price data. It is, however, difficult to reconcile the rather large income elasticities obtained from most cross-sections with the position that cross-sections usually underestimate income elasticities.[20]

Effect of Large Extraneous Income Elasticity Estimates on the Estimates of Price Elasticity

Regardless of whether the income coefficient obtained from a cross-section is a biased estimate of the "true" cross-section coefficient, the use of a cross-section income elasticity that is larger than the equivalent time-series estimate will lead to an altered estimate of the price elasticity when the combined cross-section, time-series techniques are employed. Specifically, the relationship between price and income elasticities derived from constant-elasticity functions can be described as follows:[21]

$$b^*_2 = -\frac{\Sigma y x_2}{\Sigma x_2^2} + \frac{\Sigma x_1 x_2}{\Sigma x_2^2}\,\hat{b}_1 \qquad (11)$$

where b^*_2 is the price elasticity, $\hat{b}_1$ the cross-section income elasticity, and all values are again measured as deviations from their means. Obviously, the estimate of the price elasticity will be modified by an incorrect estimate of the income elasticity as long as price and income are correlated. If income, x_1, and price, x_2, are positively related, the effect of overestimating the income elasticity, $\hat{b}_1$, will clearly be to overestimate the price elasticity, b^*_2, as well. Though there are no compelling *a priori* reasons to suppose that relative price and real income are positively correlated, available evidence indicates that such is more often than not the case. Therefore, the combined techniques would in a majority of instances result in an overestimate of the price elasticities.

Broadly speaking, a comparison of pure time-series estimates of price elasticities with those derived from combined use of cross-section and time series bears out this conclusion. Tobin, for example, found a price elasticity of .27 when using time series alone as compared with an estimate of .53 obtained from the joint time-series, cross-section analysis. If we assume that consumers in Sweden and England behave in roughly comparable fashion, a similar conclusion emerges from a comparison of the price elasticities estimated by Wold using only time series with those estimated by Stone using the combined cross-section, time-series methods. As shown in Table 4, the straightforward time-series estimate is less than the cross-section estimate for all similar food categories investigated by both Stone and Wold, except for butter, margarine, and milk. Butter and margarine are, moreover, readily explicable exceptions, since the prices of these products fell with increases in income. Furthermore, the milk case is of somewhat doubtful validity because the estimate of the price elasticity is crucially dependent on which other variables are included in the equation; specifically, introduction of the price of home-produced beef and veal in Stone's analysis raises the English price elasticity for fresh milk to over .40.

Some conclusions about the possible bias of the price elasticities can also be inferred from certain elementary considerations about the character of the time series employed. In par-

[19] This is really a variation of the errors-in-observation source of bias noted earlier and in a different context by Professor Guy H. Orcutt, "Measurement of Price Elasticities in International Trade," this REVIEW, XXXII (May 1950), 117–32.

[20] Empirical evaluation of the importance of systematic and random deviations from permanent expected income would be possible with consecutive cross-sections on the same individuals for one of more complete business cycles. Professor Friedman, in "Savings and the Balance Sheet," *Bulletin of the Oxford University Institute of Statistics*, XIX (May 1957), 136, has recently made a similar observation.

[21] See Wold and Juréen, 332. The usual expectation is that "own" price elasticities will be negative, in line with the convention that the elasticity is to be reported as a positive number. Therefore, the entire expression (obtained by ignoring *a priori* signs) has been multiplied by minus one.

TABLE 4.—COMPARISON OF OWN PRICE ELASTICITIES FOR SELECTED FOOD PRODUCTS

	Stone estimates using extraneous income estimators,[a] England	Wold estimates using time series only, Sweden	
	1920–38	1921–39	1926–39
Beef (pork prices not in regression)	.55[b]	.00	. .
Beef (pork prices in regression)	. .	.50	. .
Pork	.67	.45	. .
Butter	.38	.94	.88
Margarine	.06	2.18	.79
Fresh milk	.05 }		. .
Condensed milk	.60 }	.28	. .
Cream	1.26 }		. .
Flour	.79	.15	. .
Sugar and syrup	.42	.11	. .

[a] Where Stone has reported results from more than one regression for a given product, the regression that includes variables most similar to Wold's has been used. The butter and margarine regressions are for the years 1921–38.

[b] For both imported beef and veal.

SOURCE: Herman Wold and Lars Juréen, *Demand Analysis* (New York, 1953), 277–94; and Richard Stone, *The Measurement of Consumers' Expenditure and Behavior in the United Kingdom 1920–1938* (Cambridge, England, 1954), 322–27.

ticular, price elasticities will be influenced by the choice of price indexes, just as the income elasticities are. For example, if a Laspeyres index is used as a deflator we have already noted that the dependent variable will reflect quality as well as quantity changes, but use of a Laspeyres index as an independent (own price) variable will not reflect price changes due to quality composition changes; consequently, the price elasticity will be underestimated if a Laspeyres index is used for both purposes. On the other hand, if a Paasche index is used as the independent variable with a dependent variable free of quality effects, obtained either by direct measurement of quantity changes or by employing average value deflation of type (a), the result will be an overestimate of the price elasticity because the Paasche price index will reflect changes in the different qualities consumed. Finally, if deflation of type (b), (c), or (d) is used with a Paasche index as an independent variable, both the dependent and independent variables will reflect quality changes and to approximately the same degree because the dependent variable under such conditions will be essentially a Paasche quality-influenced quantity index. Under such conditions, the price index will actually be measuring improvements in real income, thus spuriously injecting a positive relation between price and quantity that would reduce the usual negative relationship between these variables. In fact, if the quality effects were sufficiently pronounced, a positive relationship between price and quantity might even be observed. It is also obvious that using a price variable that reflects real income variation will increase the intercorrelation between real income and the price variable, which in turn means that the time series estimate of the income elasticity will be reduced. *In general, the only admissible procedure would appear to be the use of "pure" price indexes that do not reflect quality changes, with straightforward quantity series as dependent variables.*

In practice, Wold employs the combination of a reasonably pure dependent quantity variable and a Paasche type index; this should result in an overestimate of the price elasticity. Stone, as already noted, uses chained ideal indexes and quantity series some of which reflect quality changes while others do not; in cases where Stone has a quantity variable that reflects quality changes, he will therefore get an underestimate of the price elasticity and, conversely, an overestimate in instances where the quantity variable does not reflect quality changes.[22] When Stone uses a quantity variable that reflects quality changes, he at the same time uses a chained ideal index price variable. This means that he has both a dependent and independent variable that reflect quality changes and that the estimates of the price elasticities will, *ceteris paribus*, be lower than they would otherwise be. On the other hand, when Stone uses a fixed weight, Laspeyres type index with dependent variables that do not reflect quality changes, the resulting price elasticities need not be biased on this account.

As pointed out elsewhere,[23] there are many reasons why time-series estimates of price elasticities might be biased downward. In particular, errors of observation in the price series or the existence of a simultaneous supply re-

[22] These differences in method could explain, of course, some of the positive differences between Stone's and Wold's price elasticities reported in Table 4; only in the case of pork and sugar and syrup, however, are the categories sufficiently heterogeneous that these effects might be reasonably important.

[23] Arnold C. Harberger, *Econometrica*, XXIII (April 1955), 217–18 and Guy H. Orcutt, *ibid.*, 117–32.

lationship between quantity and price that results in a positive relationship between price and the error term in the demand equation will result in least-squares estimates that tend to underestimate the price elasticity. These influences, and the presence of any of those previously cited causes that might create a downward bias in the price elasticities, will offset to some extent the upward bias created by using overly large income elasticities. The net effect of all these conflicting influences cannot be rigorously determined from *ex-ante* considerations, but the previously reported empirical results would indicate that over-estimation, caused primarily by the use of high cross-section income elasticities, is the more likely outcome.

In sum, great care should be exercised in utilizing cross-section parameter estimates jointly with time series. In particular, careful thought must be given to the possibility that a cross-section estimate is likely to measure very different influences from those represented by time-series movements. Clearly, there is such a thing as being too extraneous.

MULTICOLLINEARITY IN REGRESSION ANALYSIS: THE PROBLEM REVISITED

Donald E. Farrar and Robert R. Glauber *

TO MOST economists, the single equation least-squares regression model, like an old friend, is tried and true. Its properties and limitations have been extensively studied and documented and are, for the most part, well-known. Any good text in econometrics can lay out the assumptions on which common versions of the model are based and provide a reasonably coherent — perhaps even a lucid — discussion of problems that arise as particular assumptions are violated. A short bibliography of definitive papers on such classical problems as non-normality, heteroscedasticity, serial correlation, feedback, etc., completes the job.

As with most old friends, however, the longer one knows least squares, the more one learns about it. An admiration for its robustness under departures from many assumptions is sure to grow. The admiration must be tempered, however, by an appreciation of the model's sensitivity to certain other conditions. The requirement that explanatory variables be truly independent of one another is one of these.

Proper treatment of the model's classical problems ordinarily involves two separate stages: detection and correction. The Durbin-Watson test for serial correlation, combined with Cochrane and Orcutt's suggested first differencing procedure, is an obvious example.[1] Bartlett's test for variance heterogeneity followed by a data transformation to restore homoscedasticity is another.[2] No such "proper treatment" has been developed, however, for problems that arise as multicollinearity is encountered in regression analysis.

Attention will focus here on what we consider to be the first step in a proper treatment of the multicollinearity problem — its detection, or diagnosis. Economists are coming more and more to agree that the second step, correction, requires the generation of additional information.[3] Just how this information is to be obtained depends largely on the tastes of an investigator and on the specifics of a particular problem. It may involve additional primary data collection, the use of extraneous parameter estimates from secondary data sources, or the application of subjective information through constrained regression, or through Bayesian estimation procedures. Whatever its source, however, selectivity — and thereby efficiency — in generating the added information requires a systematic procedure for detecting its need — i.e., for detecting the existence, measuring the extent, and pinpointing the location and causes of multicollinearity within a set of independent variables. Measures are proposed here that, in our opinion, fill this need.

The paper's basic organization can be outlined briefly as follows. In the next section the multicollinearity problem's basic, formal nature is developed and illustrated. A discussion of historical approaches to the problem follows. With this as background, an attempt is made to define multicollinearity in terms of departures from a hypothesized statistical condition, and

* The authors are Associate Professor of Finance at the Sloan School of Management, M.I.T., and Assistant Professor of Business Administration at the Harvard Business School, respectively. We are indebted to Professor John R. Meyer for introducing us to the multicollinearity problem and for advice and encouragement during the present effort to place it in perspective, and to Professors John Lintner and Robert Schlaifer for their comments and criticisms. Responsibility for specific interpretations, especially erroneous ones, remains our own.

This research was supported by the Institute of Naval Studies, of which both authors were members at the time the work was conducted, and by grants from the Ford Foundation to both the Sloan School of Management and the Harvard Business School. Computation time and facilities were provided by the Computation Centers of Harvard and M.I.T.

[1] J. Durbin and G. S. Watson, "Testing for Serial Correlation in Least Squares Regression," *Biometrika*, 37–38, (1950–1951); and C. Cochrane and G. H. Orcutt, "Application of Least Squares Regression to Relationships Containing Autocorrelated Error Terms" *Journal of the American Statistical Association*, 44 (1949).

[2] F. David and J. Neyman, "Extension of the Markoff Theorem on Least Squares," *Statistical Research Memoirs*, II (London, 1938).

[3] J. Johnston, *Econometric Methods* (McGraw-Hill, 1963), 207; J. Meyer and R. Glauber, *Investment Decisions, Economic Forecasting, and Public Policy* (Division of Research, Graduate School of Business Administration, Harvard University, 1964), 181 ff.

to fashion a series of hierarchical measures — at each of three levels of detail — for its presence, severity, and location in a set of data. The measures are developed in terms of a generalized, multivariate normal, linear model. A pragmatic interpretation of resulting statistics as measures of sample properties, rather than as a basis for inferences concerning population characteristics, is advocated. A numerical illustration and a summary complete the exposition.

The Multicollinearity Problem

Nature and Effects

The purpose of regression analysis is to estimate the parameters of a dependency, not an interdependency, relationship. We define first,[4]

y, X as a sample of N observations on one dependent and n independent variables, each of which is normalized (by sample size and standard deviation) to unit length. (X^tX), accordingly, is a zero order correlation matrix.

b as a vector of true (structural) coefficients,

u as a true (unobserved) error term, with distributional properties specified by the general linear model,[5] and

σ_u^2 as the underlying, population variance of u;

and presume that y and X are related to one another through the linear form

$$y = Xb + u. \qquad (1)$$

Least-squares regression analysis leads to estimates

$$b' = (X^tX)^{-1}X^ty,$$

with variance-covariance matrix

$$V(b') = \sigma_u^2(X^tX)^{-1},$$

that, in a variety of senses, best reproduces the hypothesized dependency relationship (1).

Multicollinearity, on the other hand, is viewed here as an interdependency condition that can exist quite apart from the nature, or even the existence, of dependence between X and y. It is both a facet and a symptom of poor experimental design. Multicollinearity constitutes a threat — and often a very serious threat — both to the proper specification and the effective estimation of the type of structural relationship commonly sought through the use of regression techniques.

Estimation

Difficulties associated with a multicollinear set of data depend, of course, on the severity of the problem. As interdependence among explanatory variables X grows, the correlation matrix (X^tX) approaches singularity, and elements of the inverse matrix $(X^tX)^{-1}$ explode. In the limit, perfect linear dependence within an independent variable set leads to perfect singularity on the part of (X^tX) and to a completely indeterminate set of parameter estimates b'. In a formal sense, diagonal elements of the inverse correlation matrix $(X^tX)^{-1}$ that correspond to linearly dependent members of X become infinite. Variances for the affected variables' regression coefficients,

$$V(b') = \sigma_u^2(X^tX)^{-1}$$

accordingly, also become infinite.

The mathematics, in its brute and tactless way, tells us that explained variance can be allocated completely arbitrarily between linearly dependent members of a completely singular set of variables, and almost arbitrarily between members of an almost singular set. Alternatively, the large variances on regression coefficients produced by multicollinear independent variables indicate, quite properly, the low information content of observed data, and accordingly, the low quality of resulting parameter estimates. It emphasizes one's inability to distinguish the independent contribution to explained variance of an explanatory variable that exhibits little or no truly independent variation.

In many ways, a person whose independent variable set is completely interdependent may be more fortunate than one whose data are almost so. The former's difficulty in basing his model on data that cannot support its informational requirements will be discovered — by a purely mechanical inability to invert the singular matrix (X^tX) — while the latter's problem in most cases will never be fully appreciated.

Attempts to apply regression techniques to highly multicollinear independent variables

[4] Throughout this paper vectors are indicated by lower case English letters, e.g., y and matrices by upper case English letters, e.g., X.

[5] See for example, F. Graybill, *An Introduction to Linear Statistical Models* (McGraw-Hill, 1961), ch. 5.

generally result in parameter estimates that are markedly sensitive to changes in model specification and to sample coverage. It is unnecessary to illustrate these difficulties here, for unfortunately, illustrations abound in the literature. The best known, and in many ways the most enlightening, is the original Cobb-Douglas study, to which reference will be made later in this paper.[6]

Specification

Although less dramatic and less easily detected than instability in parameter estimates, problems surrounding model specification with multicollinear data are not less real. Far from it, correct specification ordinarily is more important to successful model building than the selection of a "correct" estimating procedure.

Poor forecasts of early postwar consumption expenditures are an example. These forecasts could have been improved marginally, perhaps, by more fortunate choices of sample, computing algorithm, direction of minimization, functional form etc. Their basic shortcoming consists of a failure to recognize the importance of liquid assets to consumer behavior. No matter how cleverly a consumption function's coefficients are estimated, if it does not include liquid assets it cannot provide a satisfactory representation of early postwar United States consumer behavior. Multicollinearity, unfortunately, contributes to difficulty in the specification as well as the estimation of economic relationships.

Specification ordinarily begins in the model builder's mind. From a combination of theory, prior information, and just plain hunch, variables are chosen to explain the behavior of a given dependent variable. The job, however, does not end with the first tentative specification. Before an equation is judged acceptable it must be tested on a body of empirical data. Should it be deficient in any of several respects, the specification — and thereby the model builder's "prior hypothesis" — is modified and tried again. The process may go on for some time. Eventually, discrepancies between prior and sample information are reduced to tolerable levels and an equation acceptable in both respects is produced.

In concept the process is sound. In practice, however, the econometrician's mind is more fertile than his data, and the process of modifying hypotheses consists largely of paring-down rather than building-up model complexity. Having little confidence in the validity of his prior beliefs, the economist tends to yield too easily to a temptation to reduce his model's scope to that of his data.

Each sample, of course, covers only a limited range of experience. A relatively small number of forces is likely to be operative over, or during, the subset of reality on which a particular set of observations is based. As the number of variables extracted from the sample increases, each tends to measure different nuances of the same few basic factors that are present. The sample's basic information is simply spread more and more thinly over a larger and larger number of increasingly multicollinear independent variables.

However real the dependency relationship between y and *each* member of a relatively large independent variable set X may be, the growth of interdependence within X as its size increases rapidly decreases the stability — and, therefore, the sample significance — of each independent variable's contribution to explained variance. As Liu points out, data limitations rather than theoretical limitations are primarily responsible for a persistent tendency to underspecify (or to oversimplify) econometric models.[7] The increase in sample standard errors for multicollinear regression coefficients virtually assures a tendency for relevant variables to be discarded incorrectly from regression equations.

The econometrician, then, is in a box. Whether his goal is to estimate complex structural relationships in order to distinguish between alternative hypotheses, or to develop reliable forecasts, the number of variables required is likely to be large, and past experience

[6] C. W. Cobb and P. H. Douglas, "A Theory of Production," *American Economic Review*, XVIII, Supplement (March 1928). See also H. Menderhausen, "On the Significance of Professor Douglas' Production Function," *Econometrica*, 6 (Apr. 1938); and D. Durand, "Some Thoughts on Marginal Productivity with Special Reference to Professor Douglas' Analysis," *Journal of Political Economy*, 45 (1937).

[7] T. C. Liu, "Underidentification, Structural Estimation and Forecasting," *Econometrica*, 28 (Oct. 1960), 856.

demonstrates with depressing regularity that large numbers of economic variables from a single sample are almost certain to be highly intercorrelated. Regardless of the particular application, then, the essence of a multicollinearity problem is the same. There exists a substantial difference between the amount of information required for satisfactory model construction and that contained in a sample of data at hand.

If a model is to be retained in all its complexity, solution of the multicollinearity problem requires an augmentation of existing data to include additional information. Parameter estimates for an n-dimensional model cannot properly be based on data that contain fewer significant dimensions. Neither can such data provide a basis for discriminating among alternative formulations of the model. Even for forecasting purposes the econometrician whose data are multicollinear is in an extremely exposed position. Successful forecasts with multicollinear variables require not only the perpetuation of a stable dependency relationship between y and X, but also the perpetuation of stable interdependency relationships within X. *Both conditions are met, unfortunately, only in a context in which the forecasting problem is all but trivial.*

Although frequently advocated, the alternative of scaling down each model to fit the dimensionality of a given set of data appears equally unpromising. A set of substantially orthogonal independent variables can, in general, be specified only by discarding much of the prior theoretical information that a researcher brings to his problem. Analyses of aggregate time series containing more than one or two independent variables would virtually disappear, and forecasting models too simple to provide reliable forecasts would become the order of the day. Consumption functions that include either income or liquid assets — but not both — provide an appropriate warning.

There is, perhaps, a middle ground. All the variables in a model are seldom of equal interest. Theoretical questions ordinarily focus on a relatively small portion of an independent variable set. Cobb and Douglas, for example, are interested only in the magnitude of labor and capital coefficients, not in the impact on output of technological change. Disputes concerning alternative consumption, investment, and cost of capital models similarly focus on the relevance of, at most, one or two disputed variables. Similarly, forecasting models rely for success mainly on the structural integrity of those variables whose behavior is expected to change. In each case, certain variables are strategically important to a particular application while others are not.

Multicollinearity, then, constitutes a problem only if it undermines that portion of the independent variable set that is crucial to the analysis in question — labor and capital for Cobb and Douglas, income and liquid assets for postwar consumption forecasts. Should these variables be multicollinear, corrective action is necessary. New information must be obtained. Insight into the pattern of interdependence that undermines present data is necessary, however, if the new information is to be collected and applied effectively.

Current procedures and summary statistics do not provide effective indications of multicollinearity's presence in a set of data, let alone the insight into its location, pattern, and severity that is required if a remedy — in the form of *selective additions* to information — is to be obtained. The current paper attempts to provide appropriate "diagnostics" for this purpose.

Multicollinearity is not always viewed in this fashion. Historical approaches will both facilitate exposition and complete the necessary background for the present approach to the multicollinearity problem.

Historical Approaches

Historical approaches to multicollinearity may be organized in any of a number of ways. A very convenient organization reflects the tastes and backgrounds of two types of persons who have worked actively in the area. Econometricians tend to view the problem in a relatively abstract manner. Computer programmers, on the other hand, see multicollinearity as just one of a relatively large number of contingencies that must be anticipated and treated. Theoretical statisticians, drawing their training, experience, and data from the controlled world of the laboratory experiment, are noticeably uninterested in the problem altogether.

Econometric

Econometricians typically view multicollinearity in a very matter-of-fact — if slightly schizophrenic — fashion. They point out on the one hand that in a sense, *there is no problem*, as least squares coefficient estimates,

$$b' = \check{b} + (X^tX)^{-1}X^tu,$$

are "best linear unbiased," since the expectation of the last term is zero regardless of the degree of multicollinearity inherent in X, *if the model is properly specified and feedback is absent.* Rigorously demonstrated, this proposition is often a source of great comfort to the embattled practitioner. At times it may justify complacency.

On the other hand, econometricians recognize that multicollinearity imparts a substantial bias toward incorrect model specification,[8] and that poor specification undermines the "best linear unbiased" character of parameter estimates over multicollinear, independent variable sets.[9] Complacency, then, tends to give way to despair as one recognizes that nonexperimental data, in general, are multicollinear and that ". . . in principle nothing can be done about it."[10] Or to use Jack Johnston's words, one is ". . . in the statistical position of not being able to make bricks without straw."[11] Data that do not include the information required by an equation cannot be expected to yield it. Admonitions that new data, or additional *a priori* information, are required to "break the multicollinearity deadlock"[12] are hardly reassuring, for the gap between information on hand and information required to estimate a model fully is so often immense.

Together the combination of complacency and despair that characterizes traditional views tends to virtually paralyze efforts to deal with multicollinearity as a legitimate and difficult, yet tractable, econometric problem. There are, of course, exceptions. Two are discussed below.

Artificial Orthogonalization

The first method is proposed by Kendall,[13] and illustrated with data from a demand study by Stone.[14] Employed correctly, the method may provide a solution to the multicollinearity problem that proceeds by reducing a model's informational requirements meaningfully to the information content of existing data. On the other hand, perverse applications lead to parameter estimates that are even less satisfactory than those based on the original set of data.[15]

Given a set of interdependent explanatory variables X, and a hypothesized dependency relationship

$$y = X\,b + u,$$

Kendall proposes ". . . [to throw] new light on certain old but unsolved problems; particularly (a) how many variables do we take? (b) how do we discard the unimportant ones? and (c) how do we get rid of multicollinearities in them?"[16]

His solution, briefly, runs as follows: Defining

- X as a matrix of N observations on n multicollinear explanatory variables,
- F as a set of $m \leq n$ orthogonal components or common factors,
- U as a matrix of n derived residual (or unique) components, and
- A as a constructed set of $(m \times n)$ normalized factor loadings,

Kendall decomposes X into a set of statistically significant *orthogonal* common factors and residual components U such that

$$X = F\,A + U$$

exhausts the sample's observed variation. $X' = F\,A$, then, summarizes X's common or "significant" dimensions of variation in $m \leq n$ artificial, orthogonal variates, while for $m < n$,

[8] *Ibid.*

[9] H. Theil, "Specification Errors and the Estimation of Economic Relationships," *Review of the International Statistical Institute,* 25 (1957).

[10] H. Theil, *Economic Forecasts and Policy* (Amsterdam: North-Holland, 1962), 216.

[11] J. Johnston, *op. cit.*, 207.

[12] *Ibid.*; and H. Theil, *op. cit.*, 217.

[13] M. G. Kendall, *A Course in Multivariate Analysis* (Hafner, 1957), 70–75.

[14] J. R. N. Stone, "The Analysis of Market Demand," *Journal of the Royal Statistical Society,* CVIII (1945), 286–382.

[15] For a recent application open to this criticism see W. F. Massy, "Principal Components Regression in Exploratory Statistical Research," *Journal of the American Statistical Association,* 60, 1965.

[16] M. G. Kendall, *op. cit.*, p. 70.

U picks up what little — and presumably unimportant — residual variation remains.

Replacing the multicollinear set X by F, estimates of the desired dependency relationship now can be based on a set of thoroughly orthogonal independent variables,

$$y = Fb^* + \epsilon^*.$$

Taking advantage of the factor structure's internal orthogonality and, through the central limit theorem its approximate normality, each artificial variate's statistical significance can be tested with much greater confidence than econometric data ordinarily permit.

In some cases individual factors may be directly identified with meaningful economic phenomena through the subsets of variables that dominate their specifications. Should this be the case, each component, or factor, may be interpreted and used as a variable in its own right, whose properties closely correspond to those required by the standard regression model. In such a case the transformation permits a reformulation of the model that can be tested effectively on existing data.

In general, however, the econometrician is not so fortunate. Each component turns out to be simply an artificial, linear combination of the original variables,

$$F = X A^t,$$

that is completely devoid of economic content. In order to give meaning to structural coefficients, therefore, it is necessary to return from factor to variable space by transforming estimators A and b^* into estimates

$$b^{**} = A^t b^*$$

of the structural parameters

$$y = X b + u$$

originally sought.

In the special (component analysis) case in which all $m = n$ factors are obtained, and retained in the regression equation, ". . . [Nothing has been lost] by the transformation except the time spent on the arithmetical labor of finding it."[17] By the same token, however, nothing has been gained, for the Gauss-Markoff theorem insures that coefficient estimates b^{**} are identical to the estimates b' that would be obtained by the direct application of least squares to the original, highly unstable, set of variables. Moreover, all $m = n$ factors will be found significant and retained only in those instances in which the independent variable set, in fact, is not seriously multicollinear.

In general, therefore, Kendall's procedure derives n parameter estimates,

$$b^{**} = A^t b^*,$$

from an $m < n$-dimensional independent variable set,

$$\begin{aligned} y &= F b^* + \epsilon^*, \\ &= (X - U) A^t b^* + \epsilon^*, \end{aligned}$$

whose total informational content is both lower and less well-defined than for the original set of variables. The rank of $(X - U)$, clearly, is never greater, and usually is smaller, than the rank of X. Multicollinearity, therefore, is intensified rather than alleviated by the series of transformations. Indeed, by discarding the residual — or perhaps the "unique" — portion of an independent variable's variation, one is seriously in danger of throwing out the baby rather than the bath — i.e., independent rather than redundant dimensions of information.

Kendall's approach is not without attractions. Should factors permit identification and use as variables in their own right, the transformation provides a somewhat defensible solution to the multicollinearity problem. The discrepancy between apparent and significant dimensions (in model and data, respectively) is eliminated by a *meaningful* reduction in the number of the model's parameters. Even where factors cannot be used directly, their derivation provides insight into the pattern of interdependence that undermines the structural stability of estimates based on the original set of variables.

The shortcoming of the approach lies in its prescriptions for handling those situations in which the data do not suggest a reformulation that reduces the model's information requirements — i.e., where components cannot be interpreted directly as economic variables. In such circumstances, solution of the multicollinearity problem requires the application of *additional* information, rather than the further reduction of existing information. Methods that retain a model's full complexity while reducing the informational content of existing

[17] M. G. Kendall, *op. cit.*, 70.

data aggrevate rather than alleviate the multicollinearity problem.

Rules of Thumb

A second and more pragmatic line of attack recognizes the need to live with poorly conditioned, non-experimental data, and seeks to develop rules of thumb by which "acceptable" departures from orthogonality may be distinguished from "harmful" degrees of multicollinearity.

The term "harmful multicollinearity" is generally defined only symptomatically, that is, as the cause of *wrong signs* or other symptoms of nonsense regressions. The inadequacy of such a practice may be illustrated, perhaps, by the ease with which the same argument can be used to explain *right signs* and sensible regressions from the same basic set of data. An operational definition of harmful multicollinearity, however inadequate it may be, is clearly preferable to the methodological slight-of-hand that symptomatic definitions make possible.

The most simple, operational definition of unacceptable collinearity makes no pretense to theoretical validity. An admittedly arbitrary rule of thumb is established to constrain simple correlations between explanatory variables to be smaller than, say, $r = .8$ or $.9$. The most obvious type of pairwise sample interdependence, of course, can be avoided in this fashion.

More elaborate and apparently sophisticated rules of thumb also exist. One that has lingered in the background of econometrics for many years has recently gained sufficient stature to be included in an elementary text. The rule holds, essentially, that ". . . intercorrelation or multicollinearity is not necessarily a problem unless it is high relative to the over-all degree of multiple correlation . . ."[18] Or, more specifically, if

r_{ij} is the zero order correlation between two independent variables, and

R_y is the multiple correlation between dependent and independent variables,

multicollinearity is said to be "harmful" if

$r_{ij} \geqq R_y$.

Although its origin is unknown, the rule's intuitive appeal appears to rest on the geometric concept of a triangle formed by the end points of three vectors (representing variables y, x_1, and x_2, respectively) in N-dimensional observation space (reduced to three dimensions in figure 1). $y' = X b'$ is represented by the perpendicular (i.e., the least squares) reflection of y onto the x_1x_2 plane. Multiple correlation R_y is defined by the direction cosine between y and y', while simple correlation r_{12} is the direction cosine between x_1 and x_2. Should multiple correlation be greater than simple correlation, the triangle's base x_1x_2 is greater than its height $y\,y'$, and the dependency relationship appears to be "stable."

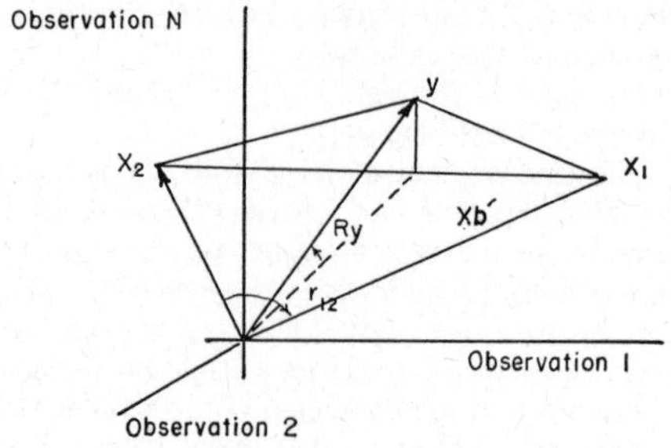

FIGURE 1

Despite its intuitive appeal the concept is highly vulnerable. On extension to multiple dimensions, for example, it breaks down entirely. Complete multicollinearity — i.e., perfect singularity — within a set of explanatory variables is quite consistent with very small pairwise correlations between members of X. A set of dummy variables whose non-zero elements accidentally exhaust the sample space is an obvious, and an aggravatingly common, example.

The rule's conceptual appeal may be rescued from absurdities of this type by extending the concept of simple correlation between independent variables to multiple correlation *within an independent variable set*. A variable x_i then, would be said to be "harmfully multicollinear" only if its multiple correlation with *other* members of the independent variable set, R_{x_i}, were greater than the dependent variable's multiple correlation with the entire set, R_y.

[18] L. R. Klein, *An Introduction to Econometrics* (Prentice-Hall, 1962), 101.

Numerous empirical counter examples remain, however, to indicate that multicollinearity is basically an *interdependency*, not a *dependency* condition. Should (X^tX) be singular — or virtually so — tight sample dependence between y and X cannot assure the structural integrity of least-squares parameter estimates; the original Cobb-Douglas studies provide an appropriate case in point.

Computer Programming

The development of large scale, high speed digital computers has had a well-recognized, virtually revolutionary impact on econometric applications. By bringing new persons into contact with the field the computer also is having a perceptible, if less dramatic, impact on econometric methodology. The phenomenon is not new. Technical specialists have called attention to matters of theoretical interest in the past — Professor Viner's famous draftsman, Mr. Wong, is a notable example.[19] More recently, the computer programmer's approach to singularity in regression analysis has begun to shape the econometrician's view of multicollinearity as well.

Specifically, the numerical estimation of parameters for a standard regression equation requires the inversion of a matrix of correlation coefficients for the independent variable set. Estimates of both slope coefficients,

$$b' = (X^tX)^{-1}X^ty,$$

and variances,

$$V(b') = \sigma_u^2(X^tX)^{-1},$$

require the operation. Should the independent variable set X be perfectly multicollinear, (X^tX), of course, is singular, and a determinate solution does not exist.

The programmer, accordingly, is required to build checks for non-singularity into standard regression routines. The test most commonly used relies on the property that the determinant of a singular matrix is zero. Defining a small, positive test value, $\epsilon > 0$, a solution is attempted only if the determinant

$$|X^tX| > \epsilon;$$

otherwise, computations are halted and a premature exit is called.

Checks for singularity may be kept internal to a computer program, well out of the user's sight. Recently, however, the determinant has tended to join b' coefficients, t-ratios, F-tests and other summary statistics as routine elements of printed output. Remembering that the determinant, $|X^tX|$, is based on a normalized, correlation matrix, its position on the scale

$$0 \leq |X^tX| \leq 1$$

yields at least heuristic insight into the degree of interdependence within an independent variable set. As X approaches singularity, of course, $|X^tX|$ approaches zero. Conversely $|X^tX|$ close to one implies a nearly orthogonal independent variable set. Unfortunately, the gradient between these limits is not well defined. As an ordinal measure of the relative orthogonality of similar sets of independent variables, however, the statistic has attracted a certain amount of well-deserved attention and use.

A single, overall measure of the degree of interdependence within an independent variable set, although useful in its own right, provides little information on which corrective action can be based. Near singularity may result from strong, sample *pairwise* correlation between independent variables, or from a more subtle and complex linkage between several members of a set. The problem's cure, of course, depends on the nature of the interaction. The determinant, per se, gives no information about this interaction.

In at least one case an attempt has been made to localize multicollinearity by building directly into a multiple regression program an index of each explanatory variable's dependence on other members of the independent variable set.[20] Recalling that (X^tX) is the matrix of simple correlation coefficients for X, and defining r^{ii} as the diagonal element of $(X^tX)^{-1}$ corresponding to the ith variable, it is well-known that

$$r^{ii} = \frac{|(X^tX)_{ii}|}{|X^tX|}$$

[19] J. Viner, "Cost Curves and Supply Curves," *Zeitschrift für Nationalökonomie*, III (1931). Reprinted in American Economic Association, *Readings in Price Theory* (Richard D. Irwin, 1952).

[20] A. E. Beaton and R. R. Glauber, *Statistical Laboratory Ultimate Regression Package* (Harvard Statistical Laboratory, 1962).

where $(X^tX)_{ii}$ denotes the correlation matrix excluding the ith variable, x_i. Should x_i be orthogonal to the remaining members of X, $|(X^tX)_{ii}| = |X^tX|$ and $r^{ii} = 1$. On the other hand, should X_i be perfectly dependent on the remaining members of X, the denominator vanishes while the numerator, since it does not contain x_i, is not affected. Thus, when x_i is perfectly dependent on the other members of X, r^{ii} — and thereby $V(b'_i) = \sigma_u r^{ii}$ — becomes infinite, pinpointing not only the existence but also the location of singularity within an independent variable set. Even though the spectrum $1 \leq r^{ii} \leq \infty$ is little explored, diagonal elements, by their size, give heuristic insight into the relative severity of redundancies, as well as their location within an independent variable set.

Armed with such basic (albeit crude) diagnostic techniques, the investigator may begin to deal with the multicollinearity problem. First, of course, the determinant $|X^tX|$ alerts him to its existence. Next, diagonal elements r^{ii} give sufficient insight into the problem's location — and therefore into its cause — to suggest the selective additions of information that are required for stable, least-squares, parameter estimates.

The Problem Revisited

Many persons, clearly, have examined one or more aspects of the multicollinearity problem. Each, however, has focused on one facet to the exclusion of others. Few have attempted to synthesize, or even to distinguish between multicollinearity's nature and effects, or its diagnosis and cure.

Those who do concern themselves with a definition of multicollinearity tend to think of the problem in terms of a discrete condition that either exists or does not exist, rather than as a continuous phenomenon whose severity is to be measured.

A good deal of confusion — and some inconsistency — emerges from this picture. Cohesion requires, first of all, a clear distinction between multicollinearity's nature and effects, and second, a definition *in terms of the former* on which diagnosis can be based.

Definition

Econometric problems ordinarily are defined in terms of discrepancies between the properties of hypothesized and sample variates. Nonnormality, heteroscedasticity and autocorrelation, for example, are defined in terms of differences between hypothesized and observed distributions of residuals. Such definitions lead directly to the development of test statistics on which detection, and an evaluation of the problem's nature and severity, can be based. Once an investigator is alerted to a problem's existence and character, of course, corrective action ordinarily constitutes a separate — and often quite straightforward — step. Such a definition would seem to be both possible and desirable for multicollinearity.

Let us define multicollinearity, then, in terms of departures from *orthogonality* in an independent variable set. Such a definition has two advantages. First, it distinguishes clearly between the problem's essential nature — which consists of a lack of independence, or the presence of interdependence among explanatory variables, — and the symptoms or effects on the dependency relationship that it produces. Second, orthogonality lends itself easily to formulation as a statistical hypothesis and, as such, leads directly to the development of test statistics, adjusted for numbers of variables and observations in X, against which the severity of departures can be calibrated. Developed in sufficient detail, such statistics may provide considerable insight into the location and pattern, as well as the severity, of interdependence that undermines the experimental quality of a given set of data.

Inferences from sample to population, of course, are possible. In general, however, little importance is attached to properties of the population from which a set of data has been drawn. Attention focuses largely, if not entirely, on the sample itself. Orthogonality provides a standard, and distributional properties a yardstick, against which one facet of experimental quality may be measured. Multicollinearity as viewed here is a sample rather than a population characteristic.[21]

[21] Interest that does exist in populations per se centers around the efficiency of continued data collection efforts. Should a particular set of data — e.g., a set of aggregate,

Diagnosis

Once a definition is in hand, multicollinearity ceases to be so inscrutable. Add a set of distributional properties and departures from orthogonality can be calibrated in a variety of ways, at several levels of detail.

To derive statistics with known distributions, specific assumptions are required about the nature of the population that generates sample values of X. As existing distribution theory is based almost entirely on assumptions that X is multivariate normal, it is convenient to retain the assumption here. Common versions of least-squares regression models, and tests of significance based thereon, also are based on multivariate normality. Questions of dependence and interdependence in regression analysis, therefore, may be examined within the same statistical framework.

Should the assumption prove unnecessarily severe its probabilistic implications can be relaxed informally. For formal purposes, however, multivariate normality's strength and convenience is essential, and underlies everything that follows.

General

The heuristic relationship between orthogonality and the determinant of a matrix of sample zero-order correlation coefficients

$$0 \leq |X^tX| \leq 1$$

has been discussed under computer programming approaches to singularity, above. Should it be possible to attach distributional properties under an assumption of parental orthogonality to the determinant $|X^tX|$, or to a convenient transformation of $|X^tX|$, the resulting statistic could provide a useful first measure of the presence and severity of multicollinearity within an independent variable set.

Presuming X to be multivariate normal, such properties are close at hand. As shown by Wishart, sample variances and covariances are jointly distributed according to the frequency function that bears his name.[22] Working from the Wishart distribution, Wilks, in an analytical tour de force, is able to derive the moments and distribution (in open form) of the determinant of sample covariance matrices.[23] Employing the additional assumption of underlying orthogonality, he then obtains the moments and distribution of determinants for sample correlation matrices $|X^tX|$ as well. Specifically the kth moment of $|X^tX|$ is shown to be

$$M_k(|X^tX|) = \frac{\left[\Gamma\left(\frac{N-1}{2}\right)\right]^{n-1} \prod_{i=2}^{n} \Gamma\left(\frac{N-i}{2}+k\right)}{\left[\Gamma\left(\frac{N-1}{2}+k\right)\right]^{n-1} \prod_{i=2}^{n} \Gamma\left(\frac{N-i}{2}\right)}, \quad (2)$$

where as before, N is sample size and n the number of variables.[24]

In theory, one ought to be able to derive the density function for $|X^tX|$ from (2), and in open form it is indeed possible. For $n > 2$, however, explicit solutions for the distribution of $|X^tX|$ have not been obtained.

Bartlett, however, by comparing the lower moments of (2) with those of the Chi Square distribution, obtains a transformation of $|X^tX|$,[25]

$$\chi^2_{|X^tX|}{}^{(\nu)} = -\left[N - 1 - \tfrac{1}{6}(2n+5)\right] \log |X^tX|, \quad (3)$$

that is distributed approximately as Chi Square with $\nu = \frac{1}{2}n(n-1)$ degrees of freedom.

In this light, the determinant of intercorrelations within an independent variable set takes on new meaning. No longer is interpretation limited to extremes of the range $0 \leq |X^tX| \leq 1$. By transforming $|X^tX|$ into an approximate Chi Square statistic, a meaningful scale is provided against which departures from orthogonality, and hence the gradient between singularity and orthogonality, can be calibrated. Should one accept the multivariate normality assumption, of course, probability levels provide a *cardinal* measure of the extent to which X is interdependent. Even without such a scale, transformation to a variable whose distribution is known, even approximately — by standardizing for sample size and number of

annual, time-series observations — be hopelessly multicollinear, further samples are likely to be similarly affected. More efficient data collection is likely to require either different sampling methods or entirely different data sources.

[22] J. Wishart, "The Generalized Product Moment Distribution in Samples from a Multivariate Normal Population," *Biometrika,* 20A (1928).

[23] S. Wilks, "Certain Generalizations in the Analysis of Variance," *Biometrika,* 24 (1932), 477.

[24] *Ibid.*, 492.

[25] M. S. Bartlett, "Tests of Significance in Factor Analysis," *British Journal of Psychology, Statistical Section,* 3 (1950), 83.

variables — offers a generalized, *ordinal* measure of the extent to which quite different sets of independent variables are undermined by multicollinearity.

Localization

Determining that a set of explanatory variables departs substantially from internal orthogonality is a first step, but only a first step in the analysis of multicollinearity proposed here. If information is to be applied efficiently to alleviate the problem, localization measures are required to specify accurately the variables most severely undermined by interdependence.

To find the basis for one such measure we return to notions developed earlier, by computer programmers and econometricians. As indicated, both use diagonal elements of an inverse correlation matrix, r^{ii}, in some form, as measures of the extent to which particular explanatory variables are affected by multicollinearity.

Intuition suggests that discrepancies between hypothesized and sample orthogonality may be tested through this statistic.

Elements of the necessary statistical theory are developed by Wilks, who obtains the distribution of numerous determinental ratios of variables from a multivariate normal distribution.[26] Specifically, for the matrix (X^tX), defining h principal minors

$$|X^tX|_i \text{ for } i = 1, \ldots, h, \quad (4)$$

such that no two contain the same diagonal element, r_{ii}, but that each r_{ii} enters one principal minor, Wilks considers the variable

$$Z = \frac{|X^tX|}{\prod_{i=1}^{h} |X^tX|_i}.$$

For any arbitrary set of h principal minors (4), he then obtains both the moments and distribution of Z. For the special case of interest here, let us form principal minors such that

$h = 2$, $|X^tX|_1 = r_{ii} = 1$, and $|X^tX|_2 = |(X^tX)_{ii}|$, then

$$Z_{\bullet} = \frac{|X^tX|}{1 \times |(X^tX)_{ii}|} = \frac{1}{r^{ii}}.$$

Defining $\nu_1 = N - n$ and $\nu_2 = n - 1$, it follows from Wilks' more general expression that the density function for $Z_{\bullet}$ can be written as,

$$f(Z_{\bullet}) = \frac{\Gamma(\frac{\nu_1 + \nu_2}{2})}{\Gamma(\frac{\nu_1}{2})\Gamma(\frac{\nu_2}{2})} Z_{\bullet}^{1/2(\nu_1 - 2)} (1 - Z_{\bullet})^{1/2(\nu_2 - 2)}. \quad (5)$$

Wilks notes that $Z_{\bullet}$, as defined, is equal to $1 - R_{x_i}^2$.[27] To obtain a more convenient (i.e., a tabulated) distribution, however, a change of variables is required. Consider the new variate,

$$\omega = (\frac{1}{Z_{\bullet}} - 1)\frac{\nu_1}{\nu_2} = (r^{ii} - 1)\frac{\nu_1}{\nu_2}, \quad (6)$$

and note that

$$Z_{\bullet} = (\frac{\nu_2}{\nu_1}\omega + 1)^{-1}. \quad (7)$$

$$\left|\frac{dZ_{\bullet}}{d\omega}\right| = (\frac{\nu_2}{\nu_1}\omega + 1)^{-2}(\frac{\nu_2}{\nu_1}), \quad (8)$$

where the vertical bars in (8) denote absolute value. Substituting (7) into (5) and multiplying by (8), we have the density function of ω,

$$g(\omega) = \frac{\Gamma(\frac{\nu_1 + \nu_2}{2})}{\Gamma(\frac{\nu_1}{2})\Gamma(\frac{\nu_2}{2})}(\frac{\nu_2}{\nu_1}\omega + 1)^{1/2(2-\nu_1)}$$
$$(1 - [\frac{\nu_2}{\nu_1}\omega + 1]^{-1})^{1/2(\nu_2 - 2)}[(\frac{\nu_2}{\nu_1}\omega + 1)^{-2}(\frac{\nu_2}{\nu_1})]$$
$$= \frac{\Gamma(\frac{\nu_1 + \nu_2}{2})}{\Gamma(\frac{\nu_1}{2})\Gamma(\frac{\nu_2}{2})}(\frac{\nu_2}{\nu_1}\omega + 1)^{-1/2(\nu_1 + \nu_2)} \omega^{1/2(\nu_2 - 2)}(\frac{\nu_2}{\nu_1})^{1/2\nu_2},$$

which can be recognized as the F-distribution with ν_1 and ν_2 degrees of freedom.[28]

The transformation

$$\omega = (r^{ii} - 1)(\frac{N - n}{n - 1}), \quad (9)$$

then, can be seen to be distributed as F with $N - n$ and $n - 1$ degrees of freedom. Defining $R_{x_i}^2$ as the squared multiple correlation between X_i and the other members of X, this result can be understood most easily by recalling that

$$r^{ii} = \frac{1}{1 - R_{x_i}^2}.$$

[26] S. Wilks, *op. cit.*, especially 480–482 and 491–492.

[27] *Ibid.*, 493.

[28] F. Graybill, *op. cit.*, 31.

Therefore; $(r^{ii} - 1)$ equals $\frac{R_{x_i}^2}{1 - R_{x_i}^2}$; and ω (as defined in equations (6) and (9) above), except for a term involving degrees of freedom, is the ratio of explained to unexplained variance. It is not surprising then, to see ω distributed as F.

As regards the distribution of (9), the same considerations discussed in the preceding section are relevant. If X is jointly normal, (9) is distributed exactly as F, and its magnitude provides a cardinal measure of the extent to which individual variables are affected by multicollinearity. If normality cannot be assumed, (9) still provides an ordinal measure, adjusted for degrees of freedom, of x_i's dependence on other variables in X.

Having established which variables in X are substantially multicollinear, it generally proves useful to determine in greater detail the pattern of interdependence between affected members of the independent variable set. An example, perhaps, will illustrate the information's importance. Suppose (9) is large in a hypothetical sample only for x_1, x_2, x_3, and x_4, indicating these variables to be significantly multicollinear, but only with each other, the remaining variables $x_5, \ldots, x_n$ being essentially uncorrelated, both with each other and with $x_1, \ldots, x_4$. Suppose further that all four variables, $x_1, \ldots, x_4$ are substantially intercorrelated with each of the other three. If well-determined estimates are desired for this subset, additional information must be obtained for at least three of $x_1, \ldots, x_4$.

Alternatively, suppose that x_1 and x_2 are highly correlated, x_3 and x_4 also are highly correlated, but that all other intercorrelations among the four, and with other members of X, are small. In this case, additional information must be obtained for only two variables — x_1 or x_2, and x_3 or x_4. Clearly, then, the efficient solution of multicollinearity requires detailed information about the *pattern* as well as the existence, severity, and location of intercorrelations within a subset of interdependent variables.

To gain insight into the pattern of interdependence in X, a straightforward transformation of off-diagonal elements of the inverse correlation matrix $(X^tX)^{-1}$ is both effective and convenient. Its development may be summarized briefly, as follows.

Consider a partition of the independent variable set

$$X = [X^{(1)}X^{(2)}]$$

such that variables x_i and x_j constitute $X^{(1)}$, and the remaining $n - 2$ variables $X^{(2)}$. The corresponding matrix of zero order correlation coefficients, then, is partitioned such that

$$(X^tX) = \begin{pmatrix} R_{11} & R_{12} \\ R_{21} & R_{22} \end{pmatrix}$$

where R_{11}, containing variables x_i and x_j, is of dimension 2×2 and R_{22} is $(n-2) \times (n-2)$. Elements of the inverse correlation matrix R_{11}^{-1} corresponding to $X^{(1)}$, then, can be expressed without loss of generality as elements of the matrix [29]

$$R_{11}^{-1} = (R_{11} - R_{12}R_{22}^{-1}R_{21})^{-1}.$$

Before inversion, the single off-diagonal element of

$$(R_{11} - R_{12}R_{22}^{-1}R_{21})$$

may be recognized as the partial covariance of x_i and x_j, holding constant $X^{(2)}$, the other members of the independent variable set. On normalizing in the usual fashion — i.e., dividing by square roots of corresponding diagonal elements — partial correlation coefficients between x_i and x_j can be obtained.[30]

For the special case considered here, where $X^{(1)}$ contains only two variables and R_{11}, accordingly is 2×2, it also can be shown that corresponding *normalized* off-diagonal elements of $(R_{11} - R_{12}R_{22}^{-1}R_{21})$ and its inverse $(R_{11} - R_{12}R_{22}^{-1}R_{21})^{-1}$ differ from one another only by sign. It follows, therefore, that by a change of sign, normalized off-diagonal elements of the inverse correlation matrix $(X^tX)^{-1}$ yield *partial correlations* among members of the independent variable set. That is, defining $r_{ij.}$ as the coefficient of partial correlation between x_i and x_j, other members of X held constant, and r^{ij} as elements of $(X^tX)^{-1}$, as above, it follows that

$$r_{ij.} = \frac{-r^{ij}}{\sqrt{r^{ii}}\sqrt{r^{jj}}}.$$

[29] G. Hadley, *Linear Algebra* (Addison-Wesley, 1961), 107 and 108.

[30] T. W. Anderson, *An Introduction to Multivariate Statistical Analysis* (John Wiley, 1958).

Distributional properties under a hypothesis of orthogonality, of course, are required to tie up the bundle. Carrying forward the assumption of multivariate normality, such properties are close at hand. In a manner exactly analogous to the simple (zero order) correlation coefficient, the statistic

$$t_{ij.}(\nu) = \frac{r_{ij.}\sqrt{N-n}}{\sqrt{1-r_{ij.}^2}}$$

may be shown to be distributed as Student's t with $\nu = N - n$ degrees of freedom.[31]

An exact, cardinal interpretation of interdependence between x_i and x_j as members of X, of course, requires exact satisfaction of multivariate normal distributional properties. As with the determinant and diagonal elements of $(X^tX)^{-1}$ that precede it, however, off-diagonal elements — transformed to $r_{ij.}$ or $t_{ij.}$ — provide useful ordinal measures of collinearity even in the absence of such rigid assumptions.

Illustration

A three-stage hierarchy of increasingly detailed tests for the presence, location, and pattern of interdependence within an independent variable set X has been proposed. In order, the stages are:

1) Test for the presence and severity of multicollinearity anywhere in X, based on the approximate distribution of determinants of sample correlation matrices, $|X^tX|$, from an orthogonal underlying population.
2) Test for the dependence of particular variables on other members of X based on the exact distribution, under orthogonality, of diagonal elements of the inverse correlation matrix, $(X^tX)^{-1}$.
3) Examine the pattern of interdependence among X through the distribution, under orthogonality, of off-diagonal elements of the inverse correlation matrix, $(X^tX)^{-1}$.

In many ways such an analysis, based entirely on statistics generated routinely during standard regression computations, may serve as a substitute for the formal, thorough (and time-consuming) factor analysis of an independent variable set. It provides the insight required to detect, and if present to identify, multicollinearity in X. Accordingly, it may serve as a starting point from which the additional information required for stable, least-squares estimation can be sought. An illustration will perhaps help to clarify the procedure's mechanics and purpose, both of which are quite straightforward.

In a series of statistical cost analyses for the United States Navy, an attempt was made to measure the effect on maintenance cost of such factors as ship age, size, intensity of usage (measured by fuel consumption), time between successive overhauls, and such discrete, qualitative characteristics as propulsion mode (steam, diesel, nuclear), complexity (radar picket, guided missile, etc.), and conversion under a recent Fleet Rehabilitation and Modernization, (FRAM) program. Equations have been specified and estimated on various samples from the Atlantic Fleet destroyer force that relate logarithms of repair costs to logarithms of age, displacement, overhaul cycle, and fuel consumption, and to discrete (0,1) dummy variables for diesel propulsion, radar picket, and FRAM conversion.[32]

Stability under changes in specification, direction of minimization, and sample coverage have been examined heuristically by comparing regression coefficients, determinants of correlation matrices $|X^tX|$, and diagonal elements of $(X^tX)^{-1}$, from different equations. The sensitivity of certain parameters under such changes (e.g., fuel consumption) and the stability of others (e.g., age and overhaul cycle) have been noted in the past.

By performing an explicit analysis for interdependence in X, such information could have been obtained more quickly, directly, and in greater detail. Consider, for example, the seven-variable equation summarized in table 1. Multiple correlation and associated F-statistics, with t-ratios for the relationship between dependent and independent variables, show dependence between y and X to be substantial.

Measures of interdependence within X, beginning with the approximate Chi Square transformation for the matrix of correlation coefficients over the entire set,

[31] F. Graybill, *op. cit.*, 215 and 208.

[32] D. Farrar and R. Apple, "Some Factors that Affect the Overhaul Cost of Ships," *Naval Research Logistics Quarterly,* 10 (1963); and "Economic Considerations in Establishing an Overhaul Cycle for Ships, *Naval Engineers Journal,* 77 (1965).

TABLE 1. — OVERHAUL COST EQUATION, UNITED STATES NAVY DESTROYERS

Measures of Dependence

$R_y^2 = .80$ $F_y\,(7,88) = 56$

$\log y = 4.81$	$+\ .34 \log x_1$	$+\ .40 \log x_2$	$-\ .79 \log x_3$	$+\ .05 \log x_4$	$-\ .03\, x_5$	$+\ .11\, x_6$	$-\ .16\, x_7$
$t\,(88) =$	11.4	5.4	8.7	0.5	3.5	2.5	2.5
Cost/Year	Age	Size	Cycle	Fuel	Diesel	Radar	FRAM

Measures of Interdependence

$\chi^2_{|X^tX|}\,(21) = 261$

$F_{x_i}\,(6,89) =$	6.3	19.9	6.3	47.5	47.1	12.7	4.8

Pattern of Interdependence

Partial $r_{ij.}$ below diagonal — Multiple $R_{x_i}^2$ on diagonal — Partial $t_{ij.}$ (89) above diagonal.

	Age	Size	Cycle	Fuel	Diesel	Radar	FRAM
Age	.30	1.27	2.01	−3.57	1.27	4.72	3.38
Size	.13	.57	2.60	3.44	−2.03	.78	−1.27
Cycle	.21	.27	.30	.82	1.15	−3.51	.59
Fuel	−.35	.34	.09	.76	−8.77	3.13	4.06
Diesel	−.27	−.21	.12	−.68	.76	5.51	2.68
Radar	.45	.08	−.35	.31	.50	.46	−2.55
FRAM	.34	−.13	.06	.40	.27	−.26	.24

SOURCE: D. Farrar and R. Apple, *op. cit.*
Sample Size, $N = 96$.
y = Overhaul Cost (thousands of dollars/year).
x_1 = Age (years).
x_2 = Size (displacement, thousands of tons).
x_3 = Overhaul Cycle (years).
x_4 = Fuel Consumption (standardized).
x_5 = 1 if diesel propulsion,
= 0 if not.
x_6 = 1 if radar picket,
= 0 if not.
x_7 = 1 if FRAM,
= 0 if not.

$$\chi^2_{X^tX}\,(21) = 261$$

quickly alert one, however, to the existence of substantial multicollinearity in X.

Multiple correlations and associated F-statistics within X (used to measure each explanatory variable's dependence on other members of the set) show x_1, x_3, and x_7, (age, cycle and FRAM conversion) to be relatively stable; x_2 and x_6 (size and radar picket) to be moderately affected by multicollinearity; and x_4 and x_5 (fuel consumption and diesel propulsion) to be extremely multicollinear.

Off-diagonal partial correlations and associated t-ratios show a linkage involving fuel consumption, diesel propulsion, and radar picket to lie at the heart of the problem.

The next step is up to the model builder. Should his purpose be to provide forecasts or to suggest policy changes that require reliable information about structural relationships between repair cost and either age or overhaul frequency, the job already is done. Dependence between y and x_1, x_3 is strong, and interdependence between these (explanatory) variables and other members of X is weak. The experimental quality of this portion of the data is high and estimates, accordingly, are likely to be stable.

Should one's purpose be to make forecasts or policy proposals that require accurate knowledge of the link between repair cost and fuel consumption, propulsion mode, or radar picket, corrective action to obtain more substantial information is required. In this particular case, sample stratification may help to overcome the problem. In other instances more strenuous efforts, such as additional primary data collection, extraneous parameter estimates from secondary data sources, or the direct application of subjective information, may be necessary.

In any case, efficient corrective action requires selectivity, and selectivity requires information about the nature of the problem to be handled. The procedure outlined here provides such information. It produces detailed diagnostics that can support the selective acquisition of information required for effective treatment of multicollinearity in regression analysis.

Summary

A point of view as well as a collection of techniques is advocated here. The techniques — in this case a series of diagnostics — can be formulated and illustrated explicitly. The spirit in which they are developed, however, is more difficult to convey. Given a point of view, techniques that support it may be replaced quite easily; the converse seldom is true. An effort will be made, therefore, to summarize our approach to multicollinearity and to contrast it with alternative views of the problem.

Multicollinearity as defined here is a statistical, rather than a mathematical condition. As such, one thinks, and speaks, in terms of the problem's *severity* rather than of its *existence* or non-existence.

As viewed here, multicollinearity is a property of the independent variable set alone. No account whatever is taken of the extent, or even the existence, of dependence between y and X. It is true, of course, that the *effect* on estimation and specification of interdependence in X — reflected by variances of estimated regression coefficient, and a tendency toward misspecification — also depends partly on the strength of dependence between y and X. In order to *treat* the problem, however, it is important to distinguish between *nature* and *effects*, and to develop diagnostics based on the former. In our view an independent variable set X is not less multicollinear if related to one dependent variable than if related to another, even though its effects may be more serious in one case than the other.

Of multicollinearity's effects on the structural integrity of estimated econometric models — estimation instability and structural misspecification — the latter, in our view, is the more serious. Sensitivity of parameter estimates to changes in specification, sample coverage, etc., is reflected at least partially in the standard deviations of estimated regression coefficients. No indication at all exists, however, of the bias imparted to coefficient estimates by incorrectly omitting a relevant, yet multicollinear, variable from an independent variable set.

Historical approaches to multicollinearity are almost unanimous in presuming the problem's solution to lie in deciding which variables to keep and which to drop from a model. That the gap between a model's informational requirements and a set of data's informational content can be reduced by increasing available information, as well as by reducing model complexity, is all too seldom considered.[33]

A major aim of the present approach, on the other hand, is to provide sufficiently detailed insight into the location and pattern of interdependence within a set of independent variables that strategic additions of information become not only a theoretical possibility, but also a practically feasible course of action.

Selectivity, however, is emphasized. This is not a counsel of perfection. The purpose of regression analysis is to estimate the structure of a dependent variable, y's, dependence on a *pre-selected* set of independent variables X, not to select an orthogonal independent variable set.

Structural integrity over an entire set, admittedly, requires both complete specification and internal orthogonality. One cannot obtain reliable estimates for an entire n-dimensional structure, or distinguish between competing n-dimensional hypotheses, with fewer than n significant dimensions of independent variation. Yet all variables are seldom equally important. Only one — or at most two or three — strategically important variables are ordinarily present in a regression equation. With complete specification and detailed insight into the location and pattern of interdependence in X, structural instability within the critical subset can be evaluated and, if necessary, corrected. Multicollinearity among non-critical variables can be tolerated. Should critical variables also be affected, additional information to provide coefficient estimates either for the essential

[33] H. Theil, *op. cit.*, 217 and J. Johnston, *op. cit.*, 207 are notable exceptions on a theoretical plane. In applied work the popularity of cross-sectional over time-series data may be traced in part to the former's great informational content. See for example, S. Prais and H. Houthakker, *The Analysis of Family Budgets* (Cambridge, England, 1955); J. Meyer and E. Kuh, *The Investment Decision: An Empirical Analysis* (Harvard University, 1957); G. Orcutt, et al., *Microanalysis of Socioeconomic Systems: A Simulation Study* (Harper, 1961); and J. R. N. Stone, *The Measurement of Consumers' Expenditure and Behavior in the United Kingdom* (Cambridge, England, 1954).

variables directly, or for those members of the set on which they are principally dependent, is required. Detailed diagnostics for the pattern of interdependence that undermines the experimental quality of X permits such information to be developed and applied both frugally and effectively.

Insight into the pattern of interdependence that affects an independent variable set can be provided in many ways. The entire field of factor analysis, for example, is designed to handle such problems.[34] Advantages of the measures proposed here are two-fold. The first advantage is pragmatic: While factor analysis involves extensive separate computations, the present set of measures relies entirely on transformations of statistics, such as the determinant $|X^tX|$ and elements of the inverse correlation matrix, $(X^tX)^{-1}$, that are generated routinely during standard regression computations. The second is that of symmetry: Questions of dependence and interdependence in regression analysis are handled in the same conceptual and statistical framework. Variables that are internal to a set X for one purpose are viewed as external to a subset of it for another. In this vein, tests of interdependence are approached as successive tests of each independent variable's dependence on other members of the set.

[34] For an application of principal components analysis to interdependence among explanatory variables, see J. Meyer and G. Kraft, "The Evaluation of Statistical Costing Techniques as Applied in the Transportation Industry," *American Economic Review,* LI (May 1961).

Persons of Bayesian bent who object to the use of probability levels in any form — either as measures of sample properties or as a basis for inference about population characteristics — may prefer mathematical to statistical measures of interdependence. Accordingly, determinants and multiple correlation and partial correlation coefficients are available. Their use is most defensible where extremely large sample sizes insure extremely small probability levels. Probabilistic measures such as Chi Square, F, and t transformations, on the other hand, may be preferred by others — especially where small samples increase a measure's sensitivity to available degrees of freedom. In either case, the conceptual and computational apparatus of regression analysis may be used to provide a quick and simple, yet serviceable, substitute for the factor analysis of an independent variable set.

It would be pleasant to conclude on a note of triumph that the problem has been solved and that no further "revisits" are necessary. Such a feeling, clearly, would be misleading. Diagnosis, although a necessary first step, does not insure cure. No miraculous "instant orthogonalization" can be offered.

We do, however, close on a note of optimism. The diagnostics described here offer the econometrician a place to begin. In combination with a spirit of selectivity in obtaining and applying additional information, multicollinearity may return from the realm of impossible to that of difficult, yet tractable, econometric problems.

THE FITTING OF STRAIGHT LINES WHEN BOTH VARIABLES ARE SUBJECT TO ERROR

ALBERT MADANSKY

Consider the situation where X and Y are related by $Y=\alpha+\beta X$, where α and β are unknown and where we observe X and Y with error, i.e., we observe $x=X+u$ and $y=Y+v$. Assume that $Eu=Ev=0$ and that the errors (u and v) are uncorrelated with the true values (X and Y). We survey and comment on the solutions to the problem of obtaining consistent estimates of α and β from a sample of (x, y)'s, (1) when one makes various assumptions about properties of the errors and the true values other than those mentioned above, and (2) when one has various kinds of "additional information" which aids in constructing these consistent estimates. The problems of obtaining confidence intervals for β and of testing hypotheses about β are not discussed, though approximate variances of some of the estimates of β are given.

1. INTRODUCTION

IF A physicist, say, were to give a statistician a set of observations on two variables, tell him that *only one* of the two variables is subject to "error" (where this "error" may be due to either errors in observation or random variation, or perhaps both), and ask him to "fit a straight line to the data," the statistician would only have to know how the observations were obtained, certain properties of the variables, that a linear relation exists, and the use to which the line is to be put, and, in the light of this information, he could fit the desired straight line to the data. If the same physicist were to come to the statistician with a set of observations on two variables and were to say that there were errors made in observing *both* of the variables, he would be surprised to hear the statistician request, in addition to the information mentioned above (which the physicist is presumably able to give the statistician quite readily), either more information on the range or standard deviation of the errors, observations on a third set of variables related to the other two, or replications of observations on each independent variable. In addition, he would be astounded to see the statistician quake if he were to mention that he believed the errors to be distributed normally.

To the physicist's eye, the situation in which both variables are subject to error does not seem to be quite as intractable as the statistician makes it out to be. If he plots the data, he could certainly plot an "eye-line" which, although it may not be the "best" line (in some sense), may be pretty close to the best line to be found by a statistician. If he knew of the method of least squares, he might argue that there are cases where for a large sample the estimate of the slope of the line relating Y to X lies between the least squares estimate of the slope of the line relating the observed y to the observed x and the reciprocal of the least squares estimate of the slope of the line relating the observed x to the observed y,[1] and hence an averaging of these two quantities calculated from the observations would lead to an "estimate" of the true slope. Hence to the physicist the only job left for the statistician is to make a more precise estimate than the one the physicist has already made, that is, use an estimator with known "nice" properties (e.g., consistency), and attach a standard error to the estimate made.

Assuming that the physicist's initial shock upon hearing that although he has an "estimate," the statistician doesn't, is over, and that the physicist is willing to hear what the statistician has to say for himself, what sort of things would the statistician like to know? As in the situation in which there were no errors in either variable, or where only one variable was subject to error, he would like to know the answers to some preliminary questions designed to give him an understanding of the problem. First of all, he would like to know something about the situation out of which the observations arose, e.g., were the observations random pairs? Is the underlying linear relationship symmetric in X and Y (in a sense to be defined later) or not? Secondly, he would like to know the use to which the linear relation is to be put, e.g., does the physicist merely want an estimate of the parameters of the linear relation? Or is he trying to predict something by using the relation? Or does he want to test some hypothesis about one or more of the values of the parameters of the linear equations? Finally, the statistician would like to know the characteristics of the underlying true variables, e.g., are they fixed numbers? Or are they random? If so, what can we assume about their distribution? With this preliminary information, the statistician can then determine the type of relationship in which the physicist is interested . . . and then it only *may* be possible to obtain a consistent estimate of the linear relationship. Besides this orientation information which the physicist is prepared to give the statistician, the statistician, as we shall soon see, will probably also need technical information about the errors which the physicist is probably unprepared to give, because he doesn't expect to be asked for such information.

[1] For a proof of this sometimes useful fact, cf. [16] and [29].

1.1. *Regression, Structural and Functional Relationships*

What are the possible situations out of which the observations arise? One situation is the following: Let X and Z be the true values which we are trying to observe. Suppose the distribution of Z given X is normal with mean $\alpha+\beta X$ and variance σ^2. Then, regardless of whether X is a random or a fixed variable, we can write, for fixed X, $Z|X=\alpha+\beta X+t$ where t is normally distributed with mean zero and variance σ^2. (So far, this is the ordinary linear regression situation with no errors in observing either variable. Rather, Z is subject to random variation.) However, we do not observe $z=Z$ or $x=X$ but instead $z=Z+v$ and $x=X+u$. If we let $Y=\alpha+\beta X$, then our observation on Z for a given X (but not for a given x) can be written as $y=Y+t+v$. It is assumed that $Eu=Ev=0$ and that u, v, and t are uncorrelated with each other and with X and Y. This situation is usually called the *regression* situation [21, 27]. It is essential that $t\neq 0$ for this model. The case where $t=0$ is considered separately.

One important property of the situation when X is a random variable is its asymmetry. By this I mean that although $Y=E(Z|X)=\alpha+\beta X$, the expression $X=(Y-\alpha)/\beta$, a result of algebraic manipulation of the original equation, is not a meaningful relation in this context. The only meaningful "inverse relation" here is $Y'=E(X|Z)$. In particular, when the joint distribution of X and Z is bivariate normal, then $E(X|Z)=\gamma+\delta Z$, which is not the result of solving the equation $Y=\alpha+\beta X$ for X. Another important point to note is that when we write $y=Y+t+v$, we must distinguish between t and v. The variable v is an error of observation which we presumably may be rid of by making finer and finer observations, whereas even if we were rid of v, we would never be rid of t. The variable t is inextricably tied up to the distribution of Z given X. The variable v is what Tukey [45] would call "fluctuation" and t is what he would call the "individual part" of an observed quantity. Finally, one should note that it makes no difference in the case in which there is no error in X whether we fix X and observe $Z|X$ or choose random pairs of observations, for in either case, in the relation $Y=E(Z|X)=\alpha+\beta X$, X is not treated as a random variable in considering the linear relationship of interest, namely the expectation of Z given X.

When X is observed with error, we can still select our pairs of observations either as random pairs or by fixing the value of x and observing the corresponding y. For example, suppose we wish to estimate β, the density of iron, by making use of the relation MASS $=\beta$ VOLUME. We can either select pieces of iron at random, so that our pairs of observations are random, or select pieces of iron of predetermined volumes, where the volumes are measured by some technique which yields the true volume of a piece of iron plus some random error. In this case, it makes a great deal of difference whether or not we can fix x in obtaining our observations, as we shall see later.

Another situation in which one might be interested in a linear relation between variables X and Y is the following. Let X and Y be the true values which we are trying to observe, and let them be linearly related by $Y=\alpha+\beta X$. In this case X, and hence Y, may be either random or nonrandom variables. We observe $y=Y+v$ and $x=X+u$. Again, it is assumed that $Eu=Ev=0$ and further that in situations where X and Y are random variables, $EYv=EXu=0$. If X is a random variable, the relation $Y=\alpha+\beta X$ is usually called a structural relation. (However, Lindley [27] calls this a functional relation. It is in this situation that "confluence analysis" [17, p. 525] is applied.) $Y=\alpha+\beta X$ has been called a *functional* relation by Kendall [21, 22] when X is not random. One immediately notes that this latter situation is a degenerate case of the regression situation, in that here $t=0$. One also notes that this situation is symmetric in that $X=(Y-\alpha)/\beta=\gamma+\delta Y$ is an equally meaningful way of writing the relation $Y=\alpha+\beta X$ in this context.

In any given situation, though, it may be difficult to determine whether to treat the relation as structural or functional. In the above example, for instance, we might interpret the linear relation as a functional relation by assuming that the pieces of iron we use are not a random sample from the population of pieces of iron, but merely what iron we had available and that, for a given piece of iron, there is a true mass and a true volume which we observe with random error due to the inaccuracies of our measuring devices. On the other hand, we might assume that the iron we had available was a random sample from the population of pieces of iron, so that the true mass and true volume of any piece of iron is a random variable. The determination of whether one treats the relation as structural or as functional depends on what sort of inferences one wishes to make. In this case, our treatment depends on whether we wish to estimate the density of iron or the density of the iron in our backyard.

What are some of the reasons for wanting to estimate α and β? We may be interested in estimating α and β because we are interested in the structural relation between two variables and hence these values are of intrinsic interest to us. For example, we may be considering the relation MASS $=\beta\cdot$VOLUME for a given element and desire to estimate β, the density of the element. Or we may have some hypothesis about the values of α and β and might need estimates of these quantities for use in the statistic to be used to test this hypothesis. Or we might be interested in estimating α and β for predictive purposes. That is to say, we may at some future time want to observe a value of X without error and use the relation $Y=\alpha+\beta X$ to predict Y from this X. From the symmetry of the structural and functional relations, if we want to do so, we can also observe a Y without error and predict X from the equation $X=(Y-\alpha)/\beta$. This, however, cannot be done in the regression situation, as has been pointed out earlier.

One should note that there is another problem in this context which is also called the prediction problem. This is the situation in which one can never hope to observe X or Y without error, and hence is only interested in predicting $Ey=Y$ for a new observed $x=X+u$. But this is just the case in which the least-squares regression of y on x works, for our independent variable is no longer X but instead x, which is observed without error. In this case, the statistician has no difficulty in estimating the parameters of the linear relation of interest. (Cf. [11, 27, 48] on this point. The confusion here is a result of and a good example of the confusion between regression and structure-function.)

1.2. *Least Squares and Maximum Likelihood Estimation*

I have spent some time outlining the preliminary information necessary to the statistician before he can undertake to estimate a linear relation between two variables observed with or without error. But once the statistician has this preliminary information, thereby ascertaining what type of linear relationship obtains, he still cannot estimate the linear relationship when both variables are observed with error.

Let us say that we observe $x_i = X_i + u_i$ and $y_i = Y_i + v_i$ where $Y_i = \alpha + \beta X_i$, and assume that $Eu_i = Ev_i = 0$, that the errors (u_i and v_i) are uncorrelated with each other and with the true values (X_i, Y_i), that our successive observations are independent, and that Var $X_i = \sigma_X^2$, Var $u_i = \sigma_u^2$, Var $v_i = \sigma_v^2$, Var $x_i = \sigma_x^2$, Var $y_i = \sigma_y^2$, and Var $Y_i = \sigma_Y^2$ for all i. Then using ordinary least squares techniques (i.e., minimizing $\sum w_i(y_i - \alpha - \beta x_i)^2$ where w_i is the reciprocal of the variance of $y_i - \alpha - \beta x_i$ given x_i, i.e., $w_i = 1/\sigma_v^2$) is not correct, for use of this method yields efficient, consistent estimates of $\beta/(1 + (\sigma_u^2/\sigma_X^2))$, not of β. By using ordinary least squares techniques, we are only minimizing "vertical" error, error in the y direction. Our situation is such that we also have "horizontal" error which should be taken into account in estimating β. To use least squares estimation correctly, as Lindley [27] points out, one should take account of both errors by minimizing

$$\sum_{i=1}^{n} w_i(\beta)(y_i - \alpha - \beta x_i)^2$$

where the $w_i(\beta)$'s are proportional to the reciprocals of the variance of $y_i - \alpha - \beta x_i$ given X_i, i.e., $w_i(\beta) = k/(\sigma_v^2 + \beta^2\sigma_u^2)$, where k does not depend on i.

If we knew $\lambda = \sigma_v^2/\sigma_u^2$, then Var $(y_i - \alpha - \beta x_i) = \sigma_v^2 + \beta^2\sigma_u^2 = (\lambda + \beta^2)\sigma_u^2$. Hence if $w_i(\beta) = 1/(\lambda + \beta^2)$, we could minimize $\sum w_i(\beta)(y_i - \alpha - \beta x_i)^2$ with respect to β quite readily, and obtain equation (3) below as our estimate of β. Lindley points out that this is the same estimate as that obtained by minimizing the distance between (x_i, y_i) and (X_i, Y_i) for all i. The method of weighted least squares, with weights depending on β, will also give an estimate of β if either σ_u^2 or σ_v^2, or both, rather than $\lambda = \sigma_v^2/\sigma_u^2$, is known. If one assumes that X, Y, u, and v are each normally distributed, with $Eu = Ev = Euv = EXu = EXv = EYu = EYv = 0$, then, as will be seen later, the method of maximum likelihood will give the same estimate as that obtained by the method of weighted least squares, whatever one of the above assumptions is made about σ_u^2 and σ_v^2, but not without one of these assumptions. Thus, to use standard statistical techniques of estimation to estimate β, one needs additional information about the variance of the errors.

Let us see exactly where the difficulty arises in using the aforementioned techniques. I shall consider the structural relation in detail here. The analysis of the regression situation is given by Lindley [27], and of the functional relation by Kendall [21].

Suppose we observe a random sample, $(x_1, y_1), \cdots, (x_n, y_n)$. Let $Ex_i = EX_i = \mu$, $Ey_i = EY_i = E(\alpha + \beta X_i) = \alpha + \beta\mu$, $\sigma_x^2 = \sigma_X^2 + \sigma_u^2$, $\sigma_y^2 = \beta^2\sigma_X^2 + \sigma_v^2$, and

Cov $(x_i, y_i) = \beta\sigma_X^2$. Let the x_i and y_i be normally distributed with these parameters. We then have six parameters, namely μ, σ_X^2, σ_u^2, σ_v^2, α, and β. (Note that we already have assumed Cov $(u_i, v_i) = 0$.) Our sufficient statistic is a quintuple, namely $(\sum x, \sum y, \sum x^2, \sum y^2, \sum xy)$. We are mainly interested in estimating $\beta = \text{Cov}(X, Y)/\sigma_X^2$. But we can only estimate μ, $\alpha+\beta\mu$, $\sigma_x^2 = \sigma_X^2 + \sigma_u^2$, $\sigma_y^2 = \sigma_Y^2 + \sigma_v^2$, and Cov $(x, y) = \beta\sigma_X^2 = \text{Cov}(X, Y)$. The maximum likelihood estimates of the parameters of the distribution of (X, Y) are $\hat{\mu} = \bar{x}$, $\hat{\alpha} = \bar{y} - \hat{\beta}\bar{x}$, $\hat{\sigma}_X^2 = \hat{\sigma}_x^2 - \hat{\sigma}_u^2$, $\hat{\sigma}_Y^2 = \hat{\sigma}_y^2 - \hat{\sigma}_v^2$, and $\widehat{\text{Cov}}(X, Y) = \widehat{\text{Cov}}(x, y)$. But $\sigma_Y^2 = \beta^2\sigma_X^2$, so, disregarding the equations in $\hat{\alpha}$ and $\hat{\mu}$, our equations become:

$$\hat{\sigma}_x^2 = \hat{\sigma}_X^2 + \hat{\sigma}_u^2, \qquad \hat{\sigma}_y^2 = \hat{\beta}^2\hat{\sigma}_X^2 + \hat{\sigma}_v^2,$$

and

$$\widehat{\text{Cov}}(x, y) = \hat{\beta}\hat{\sigma}_X^2.$$

We therefore have three equations in four unknowns, namely $\hat{\beta}$, $\hat{\sigma}_X^2$, $\hat{\sigma}_u^2$, and $\hat{\sigma}_v^2$. Hence if we knew either σ_u^2, σ_v^2, or σ_v^2/σ_u^2 and were sure that Cov $(u_i, v_i) = 0$, we could estimate β. With this estimate of β, we can always estimate α by $\hat{\alpha} = \bar{y} - \hat{\beta}\bar{x}$.

If σ_v^2 is known, we have from the above equations

$$\hat{\beta} = \frac{\sum_{i=1}^{n}(y_i - \bar{y})^2 - n\sigma_v^2}{\sum_{i=1}^{n}(x_i - \bar{x})(y_i - \bar{y})}. \tag{1}$$

If σ_u^2 is known,

$$\hat{\beta} = \frac{\sum_{i=1}^{n}(x_i - \bar{x})(y_i - \bar{y})}{\sum_{i=1}^{n}(x_i - \bar{x})^2 - n\sigma_u^2}. \tag{2}$$

If $\lambda = \sigma_v^2/\sigma_u^2$ is known, β is estimated by

$$\hat{\beta} = \frac{\sum_{i=1}^{n}(y_i-\bar{y})^2 - \lambda\sum_{i=1}^{n}(x_i-\bar{x})^2 + \left\{\left[\sum_{i=1}^{n}(y_i-\bar{y})^2 - \lambda\sum_{i=1}^{n}(x_i-\bar{x})^2\right]^2 + 4\lambda\left[\sum_{i=1}^{n}(x_i-\bar{x})(y_i-\bar{y})\right]^2\right\}^{1/2}}{2\sum_{i=1}^{n}(x_i-\bar{x})(y_i-\bar{y})}. \tag{3}$$

(Lindley's estimate [27] is incorrect. See Appendix and [6].) One can easily verify directly that the method of weighted least squares estimation yields the same estimate of β. Smith ([40], p. 12) gives an elegant verification of this.

If both σ_u^2 and σ_v^2 are known, we need not compute λ but instead can use these bits of information separately and obtain another estimate of β, namely

$$\hat{\beta} = \sqrt{\frac{\sum_{i=1}^{n} (y_i - \bar{y})^2 - n\sigma_v^2}{\sum_{i=1}^{n} (x_i - \bar{x})^2 - n\sigma_u^2}}, \tag{4}$$

where sgn $(\hat{\beta}) = \text{sgn}\ [\sum x_i y_i - \sum x_i \sum y_i / n]$.

This can easily be derived from the above equations (cf. also [39]). Here, however, neither (1), (2), (3), nor (4) are maximum likelihood estimates of β. The only optimal property these estimates are known to have is consistency. The solution of the maximum likelihood equations for $\hat{\beta}$ and $\hat{\sigma}_X{}^2$, when both $\sigma_u{}^2$ and $\sigma_v{}^2$ are known, hasn't yet been determined.

If both $\sigma_u{}^2$ and $\sigma_v{}^2$ are known, we may assume that Cov $(u, v) \neq 0$. We then have three maximum likelihood equations in three unknowns, and (4) above is the maximum likelihood estimate of β. In this case,

$$\hat{\text{Cov}}\,(u, v) = \hat{\text{Cov}}\,(x, y) - \frac{1}{n}\sqrt{\left(\sum_{i=1}^{n} (y_i - \bar{y})^2 - n\sigma_v{}^2\right)\left(\sum_{i=1}^{n} (x_i - \bar{x})^2 - n\sigma_u{}^2\right)}.$$

It has been suggested (Allen [2]) that knowledge of λ is better than knowledge of either $\sigma_u{}^2$ or $\sigma_v{}^2$ or both, for if, for example, $\sigma_u{}^2$ is known, it may be that $\hat{\sigma}_x{}^2$, being a random variable, will be less than $\sigma_u{}^2$, an absurd result. If, on the other hand, only λ were known, we would not be led to such an absurdity. However, if we modify estimates (1), (2), and (4), so that if

$$\sum_{i=1}^{n} (y_i - \bar{y})^2 - n\sigma_v{}^2 < 0$$

we take $\hat{\beta} = 0$, and if

$$\sum_{i=1}^{n} (x_i - \bar{x})^2 - n\sigma_u{}^2 < 0,$$

we take $\hat{\beta} = \infty$, no absurd results will be obtained.

The case in which both $\sigma_u{}^2$ and $\sigma_v{}^2$ are known is an over-identified situation (since only knowledge of their ratio is necessary for identifiability). In this case, it would seem reasonable to use all the available information in the hope of achieving a small variance of the estimate of β. The example of Section 8 bears out this contention that estimate (4) is the "best" one (in the sense of smallest variance) to use when both $\sigma_u{}^2$ and $\sigma_v{}^2$ are known.

To obtain the asymptotic variances of estimates (1) and (2), one can use the formula of Section 6, noting that essentially these estimates are ratios of cumulants. Also, one can easily see that the asymptotic variance of estimate (4) is $(4\beta)^{-1}$ times the asymptotic variance of the square of estimate (4), which can be computed via the formula of Section 6.

Creasy [6] has shown that

$$\hat{\phi} \pm \frac{1}{2}\sin^{-1}\frac{2t_\gamma(n-2)\lambda^{1/2}\sqrt{\sum (x_i-\bar{x})^2 \sum (y_i-\bar{y})^2 - [\sum (x_i-\bar{x})(y_j-\bar{y})]^2}}{\sqrt{n-2}\sqrt{[\lambda \sum (x_i-\bar{x})^2 - \sum (y_i-\bar{y})^2]^2 + 4\lambda[\sum (x_i-\bar{x})(y_i-\bar{y})]^2}}$$

are $100\gamma\%$ confidence limits for $\phi = \tan^{-1} \lambda^{-1/2}\beta$, where $\hat{\phi}$ is the arc tangent of $\lambda^{-1/2}$ times estimate (3) and $t_\gamma(n-2)$ is the $t(n-2)$-distributed random variable exceeded in absolute value with probability γ. Let ϕ_U and ϕ_L denote the upper and lower of these limits. We suggest that a rough estimate of the variance of estimate (3) is max $((\tan \phi_U - \tan \hat{\phi})^2/4\lambda^{-1}, (\tan \phi_L - \tan \hat{\phi})^2/4\lambda^{-1})$, where $\gamma = .95$.

So far, all I have pointed out is that we could not have solved the aforementioned equations for maximum likelihood estimates of β without additional information. Three questions arise:

(1) Can we estimate these parameters in the normal case without using additional information by some method other than least squares or maximum likelihood?

(2) If we cannot, what other kinds of information, besides knowledge of σ_u^2, σ_v^2, or λ, can be used to obtain an estimate of β in the normal case?

(3) Do we also need additional information in applying the method of maximum likelihood in estimating β if we assume that the x's and y's are not normally distributed?

As to question 1, the difficulty we had in estimating β is really rooted in the problem of identifiability. Briefly, a set of parameters is nonidentifiable if more than one set of parameters can give rise to the same distribution of the observed random variables. For example, in our case the parameters

σ_X^2	σ_u^2	σ_v^2	β	α
$\frac{1}{2}$	$\frac{1}{2}$	$\frac{1}{2}$	1	$\nu - \mu$
$\frac{1}{3}$	$\frac{2}{3}$	$\frac{1}{4}$	$\frac{3}{2}$	$\nu - \frac{3}{2}\mu$

lead to the same distribution of x and y, namely a normal distribution with $Ex = \mu$, $Ey = \nu$. $\sigma_x^2 = \sigma_y^2 = 1$, and $\rho(x, y) = 1/2$. Reiersol [37] has answered question 1 (cf. also [2, 32, 43]) by proving that if u and v are each normally distributed, then α and β are nonidentifiable if and only if X and Y are constants or normally distributed. What this means is that one cannot estimate α and β at all when the errors are normally distributed in any functional relation, in the regression situation, or in a structural relation where X and Y are normally distributed unless one has additional information sufficient to make these parameters identifiable. Without such information, there is no way of telling two sets of parameters apart by considering the distribution they define. In [24], Kiefer and Wolfowitz answer question 3 by proving that in identifiable cases, the maximum likelihood estimates of the regression parameters are in fact strongly consistent, i.e., with probability one they converge to the true parameters as n approaches infinity.

The rest of this paper is divided into two parts. In the first (Sections 2–5), we will deal with the problem of what other methods of estimating β (and hence α by $\hat{\alpha} = \bar{y} - \hat{\beta}\bar{x}$) exist in the unidentifiable case using other kinds of information. In the second part (Sections 6–7), we will deal with various estimates of β in the identifiable case when the distributions of X and Y are unknown so that the method of maximum likelihood cannot be applied. Finally, an example of the use of these estimates will be given.

2. THE METHOD OF GROUPING

A suggested method of solving the problem of estimating β in the functional relation situation when both variables are observed with error is the method of grouping (sometimes called the method of group averages [31], and known by many other names, cf. [8, p. 137]). The method in simplest form consists of ordering the observed pairs (x_i, y_i) (in a manner to be described later), selecting proportions p_1 and p_2 such that $p_1+p_2 \leq 1$, placing the first np_1 pairs in one group (G_1) and the last np_2 pairs in another group (G_3), discarding G_2, the middle group of observations (if $p_1+p_2<1$), and estimating β by

$$b = \frac{p_1^{-1} \sum_{G_1} y_i - p_2^{-1} \sum_{G_3} y_i}{p_1^{-1} \sum_{G_1} x_i - p_2^{-1} \sum_{G_3} x_i}.$$

Good graphical explanations of the intuitive rationale behind this estimate are given in [15] and [31]. The mathematical rationale behind the use of this estimate can be seen by examining the first two moments of

$$b_1 = \left(p_1^{-1} \sum_{G_1} x_i - p_2^{-1} \sum_{G_3} x_i\right) \Big/ n$$

and

$$b_2 = \left(p_1^{-1} \sum_{G_1} y_i - p_2^{-1} \sum_{G_3} y_i\right) \Big/ n.$$

Let

$$\beta_1 = \left(p_1^{-1} \sum_{G_1} X_i - p_2^{-1} \sum_{G_3} X_i\right) \Big/ n$$

and

$$\beta_2 = \left(p_1^{-1} \sum_{G_1} Y_i - p_2^{-1} \sum_{G_3} Y_i\right) \Big/ n = \beta\left(p_1^{-1} \sum_{G1} X_i - p_2^{-1} \sum_{G_3} X_i\right) \Big/ n.$$

Then $\beta = \beta_2/\beta_1$. If the grouping is independent of the errors, then

$$\text{Var}\,(b_1 - \beta_1) = \frac{1}{n^2} \text{Var}\left[p_1^{-1} \sum_{G_1} u_i - p_2^{-1} \sum_{G_3} u_i\right] = \sigma_u^2(p_1^{-1} + p_2^{-1})/n$$

and

$$\text{Var}\,(b_2 - \beta_2) = \sigma^2_v(p_1^{-1} + p_2^{-1})/n.$$

We see that as $n \to \infty$, $b_1 \to \beta_1$ and $b_2 \to \beta_2$ in probability. Then $b = b_2/b_1$ would be a consistent estimate if only (1) the grouping is independent of the errors, and (2) we can be sure that as $n \to \infty$, b_1 does not approach zero. Condition (2) is essentially Wald's condition, [47], namely

$$\liminf_{n\to\infty} \left| \left(\sum_{G_1} p_1^{-1}X_i - \sum_{G_3} p_2^{-1}X_i \right) \Big/ n \right| > 0.$$

To determine when these conditions hold, we must examine possible procedures by which one assigns each observation (x_i, y_i) to one of the groups. Clearly, if the observations were assigned to each of the groups at random, then $E\sum_{G_1}p_1^{-1}X_i$ would equal $E\sum_{G_3}p_2^{-1}X_i$, and so the second condition would not be satisfied, though the first would. On the other hand, if we knew the magnitude of the X_i's, ranked the (x_i, y_i)'s by the magnitude of the corresponding X_i's, placed the first np_1 in G_1, the last np_2 in G_3, and discarded the rest, both conditions would be satisfied and we could estimate β (cf. [41] in this regard). But it is a rare occasion when we know the relative magnitude but not the actual value of each of the X_i's.

We can, however, order the (x_i, y_i)'s by the magnitude of the x_i's quite easily. This method of ordering simulates the method of ordering by magnitude of the X_i's. But using this ordering procedure and basing the grouping on it does not guarantee the consistency of b, since this method of grouping may not be independent of the errors. What would be of interest are necessary and sufficient conditions for

$$b = \frac{p_1^{-1}\sum_{G_1} y_i - p_2^{-1}\sum_{G_3} y_i}{p_1^{-1}\sum_{G_1} x_i - p_2^{-1}\sum_{G_3} x_i}$$

to be a consistent estimate of β, when the grouping is based on ordering the observations on the basis of the x_i's and using the first np_1 and the last np_2.

Neyman and Scott [34] have found a necessary and sufficient condition for the consistency of b in the structural relation situation. The condition follows.

Let x_{p_1}, x_{1-p_2} be the p_1 and $(1-p_2)$ percentile points of $F(x)$, the distribution of x. If $[\mu, \nu]$ is the shortest interval such that $\Pr\{\mu \leq u \leq \nu\} = 1$, i.e., if $\nu - \mu$ is the range of u, then b is a consistent estimate of β if and only if

$$\Pr\{x_{p_1} - \nu < X \leq x_{p_1} - \mu\} = \Pr\{x_{1-p_2} - v < X < x_{1-p_2} - \mu\} = 0.$$

Intuitively, b is a consistent estimate of β if and only if the range of X has "gaps" of "sufficient length" at "appropriate places" (determined by p_1 and p_2) where X has probability zero of occurring. Only in this event can one be sure that as $n \to \infty$ the points which are misgrouped with respect to the X's do not contribute to tending $\text{plim}_{n\to\infty}\, b$ away from β.

Practically speaking, what does this condition mean? It means first of all that we must know the range of the error in x and above all that this range be finite, for if the range were infinite in both directions, the condition becomes $\Pr\{-\infty \leq X \leq +\infty\} = 0$, which is never satisfied. In most practical situations, one doesn't know the distribution of u and usually relies on the central limit theorem and assumes that u is normally distributed. Since the normal distribution has an infinite range, one sees from the above that this method cannot be used when the errors are normally distributed (as we knew also from Reiersol's theorem).

Besides a knowledge of the range of u, one must also know the p_1 and $(1-p_2)$ per cent points of the distribution of x and the range in which X has probability zero of occurring. If, for instance, X is distributed continuously from $-\infty$ to $+\infty$, then again b is not a consistent estimate of β. We see, then, that this method leads to consistency in very exceptional cases only.

In the functional relation situation, we can specialize the Neyman-Scott condition and see that we need only know the range of u to use b as a consistent estimate of β. In that case, if the range of u is finite, we can use nonrandom sampling of our x's in such a way that no x be observed in the intervals $[x_{p_1}-\nu,\ x_{p_1}-\mu]$ and $[x_{1-p_2}-\nu,\ x_{1-p_2}-\mu]$. Our grouping procedure would then be: (i) order the (x_i, y_i)'s by magnitude of x_i; (ii) place (x_i, y_i) in G_1 if $x_i \leq x_{p_1}$, in G_2 if $x_{p_1} < x_i \leq x_{1-p_2}$, and in G_3 if $x_i > x_{1-p_2}$. In this case, b is a consistent estimate of β.

One need not know the range of u precisely to "estimate" β. If one knows only that there exists a δ such that $\Pr\{|u| \geq \delta\}$ is negligible (e.g., if u is normally distributed, then $\delta = 4\sigma$, say), and if the number of x_i's in the intervals $[x_{p_1}-\delta,\ x_{p_1}+\delta]$ and $[x_{1-p_2}-\delta,\ x_{1-p_2}+\delta]$ is also very small, then even though the grouping is strictly speaking not independent of the u_i's, there is a high probability that the grouping by the aforementioned procedure will insure that the order of the x_i's is the same as the order of the X_i's. As we saw earlier, this is precisely the situation that we want, and so we may be satisfied with this procedure even though the estimate obtained by this method is not consistent.

In contrasting the Neyman-Scott necessary and sufficient condition with Wald's sufficient conditions for consistency, one should notice the following. If Wald's condition (2) is violated, b diverges wildly; if the Neyman-Scott condition is violated, b might still converge in probability to some limit, but not to β. Still, for small samples, b might be an "adequate" estimate of β even though the Neyman-Scott condition does not hold. The consistency property of b is not of great interest if one is dealing with a small sample, for in that case we cannot be sure that b is "close to" β at all. Only as n becomes very large are we more sure that b is within ϵ of β.

Of greater interest is the relative efficiency of b for different values of p_1 and p_2. Nair and Shrivastava [31] and Bartlett [4] have considered the case in which X is uniformly distributed and observed without error and have shown that if one compares b, the estimate based on the method of grouping, with $\hat{b}$, the estimate based on least squares, one finds that Var $\hat{b}$/Var b, the efficiency of b, is maximum when $p_1 = p_2 = 1/3$. The efficiency of b in that case is 89%. In [42] Theil and van Yzeren have shown that if X, measured without error, has a Beta distribution, then the method of grouping is most efficient if $p_1 = p_2 = .3$. The efficiency depends on the parameters of the Beta distribution, is not appreciably affected by deviations from symmetry, and the maximal efficiency is of the order of .85. They also show that for the symmetric triangular distribution of X, $p_1 = p_2 = .28$ is most efficient and if X has a normal distribution $p_1 = p_2 = .27$ is most efficient. In [15], Gibson and Jowett give the following rules for grouping for various distributions of X and the corresponding efficiency.

Description	$f(x)$	Range of x	p_1	p_2	Efficiency
Normal	$(2n)^{-\frac{1}{2}} e^{-x^2/2}$	$-\infty < x < \infty$	.27	.27	.81
Rectangular	$\frac{1}{2}$	$-1 < x < 1$	.33	.33	.89
Bell-shaped	$\frac{3}{4}(1-x^2)$	$-1 < x < 1$	.31	.31	.86
U-shaped	$\frac{10}{9}(\frac{1}{4}+x^4)$	$-1 < x < 1$	.39	.39	.93
J-shaped	e^{-2-x}	$-2 < x < \infty$	.45	.15	.79
Skew	$96x^3e^{-x/2}$	$0 < x < \infty$	.36	.19	.80

Nair and Banerjee [30] collected evidence from model sampling in a functional relation situation which showed that when both variables are subject to error, the grouping method in which $p_1 = p_2 = 1/3$ gave a more efficient estimate of β than the estimate based on $p_1 = p_2 = 1/2$. Their model was one in which the X's were one unit apart, and u and v, the random errors added to the X's and Y's were normally distributed with $\sigma = .1$. In other words, although their model did not satisfy the Neyman-Scott requirement for consistency, it did satisfy the approximate small sample condition given above for obtaining a grouping in which the rank of x_i is the same as the rank of X_i, since $x_i \leq X_i + \delta = X_i + .4$, $x_{i+1} \geq X_{i+1} - \delta = X_i + 1 - .4 = X_i + .6$, approximately. This lends some credence to the belief that in the case in which b is consistent, it is most efficient if based on $p_1 = p_2 = 1/3$. However, in our example of Section 8, the estimate based on $p_1 = p_2 = 1/2$ was more efficient than that based on $p_1 = p_2 = 1/3$.

To obtain an approximate estimate of the standard deviation of b, the following procedure may be used. Let

$$\bar{x}_1 = \frac{\sum_{G_1} x_j}{np_1}, \qquad \bar{x}_2 = \frac{\sum_{G_2} x_j}{n(1 - p_1 - p_2)}, \qquad \bar{x}_3 = \frac{\sum_{G_3} x_j}{np_2}.$$

Define $\bar{y}_1$, $\bar{y}_2$, and $\bar{y}_3$ similarly. Let

$$\begin{aligned}(n-2)S_x^2 = {} & \sum_{G_1} (x_i - \bar{x}_1)^2 + \sum_{G_2} (x_i - \bar{x}_2)^2 + \sum_{G_3} (x_i - \bar{x}_3)^2 \\ & + \delta(\bar{x}_1 + \bar{x}_3 - 2\bar{x}_2)^2(p_1^{-1} + p_2^{-1} + 4(1 - p_1 - p_2)^{-1}/n.\end{aligned}$$

$$\begin{aligned}(n-2)S_y^2 = {} & \sum_{G_1} (y_i - \bar{y}_1)^2 + \sum_{G_2} (y_i - \bar{y}_2)^2 + \sum_{G_3} (y_i - \bar{y}_3)^2 \\ & + \delta(\bar{y}_1 + \bar{y}_3 - 2\bar{y}_2)^2(p_1^{-1} + p_2^{-1} + 4(1 - p_1 - p_2)^{-1})/n,\end{aligned}$$

and

$$\begin{aligned}(n-2)S_{xy} & \\ = {} & \sum_{G_1} (x_i - \bar{x}_1)(y_i - \bar{y}_1) + \sum_{G_2} (x_i - \bar{x}_2)(y_i - \bar{y}_2) + \sum_{G_3} (x_i - \bar{x}_3)(y_i - \bar{y}_j) \\ & + \delta(\bar{x}_1 + \bar{x}_3 - 2\bar{x}_2)(\bar{y}_1 + \bar{y}_3 - 2\bar{y}_3)(p_1^{-1} + p_2^{-1} + 4(1 - p_1 - p_2)^{-1})/n,\end{aligned}$$

where

$$\delta = \begin{cases} 0 & \text{if } p_1 + p_2 = 1 \\ 1 & \text{otherwise.} \end{cases}$$

Let $t_0^2 = t_{.95}^2(n-2)$, the square of the $t(n-2)$ distributed random variable exceeded in absolute value with probability .05, and $c = n(p_1^{-1}+p_2^{-1})t_0^2$. Define

$$b^* = \frac{[n^2 b_1 b_2 - cS_{xy}] + \{c^2(S_{xy}^2 - S_x^2 S_y^2) + cn^2(b_1^2 S_y^2 + b_2^2 S_x^2 - 2b_1 b_2 S_{xy})\}^{1/2}}{n^2 b_1^2 - cS_x^2}.$$

Then, since b^* is an upper 95% confidence limit on b (cf. [4][2]), $(b^* - b)/t_0$ gives a rough estimate of the standard deviation of b.

A variant of the method of grouping which gets by with a little less information is the following. Fix two numbers r and s such that $r \leq s$ and $\Pr\{x \leq r\} > 0$, $\Pr\{x > s\} > 0$. Divide the observations into groups corresponding to whether $x_i \leq r$, $r < x_i \leq s$, or $x_i > s$, and let the number of observations in G_i be n_i. For this procedure, Neyman and Scott have shown that

$$b = \frac{n_1^{-1} \sum_{G_1} y_i - n_3^{-1} \sum_{G_3} y_i}{n_1^{-1} \sum_{G_1} x_i - n_3^{-1} \sum_{G_3} x_i}$$

is a consistent estimate of β if and only if

$$\Pr\{r - \nu < X \leq r - \mu\} = \Pr\{s - \nu < X \leq s - \mu\} = 0,$$

where $\mu - \nu$ is the range of u. In this case, we do not need any information on specific points of the distribution of x, as we did before. However, the more restrictive conditions remain with us, and we see that this variant of the grouping procedure leads to consistent estimates in the same exceptional cases as in the previous grouping method.

By far the most important, useful, and valid application of the method of grouping arises when one has some extra-data grouping criterion which is correlated with X but not with u. For example, one might be interested in the linear relationship between yield strength and hardness of steel, where each of these variables is subject to errors of observation. If one knew that he had two groups of pieces of steel, each group forged at a different heat, then this bit of information would be a good grouping criterion. This is quite different from the aforementioned methods of grouping, in that here we need not worry about such problems as the relation of the order of the x_i's to the order of the X_i's. As long as this grouping criterion is correlated with X but not with u, Wald's conditions (1) and (2) are met and b is a consistent estimate of β.

This review of the idea of grouping is by no means complete. What I have so far discussed in detail is the outgrowth of a particular estimate due to Wald. Other estimates based on the idea of grouping will be discussed later, after we discuss the use of components of variance in regression analysis.

3. USE OF INSTRUMENTAL VARIABLES

Another method of obtaining consistent estimates of β which has received extensive consideration is a method based on the use of what is sometimes called "instrumental sets of variables." These instrumental sets of variables

[2] Bartlett considers only the case where $p_1 = p_2$. His $k = np_1 = np_2$ in our notation. The first equation [4, p. 210] contains an error, in that the term $4/(n-k)$ should read $4/(n-2k)$.

are merely an additional set of variables closely related to X and Y, the "investigational set" of variables. For example, if we were interested in the linear relation between the quantity of butter available and the price of butter, possible instrumental sets of some interest would be the quantity of margarine available, the price of margarine, or both. Use of this instrumental set of variables is just another example of the different kinds of additional information useful in estimating β.

The major difficulty in using this approach is to find such a variable which is independent of the u's and correlated with the X's. If we are not really interested in observing the instrumental variable for its own sake, we are confronted with the problem of the additional cost of obtaining information on the instrumental set. If the instrumental set is highly correlated with the investigational set, we are faced with the question, "Shouldn't the instrumental set also be included in the relation of interest?" For example, in the price-quantity of butter example, perhaps our relation should be $P_B=\alpha+\beta Q_B+\gamma P_M$ where P_B, Q_B, and P_M are the price of butter, quantity of butter, and price of margarine, respectively.

We shall discuss two types of instrumental variables useful in facilitating the estimation of β. The first set of instrumental variables is a set of observations on two linearly related variables where the parameters of the linear relation are known, and where the variables are observed with error. The second set of instrumental variables is a set of error-free observations on one random variable. In this latter case, we shall give one estimate of β in this section and defer another estimate of β to Section 4, as it can best be understood in the context of that section.

3.1. *Two Linearly Related Instrumental Variables Observed with Error*

Reiersol [36] considers the case in which one knows the constants γ_1 and γ_2 of the relation $\gamma_1 Z_1+\gamma_2 Z_2=0$ between two sets of instrumental variables, Z_1 and Z_2. For convenience, let us change notation for the moment. Let $X=X_1$, $Y=X_2$, and rewrite the structural relation $Y=\beta X$ as $\beta_1 X_1+\beta_2 X_2=0$ where $\beta=-\beta_1/\beta_2$ and $EX_1=EX_2=0$.[3] Also, let $u=u_1$, $v=u_2$, $x=x_1$, and $y=x_2$. Consider the situation in which we observe the instrumental set with error, i.e., $z_j=Z_j+w_j$, $j=1, 2$. Our observations are the quadruples $(x_{1i}, x_{2i}, z_{1i}, z_{2i})$, $i=1, \cdots, n$. Assume, as usual, that the errors in all our variables are uncorrelated with the true values. Define $\lambda_i=E(u_i w_i)=E(u_i z_i)=E(x_i w_i)$, $\tilde{\mu}_{ij}=E(X_i z_j)$, and $\mu_{ij}=E(x_i z_j)$. Then $\beta_1 X_1+\beta_2 X_2=0$ implies that $\beta_1 E(z_j X_1)+\beta_2 E(z_j X_2)=0$, or $\beta_1\tilde{\mu}_{1j}+\beta_2\tilde{\mu}_{2j}=0$. If we define $B=(\beta_1, \beta_2)$ and

$$\tilde{\mu} = \begin{pmatrix} \tilde{\mu}_{11} & \tilde{\mu}_{12} \\ \tilde{\mu}_{12} & \tilde{\mu}_{22} \end{pmatrix},$$

then $B\tilde{\mu}=0$. But $\tilde{\mu}=\mu-\lambda$ where

$$\mu = \begin{pmatrix} \mu_{11} & \mu_{12} \\ \mu_{21} & \mu_{22} \end{pmatrix},$$

[3] If we define $X_i'=X_i-\bar{X}$ and $Y_i',=Y_i-\overline{Y}$, we see that $X_i'=\beta Y_i'$, or $\beta_1 X_i'+\beta_2 Y_i'=0$ for all i, where $\beta=-\beta_1\beta_2$ and $EX_i'=EY_i'=0$. Since we know how to estimate α once β is estimated, we can, without loss of generality, consider the above homogeneous linear relation.

and

$$\lambda = \begin{pmatrix} \lambda_1 & 0 \\ 0 & \lambda_2 \end{pmatrix},$$

so that $B(\mu-\lambda)=0$. It is also evident that $\tilde{\mu}_{i1}\gamma_1+\tilde{\mu}_{i2}\gamma_2=0$. If we define $\Gamma=(\gamma_1, \gamma_2)$, then $\tilde{\mu}\Gamma'=(\mu-\lambda)\Gamma'=0$. But

$$(\mu - \lambda)\Gamma' = \begin{pmatrix} \gamma_1\mu_{11} + \gamma_2\mu_{12} - \gamma_1\lambda_1 \\ \gamma_2\mu_{12} + \gamma_2\mu_{22} - \gamma_2\lambda_2 \end{pmatrix} = \begin{pmatrix} 0 \\ 0 \end{pmatrix}$$

implies that $\lambda_i=(\mu\Gamma')_i/\gamma_i$, where $(\mu\Gamma')_i$ is the i-th element of the vector $\mu\Gamma'$. One sees that

$$\mu - \lambda = \begin{pmatrix} -(\mu_{12}\gamma_1)/\gamma_2 & \mu_{12} \\ \mu_{21} & -(\mu_{21}\gamma_1)/\gamma_2 \end{pmatrix},$$

and hence $B(\mu-\lambda)=0$ implies that $\beta_2\mu_{21}=(\beta_1\mu_{12}\gamma_2)/\gamma_1$ and so $\beta=-\beta_1/\beta_2=-(\gamma_1\mu_{21})/(\gamma_2\mu_{12})$. Since we know γ_1 and γ_2, and since

$$m_{12} = \left(\sum_{i=1}^{n} x_{1i}z_{2i}\right)\Big/ n \quad \text{and} \quad m_{21} = \left(\sum_{i=1}^{n} x_{2i}z_{1i}\right)\Big/ n$$

are consistent estimates of μ_{12} and μ_{21}, respectively, β is estimated by $-(\gamma_1 m_{21})/(\gamma_2/m_{12})$, provided that Cov $(z, x)\neq 0$.

3.2. *One Instrumental Variable Observed without Error*

The great difficulty with the above method is that we not only need a pair of instrumental variables, but also a knowledge of the linear relation between them. Let us consider the case in which we have observations on only one instrumental variable, say Z, and where, in contrast to the Reiersol situation, Z is observed without error. Consider once again the relation $\beta_1X_i+\beta_2Y_i=0$, where $\beta=-\beta_1/\beta_2$, multiply it by Z_i/n and sum over all i, to obtain the expression

$$\left(\beta_1 \sum_{i=1}^{n} Z_iX_i + \beta_2 \sum_{i=1}^{n} Z_iY_i\right)\Big/ n = 0.$$

Call the left hand side $\beta_1\eta_X+\beta_2\eta_Y$. Consider the same expression with y and x substituted for Y and X, and call the left hand side $\beta_1\eta_x+\beta_2\eta_y$. Then

$$\eta_y - \eta_Y = \left(\sum_{i=1}^{n} Z_iv_i\right)\Big/ n \quad \text{and} \quad \eta_x - \eta_X = \left(\sum_{i=1}^{n} Z_iu_i\right)\Big/ n.$$

$E(\eta_x-\eta_X)=E(\eta_y-\eta_Y)=0$ and Var $(\eta_x-\eta_X)=0(1/n)$, Var $(\eta_y-\eta_Y)=0(1/n)$. Hence $\eta_y-\eta_Y$ and $\eta_x-\eta_X$ converge to zero in probability so that $\beta_1\eta_x+\beta_2\eta_y=0$ is a consistent estimate of the true relation, and

$$b = \frac{\sum_{i=1}^{n} Z_iy_i}{\sum_{i=1}^{n} Z_iy_i}$$

is an estimate of $\beta = -\beta_1/\beta_2$, provided that

$$\sum_{i=1}^{n} Z_i x_i$$

doesn't approach zero as $n \rightarrow \infty$, i.e., Cov $(Z, x) \neq 0$.

Besides obtaining this estimate of β, Geary [14] also derives the exact distribution of a function of b, when X, Y, and Z are normally distributed. He finds that

$$\phi(b)db = \frac{\left(\frac{n-2}{2}\right)!}{\left(\frac{n-3}{2}\right)!\sqrt{\pi}} (1 + y^2)^{-n/2} dy$$

where

$$y = \left\{\frac{\mu_{33}(\mu_{22}b^2 - 2\mu_{12}b + \mu_{11})}{(\mu_{23}b - \mu_{13})^2} - 1\right\}^{-1/2},$$

where $EX = EY = EZ = 0$ and $\mu_{11} = EY^2$, $\mu_{22} = EX^2$, $\mu_{33} = EZ^2$, $\mu_{12} = EXY$, $\mu_{13} = EYZ$, and $\mu_{23} = EXZ$. We see, then, that y is distributed as $(n-1)^{-1/2}t(n-1)$, where $t(n-1)$ is a random variable with a t-distribution with $n-1$ degrees of freedom.

We can obtain the approximate variance of b as follows. Write

$$\begin{aligned} W^2 \simeq & \left\{\frac{\mu_{33}(\mu_{22}\beta^2 - 2\mu_{12}\beta + \mu_{11})}{(\mu_{23}\beta - \mu_{13})^2} - 1\right\}^{-1} \\ & + \left\{\frac{2\mu_{23}(\mu_{23}\beta - \mu_{13})}{\mu_{33}(\mu_{22}\beta^2 - 2\mu_{12}\beta + \mu_{11}) - (\mu_{23}\beta - \mu_{13})^2} \right. \\ & \left. - \frac{2(\mu_{23}\beta - \mu_{13})^2[(\mu_{22}\mu_{33} - \mu_{23})^2\beta - (\mu_{12}\mu_{33} - \mu_{13}\mu_{23})]}{[\mu_{33}(\mu_{22}\beta^2 - 2\mu_{12}\beta + \mu_{11}) - (\mu_{23}\beta - \mu_{13})^2]^2}\right\}(b - \beta) \\ = & A + B(b - \beta), \end{aligned}$$

say, so that Var $b \simeq$ Var $W^2/B^2 = 2(n-2)/(n-3)^2(n-5)B^2$, $n > 5$, since W^2 is distributed as $(n-1)^{-1}F(1, n-1)$.

It is worth noting that if Z_i can take values 1, -1, and 0 depending on i but independent of the u's, then this estimate results in the grouping estimate. This is, of course, a quantification of the application of the method of grouping when the extra-data grouping criterion is correlated with X but not with u. Durbin [10] suggests that if the order of the x's is the same as the order of the X's, then a better instrumental variable would be $Z_i = i$ where the x_i's are ordered by magnitude. This variable will lead to a more efficient estimate than that of the method of grouping. Finally, the procedure of Section 6 may be construed as an example of estimation by means of instrumental variables, where the instrumental variable is just some power of x.

The same estimate has been obtained in an unpublished paper of Tukey by the following consideration. Cov $(Z,\ y-bx)=\text{Cov}\ (Z,\ \alpha+\beta X+v-bX-bu)$ $=(\beta-b)$ Cov (Z, X) is zero if and only if $b=\beta$. Thus, we can estimate β by the value of b for which the slope of the regression of Z on $y-bx$ is zero. But if one considers the sum of squares of deviations due to regression of Z on $y-bx$, one sees that

$$b = \frac{\sum_{i=1}^{n} Z_i y_i}{\sum_{j-1}^{n} Z_i x_i}$$

makes this quantity zero. The idea is the same as that of Geary, who also formmally considers the sample covariance of Z with $y-bx$ to obtain his estimate. However, Tukey's method of motivating this estimate by considering the analysis of variance in regression technique is different. In our next section, we shall see what more can be obtained from considering linear relations with errors in both variables in the light of the analysis of variance.

4. USE OF VARIANCE COMPONENTS

4.1. *Replication of Observations*

Let us now consider the situation in which we have another kind of additional information, namely, where we know that we have N_i observations x_{ij} on each of nX_i's. If we have the situation in which $y_{ij}=Y_i+v_{ij}$ and $x_{ij}=X_i+u_{ij}$, and if the usual assumptions of independence are made, then one can perform a one-criterion analysis of variance on the x's and the y's, and from this obtain an estimate of β. The simplest way of describing the procedure is to exhibit the anova table.

	Source	Mean Square	Expected Mean Square
Between Sets	I	$\sum_{i=1}^{n} N_i(\bar{x}_{i\cdot}-\bar{x}_{\cdot\cdot})^2/(n-1)$	$\sigma_u^2+\left[\left(N^2-\sum_{i=1}^{n} N_i^2\right)\Big/(nN-N)\right]\sigma_X^2$
	II	$\sum_{i=1}^{n} N_i(\bar{x}_{i\cdot}-\bar{x}_{\cdot\cdot})(\bar{y}_{i\cdot}-\bar{y}_{\cdot\cdot})/(n-1)$	$\text{Cov}(u, v)+\left[\left(N^2-\sum_{i=1}^{n} N_i^2\right)\Big/(nN-N)\right]\beta\sigma_X^2$
	III	$\sum_{i=1}^{n} N_i(\bar{y}_{i\cdot}-\bar{y}_{\cdot\cdot})^2/(n-1)$	$\sigma_v^2+\left[\left(N^2-\sum_{i=1}^{n} N_i^2\right)\Big/(nN-N)\right]\beta^2\sigma_X^2$
Within Sets	IV	$\sum_{i=1}^{n}\sum_{j=1}^{Ni}(x_{ij}-\bar{x}_{i\cdot})^2/(N-n)$	σ_u^2
	V	$\sum_{i=1}^{n}\sum_{j=1}^{Ni}(x_{ij}-\bar{x}_{i\cdot})(y_{ij}-\bar{y}_{i\cdot})/(N-n)$	$\text{Cov}(u, v)$
	VI	$\sum_{i=1}^{n}\sum_{j=1}^{Ni}(y_{ij}-\bar{y}_{i\cdot})^2/(N-n)$	σ_v^2

where

$$\bar{x}_{i\cdot} = \sum_{j=1}^{N_i} x_{ij}/N_i, \qquad \bar{y}_{i\cdot} = \sum_{j=1}^{N_i} y_{ij}/N_i, \qquad \bar{x}_{\cdot\cdot} = \sum_{i=1}^{n}\sum_{j=1}^{N_i} x_{ij}/N,$$

$$\bar{y}_{i\cdot\cdot} = \sum_{i=1}^{n}\sum_{j=1}^{N_i} y_{ij}/N, \quad \text{and} \quad N = \sum_{i=1}^{n} N_i.$$

One sees, then, that (II−V)/(I−IV), (III−VI)/(II−V), and

$$\sqrt{\frac{\text{III} - \text{VI}}{\text{I} - \text{IV}}}$$

converge in probability to β as $n \to \infty$ and $N_i \to \infty$ for some i. These estimates, along with similar estimates in other situations (to be described later), are due to Tukey [45]. (One should note that though we write σ_X^2 in the anova table, we do not mean to imply that this procedure is only applicable to structural relations. For functional relations, read

$$\left[\left(N^2 - \sum_{i=1}^{n} N_i^2\right) \Big/ (nN - N)\right]\sigma_X^2 \text{ as } \left[\sum_{i=1}^{n} N_i(X_i - \overline{X})^2\right] \Big/ (n-1),$$

where

$$\overline{X} = \sum_{i=1}^{n} N_i X_i / N.$$

Another estimate in this situation is one given by Housner and Brennan [18]. They argue as follows. Consider the expression $b_{ijkl} = (y_{ij} - y_{kl})/(x_{ij} - x_{kl})$, $x_{ij} \neq x_{kl}$. Since $y_{ij} = \alpha + \beta x_{ij} + v_{ij} - \beta u_{ij}$, $(x_{ij} - x_{kl})b_{ijkl} = \beta(x_{ij} - x_{kl}) + (v_{ij} - v_{kl}) - \beta(u_{ij} - u_{kl})$, so that

$$\beta = \frac{y_{ij} - y_{kl}}{x_{ij} - x_{kl}} - \frac{(v_{ij} - v_{kl}) - \beta(u_{ij} - u_{kl})}{x_{ij} - x_{kl}},$$

for all i, j, k, l, $x_{ij} \neq x_{kl}$. Summing over all combinations of points (where $i \neq k$) and ignoring the term involving the errors (since it converges to zero in probability), they obtain the estimate

$$b = \frac{\sum_{i=1}^{n} \bar{y}_i N_i \left(\sum_{j=1}^{n} N_j - 2\sum_{j=1}^{i} N_j + N_i\right)}{\sum_{i=1}^{n} \bar{x}_i N_i \left(\sum_{j=1}^{n} N_j - 2\sum_{j=1}^{i} N_j + N_i\right)}.$$

This estimate approaches β in probability as $N_i \to \infty$ for at least two distinct values of i. (Since the optimum efficiency of this estimate may depend on the omission of some of the combinations of points from consideration, this estimate has been considered as a variant of the method of grouping.)

We have here two approaches by which to obtain consistent estimates of β when we know that we have replications of observations on each X_i.[4] When should these estimates be used? First of all, if we really believe the relation is linear, the optimum allocation of observations would be at two points. Hence, since the estimate based on variance components approaches β in probability only as both $n \to \infty$ and at least one $N_i \to \infty$, the Housner-Brennan estimate, which approaches β in probability as $N_i \to \infty$ for at least two distinct values of i (i.e., whose consistency is independent of n), is to be preferred. If we do not believe that the underlying structure is linear, but are only trying to approximate some function in a small area of its range by a linear function, it may be more advisable to increase n at the expense of decreasing N_i to as little as 2. In this case, the Tukey components in regression estimate is the better.

4.2. *The Method of Grouping*

The same anova table can be looked at from the point of view of grouping. If our observations are divided into r groups in some manner independent of the errors in observation of x, after changing n to r, N_i to n_i, and N to n in the above table, we can interpret the "between" mean square as a mean square between groups and the "within" mean square as a mean square within groups. We still have the same three estimates of β, namely $b_1 = (\text{II} - \text{V})/(\text{I} - \text{IV})$, $b_2 = (\text{III} - \text{VI})/(\text{II} - \text{V})$, and

$$b_3 = \sqrt{\frac{\text{III} - \text{VI}}{\text{I} - \text{IV}}}.$$

In particular, if $r = 2$, we have in b_1, b_2, and b_3 competitors of any grouping estimate of Section 3 using all the data. However, to use these estimates one need only assume that the grouping is independent of the errors in x, and not all that the Neyman-Scott result asks us to assume, so that for all practical purposes, the only grouping estimate in competition with b_1, b_2, and b_3 is the one in which one groups the data by means of some criterion correlated with X but not with u. No one has yet compared the asymptotic variances of these two types of estimates. Use of Tukey's estimate of the asymptotic variances of b_1, b_2, and b_3 (cf. Section 4.3) in the example of Section 8 shows that each of these estimates has smaller variance than the grouping estimate when $p_1 = p_2 = 1/2$. However, Tukey's estimator of these asymptotic variances is very poor when $r = 2$, and so one should not generalize too hastily from this observation.

4.3. *Use of Instrumental Variables*

Finally, we can look at the situation in which we observe an instrumental variable Z without error from the components in regression point of view. Consider the following anova table.

[4] In this case, also, the solution of the maximum likelihood equation for β has not been expressed in closed form. Analogous to the results of Section 1.2, we see that

$$\frac{\left(\text{III} - \frac{\text{VI}}{\text{IV}}\,\text{I}\right) + \left\{\left(\frac{\text{VI}}{\text{IV}}\,\text{I} - \text{III}\right)^2 + 4\,\frac{\text{VI}}{\text{IV}}\,(\text{II})^2\right\}^{1/2}}{2\,\text{II}}$$

is also a consistent estimate of β.

Source		Mean Square
Regression on Z	I	$\left[\sum_{i=1}^{n}(x_i-\bar{x})(Z_i-\bar{Z})\right]^2 \Big/ \sum_{i=1}^{n}(Z_i-\bar{Z})^2$
	II	$\left[\sum_{i=1}^{n}(x_i-\bar{x})(Z_i-\bar{Z})\right]\left[\sum_{i=1}^{n}(y_i-\bar{y})(Z_i-\bar{Z})\right] \Big/ \sum_{i=1}^{n}(Z_i-\bar{Z})^2$
	III	$\left[\sum_{i=1}^{n}(y_i-\bar{y})(Z_i-\bar{Z})\right]^2 \Big/ \sum_{i=1}^{n}(Z_i-\bar{Z})^2$
Balance	IV	$\left\{\sum_{i=1}^{n}(x_i-\bar{x})^2-\left[\sum_{i=1}^{n}(x_i-\bar{x})(Z_i-\bar{Z})\right]^2 \Big/ \sum_{i=1}^{n}(Z_i-\bar{Z})^2\right\} \Big/ (n-2)$
	V	$\left\{\sum_{i=1}^{n}(x_i-\bar{x})(y_i-\bar{y})-\left[\sum_{i=1}^{n}(y_i-y)(Z_i-\bar{Z})\right]\left[\sum_{i=1}^{n}(x_i-\bar{x})(Z_i-\bar{Z})\right] \Big/ \sum_{i=1}^{n}(Z_i-\bar{Z})^2\right\} \Big/ (n-2)$
	VI	$\left\{\sum_{i=1}^{n}(y_i-\bar{y})^2-\left[\sum_{i=1}^{n}(y_i-\bar{y})(Z_i-\bar{Z})\right]^2 \Big/ \sum_{i=1}^{n}(Z_i-\bar{Z})^2\right\} \Big/ (n-2)$

Source		Expected Mean Square
Regression on Z	I	$\sigma_x^2+B^2\sum_{i=1}^{n}(Z_i-\bar{Z})^2$
	II	$\mathrm{Cov}(x, y)+\beta B^2\sum_{i=1}^{n}(Z_i-\bar{Z})^2$
	III	$\sigma_y^2+\beta^2B^2\sum_{i=1}^{n}(Z_i-\bar{Z})^2$
Balance	IV	σ_x^2
	V	$\mathrm{Cov}(x, y)$
	VI	σ_y^2

Here B is the slope of the regression of x on Z. We see then that

$$(\mathrm{I}-\mathrm{IV}) \Big/ \left(\sum_{i-1}^{n}(Z_i-\bar{Z})^2\right)$$

is an estimate of B^2,

$$(\mathrm{II}-\mathrm{V}) \Big/ \left(\sum_{i=1}^{n}(Z_i-\bar{Z})^2\right)$$

is an estimate of βB^2, and

$$(\mathrm{III}-\mathrm{VI}) \Big/ \left(\sum_{i=1}^{n}(Z_i-\bar{Z})^2\right)$$

is an estimate of β^2B^2. Hence (II$-$V)/(I$-$IV), (III$-$VI)/(II$-$V), and

$$\sqrt{\frac{\mathrm{III}-\mathrm{VI}}{\mathrm{I}-\mathrm{IV}}}$$

are all estimates of β, provided that the denominators of these estimates do not approach zero as $n \to \infty$, i.e., $B \neq 0$.

In all three situations, replications, grouping, and use of an instrumental variable, we have, from this approach, three different estimates of β. Let us examine the variance of the two estimates easiest to compute, b_1 and b_2, to determine when each of them should be used. I shall use the approximate relations $(\mathrm{II}-\mathrm{V}) \simeq \beta(\mathrm{I}-\mathrm{IV})$ and $(\mathrm{III}-\mathrm{VI}) \simeq \beta^2(\mathrm{I}-\mathrm{IV})$ in this comparison. Using 28.4 of [7], we see that

$$(1) \quad \sigma^2\left(\frac{\mathrm{II}-\mathrm{V}}{\mathrm{I}-\mathrm{IV}}\right) \simeq \frac{1}{k^2}\sigma^2_{\mathrm{II-V}} + \beta\frac{\beta^2k^2}{k^4}\sigma^2_{\mathrm{I-IV}} - 2\beta\frac{k}{k^3}\,\mathrm{Cov}\,(\mathrm{II}-\mathrm{V}, \mathrm{I}-\mathrm{IV})$$

$$(2) \quad \sigma^2\left(\frac{\mathrm{III}-\mathrm{VI}}{\mathrm{II}-\mathrm{V}}\right) \simeq \frac{1}{\beta^2k^2}\sigma^2_{\mathrm{III-VI}} + \frac{\beta^4k^2}{\beta^4k^4}\sigma^2_{\mathrm{II-V}} - \frac{2\beta^2k}{\beta^3k^3}\,\mathrm{Cov}\,(\mathrm{II}-\mathrm{V}, \mathrm{III}-\mathrm{VI})$$

$$\begin{aligned}
(1)\text{–}(2) &= \frac{\beta^2}{k^2}\sigma^2_{\mathrm{I-IV}} - \frac{1}{\beta^2k^2}\sigma^2_{\mathrm{III-VI}} - \frac{2\beta}{k^2}(\mathrm{Cov}\,(\mathrm{II}-\mathrm{V}, \mathrm{I}-\mathrm{IV}-\mathrm{III}+\mathrm{VI}))\\
&\simeq \frac{\beta^2}{k^2}\sigma^2_{\mathrm{I-IV}} - \frac{1}{\beta^2k^2}\sigma^2_{\mathrm{III-VI}} - \frac{2\beta}{k^2}(1-\beta^2)(\mathrm{Cov}(\mathrm{II}-\mathrm{V}, \mathrm{I}-\mathrm{IV}))\\
&\simeq \frac{\beta^2}{k^2}\sigma^2_{\mathrm{I-IV}} - \frac{1}{\beta^2k^2}\sigma^2_{\mathrm{III-VI}} - \frac{2\beta(1-\beta^2)}{k^2}\beta\sigma^2_{\mathrm{I-IV}}\\
&= \frac{\beta^2 - 2\beta^2 + 2\beta^4}{k^2}\sigma^2_{\mathrm{I-IV}} - \frac{1}{\beta^2k^2}\sigma^2_{\mathrm{III-VI}}\\
&\simeq \frac{-\beta^2 + 2\beta^4}{k^2}\sigma^2_{\mathrm{I-IV}} - \frac{\beta^2}{k^2}\sigma^2_{\mathrm{I-IV}} > 0\\
&\leftrightarrows \beta^2 > 1
\end{aligned}$$

where k is either

$$B^2 \sum_{i=1}^{n} (Z_i - \bar{Z})^2$$

(in the instrumental variable case),

$$\left[\left(N^2 - \sum_{i=1}^{n} N_i^2\right) \Big/ (nN - N)\right]\sigma_X^2$$

(in the replication situation), or

$$\left[\left(n^2 - \sum_{i=1}^{n} n_i^2\right) \Big/ (rn - n)\right]\sigma_X^2$$

(in the grouping situation). We see, then, that b_2 is a better estimate of β than b_1 if we know that $|\beta| > 1$, and that b_1 is better if $|\beta| < 1$. An idea as to whether or not $|\beta| > 1$ can be obtained from plotting the observations.

In [45] Tukey gives the approximate variance of b_1 and b_2. Since b_3 is the geometric mean of b_1 and b_2, the approximate variance of b_3 can be determined by 28.4 of [7]. We shall give the approximate variance of b_1; the changes which must be made to obtain Var b_2 are obvious.

$$\operatorname{Var} b_1 \simeq \frac{\dfrac{\mathrm{I}(\mathrm{III} - 2\mathrm{II}b_1 + \mathrm{I}b_1^2)}{\mathrm{df}(\mathrm{I})} + \dfrac{\mathrm{IV}(\mathrm{VI} - 2\mathrm{V}b_1 + \mathrm{IV}b_1^2)}{\mathrm{df}(\mathrm{IV})}}{(\mathrm{I} - \mathrm{IV})^2},$$

where

$$\mathrm{df}(\mathrm{I}) = \begin{cases} n - 1 & \text{in case of replications} \\ r - 1 & \text{in case of grouping} \\ 1 & \text{in case of instrumental variables} \end{cases}$$

and

$$\mathrm{df}(\mathrm{IV}) = \begin{cases} N - n & \text{in case of replications} \\ n - r & \text{in case of grouping} \\ n - 2 & \text{in case of instrumental variables.} \end{cases}$$

This approxination is good for large df(I). Hence it will not be too good in the usual cases of grouping, where r is very small, or when one has an instrumental variable. For this reason, the estimated variances via this method are not given in Table 200.

5. THE BERKSON MODEL

So far, we have considered the case in which either (x, y) was a random pair or the special case where (x, y) was chosen so that the grouping method was (at least approximately) applicable. There is, however, another model, due to Berkson, [5], (cf. also [22] and [28]), wherein instead of trying to observe a given X_i but actually observing $x_i = X_i + u_i$, we fix our x_i's and observe y_i for each fixed x_i. This process of fixing one's x_i's can be done quite easily in the laboratory sciences, where, for example, if one wished to estimate an Ohm's law constant (e.g., a resistance), one could fix the x_i's by setting the dial of the ammeter (presumably the cause of the errors in observing X_i) at predetermined settings. Then, for each fixed x (e.g., for each fixed current reading), there are a number of X's which could have given rise to the particular x which is observed; also for each X there is a probability that the observed fixed x is an observation on that X with error u. The X's are now random variables distributed about the fixed x with error u, i.e., $X = x + u$ where u is independent of x (and *not* of X).

We now observe $y = \alpha + \beta x + \beta u + v$ and here both βu and v are independent of x. Hence we have the situation in which our relation is $y = \alpha + \beta x + w$ where $w = \beta u + v$ and w is *independent* of x. If we assume $Eu = Ev = 0$, then $Ey = \alpha + \beta x$. x is now a fixed number rather than a random variable, and we know that for this situation the least squares estimate of β is

$$b = \frac{\sum_{i=1}^{n} (x_i - \bar{x})(y_i - \bar{y})}{\sum_{i=1}^{n} (x_i - \bar{x})^2}.$$

This technique works not only in the structure-function situation, but also in the regression situation, for the distinction in errors in y makes no difference in this case.

The real significance of the Berkson model lies not in the estimator of β but rather in the implications of the model to the design of experiments intended to yield data from which β may be estimated. In contrast to the problems in estimating β described above when (x, y) is a random pair, we see that if our physicist can fix his x's, the statistician has no problem in estimating the linear relation of interest.

6. ESTIMATION VIA CUMULANTS

Consider the homogeneous linear relation $\beta_1 X + \beta_2 Y = 0$ where $\beta = -\beta_1/\beta_2$ and X and Y are random variables whose expectation is zero. That is, let us consider a structural relation where the intercept is zero. Geary [12, 13] noticed that since $Y = \beta X$, the bivariate cumulant of X and Y of order c_1, c_2+1, namely $\kappa(c_1, c_2+1)$, was equal to $\beta\kappa(c_1+1, c_2)$. Also, if $c_1, c_2 > 0$, $K(c_1, c_2)$, the cumulant of the distribution of the x's and y's, is equal to $\kappa(c_1, c_2)$. This is evident from the following properties of bivariate cumulants (cf. Kendall [23], Kaplan [20], and Lindley [27]): (a) the cumulant of a sum of independent random variables is the sum of the cumulants of the variables, and (b) the bivariate cumulant of any order c_1+c_2 (where both $c_1, c_2>0$) of independent random variables is zero. Since $\mathrm{Cov}(u, X) = \mathrm{Cov}(v, Y) = \mathrm{Cov}(u, v) = 0$, $K(c_1, c_2) = \kappa(c_1, c_2) + [(c_1, c_2)\text{-th cumulant of } X \text{ and } u] + [(c_1, c_2)\text{-th cumulant of } Y \text{ and } v] + [(c_1, c_2)\text{-th cumulant of } u \text{ and } v] = \kappa(c_1, c_2) + 0 + 0 + 0 = \kappa(c_1, c_2)$. Hence, since $k(c_1, c_2)$, the sample k-statistic, is an unbiased consistent estimate of $K(c_1, c_2)$, we see that

$$\hat{\beta} = \frac{k(c_1, c_2 + 1)}{k(c_1 + 1, c_2)}$$

is a consistent estimate of β if $k(c_1+1, c_2)$ does not approach zero.

This estimate has not used any additional information and hence by the identifiability result we know that in the case of normality it must fail. This is certainly correct, for in the normal distribution, all cumulants of degree three or higher are zero, and since $c_1>0$, $c_2>0$, and cumulants of order c_1+c_2+1 are used, we cannot estimate β by this method in the normal case.

Another problem in using this method is that of what order cumulants to use, for this method provides us, in the, non-normal case, with an infinity of estimates based on the different orders of the cumulants used. Geary suggests that cumulants of lowest order be used because of ease of computation. Even so, one should know something about the shape of the joint distribution of x and y, for all odd cumulants of a symmetric distribution are zero, and hence cannot be used to estimate β.

A better measure of what order cumulants to be used is the variance of the estimates based on different orders. To be on the safe side, fourth order cumulants should be used to estimate β if nothing is known about the joint distribution of x and y, since the distribution may be symmetric and then use of third order cumulants will not yield an estimate of β. However, one should note that inaccuracy in estimation of cumulants generally increases rapidly with order, and, coupled with the fact that this general method of estimation breaks down in the normal case, one is not very likely to use it to estimate β.

One method of improving estimation via cumulants is to pool estimates of β based on different values of c_1, c_2. The linear combination of estimates $\hat{\beta}(c_1, c_2)$ and $\hat{\beta}(c_1^*, c_2^*)$ which has minimum variance is the combination $\alpha\hat{\beta}(c_1, c_2) + (1-\alpha)\hat{\beta}(c_1^*, c_2^*)$, where

$$\alpha = \frac{V(\hat{\beta}(c_1^*, c_2^*)) - \operatorname{Cov}(\hat{\beta}(c_1, c_2), \hat{\beta}(c_1^*, c_2^*))}{V(\hat{\beta}(c_1, c_2) - \hat{\beta}(c_1^*, c_2^*))}.$$

To facilitate this averaging, the asymptotic variance of $\hat{\beta}(c_1, c_2)$ and the asymptotic covariance of $\hat{\beta}(c_1, c_2)$ and $\hat{\beta}(c_1^*, c_2^*)$ should be determined. But, using the multivariate extension of 28.4 of [7],

$$\mathrm{V}\left[\frac{k(c_1, c_2+1)}{k(c_1+1, c_2)}\right] \simeq \beta^2\left[\frac{\mathrm{V}(k(c_1, c_2+1))}{\kappa^2(c_1, c_2+1)} + \frac{\mathrm{V}(k(c_1+1, c_2))}{\kappa^2(c_1+1, c_2)} - \frac{2C(k(c_1, c_2+1), k(c_1+1, c_2))}{\kappa(c_1, c_2+1)\kappa(c_1+1, c_2)}\right],$$

and

$$C\left[\frac{k(c_1, c_2+1)}{k(c_1+1, c_2)}, \frac{k(c_1^*, c_2^*+1)}{k(c_1^*+1, c_2^*)}\right]$$
$$\simeq \beta^2\left[\frac{C(k(c_1, c_2+1), k(c_1^*, c_2^*+1))}{\kappa(c_1, c_2+1)\kappa(c_1^*, c_2^*+1)} + \frac{C(k(c_1+1, c_2), k(c_1^*+1, c_2^*))}{\kappa(c_1+1, c_2)\kappa(c_1^*+1, c_2^*)} - \frac{C(k(c_1, c_2+1), k(c_1^*+1, c_2^*))}{\kappa(c_1, c_2+1)\kappa(c_1^*+1, c_2^*)} - \frac{C(k(c_1+1, c_2), k(c_1^*, c_2^*+1))}{\kappa(c_1+1, c_2)\kappa(c_1^*, c_2^*+1)}\right],$$

and each of these variances and covariances can be determined using the procedure of [20].

Estimation of β via moments rather than cumulants has also been considered. Since the ideas behind and the problems besetting this method are similar to those presented above, I shall only refer the reader to [9] and [38] for a fuller discussion of these estimates.

7. ESTIMATION IN IDENTIFIABLE CASES

An entirely different approach to the problem of estimating β in the linear structural relation is taken by Neyman [33]. He first rewrites the equation

$Y=\alpha+\beta X$ in polar coordinates as $X\cos\theta^*+Y\sin\theta^*=P$ where $\theta^*=\tan^{-1}\beta$ and $-\pi/2<\theta^*\leq\pi/2$. Neyman then finds a consistent estimate of

$$\theta=\begin{cases}0 & \text{if } \theta^*=\pi/2\\ \theta^* & \text{otherwise}\end{cases}$$

when the following conditions are true: (i) X and Y follow an arbitrary non-normal distribution, and (ii) $u=u'+u''$ and $v=v'+v''$ where (a) u', v' are independent, (b) u', v' are independent of X and Y, (c) u' and v' are arbitrarily distributed, (d) (u'', v'') is distributed in an arbitrary bivariate normal distribution, and (e) (u'', v'') are independent of X, Y, u', and v'. Condition (i) is due to the identifiability result of Reiersol and the fact that Neyman uses no additional information in arriving at his estimate.

Since a good presentation of Neyman's estimate is given in [33] and the procedure is lengthy and complex, the reader is referred to [33] for a detailed exposition of this estimate. This estimate is motivated by and based on the properties of non-normal characteristic functions, i.e., characteristic functions of distributions not satisfying the Reiersol necessary and sufficient condition for identifiability.

There are quite a few problems to be faced in applying this method to practical situations. Aside from a lack of criteria on how to make certain choices before commencing to use Neyman's procedure, there is the possibility that one may end up estimating $\theta=0$, in which case an estimate for θ^* (and hence β) is indeterminate.

Wolfowitz ([49, 50, 51, 52]) employs another technique, the minimum distance method, to estimate α and β for both structural and functional relations when the conditions for identifiability are met. The only difference between Wolfowitz's assumptions and those of Neyman above are that u and v cannot be expressed as the sum of two components, one normally and the other arbitrarily distributed. Rather, Wolfowitz assumes that u and v are jointly normally distributed with zero means and independent of X and Y. On the other hand, Wolfowitz estimates β for all values of β, in contrast to Neyman's estimate of $\beta=\tan\theta^*$ only for $\theta^*\neq 0$. The fundamental idea behind the estimate is the following. The estimates of α and β, $\hat{\alpha}$ and $\hat{\beta}$, say, are chosen so that the empiric distribution function of the observations and the true distribution function of the random variables $\{(x_i, y_i), i=1, \cdots, n\}$ when $\hat{\alpha}$ and $\hat{\beta}$ replace α and β in this distribution function are "closest" in a sense defined in these papers.

For the functional relation, intuitively speaking, if (I), the X_i's do not go off to infinity "too fast," and (II), the "empiric distribution" of the (non-random) X's does not get "too close" to some normal distribution with zero mean, then α and β are strongly consistent estimates of α and β. In [49], Wolfowitz gives sufficient conditions for I and II to be satisfied which are not difficult to meet, so that conditions I and II are usually satisfied. In particular, if the X_i's are random variables with some non-normal distribution, then conditions I and II are met with probability one and so the result for the structural relation is a special case of the result for the functional relation.

8. AN EXAMPLE

Let us now consider a case in which an estimate of the parameter β in the linear relation between two variables observed with error is desired. We are concerned with estimating the linear relationship between the Brinell hardness and the yield strength of artillery shells. Shells were manufactured from two different heats of steel, a random sample of 25 shells manufactured from each of the two heats of steel was taken, and the Brinell hardness and yield strength of the 50 shells were measured. Brinell hardness was measured by making a dent in each shell with a device connected to a dial from which the "hardness" in appropriate units is read. Besides variation in the force applied in making the dent, we have errors in this measurement from two other sources, inhomogeneity of the steel shell with respect to hardness and error in reading of the Brinell dial. Yield strength was measured by taking a piece of steel of specified length, width, and breadth, pulling it from two sides with constant pressure for a given period of time, and converting the new dimension into a measure of yield strength. Errors in this measurement are due again to inhomogeneity of the steel and to other errors of mensuration. The data appear in Table 198.

TABLE 198

Low Heat		High Heat	
Yield Strength	Brinell Hardness	Yield Strength	Brinell Hardness
x	y	x	y
229	845	277	900
230	810	285	800
235	750	285	815
235	750	285	815
235	755	285	925
235	755	285	965
235	765	285	970
235	795	285	970
235	795	285	975
235	930	285	975
239	905	285	975
241	760	285	1,010
241	760	285	1,030
241	760	285	1,045
241	795	285	1,150
241	800	285	1,160
241	805	293	940
241	815	293	1,005
241	825	293	1,005
241	825	293	1,015
241	835	293	1,040
241	870	302	935
241	875	302	1,075
241	960	302	1,095
241	1,050	321	1,140

We have been told that σ_u^2 and σ_v^2 are approximately 50 and 7500, respectively. Using this information, we obtain the four least squares estimates of Section 1,

$$(1)\quad b = 3.536$$

$$(2)\quad b = 2.738$$

$$(3)\quad b = 3.475$$

$$(4)\quad b = 3.112.$$

To use some of the other estimation techniques, we must make some interpretations about our underlying model. One interpretation is that each piece of steel is really different and has its own true Brinell hardness and its own true yield strength. We can immediately apply the method of grouping to this case, as we have a natural extra-data grouping criterion here, the heat at which the various pieces of steel were tempered. (Actually, since σ_u^2 is 50 and since the 25th largest x_i was 241 and the 26th was 277, about 4σ apart, the approximate grouping procedure applied here as well.) The Wald estimate based on all 50 observations, 25 in each group, was $b=3.204$, and, after discarding the middle 1/3 of the observations and using 17 observations per group, $b=4.256$. The Tukey procedure yields the following mean squares:

I	33,385.28	IV	48.425
II	106,977.6	V	217.56
III	342,792.0	VI	7,370.0

so that $(\text{II}-\text{V})/(\text{I}-\text{IV})=3.20$, $(\text{III}-\text{VI})/(\text{II}-\text{V})=3.142$,

$$\sqrt{\frac{\text{III} - \text{VI}}{\text{I} - \text{IV}}} = 3.172,$$

and the estimate of β given by the estimator in the footnote of Section 4.1 is 3.427.

If we interpret the situation so that for each piece of steel manufactured at the same heat there is the same "true" Brinell hardness and yield strength, we see that we have 25 replications on each of two values of X. As we saw before, the previous anova table for grouping can also be considered in a new light and interpreted for replications, and so we obtain the same estimation by the components in regression technique when adopting this point of view. Upon applying the Housner and Brennan estimate to this case, we find that our estimate of β is 3.204, exactly the same estimate as Wald's. This is so in this case because there are only two X's (corresponding to two groups), and the Housner-Brennan estimate eliminates no observations in its summation over all sample points.

It is of interest to see how these estimates compare with some of the others mentioned above. The least squares regression of y on x (which would be the Berkson estimate if this model were Berksonian) yields $b=3.288$. Berkson [5] shows that

$$\text{Var } b = \frac{\sigma_v^2 + \beta^2 \sigma_{u'}^2}{n\sigma_x^2},$$

where $\sigma_{u'}^2$ is the variance of u when x is measured as a controlled observation. If we assume that $\sigma_{u'}^2 = \sigma_u^2$, then an estimate of the standard deviation of b is .47. Using third order cumulants, Geary's estimate of β is 5.66; using fourth order cumulants we find that $k_{22}/k_{31} = 3.326$ and $k_{13}/k_{22} = 4.538$. If we use $Z_i = i$ as our instrumental variable, with the x_i's ordered by magnitude, we find that $b = 3.462$. Finally, in computing the Neyman estimate for a particular choice of characteristic functions used in his procedure, the estimate of θ was 0, and the estimate of β was indeterminate.

To summarize, following are the estimates of the slope of the linear relation and, where computed, estimates of the standard deviation of the estimated slope.

TABLE 200

Method	Estimate of β	Standard Deviation of Estimate
Least squares y on x	3.288	.47
Least squares knowing σ_u^2	3.536	.41
Least squares knowing σ_v^2	2.738	.62
Least squares knowing $\lambda = \sigma_u^2/\sigma_v^2$	3.475	.49
Least squares knowing σ_u^2 and σ_v^2	3.112	.25
Grouping, $p_1 = p_2 = 1/2$	3.204	.22
Grouping, $p_1 = p_2 = 17/50$	4.256	.60
Instrumental variable $Z_i = i$	3.969	.29
Components of variance 1	3.202	—
Components of variance 2	3.142	—
Components of variance 3	3.172	—
Components of variance 4	3.427	—
Cumulants—3rd order	5.660	3.1
Cumulants—4th order (1)	4.538	—
Cumulants—4th order (2)	3.326	—

In this particular case, another consistent estimate of β, namely $\bar{y}/\bar{x} = 3.434$, should also be considered, for we can assume that when $X = 0$, $Y = 0$, so that $\alpha = 0$. The estimated asymptotic standard deviation of $\bar{y}/\bar{x}$ is .04, and so this is a good estimate of β. It is this peculiarity of the example which lessens its value. Nevertheless, the differences between the various estimates presented in this paper are illustrated by the example considered.

9. APPENDIX

Lindley gives

$$\hat{\beta} = \frac{\sum_{i=1}^{n} (y_i - \bar{y})^2 - \lambda \sum_{i=1}^{n} (x_i - \bar{x})^2}{2 \sum_{i=1}^{n} (x_i - \bar{x})(y_i - \bar{y})} \tag{1}$$

$$+\sqrt{\left[\frac{\sum_{i=1}^{n}(y_i-\bar{y})^2-\lambda\sum_{i=1}^{n}(x_i-\bar{x})^2}{2\sum_{i=1}^{n}(x_i-\bar{x})(y_i-\bar{y})}\right]^2+\lambda}$$

as his estimate of β when $\lambda=\sigma_v^2/\sigma_u^2$ is known. If we let

$$\gamma=\frac{\sum_{i=1}^{n}(y_i-\bar{y})^2-\lambda\sum_{i=1}^{n}(x_i-\bar{x})^2}{2\sum_{i=1}^{n}(x_i-\bar{x})(y_i-\bar{y})},$$

we rewrite (1) as

$$\hat{\beta}=\gamma+\sqrt{\gamma^2+\lambda},$$

which can never be less than zero, and hence is an incorrect estimate of β. He arrives at this estimate by solving the following quadratic equation (where for convenience the x's and y's are measured from their means):

$$\hat{\beta}^2\left(\sum_{i=1}^{n}x_iy_i\right)+\hat{\beta}\sum_{i=1}^{n}(\lambda x_i^2-y_i^2)-\left(\sum_{i=1}^{n}\lambda x_iy_i\right)=0.$$

We obtain

$$(2)\quad \hat{\beta}=\frac{\sum_{i=1}^{n}y_i^2-\lambda\sum_{i=1}^{n}x_i^2\pm\sqrt{\left(\sum_{i=1}^{n}\lambda x_i^2-y_i^2\right)^2+4\lambda\left(\sum_{i=1}^{n}x_iy_i\right)^2}}{2\sum_{i=1}^{n}x_iy_i}.$$

By algebraic manipulation, (2) can be put into form (1), except for a possible minus sign before the radical. Lindley then asserts that using the positive sign yields a maximum likelihood estimate, whereas using the negative sign yields a minimum likelihood estimate. In form (2), this is true; in form (1) this is clearly not true, by the above argument.

That the plus sign is correct in (2) can easily be seen by considering the equation

$$\hat{\rho}(x,y)=\frac{\hat{\beta}\hat{\sigma}_X^2}{\hat{\sigma}_y\hat{\sigma}_x}.$$

Since

$$\hat{\rho}(x,y)=\frac{\sum_{i=1}^{n}x_iy_i}{\left(\sum_{i=1}^{n}x_i^2\sum_{i=1}^{n}y_i^2\right)^{1/2}},$$

we see that

$$\text{signum } [\hat{\rho}(x, y) = \text{sgn}\left(\sum_{i=1}^{n} x_i y_i\right).$$

Since $\hat{\sigma}_X{}^2/\hat{\sigma}_y\hat{\sigma}_x$ is positive, we have that

$$\text{sgn}\left(\sum_{i=1}^{n} x_i y_i\right) = \text{sgn } \hat{\beta}.$$

Therefore, if form (1) is used, the rule would be to use a minus sign before the square root if

$$\sum_{i=1}^{n} x_i y_i < 0,$$

and a plus sign otherwise. In form (2),

$$\text{sgn}\left(\sum_{i=1}^{n} x_i y_i\right) = \text{sgn } \hat{\beta}$$

if and only if the numerator is positive, which is only when the plus sign is used.

The least squares estimate of β when $\lambda = \sigma_v{}^2/\sigma_u{}^2$ is known has appeared independently innumerable times with the earliest appearance in 1879, [26],[5] and the latest in 1946 [3]. Lindley [27], Tintner [44], and Zucker [53] refer to many of these papers. In searching through the literature on this subject, we find that form (1) of $\hat{\beta}$ is cited only in [18, 19, 26, 27].

One should note, though, that some of the papers referred to in [27] and [53] derive the least squares estimate of tan 2θ, where $\beta = \tan\,\theta$, when $\lambda = 1$. They find that

$$\tan\, 2\hat{\theta} = \frac{2\hat{\rho}(x, y)\hat{\sigma}_\lambda\hat{\sigma}_y}{\hat{\sigma}_x{}^2 - \hat{\sigma}_y{}^2}$$

but do not solve for $\hat{\beta}$ using the relation

$$\tan\, 2\hat{\theta} = \frac{2\tan\,\hat{\theta}}{1 - \tan^2\,\theta^2} = \frac{2\hat{\beta}}{1 - \hat{\beta}^2}\,.$$

If they had done so, they would have to solve

$$\left(\sum_{i=1}^{n} x_i y_i\right)\hat{\beta}^2 + \left(\sum_{i=1}^{n} x_i{}^2 - \sum_{i=1}^{n} y_i{}^2\right)\hat{\beta} - \sum_{i=1}^{n} x_i y_i = 0$$

for β, the same quadratic as above when $\lambda = 1$.

Pearson [35] was one who estimated tan 2θ but then argued that "the best-fitting straight line for the system of points coincides in direction with the major axis of the correlation ellipse." But the direction of the major axis of the correlation ellipse depends only on

---

[5] 1878, [1], when λ was assumed equal to 1.

$$\operatorname{sgn}\left(\sum_{i=1}^{n} x_i y_i\right).$$

Hence Pearson's estimate is equivalent to form (2) when $\lambda=1$. In none of the others papers do I find such an argument.

This estimate is also well known to econometricians (cf. [10, 25, 44] and also [46]) in the following guise. Consider the linear relation $Y_1+\alpha_2 Y_2+\cdots+\alpha_m Y_m=0$, where each of the Y_i's is observed with error, i.e., $y_{ij}=Y_i+u_{ij}$ is observed, $j=1,\cdots,n$. Let ξ be the $n\times m$ matrix of y_{ij}'s, let V be the $m\times m$ covariance matrix of the u_i's, and assume that $V^*=kV$ is known. Then if $a=(1,a_2,\cdots,a_m)$ denotes the maximum likelihood estimate of $\alpha=(1,\alpha_2,\cdots,\alpha_n)$, a is the solution of the equation $(\xi'\xi-\theta V^*)a'=0$, where θ is the smallest root of $|\xi'\xi-\theta V^*|=0$.

In our case,

$$\xi'\xi = \begin{bmatrix} \sum_{i=1}^{n} y_i^2 & \sum_{i=1}^{n} x_i y_i \\ \sum_{i=1}^{n} x_i y_i & \sum_{i=1}^{n} x_i^2 \end{bmatrix}, \qquad V = \sigma_u^2\begin{pmatrix}\lambda & 0\\ 0 & 1\end{pmatrix}, \qquad k = 1/\sigma_u^2,$$

$$\theta = \frac{\lambda\sum_{i=1}^{n} x_i^2 + \sum_{i=1}^{n} y_i^2 - \sqrt{\left(\lambda\sum_{i=1}^{n} x_i^2 - \sum_{i=1}^{n} x_i^2\right)^2 + 4\lambda\left(\sum_{i=1}^{n} x_i y_i\right)^2}}{2\lambda},$$

and our estimate of β, $-a_2$, is equation (2) above.

One final note should be made with regard to the literature on least squares estimation of β. As was pointed out earlier, weighted least squares as defined in 1.1 is appropriate here. Zucker, though, gives estimates based on various other "least squares" approaches, all of which are not consistent estimates of β. The estimate she calls k_p is equivalent to the "least squares" estimate when $\lambda=1$. The estimate she calls $k_{p-\sigma}$ is equal to k_p for functional relations; for structural relations it is not a consistent estimate of β.

REFERENCES

[1] Adcock, R. J., "A problem in least squares," *The Analyst*, 5 (1878), 53–54.

[2] Allen, R. G. D., "Assumptions of linear regression," *Economica*, 6 (1939), 199–204.

[3] Austen, A. E. W., and H. Pelzer, "Linear curves of best fit," *Nature*, 157 (1946), 693–694.

[4] Bartlett, M. S., "Fitting a straight line when both variables are subject to error," *Biometrics*, 5 (1949), 207–212.

[5] Berkson, J., "Are there two regressions?" *Journal of the American Statistical Association*, 45 (1950), 164–180.

[6] Creasy, M. A., "Confidence limits for the gradient in the linear functional relationship," *Journal of the Royal Statistical Society, Series B*, 18 (1956), 65–69.

[7] Cramer, H., *Mathematical Methods of Statistics*, Princeton University Press, Princeton, New Jersey, 1951.

[8] Deming, W. E., *Statistical Adjustment of Data*, John Wiley and Sons, New York, 1943.

[9] Drion, E. F., "Estimation of the parameters of a straight line and of the variances of the variables, if they are both subject to error," *Indagationes Math.*, 13 (1951), 256–260.

[10] Durbin, J., "Errors in variables," *Revue de l'Institut International de Statistique*, 22 (1954), 23–32.

[11] Eisenhart, C., "Interpretation of certain regression methods and their use in biological and industrial research," *Annals of Mathematical Statistics*, 10 (1939), 162–186.

[12] Geary, R. C., "Inherent relations between random variables," *Proc. Royal Irish Academy*, 47 (1942), 63–76.

[13] Geary, R. C., "Relations between statistics: the general and the sampling problem when the samples are large," *Proc. Royal Irish Academy*, 49 (1943), 177–196.

[14] Geary, R. C., "Determination of linear relations between systematic parts of variables with errors of observation the variances of which are unknown," *Econometrica*, 17 (1949), 30–59.

[15] Gibson, W. M., and G. H. Jowett, "'Three-group' regression analysis. Part I. Simple regression analysis," *Applied Statistics*, 6 (1957), 114–122.

[16] Gini, C., "Sull'interpolazione di una retta quando i valori della variabile indipendente sono affetti da errori accidentali," *Metron*, 1 (1921), 63–82.

[17] Hald, A., *Statistical Theory with Engineering Applications*, John Wiley and Sons, New York, 1952.

[18] Housner, G. W., and J. F. Brennan, "Estimation of linear trends," *Annals of Mathematical Statistics*, 19 (1948), 380–388.

[19] Jessop, W. N., "One line or two?' *Applied Statistics*, 2 (1952), 131–137.

[20] Kaplan, E. L., "Tensor notation and the sampling cumulants of k-statistics," *Biometrika*, 39 (1952), 319–323.

[21] Kendall, M. G., "Regression, structure, and functional relationships, Part I," *Biometrika*, 38 (1951), 11–25.

[22] Kendall, M. G., "Regression, structure, and functional relationships, Part II," *Biometrika*, 39 (1952), 96–108.

[23] Kendall, M. G., *The Advanced Theory of Statistics*, Vol. I, Charles Griffin and Co., Ltd. London, 1948.

[24] Kiefer, J., and J. Wolfowitz, "Consistency of the maximum likelihood estimator in the presence of infinitely many incidental parameters," *Annals of Mathematical Statistics*, 27 (1956), 887–906.

[25] Koopmans, T. C., *Linear Regression Analysis of Economic Time Series*, DeErven F. Bohn, Haarlem, Netherlands, 1937.

[26] Kummel, C. H., "Reduction of observed equations which contain more than one observed quantity," *The Analyst*, 6 (1879), 97–105.

[27] Lindley, D. V., "Regression lines and the linear functional relationship," *Jour. Royal Stat. Soc., Supp.*, 9 (1947), 219–244.

[28] Lindley, D. V., "Estimation of a functional relationship," *Biometrika*, 40 (1953), 47–49.

[29] Moran, P. A. P., "A test of significance for an unidentifiable relation," *Journal of the Royal Statistical Society, Series B*, 18 (1956), 61–64.

[30] Nair, K. R., and K. S. Banerjee, "Note on fitting of straight lines if both variables are subject to error," *Sankhya*, 6 (1942), 331.

[31] Nair, K. R., and M. P. Shrivastava, "On a simple method of curve fitting," *Sankhya*, 6 (1942), 121–132.

[32] Neyman, J., "Remarks on a paper by E. C. Rhodes," *Journal of the Royal Statistical Society*, 100 (1937) ,50–57.

[33] Neyman, J., "Existence of consistent estimate of the directional parameter in a linear structural relation between two variables," *Annals of Mathematical Statistics*, 22 (1951), 496–512.

[34] Neyman, J., and E. L. Scott, "On certain methods of estimating the linear structural relation," *Annals of Mathematical Statistics*, 22 (1951), 352–361, Correction, *Annals of Mathematical Statistics*, 23 (1952), 115.

[35] Pearson, K., "On lines and planes of closest fit to systems of points in space," *Phil. Mag.*, 2 (1901), 559–572.

[36] Reiersol, O., "Confluence analysis by means of instrumental sets of variables," *Arkiv for Matematik, Astronomi Och Fysik*, 32 (1945), 1–119.
[37] Reiersol, O., "Identifiability of a linear relation between variables which are subject to error," *Econometrica*, 18 (1950), 375–389.
[38] Scott, E. L., "Note on consistent estimates of the linear structural relation between two variables," *Annals of Mathematical Statistics*, 21 (1950), 284–288.
[39] Seares, F. H., "Regression lines and the functional relation," *Astrophysical Journal*, 100 (1944), 255–263.
[40] Smith, H. F., *Estimating a Linear Functional Relation*. ASTIA Document No. 85543 (unclassified).
[41] Theil, H., "A rank invariant method of linear and polynomial regression analysis," *Indagationes Math.*, 12 (1950), 85–91.
[42] Theil, H., and van Yzeren, J., "On the efficiency of Wald's method of fitting straight lines," *Revue de l'Institut International de Statistique*, 24 (1956), 17–26.
[43] Thomson, G. H., "A hierarchy without a general factor," *British Journal of Psychology*, 8 (1916), 271–281.
[44] Tintner, G., *Econometrics*, John Wiley and Sons, New York, 1952.
[45] Tukey, J. W., "Components in regression," *Biometrics*, 7 (1951), 33–70.
[46] van Uven, M. J., "Adjustment of N points (in n-dimensional space) to the best linear (n-1)-dimensional space," *Koninklijke Akadamie van Wetenschappen te Amsterdam, Proceedings of the Section of Sciences*, 33 (1930), 143–157, 307–326.
[47] Wald, A., "Fitting of straight lines if both variables are subject to error," *Annals of Mathematical Statistics*, 11 (1940), 284–300.
[48] Winsor, C. P., "Which regression?" *Biometrics Bulletin*, 2 (1946), 101–109.
[49] Wolfowitz, J., "Consistent estimators of the parameters of a linear structural relation," *Skandinavisk Actuarietidskrift*, (1952), 132–151.
[50] Wolfowitz, J., "Estimation by the minimum distance method," *Annals of the Institute of Statistical Mathematics*, 5 (1953), 9–23.
[51] Wolfowitz, J., "Estimation of the components of stochastic structures," *Proceedings of the National Academy of Sciences*, 40 (1954), 602–606.
[52] Wolfowitz, J., "The minimum distance method," *Annals of Mathematical Statistics*, 28 (1957), 89–110.
[53] Zucker, L. M., "Evaluation of slope and intercept of straight lines," *Human Biology*, 19 (1947), 231–259.

Erratum

p. 230, line 9 from bottom change "with u" to "with u or v".

THE ESTIMATION OF ECONOMIC RELATIONSHIPS USING INSTRUMENTAL VARIABLES

BY J. D. SARGAN

1. INTRODUCTION

THE USE OF INSTRUMENTAL variables was first suggested by Reiersøl [**13, 14**] for the case in which economic variables subject to exact relationships are affected by random disturbances or measurement errors. It has since been discussed for the same purpose by several authors, notably by Geary [**9**] and Durbin [**7**]. In this article the method is applied to a more general case in which the relationships are not exact, so that a set of ideal economic variables is assumed to be generated by a set of dynamic stochastic relationships, as in Koopmans [**12**], and the actual economic time series are assumed to differ from the ideal economic variables because of random disturbances or measurement errors. The asymptotic error variance matrix for the coefficients of one of the relationships is obtained in the case in which these relationships are estimated using instrumental variables. With this variance matrix we are able to discuss the problem of choice that arises when there are more instrumental variables available than the minimum number required to enable the method to be used. A method of estimation is derived which involves a characteristic equation already considered by Hotelling in defining the canonical correlation [**10**]. This method was previously suggested by Durbin [**7**].

The same estimates would be obtained by the maximum-likelihood limited-information method if all the predetermined variables which are assumed subject to disturbances or errors were treated as if they were jointly determined, and the instrumental variables treated as if they were predetermined variables. Such a procedure was suggested by Chernoff and Rubin [**5**]. It is possible to use the smallest roots of the characteristic equation for significance tests in exactly the same way as when using the maximum-likelihood method, and similar confidence regions can be defined.

All the results listed so far depend on the use of asymptotic approximations. A few calculations were made by the author on the order of magnitude of the errors involved in this approximation. They were found to be proportional to the number of instrumental variables, so that, if the asymptotic approximations are to be used, this number must be small.

2. THE STRUCTURE OF RANDOM SHOCKS AND DISTURBANCES

This article is concerned with a model in which there exist both disturbances with properties first outlined by Frisch [**8**] and random shocks as in the models used by Koopmans and others [**12**]. The only problem which will be considered is that of determining the coefficients of a single relationship.

The actual time series with which the economist is concerned are represented by x_{it}, $i = 1 \ldots n$, $t = 1 \ldots T$, and are assumed to be of the form

$$x_{it} = x'_{it} + x''_{it} \tag{2.1}$$

where x'_{it} is the systematic part of the variable and x''_{it} accounts for the measurement error and the random disturbances.

The x'_{it}, except for a few which have no measurement error (the constant term, the trend and the seasonal components), are either exogenous variables, or, if endogenous, are assumed to have been generated by a stochastic model of the kind considered by Koopmans [12]. The relationship under consideration will then be written

$$\sum_{i=1}^{n} a_i x'_{it} = \varepsilon_t \tag{2.2}$$

where ε_t, the random shock, is assumed to be independent of the systematic parts of all the predetermined variables.

We now assume that there are some predetermined variables whose measurement errors are independent of the measurement errors of all the variables in the relationship, and of the random shock. This requirement excludes certain categories of predetermined variables: those in the relationship (unless they have no measurement error), lagged values of variables in the relationship (unless one makes the unrealistic assumption that measurement errors are not autocorrelated), and any predetermined variable which is estimated from the same data as one of the variables in the relationship. Thus, it is necessary that the sources of data used for estimating the instrumental variables should be largely independent of those used to estimate the variables in the relationship. The instrumental variables will be denoted by u_{jt}, $j = 1, \ldots, N$.

If

$$\sum_{i=1}^{n} a_i x_{it} = E_t \tag{2.3}$$

it follows from (2.1) and (2.2) that

$$E_t = \varepsilon_t + \sum_{i=1}^{n} a_i x''_{it}. \tag{2.4}$$

E_t will be called the residual, and it follows from (2.4) and the discussion above that it is independent of all the instrumental variables. The notation used takes no account of the fact that some of the instrumental variables may be in the relationship. As noted above such variables must have zero measurement error, and this restricts them in practice mainly to the constant term or trend or seasonal factors.

In this notation, then, Reiersøl's method amounts to positing a zero sample covariance between the residual and each instrumental variable. One therefore obtains the following equations:

$$\frac{1}{T}\sum_{t=1}^{T} E_t u_{jt} = 0, \qquad (j = 1, \ldots, N), \tag{2.5}$$

or

$$\sum_{i=1}^{n} a_i \left(\frac{1}{T} \sum_{t=1}^{T} x_{it} u_{jt} \right) = 0, \qquad (j = 1, \ldots, N).$$

Equations (2.5) provide N equations for the n—1 ratios of the coefficients, so that if $N = n—1$ they give a unique set of estimates of the coefficients a_i.

The interpretation of the "ideal economic variable" and of the "disturbance" is a little difficult. Probably the simplest interpretation is to suppose that, if the data were available for sufficiently short periods, it would be possible to use a model in which each equation explains how some class of economic agents determine the value of one variable as a function of the previous values of other variables. Then it will be assumed that the "ideal economic variables" are the actual variables to which the economic agents react. At the same time a random component or shock is used in the model equation to represent all those factors which affect the variable being determined by the relationship, including factors which are not easy to measure or to represent numerically, factors which have individually such a small effect that they are not worth attempting to measure, and a catch-all factor providing for the economist's ignorance of human relationships and other social, institutional, and technological factors. The random component is treated like a random variable and is assumed to be independent of the other variables (the lagged variables) in the relationship.

It is not necessarily true that the determined variable is also an ideal economic variable in the sense that it is exactly equal to the variable to which some other economic agent later reacts, or that if an economic variable appears as a cause in two different equations the appropriate values of the ideal economic variable are the same. It will be assumed that if there are differences they can be absorbed into the random shock, or equation error.

Owing to lack of data and the need to simplify the estimation problem this ideal model must be replaced by a simpler model in which short lags must be ignored or approximated by distributed lags. The ideal economic variables of this simpler model correspond to the ideal economic variables of the ideal model. The disturbances or non-systematic parts of the variables, being the differences between the actual times series and the ideal economic variables, can be regarded as really measurement errors perhaps partly due to differences in definition. It is not easy to justify the basic assumption concerning these errors, namely, that they are independent of the instrumental variables. It seems likely that they will vary with a trend and with the trade cycle. In so far as this is true the method discussed here will lead to biased estimates of the coefficients. Nothing can be done about this since presumably, if anything were known about this type of error, better estimates of the variables could be produced. It must be hoped that the estimates of the variables are sufficiently accurate, so that systematic errors of this kind are small.

In any case it will be noted that the method of this article uses the minimum assumption about the measurement error. There is no need to assume, for example, that the errors on the variables in the equation are independent of each other, and the estimated coefficients are still consistent even if the errors are autocorrelated.

Throughout this paper it will be assumed that the E_t are not autocorrelated.

3. THE ASYMPTOTIC COVARIANCE MATRIX

The main results of this article will be concerned with the asymptotic properties of the estimates. The following general notation will be used. The sample covariance matrix of the variables in the relationship will be denoted by M_{xx}; the sample covariance matrix of the instrumental variables will be denoted by M_{uu}; and the sample covariance matrix between a variable in the relationship and an instrumental variable will be denoted by M_{xu}.

The asymptotic limit of a sample function of variables will be denoted by placing a bar over the corresponding symbol. Thus $\bar{M}_{xu}$, representing the probability limit of M_{xu}, will be equal to the stationary limit of $\mathscr{E}\,(x_t' u_t)$ providing that the model is not explosive, and similarly for the other covariance matrices.

Considering first the case in which $N = n{-}1$ it is convenient to introduce the functions

$$w_j = \frac{1}{\sqrt{T}} \sum_{r=1}^{T} E_t u_{jt}, \qquad (j = 1, \ldots, N).$$

For finite T, the w_j are not usually normally distributed. But their asymptotic joint distribution is normal. From a direct expansion of the w_j and w_k and the fact that E_t is independent of u_{jt}', for $t \geqslant t'$ and of E_t', for $t \neq t'$, it follows that

$$\mathscr{E}\,(w_j w_k) = \mathscr{E}\left(\frac{1}{T}\sum_{t=1}^{T} u_{jt} u_{kt}\right)\sigma^2 = \mathscr{E}\,(M_{uu})_{jk}\,\sigma^2$$

with

$$\sigma^2 = \mathscr{E}\,(E_t{}^2)$$

so that

$$\mathscr{E}(\bar{w}_j \bar{w}_k) = (\bar{M}_{uu})_{jk}\sigma^2.$$

We adopt the standardization that the mth parameter (an arbitrary parameter) be equal to unity. We then denote by a_m the vector of the n—1 parameters which are not assumed equal to 1, by M_{xum} the $N \times N$ matrix M_{xu} with its mth row missing and by q_m the vector whose jth component is equal to

$$\frac{1}{T}\sum_{t=1}^{T} x_{mt} u_{jt}.$$

Then the estimate derived from (2.5) can be written

$$\hat{a}_m = -q_m\, M^{-1}_{xum}$$

where the $\hat{a}_m$ is obtained from the estimated vector by the omission of the unit in the mth position.

Now,

$$\sum_{i=1}^{n} a_i \left(\sum_{t=1}^{T} x_{it} u_{jt}\right) = \sum_{t=1}^{T} E_t u_{jt} = w_j \sqrt{T},$$

and this can be written in terms of the previously defined vectors

$$\sqrt{T}(a_m M_{xum} + q_m) = w$$

where w is the vector with components equal to w_j.

From this it follows that

$$\sqrt{T}(a_m - \hat{a}_m) = w M^{-1}_{xum}.$$

Asymptotically $\sqrt{T}(a_m - \hat{a}_m)$ is distributed like $\bar{w}\bar{M}^{-1}_{xum}$ and its asymptotic variance-covariance matrix is given by:

$$\bar{M}^{-1}_{uxm}\, \mathscr{E}(\bar{w}'\bar{w})\, M^{-1}_{xum} = \sigma^2\, (\bar{M}^{-1}_{uxm}\, \bar{M}_{uu}\, \bar{M}^{-1}{}_{xum}).$$

4. THE REDUCED SET OF INSTRUMENTAL VARIABLES

In general there will be more instrumental variables available than the number of parameters to be determined. Then there arises a problem of choice as to which set of instrumental variables should be used. More generally, one may consider the problem of choosing $n-1$ linear transformations of the available N instrumental variables, so as to provide a reduced set of instrumental variables.

This reduced set of instrumental variables will be denoted by u^*_{it}, $i = 1 \ldots n-1$, and it will be assumed that

$$u^*_{it} = \sum_{j=1}^{N} \theta_{ij} u_{jt}.$$

The problem is then to choose an optimum set of u^*_{it}. It is clear that if any particular set of u^*_{it} is considered any linear transformation of this set is an equivalent set in the sense that it will lead to the same estimates of the coefficients a_i. The choice of the optimum set will be made only with reference to the asymptotic covariance matrix of the estimates of the coefficients.

From the results of the previous section it follows that the asymptotic variance matrix is given by

$$(T\bar{V}_m) = \sigma^2 ((\theta M_{uxm})^{-1} (\theta M_{uu} \theta') (M_{xum} \theta')^{-1})$$

where $\theta = \theta(_{ij})$. Now, if the elements of this matrix are denoted by V_{ij} it is convenient to introduce an arbitrary positive definite weighting matrix c_{ij} and to determine the θ_{ij} so as to minimise

$$\sum_{i=1}^{n-1} \sum_{j=1}^{n-1} c_{ij} V_{ij} = \text{tr}\ (cV)$$

$$= \text{tr}[c(\theta \bar{M}_{uxm})^{-1} (\theta \bar{M}_{uu}\theta') (\bar{M}_{xum}\theta')^{-1}]$$

$$= \text{tr}\ [(\bar{M}_{xum}\theta')^{-1} c(\theta \bar{M}_{uxm})^{-1} (\theta \bar{M}_{uu}\theta')]\ .$$

Now, the optimum θ will be indeterminate to the extent that a linear transformation can be applied on the left. Further restrictions must, therefore, be imposed on the θ_{ij} to make the solution determinate, and the following seem the most appropriate restrictions.

$$(\theta \bar{M}_{uxm})c^{-1}(\bar{M}_{xum}\theta') = I,$$

$$\theta \bar{M}_{uu}\theta' = \text{a diagonal matrix.}$$

The problem is then to minimise $\text{tr}(\theta \bar{M}_{uu}\theta')$ subject to these conditions. A conventional minimisation using Lagrange multipliers then shows that the rows of θ are characteristic vectors satisfying the equations

$$\bar{M}_{uu}v' = \lambda\ (\bar{M}_{uxm}\, c^{-1}\bar{M}_{xum})\ v'.$$

Thus,

$$\bar{M}_{uu}\theta' = (\bar{M}_{uxm}\, c^{-1}\bar{M}_{xum})\ \theta'\ \Delta,$$

where Δ is the diagonal matrix of characteristic roots. Thus,

$$\theta' = (\bar{M}_{uu}^{-1} \bar{M}_{uxm}) (c^{-1} \bar{M}_{xum}\theta' \Delta).$$

The last pair of parentheses enclose a product matrix which is a square $n-1 \times n-1$ matrix, so that θ' is a linear transformation of $\bar{M}_{uu}^{-1} \bar{M}_{uxm}$. It follows that the optimum transformation matrix θ can be more simply taken to be

(4.1) $$\theta = \bar{M}_{xum} \bar{M}_{uu}^{-1}.$$

With this value of θ the asymptotic variance matrix is

(4.2) $$(\overline{TV}_m) = \sigma^2 (\bar{M}_{xum} \bar{M}_{uu}^{-1} \bar{M}_{uxm})^{-1}.$$

Since the optimum value of θ is independent of the matrix c it follows that c can be allowed to tend to a semi-definite matrix. In particular it follows that this choice of θ minimised the asymptotic variance of any linear function of the estimates.

Now of course the matrices $\bar{M}_{uu}$ and $\bar{M}_{xum}$ are unknown, but they are the asymptotic limits of M_{uu} and M_{xum}. This suggests that the transformation $\theta = M_{xum} M_{uu}^{-1}$ should be considered. The corresponding estimates are given by

$$\hat{a}_m M_{xum} M_{uu}^{-1} M_{uxm} = -q_m M_{uu}^{-1} M_{uxm}.$$

Provided $\bar{M}_{xum} \bar{M}_{uu}^{-1} \bar{M}_{uxm}$ is nonsingular these estimates have indeed an asymptotic variance matrix equal to (4.2). This variance matrix is the probability limit of

(4.3) $$s^2 (M_{xum} M_{uu}^{-1} M_{uxm})^{-1}$$

where

$$s^2 = \frac{\sum_{t=1}^{T} \left(\sum_{i=1}^{n} \hat{a}_i \times x_{it} \right)^2}{T}.$$

From these results the advantage of adding one new instrumental variable can be discussed. It is clear that eliminating one variable from a set of instrumental variables is equivalent to obtaining the optimum subject to the condition that the coefficients of one of the instrumental variables are zero, so that eliminating that variable cannot improve the asymptotic variance matrix. It follows that the addition of a new instrumental variable will improve the variance matrix unless the partial correlation between each variable in the relationship and the new instrumental variable is zero after the effects of the other instrumental variables have been allowed for. In practice the addition of a new instrumental variable will usually improve the estimated variance matrix (4.3) unless it leads to an increase in s. However, the improvements are usually small after the first three or four instrumental variables have been added. Thus there may be no great advantage in increasing the number of instrumental variables, and from the later discussion it emerges that the estimates have large biases if the number of instrumental variables becomes too large. We return to this problem of whether there are advantages or disadvantages in using a large number of instrumental variables in our conclusions.

Now it is clear that for each m a different set of estimates is obtained, and that these can be summarised by saying that they are obtained from the set of n equations

$$(M_{xu}\, M_{uu}^{-1}\, M_{ux})\, \hat{a} = 0 \tag{4.4}$$

upon deleting the mth equation. In Section 7 it will be shown that in fact these estimates of $\hat{a}$ will differ asymptotically by quantities of order $1/T$ provided that $|\bar{M}_{xu}\, \bar{M}_{uu}^{-1}\, \bar{M}_{ux}|$ is of rank n—1.

5. THE CANONICAL CORRELATION APPROACH

The symmetrical equations (4.4) immediately suggest the canonical correlation equations introduced by Hotelling [**10**]. In the latter analysis the intercorrelation between two sets of variables is considered, and it is shown that there are linear transformations of the two sets such that the transformed sets have the following property: The variance matrix for two variables both in the same set is the unit matrix, and the covariance between two variables, one from each set, is zero unless both have the same suffix when it is a canonical correlation.

This analysis can be applied to the present problem by taking the variables in the relationship as one set of variables, and the instrumental variables as the other set of variables. If there is actually a relationship between the variables whose residual is independent of the instrumental variables, then one linear transformation of the variables in the relationship will have zero correlation with all the instrumental variables. It follows that the smallest population canonical correlation is zero. This suggests that the smallest sample correlation should be small, and that the corresponding transformation provides an estimate of the relationship's coefficients. In fact the sample correlation coefficient is the square root of the characteristic root λ of the equation

$$(M_{xu}\, M_{uu}^{-1}\, M_{ux} - \lambda\, M_{xx})\, \hat{a}' = 0. \tag{5.1}$$

The characteristic vector is an estimate of the coefficients of the corresponding linear transformation, and, when λ is the smallest root, this provides an estimate of the coefficients of the economic relationship.

If there are two or more small canonical correlations it is clear that the estimates of the coefficients will be rather badly determined, since any linear combination of the two characteristic vectors will be nearly independent of all the instrumental variables. There will be no way of deciding between these different possible vectors unless one has some information about the relationship other than the variables it contains and the independence between the residual and the present set of instrumental variables.

6. A MINIMAX APPROACH

The general properties of the canonical correlation suggest the following alternative derivation. If a_i is any possible set of coefficients, the linear combination

$$\sum_{i=1}^{N} b_i u_{it}$$

is considered which has the maximum correlation with

$$\sum_{i=1}^{n} a_i x_{it}.$$

Then the a_i are chosen to minimise this maximum correlation.

It is clear that the correlation studied can be written vectorally as

$$\varrho^2 = \frac{(aM_{xu}b')^2}{(aM_{xx}a')\,(bM_{uu}b')}.$$

If a is given, ϱ^2 is maximised for the values of b satisfying

$$M_{ux}a = \mu M_{uu}b$$

and then

$$\varrho^2 = \frac{a(M_{xu}\,M_{uu}^{-1}\,M_{ux})\,a'}{a\,M_{xx}\,a'}.$$

Now, the minimum value for ϱ^2 with respect to a, is equal to the smallest root of the characteristic equation

$$(M_{xu}\,M_{uu}^{-1}\,M_{ux} - \lambda\,M_{xx})\,a' = 0.$$

This analysis suggests again that the value of λ would be a suitable criterion for the presence of a relationship of the suggested type.

This approach to the problem is similar to that of Durbin [7] who considers specifically the case in which only one of the variables in the relationship is jointly determined, all the other variables in the relationship being predetermined variables with measurement errors. He suggests that the appropriate procedure is to minimise the canonical correlation between the single variable E_t, which is the residual of the relationship, and the set of variables $u_{jt}, j = 1, \ldots, N$. This canonical correlation is given in the previous notation by

$$T \varrho^2 = \frac{w\, M_{uu}^{-1}\, w'}{s^2}$$

or

$$\varrho^2 = \frac{a\, M_{xu}\, M_{uu}^{-1}\, M_{ux}\, a'}{a\, M_{xx}\, a'}.$$

Thus Durbin's method is equivalent to the method developed here, although he has apparently only considered the restricted case in which n—1 of the variables x_{it} can be expressed as linear functions of the u_{jt} of the form

$$x_{it} = \sum_{j=1}^{N} \beta_{ij}\, u_{jt} + \eta_{it} \qquad (i = 2, \ldots, n)$$

and the η_{it} are all random variables independent of all previous variables in the model and non-autocorrelated. These are clearly more restrictive assumptions than those used in this article.

7. THE ASYMPTOTIC DISTRIBUTION OF THE SMALLEST CHARACTERISTIC ROOT

In this section the distribution of the smallest root of (5.1) is considered on the assumption that $\bar{M}_{xu}$ is of rank n—1, so that only one population characteristic root is zero.

Now there will be a unique matrix H which will satisfy the equation $HH' = M_{uu}^{-1}$ and a suitable arbitrary set of linear restrictions of number $\frac{1}{2}N(N-1)$. It follows that $\overline{HH'} = \bar{M}_{uu}^{-1}$, and, if $t = wH/\sigma$, then $\bar{t} = \overline{wH}/\sigma$. Thus the components of $\bar{t}$ are all asymptotically independently normally distributed with unit variance.

arbitrary Now, if

$$\frac{a\, M_{xu}\, M_{uu}^{-1}\, M_{ux}\, a'}{a\, M_{xx}\, a'}$$

is considered as a function of a, the smallest characteristic root λ_1 is its minimum. Hence:

$$T\, \lambda_1 \leqslant \frac{T\, a\, M_{xu}\, M_{uu}^{-1}\, M_{ux}\, a'}{a\, M_{xx}\, a'} = F\,(a)$$

and

$$T\,(a\, M_{xu}\, M_{uu}^{-1}\, M_{ux}\, a') = w\, M_{uu}^{-1}\, w'$$

and, of course,

$$\text{plim}\,(a\, M_{xx}\, a') = \sigma^2.$$

Thus the asymptotic distribution of $F(a)$ is the same as that of

$$\sum_{i=1}^{N} t_i^2$$

and, since the latter is a continuous function of the t_i, it follows that

$$\overline{F}(a) = \sum_{i=1}^{N} \overline{t}_i^2.$$

This has a χ^2 distribution of N degrees of freedom, so that λ is asymptotically of order $1/T$.

Now, if $\overline{M}_{xu}\, \overline{M}_{xu}^{-1}\, \overline{M}_{ux}$ is of rank n—1, there is a unique a satisfying

$$(\overline{M}_{xu}\, \overline{M}_{uu}^{-1}\, \overline{M}_{ux})\, a' = 0$$

and $\operatorname{plim}_{T\to\infty} \hat{a} = a$.

From the equations determining them and the previous result it follows that if $\hat{a}$ is suitably standardised it differs asymptotically from $\hat{a}_m$ by quantities of order $1/T$. The asymptotic error variance matrix of $\hat{a}_m$ shows $\Delta a = a - \hat{a}$ is of order $1/\sqrt{T}$.

Now

$$\begin{aligned} & a\,(M_{xu}\, M_{uu}^{-1}\, M_{ux} - \lambda_1\, M_{xx})\, a' \\ &= (\hat{a} + \Delta a)\,(M_{xu}\, M_{uu}^{-1}\, M_{ux} - \lambda_1\, M_{xx})\,(\hat{a}' + \Delta a') \\ &= \Delta a\,(M_{xu}\, M_{uu}^{-1}\, M_{ux} - \lambda_1\, M_{xx})\,\Delta a', \end{aligned}$$

using

$$(M_{xu}\, M_{uu}^{-1}\, M_{ux} - \lambda_1\, M_{xx})\,\hat{a}' = 0$$

so that

$$\lambda_1 = \frac{a\, M_{xu}\, M_{uu}^{-1}\, M_{ux}\, a' - \Delta a(M_{xu}\, M_{uu}^{-1}\, M_{ux})\,\Delta a}{a\, M_{xx}\, a' - \Delta a(M_{xx})\,\Delta a'}.$$

Now, since Δa is asymptotically zero, it follows that

$$\operatorname*{plim}_{T\to\infty}\,(a\, M_{xx}\, a' - \Delta a(M_{xx})\,\Delta a') = \sigma^2$$

so that the asymptotic distribution of $T\lambda_1$ is the same as that of

$$\frac{T(a\, M_{xu}\, M_{uu}^{-1}\, M_{ux}\, a')}{\sigma^2} - \frac{T(\Delta a\,(M_{xu}\, M_{uu}^{-1}\quad {}_{x})\,\Delta a')}{\sigma^2}. \tag{7.1}$$

Now, if Δa is replaced by $a_m - \hat{a}_m$, the difference in (7.1) is easily seen to be of order $1/\sqrt{T}$. Hence, no difference will be produced in the asymptotic distribution of (7.1). Both a_m and $\hat{a}_m$ are standardised so that their mth components are unity. In the second part of (7.1) will only appear those terms which do not involve these components. Further, the components of $\sqrt{T}\,(a_m - \hat{a}_m)$ can be represented as linear functions of the w_t. They are asymptotically jointly normally distributed with variance matrix equal to

$$\frac{\sigma^2}{T}\,(\bar{M}_{xum}\,\bar{M}_{uu}^{-1}\,\bar{M}_{uxm})^{-1}.$$

Thus, as before, a linear transformation of the w_t can be defined so that

$$\frac{T}{\sigma^2}\,(a\,M_{xu}\,M_{uu}^{-1}\,M_{ux}\,a') = \sum_{i=I}^{N} t_i^2$$

$$\frac{T}{\sigma^2}\,(a_m - \hat{a}_m)\,(M_{xu}\,M_{uu}^{-1}\,M_{ux})\,(a_m' - \hat{a}_m') = \sum_{i=1}^{n-1} t_i^2$$

then $$(\overline{T\lambda_1}) = \sum_{i=n}^{N} (\bar{t}_i)^2$$

where all the t_i are normally and independently distributed with unit variance, so that $(\overline{T\lambda_1})$ is distributed as χ^2 with $N - n + 1$ degrees of freedom.

This provides a significance test for the hypothesis that there is a relationship between the suggested variables with a residual independent of all the instrumental variables.

This is a suitable test even when $\bar{M}_{xu}$ is of rank less than n—1 since it can be shown that in this case the probability of rejecting the hypothesis will be less than in the other case.

8. THE A PRIORI UNIDENTIFIED CASE

The results of the previous section depend on the assumption that $\bar{M}_{xu}$ is of rank $n - 1$. If its rank is less than this, the relationship will be said to be a priori unidentified. At least two of the population characteristic roots are then zero and the equation

$$(\bar{M}_{xu}\,\bar{M}_{uu}^{-1}\,\bar{M}_{ux})\,a' = 0$$

no longer has a unique solution.

Let us now assume that $\bar{M}_{xu}$ is of rank $n - 2$ and that there is no serial correlation for any linear combination ax'_t which corresponds to the double-zero characteristis root. If λ_1 and λ_2 are the two smallest sample characteristic roots, one may prove, by the methods of the last section, that $T(\lambda_1 + \lambda_2)$ is asymptotically distributed as χ^2 with $2\ (N - n + 2)$ degrees of freedom.

This result can now be used as an approximate significance test of the hypothesis that the relationship is a priori unidentified and that any possible relationship has a non-autocorrelated residual. This hypothesis is not very likely to be true a priori since even if there is a relationship between the suggested variables with a non-autocorrelated residual it is unlikely that there would be a second combination of these variables not only independent of all the instrumental variables but non-autocorrelated as well. In practice the significance test fairly often indicates that the hypothesis may be true, but this is probably because the smallest non-zero root of the population characteristic equation is small, the corresponding residual is not very highly autocorrelated and T is not large enough to make $T(\lambda_1 + \lambda_2)$ significant. The use of the test, however, provides a useful qualitative answer as to whether the estimates are reasonably well identified, although as noted in Section 12 the fact that the estimates are well identified does not necessarily mean that they have reasonably small standard errors.

9. ON THE USE OF VARIABLES IN THE RELATIONSHIP AS INSTRUMENTAL VARIABLES

It is now worthwhile to introduce a notation which explicitly recognises that some of the variables in the relationship may be used as instrumental variables. As noted in Section 2 this is only possible if they are predetermined variables with zero measurement errors. The most important variables which are of this type are those representing the constant term, the trend, and seasonal factors. It is convenient to use a notation very similar to that used by Anderson [3].

Let H and K^* be, respectively, the number of variables in the relationship which cannot and which can be used as instrumental variables ($K^* + H = n$). Let K^{**} be the number of instrumental variables not in the relationship ($K^{**} + K^* = N$).

Let the variables in the relationship which cannot be used as instrumental variables be denoted by $y_{it'}$, $i = 1, \ldots, H$; let the instrumental variables in the relationship be denoted by u^*_{it}, $i = 1, \ldots, K^*$; and let the other instrumental variables be denoted by u_{it}, $i = 1, \ldots, K^{**}$. Then M_{uu} can be partitioned as below

$$M_{uu} = \left(\begin{array}{c|c} M_{u^*\,u^*} & M_{u^*\,u^{**}} \\ \hline M_{u^{**}\,u^*} & M_{u^{**}\,u^{**}} \end{array}\right).$$

Similarly,

$$M_{xu} = \left(\frac{M_{yu}}{M_{u^*\,u}}\right) = \left(\begin{array}{c|c} M_{yu^*} & M_{yu^{**}} \\ \hline M_{u^*\,u^*} & M_{u^*u^{**}} \end{array}\right),$$

and

$$M_{xx} = \left(\frac{M_{yy}}{M_{u^*y}} \middle| \frac{M_{yu^*}}{M_{u^*u^*}}\right).$$

Now clearly

$$M_{u^*u} M_{uu}^{-1} = (I \mid 0)$$

so that

$$M_{xu} M_{uu}^{-1} = \left(\frac{M_{yu}}{M_{u^*u}}\right) M_{uu}^{-1} = \left(\frac{M_{yu} M_{uu}^{-1}}{I \mid 0}\right).$$

Thus

$$M_{xu} M_{uu}^{-1} M_{ux} = \left(\frac{M_{yu} M_{uu}^{-1} M_{uy}}{M_{u^*y}} \middle| \frac{M_{yu} M_{uu}^{-1} M_{uu^*}}{M_{u^*u^*}}\right)$$

$$= \left(\frac{M_{yu} M_{uu}^{-1} M_{uy}}{M_{u^*y}} \middle| \frac{M_{yu^*}}{M_{u^*u^*}}\right).$$

Writing $\hat{a} = (\hat{b} \mid \hat{c})$ equations (5.1) take the form

$$\left(\frac{M_{yu} M_{uu}^{-1} M_{uy}}{M_{u^*y}} \middle| \frac{M_{yu^*}}{M_{u^*u^*}}\right) \left(\frac{\hat{b}'}{\hat{c}'}\right) = \lambda \left(\frac{M_{yy}}{M_{u^*y}} \middle| \frac{M_{yu^*}}{M_{u^*u^*}}\right) \left(\frac{\hat{b}'}{\hat{c}'}\right)$$

or

$$(M_{yu} M_{uu}^{-1} M_{uy} - \lambda M_{yy})\, \hat{b}' + (1 - \lambda)\, M_{yu^*}\, \hat{c}' = 0 \tag{9.1}$$

and

$$(1 - \lambda)\, (M_{u^*y}\, \hat{b}' + M_{u^*u^*}\, \hat{c}') = 0. \tag{9.2}$$

It follows that in this case K^* of the canonical correlations are unity, the corresponding canonical transformations being those for which $\hat{b} = 0$. For the other canonical correlations $\lambda < 1$, and it is then possible to solve equations (9.2) for $\hat{c}$ in terms of $\hat{b}$ in the form

$$\hat{c}' = - M_{u^*u^*}^{-1} M_{u^*y}\, \hat{b}'.$$

Substituting in equations (9.1) and rearranging, we obtain

$$(M_{yu}M_{uu}^{-1}M_{uy} - M_{yu^*}M_{u^*u^*}^{-1}M_{u^*y})\hat{b}' = \lambda(M_{yy} - M_{yu^*}M_{u^*u^*}^{-1}M_{u^*y})\hat{b}'). \tag{9.3}$$

This has eliminated the roots $\lambda = 1$ from the characteristic equation, and so has reduced the degree of the characteristic equation to H.

10. THE CONFIDENCE REGIONS

It is now possible to derive two confidence regions for the unknown coefficients of the relationship. We use the notation

$$F_1(a) = \frac{T}{\sigma^2}(bM_{yy}b' + 2cM_{u^*y}b' + cM_{u^*u^*}c')$$

$$= \frac{T}{\sigma^2}(aM_{xx}a') = \sum_{t=1}^{T} \frac{E_t^2}{\sigma^2}$$

and has a χ^2 distribution with T degrees of freedom.
Similarly,

$$F_2(a) = \frac{T}{\sigma^2}(b\,M_{yu}M_{uu}^{-1}M_{uy}b' + 2cM_{u^*y}b' + cM_{u^*u^*}c')$$

$$= \frac{T}{\sigma^2}(aM_{xu}M_{uu}^{-1}M_{ux}a')$$

and from the argument of Section 7 it follows that asymptotically $F_2(a)$ is distributed as χ^2 with $K^* + K^{**}$ degrees of freedom. But the argument of Section 7 can be repeated for only the instrumental variables in the relationship, and it will then be found that

$$F_3(a) = \frac{T}{\sigma^2}(bM_{yu^*}M_{u^*u^*}^{-1}M_{u^*y}b' + 2c\,M_{u^*y}b' + cM_{u^*u^*}c')$$

$$= \frac{T}{\sigma^2}(aM_{xu^*}M_{u^*u^*}^{-1}M_{u^*x}a')$$

is asymptotically distributed as χ^2 with K^* degrees of freedom. Further, it can be shown by the methods of Section 7 that $F_1 - F_2$, $F_2 - F_3$, and F_3 are all asymptotically independent of each other and are therefore all asymptotically distributed as independent χ^2's with $T - K^* - K^{**}$, K^{**}, and K^* degrees of freedom, respectively.

Thus $F^2/(F_1 - F_2)$ is asymptotically distributed as the ratio of two independent χ^2's and so

$$\varphi_1 = \frac{F_2}{F_1 - F_2}\left(\frac{T - K^* - K^{**}}{K^* + K^{**}}\right)$$

is distributed as the ratio of two independent estimates of the same variance based upon samples with degrees of freedom N and $T - N$ respectively. A confidence region can now be used representing all values of b and c which satisfy the inequality

$$\frac{b\,M_{yu}M_{uu}^{-1}M_{uy}b' + 2\,b\,M_{yu^*}c' + c\,M_{u^*u^*}c'}{b\,(M_{yy} - M_{yu}M_{uu}^{-1}M_{uy})\,b'} = \frac{F_2}{F_1 - F_2} \leqslant \varphi_{1L}\,\frac{N}{T - N}$$

where φ_{1L} is a limit which is likely to be exceeded with only a small probability, say 5%. Then, if we consider the possibility that the actual values of b and c correspond to a point outside the confidence region, it is clear that the probability of the sample φ_1 being greater than φ_{1L} would be less than 5%. Thus, using this criterion, it is unlikely that the data could have been produced if the relationship had coefficients corresponding to a point outside the confidence region. This type of confidence region will be referred to as a confidence region of Type I.

In the same way $(F_2 - F_3)/(F_1 - F_2)$ is distributed asymptotically as the ratio of two independent χ^2's and so

$$\varphi_2 = \frac{F_2 - F_3}{F_1 - F_2}\left(\frac{T - K^* - K^{**}}{K^{**}}\right)$$

is asymptotically distributed as the ratio of two independent variance estimates of degrees of freedom K^{**} and $T - N$ and, if φ_{2L} is an appropriate limit,

$$\left(\frac{F_2 - F_3}{F_1 - F_2} = \frac{b\,(M_{yu} M_{uu}^{-1} M_{yu} - M_{uy^*} M_{u^*u^*}^{-1} M_{u^*y})\,b'}{b\,(M_{yy} - M_{yu} M_{uu}^{-1} M_{uy})\,b'} \leqslant \frac{K^{**}\,\varphi_{2L}}{T - N}\right)$$

provides an appropriate confidence region for the components of b, which is usually more useful than the region of Type I since the coefficients c are usually not very interesting. For computational purposes it is often useful to rewrite the last equation in the form

$$\left(\frac{b\,(M_{yu} M_{uu}^{-1} M_{uy} - M_{yu^*} M_{u^*u^*}^{-1} M_{u^*y})\,b'}{b\,(M_{yy} - M_{yu^*} M_{u^*u^*}^{-1} M_{u^*y})\,b'} \leqslant \frac{K^{**}\,\varphi_{2L}}{T - N + K^{**}\,\varphi_{2L}}\right).$$

This type of region will be referred to as the Type II confidence region.

These confidence regions are exact for finite T provided all the instrumental variables are completely exogenous, that is, provided all the u_{it} are independent of all the $E_{t'}$ for all t and t'. Otherwise, they are only accurate as $T \to \infty$. It is to be noted that they are valid even in the a priori unidentified case, although in this case they will usually be hyperbolic conics or hyperconics. Thus they are certainly usable in the more usual almost-unidentified case. Further, in view of the asymptotic approximation, they are equally well defined by the conditions that $T\,F_2/F_1$ and $T\,(F_2 - F_3)/(F_1 - F_3)$ are distributed as χ^2's with N and K^{**} degrees of freedom.

It is also noteworthy that these regions depend upon the assumption that the residuals are non-autocorrelated. If the residuals are positively autocorrelated the confidence regions (and of course the computed standard errors) will understate the indeterminacy of the coefficients.

11. THE ACCURACY OF THE ASYMPTOTIC APPROXIMATION

The previous sections have been concerned only with the purely theoretical problems of the asymptotic behaviour of the estimates. In practice T is unlikely to be greater than 100, and in some cases it may be necessary to attempt estimation where T is as small as 15, so that the usefulness of the asymptotic approximations depends upon their accuracy for finite T. It is very difficult to work out the actual distributions of the sample functions that have been used for finite T, and an obviously simpler approach is to attempt to calculate some of the important properties of these distributions (e.g., their moments).

The author has derived the expressions for the first and second moments for the case in which the variables are generated by linear stochastic models of the type considered by Koopmans et al. [**12**], disturbed by measurement errors, and with all random elements normally distributed. The calculations are, however, too lengthy to be reproduced here.

The general conclusion is that the biases in the estimates $\hat{a}$ and $T\lambda$ are both of order $N/T\bar{\lambda}_2$ where $\bar{\lambda}_2$ is the square of the smallest non-zero population canonical correlation coefficient. The biases are of course large when $\bar{\lambda}_2$ is small, that is, when the relationship is almost unidentified.

Likewise, it is found that the size of the biases in the confidence regions is not, to a first approximation, dependent on $\bar{\lambda}_2$ but is still proportional to N. This means that even when T is large, of order 100, N must be limited if the asymptotic approximation is to be satisfactory. One may consider as a necessary requirement that $N \leqslant T/20$. This, indeed, limits severely the number of instrumental variables which may be used.

The approximation obtained by regarding $w\ M_{uu}^{-1}\ w'/\sigma^2$ as distributed as χ^2 with N degrees of freedom gives a distribution for the variable which is biased in a positive direction. In particular, confidence regions based on it will be too large, and significance tests based indirectly on it will have too large a chance of accepting a suggested form of relationship. A simple change, which would probably reduce the bias considerably, is to assume that

$$\frac{T + 4\ N}{\sigma^2}\,(a\ M_{xu}\ M_{uu}^{-1}\ M_{ux}\ a')$$

is distributed as χ^2 with N degrees of freedom.

12. A COMPARISON WITH ALTERNATIVE METHODS: (1) LEAST SQUARES

In discussing the use of least squares to estimate the coefficients of a relationship it is convenient to denote the dependent variable by y_t, and the remaining variables by z_{it}, $i = 1, \ldots, p$. The relationship may then be written

$$(12.1) \qquad y_t = \sum_{i=1}^{P} a_i z_{it} + \varepsilon_t \qquad (t = 1, \ldots, T).$$

and the least squares equations can be written

$$(12.2) \qquad m_{yz} = \hat{a} M_{zz}$$

where

$$m_{yz} = \frac{1}{T} \sum_{t=1}^{T} y_t z_{it}$$

and

$$M_{zz} = \frac{1}{T} \sum_{t=1}^{T} z_{it} z_{jt}.$$

Now, multiplying each of equations (12.1) by z_{jt} and summing, we obtain

$$\sum_{t=1}^{T} y_t z_{jt} = \sum_{i=1}^{P} a_i \sum_{t=1}^{T} z_{it} z_{jt} + \sum_{t=1}^{T} \varepsilon_t z_{jt}$$

or

$$m_{yz} = a M_{zz} + v$$

where

$$v = \frac{1}{T} \sum_{t=1}^{T} \varepsilon_t z_{jt}$$

so that

$$(\hat{a} - a) M_{zz} = v.$$

Now let

$$\mathscr{E}(M_{zz}) = A_{zz}.$$

It will be assumed that the variables are stationary so that A_{zz} is independent of T. Let $M_{zz} - A_{zz} = Z_{zz}$.

Then

$$(12.3) \qquad A_{zz} (\hat{a}' - a') = v' - Z_{zz} (\hat{a}' - a').$$

Now, in the asymptotic approximation the second term has a probability limit of zero. If $\mathscr{E}(\overline{v}) = u$ is not zero, then asymptotically the biases in the estimates $\hat{a}$ can be taken as

$$(12.4) \qquad \mathscr{E}(\hat{a}' - a') = A_{zz}^{-1} u'.$$

It is now convenient to write $|A_{zz}| = \Delta$ and to denote the elements of the matrix adjugate to A_{zz} by Δ_{ij}. One may also write $u_i = \sigma_i \sigma \varrho_i$ where σ_i is the standard deviation of Z_{it}, σ the standard deviation of ε_t, and ϱ_i the correlation coefficient between Z_{it} and ε_t. Assuming that the variables are standardised so that $\sigma_i = 1$, the above equation (12.4) can be written

$$\Delta\,(\mathscr{E}(\hat{a}_i - a_i)) = (\sum_{j=1}^{P} \Delta_{ij}\,\varrho_j)\,\sigma.$$

An upper bound on the bias can be obtained by noting that $|\varrho_j| \leqslant 1$ and $\sigma^2 = 1 - R^2$, R being the multiple correlation coefficient. Also

$$\max_{i,j}\left(\frac{\Delta^2_{ij}}{\Delta^2}\right) = \max_{i}\left(\frac{\Delta_{ii}}{\Delta}\right)^2 = \left(\frac{1}{1 - R^2_m}\right)^2$$

where R_m is the maximum multiple correlation between any z_{it} and the other independent variables. From the properties of the multiple correlations one has $R_m \leqslant R$. Thus the bias is certainly less than

$$\frac{p\sqrt{1-R^2}}{1-R^2_m} \leqslant \frac{p}{\sqrt{1-R^2_m}} \leqslant \frac{p}{\sqrt{1-R^2}}.$$

The bias may become large if R_m is near unity or, in other words, if there is some Δ_{ii} which is large compared with Δ. Δ is then almost singular.

Returning to the notation of the previous sections, dropping the distinction between dependent and independent variables and denoting all the variables in the relationship by x_{it}, $i = 1, \ldots, n$, the biases will be large when the matrix $\bar{M}_{xx}$ is approximately of rank $n - 2$ or less. When this is true it is usual to say that the variables are confluent. In this case, even if the conditions are fulfilled which make the least squares estimates consistent, that is, even if $\varrho_i = 0$ for all i, the standard error of the estimates will still be large. When these conditions are not fulfilled it is clear by using equations (12.3) that the variance of the estimates is also large.

From the results of the previous sections it follows that if the instrumental variables have been correctly chosen their estimates are always consistent, in the sense that their biases tend to zero as T becomes infinite provided that the relationship is a priori identified. However, if the variables in the relationship are confluent so that $\bar{M}_{xx}$ is almost of rank $n - 2$ or less, it can be shown that the standard errors of the estimates are still large.

To show this it is convenient to return to the notation and results of Section 4. Adopting again the normalisation $a_m = 1$ for arbitrary m, the asymptotic error variance matrix of the estimates of the instrumental variables is

$$V_m = \frac{\sigma^2}{T}\,(\bar{M}_{xum}\,\bar{M}^{-1}_{uu}\,\bar{M}_{uxm})^{-1}$$

and the corresponding error variance matrix, which would be obtained for the least squares estimates on the assumption that the method is usable, would be

$$V^*_m = \frac{\sigma^2}{T} (\bar{M}^{-1}_{xxm})$$

where $\bar{M}_{xxm}$ means $\bar{M}_{xx}$ with the mth row and column omitted. If γ is any vector with $n - 1$ components, the function $\gamma\, \hat{a}'_m$ will have an asymptotic variance

$$\frac{\sigma^2}{T} (\gamma\, (\bar{M}_{xum}\, \bar{M}^{-1}_{uu}\, \bar{M}_{uxm})^{-1} \gamma').$$

But, if instead the a_m are assumed to have a variance matrix equal to that appropriate to least squares estimates, $\gamma\, \hat{a}'_m$ will have a variance

$$\frac{\sigma^2}{T} (\gamma\, \bar{M}^{-1}_{xxm}\, \gamma').$$

If a canonical correlation transformation is now introduced, and if H is the transformation matrix of $\bar{M}_{xxm}$, it follows that

$$H\, \bar{M}_{xxm}\, H' = I.$$

If then $H\gamma' = \delta$, it follows that

$$\gamma\, \bar{M}^{-1}_{xxm}\, \gamma' = \delta\delta' = \sum_{i=1}^{n-1} \delta_i^2,$$

and

$$\gamma\, (\bar{M}_{xum}\, \bar{M}^{-1}_{uu}\, \bar{M}_{uxm})\, \gamma' = \sum_{i=1}^{n-1} \frac{\delta_i^2}{\varrho_i^2}$$

where the ϱ_i are the canonical correlations. Thus, unless $\delta_i = 0$ except when $\varrho_i = 1$ $\gamma\, V_m \gamma' > \gamma\, V^*_m \gamma'$ and in any case $\gamma\, V_m \gamma' \geqslant \gamma\, V^*_m \gamma'$. Thus, the standard error of $\gamma\, \hat{a}'_m$ is usually greater than would have been obtained if the least squares method could be used. And, in particular, if the variables are confluent so that the least squares standard errors are large, the standard errors using instrumental variables will be even larger.

Theoretically then, if the asymptotic properties of the two kinds of estimates are compared, the instrumental variables method (provided the relationship is a priori identified) is the better, since the estimates are consistent, whereas the least squares estimates are not. However, for finite T, the advantage of using the instrumental variables method is less certain, since the instrumental variables estimates may have large biases especially in the almost unidentified case and in the event the number of instrumental variables is large.

The best practical test is obtained by comparing the results yielded by the two methods in practical cases. Let us suppose that, using a minimum of instrumental variables, confidence regions are obtained (these are still reasonably good approximations even in the almost unidentified case) and that the least squares estimates lie outside the confidence regions. This is sufficient evidence to show that the least squares estimates are probably significantly biased. In practice this happens when it would be expected theoretically, i.e., when there are at least two important jointly determined variables, or when some of the variables treated as independent in applying the method of least squares have large and obvious random variations.

13. A COMPARISON WITH ALTERNATIVE METHODS: (2) THE LIMITED-INFORMATION MAXIMUM-LIKELIHOOD METHOD

It is clear from a comparison of the equations (9.3) and the similar equations of the limited-information maximum-likelihood (L.I.M.L.) method as formulated by Anderson and Rubin [**1**, **2**] that the two methods are in practice very similar. Indeed the equations (9.3) can be easily transformed to the form

$$(M_{yy} - M_{yu} M_{uu}^{-1} M_{uy})\, \hat{b}' = \mu(M_{yy} - M_{yux} M_{u^*u^*}^{-1} M_{u^*y})\, \hat{b}'$$

where $\mu = 1/(1 - \lambda)$.

This differs from the L.I.M.L. equations only by the replacement of z, representing all the predetermined variables, with u, representing the instrumental variables. Indeed the L.I.M.L. method is equivalent to using the instrumental variables method with all the predetermined variables in the model used as instrumental variables. This procedure is reasonable since an essential assumption of the L.I.M.L. method is that there are no measurement errors. As argued in Section 2, it is then possible to use the predetermined variables in the relationship as instrumental variables. The difference between the two methods can be summarised as below.

(*i*) The L.I.M.L. method strictly interpreted requires that all predetermined and exogenous variables which occur in any relationship in the model should be used. The instrumental variables approach is wider in allowing the use of any suitable predetermined variable whether it occurs in any relationship or not.

(*ii*) The instrumental variable method, however, is narrower in not allowing the use of any predetermined variables occurring in the actual relationship being studied, unless it has no measurement error or disturbance, for the reasons discussed in Section 2. It is also suggested in Section 2 that it is probably not wise to use lagged values of a variable appearing in the relationship as instrumental variables.

With both methods practical difficulties of computation and theoretical considerations concerning the biases make it worthwhile in practice to use only a small selection of the vast number of possible predetermined variables or instrumental variables.

Alternatively, it may be said that the instrumental variables method consists in modifying the L.I.M.L. method by treating those predetermined variables in the relationship which have measurement errors as if they were jointly determined variables. This method of treating variables with measurement errors has already been suggested by Chernoff and Rubin [**5**].

14. SOME GENERAL CONCLUSIONS

From the previous results and from quite a large amount of work carried out by the author to test the method in practice, part of which it is hoped will be published later, several tentative conclusions may be drawn:

(*i*) The use of the instrumental variables method will produce consistent estimates of coefficients even when large measurement errors are apparent.

(*ii*) Better results may appear to be obtained if an attempt is made to reduce measurement errors somewhat. One may, for example, smooth the series containing obvious random errors by use of moving averages. Such a process, however, often increases the autocorrelation of the residual.

(*iii*) The use of the limited-information maximum-likelihood method is likely to produce, and in practice has produces, biased estimates when there are large measurement errors in any of the predetermined variables in the relationship. The least squares method is likely to produce large biases when there are large measurement errors, or when some of the independent variables are not predetermined variables and the relationship is confluent.

(*iv*) The use of large numbers of instrumental variables may not improve the accuracy of the estimates. In practice, the effect of increasing the number of instrumental variables has been tried by the author. It has been found that if the first few instrumental variables are well chosen, there is usually no improvement, and even a deterioration, in the confidence regions as the number of instrumental variables is increased beyond three or four. This might have been expected a priori from a study of the results achieved by Stone [**15**] and others when applying factor analysis to economic time series. It has usually been found that three general factors were obtained corresponding to a linear trend, the ten year business cycle, and the rate of change of the ten year cycle. Now, if all the variables in the relationship and all the instrumental variables together can be approximately analysed in this way, the maximum number of coefficients that can be simultaneously determined is three, and the addition of instrumental variables after the third will not improve the accuracy. If, however, there are large random effects (of the same order of magnitude as the cyclical movements) such as strikes, wars etc., and if the residual of the relationship can be regarded as independent of the random effects then this might allow the determination of further coefficients. The latter assumption is, however, very rarely realistic.

In practice, when data covering less than twenty years are used, it seems appropriate to use three instrumental variables: a linear trend, a lagged variable that leads in the trade cycle, and a lagged variable that lags with reference to the trade cycle. Analyses of single economic time series indicate that if longer periods of time were studied a factor analysis might disclose more general factors, for example, another factor corresponding to a parabolic trend, and two more factors to represent the building cycle. To some extent, this gain might be cancelled by the need to introduce more complicated trends into the relationship.

REFERENCES

[1] ANDERSON, T. W. AND H. RUBIN: "Estimation of the Parameters of a Single Equation in a Complete Set of Stochastic Equations," *Annals of Mathematical Statistics*, Vol. 20, 1949, pp. 46-65.

[2] ANDERSON AND RUBIN: "The Asymptotic Properties of Estimates of the Parameters of a Single Equation in a Complete System of Stochastic Equations," *Annals of Mathematical Statistics*, Vol. 21, 1950, pp. 570-592.

[3] ANDERSON, T. W.: "Estimation of the Parameters of a Single Equation by the Limited Information Maximum-Likelihood Method," *Cowles Commission Monograph* 10, 1950, pp. 311-322.

[4] ———: "The Asymptotic Distribution of Certain Characteristic Roots and Vectors," *Proceedings of the Second Berkeley Symposium on Mathematical Statistics and Probability*, 1950, pp. 103-130.

[5] CHERNOFF, H. AND H. RUBIN: "Asymptotic Properties of Limited Information Estimates under Generalised Conditions," *Cowles Commission Monograph* 14, 1953, pp. 200-212.

[6] CRAMER, H.: *Mathematical Methods of Statistics*, 1946.

[7] DURBIN, J.: "Errors in Variables," *Review of Institute of International Statistics*, Vol. 22, 1954, pp. 23-54.

[8] FRISCH, R.: *Statistical Confluence Analysis by Means of Complete Regression Systems*, 1934.

[9] GEARY, R. C.: "Studies in Relations between Economics Time Series", *Journal of the Royal Statistical Society, Series B*, Vol. 10, 1949, pp. 158-172.

[10] HOTELLING, H.: "Relations between Two Sets of Variables," *Biometrika* Vol. 28, 1936, pp. 321-335.

[11] HSU, P. L.: "On the Limiting Distribution of Roots of a Determinantal Equation," *Journal of the London Mathematical Society*, Vol. 16, 1941, pp. 183-194.

[12] KOOPMANS, T. C., H. RUBIN, AND R. B. LEIPNIK: "Measuring the Equation Systems of Dynamic Economics," *Cowles Commission Monograph 10*, pp. 52-237.

[13] REIERSØL, O.: "Confluence Analysis by Means of Lag Moments and Other Methods of Confluence Analysis," *Econometrica*, Vol. 9, no. 1, 1941, pp. 1-23.

[14] ———: *Confluence Analysis by Means of Sets of Instrumental Variables*, 1945.

[15] STONE, R.: "On the Interdependence of Blocks of Transactions," *Journal of the Royal Statistical Society Supplement* 8, 1947, pp. 1-13.

[16] TURNBULL, H. W. AND A. C. AITKEN: *An Introduction to the Theory of Canonical Matrices*, 1938.

THE VALIDITY OF CROSS-SECTIONALLY ESTIMATED BEHAVIOR EQUATIONS IN TIME SERIES APPLICATIONS[1]

BY EDWIN KUH

Regression estimates from cross-section and time series sample data are often different. Some reasons why these discrepancies arise are presented, along with quantative results for three investment functions, explaining investment by gross internal funds and the firm's capital stock, and using individual firm observations. A substantial analytical advantage can be gained from having both time series and cross-sections for an identical group of firms so that the error variance structure for estimates based on both sorts of data can be analysed efficiently.

INTRODUCTION

WHILE AT one time glamorous new discoveries in estimation methods held the postwar econometric limelight, recent second thoughts about the quality and the nature of aggregate economic data have lead to increased exploitation of micro-data, particularly cross-sections. This tendency to place greater reliance on disaggregated information was heavily influenced by two factors. The first influence was the frequent occurrence of collinearity in time series, a handicap which appeared to be less severe in cross-sections. The second major impetus was the desire to construct more complicated behavior models. Because so many aggregative economic hypotheses are scale models of microeconomic behavior, hypothesis tests based on cross-sections or other micro information were quite appealing.[2]

In the last several years, however, doubts have been voiced about the suitability and comparability of estimates from different kinds of data, micro or aggregate, cross-section or time series. This paper is an assessment of regression coefficients and error variance estimates from cross-sections and time series, which offers partial documentation on the side of the skeptics.[3] Empirical illustrations are drawn from a study of investment behavior using micro observations on firms in capital goods producing industries. Results from numerous regression estimates for the identical group of firms both in time series and cross-sections provide the basic evidence, so

[1] Paper delivered December 29, 1957, at the Econometric Society Meetings. This research has been financed in part by the Sloan Research Fund. I wish to thank Gregory Chow, Jean Crockett, Guy Orcutt, John Meyer, Robert Solow and the Harvard Seminar in Quantitative Economics for helpful criticisms on earlier versions of this paper.

[2] A third reason, really the reverse of the second, is that increased flows of sample survey information challenged the ingenuity of many investigators.

[3] The main criterion of judgment will be prediction, either in the sense of forecasting into subsequent periods, or hypothetical predictions, for instance, about what would happen given a hypothetical policy change.

that extraneous influences arising out of sample differences do not obscure the analysis.

Subsequent remarks fall into four main sections. In the first there are some comments on the estimated regression functions and their theoretical justification. In the second section there are outlined various important features of the sample and of the variables and of the processing of the data. In the third, some results are presented regarding the structure of error variances and the manner in which these differ between cross-sections and time series. In the fourth section contrasts are drawn between estimates of cross-section and time-series coefficients and some of the key reasons for the observed discrepancies are indicated.

1. REGRESSION MODELS

Gross investment is the dependent variable while gross retained profits (net retained income plus depreciation expense) with different lags and the firm's gross capital stock at the beginning of year t are the explanatory variables. Since this paper is limited to certain statistical implications of the model, I shall at this time restrict myself to a few sparse observations in justification of these particular explanatory variables. Theoretical and empirical work by Tinbergen, Kalecki, Tsiang, Klein, John Meyer, myself and others has indicated that, at least in the short run, profits are an important variable in determining the actual rate of investment in the manufacturing sector. On the demand side, profits are an expectational variable and possibly, what is more important, on the supply side, short-run investment timing will be strongly influenced by profits, which are major sources of funds.[4] Because of the limited availability of funds to the firm (i.e., credit rationing), capital market imperfections, or the desire of the firm to avoid external financing, the profit variable has often been considered a crucial short-run variable.

The introduction of capital stock into the equation recognizes effects that happen to conflict on *a priori* grounds. A negative sign reflects the depressing effects on investment of a larger capital stock. In capacity-acceleration models, a negative capital stock coefficient may be interpreted

[4] Jan Tinbergen, *Statistical Testing of Business Cycle Theories*, Vol. 1, New York, 1938, Michael Kalecki, "A New Approach to the Theory of the Business Cycle," *Review of Economic Studies*, Vol. 16, 1949-1950, S.C. Tsiang, "Accelerator Theory of the Firm, and the Business Cycle," *Quarterly Journal of Economics*, 65:325-341 (August 1951), Lawrence Klein, *Economic Fluctuations in the United States*, 1921-1941, 1950 and "Studies in Investment Behavior," *Conference on Business Cycles*, 1951, and John R. Meyer and Edwin Kuh, *The Investment Decision: An Empirical Study*, 1957. While regression results have also been obtained for a capacity-accelerator model, in order to save time and reduce the complexity of presentation, these results will be reported at a later date.

theoretically as a reaction coefficient. Because of the strong empirical relation between output and profit, the same interpretation can be applied, with minor qualifications, to the formulations of this paper.[5] A positive sign, on the other hand, indicates that more gross investment is required, the larger the existing capital stock, to replace worn or obsolescent facilities.

Results for three regression equations are presented. The dependent variable, annual investment, and the independent variable, beginning-of-year capital stock, are the same in all three regressions. In the first equation current profits appears as an independent variable, in the second equation last year's profits is an independent variable, and in the final equation the average of current and lagged profits is an independent variable:[6]

$$I_t = a_0 + a_1 P_t + a_2 K_{t-1} + a_3 C, \tag{1}$$

$$I_t = a_0 + a_1 P_{t-1} + a_2 K_{t-1} + a_3 C, \tag{2}$$

$$I_t = a_0 + a_1 \{[(P_t + P_{t-1})] \div 2\} + a_2 K_{t-1} + a_3 C, \tag{3}$$

where I is investment, P is gross retained profit, K is capital stock, and C is a capital intensity index.

2. DATA

The sample consists of seventy-three capital goods producing firms with complete records on investment and explanatory variables over the period 1935—1955, excluding the war years 1942—1945. The initial year, 1935, was selected because of data availability, since the Securities and Exchange Commission records of investment outlays were relatively complete in that year for the first time. Extremely large firms were eliminated so that the firms included range from quite small to medium-sized; in 1953 most had gross fixed assets valued in the neighborhood of \$30 to \$50 million dollars. This is a "selective sample" which includes capital goods producing firms that have registered securities outstanding,

[5] See Hollis Chenery, "Overcapacity and the Acceleration Principle," *Econometrica*, January 1952, pp. 1-28, and Franco Modigliani, "Comment on Capacity, Capacity Utilization and the Acceleration Principle" (by Bert Hickman), in *Problems of Capital Formation, Studies in Income and Wealth*, Vol. 19, 1957, pp. 450-463.

[6] The capital intensity index is a cross-section type variable which could only influence time-series intercept estimates. The capital intensity measure is the average of sales to gross fixed assets for three years of high capacity utilization rates, 1948, 1952 and 1953. In a cross-section, this variable represents the hypothesis that high capital intensity firms will, *ceteris paribus*, invest more than firms of low capital intensity. This estimate of a reciprocal of a capital coefficient is analogous to methods used on the Leontief Project, explained more fully by Robert N. Grosse, "The Structure of Capital," *Studies in The Structure of the American Economy*, by Wassily W. Leontief and others, 1953, pp. 185-242.

which were not too active in the sphere of mergers and, generally speaking, were medium-sized.

Space does not permit more than brief comment on the steps undertaken to remedy the distorting influence of price level variations. The flow variables, investment and gross retained earnings (depreciation charges plus retained net profit), were price deflated by a capital goods price index. The remaining influential variable, gross fixed assets, was placed on a constant dollar base by a fairly elaborate process.[7]

3. ERROR VARIANCE COMPOSITION

The translation of cross-section estimates into useful aggregate predictions should be quite easy, it is sometimes thought, because the independent errors will tend to cancel each other and thereby eliminate much of the cross-section error variance. Therefore, the relative error variance will decrease as more and more firms are included in the aggregate. Even though individual variances are additive (plus or minus covariance terms), the relative prediction error will decrease as sample size increases. That is, the relative prediction error is given by $\sigma_e/\bar{Y} = \sigma_{ej}/\sqrt{N}\bar{Y}_j$, where N is the sample size, σ_e is the regression standard error of estimate, $\bar{Y}_j$ is the mean of the dependent variable and, for each firm, σ_{ej} is the same. When observations are averaged, it follows directly that $\sigma_e = \sigma_{ej}/\sqrt{N}$. These presumptions break down if the errors in fact are not independent but instead are persistent, autocorrelated characteristics of the individual firms in the sample. If much of the unexplained variance is systematic and non-random, the cross-section relative prediction error will not be a decreasing function of the number of firms according to the square-root relation, and the cross-section error variance will systematically overstate the variability of the time series.

a. Decomposition of errors

With a rectangular array of data available, we can estimate these persistent individual firm effects and their influence on the cross-section residual variance. The hypothesized regression equation can be expressed as follows:

(4) $Y_{jt} = a_0 + a_1X_{1jt} + a_2X_{2jt} + \dots + a_kX_{kjt} + \varepsilon_{jt} \quad (j = 1, \dots, J; t = 1, \dots, T)$,

where j indicates the firm and t is time in years.

[7] It can be summarized by stating that additions to the base year's fixed assets in constant dollars were computed by adding investment, deflated by a price index of capital goods, and subtracting estimated retirements corrected for price changes since the time of acquisition. The price index used for this latter purpose is in effect the reciprocal of a replacement-cost price index. The net result of these operations is a constant-dollar gross fixed asset or real capital stock estimate. Fuller details are given in the Appendix.

In this regression equation the error term ε_{jt} is usually specified to be a random variable distributed independently of the included variables. But let us redefine ε_{jt} according to equation (5)

$$\varepsilon_{jt} = \gamma_j + \nu_{jt}, \tag{5}$$

which consists of two additive parts, the first, γ_j, representing a constant individual-firm effect mentioned above, and the second, ν_{jt}, symbolizing a random variable which varies through time.

The squared residual ε_{jt} redefined by equation (5) can be represented as

$$\varepsilon_{jt}^2 = 2\gamma_j \, \nu_{jt} + \gamma_j^2 + \nu_{jt}^2. \tag{6}$$

With no loss of generality we may assume that both γ_j and ν_{jt} have zero means so that the within-cell error sum of squares would be represented by

$$\sum_{j=1}^{J} \varepsilon_{jt}^2 = 2 \sum_{j=1}^{J} \gamma_j \, \nu_{jt} + \sum_{j=1}^{J} \gamma_j^2 + \sum_{j=1}^{J} \nu_{jt}^2. \tag{7}$$

Can we actually estimate the γ_j^2 and ν_{jt}^2 components separately, as well as the covariance term? Provided the same firms are in every observation period, we can compute the average residual for a particular firm by averaging that firm's residual across years to supply an estimate of γ_j.[8] In addition, when the γ_j has been computed as the average residual for a firm in different cross-sections, the covariance term, involving $\gamma\nu$ will be identically zero for all cross-sections combined, so that

$$\sum_t^T \sum_j^J \varepsilon_{jt}^2 = T \sum_j \gamma_j^2 + \sum_t \sum_j \nu_{jt}^2. \tag{8}$$

Within any particular cross-section, the interaction or covariance component of $\sum_j \hat{\varepsilon}_{jt}^2$ can be estimated from the sample data since $\hat{\nu}_{jt} \equiv \hat{\varepsilon}_{jt} - \hat{\gamma}_j$.

From this analysis the relative importance of systematic firm effects can be exhibited in a variety of ways. One of the more illuminating ways will be to show their relative importance by computing

$$\sum_t^T \sum_j^J \hat{\gamma}_j^2 \div \sum_t^T \sum_j^J \hat{\nu}_{jt}^2 \tag{9}$$

for all three equations, as indicated in Part A of Table I. These numbers affirm in precise form what we might have suspected: that the individual firm effects are important, being, in the present instance, one-quarter to one-third as large as the time-varying errors.

Further interesting implications of a cyclical nature are evident in

[8] Of course, the double summation over all individual γ_j and years will be identically zero provided the residuals have been computed from least squares regressions.

TABLE I

Measurements on the Importance of Time Constant and Time Varying Errors

(γ_j = Time Constant Error; v_{jt} = Time Varying Error)

PART A

Total Squared Time Constant Error Sum of Squares as a Percent of Total Time Varying Error Sum of Squares

Equation 1	.2430
Equation 2	.3290
Equation 3	.2860

PART B

Relative Annual Importance of Time Constant Errors and Correlation Between Time Constant Errors and Time Varying Errors

(Significance levels: 5% = r; 1% = r**)*

	Equation 1		*Equation 2*		*Equation 3*	
	$r_{\gamma v}$	$\Sigma \gamma_j^2/\Sigma v_{jt}^2$	$r_{\gamma v}$	$\Sigma \gamma_j^2/\Sigma v_{jt}^2$	$r_{\gamma v}$	$\Sigma \gamma_j^2/\Sigma v_{jt}^2$
1935	—.8438**	.7645				
1936	—.0487	.4453	—.1181	.6309	—.1343	.5327
1937	—.5483**	.4707	—.7128**	.4878	—.6655**	.4589
1938	—.6603**	.5836	—.7600**	.6094	—.7338**	.5591
1939	—.8150**	1.2600	—.8599**	1.4548	—.8555**	1.3386
1940	—.6240**	.7426	—.7380**	.8952	—.7077**	.8602
1941	—.8542**	.8678	—.8457**	.8970	—.8773**	.8693
1946	.0580	.3477				
1947	.3994**	.1624	.3147**	.2437	.2680*	.1842
1948	.0399	.2394	.0229	.3977	—.0091	.2963
1949	—.3778**	.4550	—.4134**	.6400	—.3951**	.5425
1950	—.0514	.4912	.3268**	.5658	.1290	.5853
1951	.6902**	.1327	.3733**	.3143	.6242**	.2222
1952	.5057**	.0500	.6932**	.0771	.6777**	.0662
1953	.3859**	.1541	.5230**	.1871	.4315**	.1925
1954	—.0429	.2638	—.1331	.2844	—.1118	.2864
1955	—.2474	.0323	—.1281	.4101	—.2241	.3457
$\bar{r}$	—.2439		—.2402		—.2489	

PART C

Variance Analysis

$$F = \frac{\sum_t^T \sum_j^J \gamma_j^2 / J}{\sum_t^T \sum_j^J v_{jt}^2 / [T(J-k-1)-J]} = \frac{\sum_t^T \sum_j^J \gamma_j^2 / 73}{\sum_t^T \sum_j^J v^2 / (69\,T-73)}$$

	Actual F	*Critical F (1/2% significance level[a])*
Equation 1	3.662	1.71
Equation 2	4.336	1.71
Equation 3	3.769	1.71

[a] Linear interpolation between values for numerator degrees of freedom 60 and 120 and 120 denominator degrees of freedom. Because of the large excess of sample over critical test values, any further refinement appeared unnecessary. Actual denominator degrees of freedom are 1100 for equation 1 and 962 for equations 2 and 3. Even if the time errors were autocorrelated so that we could claim only one degree of freedom for each ten unconstrained observations, for example, all the sample F ratios would remain significant at the 1/2% level.

Part B of Table I. The first column for each equation shows the simple correlation within each year between the firm effect, γ_j, and the time-varying error, v_{jt}. These correlations are strongly negative in nearly all prewar years and, except for negative values in 1949 and 1955, moderately positive in the postwar years. This bimodal distribution, not surprisingly, led to very large χ^2 values and strong indications, therefore, of inter-year heterogeneity. The economic implication of these results would seem to be that in periods of underutilized capacity, "errors," (representing all factors other than the included variables) of the two kinds specified are offsetting in their effects. In the boom periods characterizing the postwar scene, the excluded forces (both firm effects and dynamic "shocks") were mutually reinforcing.[9]

One-way analysis of variance offers an efficient test procedure to contrast the relative importance of these different error effects. In Part C of Table I, the firm averages are the column effects, which can be tested against the time-varying error sum of squares.[10] The results once again speak for themselves: the divergences among firm effects which are independent of time are substantial and highly significant.

b. *Actual effects of averaging*

We shall next evaluate how the averaging of observations described at the beginning of this section can actually reduce the standard error of estimate, which depends in large measure on the extent to which the errors in cross-sections do or do not contain autocorrelated individual-firm effects. To do so, some computations were made using standard errors of estimate from the annual cross-sections and from the time series based on individual firm observations, on the one hand, and the standard errors of estimate based on averaged data, on the other. The averaged data are, first, averages of firm observations over time which can then be used for a cross-section regression, and, second, annual averages across firms which thereby yield average values which are time series observations. The actual "typical" standard error of estimate, which represents an error estimate using unaveraged data, was computed by averaging individual (firm or year) variances and is reported in column (1) of Table II. When divided through by the square root of the number of items in the aggregated observations, we obtain a prediction, shown in column (2) of the regression standard error we would observe if the individual

[9] This conclusion follows from the additional proposition that the regressions corresponding to this correlation are homogeneous. Because Var γ_j is constant in every year and $\Sigma \Sigma \gamma_j v_{jt} = 0$, interpretation of these correlations must be undertaken with extreme caution.

[10] As mentioned earlier in the text, the covariance term $\Sigma \Sigma \gamma_j v_{jt} = 0$ for all cells, so that the two sums of squares are independently distributed.

TABLE II

PREDICTED AND ACTUAL REDUCTIONS IN STANDARD ERRORS OF ESTIMATE ATTRIBUTABLE TO AVERAGING OF OBSERVATIONS

A. *Cross-Sections*

Equation	Unaveraged Data "Typical" $\hat{\sigma}_e$ (1)	Predicted[a] $\hat{\sigma}_e$ (2)	Actual[b] $\hat{\sigma}_e$ (3)	Difference (4)=(3)−(2)	Difference ÷ Unaveraged $\hat{\sigma}_e$ (5)=(4)÷(1)	Actual $\hat{\sigma}_e$ ÷ Predicted $\hat{\sigma}_e$ (6)=(3)÷(2)
1A	$2155	$523	$1228	$705	.327	2.358
2A	2306	595	1323	728	.316	2.223
3A	2219	573	1307	743	.335	2.281

B. *Time Series*

1B	1981	232	455	223	.112	1.861
2B	2122	248	433	185	.087	1.746
3B	1972	231	413	182	.092	1.788

Ratio of Cross-Section to Time Series Relative Difference (Column 5A number divided by corresponding element in Column 5B)	Ratio of Cross-Section to Time Series Differences (Column 4A number divided by corresponding element in Column 4B)	Ratio of Cross-Section to Time Series Actual $\hat{\sigma}_e$ ÷ Predicted $\hat{\sigma}_e$ (Column 6A number ÷ by corresponding element in Column 6B)
Row 1A ÷ 1B = 2.920	Row 1A ÷ 1B = 3.161	Row 1A ÷ 1B = 1.202
2A ÷ 2B = 3.632	2A ÷ 2B = 3.935	2A ÷ 2B = 1.273
3A ÷ 3B = 3.641	3A ÷ 3B = 4.033	3A ÷ 3B = 1.276

[a] Predicted $\hat{\sigma}_e^2$ is computed by adding up individual error sums of squares (year errors in the cross-section case, firm constant errors in the time series case) and dividing by degrees of freedom, to provide the typical $\hat{\sigma}_e$ shown in column (1). This "typical" error variance for *unaveraged* data is then divided by N (the number of items averaged to provide one sample observation) to obtain the square of column (2), predicted $\hat{\sigma}_e$. For cross-sections, $N=17$ for equation (1), and $N=15$ for equations (2) and (3). For time series, $N=73$ in all instances. The square roots of all results were then obtained to provide standard errors of estimate.

[b] Actual $\hat{\sigma}_e$ is simply the regression standard error of estimate computed from averaged data.

errors were truly independent. In column (3) are the actual results, where the standard error is from the regression equation estimated from averaged data. These results are shown for both cross-section and time series, and the difference between the predicted and the actual standard errors of estimate are shown in column (4).

Column (5) presents a comparison of relative errors, measured by dividing the "actual" error (4) by the original unaveraged "typical" standard error (1). In all three regressions the relative error for cross-sections is about 3 to 3.5 times greater than that for the time series (indicated by the first

TABLE III

COMPARISON OF CROSS-SECTION AND TIME SERIES SLOPE REGRESSION COEFFICIENTS FOR INVESTMENT EQUATION*

A. AVERAGED DATA

Equation		Independent Variables: Retained Profit	Independent Variables: Capital Stock $(t-1)$	Multiple Correlation
		(t)		
(1)	Cross-section	.518 (.123)	.028 (.011)	.862
	Time series	.202 (.274)	.098 (.040)	.842
		$(t-1)$		
(2)	Cross-section	.618 (.137)	.022 (.012)	.852
	Time series	.289 (.260)	.088 (.036)	.854
		$[(t)+(t-1)]\div 2$		
(3)	Cross-section	.565 (.128)	.025 (.011)	.856
	Time series	.520 (.333)	.062 (.043)	.868

B. WEIGHTED REGRESSION, UNAVERAGED DATA

Equation		Independent Variables: Retained Profit	Independent Variables: Capital Stock $(t-1)$	Multiple Correlation
		(t)		
(1)	Cross-section	.477 (.034)	.032 (.004)	.682
	Time series	.222 (.036)	.068 (.007)	.419
		$(t-1)$		
(2)	Cross-section	.494 (.036)	.033 (.004)	.672
	Time series	.263 (.041)	.064 (.008)	.413
		$[(t)+(t-1)]\div 2$		
(3)	Cross-section	.646 (.041)	.016 (.005)	.699
	Time series	.395 (.049)	.049 (.009)	.436

* The "pure" cross-section type variable, designed to measure inter-firm capital intensity variability, is not included. Standard errors of regression coefficients are in parentheses.

column in the lower half of Table II.[11] This illustrates how individual-firm effects tend to nullify the desirable results of increasing sample size and/or averaging, so that presuming errors will cancel out in the aggregate for cross-sections can indeed be dangerous. Some of them will, but many will not, as these results clearly indicate.[12]

4. COMPARISON OF CROSS-SECTION AND TIME SERIES ESTIMATED COEFFICIENTS

The simplest way to compare regression coefficients from cross-sections and from time series is to average individual firm data and then compare regression coefficients estimated from this averaged information. This has been done in the top half of Table III. The cross-section estimates are obtained by averaging either 15 or 17 annual observations per firm, which yields 73 observations per variable. To get the time series estimates, observations across the 73 firms in a given year are averaged to provide 15 or 17 annual averaged observations. In Part A of Table III results so computed are shown for equations with different profit-lag structures.[13] In all cases, capital stock is recorded at the beginning of the current year. It will be recalled that the current year's value in the first equation is gross retained profits and in the second equation is last year's gross retained profit, while in the third equation it is the average of current and lagged profit.

[11] Different ways of measuring relative error, involving columns (4) and (6) are indicated in the last two columns of the lower half of Table II. Suffice it to mention here that column (6) shows the least per cent difference, although, qualitatively, of course, the direction of change is the same for all three measures.

[12] This conclusion must be qualified to the extent that regression coefficients are not truly homogeneous (see E. Kuh, *op. cit.*). Further, an alternative method of evaluating firm effects—the use of dummy firm variables—has much to recommend it, but has not yet been tackled. The definition of $\varepsilon_{jt} = \gamma_j + \nu_{jt}$ should for the sake of completeness include time-constant effects, (analogous to firm effects), i.e., excluded variables that differ among time periods but which are the same to all firms at each point of time (capital goods prices, for instance). This fraction of the time series error variability will not be reduced upon aggregation according to the square root relation, just as the γ_j fraction will not be reduced in cross-sections. It is, however, a less important source of variation relative to γ_j so that the cross-section, time series contrasts of Table II are not much influenced. Define $\sum_{j=1}^{J} \varepsilon'_{jt}/J$ as the average time-constant effect where ε'_{jt} is the time series residual for firm j in year t. This variable accounted for about 7% of the time series total individual error sums of squares. As a last necessary qualification, it should be observed that time series errors, too, have some autocorrelation, but not to the same relative extent as cross-sections in the present sample.

[13] Concerning general questions of identification and other purely statistical properties of this type of regression model, the reader should see John Meyer and Edwin Kuh, *op. cit.*, Chapter 5, and Edwin Kuh, *op. cit.*

a. Actual comparisons

One of the first points to note in this comparison of cross-sections and time series, is that the capital stock regression coefficient is always positive and larger on time series than on cross-sections.

We next turn to the relative magnitudes of the regression coefficient for the profit variable. In equations (1) and (2) the fact is starkly apparent that the cross-section regression slope is typically about twice as large as the corresponding time series estimate. When we turn to the final equation (3), the change in the lag structure appreciably increases the time series estimate to approximate equality with the cross-section.

A slightly more complicated method which eliminates some (but not all) aggregation bias is also available for comparisons between cross-section and time series estimated coefficients. Instead of aggregating data we may aggregate product moments of the data in order to get a weighted average regression coefficient, which eradicates the aggregation bias effects of different intercepts among individual regressions.[14] In this case too, shown in Part B of Table III, the difference between cross-section and time series estimates remains pronounced; the prior results were not accidents attributable to aggregation peculiarities. In fact, it is more pronounced than in the case of the averaged information. Even the average of the past and current values of profit in equation (3) does not tend to reduce the discrepancy between the cross-section and the time series estimates as was the case with averaged data. The major conclusion in both cases is that the time-series profit slope is less and often substantially less than the cross-section estimates, while the reverse is true for the capital stock variable.[15]

b. Sources of discrepancies

One reason the estimates differ (and in this study one cannot point to the fact that the estimates depend upon different information with different quantitative implications) is that cross-sections typically will reflect

[14] This is done in the following fashion: take all product moments as deviations from the mean, i.e., the usual entries in a single moment matrix, and aggregate these moments over cells so that we have a regression which is termed the "cell mean corrected" regression in the analysis of covariance. This regression was acquired incidental to computations required for an analysis of covariance reported upon earlier in "A Time-Series Approach to Cross-Section Investment Behavior." (See abstract, *Econometrica*, Vol. 25, No. 4, October 1947, p. 609). The time-series weighted regression coefficients were computed from summed moments from which the average firm effects had been removed while the cross-section estimates have had year effects removed. (See A. M. Mood, *Introduction to the Theory of Statistics*, pp. 351-2.)

[15] While the coefficients diverge in opposite directions in the present case, no "law of compensating errors" can be called upon to support those wishing to use the regressions interchangeably.

long-run adjustments whereas annual time series will tend to reflect shorter run reaction.[16] Because disequilibrium among firms tends to be synchronized in response to common market forces and the business cycle, many disequilibrium effects wash out (or appear in the regression intercept) so that the higher cross-section slope estimates can be interpreted as long-run coefficients. The fully adjusted response will typically show a higher coefficient than an incompletely adjusted response. Since the cross-section data will also contain some short-run disturbances, however, these coefficients will only approximate fully adjusted long-run coefficients.

Thus, dynamic specification errors that bias time-series estimates downwards will be less observable in cross-sections. Suppose that the explanatory variables operate according to a pattern of distributed lags:

$$I_t = a + b_0X_t + b_1X_{t-1} + \dots b_nX_{t-n} + cK_{t-1} + \varepsilon_t. \tag{10}$$

If, for example, terms beyond a_1 are neglected, a_1, which represents only a part of the reaction, will be a small number compared to the total, long-run reaction coefficient.[17] Least-squares bias, which arises from high partial correlations between the excluded and included variables should not ordinarily be large, since the X_{t-i} are likely to have almost equally strong simple correlations with both X_t *and* K_{t-1}. On cross-sections, behavior is less explicitly dynamic: inter-firm variability is reflected by the observed variables and their coefficients so that inter-firm excluded factors rather than intra-firm dynamic factors dominate. That is, inter-firm dynamic specification difficulties will be less since market or cyclical factors largely common to all firms in an industry will not affect inter-firm variability and will hence exert a minor influence on cross-section estimates. In particular, we should *a priori* expect the cross-section negative reaction coefficient to be larger than the shorter-run time series estimate, a proposition that perhaps explains much of the observed phenomenon that the time-series capital stock coefficients are typically more positive than the corresponding cross-section estimates, given a similar depreciation effect on both cross-sections and time series.

How important the individual cross-section biases actually can be is indicated by Table IV for Equation (1) only.[18] Using the decomposed residual estimates of γ_j and v_{jt}, partial correlations between each of these

[16] In the case of food demand functions, response mechanism and the difficulties inherent in combining qualitatively different data are discussed by Edwin Kuh and John Meyer, "How Extraneous Are Extraneous Estimates?", *Review of Economics and Statistics*, November 1957, pp. 380-93.

[17] Some problems of distributed lags and their measurement have been adroitly handled by L. Koyck, *Distributed Lags and Investment Analysis*, Amsterdam, 1954.

[18] Limitations of time and money precluded computation of estimates for the other equations.

TABLE IV

CROSS-SECTION PARTIAL CORRELATIONS OF ESTIMATED ERROR TERMS WITH INDEPENDENT VARIABLES, EQUATION 1

(Significance levels: 5% = r^*; 1% = r^{**})

Years	$r_{\gamma 1.23}$ (1)	$r_{\gamma 2.13}$ (2)	$r_{\nu 1.23}$ (3)	$r_{\nu 2.13}$ (4)
1935	—.3415**	—.0107	.2964*	.0092
1936	—.4010**	—.1338	.2612*	.0832
1937	—.2581*	—.1587	.1747	.1062
1938	—.0668	—.0148	.0506	.0112
1939	—.2737*	—.0453	.3087**	.0517
1940	—.2354*	—.0667	.2024	.0569
1941	—.1611	—.0442	.1497	.0410
1946	.0242	.0386	—.0141	—.0225
1947	.0658	.0549	—.0264	—.0220
1948	.0268	.0124	—.0131	—.0061
1949	—.1813	—.1090	.1213	.0725
1950	—.4590**	—.3400**	.3150**	.2262
1951	—.0392	—.0379	.0142	.0137
1952	—.3766**	—.3027**	.0795	.0622
1953	—.3821**	—.3228**	.1391	.1151
1954	—.2216	—.2182	.1061	.1044
1955	—.2629*	—.2316	.1166	.1020
Prewar Average[a]	—.2482	—.0677	.2062	.0513
Postwar Average[a]	—.1805	—.1456	.0838	.0645
Grand Average[a]	—.2084	—.1135	.1342	.0591

Note: Variable Designations: variable 1 is retained profit;
γ = Time constant error; variable 2 is capital stock;
ν = Time varying error; variable 3 is capital intensity measure.

[a] Since the correlations are rather small, straight arithmetic averages were computed instead of using Fisher's Z transformation.

error components with the included variables, retained profit and capital stock, were computed. Large partial correlations, of course, indicate large biases. In only a few years were either $\hat{\gamma}_j$ or $\hat{\nu}_{jt}$ significantly correlated with the capital stock variable and then those were only postwar years, while the error terms' partial correlations with profit were often highly significant. Although these latter correlations were significant they were of opposite signs prewar (see Table IV), so that the net bias effects were small.

Postwar, a clearly different pattern emerged. While firm effects that are independent of time remained significantly correlated (although relatively less often than prewar), the time-varying errors were negligible in all years except 1950. Postwar, therefore, the combined effect of both errors was to bias downward the estimate of the profit coefficient in the cross-section regression.[19] As a last point, the partial correlations of the time-varying error with profit were noticeably less than the non-time-varying errors, the former differing significantly from zero at the 5% level in only four years and the latter displaying significant correlation in nine out of 17 years. Thus, the cross-section biases were especially strong, while time series biases were not.

These observations on cross-section bias lend support to the rather obvious, but pertinent proposition that the biases from excluded variables can be strikingly different in time series and cross-sections. Therefore, the propriety for prediction purposes of applying in one context behavior relations estimated in another context is highly questionable. To the extent that these biases are inherent in the time reaction mechanism, we shall want to preserve estimation biases, and we could cause positive damage by importing static inter-firm bias into a time series frame of reference. In short, sources of biases differ and often may be rather stable. We should, therefore, preserve such biases until more appropriate specification can reduce bias in its relevant temporal context.

Cross-section and time series estimates will usually differ for the reasons given above. For prediction purposes, however, it is most important that the numerical value of differences between estimates be ascertained. If the time series estimate is some function of the typical cross-section estimate, one estimate can be translated into the other irrespective of the causal factors that determined the discrepancy. When such systematic relations can be found, the predicting statistician will have an extremely valuable tool. In this context, cross-sections have two advantages. First, should the relations which generated the observations undergo a structural change, the estimates could be revised immediately upon discovery that the cross-section relationships had altered, unless the function translating cross-section into time series estimates changed at the same time. Time series could not be used so efficiently for this purpose because of the necessarily long time interval that must pass before assurance can be given that a change had occurred. The more variable are the cross-section estimates, however, the weaker does this proposition become. Second, cross-sections typically have many more degrees of freedom than time series and often the independent variation is greater. On this account heavier reliance on coefficients estimated on cross-sections is warranted.

[19] If this interpretation is correct, the "true" difference between the time-series and cross-section slopes may be greater than that presently observed. First differencing would, of course, eliminate the γ_j so that bias from this source would be negligible. Similarly, the effects of firms on the error variance would vanish. The advisability of first differences, however, hinges on a number of additional considerations not all of which are favorable to its adoption.

What should be stressed, however, is that cross-sections cannot be used successfully to make time series predictions unless a systematic relationship between the cross-section and time series estimates has been firmly established. Only when joint information is available and empirical relations are established between the two types of information will it be possible to make inferences from one type of data to the other without other major sources of variation (e.g., quality of data, type of data) obscuring the causes of observed discrepancies.

5. CONCLUSIONS

Throughout this paper I have insisted upon the proposition that understanding the time series implications of a single cross-section requires sequential observations on the same individuals in a number of different time periods. Other possible data compositions that frequently arise in practice include those with different individuals in a number of consecutive time periods for sample surveys, and cross-section samples at separate points of time linked by aggregates for the intervening periods. Until a great deal more has been learned about how cross-sections and time series are related, however, a rectangular array of data is essential to the full understanding of the systematic interrelations between the different sample types. Observations on individuals at only one or a few points of time will often be structurally incomplete because the observations in a given cross-section are likely to be affected by prior observations.[20] More important, with a rectangular array of data, inference from time series residuals about the cross-section behavior can be drawn, and *vice versa*. Many relevant hypotheses about the structure of error distributions in cross-sections and hence about the joint time series, cross-section structure depend upon completeness of information.

We have attempted to illustrate these generalizations by the evidence already presented. This evidence from a particular study with a limited set of variables for the period 1935-1955 leads to the following empirical propositions:

1. The error variances in cross-sections overestimate the variability actually present in the independent time series error. The extent of overestimation is difficult to ascertain unless we have a rectangular set of observations. In the present case, as reported in Table I, it is seen that irrelevant, "pure cross-section variability" amounts to slightly more than one quarter of the time-varying unexplained variance. Thus, while it is true that this source of variability will not affect the time series variance, we cannot

[20] This point has been explicitly recognized in the late 1940 studies of consumption behavior by James Duesenberry and Franco Modigliani and also in the more recent work of Modigliani and Brumberg and Milton Friedman.

evaluate how much cross-section errors will in fact diminish through increased sample size or aggregation unless both time series and cross-section information has been used according to procedures suggested above.

2. For the investment function considered the cross-section estimates of the profit coefficient are typically almost twice as large as the corresponding time series estimates, while the capital stock coefficients are substantially smaller. Although differences among coefficients were found in estimates from aggregate data, it is shown that the differences could not be attributed to certain aggregation biases, since the weighted regression coefficients, which do not suffer to the same extent from dangers inherent in the aggregation process, displayed similar behavior. Quantitatively, estimates in both cases yield quite similar results.

3. While the estimates of biases in the cross-sections from individual-firm effects could themselves only be estimated in a biased way, the results reported in Table IV clearly reveal the possibility of substantial cross-section bias. It is furthermore highly unlikely that the biases which influenced the cross-section estimates can be qualitatively or quantitatively of the same sort that effect the time series estimates. Because, in any realistic situation, estimating equations typically will be incorrectly specified, certain time series biases will do no damage if the underlying structure does not change and they therefore ought to be preserved. We are almost certain to be mislead if the incorrectly specified cross-section estimates with their particular, and often irrelevant biases, are utilized in a time series context.

In general, we cannot estimate dynamic coefficients from cross-sections with any degree of confidence unless there is supporting time series information to assure us that the biases analyzed throughout this paper do not distort the estimated coefficients and variances in the particular cross-section. Only when we have supporting micro time series can cross-sections be used safely in a time series context. We must conclude that estimates of micro or macro dynamic effects, cannot typically rely upon cross-section estimates. This does not reduce or eliminate the usefulness of cross-sections for testing many kinds of hypotheses. It does suggest that the estimated coefficients be used with the greatest circumspection in their application to time series processes.

APPENDIX

Price Corrections

A. GENERAL PURPOSE PRICE DEFLATOR

Except for the capital stock, which required special deflating procedures, the basic variables were converted to constant 1953 dollars by deflation by the two implicit price deflators, non-residential construction and producers durable equipment, contained in the *1954 National Income Supplement.*[21] The two implicit price indexes have been combined by using current weights for the corresponding categories. The major purpose of this price deflator was not to take account of relative price changes, but, instead, to correct for variations in the absolute price level. Since these firms are predominently capital goods producers, it seemed feasible to use a single deflator for all the series (except capital stock) so that no suspicion would exist that some empirical results could be ascribed to the use of different indexes for the different series.

B. REPLACEMENT PRICE INDEX AND THE CAPITAL STOCK DEFLATION

Construction of a time series on a firms capital stock presents a number of formidable problems. The most vexatious is that the value productivity of older capital stock will as a rule decline through time. We have done little about this. Only on the "one horse shay" hypothesis about behavior would it be possible to ignore declining value productivity.

A second major problem relates to the treatment of retirements out of the capital asset açcount. The procedure actually applied to a typical firm is the following. Fixed assets as of the end of 1934 were revalued in terms of 1929 prices, on the assumption that both retirements and additions at cost were comparatively minor in the years intervening between 1929 and the end of 1934. The next step was to split the change in the book value of gross fixed assets into two components. The first part is investment, a figure obtained from published records. The retirements and/or fixed asset sales figure was then found by subtracting the change in the gross fixed asset account over the year from the investment of the same period. Provided capital losses and

TABLE V

POSTWAR CAPITAL GOODS RETIREMENT COST INDEX

(1953 = 1000*)

Year	Retirement Index
1946	513
1947	521
1948	528
1949	568
1950	545
1951	560
1952	575
1953	590
1954	625
1955	624

* In this context, 1953 = 1000 means that capital goods retired from a firm's property account were valued on the average at 1953 prices.

[21] *1954 National Income Supplement to the Survey of Current Business*, U.S. Department of Commerce, Office of Business Economics, p. 216. Indexes for the subsequent two years were derived from *Economic Report of the President*, 1956, Tables D1-D3, pp. 165-8.

revaluations generally were of small magnitude relative to the original dollar value of retirements, this procedure will yield a close estimate of the correct retirements and sales figure. Most property account revaluations that occurred in the 1930's were concentrated in the first three to four years of the period with the possible exception of 1934.

Then the gross investment figure in constant dollars introduced into the property accounts by deflating the additions-at-cost figure with the price index outlined in previous paragraphs of this appendix. The thorny problem remains: how are we to account for removals from the property account since these removals or sales were entered in original dollars representing many different price levels? The approach adopted was to construct a replacement (i.e., original dollar) price index in which Fabricant's estimates of the age distribution of assets presented in *Capital Consumption and Adjustment,* p. 181, were used to weight price indexes of the original year of purchase. This weighted index was used as a deflator for a dollar value of retirements from the property account.

Table V shows the replacement cost index in terms of 1953 dollars, computed only for the post-war period of rapid price increases when retirements had originally been purchased in years of much lower price levels. Throughout the 1930's and early 1940's, it was assumed, retirements were in 1929 prices, since so little investment took place during the 1930's and since what was invested probably was not retired during the same period.

The final step in computing a constant-price fixed-asset value estimate is to reconstitute the change in the gross property account in terms of constant dollars, adding in deflated investment and subtracting out deflated estimated requirements. This amount is added to the previous year's gross property account which, is either (a) the initial year 1934 expressed in 1929 prices or (b) the accumulated sum of changes adjusted in the manner just described. The next year's dollar change in the property account is split into additions on the one hand and retirements on the other; these components are deflated and then reconstituted into the change of gross property accounts in constant dollars; and this figure is added to the "real" gross property account; etc.

USE OF DUMMY VARIABLES IN REGRESSION EQUATIONS

DANIEL B. SUITS

The use of dummy variables requires the imposition of additional constraints on the parameters of regression equations if determinate estimates are to be obtained. Among the possible constraints the most useful are (a) to set the constant term of the equation to zero, or (b) to omit one of the dummy variables from the equation. In working with a single system of classes either constraint can be used, and results from the application of one are readily derived from those obtained from the other. If several systems of classes are involved the best procedure is to delete one dummy variable from each system.

THE dummy variable is a simple and useful method of introducing into a regression analysis information contained in variables that are not conventionally measured on a numerical scale, e.g., race, sex, region, occupation, etc. The technique itself is not new but, so far as I am aware, there has never been any exposition of the procedure. As a consequence students and researchers trying to use dummy variables are sometimes frustrated in their first attempts. It is the purpose of this note to point out very briefly some of the problems encountered in the use of dummy variables and some of the alternative procedures available. A few concluding remarks will be directed to the more general application of the dummy variable, to include its use in the analysis of the influence of variables already conventionally scaled.

1. A SINGLE SYSTEM OF CLASSES

Let us suppose we are concerned with the regression of a numerically scaled dependent variable Y, on a set of numerical independent variables X_1, X_2, etc.; furthermore the population is partitioned into mutually exclusive classes, and we know to which class each item of the sample belongs. We want to study not only the influence of X_1, X_2, etc. on Y but also the effect of class membership. To fix ideas and simplify the presentation let us suppose the dependent variable to be the number of pounds of sweet potatoes consumed by a family. We wish to study the relationship between this and family income, X, and also to determine the influence of the region in which the family lives. For this purpose suppose we have a three region classification of families: Eastern, Southern, and Western.

Since region is not a conventionally scaled attribute we must somehow supply it with numerical values if we are to introduce it into a regression equation. To do this we define three dummy variables, R_1, R_2, R_3, with the property that $R_i=1$ if the item belongs to the ith region; otherwise $R_i=0$. These variables may then be put in the regression as variables in good standing provided the proper steps are taken to insure that the solution of the normal equations will be determinate.

The natural inclination is to set up a regression model of the form

$$Y = aX + b_{11}R_1 + b_{12}R_2 + b_{13}R_3 + c_1 + u \tag{1.1}$$

but it is immediately clear that this would be a mistake. The optimum estimates of c_1 and the b_{1i} are indeterminate. To demonstrate this we need only recall that for each item in the sample, one and only one of the R_i has the value 1, the others being equal to 0. Thus any arbitrary number added to each of the b_{1i} and subtracted from c_1 leaves the value of Y identically unaffected. To look at the matter another way, there is perfect linear multiple correlation among the R_i; any attempt to estimate the regression parameters of (1.1) will fail because of singularity in the moments matrix. To obtain determinate estimates of the parameters of (1.1) we must impose an additional constraint. This can be done, for example, by pre-assigning a value to one of the b_{1i}, or to their average, or to c_1, etc.

Among the possibilities there are two that are particularly useful. (a) We may set $c_1 = 0$. The effect of this preassignment is to convert (1.1) into the homogeneous form

$$Y = aX + b_{21}R_1 + b_{22}R_2 + b_{23}R_3 + u, \tag{1.2}$$

the coefficients of which may be estimated in the usual way. It will be recalled that the normal equations used to estimate the regression coefficients of a homogeneous form involve moments around zero, rather than around means. This saves a step in calculation. Moreover, slnce $R_iR_j = 0$ for all $i \neq j$, the matrix of moments among the dummy variables is diagonal. Placing this diagonal matrix at the top of a Doolittle format makes the hand calculation of the forward solution particularly easy. (b) A convenient alternative to (a) is to set one of the $b_{1i} = 0$. The one selected may be designated without loss of generality as b_{13}, and (1.1) is converted into

$$Y = aX + b_{31}R_1 + b_{32}R_2 + c_3 + u. \tag{1.3}$$

This form is an ordinary nonhomogeneous regression equation in which R_3 does not appear as an independent variable. Dropping out the variable R_3 does not, of course, reduce the amount of information incorporated in the analysis since its values are identically derivable from R_1 and R_2.

Since (1.2) and (1.3) represent merely different constraints imposed on (1.1), they necessarily yield identical estimates of Y; and while the direct interpretation of the two versions differ, parameter estimates for one are readily derived from those obtained for the other. The b_{2i} of (1.2) measure regional influences as deviations from zero; and (1.2) can be interpreted as a linear regression of Y on X, the intercept of which (b_{2i}) varies from region to region. By adding $-b_{23}$ to each of the b_{2i} of (1.2) and $+b_{23}$ to the (zero) constant term of (1.2), we obtain form (1.3). Thus $b_{3i} = b_{2i} - b_{23}$, and the b_{3i} measure regional shifts in the regression of Y on X as deviations from the intercept of region 3 taken as a base.

Since the parameters of the two forms are related by a linear transformation, so are the variances and covariances of the parameter estimates. In particular it may be noted that the variances of the estimates of the b_{3i} in (1.3) may be readily calculated from the variance-covariance matrix of the estimates of the b_{2i} in (1.2) by the usual formula for the variance of the difference between two random variates.[1]

2. INTERACTIONS

In addition to regional shifts in the intercept of the regression of Y on X we may also be interested in regional variation in slope. This may be investigated by introducing an interaction term involving X and the dummy variables. A regression model with this interaction is represented as

$$Y = (a + d_1R_1 + d_2R_2 + d_3R_3)X + b_1R_1 + b_2R_2 + b_3R_3 + c + u. \quad (2.1)$$

The problem of indeterminacy arises among the d_i and a as well as among the b_i and c, and it is necessary to impose two constraints on (2.1). The same convenient alternatives present themselves and we may either set $a=c=0$, or, for some i, set $d_i=b_i=0$. One could, of course, elect to set $a=0$ and, say, $b_3=0$. This would yield a determinate solution but would be awkward to interpret, and one should either formulate both interaction term and direct regional effects as homogeneous forms, or should drop one of the dummy variables from the equation. The differences in interpretation of these alternatives correspond to those of section 1.

3. SEVERAL SYSTEMS OF CLASSES

Considerations similar to those outlined above hold for situations in which a number of different classifications are investigated simultaneously. In the demand for sweet potatoes of section 1, for example, the items of the sample may be assigned to, say, occupational and racial classes.

In the general case we have t systems of classification, of which the ith contains k_i mutually exclusive classes. We define t sets of dummy variables $R_{ij}(i=1, 2, \cdots, t; j=1, 2, \cdots, k_i)$ so that $R_{ij}=1$ if the item belongs to the jth class of the ith system; in all other cases $R_{ij}=0$. The generalization of (1.1) is then

$$Y = aX + \sum_{i=1}^{i=t} \sum_{j=1}^{j=k_i} b_{ij}R_{ij} + c + u. \quad (3.1)$$

It is clear that for any set of constants $b_i^*(i=1, 2, \cdots, t)$ and c^* such that $\sum_{i=1}^{i=t} b_i^*+c^*=0$, Y is identically unaffected by the substitution of $b_{ij}+b_i^*$ and $c+c^*$ in place of b_{ij} and c in (3.1), and determinate results again require a system of constraints. This is most easily arranged by dropping out one dummy variable from each set; i.e. select a j_i for each system of classes i, and pre-assign $b_{ij_i}=0$ $(i=1, 2, \cdots, t)$. This is a generalization of procedure (b) of section 1.

---

[1] More generally, let $V=(v_{ij})$ be the variance-covariance matrix of parameter estimates of (1.2) so arranged that $i, j=1, 2, \cdots, k$ are associated with conventionally scaled variables, and $i, j=k+1, \cdots, n$ with dummy variables. Without loss of generality let $i, j=n$ be associated with that dummy variable which appears in (1.2) but not in (1.3). Let A be a matrix obtained from a unit matrix by subtracting the nth row from each of the rows $k+1, k+2, \cdots, n-1$. Then if V^* is the variance-covariance matrix of parameter estimates of (1.3), $V^*=AVA'$.

4. BROADER ASPECTS OF DUMMY VARIABLES

One occasionally encounters suspicion of dummy variables and a feeling that somehow something not quire respectable is involved in their use. Although this reference to other uses of dummy variables sometimes has practical application it is intended primarily to dispel this feeling. Perhaps part of the trouble lies in the use of the term "dummy" variable. There is nothing artificial about such variables; indeed in a fundamental sense they are more properly scaled than conventionally measured variables. If we conceive the task of regression analysis to be that of providing an estimate of a dependent variable, given certain information, the use of linear regression yields biased estimates in the event of curvature. By partitioning the scale of a conventionally measured variable into intervals and defining a set of dummy variables on them, we obtain unbiased estimates since the regression coefficients of the dummy variables conform to any curvature that is present.

This procedure can be fruitfully applied to a variable like age, the influence of which is frequently U-shaped. Attempts to use chronological age as a linear variable may lead not only to the bias mentioned above, but to the failure of the variable to show significance in the regression. Although we sometimes resort to the use of a quadratic form in age to capture this curvature, there is little additional difficulty and in general better results in the application of a system of dummy variables defined by age classes.

TESTS OF EQUALITY BETWEEN SETS OF COEFFICIENTS IN TWO LINEAR REGRESSIONS[1]

BY GREGORY C. CHOW

Having estimated a linear regression with p coefficients, one may wish to test whether m additional observations belong to the same regression. This paper presents systematically the tests involved, relates the prediction interval (for $m = 1$) and the analysis of covariance (for $m > p$) within the framework of general linear hypothesis (for any m), and extends the results to testing the equality between subsets of coefficients.

1. INTRODUCTION

THE MODEL of normal linear regression has often been widely applied to the measurement of economic relationships. In studies of the consumption function, the mean of consumption is assumed to be a linear function of income and other variables. In studies of consumer demand, the quantity of a commodity is regressed linearly on its price, income, and perhaps the price of an important complement or substitute. In studies of business investment, linear regressions on profits, sales, liquid asset holdings, and the interest rate, have been estimated. Other notable examples include empirical studies of dividend policy, of prices of corporate stocks, and of cost and supply functions.

When a linear regression is used to represent an economic relationship, the question often arises as to whether the relationship remains stable in two periods of time, or whether the same relationship holds for two different groups of economic units. Is the consumption pattern of the American people today the same as it was before World War II? Do the firms in the steel industry and the firms in the chemical industry have similar dividend policies? Statistically these questions can be answered by testing whether two sets of observations can be regarded as belonging to the same regression model.

Often there is no economic rationale in assuming that two relationships are completely the same. It may be more reasonable to suppose that only parts of the relationships are identical in two periods, or for two groups. Maybe the price elasticity of demand for a certain food product has not changed since World War II, while the income elasticity has changed. Maybe the investments of two groups of firms are affected in the same manner by profits, but not by liquid assets. Statistically, we are asking whether subsets of coefficients in two regressions are equal.

[1] An early draft of this paper has been revised after helpful comments from William Kruskal, Edwin Kuh, and David L. Wallace, to all of whom I am grateful.

To state our problems more formally, let y be the dependent variable, and $x_1, x_2, \ldots, x_p$ be the explanatory variables. Assume that there is a sample of n observations. These observations are governed by a model of normal linear regression. In matrix notations, the model is:

$$\begin{bmatrix} y_1 \\ y_2 \\ \cdot \\ \cdot \\ \cdot \\ y_n \end{bmatrix} = \begin{bmatrix} x_{11}\, x_{12} \ldots x_{1p} \\ x_{21}\, x_{22} \ldots x_{2p} \\ \\ \cdot \quad \cdot \quad \cdot \\ \\ x_{n1} x_{n2} \ldots x_{np} \end{bmatrix} \begin{bmatrix} \beta_1 \\ \beta_2 \\ \cdot \\ \cdot \\ \cdot \\ \beta_p \end{bmatrix} + \begin{bmatrix} \varepsilon_1 \\ \varepsilon_2 \\ \cdot \\ \cdot \\ \cdot \\ \varepsilon_n \end{bmatrix}.$$

Here the x's are p fixed variates. The β's are the regression coefficients—β_1 is the intercept if x_1 is set identically equal to one. The ε's are independent and normally distributed, each with mean zero and standard deviation σ. Assuming $n > p$ and nonsingularity of the X matrix, we can estimate the parameters $\beta_1, \beta_2, \ldots, \beta_p$ and σ. Our problems are the testing of whether m additional observations are from the same regression as the first sample of n observations, and the testing of whether subsets of coefficients in the two regressions are identical. The present paper is devoted to a systematic and unified treatment of these tests.

To test the hypothesis that both samples belong to the same regression, the well-known prediction interval [**8**] can be used when the number m of observations in the second sample equals one, and the analysis of covariance [**7**] can be used when $m > p$. We will present two tests for the case $2 \leqslant m \leqslant p$. The first test, to be presented in Section 2, is based on a prediction interval for the mean of m additional observations. The second test is an F test, to be developed in Section 3. The relationship among this F test, the prediction interval, and the analysis of covariance will be explained in Section 4. In Section 5, our results will be extended to testing the equality between subsets of regression coefficients in the two regressions. Two examples of econometric applications are given in Section 6. These examples are concerned with the temporal stability of a statistical demand function for automobile ownership, and of a statistical demand function for new automobiles. It was through these examples that I became interested in the tests presented in this paper.

2. PREDICTION INTERVAL FOR THE MEAN OF m ADDITIONAL OBSERVATIONS

It is straightforward to extend the prediction interval idea from one observation to the arithmetic mean of m observations.

First, let us rewrite the model in Section 1 briefly as

$$y_1 = X_1\beta_1 + \varepsilon_1 \tag{1}$$

where both y_1 and ε_1 are column vectors with n elements, X_1 is a nonsingular n by p matrix, and β_1 is the column vector of the p regression coefficients. The subscript 1 denotes the first sample of n observations. The least-squares estimator of β_1 from this first sample is given by:

$$b_1 = (X_1'X_1)^{-1} X_1' y_1 = \beta_1 + (X_1'X_1)^{-1} X_1' \varepsilon_1 \tag{2}$$

$X_1'X_1$ is the cross-product matrix of the p x's from the first sample.

Let the m additional observations y_2 of the dependent variable be specified by the model

$$y_2 = X_2\beta_2 + \varepsilon_2 \, . \tag{3}$$

X_2 is a nonsingular m by p matrix, with its m rows representing the m new observations on the p explanatory variables. ε_2 is normally distributed with the covariance matrix $I\sigma^2$. If we form the difference between the vector y_2 and the vector of predictions based on the regression estimated by the first n observations, we have, incorporating the relations (2) and (3),

$$d = y_2 - X_2b_1 = X_2\beta_2 - X_2\beta_1 + \varepsilon_2 - X_2(X_1'X_1)^{-1} X_1'\varepsilon_1 \, . \tag{4}$$

The expectation of d is

$$E(d) = X_2\beta_2 - X_2\beta_1 \, . \tag{5}$$

Because of the independence of ε_2 and ε_1, the covariance matrix of d becomes

$$\begin{aligned} \text{Cov}\,(d) &= \text{Cov}\,(\varepsilon_2) + \text{Cov}\,[X_2(X_1'X_1)^{-1} X_1'\varepsilon_1] \\ &= I\sigma^2 + X_2(X_1'X_1)^{-1} X_1'(\text{Cov}\,\varepsilon_1)\ X_1(X_1'X_1)^{-1} X_2' \\ &= [I + X_2(X_1'X_1)^{-1} X_2']\sigma^2 \, . \end{aligned} \tag{6}$$

In the special case when $m = 1$, both y_2 and d become scalars, and X_2 becomes a row vector. From (6), the variance of d in this special case will be

$$\text{Var}\,(d) = [1 + X_2(X_1'X_1)^{-1} X_2']\sigma^2 \tag{7}$$

σ^2 can be estimated by s^2, the (unbiased) square of the standard error from the first n observations. Under the null hypothesis that $\beta_2 = \beta_1 = \beta$ the expectation of d given in (5) will be zero, and the ratio

$$\frac{d^2}{[1 + X_2(X_1'X_1)^{-1} X_2']\ s_1^2} \tag{8}$$

will be distributed as $F(1, n - p)$. This test, which is based on the prediction interval for one new observation, can be found in [**8**].

When we have m new observations and thus m differences $d_1, d_2, \ldots, d_m$, we may consider the average.

$$\bar{d} = \frac{1}{m} \sum_{i=1}^{m} d_i \tag{9}$$

Given the covariance matrix of d in (6) above, the variance of $\bar{d}$ is

$$\text{Var}(\bar{d}) = \frac{1}{m^2} \text{Var}\left[\sum_{i=1}^{m} d_i\right] = \frac{\sigma^2}{m^2}\left\{[1 \ldots 1]\ [I + X_2(X_1'X_1)^{-1} X_2'] \begin{bmatrix}1\\ \vdots \\ 1\end{bmatrix}\right\} \tag{10}$$

Similarly, under the null hypothesis that $\beta_2 = \beta_1$,

$$\frac{\bar{d}^2}{\left\{[1 \ldots 1]\ [I + X_2(X_1'X_1)^{-1} X_2'] \begin{bmatrix}1\\ \vdots \\ 1\end{bmatrix}\right\} \frac{s_1^2}{m^2}} \tag{11}$$

will be distributed as $F(1, n - p)$.

The use of a $\bar{d}$ test can be found in reference [**4**], although the formula given in the Appendix of this reference is incorrect.[2] There is little rationale in using $\bar{d}$ for the purpose of testing. The test is obviously weak against a number of alternative hypothesis. One can envisage many situations in which $\bar{d}$ is small, not because the new m observations have come from the same regression, but because their deviations cancel out. The usefulness of deriving the distribution of $\bar{d}$ lies probably more in the construction of prediction intervals for the mean of additional observations—in so far as the mean is of interest.

3. USE OF F RATIO FOR TESTING THAT $E(d)$ IS A ZERO VECTOR

Instead of changing the null hypothesis $\beta_2 = \beta_1 = \beta$ to the hypothesis $E(\bar{d}) = 0$, consider the quadratic form $d'\,(\text{Cov}\, d)^{-1}\, d$. It follows from(4) and (6) that

$$d'(\text{Cov}\, d)^{-1} d = [\beta_2' X_2' - \beta_1' X_2']\ [I + X_2(X_1'X_1)^{-1} X_2']^{-1}\ [X_2\beta_2 - X_2\beta_1]\ \frac{1}{\sigma^2} + \tag{12}$$

$$[\varepsilon_1' \varepsilon_2'] \begin{bmatrix}-X_1(X_1'X_1)^{-1} X_2' \\ I\end{bmatrix} [I + X_2(X_1'X_1)^{-1} X_2']^{-1} [-X_2(X_1'X_1)^{-1} X_1' \quad I] \begin{bmatrix}\varepsilon_1 \\ \varepsilon_2\end{bmatrix} \frac{1}{\sigma^2}$$

The last term is a quadratic form in $\begin{bmatrix}\varepsilon_1 \\ \varepsilon_2\end{bmatrix}$ with rank m—note that $[I + X_2 (X_1'X_1)^{-1} X_2']^{-1}$ is m by m. It will be equal to $d'(\text{Cov}\ d)^{-1} d$ under the null hypothesis that $\beta_2 = \beta_1$, as can easily be seen from (12). Therefore under the null hypothesis, $d'(\text{Cov}\ d)^{-1} d$ will follow $\chi^2(m)$ distribution; whereas under the alternative hypothesis $\beta_2 \neq \beta_2$, $d'(\text{Cov}\ d)^{-1} d$ will follow a noncentral χ^2 distribution.

[2] I am indebted to Robert Solow for pointing out this reference and the errors therein.

It is well known that the square of the standard error from the first regression, s_1^2, times $(n - p)/\sigma^2$, follows $\chi^2(n - p)$. This $\chi^2(n - p)$ is independent of $d = y_2 - X_2 b_1$. s_1^2 is independent of b_1 and is certainly independent of y_2. Therefore, under the null hypothesis, the ratio

$$\text{(13)} \qquad \frac{d'(\text{Cov } d)^{-1} d \dfrac{1}{m}}{\dfrac{s_1^2 (n-p)}{\sigma^2} \cdot \dfrac{1}{(n-p)}} = \frac{d'[I + X_2(X_1'X_1)^{-1} X_2']^{-1} d}{s_1^2 m}$$

will follow $F(m, n - p)$. Since the numerator of (13) will have a non-central χ^2 distribution when $\beta_2 \neq \beta_1$, the upper-tail F test can appropriately be used. Clearly the test (13) reduces to the prediction interval (8) when $m = 1$.

4. RELATIONSHIPS OF PREDICTION INTERVAL AND ANALYSIS OF COVARIANCE TO THEORY OF LINEAR HYPOTHESES

This section shows the relationships among the F test of (13), the prediction interval for one additional observation, and the analysis of covariance (for $m > p$). All three methods are special applications of the theory of testing general linear hypotheses. It will therefore be convenient to summarize first the theory of linear hypotheses as applied to testing the homogeneity of the (entire) sets of coefficients in two regressions. The size m of the second sample will first be assumed to be larger than p, and then reduced to one.

In our context, the model of general linear hypotheses takes the form[3]

$$\text{(14)} \qquad \begin{aligned} y_1 &= X_1\beta_1 + 0\,\beta_2 + \varepsilon_1 \\ y_2 &= 0\,\beta_1 + X_2\beta_2 + \varepsilon_2 \end{aligned}$$

or

$$\begin{bmatrix} y_1 \\ y_2 \end{bmatrix} = \begin{bmatrix} X_1 & 0 \\ 0 & X_2 \end{bmatrix} \begin{bmatrix} \beta_1 \\ \beta_2 \end{bmatrix} + \begin{bmatrix} \varepsilon_1 \\ \varepsilon_2 \end{bmatrix}.$$

Under the null hypothesis (H_o: $\beta_1 = \beta_2 = \beta$), the model becomes

$$\text{(15)} \qquad \begin{bmatrix} y_1 \\ y_2 \end{bmatrix} = \begin{bmatrix} X_1 \\ X_2 \end{bmatrix} \beta + \begin{bmatrix} \varepsilon_1 \\ \varepsilon_2 \end{bmatrix}.$$

The sum of squares of the residuals under H_o will be shown to equal the sum of squares of residuals under the alternative hypothesis (H_a: $\beta_1 \neq \beta_2$) plus the sum of squares of the deviations between the two sets of estimates of y under these two hypotheses. The ratio between the latter two sums, adjusted for their numbers of degrees of freedom, will be shown to follow an F distribution if the null hypothesis is true.

[3] The developments here follow, and are special applications of, Kempthorne [**6**].

If the null hypothesis is true, the least-squares (also maximum likelihood) estimator of β, denoted by b_o, is

$$\text{(16)} \qquad b_o = \left[(X_1' \, X_2')\begin{pmatrix}X_1\\X_2\end{pmatrix}\right]^{-1} [X_1' \, X_2'] \begin{bmatrix}y_1\\y_2\end{bmatrix}$$

$$= [X_1'X_1 + X_2'X_2]^{-1} [X_1' \, X_2'] \begin{bmatrix}y_1\\y_2\end{bmatrix} = \beta + [X_1'X_1 + X_2'X_2]^{-1} [X_1' \, X_2'] \begin{bmatrix}\varepsilon_1\\\varepsilon_2\end{bmatrix}.$$

The residuals from this regression are:

$$\text{(17)} \qquad \begin{bmatrix}y_1\\y_2\end{bmatrix} - \begin{bmatrix}X_1\\X_2\end{bmatrix} b_o = \begin{bmatrix}X_1\\X_2\end{bmatrix}\beta + \begin{bmatrix}\varepsilon_1\\\varepsilon_2\end{bmatrix} - \begin{bmatrix}X_1\\X_2\end{bmatrix}\beta$$

$$- \begin{bmatrix}X_1\\X_2\end{bmatrix} [X_1'X_1 + X_2'X_2]^{-1} [X_1' \, X_2'] \begin{bmatrix}\varepsilon_1\\\varepsilon_2\end{bmatrix}$$

$$= \left[I - \begin{pmatrix}X_1\\X_2\end{pmatrix} (X_1'X_1 + X_2'X_2)^{-1} (X_1' \, X_2')\right] \begin{bmatrix}\varepsilon_1\\\varepsilon_2\end{bmatrix}.$$

The sum of squares of the residuals under H_o can be written as

$$\text{(18)} \qquad \left\|\begin{pmatrix}y_1\\y_2\end{pmatrix} - \begin{pmatrix}X_1\\X_2\end{pmatrix} b_o\right\|^2 = \left[\begin{pmatrix}y_1\\y_2\end{pmatrix} - \begin{pmatrix}X_1\\X_2\end{pmatrix} b_o\right]' \left[\begin{pmatrix}y_1\\y_2\end{pmatrix} - \begin{pmatrix}X_1\\X_2\end{pmatrix} b_o\right]$$

$$= [\varepsilon_1'\varepsilon_2'] \left[I - \begin{pmatrix}X_1\\X_2\end{pmatrix} (X_1'X_1 + X_2'X_2)^{-1} (X_1' \, X_2')\right] \begin{bmatrix}\varepsilon_1\\\varepsilon_2\end{bmatrix}.$$

Since these residuals are from a regression of $n + m$ observations on p explanatory variables, the quadratic form (18) in the ε's has rank $n + m - p$.[4]

If the alternative hypothesis (H_a: $\beta_1 \neq \beta_2$) is true, we are back to the model (14), and the least-squares estimators of β_1 and β_2 are

$$\text{(19)} \qquad \begin{bmatrix}b_1\\b_2\end{bmatrix} = \begin{bmatrix}X_1'X_1 & 0\\0 & X_2'X_2\end{bmatrix}^{-1} \begin{bmatrix}X_1' & 0\\0 & X_2'\end{bmatrix} \begin{bmatrix}y_1\\y_2\end{bmatrix} = \begin{bmatrix}(X_1'X_1)^{-1} X_1' y_1\\(X_2'X_2)^{-1} X_2' y_2\end{bmatrix}.$$

The residuals under H_a will be

$$\text{(20)} \qquad \begin{bmatrix}y_1 - X_1b_1\\y_2 - X_2b_2\end{bmatrix} = \begin{bmatrix}[I - X_1 (X_1'X_1)^{-1} X_1'] \, \varepsilon_1\\ [I - X_2 (X_2'X_2)^{-1} X_2'] \, \varepsilon_2\end{bmatrix}.$$

Similarly, the sum of squares of these residuals will be

$$\text{(21)} \qquad \left\|\begin{matrix}y_1 - X_1b_1\\y_2 - X_2b_2\end{matrix}\right\|^2 = ||y_1 - X_1b_1||^2 + ||y_2 - X_2b_2||^2$$

$$= \varepsilon_1'[I - X_1(X_1'X_1)^{-1} X_1']\varepsilon_1 + \varepsilon_2' \, [I - X_2(X_2'X_2)^{-1} X_2']\varepsilon_2 .$$

Since the last two quadratic forms have ranks $n - p$ and $m - p$ respectively, and since ε_1 and ε_2 are independent, the rank of the quadratic form (21) will be $n + m - 2p$.

[4] For a proof of this, see Kempthorne [**6**].

Now the sum of squares (18) under H_o will be decomposed into the sum of squares (21) under H_a plus the sum of squares of the differences

$$[X_1b_1 - X_1b_o] \text{ and } [X_2b_2 - X_2b_o] .$$

First start from the identity

$$\text{(22)} \qquad \begin{bmatrix} y_1 - X_1b_o \\ y_2 - X_2b_o \end{bmatrix} = \begin{bmatrix} y_1 - X_1b_1 \\ y_2 - X_2b_2 \end{bmatrix} + \begin{bmatrix} X_1b_1 - X_1b_o \\ X_2b_2 - X_2b_o \end{bmatrix} .$$

Summing the squares of the elements on both sides of (22) gives

$$\text{(23)} \qquad \left\| \begin{matrix} y_1 - X_1b_o \\ y_2 - X_2b_o \end{matrix} \right\|^2 = \left\| \begin{matrix} y_1 - X_1b_1 \\ y_2 - X_2b_2 \end{matrix} \right\|^2 + \left\| \begin{matrix} X_1b_1 - X_1b_o \\ X_2b_2 - X_2b_o \end{matrix} \right\|^2$$

because the cross-product term on the right side of (23) can easily be seen to be zero. To economize space, (23) will also be written as

$$\text{(24)} \qquad Q_1 = Q_2 + Q_3 .$$

We will proceed to show that the rank of the quadratic form Q_3 can at most be p. From (16) and (19), it follows that

$$\text{(25)} \qquad [X_1'X_1 + X_2'X_2]b_o = X_1'y_1 + X_2'y_2 = X_1'X_1b_1 + X_2'X_2b_2$$

which implies

$$\text{(26)} \qquad b_2 - b_o = -(X_2'X_2)^{-1} X_1'X_1 (b_1 - b_o) .$$

Substituting (26) into Q_3, we have

$$\text{(27)} \qquad Q_3 = \left\| \begin{matrix} X_1(b_1 - b_o) \\ -X_2(X_2'X_2)^{-1} X_1'X_1(b_1 - b_o) \end{matrix} \right\|^2$$

$$= [b_1' - b_o'] [X_1' \; -X_1'X_1(X_2'X_2)^{-1} X_2'] \begin{bmatrix} X_1 \\ -X_2(X_2'X_2)^{-1} X_1'X_1 \end{bmatrix} [b_1 - b_o] .$$

(27) is a quadratic form in $b_1 - b_o$ and therefore cannot have rank higher than p. But $b_1 - b_o$ is a linear transformation of the ε's, as can be shown from (2) and (16):

$$\text{(28)} \quad b_1 - b_o = \beta_1 - \beta + \{[(X_1'X_1)^{-1}X_1' \, 0] - [X_1'X_1 + X_2'X_2]^{-1}[X_1' \; X_2']\} \begin{bmatrix} \varepsilon_1 \\ \varepsilon_2 \end{bmatrix} .$$

Under the null hypothesis $\beta_1 = \beta_2 = \beta$, Q_3 will thus be a quadratic form in the ε's with a maximum rank of p. From (28), we also see that Q_3 will tend to be larger when the null hypothesis is not true.

It has already been observed that the rank of Q_2 is $m + n - 2p$. Since the rank of Q_1 is smaller than or equal to the rank of Q_2 plus the rank of Q_3, the rank of Q_3 must be p. Under the null hypothesis Q_2 and Q_3 will be distributed independently as $\chi^2(m + n - 2p)\sigma^2$ and $\chi^2(p)\sigma^2$. While the distribution of Q_3 is affected if H_o does not hold, Q_2 will have the same distribution regardless. We thus can test H_o by the F ratio

$$(29) \qquad F(p, m+n-2p) = \frac{Q_3/p}{Q_2/(m+n-2p)}$$
$$= \frac{||X_1b_1 - X_1b_o||^2 + ||X_2b_2 - X_2b_o||^2}{||\ y_1 - X_1b_1\ ||^2 + ||\ y_2 - X_2b_2\ ||^2} \cdot \frac{(m+n-2p)}{p}.$$

(29) is the standard analysis-of-covariance test when $m > p$.[5]

A few remarks will suffice to indicate the application of the theory of linear hypotheses to the case $m \leqslant p$. Let us rewrite (23) as

$$(30) \quad \left\|\begin{matrix} y_1 - X_1b_o \\ y_2 - X_2b_o \end{matrix}\right\|^2 = ||y_1 - X_1b_1||^2 + ||X_1b_1 - X_1b_o||^2 + ||y_2 - X_2b_2||^2 + ||X_2b_2 - X_2b_o||^2$$

Our models for H_o and H_a are (15) and (14), as before. The sum of squares under H_o is clearly Q_1 whether $m > p$ or $m \leqslant p$. The sum of squares under H_a will become $||y_1 - X_1b_1||^2$ when $m \leqslant p$—this can be seen either by evaluating the sum of squares of the residuals from regression (14) or by noting that the residuals from the second sample will simply be zero. Regardless of the size m, $||y_1 - X_1b_1||^2$ will be distributed as $\chi^2(n-p)\sigma^2$ and will be independent of the sum of the other three terms on the right side of (30). The sum of these three terms equals

$$||X_1b_1 - X_1b_o||^2 + ||y_2 - X_2b_o||^2$$

even if b_2 is undefined. When $m \leqslant p$, we can test H_o by the ratio

$$(31) \qquad F(m, n-p) = \frac{||X_1b_1 - X_1b_o||^2 + ||y_2 - X_2b_o||^2}{||y_1 - b_1X_1||^2} \cdot \frac{(n-p)}{m}.$$

When $m > p$, (31) remains valid. However, using (31) instead of (29) in this situation would amount to taking a part of Q_1, i.e., $||y_2 - X_2b_2||^2$, which is not affected by the inequality between β_1 and β_2, and placing it in the numerator of the F ratio. This would reduce the power of the test.

The theory of linear hypotheses has now been applied to testing the homogeneity of two regressions. To provide a link between the analysis of covariance (29) and the prediction interval (8), we will point out that the test (13) in Section 3, including its special case (8), is identical with the test (31). The proof of this identity requires only the proof that

$$(32) \qquad d'[I + X_2(X_1'X_1)^{-1}X_2']^{-1}\,d = ||X_1b_1 - X_1b_o||^2 + ||y_2 - X_2b_o||^2.$$

[5] Additional references on the analysis of covariance include [**1**], [**5**], [**9**], and [**10**]. [**1**] is a special issue devoted to the analysis of covariance mainly for the design of experiments.

From (25), we deduce

$$(33) \qquad b_1 = [I + (X_1'X_1)^{-1} X_2'X_2]b_o - (X_1'X_1)^{-1} X_2'y_2 .$$

Substitute (33) into d:

$$(34) \qquad d = y_2 - X_2b_1 = [I + X_2(X_1'X_1)^{-1} X_2'] [y_2 - X_2b_o] .$$

Given (34), we evaluate the quadratic form

$$(35) \quad d'[I + X_2(X_1'X_1)^{-1} X_2']^{-1} d = [y_2' - b_o'X_2'] [I + X_2(X_1'X_1)^{-1} X_2'] [y_2 - X_2b_o]$$

$$= [y_2' - b_o'X_2'] [y_2 - X_2b_o] + [y_2'X_2 - b_o'X_2'X_2] (X_1'X_1)^{-1} [X_2'y_2 - X_2'X_2b_o].$$

Our proof of (32) will be complete by observing the relationship, based on (25), that

$$(36) \qquad X_2'y_2 - X_2'X_2b_o = - [X_1'X_1b_1 - X_1'X_1b_o] .$$

5. TESTS OF EQUALITY BETWEEN SUBSETS OF COEFFICIENTS IN TWO REGRESSIONS

The results given so far, as summarized by (29) and (31), will now be extended to testing the equality between subsets of coefficients in two regressions. As before, we will first examine the case $m > p$.

Under the alternative hypothesis, our model is

$$(37) \qquad \begin{aligned} y_1 &= X_1\beta_1 + \varepsilon_1 = Z_1\gamma_1 + W_1\delta_1 + \varepsilon_1 , \\ y_2 &= X_2\beta_2 + \varepsilon_2 = Z_2\gamma_2 + W_2\delta_2 + \varepsilon_2 , \end{aligned}$$

or

$$\begin{bmatrix} y_1 \\ y_2 \end{bmatrix} = \begin{bmatrix} Z_1 & 0 & W_1 & 0 \\ 0 & Z_2 & 0 & W_2 \end{bmatrix} \begin{bmatrix} \gamma_1 \\ \gamma_2 \\ \delta_1 \\ \delta_2 \end{bmatrix} + \begin{bmatrix} \varepsilon_1 \\ \varepsilon_2 \end{bmatrix},$$

where the coefficients β_1 are divided into γ_1 and δ_1, the matrix X_1 is correspondingly divided into Z_1 and W_1, and similarly for β_2 and X_2. Let γ_1 and γ_2 be column vectors of q elements each; and δ_1 and δ_2 be column vectors of $p - q$ elements each. The subsets of coefficients to be tested are γ_1 and γ_2.

The null hypothesis is $\gamma_1 = \gamma_2 = \gamma$, implying the model

$$(38) \qquad \begin{bmatrix} y_1 \\ y_2 \end{bmatrix} = \begin{bmatrix} Z_1 & W_1 & 0 \\ Z_2 & 0 & W_2 \end{bmatrix} \begin{bmatrix} \gamma \\ \delta_1 \\ \delta_2 \end{bmatrix} + \begin{bmatrix} \varepsilon_1 \\ \varepsilon_2 \end{bmatrix}.$$

Under the null hypothesis, the least-squares estimators of the coefficients are

$$(39)\qquad \begin{bmatrix} c_0 \\ d_{10} \\ d_{20} \end{bmatrix} = \begin{bmatrix} Z_1'Z_1 + Z_2'Z_2 & Z_1'W_1 & Z_2'W_2 \\ W_1'Z_1 & W_1'W_1 & 0 \\ W_2'Z_2 & 0 & W_2'W_2 \end{bmatrix}^{-1} \begin{bmatrix} Z_1' & Z_2' \\ W_1' & 0 \\ 0 & W_2' \end{bmatrix} \begin{bmatrix} y_1 \\ y_2 \end{bmatrix}.$$

The sum of squares of the residuals under H_o, analogous to (18), will be

$$(40)\quad [\varepsilon_1'\varepsilon_2'] \left[I - \begin{pmatrix} Z_1 & W_1 & 0 \\ Z_2 & 0 & W_2 \end{pmatrix} \begin{pmatrix} Z_1'Z_1 + Z_2'Z_2 & Z_1'W_1 & Z_2'W_2 \\ W_1'Z_1 & W_1'W_1 & 0 \\ W_2'Z_2 & 0 & W_2'W_2 \end{pmatrix}^{-1} \begin{pmatrix} Z_1' & Z_2' \\ W_1' & 0 \\ 0 & W_2' \end{pmatrix} \right] \begin{bmatrix} \varepsilon_1 \\ \varepsilon_2 \end{bmatrix}$$

with $m + n - 2p + q$ degrees of freedom.

Under the alternative hypothesis $\gamma_1 \neq \gamma_2$, the least-squares estimators are

$$(41)\qquad \begin{bmatrix} c_1 \\ c_2 \\ d_1 \\ d_2 \end{bmatrix} = \begin{bmatrix} Z_1'Z_1 & 0 & Z_1'W_1 & 0 \\ 0 & Z_2'Z_2 & 0 & Z_2'W_2 \\ W_1'Z_1 & 0 & W_1'W_1 & 0 \\ 0 & W_2'Z_2 & 0 & W_2'W_2 \end{bmatrix}^{-1} \begin{bmatrix} Z_1' & 0 \\ 0 & Z_2' \\ W_1' & 0 \\ 0 & W_2' \end{bmatrix} \begin{bmatrix} y_1 \\ y_2 \end{bmatrix}.$$

The sum of squares of the residuals under H_a, which is identical with (21), will have $m + n - 2p$ degrees of freedom.

As before, the sum of squares under H_o can be broken up into the sum of squares under H_a plus the sum of squares of the differences between the two sets of estimates of y, namely,

$$(42)\qquad \left\| \begin{pmatrix} y_1 \\ y_2 \end{pmatrix} - \begin{pmatrix} Z_1 & W_1 & 0 \\ Z_2 & 0 & W_2 \end{pmatrix} \begin{pmatrix} c_0 \\ d_{10} \\ d_{20} \end{pmatrix} \right\|^2 = \left\| \begin{pmatrix} y_1 \\ y_2 \end{pmatrix} - \begin{pmatrix} Z_1 & 0 & W_1 & 0 \\ 0 & Z_2 & 0 & W_2 \end{pmatrix} \begin{pmatrix} c_1 \\ c_2 \\ d_1 \\ d_2 \end{pmatrix} \right\|^2$$

$$+ \left\| \begin{pmatrix} Z_1 & 0 & W_1 & 0 \\ 0 & Z_2 & 0 & W_2 \end{pmatrix} \begin{pmatrix} c_1 \\ c_2 \\ d_1 \\ d_2 \end{pmatrix} - \begin{pmatrix} Z_1 & W_1 & 0 \\ Z_2 & 0 & W_2 \end{pmatrix} \begin{pmatrix} c_0 \\ d_{10} \\ d_{20} \end{pmatrix} \right\|^2$$

or

$$Q_1^* = Q_2 + Q_3^*.$$

We will omit the proof that each of the cross-products on the right side of (42) is zero, but will indicate following identity which may be used in the proof:

$$(43)\qquad \begin{bmatrix} Z_1 & W_1 & 0 \\ Z_2 & 0 & W_2 \end{bmatrix} = \begin{bmatrix} Z_1 & 0 & W_1 & 0 \\ 0 & Z_2 & 0 & W_2 \end{bmatrix} \begin{bmatrix} I & 0 & 0 \\ I & 0 & 0 \\ 0 & I & 0 \\ 0 & 0 & I \end{bmatrix}.$$

Given that the ranks of Q_1^* and Q_2 are respectively $m + n - 2p + q$ and $m + n - 2p$, the rank of Q_3^* must be q once it can be shown that it is at most q. To show the maximum rank of Q_3^*, we first define $y_{1\cdot}$ as the residuals of the regression of y_1 on W_1, $Z_{1\cdot}$ as the residuals of Z_1 on W_1, and similarly for $y_{2\cdot}$ and $Z_{2\cdot}$. Then it can be proved that

$$(44) \qquad \begin{bmatrix} c_1 \\ c_2 \end{bmatrix} = \begin{bmatrix} (Z_{1\cdot}'Z_{1\cdot})^{-1} Z_{1o}'y_{1\cdot} \\ (Z_{2\cdot}'Z_{2\cdot})^{-1} Z_{2\cdot}'y_{2\cdot} \end{bmatrix}$$

and

$$45) \qquad \begin{bmatrix} d_1 \\ d_2 \end{bmatrix} = \begin{bmatrix} (W_1'W_1)^{-1}W_1'y_1 \\ (W_2'W_2)^{-1}W_2'y_2 \end{bmatrix} - \begin{bmatrix} (W_1'W_1)^{-1}W_1'Z_1c_1 \\ (W_2'W_2)^{-1}W_2'Z_2c_2 \end{bmatrix}.$$

Rather than digressing to complete the proofs of (44) and (45), we simply indicate that essentially they involve partitioning the matrix of the cross-products of the explanatory variables in (41) into four blocks and then inverting the partitioned matrix. The same method will also prove

$$(46) \qquad c_0 = [Z_{1\cdot}'\, Z_{1\cdot} + Z_{2\cdot}'\, Z_{2\cdot}]^{-1}\, [Z_{1\cdot}'\, Z_{2\cdot}'] \begin{bmatrix} y_{1\cdot} \\ y_{2\cdot} \end{bmatrix}$$

and

$$(47) \qquad \begin{bmatrix} d_{10} \\ d_{20} \end{bmatrix} = \begin{bmatrix} (W_1'W_1)^{-1}W_1'y_1 \\ (W_2'W_2)^{-1}W_2'y_2 \end{bmatrix} - \begin{bmatrix} (W_1'W_1)^{-1}W_1'Z_1c_0 \\ (W_2'W_2)^{-1}W_2'Z_2c_0 \end{bmatrix}.$$

Using (45) and (47), we can rewrite the vector of the differences between the estimates of y under H_a and under H_o:

$$(48) \qquad \begin{bmatrix} Z_1 & 0 & W_1 & 0 \\ 0 & Z_2 & 0 & W_2 \end{bmatrix} \begin{bmatrix} c_1 \\ c_2 \\ d_1 \\ d_2 \end{bmatrix} - \begin{bmatrix} Z_1 & W_1 & 0 \\ Z_2 & 0 & W_2 \end{bmatrix} \begin{bmatrix} c_0 \\ d_{10} \\ d_{20} \end{bmatrix}$$

$$= \left[I - \begin{pmatrix} W_1(W_1'W_1)^{-1}\, W_1' & 0 \\ 0 & W_2(W_2'W_2)^{-1}W_2' \end{pmatrix} \right] \begin{bmatrix} Z_1(c_1 - c_0) \\ Z_2(c_2 - c_0) \end{bmatrix}.$$

The developments from now on will correspond to the developments of (25), (26), (27), and (28) in Section 4. From (44) and (46), it follows that

$$(49) \quad [Z_{1\cdot}'\, Z_{1\cdot} + Z_{2\cdot}'\, Z_{2\cdot}]\; c_0 = Z_{1\cdot}'\, y_{1\cdot} + Z_{2\cdot}'\, y_{2\cdot} = Z_{1\cdot}'\, Z_{1\cdot}\, c_1 + Z_{2\cdot}'\, Z_{2\cdot}\, c_2$$

which corresponds to (25). (49) can be used to express $c_2 - c_0$ as a linear tranformation of $c_1 - c_0$, a transformation similar to the one in (26). Replacing $c_2 - c_0$ in (48) by this transformation of $c_1 - c_0$, we will observe that Q_3^* is a quadratic form in $c_1 - c_0$, with maximum rank q. A further step analogous to (28) will show that Q_3^* tends to be larger when $\gamma_1 \neq \gamma_2$. We therefore have

$$(50) \qquad F(q, m+n-2p) = \frac{Q_3^*/q}{Q_2/(m+n-2p)}$$

$$= \frac{||Z_1c_1 + W_1d_1 - Z_1c_0 - W_1d_{10}||^2 + ||Z_2c_2 + W_2d_2 - Z_2c_0 - W_2d_{20}||^2}{||y_1 - Z_1c_1 - W_1d_1||^2 + ||y_2 - Z_2c_2 - W_2d_2||^2} \times \frac{(m+n-2p)}{q}.$$

The remaining case for examination is $(p - q) \leqslant m \leqslant p$. As long as $m \geqslant (p - q)$, least-squares estimators under H_o can be obtained by (39), but not when $m < (p - q)$ because $W_2'W_2$ will then be singular. The sum of squares of the residuals under H_o will still be Q_1^*. The sum of squares of the residuals under H_a will be $||y_1 - Z_1c_1 - W_1d_1||^2$ with $n - p$ degrees of freedom. Corresponding to (31), we have

$$(51) \qquad F(m-p+q, n-p) = \frac{||Z_1c_1 + W_1d_1 - Z_1c_0 - W_1d_{10}||^2 + ||y_2 - Z_2c_0 - W_2d_{20}||^2}{||y_1 - Z_1c_1 - W_1d_1||^2} \cdot \frac{(n-p)}{(m-p+q)}.$$

The results of this paper, which are really contained in (50) and (51), can be summarized briefly. To test the equality between sets of coefficients in two linear regressions, we obtain the sum of squares of the residuals assuming the equality, and the sum of squares without assuming the equality. The ratio of the difference between these two sums to the latter sum, adjusted for the corresponding degrees of freedom, will be distributed as the F ratio under the null hypothesis. This latter sum of squares will be computed only from the first sample of n observations when the second sample is not large enough for computing a separate regression. We have attempted to show how the theory of general linear hypotheses is applied to our problem and how the prediction interval and the analysis of covariance are related to each other and to the theory of general linear hypotheses. While we have dealt with the comparison of coefficients in only two regressions, the proofs of (29) and (50) can obviously be generalized to the case of many regressions.

6. EXAMPLES

To illustrate how some of the tests given above are applied, one numerical example for each of (29) and (31) will now be provided. These examples originated in a study of the demand for automobiles in the United States [**2**]. We will not here go into the economic justifications of them as they are contained in the reference cited. The study utilizes annual observations on the following variables:

X_t, ownership of automobiles measured in "new-car equivalents" per capita at the end of year t. The unit is per cent of a new-car equivalent per capita.
X_t^1, purchase of new cars during year t, with the same unit of measurement as above.
P_t, relative price index of automobile stock, with 1937 as 100.
I_{dt}, real disposable income per capita in 1937 dollars.
I_{et}, real "expected" income per capita in 1937 dollars used by Milton Friedman in his *A Theory of the Consumption Function* (Princeton: Princeton University Press, 1957).

A statistical demand function for automobile ownership computed from observations of 33 years from 1921 to 1953 is

$$\text{(X1e)} \quad \begin{aligned} \dot{X}_t = -.7247 - &.048802\, P_t + .025487\, I_{et}, \quad && R^2 = .895, \\ &(.004201) \qquad (.001747) && s = .618. \end{aligned}$$

A statistical demand function for new purchase computed from observations of 28 years, from 1921 to 1953 but excluding 1942 to 1946, is

$$\text{(4s)} \quad \begin{aligned} \dot{X}_t^1 = .07791 - &.020127\, P_t + .011699\, I_{dt} - .23104\, X_{t-1}, && R^2 = .858, \\ &(.002648) \qquad (.001070) \qquad (.04719) && s = .308. \end{aligned}$$

Four years after the study had been made, four additional observations were available for testing whether these demand functions remained stable over time. Since four observations are sufficient for computing a separate regression of the form (X1e), test (29) was used. To determine the stability of (4s), test (31) was used. The follow-up study is described more thoroughly in [**3**]. Before presenting the analysis of covariance (29) for the demand function (X1e), we exhibit here the estimated values of the dependent variable together with the deviations of the observed values from the estimated values.

	1954	1955	1956	1957
X_t estimated from (X1e)	12.665	12.993	13.328	13.025
X_t observed minus estimated	—.613	.079	.102	.437

The residuals of the observed values from the estimated values are very small, as compared with the standard error of .618. They do not indicate any shifts in the pattern of demand for automobile ownership during the four years 1954 to 1957.

We will now proceed with the analysis of covariance (29). The method involved can be described very simply. Suppose that n observations are used to estimate a regression with p parameters ($p - 1$ coefficients plus one intercept). Suppose also that there are m additional observations, and we are interested in deciding whether they are generated by the same regression model as the first n observations. To perform the analysis of covariance, we need the following sums of squares:

A, sum of squares of $n + m$ deviations of the dependent variable from the regression estimated by $n + m$ observations, with $n + m - p$ degrees of freedom.
B, sum of squares of n deviations of the dependent variable from the regression estimated by the first n observations, with $n - p$ degrees of freedom.
C, sum of squares of m deviations of the dependent variable from the regression estimated by the second m observations, with $m - p$ degrees of freedom.

From (29), the ratio of $(A - B - C)/p$ to $(B + C)/(n + m - 2p)$ will be distributed as $F(p, n + m - 2p)$ under the null hypothesis that both groups of observations belong to the same regression model. For testing the demand function (X1e), the sum of squares A is 10.1155, and $B + C$ is 9.6130. The ratio $F(3,26)$ is therefore 0.45. In order to interpret the new observations as coming from a different structure at the 5 per cent level of significance, F would have to be at least 2.98. Our impression from examining the four deviations that there was no change in structure is strongly confirmed.

The following is a comparison of the estimated and the observed values of the dependent variable of demand function (4s).

	1954	1955	1956	1957
X_t^1 estimated from (4s)	3.452	3.730	3.630	3.270
X_t^1 observed minus estimated	—.044	.608	—.087	.226

Again, inspection of the residuals reveals that they are not large relative to 0.308, the standard error of estimate for (4s). The year 1955 is an exception, where we find the residual to be twice as large as the standard error. To apply test (31), we compute the sum of squares A of the 32 deviations from the regression including the four new observations, with 32—4 or 28 degrees of freedom. A turns out to be 2.6444 numerically. The sum of squares B of the 28 deviations from the regression of the original set of observations turns out to be 2.2818, with 24 degrees of freedom. The sum of squares C vanishes as long as the number m of new observations does not exceed the number of parameters p. According to (31), the F ratio is the ratio of $(A - B)/4$ to $B/24$, or 0.95 numerically. Therefore, we accept the null hypothesis that automobile purchases in the years 1954 to 1957 were governed by the same relationship as before.

REFERENCES

[1] *Biometrics*, Vol. XIII, No. 3, September, 1957.

[2] Chow, Gregory C.: *Demand for Automobiles in the United States*, (Amsterdam: North-Holland Publishing Co., 1957).

[3] ———: "Statistical Demand Functions for Automobiles and Their Use for Forecasting," pp. 147–78, *The Demand for Durable Goods*, ed. by A. C. Harberger, (Chicago: University of Chicago Press, 1960).

[4] Davis, Tom E.: "The Consumption Function as a Tool of Prediction," *The Review of Economics and Statistics*, Vol. XXXIV, No. 3, August, 1952, p. 270.

[5] Friedman, Milton.: "Testing the Significance Among a Group of Regression Equations," *Econometrica*, Vol. V (1937), p. 194–5.

[6] Kempthorne, Oscar: *The Design and Analysis of Experiments*, (New York: John Wiley & Sons, Inc., 1952), pp. 54–66.

[7] Kendall, Maurice G.: *The Advanced Theory of Statistics*, (London: Charles Griffin and Company, Limited, 1946), Vol. II, pp. 242 ff.

[8] Mood, Alexander M.: *Introduction to the Theory of Statistics*, (New York: McGraw-Hill Book Company, Inc., 1950), pp. 304–5.

[9] Wallis, W. A.: "The Temporal Stability of Consumption Patterns," *The Review of Economic Statistics*, Vol. XXIV (1942), pp. 177–83.

[10] Welch, B. L.: ,,Some Problems in the Analysis of Regression Among *k* Samples of Two Variables," *Biometrika*, Vol. XXVII (1935), pp. 145–60.

SIMULTANEOUS EQUATIONS

METHODS OF MEASURING THE MARGINAL PROPENSITY TO CONSUME[1]

TRYGVE HAAVELMO

This study deals with statistical principles and methods of deriving estimates of the marginal propensity to consume, from time series of total consumption, income, and investment.

It is shown that the method of obtaining the marginal propensity to consume by correlating consumers' expenditure with income is inconsistent with an important branch of current economic theory: the method tends to overestimate the marginal propensity to consume. If, as in some important modern economic theories, investment is regarded as an independent, autonomous variable, the corresponding correct statistical procedure is, first, to obtain the "multiplier" by correlating income with investment, and then, from this estimate of the multiplier, to calculate the marginal propensity to consume. (These results follow from the general principles of the "Simultaneous-Equations Approach," as developed by the Cowles Commission for Research in Economics.)

Some theoretical results are given also for the alternative case where investment is, in part, induced by changes in income.

Numerical illustrations show the results of applying the theoretical formulae to U. S. statistics of consumption, income, and investment, for the interwar period.

1. INTRODUCTION

THE marginal propensity to consume and its companion, the multiplier, are of central importance in modern theories of macroeconomics. The intense interest in these parameters derives largely from the importance that modern theories (and many older ones too) attach to the rate of investment as a primary factor in determining the levels of income and employment. In some theories investment is considered as an autonomous variable, an impressed force. (E.g. Schumpeter's theory of innovations.) Other theories, while operating with the notion of induced investment, imply, nevertheless, that current investment is, in part at least, an autonomous variable, its main determinants being such "external" factors as growth of population, new

[1] Cowles Commission Papers, New Series, No. 22. Some of the methods discussed below were developed in connection with a study of the demand for agricultural products, now in progress at the Department of Economics, The University of Chicago. The author is indebted to his colleagues at the Cowles Commission for many helpful suggestions.

inventions, wars, etc., or *past* values of some other economic variables, such as profit, sales, or capital accumulation. It is in line with these ideas that attempts to derive, statistically, the marginal "propensity to invest" apparently have met with little success. The current view on the subject is probably well expressed in the following statement by Alvin H. Hansen: "Thus, the statistical data during the last two decades tend to support the thesis that the active dynamic factor in the cycle is investment, with consumption assuming a passive, lagging role."[2] Qualifying this statement somewhat, he continues: "For the most part, spontaneous expenditures—expenditures not caused by a prior rise in income—are likely to be made on investment goods or upon durable consumers' goods, but not upon other forms of consumption.

"It does not follow, however, that all investment is spontaneous. Much of it is, in fact, induced. It is, however, quite impossible to determine statistically what part is spontaneous and what part is induced."[3] Many economists would agree with Paul A. Samuelson's statement that "In behavior it [i.e., investment][4] is sporadic, volatile, and capricious. Its effective determinants are almost completely independent of current statistical factors (level of income, etc.)."[5]

If this is the current view on the role of investment, it is somewhat surprising to find that current attempts to derive, statistically, the marginal propensity to consume approach the problem by correlating consumers' expenditures with income.[6] This procedure is inconsistent with the view that investment is the autonomous determinant of income. We should, instead, take the regression of income *on investment*, to obtain the multiplier, and from this estimate of the multiplier we should derive the marginal propensity to consume. This idea, I am sure, is not new, but it might perhaps be useful to set down the arguments involved in somewhat more rigorous terms. I shall also give some numerical results, as illustrations.

2. ESTIMATION OF THE CONSUMPTION FUNCTION WHEN INVESTMENT IS AN AUTONOMOUS VARIABLE

In this Section we shall be concerned with the following observable time series:

[2] Alvin H. Hansen, *Fiscal Policy and Business Cycles*, New York, 1941, p. 50.

[3] *Op. cit.*, pp. 62–63.

[4] Author's remark.

[5] Paul A. Samuelson: "Full Employment After the War," in *Postwar Economic Problems*, edited by S. E. Harris, New York, 1943, p. 41.

[6] See, for example, Arthur Smithies, "Forecasting Postwar Demand: I," *Econometrica*, Vol. 13, 1945. No. 1, pp. 4–6, Jacob L. Mosak, "Forecasting Postwar Demand: III," *Econometrica*, Vol. 13, 1945, No. 1, p. 44, and others, too numerous to be mentioned here.

c_t = consumers' expenditure, in constant dollars per capita,
y_t = disposable income, in constant dollars per capita,
z_t = investment expenditures, in constant dollars per capita.

The term investment, as used here, is defined as the difference between disposable income and consumers' expenditure. (In terms of current statistical measurements by the U. S. Department of Commerce investment, as defined here, would be equal to private net investment minus corporate savings plus Government deficits. Cf. Section 4 below.) This means that we impose the exact relationship

$$y_t = c_t + z_t. \tag{2.1}$$

We assume further that the consumption function is a linear function of disposable income, but that this function is subject to random shifts. Let this function be

$$c_t = \alpha y_t + \beta + u_t \tag{2.2}$$

where α and β are constants, and u_t is the random element in consumers' behavior. The problem is to estimate the true values of α and β, by means of a certain number of observations of the time series c_t, y_t, and z_t. The u's are not observable.

The model, as it stands, is not complete. It does not determine the levels of income, consumption, and investment, even if we knew the true values of α and β. There are three variables, y, c, z, and only two equations, (2.1) and (2.2). For the same reason the model does not as yet tell us how to proceed statistically in order to estimate α and β. The model, as it stands, does not determine how the joint probability distribution of the observable variables c_t and y_t depends on α and β, and, therefore, does not determine the appropriate type of estimation formulae to be used. It is necessary to complete the model in such a way that the problem of estimating α and β becomes a well-defined statistical problem. For this purpose we add the following assumptions:

a) The random variable u_t has expected value $E(u_t)=0$, and variance $E(u_t^2)=\sigma_u^2$ for every value of t. The u's are serially uncorrelated, i.e. $E(u_t u_{t-\tau})=0$ for $\tau \neq 0$.

b) The time series z_t, $t=1, 2, \cdots$, is autonomous in relation to c_t and y_t. This condition is fulfilled if either

b.1) the sequence z_t is a sequence of given numbers, in which case automatically $E(z_t u_t)=z_t E(u_t)=0$ (by a), or if

b.2) each z_t is a random variable which is stochastically independent of u_t.

If the assumption b.1) is adopted we shall impose the condition that

$$\text{(2.3)}\qquad \lim_{N\to\infty} m_{zz} \equiv \lim_{N\to\infty} \frac{1}{N}\sum_{t=1}^{t=N}\left(z_t - \frac{1}{N}\sum_{t=1}^{t=N} z_t\right)^2 = \bar{m}_{zz},$$

where $\bar{m}_{zz}$ is a positive, finite number. Therefore

$$\text{(2.4)}\qquad Nm_{zz} \to \infty \quad \text{as} \quad N \to \infty.$$

Similarly, if the assumption b.2) is adopted, we shall assume that

$$\text{(2.5)}\qquad \operatorname*{plim}_{N\to\infty} \frac{1}{N}\sum_{t=1}^{t=N}\left(z_t - \frac{1}{N}\sum_{t=1}^{t=N} z_t\right)^2 = \bar{m}_{zz}$$

where $\bar{m}_{zz}$ is positive and finite.[7] These assumptions are used in the analysis of the large-sample properties of the estimates discussed below.

Let us assume that the conditions a) and b.1) are fulfilled. And consider any onė of the following two relations derived from (2.1) and (2.2),

$$\text{(2.6)}\qquad c_t = \frac{\alpha}{1-\alpha} z_t + \frac{\beta}{1-\alpha} + \frac{u_t}{1-\alpha}$$

$$\text{(2.7)}\qquad y_t = \frac{1}{1-\alpha} z_t + \frac{\beta}{1-\alpha} + \frac{u_t}{1-\alpha}.$$

Under the assumptions made, each of these two equations satisfies the conditions of the Markoff theorem on least squares, when z_t is considered as the independent variable.[8] In the following we shall use the moment notations

$$\text{(2.8)}\qquad m_{pq} = \frac{1}{N}\sum_{t=1}^{t=N}\left(p_t - \frac{1}{N}\sum_{t=1}^{t=N} p_t\right)\left(q_t - \frac{1}{N}\sum_{t=1}^{t=N} q_t\right)$$

$$\text{(2.9)}\qquad m_p = \frac{1}{N}\sum_{t=1}^{t=N} p_t.$$

Using well-known formulae from ordinary regression theory, and writing b. u. est. as an abbreviation for "best unbiased estimate,"[9] we can then make the following statements.

[7] "plim" means "the probability limit of". A statistic T_N, say, calculated from a sample of N observations, is said to have the probability limit A if the probability of $|T_N - A| > \epsilon$ approaches zero when N approaches infinity, for every fixed value of $\epsilon > 0$. A statistic T_N having this property is said to be a *consistent* estimate of A, or, to converge stochastically to A.

[8] See, e.g., F. N. David and J. Neyman, "Extension of the Markoff theorem on least squares," *Statistical Research Memoirs, II*, London, 1938, pp. 105–116.

[9] An estimate is said to be unbiased if its expected value is equal to the true parameter. An estimate is said to be a "best unbiased" estimate if its variance is smaller than that of any other unbiased estimate that is linear in the random variables involved.

$$\text{(2.10)} \qquad \frac{m_{cz}}{m_{zz}} = \text{b.u. est. of } \frac{\alpha}{1-\alpha}$$

$$\text{(2.11)} \qquad \frac{m_{yz}}{m_{zz}} = \text{b.u. est. of } \frac{1}{1-\alpha}$$

$$\text{(2.12)} \qquad \frac{m_{zz}m_c - m_{cz}m_z}{m_{zz}} = \text{b.u. est. of } \frac{\beta}{1-\alpha}\cdot$$

We also have

$$\text{(2.13)} \quad s^2 = \frac{N}{N-2} \; \frac{m_{yy}m_{zz} - m^2_{yz}}{m_{zz}} = \text{an unbiassed estimate of } \frac{\sigma_u^{\,2}}{(1-\alpha)^2}\cdot$$

Under the assumption (2.3) these estimates are *consistent,* that is, any one of the estimates (2.10)–(2.13) has the property that the probability of the estimate deviating more than an arbitrary ϵ from the true parameter approaches zero as N approaches infinity. Since α and β are continuous functions of $1/(1-\alpha)$ and $\beta/(1-\alpha)$ when $\alpha \neq 1$, we also know that the estimates, $\hat{\alpha}$ and $\hat{\beta}$, of α and β, derived[10] from (2.10) or (2.11), and (2.12), will have the following properties.

$$\text{(2.14)} \qquad \hat{\alpha} = \frac{m_{cz}}{m_{yz}} = \text{cons. est. of } \alpha$$

$$\text{(2.15)} \qquad \hat{\beta} = \frac{m_{yz}m_c - m_{cz}m_y}{m_{yz}} = \text{cons. est. of } \beta.$$

The "estimates" of α and β obtained by the commonly used procedure of taking the least squares regression of c_t on y_t do not possess this property. Let us denote these "estimates" by a and b, respectively. Then we have

$$\text{(2.16)} \qquad a = \frac{m_{cy}}{m_{yy}}$$

[10] In the present model, as well as in the model discussed in Section 4 below, the problem of obtaining estimates of the structural coefficients α and β from the regression coefficients in (2.10), or (2.11) and (2.12) happens to be particularly simple, because we have exactly two independent equations defining the estimates of α and β, namely (2.10) and (2.12), or (2.11) and (2.12). [(2.10) and (2.11) give identical estimates of α]. In more general systems of structural equations the situation may be much more complicated: There may be more independent equations of the type (2.11)–(2.12) than there are structural parameters, or there might be too few such equations (as, e.g., in Section 3 below, if q_t is not observable). In such cases different, and—in general—much more laborious estimation procedures are required. For further discussion on this point see, e.g., Tjalling Koopmans, "Statistical Estimation of Simultaneous Economic Relations," *Journal of the American Statistical Association*, Vol. 40, 1945, pp. 458–459.

$$(2.17) \qquad b = \frac{m_{yy}m_c - m_{cy}m_y}{m_{yy}}.$$

These "estimates" a and b are not consistent estimates of α and β. This is seen as follows. Using (2.1) and (2.2) we obtain

$$(2.18) \qquad a = \frac{\alpha m_{zz} + (1 + \alpha)m_{zu} + m_{uu}}{m_{zz} + 2m_{zu} + m_{uu}}.$$

From our assumptions it follows that $m_{zu} \to 0$ and $m_{uu} \to \sigma_u^2$ as $N \to \infty$. Thus, for sufficiently large samples, the statistic a approaches, stochastically, the limit

$$(2.19) \qquad \operatorname*{plim}_{N\to\infty} a = \frac{\alpha + \dfrac{\sigma_u^2}{\overline{m}_{zz}}}{1 + \dfrac{\sigma_u^2}{\overline{m}_{zz}}} > \alpha \quad \text{when} \quad 0 < \alpha < 1.$$

Similarly, b will approach the limit

$$(2.20) \qquad \operatorname*{plim}_{N\to\infty} b = \frac{\beta - \dfrac{\sigma_u^2}{\overline{m}_{zz}} m_z}{1 + \dfrac{\sigma_u^2}{\overline{m}_{zz}}} < \beta \quad \text{when} \quad m_z > -\beta.$$

Suppose now that we substitute assumption b.2) for b.1), letting the z's be random variables in repeated samples. Then the exact conditions of the Markoff theorem are no longer fulfilled. But under the assumption (2.5), all the statements above concerning consistency and limit values of the estimates remain valid.

Thus, we reach the following conclusion: If investment, z_t, is an autonomous variable, and if $0<\alpha<1$, $m_z>-\beta$, the least squares' regression of c_t on y_t leads to an "estimate," a, of α that has a systematic positive bias, and an "estimate," b, of β that has a systematic negative bias. If we believe that investment, z_t, is an autonomous variable we should rather use, in that case, the consistent estimates (2.14) and (2.15).

Confidence limits for the estimate of α by (2.14) may be derived in the following manner. Let us assume that the distribution of the u's is approximately normal, and that the z's are not random variables. Then the ratio

$$(2.21) \qquad t = \frac{\dfrac{m_{yz}}{m_{zz}} - \dfrac{1}{1-\alpha}}{\dfrac{s}{\sqrt{Nm_{zz}}}}$$

has the "Student" t-distribution, with N-2 degrees of freedom. Choosing a certain level of significance, say 5 per cent, we obtain confidence limits for $1/(1-\alpha)$. From these limits we can then derive confidence limits for α itself although, admittedly, this is not the only possible way of obtaining such confidence limits. The choice of confidence interval always depends, to some extent, on the type of statement one wants to make about the unknown parameter. (E.g. one might be more anxious to make a correct statement in the case where α is near to 1 than if α is smaller.)

3. EFFECTS OF INDUCED INVESTMENT

Suppose now that the hypothesis of investment, z_t, being autonomous is not true. Suppose that, instead, the variable z_t consists of two parts, one which is related to current income, and another, q_t say, which is autonomous. Assuming linearity, this alternative can be expressed as follows.

$$(3.1) \qquad z_t = q_t + (\kappa y_t + \lambda + v_t).$$

Here the expression in parentheses represents the behavior of those investors whose investment policy depends on current income, y_t. κ and λ are constants, while v_t is a random element such that $E(v_t) = 0$, $E(v_t^2) = \sigma_v^2$, for every value of t, and also $E(v_t v_{t-\tau}) = 0$, $E(v_t u_{t-\tau}) = 0$, for $\tau \neq 0$. u_t and v_t may, however, be correlated, that is, $E(u_t v_t) = \sigma_{uv}$ may be different from zero. We shall assume that the q's satisfy a condition of the type (2.3). Thus $\bar{m}_{qq}$ is obtained from (2.3) by substituting q for z.

Suppose, first, that the series q_t could actually be observed. Then one could obtain consistent estimates of α, β, κ, and λ, by the following procedure. From (2.1), (2.2) and (3.1) we derive

$$(3.2) \qquad c_t = \frac{\alpha}{1-\alpha-\kappa} q_t + \frac{\alpha\lambda + (1-\kappa)\beta}{1-\alpha-\kappa} + \frac{\alpha v_t + (1-\kappa)u_t}{1-\alpha-\kappa}$$

$$(3.3) \qquad y_t = \frac{1}{1-\alpha-\kappa} q_t + \frac{\beta+\lambda}{1-\alpha-\kappa} + \frac{u_t + v_t}{1-\alpha-\kappa}.$$

Under the assumptions made these equations satisfy the requirements of the Markoff theorem on least squares, when q_t is taken as the independent variable. If we assume that the sequence q_t is a sequence of constants, we therefore have

$$(3.4)\qquad \frac{m_{cq}}{m_{qq}} = \text{b.u. est. of } \frac{\alpha}{1-\alpha-\kappa}$$

$$(3.5)\qquad \frac{m_{yq}}{m_{qq}} = \text{b.u. est. of } \frac{1}{1-\alpha-\kappa}$$

$$(3.6)\qquad \frac{m_{qq}m_c - m_{cq}m_q}{m_{qq}} = \text{b.u. est. of } \frac{\alpha\lambda + (1-\kappa)\beta}{1-\alpha-\kappa}$$

$$(3.7)\qquad \frac{m_{qq}m_y - m_{yq}m_q}{m_{qq}} = \text{b.u. est. of } \frac{\beta+\lambda}{1-\alpha-\kappa}.$$

These estimates are consistent. We, therefore, also have the solutions

$$(3.8)\qquad \frac{m_{cq}}{m_{yq}} = \text{cons. est. of } \alpha,$$

$$(3.9)\qquad \frac{m_{yq} - m_{cq} - m_{qq}}{m_{yq}} = \text{cons. est. of } \kappa,$$

$$(3.10)\qquad \frac{m_{yq}m_c - m_{cq}m_y}{m_{yq}} = \text{cons. est. of } \beta,$$

$$(3.11)\qquad \frac{m_{yq}(m_z - m_q) - (m_{yq} - m_{cq} - m_{qq})m_y}{m_{yq}} = \text{cons. est. of } \lambda.$$

It will be observed that the expressions (3.8) and (3.10) are analogous to (2.14) and (2.15).

In Section 2 we compared the results, a and b, of the least squares' regression of c_t on y_t with the consistent estimates, $\hat{\alpha}$ and $\hat{\beta}$, under the assumption that z_t was autonomous. We found that a and b were not consistent estimates of α and β. Now, if a part of z_t is induced the formulae (2.14) and (2.15) will, of course, not give consistent estimates either, the consistent estimates in that case being given by (3.8) and (3.10). It is of some interest to evaluate the large sample bias that would result if we were to apply (2.14) and (2.15) in the present case, and to compare this bias with the large sample bias involved in using (2.16) and (2.17). Let us consider, in particular, the estimates of α. Denote by a_1 the "estimate" of α given by (2.14) if z_t is defined by

(3.1). And let a_2 be the corresponding "estimate" obtained from (2.16). Using (2.1), (2.2), and (3.1), and the properties assumed for the random variables involved, we find

$$(3.12)\quad \begin{aligned}\operatorname*{plim}_{N\to\infty} a_1 &\equiv \operatorname*{plim}_{N\to\infty} \frac{m_{cz}}{m_{yz}} \\ &= \frac{\alpha(1-\alpha)(\overline{m}_{qq}+\sigma_v{}^2)+\kappa(1-\kappa)\sigma_u{}^2+\kappa(1-\alpha-\kappa+2\alpha\kappa)\sigma_{uv}}{(1-\alpha)(\overline{m}_{qq}+\sigma_v{}^2)+\kappa\sigma_u{}^2+(1-\alpha+\kappa)\sigma_{uv}}\end{aligned}$$

$$(3.13)\quad \begin{aligned}\operatorname*{plim}_{N\to\infty} a_2 &\equiv \operatorname*{plim}_{N\to\infty} \frac{m_{cy}}{m_{yy}} \\ &= \frac{\alpha(\overline{m}_{qq}+\sigma_v{}^2)+(1-\kappa)\sigma_u{}^2+(1-\kappa+\alpha)\sigma_{uv}}{(\overline{m}_{qq}+\sigma_v{}^2)+2\sigma_{uv}+\sigma_u{}^2}.\end{aligned}$$

It is seen that neither of these expressions is, in general, equal to α. The bias depends on the unknown parameters. If we have some a priori knowledge about some of the parameters we can make more definite statements about the bias. Thus, if we assume that $0<\alpha<1$, $0<\kappa<1$, $0<(1-\alpha-\kappa)<1$, and that $\sigma_{uv}>0$, we find that the bias of both (3.12) and (3.13) will be positive. If κ is small compared with α, and σ_{uv} also small, (3.12) will give smaller bias than (3.13), and so forth.

4. A MORE EXPLICIT MODEL

In Section 2 we defined investment z_t in such a way that $y_t=c_t+z_t$. Before making a decision upon the use of this z_t as an autonomous variable, it might be worth-while to examine its content in terms of current statistics of the gross national product and its components.

In the terminology of the U. S. Department of Commerce the gross national product, and disposable income, are defined as follows:[11] (For our purpose here the data should be interpreted as "per capita, in constant dollars.")

Gross national product = Government expenditures (excl. transfer payments)
+Gross private capital formation
+Consumers' expenditures.

Disposable income of individuals = Gross national product
−(Total business taxes+personal taxes + employment taxes −transfer payments)

[11] See, e.g., *Survey of Current Business*, May, 1942, p. 12.

−(Depreciation and depletion charges + capital outlay charged to current expense + income credited to other business reserves − revaluation of business inventories + corporate savings).

The total of the five terms in the last parentheses might be termed "gross business savings," or "withholdings." From these definitions it follows that disposable income (y_t) − consumers' expenditures $(c_t) = z_t$ = (Government expenditures + transfers − all taxes + gross private capital formation) − gross business savings. Denoting the total of the four terms in the last parentheses above by x_t, and denoting gross business savings by r_t, we have

$$y_t - c_t = z_t = x_t - r_t. \tag{4.1}$$

The quantity x_t might be called "gross investment." Gross investment is, therefore, here defined as gross private capital formation plus Government net deficit. It might now be argued that it is this "gross investment" which is the exogenous, "dynamic" element, rather than z_t. (That is, one might say that z_t is composed of two parts, one, x_t, which is autonomous, and another, $-r_t$, which is induced.)

To reach a complete model under this hypothesis one has to introduce an additional hypothesis concerning the determination of r_t. Here there might be several possible alternatives. One might, for example, think of r_t as being a function of $(x_t + c_t)$. [The quantity $(x_t + c_t)$ could be called the "gross disposable income" of the private sector of the economy.] Another alternative would be to consider r_t as a function of profits, accumulated business savings, etc. As an illustration of the methodological problems involved in dealing, statistically, with such models let us here adopt the hypothesis that r_t is a linear function of $(x_t + c_t)$. This leads us to the following model.

$$c_t = \alpha y_t + \beta + u_t \tag{4.2}$$

$$r_t = \mu(c_t + x_t) + \nu + w_t \tag{4.3}$$

$$y_t = c_t + x_t - r_t \tag{4.4}$$

$$x_t = \text{an autonomous variable.} \tag{4.5}$$

Here (4.2) is a repetition of (2.2), while (4.3) is the "business-savings" equation. μ and ν are constants to be estimated, w_t being a non-observable random variable. We assume that $E(w_t) = 0$, $E(w_t^2) = \sigma_w^2$, and

$E(w_t w_{t-\tau})=0$, $E(u_t w_{t-\tau})=0$, for $\tau \neq 0$. We do not, however, assume that u_t and w_t are necessarily independent. The sequence x_t, $t=1, 2, \cdots$ is assumed to fulfill a condition of the type (2.3).

Because of (4.4) and (4.5) there are really only two "endogeneous" variables involved. We may take these two variables to be c_t and y_t. Solving the system for c_t and y_t we obtain

$$(4.6) \quad c_t = \frac{\alpha(1-\mu)}{1-(1-\mu)\alpha} x_t + \frac{\beta - \alpha\nu}{1-(1-\mu)\alpha} + \frac{u_t - \alpha w_t}{1-(1-\mu)\alpha}$$

$$(4.7) \quad y_t = \frac{(1-\mu)}{1-(1-\mu)\alpha} x_t + \frac{(1-\mu)\beta - \nu}{1-(1-\mu)\alpha} + \frac{(1-\mu)u_t - w_t}{1-(1-\mu)\alpha}.$$

Under the assumptions made both these equations satisfy the requirements of the Markoff theorem on least squares, if x_t, $t=1, 2, \cdots$, is considered as a sequence of constants. Hence we have

$$(4.8) \quad \hat{A}_1 = \frac{m_{cx}}{m_{xx}} = \text{b.u. est. of } \frac{\alpha(1-\mu)}{1-(1-\mu)\alpha}$$

$$(4.9) \quad \hat{A}_2 = \frac{m_{yx}}{m_{xx}} = \text{b.u. est. of } \frac{(1-\mu)}{1-(1-\mu)\alpha}$$

$$(4.10) \quad \frac{m_{xx}m_c - m_{cx}m_x}{m_{xx}} = \text{b.u. est. of } \frac{\beta - \alpha\nu}{1-(1-\mu)\alpha}$$

$$(4.11) \quad \frac{m_{xx}m_y - m_{yx}m_x}{m_{xx}} = \text{b.u. est. of } \frac{(1-\mu)\beta - \nu}{1-(1-\mu)\alpha}.$$

These equations may, in turn, be solved, to obtain estimates, $\hat{\alpha}$, $\hat{\beta}$, $\hat{\mu}$, $\hat{\nu}$, of the structural parameters α, β, μ, ν, respectively. These solutions are

$$(4.12) \quad \hat{\alpha} = \frac{m_{cx}}{m_{yx}}$$

$$(4.13) \quad \hat{\beta} = \frac{m_{yx}m_c - m_{cx}m_y}{m_{yx}}$$

$$(4.14) \quad \hat{\mu} = 1 - \frac{m_{yx}}{m_{cx} + m_{xx}}$$

$$(4.15) \quad \hat{\nu} = \frac{m_{yx}(m_c + m_x) - (m_{cx} + m_{xx})m_y}{m_{cx} + m_{xx}}.$$

In a similar manner we might estimate σ_u^2, σ_w^2, and σ_{uw}. It will be noticed that the estimation formulae above are very similar to those of Section 3, although the present model has a different economic meaning.

If, as assumed, $Nm_{xx} \to \infty$ as $N \to \infty$, all the estimates above are consistent, by the same type of argument as that of Section 2.

An estimate of a parameter is in itself of little practical value unless it is accompanied by some measure of reliability. What we want is a "confidence region" for the unknown parameters: that is, if we consider all possible simultaneous values of the parameters as points in a parameter space, we want to construct a region, or set of points, which is a function of the observations, and which has a pre-assigned probability of covering the true, but unknown, parameter point. We shall indicate how such a region could be constructed in connection with the model above. We shall consider only the two "essential" parameters α and μ.

Let us first make the assumption that u_t and w_t have a joint probability distribution which is approximately normal. As before, we assume that x_t is a fixed variable. Denote by A_1 the true value of the coefficient $[\alpha(1-\mu)/(1-(1-\mu)\alpha)]$ in (4.6), and by A_2 the true value of the coefficient $[(1-\mu)/(1-(1-\mu)\alpha)]$ in (4.7). And let $\hat{A}_1$ and $\hat{A}_2$ be the corresponding estimates, as given by (4.8) and (4.9). Under the assumptions made the statistics $\hat{A}_1$ and $\hat{A}_2$ will be linear functions of normally distributed variables. $\hat{A}_1$ and $\hat{A}_2$ will, therefore, also be normally distributed. Their means will be equal to A_1 and A_2, respectively. The variance-covariance matrix of $\hat{A}_1$ and $\hat{A}_2$ will depend on σ_u^2, σ_w^2, σ_{uw}, α, and μ. It is then possible to obtain a joint confidence region for α and μ in the following manner.

Let σ_{11} and σ_{22}, and σ_{12} be the variances and the covariance of the residual random elements in (4.6) and (4.7), i.e.

$$(4.16) \qquad \sigma_{11} = E\left[\frac{u_t - \alpha w_t}{1-(1-\mu)\alpha}\right]^2$$

$$(4.17) \qquad \sigma_{22} = E\left[\frac{(1-\mu)u_t - w_t}{1-(1-\mu)\alpha}\right]^2$$

$$(4.18) \qquad \sigma_{12} = E\left[\frac{u_t - \alpha w_t}{1-(1-\mu)\alpha}\cdot\frac{(1-\mu)u_t - w_t}{1-(1-\mu)\alpha}\right].$$

If the equations (4.6) and (4.7) are fitted to the data by the method of least squares we obtain unbiased estimates, s_{11}, s_{22}, and s_{12}, of σ_{11}, σ_{22}, and σ_{12}, respectively. These estimates are

$$s_{11} = \frac{N}{N-2} \frac{m_{cc}m_{xx} - m_{cx}^2}{m_{xx}} \tag{4.19}$$

$$s_{22} = \frac{N}{N-2} \frac{m_{yy}m_{xx} - m_{yx}^2}{m_{xx}} \tag{4.20}$$

$$s_{12} = \frac{N}{N-2} \frac{m_{cy}m_{xx} - m_{cx}m_{yx}}{m_{xx}}. \tag{4.21}$$

Consider now the statistic T^2 defined by

$$T^2 = Nm_{xx} \sum_{i,j=1}^{i,j=2} s^{ij}(A_i - \hat{A}_i)(A_j - \hat{A}_j) \tag{4.22}$$

where s^{ij} denotes the inverse of the matrix s_{ij}. The distribution of the statistic T^2 is known. More specifically $\{(N-3)/[2(N-2)]\}T^2$ has the F distribution with 2 and $N-3$ degrees of freedom.[12] Choosing a certain level of significance we find the corresponding value of F in Snedecor's table.[13] Let the corresponding value of T^2 be T_0^2. All the points A_1 and A_2 in the parameter space (A_1, A_2) for which $T^2 \leqq T_0^2$ form the area of an ellipse with center at $(\hat{A}_1, \hat{A}_2)$. This is a confidence region for the parameter point (A_1, A_2).

Since the transformation from the (A_1, A_2) plane to the (α, μ) plane is continuous the confidence region derived for A_1, A_2 leads to a corresponding confidence region for α and μ. This transformation is given by the definition of A_1 and A_2. Expressing α and μ in terms of A_1 and A_2, we have

$$\alpha = \frac{A_1}{A_2} \tag{4.23}$$

$$\mu = 1 - \frac{A_2}{1 + A_1}. \tag{4.24}$$

In the next Section we shall give some numerical illustrations.

5. SOME NUMERICAL RESULTS

Some of the methods discussed in the preceding Sections have been applied to U.S. data, partly for the period 1922–41, partly for the period

[12] This fact was pointed out by Dr. T. W. Anderson of the Cowles Commission. See also S. S. Wilks, *Mathematical Statistics*, Princeton University Press, 1943, pp. 234–250.

[13] See G. W. Snedecor, *Statistical Methods*, Ames, Iowa, 1940, p. 184.

TABLE 1

U. S. DATA USED IN STUDY

Year	(1) Disposable income, dollars per capita, deflated y_t	(2) Consumers' expenditure, dollars per capita, deflated c_t	(3) $s_t = y_t - c_t$	(4) "Gross investment" dollars per capita, deflated x_t	(5) Deflator: B.L.S. Cost of Living 1935–39 = 100	(6) U. S. population millions
1922	433	394	39	—	119.7	110.1
23	483	423	60	—	121.9	112.0
24	479	437	42	—	122.2	114.1
25	486	434	52	—	125.4	115.8
26	494	447	47	—	126.4	117.4
27	498	447	51	—	124.0	119.0
28	511	466	45	—	122.6	120.5
29	534	474	60	128	122.5	121.8
1930	478	439	39	97	119.4	123.8
31	440	399	41	81	108.7	124.8
32	372	350	22	45	97.6	125.6
33	381	364	17	45	92.4	126.3
34	419	392	27	66	95.7	127.1
35	449	416	33	78	98.1	128.0
36	511	463	48	103	99.1	128.9
37	520	469	51	98	102.1	129.6
38	477	444	33	83	100.8	130.7
39	517	471	46	105	99.4	131.7
1940	548	494	54	122	100.2	132.8
41	629	529	100	165	105.2	134.0
Sums:						
1922–41	9659	8752	907	—		
1929–41	6275	5704	—	1216	—	—
Means:						
1922–41	482.95	437.60	45.35			
1929–41	482.692	438.769		93.5385		

Second order moments about mean:

1922–41:

$m_{yy} = 3249.65$ $m_{cy} = 2379.25$

$m_{cc} = 1794.35$ $m_{ys} = 870.40$

$m_{ss} = 285.55$ $m_{cs} = 584.90$

1929–41:

$m_{yy} = 4718.23$ $m_{cy} = 3413.69$

$m_{cc} = 2519.85$ $m_{yx} = 2159.62$

$m_{xx} = 1025.92$ $m_{cx} = 1537.85$

Sources of data.

Columns (1), (2), and (3): Years 1929–41 from *Survey of Current Business*, May, 1942, p. 12. Earlier years from unpublished estimates by the Department of Commerce. Deflated, per capita, figures have been calculated by means of Columns (5) and (6).

Column 4: See definition of x_t on p. 114. Years 1929–41 from *Survey of Current Business*, May, 1942, as revised in subsequent issues.

Columns (5) and (6): See, e.g., *Statistical Abstracts of the United States.* (Population figures for 1930–41 have been adjusted for underenumeration of children under 5.)

1929–41. The data used are given in Table 1.[14] Moments used in the calculations are listed in appendix to Table 1. The numerical results given below are numbered so as to correspond to the theoretical formulae given in the preceding, theoretical Sections. These results should, therefore, require little additional explanation.

A. Numerical illustrations to Section 2.

Applying formulae (2.11), (2.14) and (2.15) to the data given in Table 1, we obtain the following estimates

$$\text{(2.11.a)} \qquad \frac{1}{1-\hat{\alpha}} = 3.048 \quad \text{(The "multiplier")}$$

$$\text{(2.14.a)} \qquad \hat{\alpha} = .672 \quad \text{(The marginal propensity to consume)}$$

$$\text{(2.15.a)} \qquad \hat{\beta} = 113.1.$$

Formula (2.13), for $N=20$, gives

$$\text{(2.13.a)} \qquad s^2 = 662.82; \qquad s = 25.7$$

from which we obtain the standard error of $1/(1-\hat{\alpha}) = s/\sqrt{20m_{zz}} = .341$. From tables of the t-distribution, and choosing 5 per cent as the level of significance, we find

$$\text{(2.21.a)} \qquad -2.101 \leqq t = \frac{3.048 - \dfrac{1}{1-\alpha}}{.341} \leqq 2.101,$$

from which it follows that

$$2.33 \leqq \frac{1}{1-\alpha} \leqq 3.76.$$

The corresponding confidence interval for α is

$$.57 \leqq \alpha \leqq .73.$$

For comparison, we have calculated the least squares "estimates," a, and b, obtaining

[14] It will be noticed that, in addition to reducing the figures to a per-capita basis, we have used the Bureau of Labor Statistics cost of living index as a common deflator. By this procedure we do not, of course, mean to imply that the measure of "real investment" thus obtained is a good measure of the physical output of investment goods. The purpose of deflating the current-dollars series by the cost of living index is only to eliminate the effect of a scale factor in all prices, this scale factor being taken to be an autonomous variable. If we postulate that the absolute level of prices should not affect the real volume of consumption, investment, etc. we are—at least in point of principle—free to choose any price index as a common deflator.

(2.16.a) $a = .732$

(2.17.a) $b = 84.0.$

As one might expect [see (2.19) and (2.20)] we find that $a > \hat{\alpha}$, and $b < \hat{\beta}$. Although the difference does not appear to be very large in terms of α it is considerable in terms of the multiplier $1/(1-\alpha)$, viz. 3.048 versus 3.731.[15]

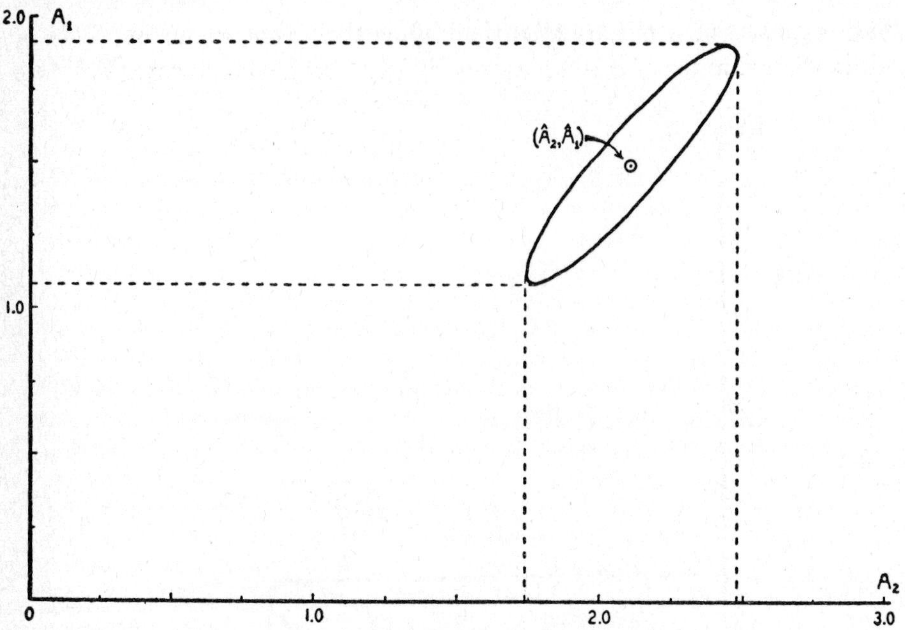

FIGURE 1. JOINT CONFIDENCE REGION FOR A_1 AND A_2.
LEVEL OF SIGNIFICANCE 5 PERCENT.

B. Numerical illustrations to Section 4.

Here we consider the model given by (4.2)–(4.5). We use data for 1929–41 only, since the present model requires that the various terms add up in the manner defined by the U. S. Department of Commerce estimates of the gross national product and its components. Consistent data in this respect are available only from 1929. The results obtained are as follows.

(4.8a) $\hat{A}_1 = 1.499$

[15] Although it is not the purpose of the present article to improve upon economic theory it is perhaps of interest to observe that, under the approach outlined above, it is possible to show that also last years' income plays a role as a variable in the consumption function. By a method similar to that used above, treating y_{t-1} as a predetermined variable, one finds $c_t = .57y_t + .16y_{t-1} + \text{const.}$, while the least squares' estimate of this equation yields $c_t = .7y_t + .05y_{t-1} + \text{const.}$

(4.9.a)	$\hat{A}_2 =$	2.105
(4.12.a)	$\hat{\alpha} =$	.712
(4.13.a)	$\hat{\beta} =$	95.05
(4.14.a)	$\hat{\mu} =$	.158
(4.15.a)	$\hat{\nu} =$	$-$ 34.30.

The estimate of α is here slightly higher than that given by (2.14.a), while the estimate of β is, correspondingly, somewhat lower. (For com-

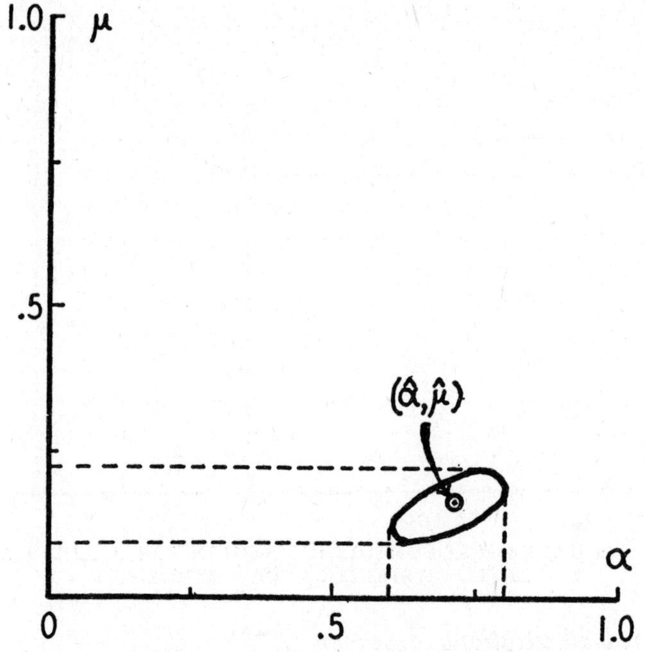

FIGURE 2. JOINT CONFIDENCE REGION FOR α AND μ, CORRESPONDING TO THE REGION IN FIGURE 1.

parison, we have also here calculated the least squares regression of c_t on y_t. The "estimate" obtained for α was .723, which in this case happens to come rather close to the estimate α above.)

We shall derive a confidence region for α and μ. For this purpose we have calculated

(4.19.a)	$s_{11} =$	253.658
(4.20.a)	$s_{22} =$	203.439
(4.21.a)	$s_{12} =$	208.538.

Now, $[(N-3)/2(N-2)]T^2$ has the "F"-distribution, $F_{2,N-3}$. In our case $N=13$. Choosing the 5 per cent level of significance, we find from Snedecor's table that $F=4.10$. The corresponding value of T^2 is then $T_0^2=9.02$. Using this and (4.19.a)–(4.21.a) we derive

$$\begin{aligned} 9.02 = 13337[&.02507(A_1 - \hat{A}_1)^2 \\ &- .05139(A_1 - \hat{A}_1)(A_2 - \hat{A}_2) + .03125(A_2 - \hat{A}_2)^2], \end{aligned} \tag{4.22.a}$$

where $\hat{A}_1$ and $\hat{A}_2$ are given by (4.8.a) and (4.9.a). (4.22.a) represents an ellipse in the parameter space of A_1 and A_2. The area covered by this ellipse is the confidence region for A_1 and A_2. It is shown in Figure 1. The corresponding confidence region for α and μ is shown in Figure 2. This latter region was derived numerically by means of the transformations defining A_1 and A_2.

GENERALIZATION OF THE RANK AND ORDER CONDITIONS FOR IDENTIFIABILITY

By Franklin M. Fisher[1]

The problem of the identifiability of a structural equation under nonlinear and nonhomogeneous restrictions on its parameters is examined. The usual results for the linear and homogeneous case are generalized and some consequences for the use of *a priori* inequalities are derived.

1

The problem of the identifiability of a single structural equation as a whole under linear homogeneous restrictions on its parameters alone was solved by Koopmans and Rubin in a now classic paper [**3**]. In another essay in the same volume, Wald [**6**] considered a far more general problem, that of the identifiability of a single parameter under restrictions with continuous first derivatives on all or some of the parameters of the system, and obtained farther reaching but perhaps less useful results.[2] This paper considers a problem intermediate in generality between the two—that of the identifiability of a single structural equation as a whole under restrictions of any form with continuous first derivatives on its parameters alone—and derives results similar to those of Koopmans and Rubin. While the approach is that of a generalization of the Koopmans-Rubin results (which follow immediately as a special case), it is clear that the problem might equally well have been treated as a specialization of the Wald results. Indeed, several of our subsidiary results are obviously similar to some of Wald's more general theorems and undoubtedly could have been derived as corollaries thereof. Aside from such intrinsic interest as it may possess, therefore, this paper provides a bridge, at least in part, between these two existing discussions.

2

Consider the system of structural equations:

$$u(t) = Ax(t) \tag{1}$$

where $u(t)$ is an $(m + 1)$ dimensional column vector of disturbances; A is an $(m + 1) \times (n + 1)$ matrix of coefficients with first row A_1, say; and $x(t)$ is an $(n + 1)$ dimensional column vector of variables. Without loss of generality, we may renumber the variables so that the first $(m + 1)$ elements of

[1] I am indebted to John R. Meyer, Gerald Kraft, Paul A. Samuelson, and Andrew Gleason for their advice and criticism at various stages of this paper. All errors are mine, however.

[2] See [**3**, pp. 106-107].

$x(t)$ are endogenous and the rest exogenous. Then A may be partitioned accordingly into:

$$A = [B \mid G] \tag{2}$$

where B is a square nonsingular matrix of rank $m + 1$. We further assume that there are no linear identities connecting the exogenous variables.

We shall be concerned exclusively with the identifiability of A_1 as a whole. Let α be an $(n + 1)$ dimensional row vector of parameters and consider the *a priori* restrictions:

$$\varphi^i(\alpha) = 0 \qquad (i = 1, \ldots, K). \tag{3}$$

We assume that these are *a priori* restrictions on the coefficients of the first equation of (1) so that they are satisfied for $\alpha = A_1$.

Let T_1 be the first row of any $(m+1) \times (m+1)$ nonsingular matrix, T, say.[3]

DEFINITION 1. A non-zero vector, T_1, is said to be *admissible* if and only if (3) is satisfied for $\alpha = T_1A$. The set of all such admissible T_1 is called *the admissible T_1-set.*

DEFINITION 2. A row vector, α, is said to be *admissible* if and only if it satisfies (3) and $\alpha = T_1A$ for some non-zero T_1. The set of all such admissible α is called *the admissible α-set.*

We must now distinguish two cases. If each of the restrictions (3) is homogeneous of some degree (not necessarily all of the same degree), then if some T_1 or α is admissible, so are all scalar multiples of that T_1 or α. Since the first equation of (1) is homogeneous in the elements of A_1, such scalar multiplication is indeed a trivial transformation. If, on the other hand, at least one of the restrictions (3) is not homogeneous of any degree, then such multiplication is not trivial. In the homogeneous case, then, we shall generally restrict our attention to points on the unit hypersphere in the $(n + 1)$-space whose axes correspond to the elements of α.

[3] Since we shall be exclusively concerned with T_1, the requirement that T be nonsingular will not concern us further in this paper save as a requirement that T_1 be non-zero. Provided that T_1 is non-zero, we can always choose the other rows of T in such a manner as to ensure its nonsingularity. For example, if the cth element of T_1 is non-zero, we can choose the other rows of T so that when the first and cth columns of T are interchanged (a procedure which does not affect the vanishing or non-vanishing of the determinant), we obtain the matrix:

$$\begin{bmatrix} T_{1c}\; T_{12} \ldots T_{1c-1}\; T_{11}\; T_{1c+1} \ldots T_{1m+1} \\ \begin{array}{c|c} 0 & \\ 0 & \\ \cdot & I_m \\ \cdot & \\ 0 & \end{array} \end{bmatrix}$$

where I_m is the $m \times m$ unit matrix. This is obviously nonsingular.

DEFINITION 3. If the restrictions (3) are not all homogeneous, A_1 is said to be *uniquely, multiply*, or *countably identifiable* under (3) if and only if the admissible T_1-set has one, a finite number, or a countable number of members, respectively.

DEFINITION 4. If the restrictions (3) are all homogeneous, A_1 is said to be *uniquely, multiply*, or *countably identifiable* under (3) if and only if the admissible T_1-set contains one, a finite number, or a countable number of rays through the origin, respectively.

DEFINITION 5. In either case, A_1 is said to be *completely identifiable* under (3) if and only if it is uniquely or multiply identifiable under (3); otherwise it is said to be *incompletely identifiable.*

DEFINITION 6. By a *δ-neighborhood* of a point is meant a hypersphere with radius δ and center at that point, unless we are speaking of a bounded set, in which case a δ-neighborhood of a point will be understood to mean the intersection of such a hypersphere with the bounded set.

DEFINITION 7. In the nonhomogeneous case, an admissible α will be said to be *locally identifiable* under (3) if and only if there exists a δ-neighborhood of that α which contains no other admissible α. In the homogeneous case, an admissible α on the unit hypersphere will be said to be *locally identifiable* if and only if there exists some δ-neighborhood of that α which contains no other admissible α on the unit hypersphere; more generally, an admissible α is locally identifiable if and only if some δ-neighborhood of that α contains no other admissible α save those on the same ray through the origin.

We use the following notation: for any matrix, M, let $\varrho(M)$ be the rank of M; let $K(M)$ be the row kernel of M, i.e., the space of all vectors which give the zero vector on post-multiplication by M.

Throughout what follows, we shall make repeated use of the theorem on linear transformations which states that the dimensionality of the range of a linear transformation plus the dimensionality of its kernel is equal to the dimensionality of its domain.[4] For our purposes, the less general form:

$$\varrho(M) + \dim K(M) = \text{number of rows of } M \tag{4}$$

will serve.

LEMMA 1. *There is a one-to-one correspondence between the admissible T_1-set and the admissible α-set.*

PROOF. It is obvious that to every admissible T_1 there corresponds one and only one admissible α and that to every admissible α there corresponds at least one admissible T_1. Suppose that more than one T_1, say T_1^1 and T_1^2, corresponded to the same admissible α so that $T_1^1A = \alpha = T_1^2A$ but $T_1^1 \neq T_1^2$.

[4] See [5, pp. 34-35].

Then $(T_1^1 - T_1^2)A = 0$ so that $(T_1^1 - T_1^2)$ is a non-zero vector in $K(A)$ and application of (4) yields $\varrho(A) \leq m$. This is impossible, however, since the sub-matrix, B, in (2) was assumed nonsingular. Hence one and only one admissible T_1 corresponds to a given admissible α and the lemma is proved.

Now define W' as the $(n + 1) \times (n - m)$ matrix whose ith row consists of the zero order least squares population regression coefficients of the ith variable on each of the exogenous variables. From (1) and the normal equations of least squares, we have:

$$AW' = 0. \tag{5}$$

Let V' be the matrix formed by the last $n - m$ rows of W'.

LEMMA 2. *V' is nonsingular and hence $\varrho(W') = n - m$.*

PROOF. V' is the matrix of the regression coefficients of the exogenous variables on themselves. It is easy to show that the determinant of V' is equal to the determinant of the correlation matrix of these same variables. This latter matrix cannot be singular, however, for it was assumed that there are no identities connecting the exogenous variables. Hence V' is nonsingular.[5]

Consider the equations:

$$\alpha W' = 0. \tag{6}$$

We prove the following theorem:

THEOREM 1. *The set of all α satisfying* (3) *and* (6) (*with the possible exception of the zero vector*) *is precisely the admissible α-set.*

[5] Lest it be thought that the discussion is overly dependent on least squares, it may be worth pointing out that the above has an exact analogy in the non-stochastic case where $u(t)$ is replaced by 0 in (1). In that case, we may choose values for $n - m$ of the variables arbitrarily, the values of the rest being determined by (1). The equivalent of Lemma 2 is then the statement that we can so choose those values in precisely $n - m$ independent ways. Every use made of W' or of (5) below has a similar parallel; indeed, it would be largely possible—though perhaps not so enlightening—to proceed without using them at all.

In this connection, Walter D. Fisher has pointed out that nothing in the discussion would be changed if our W' were replaced by the matrix $Z = \begin{bmatrix} \Pi \\ I \end{bmatrix}$, where $\Pi = -B^{-1}G$ is the matrix of reduced form coefficients, and I is the $(n - m) \times (n - m)$ unit matrix. It is easily seen from (5) that $Z = W'V'^{-1}$, so that Z and W' coincide only if the exogenous variables are uncorrelated in the population. Of course, Lemma 2 is trivial if Z is used in place of W', and the ensuing discussion remains unchanged. The reader is at liberty to think of W' as Z; however, we retain the original definition in order to emphasize the *a posteriori* character of (6) below as contrasted with the *a priori* restrictions (3). This point is particularly to be kept in mind in Section 5, below.

PROOF. (a) Clearly any admissible α satifsies (3) by definition. Further, in view of (5), $\alpha W' = (T_1A)W' = T_1(AW') = 0$ for any admissible α, so that any admissible α satisfies (6).

(b) If an α satisfies (6), it is in $K(W')$. However, Lemma 2 and (4) give $\dim K(W') = m + 1$; from (5), every row of A is in $K(W')$; and, as seen above, $\varrho(A) = m + 1$, by assumption, so that the rows of A span $K(W')$. Therefore, any non-zero α satisfying (6) can be written as $\alpha = T_1A$ for some non-zero T_1. It follows that any non-zero α satisfying (3) and (6) is admissible, and the theorem is proved.

COROLLARY TO THEOREM 1. *In view of Lemma 1, a necessary and sufficient condition that A_1 be completely identifiable in the nonhomogeneous case is that* (3) *and* (6) *admit of only a finite number of solutions. A necessary and sufficient condition for such complete identifiability in the homogeneous case is that* (3) *and* (6) *admit of only a finite number of solutions on the unit hypersphere. (Analogous statements hold for unique, multiple, and countable identifiability.)*

3

We now consider the homogeneous case in detail. Throughout this section it will be assumed that each of the restrictions (3) is homogeneous and has continuous first derivatives.

Let $\varphi'(\alpha)$ be the $(n + 1) \times K$ transpose of the Jacobian of (3) with respect to the elements of α. (That is, each column of $\varphi'(\alpha)$ corresponds to an equation of (3), each row to an element of α.)

Let $J(\alpha) = [\varphi'(\alpha) \mid W']$, so that $J(\alpha)$ is $(n + 1) \times (K + n - m)$.

LEMMA 3. *Let α^o be admissible. A sufficient condition that α^o be locally identifiable is that at least one matrix, say $L(\alpha^o)$, formed from $J(\alpha^o)$ by striking out one of the first $m + 1$ rows thereof, be of rank n.*[6]

PROOF. Without loss of generality, we may renumber the endogenous variables so that it is the first row of $J(\alpha^o)$ which is struck in securing $L(\alpha^o)$. Let α_1^o be the first element of α^o. We impose the normalization rule:

$$\alpha_1^o = 1. \tag{7}$$

Choose n independent columns from $L(\alpha^o)$ and let $M'(\alpha^o)$ be the transpose of the matrix formed by these columns. Let $N'(\alpha^o)$ be the transpose of the

[6] It would, in fact, suffice that some matrix formed from $J(\alpha^o)$ by striking out *any* row thereof be of rank n. The above construction is employed to ensure that normalization with respect to an endogenous variable is possible, this being the usual practice. In any case, Lemma 4 below ensures that this restriction makes no difference.

matrix formed by the corresponding columns of $J(\alpha^o)$. Consider the matrix:

$$Q(\alpha^o) = \left[\frac{1\,0\,0\ldots 0}{N'(\alpha^o)}\right].$$

Expanding the determinant of $Q(\alpha^o)$ by the cofactors of its first row, it is clear that $\det Q(\alpha^o) = \det M'(\alpha^o) \neq 0$ by assumption. However, $Q(\alpha)$ is the Jacobian of (7) and n equations of (3) and (6) with respect to the elements of α and, since (3), (6), and (7) all have continuous first derivatives, this is non-singular in a δ-neighborhood of α^o, since, as we have just seen, it is non-singular at α^o. It follows that these equations have a unique solution in α^o in a δ-neighborhood of α^o. However, (7) is just a normalization rule while (3) and (6) are homogeneous in the elements of α. Therefore, all other solutions of (3) and (6) alone in a δ-neighborhood of α^o must be scalar multiples of α^o, and, hence, by Theorem 1, α^o is indeed locally identifiable.

LEMMA 4. *For any α, admissible or not, at least one matrix, $L(\alpha)$, formed as in Lemma 3, has rank n if and only if $\varrho(J(\alpha)) \geq n$.*

PROOF. That $\varrho(J(\alpha)) \geq n$ if such a matrix has rank n is obvious. It remains to prove the reverse implication.

Assume that $\varrho(J(\alpha)) \geq n$ but that all matrices formed in the way described have rank less than n. Consider $L^1(\alpha)$, the matrix formed from $J(\alpha)$ by striking out the first row thereof. Since $\varrho(L^1(\alpha)) < n$, by (4), there exists a non-zero vector, say β, such that $\beta J(\alpha) = 0$ and the first element of β is zero. Note that at least one of the first $m + 1$ elements of β must be non-zero, since otherwise the last $n - m$ elements would form a non-zero vector in $K(V')$ and (4) would imply $\varrho(V') < n - m$, contradicting Lemma 2. Without loss of generality, then, we can renumber the endogenous variables so that it is the second element of β which is non-zero.

Now consider $L^2(\alpha)$, the matrix formed from $J(\alpha)$ by striking out the second row thereof. Since $\varrho(L^2(\alpha)) < n$, there exists, by (4), a non-zero vector, say π, such that $\pi J(\alpha) = 0$ and the second element of π is zero. In that case, however, β and π are clearly non-zero independent vectors in $K(J(\alpha))$ and application of (4) yields $\varrho(J(\alpha)) < n$, contrary to assumption, and the lemma is proved.

LEMMA 5. *For any α, admissible or not, $\varrho(J(\alpha)) \geq n$ if and only if $\varrho(A\varphi'(\alpha)) \geq m$.*[7]

PROOF. (a) Assume that $\varrho(J(\alpha)) \geq n$ but that $\varrho(A\varphi'(\alpha)) < m$. (4) then

[7] In the present homogeneous case, Euler's theorem ensures that for an admissible α, say $\alpha^o = T_1^o A$, T_1^o is in $K(A\varphi'(\alpha^o))$, so that $\varrho(A\varphi'(\alpha^o))$ cannot be greater than m. There is no general reason why this should be so for other, inadmissible α, however, so that $\varrho(A\varphi'(\alpha)) > m$ is a possibility for such points even in the homogeneous case. Similar remarks apply to $\varrho(J(\alpha))$.

implies the existence of at least two non-zero independent vectors, say β and π, in $K(A\varphi'(\alpha^o))$. Hence:

(8) $$(\beta A)\varphi'(\alpha) = \beta(A\varphi'(\alpha)) = 0$$

and similarly for π. Therefore, βA and πA are both in $K(\varphi'(\alpha))$ and they are both non-zero since $\varrho(A) = m + 1$. Now suppose that they are dependent. Then for some non-zero scalar, say λ:

(9) $$(\beta + \lambda\pi)A = (\beta A) + \lambda(\pi A) = 0$$

and

(10) $$(\beta + \lambda\pi) \neq 0$$

since β and π are independent. In that case, however, (9) and (4) imply $\varrho(A) < m + 1$, contrary to assumption. Hence βA and πA are independent. However, from (5):

(11) $$(\beta A)W' = \beta(AW') = 0$$

and similarly for πA. Therefore, βA and πA are both in $K(W')$, but, since they are also in $K(\varphi'(\alpha))$, they are in $K(J(\alpha))$. Therefore, dim $K(J(\alpha)) \geq 2$, and (4) gives $\varrho(J(\alpha)) < n$, contrary to assumption. Hence $\varrho(J(\alpha)) \geq n$ implies $\varrho(A\varphi'(\alpha)) \geq m$.

(b) Now assume that $\varrho(A\varphi'(\alpha)) \geq m$ but that $\varrho(J(\alpha)) < n$. (4) implies that there exist at least two independent non-zero vectors, say b and p, in $K(J(\alpha))$. However, if b and p are in $K(J(\alpha))$, they are in $K(W')$ and we saw in the proof of Theorem 1 that the rows of A span $K(W')$. Hence there exist two non-zero vectors, say β and π, such that $b = \beta A$ and $p = \pi A$. Moreover, β and π must be independent, since otherwise there would exist some non-zero scalar, say λ, for which (9) held, and the middle member of (9) is equal to $(b + \lambda p)$ which is non-zero since b and p are independent. Finally, since b and p are in $K(J(\alpha))$, they are in $K(\varphi'(\alpha))$, so that :

(12) $$\beta(A\varphi'(\alpha)) = (\beta A)\varphi'(\alpha) = b\varphi'(\alpha) = 0$$

and similarly for π. Therefore, β and π are independent non-zero vectors in $K(A\varphi'(\alpha))$ so that dim $K(A\varphi'(\alpha)) \geq 2$ and a final application of (4) gives $\varrho(A\varphi'(\alpha)) < m$, contrary to assumption. Hence $\varrho(A\varphi'(\alpha)) \geq m$ implies $\varrho(J(\alpha)) \geq n$ and the lemma is proved.

As an immediate consequence of Lemmas 3-5 we have:

THEOREM 2. *Let α^o be admissible. A sufficient condition that α^o be locally identifiable is that $\varrho(A\varphi'(\alpha^o)) = m$.*[8]

[8] It would have been entirely feasible to prove this theorem by way of another and slightly easier route than that of Lemmas 3—5, a route analogous to that followed below in the proof of the corresponding theorem in the nonhomogeneous case (Theorem 8). However, Lemmas 3—5, as well as following naturally from the preceding discussion and being needed later on, may be of interest, insofar as they show the direct relation-

We now introduce two needed concepts.

DEFINITION 8. Consider any determinant, say $D(\lambda)$, whose elements, $D(\lambda)_{ij}$, are functions of a vector of variables, λ. If it is possible, given a set of points, Σ, to renumber the rows and columns of $D(\lambda)$ so that for λ in Σ the principal minors:

$$\begin{vmatrix} D(\lambda)_{11} \end{vmatrix}, \quad \begin{vmatrix} D(\lambda)_{11} & D(\lambda)_{12} \\ D(\lambda)_{21} & D(\lambda)_{22} \end{vmatrix}, \ldots, D(\lambda)$$

are all non-zero, then $D(\lambda)$ will be said to be *Samuelsonian* over Σ.

DEFINITION 9. Consider any matrix, say $M(\lambda)$, whose elements are functions of a vector of variables, λ. If, given a set of points, Σ, the largest determinant, Samuelsonian over Σ, which can be formed by striking out rows and columns of $M(\lambda)$ is of order r, $M(\lambda)$ will be said to be *Samuelsonian of order* r over Σ, and we write $S(M(\lambda)) = r$ over Σ.

The reason for the terminology is that we are going to make use of a theorem due to Professor Samuelson to the effect that if the Jacobian determinant of n equations with respect to n variables is everywhere Samuelsonian, then the equations have a unique solution ([**4**, pp. 16-17]). Similar uniqueness holds locally if the Jacobian is Samuelsonian over some neighborhood. It is easy to show that in the case of a system of linear equations the non-vanishing of the Jacobian determinant is equivalent to the determinant being everywhere Samuelsonian. In general, however, while this is true at any particular point, it is not true over a set of points.

It is possible to prove, by analogy to the proof of Lemma 5, that $S(A\varphi'(\alpha)) \geq m$ implies $S(J(\alpha)) \geq n$ for any set of values of α. All theorems follow more simply, however, from the proof of Theorem 8, below, and the analogous proof of Theorem 2 in the present homogeneous case.

We have:

THEOREM 3. *A sufficient condition that* A_1 *be uniquely identifiable under* (3) *is that* $S(A\varphi'(\alpha)) \geq m$ *over the set of all* α.[9]

Moreover, it is easy to prove:

THEOREM 4. *A necessary and sufficient condition that* A_1 *be completely identifiable under* (3) *is that every admissible* α *on the unit hypersphere which is such that* $\varrho(A\varphi'(\alpha)) < m$ *be locally identifiable.*

---

ship between Theorem 2 and its extensions which follow and Theorem 1 and its Corollary. As Theorem 2 and its extensions are direct generalizations of the Koopmans-Rubin results, while the Corollary to Theorem 1 is a special case of Wald's work ([**6**, *Theorem 3.1*, p. 243]), proving Theorem 2 in this way illuminates the direct relationship between the two studies. We shall return to this below.

[9] I am grateful to Professor Samuelson for preserving me from error here.

PROOF. (a) *Sufficiency*. The intersection of the admissible α-set with the unit hypersphere is a bounded set. The only way, therefore, in which it can have more than a finite number of members is for some or all of them to form an infinite convergent sequence.[10] There are three possibilities:

(1) Such a sequence cannot converge to an inadmissible α. This is so, since, in view of Theorem 1, at such a point at least one of the equations (3) and (6) is not satisfied so that the value of the left-hand member of that equation differs from zero. All these left-hand members are continuous functions, however, since (6) is linear and (3) is assumed to have continuous first derivatives. Therefore, for each inadmissible point, there exists a δ-neighborhood of that point in which at least one of the equations (3) and (6) is not satisfied and which hence contains no admissible points. It follows that an infinite sequence of admissible points cannot converge to an inadmissible one.

(2) Such a sequence cannot converge to an admissible point, say α^o, where $\varrho(A\varphi'(\alpha^o)) = m$, for by Theorem 2, all such points are locally identifiable.

(3) Such a sequence cannot converge to any other admissible point, for, by assumption, all such points are also locally identifiable.

Hence no such sequence can converge so that there can only be a finite number of admissible points on the unit hypersphere. Therefore A_1 is completely identifiable.

(b) *Necessity*. Suppose that there is some admissible point on the unit hypersphere, say α^o, such that $\varrho(A\varphi'(\alpha^o)) < m$ and α^o is not locally identifiable. Then, by definition, every δ-neighborhood of α^o contains some other admissible α on the unit hypersphere. In that case, however, every δ-neighborhood of α^o must contain an infinite number of admissible α on the unit hypersphere,[11] and hence A_1 is incompletely identifiable under (3).

We also have:

COROLLARY TO THEOREM 4. *Sufficient conditions that A_1 be completely identifiable under* (3) *are that $\varrho(A\varphi'(\alpha)) = m$ for all admissible α, or,* a fortiori, *that $\varrho(A\varphi'(\alpha)) \geq m$ for all α.*

We now consider the problem of local identifiability in the case where $\varrho(A\varphi'(\alpha^o)) < m$ for an admissible α^o.

THEOREM 5. *Let α^o be an admissible α on the unit hypersphere with $\varrho(A\varphi'(\alpha^o)) < m$. A sufficient condition that α^o be locally identifiable is that there exist some δ-neighborhood of α^o such that $S(A\varphi'(\alpha)) \geq m$ over the set of all points in that neighborhood on the unit hypersphere, other than α^o itself.*

[10] See [2, p. 128].
[11] See [2, pp. 126-127].

PROOF. Suppose that α^o is not locally identifiable. Then, as before, every δ-neighborhood of α^o contains an infinite number of admissible points on the unit hypersphere which form at least one sequence converging to α^o. Consider such a sequence.

Now, consider any δ-neighborhood of one of the admissible points in the sequence which contains at least one other admissible point also in the sequence. For each such neighborhood there are two possibilities:

(1) One of the admissible points in the neighborhood on the unit hypersphere, say α^1, is such that $\varrho(A\varphi'(\alpha^1)) < m$.

(2) $\varrho(A\varphi'(\alpha)) = m$ for all admissible points in the neighborhood on the unit hypersphere. In that case, however, $S(A\varphi'(\alpha)) \ngtr m$ over the entire neighborhood, for, if it were, extension of the Samuelson theorem would ensure that the neighborhood contains only one admissible point on the unit hypersphere, contrary to assumption.

Hence $S(A\varphi'(\alpha)) \ngtr m$ over any δ-neighborhood of an admissible point on the unit hypersphere which contains some other admissible point also on the unit hypersphere.

Now, choose a $\delta > 0$. Then, by Cauchy's Fundamental Convergence Theorem, we can find a smaller $\varepsilon > 0$ such that for an admissible α far enough along in the convergent sequence, an ε-neighborhood of that α contains at least one other admissible α on the unit hypersphere, and does not contain α^o, and such that that ε-neighborhood is itself entirely contained in the δ-neighborhood of α^o defined by the δ chosen. Hence every δ-neighborhood of α^o contains at least one neighborhood on the unit hypersphere, which does not contain α^o itself, over which $S(A\varphi'(\alpha)) < m$, contrary to assumption. Therefore, α^o must be locally identifiable under the conditions assumed, and the theorem is proved.[12]

We state the following theorem without proof as being sufficiently obvious given Lemmas 3—5 and Theorem 1.

THEOREM 6. *Let α^o be an admissible α on the unit hypersphere for which $\varrho(A\varphi'(\alpha^o)) < m$. A necessary condition that α^o be locally identifiable is that there exist no δ-neighborhood of α^o for every point of which on the unit hypersphere $\varrho(A\varphi'(\alpha)) < m$.*

Combining these results with *Theorem 4*, we have:

COROLLARY TO THEOREMS 4 AND 5. *A sufficient condition that A_1 be completely identifiable under* (3) *is that for every admissible α on the unit hypersphere, say α^o, at which $\varrho(A\varphi'(\alpha^o)) < m$, there exist a δ-neighborhood of that α^o over the set of all other points in which on the unit hypersphere $S(A\varphi'(\alpha)) \geq m$.*

[12] So far as I am aware, the corresponding direct theorem on the solution of equations is a new result. It can be proved in another way by extension of the usual proofs of the Implicit Function Theorem.

COROLLARY 1 TO THEOREMS 4 AND 6. *A necessary condition that* A_1 *be completely identifiable under* (3) *is that there exist no* δ*-neighborhood of an admissible* α *on the unit hypersphere at every point of which on the unit hypersphere* $\varrho(A\varphi'(\alpha)) < m$.

COROLLARY 2 TO THEOREMS 4 AND 6. *A necessary condition that* A_1 *be completely identifiable under* (3) *is that* $\varrho(A\varphi'(\alpha))$ *be not below* m *for all* α.

Since, in the case where all the restrictions (3) are linear as well as homogeneous, the Jacobian, $\varphi'(\alpha)$, is not a function of α, so that the rank of $A\varphi'(\alpha)$ is either below m for all α or equal to m for all α,[13] and, since in this case, $\varrho(A\varphi'(\alpha)) = m$ implies $S(A\varphi'(\alpha)) = m$ over the set of all α, we may combine this last corollary with Theorem 3 to secure:

THEOREM 7. *Let each of the restrictions* (3) *be linear as well as homogeneous. A necessary and sufficient condition that* A_1 *be uniquely identifiable under* (3) *is that* $\varrho(A\varphi'(\alpha)) = m$.

This, of course, is the well known Koopmans-Rubin "rank condition."[14] What we have shown, generally speaking, is that, in the nonlinear homogeneous case, it is necessary for complete identifiability that this condition (with the equality replaced with a weak inequality) hold somewhere on the unit hypersphere and sufficient that it hold everywhere or that a stronger version hold everywhere in a δ-neighborhood of each admissible α, with the possible exception of the admissible α itself.[15]

The Koopmans-Rubin "order condition,"[16] however, generalizes more directly. Returning to the general homogeneous case and recalling that the rank of a matrix cannot increase on pre-multiplication by another matrix, we obtain:

COROLLARY 3 TO THEOREMS 4 AND 6. *A necessary condition that* A_1 *be completely identifiable under* (3) *is that there exist no* δ*-neighborhood of an admissible* α *on the unit hypersphere for every point of which on the unit hypersphere the rank of* $\varphi'(\alpha)$ (*the number of independent restrictions expressed by* (3)) *is less than* m.

COROLLARY 4 TO THEOREMS 4 AND 6. *A necessary condition that* A_1 *be completely identifiable under* (3) *is that the number of not identically dependent equations of* (3) (*the number of not identically dependent columns of* $\varphi'(\alpha)$) *be at least* m.

[13] It cannot be greater than m, since the first row of $A\varphi'(\alpha)$ here will always consist of zeros only. See footnote 7 above.

[14] [**3**, *Theorem* 2.2.2, p. 81].

[15] Of course, since the restrictions (3) are assumed to have continuous first derivatives, the weaker condition will hold in such a neighborhood if it holds at the admissible point.

[16] [**3**, *Corollary to Theorem* 2.2.2, pp. 81-82].

This last is, of course, identical with the Koopmans-Rubin "order condition" in the linear case.

This completes our discussion of the case in which each of the restrictions (3) is homogeneous.

4

We now consider the more general case. Throughout this section, it will be assumed that the restrictions (3) have continuous first derivatives but are not all homogeneous. We now no longer restrict our attention to points and neighborhoods on the unit hypersphere. As might be expected, each of the theorems of the last section has its extension here, and, as the proofs are quite similar, we shall give them only when it seems of interest to do so.

THEOREM 8. *Let α^o be admissible. A sufficient condition that α^o be locally identifiable is that $\varrho(A\varphi'(\alpha^o)) = m + 1$.*

PROOF. It would be entirely possible to prove this theorem by proving the obvious extensions of Lemmas 3-5—that is, by proving that it is sufficient for local identifiability of α^o that $\varrho(J(\alpha^o)) = n + 1$ and that this will be the case if and only if $\varrho(A\varphi'(\alpha^o)) = m + 1$. Instead, however, the following simple proof is offered for the light it sheds on the true role of the matrix $A\varphi'(\alpha)$ with which we have been so concerned.

Since α^o is admissible, there exists, by Lemma 1, a unique admissible T_1, say T_1^o, such that $\alpha^o = T_1^o A$. Moreover, since A is a linear and continuous mapping, it will suffice to prove that there is no other admissible T_1 in some δ-neighborhood of T_1^o. A sufficient condition that this be the case, however, is that the Jacobian of

$$\varphi^i(T_1 A) = 0 \qquad (i = 1, \ldots, K) \tag{13}$$

(that is, of (3)) with respect to the elements of T_1 be of rank $m + 1$ in a δ-neighborhood of T_1^o. Further, since each equation of (3) and hence of (13) is assumed to have continuous first derivatives, it will suffice that the Jacobian mentioned be of rank $m + 1$ at T_1^o. It remains only to observe that the Jacobian of (13) with respect to the elements of T_1, when evaluated at T_1^o, is precisely the transpose of $A\varphi'(\alpha^o)$, and the theorem is proved.

The reader should compare this proof with the proof of Theorem 2 above by way of Lemmas 3-5 and Theorem 1 and with Lemma 1 to see how this proof really rounds out the discussion of the role of the matrix $A\varphi'(\alpha)$. That matrix is directly (proof of Theorem 8) the transpose of the Jacobian of (3) or (13) with respect to the elements of T_1, when evaluated at an admissible T_1 and it is intimately related (Lemmas 3-5 and their extension to the non-homogeneous case) to the Jacobian of (3) and (6) with respect to the elements of α. Theorem 1 and its Corollary complete the circle through Lemma 1.

As mentioned above, the Corollary to Theorem 1 is a special case of Wald's major result, so that this group of theorems and lemmas indicates the relationship between Wald's work and the Koopmans-Rubin rank condition.

We further have:

THEOREM 9. *A sufficient condition that* A_1 *be uniquely identifiable under* (3) *is that* $S(A\varphi'(\alpha)) = m + 1$ *over the set of all* α.

THEOREM 10. *A necessary and sufficient condition that* A_1 *be* countably[17] *identifiable under* (3) *is that every admissible* α *which is such that* $\varrho(A\varphi'(\alpha)) < m + 1$ *be locally identifiable.*

COROLLARY 1 TO THEOREM 10. *A sufficient condition that* A_1 *be completely identifiable under* (3) *is that the admissible* α*-set be bounded and the conditions of Theorem* 10 *be satisfied.*

In the homogeneous case, we did not have to require that the admissible α-set be bounded, since the unit hypersphere is itself a bounded set. (See the proof of Theorem 4, above.)

COROLLARY 2 TO THEOREM 10. *Sufficient conditions that* A_1 *be countably identifiable under* (3) *are that* $\varrho(A\varphi'(\alpha)) = m + 1$ *for all admissible* α, *or*, a fortiori *that* $\varrho(A\varphi'(\alpha)) = m + 1$ *for all* α.

COROLLARY 3 TO THEOREM 10. *Sufficient conditions that* A_1 *be completely identifiable under* (3) *are that the admissible* α*-set be bounded and the conditions of the preceding corollary satisfied.*

THEOREM 11. *Let* α^o *be admissible with* $\varrho(A\varphi'(\alpha^o)) < m + 1$. *A sufficient condition that* α^o *be locally identifiable is that there exist some* δ*-neighborhood of* α^o *such that* $S(A\varphi'(\alpha)) = m + 1$ *over the set of all* α *in that neighborhood other than* α^o *itself.*

THEOREM 12. *Let* α^o *be admissible with* $\varrho(A\varphi'(\alpha^o)) < m + 1$. *A necessary condition that* α^o *be locally identifiable is that there exist no* δ*-neighborhood of* α^o *for every point of which* $\varrho(A\varphi'(\alpha^o)) < m + 1$.

COROLLARY 1 TO THEOREMS 10 AND 11. *A sufficient condition that* A_1 *be countably identifiable under* (3) *is that at each admissible* α *which is such that* $\varrho(A\varphi'(\alpha)) < m + 1$, *there exist a* δ*-neighborhood of that* α *such that* $S(A\varphi'(\alpha)) = m + 1$ *over the set of all* α *in that neighborhood save the admissible one.*

COROLLARY 2 TO THEOREMS 10 AND 11. *A sufficient condition that* A_1 *be completely identifiable under* (3) *is that the admissible* α*-set be bounded and the conditions of the preceding corollary satisfied.*

[17] See Definition 3, above.

Corollary 1 to Theorems 10 and 12. *A necessary condition that* A_1 *be countably identifiable* (*and*, a fortiori, *that it be completely identifiable*) *under* (3) *is that there exist no* δ*-neighborhood of an admissible* α *for every point of which* $\varrho(A\varphi'(\alpha)) < m + 1$.

Corollary 2 to Theorems 10 and 12. *A necessary condition that* A_1 *be countably* (*completely*) *identifiable under* (3) *is that* $\varrho(A\varphi'(\alpha))$ *be not below* $m+1$ *for all* α.

Theorem 13. *Let each of the restrictions* (3) *be linear. A necessary and sufficient condition that* A_1 *be uniquely identifiable under* (3) *is that* $\varrho(A\varphi'(\alpha)) = m + 1$.

Corollary 3 to Theorems 10 and 12. *A necessary condition that* A_1 *be countably* (*completely*) *identifiable under* (3) *is that there exist no* δ*-neighborhood of an admissible* α *for every point of which* $\varrho(\varphi'(\alpha))$ (*the number of independent restrictions expressed by* (3)) *is less than* $m + 1$.

Finally, we have:

Corollary 4 to Theorems 10 and 12. *A necessary condition that* A_1 *be countably* (*completely*) *identifiable under* (3) *is that the number of not identically dependent equations of* (3) (*the number of not identically dependent columns of* $\varphi'(\alpha)$) *be at least* $m + 1$.

5

In this section we discuss the application of the foregoing generalization of the rank condition and one of its consequences. First of all, most of the theorems of the last two sections ran in terms of the rank of the matrix $A\varphi'(\alpha)$ when evaluated at some admissible α. This sort of evaluation, however, if performed directly, might well prove somewhat tedious, since, not only does it require the explicit estimation of the last m rows of A, as it does also in the linear case,[18] but it also requires setting A_1 equal to each admissible α in turn and evaluating the rank of $A\varphi'(\alpha)$ for all other admissible α. If the number of admissible α is at all large, this could be something of a chore, to say the least.

An alternate course is open to us, however, in view of Lemmas 3-5, namely, to investigate the properties of the matrix $J(\alpha)$. Since $J(\alpha)$ is not explicitly a function of A, this is probably a more efficient approach, especially if n is small relative to m. In actual estimation work, of course, what

[18] By the way, since the determinants involved are all linear functions of the elements of the last m rows of A, the useful property of identifiability almost everywhere in the $m(n + 1)$-space of those parameters continues to hold when the rank of $A\varphi'(\alpha)$ is not identically below that required for our theorems, identically in those parameters. (See [**3**, pp. 82-83].) Unfortunately, this is not the case as regards A_1 itself.

this amounts to is that, as in the linear case, maximum likelihood methods of estimation (when they are adapted to the general case) will converge slowly and standard errors will be large when identifiability is not present for a particular set of parameters.

Secondly, until such estimation methods are adapted, in the case where A_1 is completely but multiply identifiable under (3), if it happens that (3) can be divided into two or more not necessarily disjunct subsets, such that A_1 is completely identifiable under each of them, then the number of members of the admissible α-set may be reduced, since the admissible α-set corresponding to (3) as a whole will be the intersection of the admissible α-sets corresponding to the subsets of (3).[19]

Finally, we turn to the role of inequalities in the analysis of the identifiability of a single structural equation as a whole under restrictions on its parameters alone. This role is a double one, at least potentially. First, inequalities may be used to bound the admissible α-set in cases where this is not possible analytically, so that the theorems of the last section secure complete rather than countable identifiability; or, as mentioned in [**3**, p. 97], they may be used in cases of complete but multiple identifiability to reduce the number of admissible solutions or even to secure unique identifiability. Their second use is more direct. Suppose that (3) is replaced[20] by:

$$\varphi^i(\alpha) \geq 0 \qquad (i = 1, \ldots, K). \tag{14}$$

(Strong inequalities would raise no different problems.) Adopting a procedure familiar from linear programming problems, we define K new "slack" variables, k_i, such that:

$$\varphi^i(\alpha) - k_i = 0, \quad k_i \geq 0 \qquad (i = 1, \ldots, K). \tag{15}$$

These are nonhomogeneous equations in the elements of α, but such were the subject of the last section. If, therefore, the conditions of the appropriate theorems of the last section are satisfied with (15) in place of (3),[21] Theorem 1 and the extension of Lemmas 3—5 to the nonhomogeneous case provide that we can solve (15) and (6) for each admissible α in terms of $m + 1$ of the k_i

[19] Note that, in view of what follows, it may be possible to use inequalities in this way to help reduce the size of the admissible α-set as well as to use them directly towards this end in the obvious way.

[20] Obviously, the case where both equalities and inequalities are known to obtain at the same time could be treated analogously. Treating the case where all *a priori* restrictions take the form of inequalities is slightly more convenient for expositional purposes, however.

[21] Observe that if two or more of the inequalities (14) really restrict the same function of α, these do not lead to more than one independent equation in (15). This is as it should be, since such restrictions hold less information together than does an equality in the same function of α, and the latter would be only one equation in (3).

(or, equivalently, when estimation methods have been adapted, that each admissible α can be estimated in terms of some or all of the k_i). Now set all of the k_i equal to zero and evaluate such a solution, say α^o. Further, find the partial derivative of each element of α^o with respect to each of the k_i,[22] evaluated at the same point. If these are all positive (negative) for a given element of α^o, we may conclude (ignoring higher order terms in a MacLaurin expansion) that that element of the admissible α in question lies above (below) the value calculated.[23]

Furthermore, even if higher order terms cannot be ignored, and even if all the partial derivatives of a given element of α^o with respect to the k_i are not of the same sign, they may yield some information. Just as the k_i are like the "slack" variables of linear programming, so are these derivatives like "shadow prices"; each of them shows the effect of weakening or strengthening a given inequality in (14) on the limits that can be put on some element of the admissible α in question. Thus *a priori* information, intuitive or otherwise, as to whether a given $\varphi^i(\alpha)$ in (14) is "almost zero," "not too far from zero," "very far from zero," and the like may be brought to bear on the problem.[24] In particular, this sort of analysis is likely to prove most useful when all inequalities (14) are linear ones so that, by Theorem 13, there is only one admissible α in the completely or countably identifiable case, and the solution of (15) and (6) in that admissible α is linear in the k_i, so that the "shadow prices" are constant. Such linearity is, of course, a common circumstance.

Before closing, it is probably worthwhile to discuss a problem called to my attention by Carl Christ—that of the likelihood of encountering inhomogeneous restrictions in practice. The examples that come to mind are not so satisfying as they might appear, since they generally have the property that

[22] By use of the Implicit Function Theorem, this may be done without explicit solution. This may save time by indicating what solutions are such that the remarks in the text will prove most helpful with regard to them.

[23] An oversimplified example may be of some aid here. Suppose that it is desired to estimate the consumption function:

$$C_t = a_1 Y_t + a_2 i_t$$

where C, Y, and i are consumption, income, and the rate of interest, respectively. Suppose further that, because of the accounting identity connecting income and consumption and because of other (suppressed) relations in the complete system, this equation is not identifiable but that i is exogenous. What we have been saying is exemplified by the proposition that if one is willing to prescribe $a_1 > 0$, that is, $a_1 - k = 0$, $k > 0$, one can put some limit on the possible value of a_2, possibly even discovering its sign. This is by no means a trivial proposition.

[24] In an unpublished paper, [**1**], A. C. Harberger uses intuitive belief as to somewhat different inequalities to similar effect. Of course, any maximum or minimum properties of the solutions should also be exploited.

the restriction involved is equivalent to a homogeneous restriction plus an implied normalization rule. Thus, in the example of footnote 23, if we had written $0 = \alpha_0 C_t + \alpha_1 Y_t + \alpha_2 i_t$ our restriction on the sign of α_1 would really have been a restriction on the sign of the *ratio* of α_1 to α_0 plus the normalization rule, $\alpha_0 = -1$. Using the dummy variable, k, this gives $\alpha_1 - k\alpha_0 = 0$, an homogeneous restriction. Similar remarks apply to such restrictions as requiring the parameters in a Cobb-Douglas production function to add up to one. It is frequently possible to define a new parameter in such a way as to make an apparently inhomogeneous restriction homogeneous.

There are, however, two reasons for discussing inhomogeneous restrictions nonetheless. First, such constructions as above may frequently be highly inconvenient and may exclude particular normalization rules. Thus, in the consumption function example, setting $\alpha_1 = -1$ leads to annoying complications when k is set equal to zero. Since the theorems of Section 3 only guarantee that *some* normalization rule is possible, it may be more convenient (as well as being more natural) to proceed as in footnote 23, adding the implied normalization rule explicitly (of course, adding it explicitly adds an inhomogeneous restriction so that the original inequality might just as well be left as it is). Second, it is by no means true that all inhomogeneous restrictions can be turned into homogeneous ones by means of devices such as the above. This being the case, since the theorems of Section 4 come to us with little marginal effort, it is worthwhile having them.[25]

REFERENCES

[1] HARBERGER, A. C.: *On the Estimation of Economic Parameters*, Cowles Commission Discussion Paper: Economics No. 2088, 1953 (unpublished).

[2] KAMKE, E.: *Theory of Sets* (F. Bagemihl, trans.), New York, Dover Publications, 1950.

[3] KOOPMANS, T. C., H. RUBIN, AND R. B. LEIPNIK: "Measuring the Equation Systems of Dynamic Economics," chapter II in *Statistical Inference in Dynamic Economic Models* (T. C. Koopmans, ed.), New York, John Wiley and Sons, 1950 (Cowles Commission Monograph No. 10).

[4] SAMUELSON, P. A.: "Prices of Factors and Goods in General Equilibrium," *Review of Economic Studies*, vol. XXI(1), No. 54, pp. 1-20.

[5] THRALL, R. M., AND L. TORNHEIM: *Vector Spaces and Matrices*, New York, John Wiley and Sons, 1957.

[6] WALD, A.: "Note on the Identification of Economic Relations," chapter III in *Statistical Inference in Dynamic Economic Models*.

[25] Incidentally, it is interesting to speculate on what becomes of the *a priori* restrictions of microtheory when analysis is performed on aggregates. Discussion of this problem is beyond the scope of this paper, but it is clear that we are now in a position to evaluate the effects on the identifiability of the macrosystem of the transformation of the *a priori* restrictions in the aggregation process.

ON FINITE SAMPLE DISTRIBUTIONS OF GENERALIZED CLASSICAL LINEAR IDENTIFIABILITY TEST STATISTICS*

R. L. BASMANN

In the estimation of econometric simultaneous equations models, hypothesized necessary conditions for the identifiability of a single equation usually specify the exclusion of a number of variables from the structural equation in question. If the pre-determined variables are completely exogenous, if the disturbances in the equations are jointly normally distributed, and if a moderately high degree of precision can be obtained in reduced-form estimation, then the exact finite sample distribution of the generalized classical linear *identifiability test statistic* can be closely approximated by Snedecor's F with appropriate degrees of freedom.

1. INTRODUCTION

THE purpose of this note is to make more widely known some results of a sampling experiment, Basmann [5], that have significant implications for the practical use of identifiability tests and confidence regions in econometric statistics, and that suggest potentially fruitful lines of mathematical inquiry into the question of the finite sample distributions of the former. Several conjectures about the finite sample distributions of the LVR (least variance ratio) [1, 2, 13] and GCL (generalized classical linear) [3, 14, 15] identifiability statistics have been put to test with interesting results. The derivation of these conjectures was not arbitrary. For instance, the limiting distributions of the LVR and GCL test statistics are known, [1, 2, 4, 12]; as a matter of heuristic and practical strategy, it is natural to select for initial study those finite sample distributions that possess the required limiting form and have been tabulated.[1]

Let

$$y_{.1} = Y_2\beta_2^* + X_1\gamma_1^* + X_2^*\gamma_2^* + e_{.1} \tag{1.1}$$

denote a single structural equation in a system of G structural equations. $y_{.1}$ denotes a column vector of N independent observations of an endogenous variable y_1; Y_2 denotes a matrix $(N\times\overline{G-1})$ of N independent observations of $G-1$ additional endogenous variables $y_2, y_3, \cdots, y_G$ hypothetically appearing in (1.1); X_1 denotes a matrix $(N\times K_1)$ of independent observations of *exogenous variables* (see Section 2, fin. 3) hypothetically appearing in (1.1); X_2 denotes a matrix $(N\times K_2)$, *exogenous variables* hypothetically absent from (1.1), but appearing in one or more of the reduced-form equations [13, pp. 135 ff.] corresponding to the endogenous variables $y_2, y_3, \cdots, y_G$. $\beta_2^*, \gamma_1^*, \gamma_2^*$ are column vectors of $G-1$, K_1 and K_2 components, respectively; the asterisk is used to denote population values. Finally, $e_{.1}$ denotes a column vector of N independent and identically distributed random variables with

* A part of this work was performed under Contract No. AT(45-1)-1350 between the Atomic Energy Commission and General Electric Company.

[1] A second line of attack has been inspired by the early papers of Geary [11] and Fieller [10].

$$E(e_{.1}) = 0, \tag{1.2}$$

$$E(e_{.1}e'_{.1}) = I_N\omega_{11}^*. \tag{1.3}$$

The identifiability hypothesis is

$$H_0\colon \gamma_2^* = 0. \tag{1.4}$$

We shall confine our attention to the case in which $K_2 \geq G$; that is, to over-identifying hypotheses.

Let β_2 denote a column vector of $G-1$ components defined over the space of β_2^*. Form

$$G_1(\beta_2) = (y_{.1} - Y_2\beta_2)'[I_N - X_1(X_1'X_1)^{-1}X_1'](y_{.1} - Y_2\beta_2), \tag{1.5}$$

$$G_2(\beta_2) = (y_{.1} - Y_2\beta_2)'[I_N - X(X'X)^{-1}X'](y_{.1} - Y_2\beta_2), \tag{1.6}$$

$$Q(\beta_2) = G_1(\beta_2) - G_2(\beta_2), \tag{1.7}$$

$$\phi = \frac{G_1(\beta_2) - G_2(\beta_2)}{G_2(\beta_2)} \cdot \tag{1.8}$$

GCL estimates of β_2^* are obtained by minimization of (1.7) with respect to β_2 [cf. 3]; denote these estimates by $\hat{\beta}_2$; LVR estimates of β_2^* are obtained by minimization of (1.8) [cf. 1, 2, 13]; denote these estimates by $\tilde{\beta}_2$. Finally, let

$$\hat{\phi} = \frac{G_1(\hat{\beta}_2) - G_2(\hat{\beta}_2)}{G_2(\hat{\beta}_2)}\,; \tag{1.9}$$

and

$$\tilde{\phi} = \frac{G_1(\tilde{\beta}_2) - G_2(\tilde{\beta}_2)}{G_2(\tilde{\beta}_2)} \cdot \tag{1.10}$$

If the identifiability hypothesis (1.4) is valid, then, with $N \to \infty$,

$$N\hat{\phi} \sim \chi^2, \qquad K_2 - G + 1 \text{ d.f.} \tag{1.11}$$

and

$$N\tilde{\phi} \doteqdot N \ln (1 + \tilde{\phi}) \sim \chi^2, \qquad K_2 - G + 1 \text{ d.f.} \tag{1.12}$$

under fairly general conditions [1, 2, 3, 13]. If the identifiability hypothesis (1.4) is not valid, then

$$\lim NE(\hat{\phi}) = +\infty, \tag{1.13}$$

and

$$\lim NE(\tilde{\phi}) = +\infty \tag{1.14}$$

except in a special case.[2] Consequently, the critical region (of rejection)

$$N\phi \geq \chi^2_{K_2-G+1}(\epsilon), \tag{1.15}$$

where ϕ denotes either $\hat{\phi}$ or $\tilde{\phi}$, has been proposed as a *large-sample* test of

[2] The validity of (1.4) implies that the *rank condition* holds [cf. 13, p. 138]; the converse, however, is not true.

TABLE 2a. "TRUE" REDUCED FORM EQUATIONS

$$y'_t = \pi x'_t + \eta'_t$$

	π_{i1}	π_{i2}	π_{i3}	π_{i4}	π_{i5}	π_{i6}
(2.1) $y_{t1} =$	$0.7315x_{t1}$	$-1.3424x_{t2}$	$-1.2451x_{t3}$	$+1.6965x_{t4}$		$-7.2763 + \eta_{t1}$
(2.2) $y_{t2} =$	$0.5973x_{t1}$	$-0.5136x_{t2}$	$+0.1323x_{t3}$	$+0.0447x_{t4}$		$+1.0856 + \eta_{t2}$
(2.3) $y_{t3} =$	$-0.7160x_{t1}$	$-1.5800x_{t2}$	$-0.6540x_{t3}$	$+1.1910x_{t4}$	$+0.4000$	$-10.0700 + \eta_{t3}$

TABLE 2b. VARIANCE-COVARIANCE MATRIX: REDUCED-FORM DISTURBANCES

$$\Sigma = (\sigma_{hi}) = \begin{bmatrix} 448.2882 & -63.2987 & 121.4734 \\ & 21.2150 & -20.7019 \\ & & 303.0165 \end{bmatrix}$$

TABLE 3. EXOGENOUS VARIABLES

x_1	x_2	x_3	x_4	x_5	x_6
157	64	12	79	95	1.0
170	90	25	68	72	1.0
162	67	45	67	89	1.0
166	68	24	74	81	1.0
155	56	37	70	100	1.0
159	68	12	23	98	1.0
164	61	38	51	80	1.0
147	90	10	60	72	1.0
149	54	14	23	85	1.0
163	83	15	35	79	1.0
152	50	49	87	76	1.0
170	50	14	89	86	1.0
144	88	18	21	97	1.0
141	99	32	55	97	1.0
148	97	16	47	87	1.0
141	72	25	48	103	1.0

The reduced form disturbances η_{ti} were generated from $\xi_{th} \sim n\ (0, 1)$ by the transformation:

$$\begin{aligned} \eta_1 &= 14.71815\ \xi_1 - 11.99752\ \xi_2 - 9.36609\ \xi_3 \\ \eta_2 &= 2.05985\ \xi_2 + 4.11971\ \xi_3 \\ \eta_3 &= 10.05015\ \xi_1 + 10.05015\ \xi_2 - 10.05015\ \xi_3 \end{aligned} \tag{2.1}$$

The structural equation (1.1) in Table 1 was estimated by LVR and GCL methods under the correctly specified hypothesis

$$H_0\colon \gamma_{12}^* = 0, \qquad \gamma_{13}^* = 0, \qquad \gamma_{14}^* = 0. \tag{2.2}$$

The 200 independent experimental values of $\hat{\phi}$ and $\tilde{\phi}$ have been used to test the following conjectures:

$$\text{dist. } N \ln (1 + \tilde{\phi}) \sim \chi^2,\ K_2 - \mathrm{G} + 1 \text{ d.f.}, \tag{2.3}$$

$$\text{dist. } \frac{N - K}{K_2}\, \tilde{\phi} \sim F_{K_2, N-K}, \tag{2.4}$$

$$\text{dist. } \frac{N+K}{K_2 - G + 1}\tilde{\phi} \sim F_{K_2-G+1,N-K}, \tag{2.5}$$

$$\text{dist. } N\hat{\phi} \sim \chi^2,\ K_2 - G + 1 \text{ d.f.}, \tag{2.6}$$

$$\text{dist. } \frac{N-K}{K_2}\tilde{\phi} \sim F_{K_2-G+1,N-K}, \tag{2.7}$$

$$\text{dist. } \frac{N-K}{K_2 - G + 1}\hat{\phi} \sim F_{K_2-G+1,N-K}, \tag{2.8}$$

with $N=16$, $G=3$, $K=6$, $K_2=3$. The conjectures are to be read: e.g., (2.3) the distribution of $N \ln (1+\tilde{\phi})$ can be closely approximated (numerically) by the distribution of χ^2 with K_2-G+1 degrees of freedom.

Results of tests of conjectures (2.3), (2.4), and (2.5) have been reported elsewhere in another connection [6]. Briefly, the conjectures (2.3) and (2.4) were strongly contradicted by the experimental results, which indicate that the LVR test of identifiability based on the critical region (1.15) is markedly biased against a valid identifiability hypothesis, and that the LVR test based on (1.17) is extremely biased in favor of a valid identifiability hypothesis. In the case of (2.4), the maximum deviation between the experimental distribution and the conjectured distribution was non-significant, although a slight bias in favor of the identifiability hypothesis was indicated.

In Table 4 are shown 200 independent observations of $\hat{\phi}$ arranged in order of increasing magnitude. It is believed that the values shown are correct to within one unit in the fifth decimal. The experimental mean $\bar{x}_1$ and standard deviations are shown in the heading. The empirical probability (set) function [cf. 9, pp. 56–8].

$$P_{200}\{\hat{\phi} < x\} = \frac{\nu(x)}{200}, \tag{2.9}$$

where $\nu(x)$ is the number of observed experimental values of $\hat{\phi}$ *less than* x, $x=0, .001, .002, \cdots$, is exhibited in Figure 1. Superimposed on Figure 1 are several points of the distribution functions of $\frac{1}{10}F_{1,\,10}$ and $x^2_{1/16}$.

Test of Conjecture 2.6. Since $\hat{\phi} \geq \tilde{\phi} \geq \ln (1+\tilde{\phi})$ as $\tilde{\phi} \to 0$, the unfavorable outcome of the test of conjecture (2.3), already noted, implies *a fortiori* an unfavorable outcome of the test of conjecture (2.6). Visual inspection of Figure 1 indicates a uniform and large deviation between the empirical and conjectured distribution functions, and that the critical region (1.15), $\phi=\hat{\phi}$, is strongly biased against the valid identifiability hypothesis. The maximum *absolute* deviation between the empirical probability function (2.9) and the conjectured distribution function (of $x^2_{1/16}$) is located (by visual inspection) at $x=.103$ and is approximately $d_{200}=.15$. Since the empirical probability (set) function $P_{200}(\phi<x)$, (2.9), closely approximates the empirical *distribution function* $F_{200}(x)$ defined by

$$F_{200}(x) = P_{200}\{\phi \leq x\} = \frac{n(x)}{200}, \tag{2.10}$$

TABLE 4

$\bar{x} = .13964$ $s = .33990$ med. = .05070

.00000	.00915	.05278	.15881
.00003	.00947	.05327	.15933
.00007	.01025	.05456	.16089
.00009	.01068	.05512	.16341
.00009	.01094	.05528	.16577
.00009	.01096	.05596	.17036
.00010	.01105	.05902	.17375
.00010	.01141	.05922	.17433
.00014	.01183	.05960	.17855
.00016	.01310	.06025	.18876
.00024	.01328	.06073	.19290
.00030	.01371	.06137	.19533
.00036	.01385	.06209	.19866
.00044	.01526	.06551	.20077
.00047	.01694	.06679	.20407
.00052	.01780	.06883	.21898
.00057	.01789	.07157	.21924
.00057	.01806	.07248	.22702
.00062	.01817	.07405	.23196
.00066	.01937	.07909	.23355
.00079	.01945	.08047	.23985
.00101	.02020	.08210	.25083
.00143	.02077	.08513	.25993
.00150	.02127	.08593	.26132
.00196	.02242	.08965	.27182
.00208	.02383	.09392	.28189
.00213	.02441	.09712	.29244
.00214	.02512	.09921	.30500
.00239	.02626	.10227	.30759
.00245	.02788	.10317	.32072
.00259	.03221	.10401	.32356
.00305	.03359	.10445	.33025
.00322	.03449	.10571	.35010
.00344	.03535	.11199	.35173
.00390	.03589	.11666	.35330
.00411	.03659	.11845	.36076
.00454	.03754	.11959	.38044
.00517	.03854	.12030	.41225
.00541	.03857	.12354	.42805
.00553	.03910	.12631	.43195
.00655	.04005	.12690	.46515
.00683	.04060	.12895	.49248
.00696	.04160	.12971	.54763
.00699	.04175	.13824	.58496
.00718	.04185	.14035	.59911
.00736	.04293	.14765	.81366
.00817	.04350	.14772	.87415
.00898	.04403	.15167	.99378
.00899	.04710	.15248	1.30512
.00902	.04861	.15411	4.20689

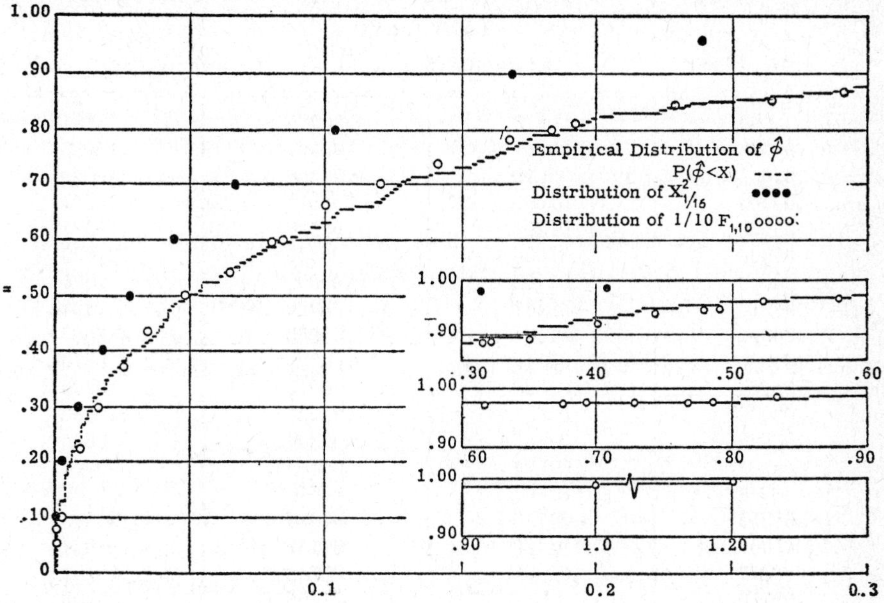

FIG. 1

where x is continuous and $n(x)$ denotes the number of observations of $\hat{\phi}$ that do not exceed x, [12], we make use of the limiting form of the Kolmogorov-Smirnov distribution in the test of this conjecture. Let $D_{200} = \sup_x |F(x) - F_{200}(x)|$ where $F(x)$ is the conjectured distribution; then

$$P\{D_{200} \geq .15\} < .01 \tag{2.11}$$

under the hypothesis that $\hat{\phi}$ is distributed like $\chi^2_{1/16}$ with one degree of freedom [cf. 8, p. 427]. This result is, as was expected, in strong contradiction to the conjecture that $16\hat{\phi} \sim \chi^2_1$. That is to say, the finite sample distribution of $16\hat{\phi}$ does not closely approximate its known large sample (asymptotic) distribution. [cf. 4, Section 5].

Test of Conjecture 2.7. A test of this conjecture would be superfluous, [cf. 6.]

Test of Conjecture 2.8. The maximum absolute deviation between the empirical probability function (2.9) in Figure 1, and the conjectured distribution is located (visually) at $x = .100$ and is approximately $d_{200} = .02$. Given that the experimental $\hat{\phi}$ is distributed as $\frac{1}{10}F_{1,10}$,

$$P\{D_{200} \geq .02\} \doteqdot 1.0. \tag{2.12}$$

A χ^2 goodness-of-fit test employing six intervals with suprema equal to the $p = .10$, .30, .50, .70, .90, points of the $\frac{1}{10}F_{1,10}$ distribution yields a criterion value

$$u = .3500, \tag{2.13}$$

from which

$$P\{\chi_5^2 \geq .3500\} > .995, \tag{2.14}$$

a result fully consistent with the result (2.12) of the Kolmogorov-Smirnov test. Visual inspection of Figure 1 leads to the conclusion that the goodness-of-fit criterion, u, would not be changed significantly by increasing the number of intervals.

The most remarkable feature of the experimental results is the almost perfect agreement between the conjectured distribution $\frac{1}{10}F_{1,10}$ and the empirical distribution of the GCL statistic $\hat{\phi}$. Indeed, even if conjecture (2.8) is valid, the extremely close fit is a rare event. For all that, the most we can validly assert is the (rather obvious) fact that the experimental results are consistent with the conjecture.

3. CONCLUSION

In the Introduction the conjectures (2.4) and (2.8) were motivated primarily on the grounds of their being consistent with the known asymptotic distributions (1.11) and (1.12) of the LVR and GCL test statistics $\tilde{\phi}$ and $\hat{\phi}$. The conjecture (2.8) was motivated, however, by more fundamental considerations intimately related to the question of what parametric conditions are sufficient to ensure that certain non-linear functions of GCL coefficient estimators $\hat{\beta}_2$, $\hat{\gamma}_1$, are approximately jointly normally distributed; these considerations involve a generalization of the early contributions of Geary [11] and Fieller [10].[4] The experimental results indicate the potential fruitfulness of further mathematical investigation of these parametric conditions.

The experimental results also indicate that it is desirable to reexamine the conclusions of empirical studies in which identifiability tests based on the critical regions (1.15) or (1.17) have been used, or in which confidence regions based on $F_{K_2,N-K}$ have been applied. Finally, it would be desirable to apply identifiability tests in some previous studies in which they have not been applied.

REFERENCES

[1] Anderson, T. W., "Estimating Linear Restrictions on Regression Coefficients for Multivariate Distributions," *Annals of Mathematical Statistics*, 22, (1951), 327–51.

[2] Anderson, T. W., and Rubin, H., "Estimation of the Parameters of a Single Equation in a Complete System of Stochastic Equations," *Annals of Mathematical Statistics*, 20, (1949), 570–82.

[3] Basmann, R. L., "A Generalized Classical Method of Linear Estimation of Coefficients in a Structural Equation," *Econometrica*, 25, (1957), 77–83.

[4] Basmann, R. L., "On the Asymptotic Distributions of Generalized Classical Linear Estimators," *Econometrica*, 28, (1960), 97–107.

[5] Basmann, R. L., "An Experimental Investigation of Some Small-Sample Properties of (GCL) Estimators of Structural Equations: Some Preliminary Results," Richland, Washington, General Electric Company, Hanford Laboratories Operation, November 21, 1958. (mimeo.)

[4] The exact joint finite sample frequency functions of the GCL estimators $\hat{\beta}_2$, γ_1 have been worked out in several leading cases. Under certain finite sample conditions their distribution functions can be closely approximated by the normal form [7, Section 3]. In the process of working through the derivations of exact distributions it is necessary to integrate the numerator of $\hat{\phi}$ (1.9) out of the joint frequency function. At that point, however, it is clear that the exact distribution of $\hat{\phi}$ can be closely (numerically) approximated by the distribution of the ratio of two independent χ^2 variables.

[6] Basmann, R. L., "An Experimental Investigation of Some Approximate Finite Sample Tests of Linear Restrictions on Matrices of Regression Coefficients," (unpublished mimeo) 1959.
[7] Basmann, R. L., *On the Exact Finite Sample Distributions of Generalized Classical Linear Structural Estimators*. TEMPO SP-91, General Electric Company, Santa Barbara, California. July 1, 1960.
[8] Birnbaum, Z. W., "Numerical Tabulation of the Distribution of Kolmogorov's Statistic for Finite Sample Size," *Journal of American Statistical Association*, 47, (1952), 425–41.
[9] Cramér, H., *Mathematical Methods of Statistics*, Princeton: Princeton University Press, 1951.
[10] Fieller, E. C., "The Distribution of the Index in a Normal Bivariate Population," *Biometrika*, 24, (1932), 428–40.
[11] Geary, R. C., "The Frequency Distribution of the Quotient of Two Normal Variates," *Journal of the Royal Statistical Society*, 93, (1930), 442–6.
[12] Kolmogorov, A. N., "Confidence Limits for an Unknown Distribution Function," *Annals of Mathematical Statistics*, 12, (1941), 461–3.
[13] Koopmans, T. C. and Hood, W. C., "The Estimation of Simultaneous Linear Economic Relationships," in *Studies in Econometric Method*, New York: John Wiley, 1953.
[14] Theil, H., "Estimation and Simultaneous Correlation in Complete Equations Systems." The Hague: Centraal Planbureau, 1953 (mimeo.).
[15] Theil, H., *Economic Forecasts and Policy*. Amsterdam: North Holland Publishing Company, 1958.
[16] Tintner, G., *Econometrics*, New York: John Wiley, 1952.

ESTIMATION OF THE PARAMETERS OF A SINGLE EQUATION IN A COMPLETE SYSTEM OF STOCHASTIC EQUATIONS[1,2]

By T. W. Anderson and Herman Rubin

1. Summary. A method is given for estimating the coefficients of a single equation in a complete system of linear stochastic equations (see expression (2.1)), provided that a number of the coefficients of the selected equation are known to be zero. Under the assumption of the knowledge of all variables in the system and the assumption that the disturbances in the equations of the system are normally distributed, point estimates are derived from the regressions of the jointly dependent variables on the predetermined variables (Theorem 1). The vector of the estimates of the coefficients of the jointly dependent variables is the characteristic vector of a matrix involving the regression coefficients and the estimate of the covariance matrix of the residuals from the regression functions. The vector corresponding to the smallest characteristic root is taken. An efficient method of computing these estimates is given in section 7. The asymptotic theory of these estimates is given in a following paper [2].

When the predetermined variables can be considered as fixed, confidence regions for the coefficients can be obtained on the basis of small sample theory (Theorem 3).

A statistical test for the hypothesis of over-identification of the single equation can be based on the characteristic root associated with the vector of point estimates (Theorem 2) or on the expression for the small sample confidence region (Theorem 4). This hypothesis is equivalent to the hypothesis that the coefficients assumed to be zero actually are zero. The asymptotic distribution of the criterion is shown in a following paper [2] to be that of χ^2.

2. A complete system of linear difference equations. In many fields of study such as economics, biology, and meteorology the occurrence of values of the observed quantities can be described in terms of a probability model which, as a first approximation, is a set of stochastic equations. Consider a (row) vector y_t of quantities which are observed at time t. Suppose that these quantities are *jointly dependent* on a vector z_t of quantities "predetermined" at time t (i.e., known without error at time t). Some of the coordinates of z_t may be coordinates

---

[1] This paper will be included in Cowles Commission Papers, New Series, No. 36.

[2] The results in this paper were presented at meetings of the Institute of Mathematical Statistics in Washington, D. C., April 12, 1946 (Washington Chapter) and in Ithaca, N. Y., August 23, 1946.

of y_{t-1}, y_{t-2}, etc.; other coordinates of z_t are quantities which are assumed given constants. The set of vectors $y_t(t = 1, 2, \cdots, T)$ are called *endogenous*. The part of the set z_t which does not consist of lagged endogenous variables is called *exogenous*; these are treated as "fixed variates." For convenience we shall think of t as indicating a point of time, although it may in many cases indicate the ordering of a sample in another dimension, or, indeed, the t may indicate simply a numbering of the observations (if z_t is entirely *exogenous*). In a dynamic economic model the endogenous variables are economic quantities such as amount of investment, interest rate, amount of consumption, etc. The exogenous variables are those quantities which are considered to be determined primarily outside the economic system, such as amount of rainfall, amount of government expenditures, time, etc.

A simple probability model may be set up on the assumption that these quantities approximately satisfy certain linear equations. Specifically the model is

$$B_{yy}y'_t + \Gamma_{yz}z'_t = \epsilon'_t \tag{2.1}$$

where ϵ_t is a (row) vector having a probability distribution with expected value zero and B_{yy} and Γ_{yz} are matrices, the former being non-singular. Primes (′) indicate transposition of vectors and matrices. If there are G jointly dependent variables, there are G component equations in (2.1); that is, there are as many equations as there are variables depending on the system. The fact that y_t and z_t do not satisfy linear equations exactly is indicated by setting the linear forms not equal to zero, but equal to random elements, called *disturbances.* We will call the component equations of (2.1) *structural* equations, for they express the structure of the system. For example, one equation involving the amount of goods consumed, the prices of these goods, the size of the national income, etc., might describe the behaviour of the consumers. Another equation involving interest rate might relate to the behaviour of investors.

It has been shown [7], [11], that in general one cannot use ordinary regression methods to estimate the matrices B_{yy} and Γ_{yz} and the parameters of an assumed distribution of the disturbances. Mann and Wald [9], for a special class of systems, and Koopmans, Rubin, and Leipnik [11], in a more general case, have obtained maximum likelihood estimates of all of the parameters for the case of the ϵ_t having a normal multivariate distribution.

Since B_{yy} is non-singular, we can rewrite (2.1) in a different form, called the *reduced form,*

$$y'_t = -B_{yy}^{-1}\Gamma_{yz}z'_t + B_{yy}^{-1}\epsilon'_t, \tag{2.2}$$

or as

$$y'_t = \Pi_{yz}z'_t + \eta'_t \tag{2.3}$$

where

$$\Pi_{yz} = -B_{yy}^{-1}\Gamma_{yz}, \tag{2.4}$$

$$\eta'_t = B_{yy}^{-1}\epsilon'_t. \tag{2.5}$$

If ϵ_t has a normal distribution, so does η_t. For a given t then, we can consider the model as specifying a distribution of y_t with conditional expected value $z_t\Pi'_{yz}$.

It is clear that we can multiply (2.1) on the left by any non-singular matrix and obtain a system of equations which defines the same distribution of y_t. On the other hand, it has been shown that the only transformations of $(B_{yy}\Gamma_{yz})$ which preserve the linearity of the system of equations are multiplications on the left by non-singular matrices. If there are a priori restrictions on $(B_{yy}\Gamma_{yz})$, the set of matrices which result in new coefficient matrices satisfying these restrictions is correspondingly decreased. If the set of admissible matric multipliers includes only diagonal matrices the system of structural equations is said to be *identified.* In this case only multiplication of all coefficients by a given constant is permitted.

Knowledge of the distribution of y_t given z_t is obviously equivalent to knowledge of Π_{yz} in (2.3) and the distribution of η_t. When the system is identified, the matrix B_{yy} and

(2.6) $$\Gamma_{yz} = -B_{yy}\Pi_{yz}$$

are determined uniquely except for multiplication on the left by a diagonal matrix. Thus identification of a system is equivalent to the possibility of inferring the structural equations from knowledge of the distribution. The estimation of all coefficients of B_{yy} and Γ_{yz} has been considered in [11].

3. A single identified equation of a complete system. In many studies the investigator may be interested only in a specific equation of the system, say,

(3.1) $$\beta_y y'_t + \gamma_z z'_t = \zeta_t,$$

where ζ_t is a scalar disturbance. The investigator may not be interested in the entire system (2.1) of which (3.1) is one component. Since a considerable amount of computation is necessary to estimate all parameters of a complete system, there arises the problem of estimating only the coefficients of a single equation. It is desirable to do this with the least possible restrictive assumptions about the part of the system which is not the selected structural equation. In order to treat the selected equation at all, we require that it is identified; that is, that there are certain restrictions on (β_y, γ_z) such that no linear combination of rows of $(B_{yy}\Gamma_{yz})$ satisfies these restrictions other than a constant times (β_y, γ_z). It is not necessary to assume that every component equation is identified; that is, that the entire system is identified.

We shall suppose that the restrictions imposed are that certain coefficients are zero. We can arrange the components of the vectors so that the restrictions are

(3.2) $$(\beta_y, \gamma_z) = (\beta, 0, \gamma, 0),$$

where

(3.3) $$\beta = (\beta^1, \cdots, \beta^H)$$

has H coefficients not assumed to be zero and

$$\gamma = (\gamma^1, \cdots, \gamma^F) \tag{3.4}$$

has F coefficients not assumed to be zero.

It will be convenient to divide the G components of y_t into two groups (in number H and $G - H$, respectively), and the K components of z_t into two groups (in number F and D respectively) according to whether or not the components enter into (3.1) with coefficients not assumed to be zero. Let

$$y_t = (x_t, r_t), \tag{3.5}$$

$$z_t = (u_t, v_t), \tag{3.6}$$

where

$$x_t = (x_{t1}, \cdots, x_{tH}), \tag{3.7}$$

$$r_t = (r_{t1}, \cdots, r_{t,G-H}), \tag{3.8}$$

$$u_t = (u_{t1}, \cdots, u_{tF}), \tag{3.9}$$

$$v_t = (v_{t1}, \cdots, v_{tD}). \tag{3.10}$$

Then the selected equation is

$$\beta x'_t + \gamma u'_t = \zeta_t . \tag{3.11}$$

Now let us see how the identification is accomplished. Partitioning Π_{yz} into H and $G - H$ rows and F and D columns as

$$\Pi_{yz} = \begin{pmatrix} \Pi^*_{xu} & \Pi_{xv} \\ \Pi_{ru} & \Pi_{rv} \end{pmatrix},$$

we can write the reduced form (2.3) as

$$x'_t = \Pi^*_{xu} u'_t + \Pi_{xv} v'_t + \delta'_t , \tag{3.12}$$

$$r'_t = \Pi_{ru} u'_t + \Pi_{rv} v'_t + \xi'_t , \tag{3.13}$$

where

$$\eta_t = (\delta_t , \xi_t).$$

Multiplying the above equation with $(\beta, 0)$ we obtain

$$\beta x'_t = \beta \Pi^*_{xu} u'_t + \beta \Pi_{xv} v'_t + \beta \delta'_t . \tag{3.14}$$

Since this must be identical to (3.11) we must have

$$\gamma = -\beta \Pi^*_{xu} , \tag{3.15}$$

$$0 = -\beta \Pi_{xv} . \tag{3.16}$$

The matrices Π^*_{xu} and Π_{xv} are defined by the distribution of x_t given u_t and v_t (for at least $K = D + F$ linearly independent values of u_t, v_t). The equation

(3.11) is identified if and only if the solution of (3.15) and (3.16) for β and γ is unique except for a constant of proportionality. This depends on the rank of Π_{xv} being $H - 1$. Thus a necessary and sufficient condition that (3.11) is identified is that the rank of x_t on v_t be $H - 1$. In particular this implies that the number of coordinates of v_t (the number of zero coefficients in γ_z) be at least $H - 1$. It can easily be shown that this condition is equivalent to requiring that the rank of the matrix obtained by selecting the $G - H$ columns of B_{yy} and the D columns of Γ_{yz} corresponding to the coefficients assumed zero in the selected equation is $G - 1$. This is the condition given by Koopmans and Rubin [11]. Other homogenous linear restrictions can be put in this form.

If the vector ϵ_t is normally distributed with mean zero the vector η_t is normally distributed with mean zero. Let the covariance matrix of δ_t be Ω_{xx}. Then the variance of $\zeta_t = \beta\delta_t'$ is

$$\sigma^2 = \beta\Omega_{xx}\beta'. \tag{3.17}$$

The constant of proportionality in β may be determined by setting the variance of ζ_t, σ^2, $= 1$; another normalization is

$$\beta^i = 1, \tag{3.18}$$

where β^i is the ith coordinate of β. In general the normalization can be written as

$$\beta\Phi_{xx}\beta' = 1, \tag{3.19}$$

where Φ_{xx} can be either a known constant or can be a known function of unknown parameters.

As an estimation procedure for β and γ and $D = H - 1$, M. A. Girschick suggested in an unpublished note that one solve equations (3.15) and (3.16) with (Π^*_{xu}, Π_{xv}) replaced by $(P^*_{xu}P_{xv})$, the sample regression of x on u and v. By these means Girschick found confidence regions (see section 8) for the parameters of a two equation system. A similar idea lies behind a method of O. Reiersøl [10].

The present paper develops a method for handling the case of $D \geq H$. In this case the rank of P_{xv} is usually H, thus giving no admissible estimate of β. The proposed method follows the approach used in discriminant problems.

In a second paper [2] the present authors shall give asymptotic properties of these estimates that give a certain justification for the use of them. Under very general assumptions concerning the v_t and the ϵ_t we prove that these estimates are consistent. These hypotheses permit the investigator to neglect some predetermined variables absent from his particular equation. Alternative assumptions include the case of the other $G - 1$ equations being non-linear. Finally, it is shown that the estimates are asymptotically normally distributed. For this result it is not necessary to assume that the disturbances are normally distributed, or even that they have identical distributions.

4. A description of the estimation procedure. In a sense the dependence of the endogenous variables x_t on the predetermined variables u_t and v_t is given by the matrix $(\Pi^*_{xu}\ \Pi_{xv})$ of regression coefficients of x_t on u_t and v_t. The interdependence of the coordinates of x_t indicated by the selected equation nullifies the dependence on v_t; that is,

$$\beta \Pi_{xv} = 0. \tag{4.1}$$

Suppose we wish to estimate β and γ from a sample of T observations: (x_1, z_1), (x_2, z_2), $\cdots$ (x_T, z_T). The information we need can be summarized in the second order moment matrices

$$M_{xx} = \frac{1}{T}\sum_{t=1}^{T} x'_t x_t, \tag{4.2}$$

$$M_{xz} = (M_{xu} M_{xv}) = \frac{1}{T}\left(\sum_{t=1}^{T} x'_t u_t \sum_{t=1}^{T} x'_t v_t\right), \tag{4.3}$$

$$M_{zz} = \begin{pmatrix} M_{uu} & M_{uv} \\ M_{vu} & M_{vv} \end{pmatrix} = \frac{1}{T}\begin{pmatrix} \sum_{t=1}^{T} u'_t u_t & \sum_{t=1}^{T} u'_t v_t \\ \sum_{t=1}^{T} v'_t u_t & \sum_{t=1}^{T} v'_t v_t \end{pmatrix}. \tag{4.4}$$

Since one coordinate of u_t may be unity there is no advantage in taking these moments about the mean. We shall find it more convenient to use instead of v_t the part of v_t that is orthogonal to u_t; that is, we shall use

$$s'_t = v'_t - M_{vu} M_{uu}^{-1} u'_t. \tag{4.5}$$

The moments are then M_{xx}, M_{xu}, M_{uu},

$$M_{xs} = M_{xv} - M_{xu} M_{uu}^{-1} M_{uv}, \tag{4.6}$$

and

$$M_{ss} = M_{vv} - M_{vu} M_{uu}^{-1} M_{uv}. \tag{4.7}$$

We can express the reduced form as

$$x'_t = \Pi_{xu} u'_t + \Pi_{xs} s'_t + \delta'_t, \tag{4.8}$$

where

$$\begin{aligned} \Pi_{xu} &= \Pi^*_{xu} + \Pi_{xv} M_{vu} M_{uu}^{-1}, \\ \Pi_{xs} &= \Pi_{xv}. \end{aligned} \tag{4.9}$$

An estimate of Π_{xs} is the regression of x on s,

$$P_{xs} = M_{xs} M_{ss}^{-1}. \tag{4.10}$$

To estimate β we take the β that makes βP_{xs} smallest in the metric determined by the moment matrix of the residuals

$$W_{xx} = M_{xx} - P_{xs} M_{ss} P'_{xs} - P_{xu} M_{uu} P'_{xu}, \tag{4.11}$$

where

(4.12) $$P_{xu} = M_{xu}M_{uu}^{-1} .$$

This is the natural generalization of least squares; the greatest weight is given to the component with least variance. This estimate is the vector satisfying

(4.13) $$(P_{xs}M_{ss}P'_{xs} - \nu W_{xx})b' = 0$$

which is associated with the smallest root of

(4.14) $$| P_{xs}M_{ss}P'_{xs} - \nu W_{xx} | = 0.$$

This is normalized and the estimate of γ is $-bP_{xu}$.

In section 5 we derive these estimates by the method of maximum likelihood under certain assumptions. Although it is assumed that the disturbances are normally distributed for this derivation, the estimates can be used in more general situations. This theory is in one sense a special case of the theory of estimating a matrix of means of a given dimensionality which is an extension of the discriminant function theory [5]. For an application of this method of estimation see [6].

5. Derivation of maximum likelihood estimates. We derive the estimates of β, γ, and σ^2 under the following assumptions:

ASSUMPTION A. *The selected structural equation*

(3.11) $$\beta x'_t + \gamma u'_t = \zeta_t$$

is one equation of a complete linear system of G stochastic equations. The equation is identified by the fact that if H is the number of coordinates in x_t there are at least $H - 1$ coordinates in v_t, the vector of predetermined variables not in (3.11) *but in the system.*

ASSUMPTION B. *At time t all of the coordinates of $z_t = (u_t, v_t)$ are given.*

ASSUMPTION C. *The coordinates of z_t are given functions of exogenous variables and of coordinates of $y_{t-1}, y_{t-2}, \cdots$. If coordinates of $y_0, y_{-1}, \cdots$ are involved in z_t, they will be considered as given numbers. The moment matrix M_{ss} is non-singular with probability one.*

ASSUMPTION D. *The disturbance vectors δ_t are distributed serially independently and normally with mean zero and covariance matrix Ω_{xx}.*

We shall consider normalizations (3.19) where Φ_{xx} may be a function of other parameters, but

(5.1) $$\partial\Phi_{xx}/\partial\beta = 0.$$

We can state the results in a theorem:

THEOREM 1. *Under assumptions A, B, C, and D the maximum likelihood estimate of β is*

(5.2) $$\hat{\beta} = b/\sqrt{b\hat{\Phi}_{xx}b'},$$

where b is the solution of

$$(4.13) \qquad (P_{xs}M_{ss}P'_{xs} - \nu W_{xx})b' = 0$$

corresponding to the smallest value of ν *and* P_{xs} *is defined by* (4.10), M_{ss} *by* (4.6), *and* W_{xx} *by* (4.11). *An estimate of* γ *based on the maximum likelihood estimate* $\hat{\Pi}_{xu}$ *is given by*

$$(5.3) \qquad \hat{\gamma} = -\hat{\beta}P_{xu} ,$$

where P_{xu} *is given by* (4.12). *The estimate of* σ^2 *is*

$$(5.4) \qquad \hat{\sigma}^2 = (1 + \nu)/b\hat{\Phi}_{xx}b'$$

if

$$(5.5) \qquad bWb' = 1.$$

We apply the method of maximum likelihood to

$$(5.6) \qquad L = (2\pi)^{-\frac{1}{2}TH} \,|\, \Omega_{xx}^{-1} \,|^{\frac{1}{2}T} \exp\left\{-\tfrac{1}{2}\sum_{t=1}^{T} (x_t - z_t\,\Pi'_{xz})\Omega_{xx}^{-1}(x'_t - \Pi_{xz}z'_t)\right.$$

under the restrictions (4.1) and (3.19). Replacing v_t by s_t and adding (4.1) and (3.19) multiplied by Lagrange multipliers λ (a vector of D coordinates) and ϕ respectively to the logarithm of L we obtain after division by T

$$(5.7) \qquad \begin{aligned} A = {} & -\tfrac{1}{2}H \log 2\pi + \tfrac{1}{2} \log |\, \Omega_{xx}^{-1} \,| + \beta\Pi_{xs}\lambda' + \phi(\beta\Phi_{xx}\beta' - 1) \\ & - \frac{1}{2T}\sum_{t=1}^{T} (x_t - u_t\Pi'_{xu} - s_t\Pi'_{xs})\Omega_{xx}^{-1}(x'_t - \Pi_{xu}u'_t - \Pi_{xs}s'_t). \end{aligned}$$

Differentiating (5.7) with respect to β, we obtain

$$(5.8) \qquad \frac{\partial A}{\partial \beta} = \Pi_{xs}\lambda' + 2\phi\Phi_{xx}\beta' .$$

Setting this equal to zero and multiplying by β, we have

$$\beta\Pi_{xs}\lambda' + 2\phi\beta\Phi_{xx}\beta' = 0.$$

By virtue of (4.1) and (3.19), the Lagrange multiplier ϕ must be zero. Hence, as far as the derivarives of (5.7) are concerned the restriction (3.19) does not enter. The setting of the derivatives of (5.7) equal to zero and (4.1) will define $\hat{\beta}$ except for a constant of proportionality which is finally determined by (3.19). For convenience in deriving the estimates we shall use the normalization

$$(5.9) \qquad \beta\Omega_{xx}\beta' = 1.$$

The derivatives of (5.7) with respect to the coordinates of Ω_{xx} , Π_{xu} , Π_{xs} , and β are set equal to zero, resulting in

$$(5.10) \qquad \begin{aligned} \hat{\Omega}_{xx} = {} & M_{xx} - M_{xs}\hat{\Pi}'_{xs} - M_{xu}\hat{\Pi}'_{xu} - \hat{\Pi}_{xs}M_{sx} \\ & - \hat{\Pi}_{xu}M_{ux} + \hat{\Pi}_{xu}M_{uu}\hat{\Pi}'_{xu} + \hat{\Pi}_{xs}M_{ss}\hat{\Pi}'_{xs} , \end{aligned}$$

$$(5.11)\qquad \hat{\Omega}_{xx}^{-1}(M_{xs} - \hat{\Pi}_{xs}M_{ss}) + \hat{\beta}'\hat{\lambda} = 0,$$

$$(5.12)\qquad \hat{\Omega}_{xx}^{-1}(M_{xu} - \hat{\Pi}_{xu}M_{uu}) = 0,$$

$$(5.13)\qquad \hat{\Pi}_{xs}\hat{\lambda}' = 0.$$

Solving (5.12) for $\hat{\Pi}_{xu}$, we obtain

$$(5.14)\qquad \hat{\Pi}_{xu} = P_{xu}$$

defined by (4.12). Solving (5.11) for $\hat{\Pi}_{xs}$, we obtain

$$(5.15)\qquad \hat{\Pi}_{xs} = P_{xs} + \hat{\Omega}_{xx}\hat{\beta}'\hat{\lambda}M_{ss}^{-1}.$$

Multiplying (5.15) by $\hat{\beta}$ and solving for $\hat{\lambda}$, we obtain

$$(5.16)\qquad \hat{\lambda} = -\hat{\beta}P_{xs}M_{ss}.$$

Substitution into (5.15) gives

$$(5.17)\qquad \hat{\Pi}_{xs} = (I - \hat{\Omega}_{xx}\hat{\beta}'\hat{\beta})P_{xs}.$$

In view of (5.14) and (5.17) we can write (5.10) as

$$(5.18)\qquad \hat{\Omega}_{xx} = W_{xx} + \hat{\Omega}_{xx}\hat{\beta}'\hat{\beta}P_{xs}M_{ss}P'_{xs}\hat{\beta}'\hat{\beta}\hat{\Omega}_{xx}.$$

Let

$$(5.19)\qquad \hat{\beta}P_{xs}M_{ss}P'_{xs}\hat{\beta}' = \mu.$$

Then multiplication of (5.18) on the right by $\hat{\beta}'$ with use of (5.9) gives

$$\begin{aligned}\hat{\Omega}_{xx}\hat{\beta}' &= W_{xx}\hat{\beta}' + \hat{\Omega}_{xx}\hat{\beta}'\hat{\beta}P_{xs}M_{ss}P'_{xs}\hat{\beta}' \\ &= W_{xx}\hat{\beta}' + \mu\hat{\Omega}_{xx}\hat{\beta}',\end{aligned}$$

that is,

$$(5.20)\qquad \hat{\Omega}_{xx}\hat{\beta}' = \frac{1}{1-\mu} W_{xx}\hat{\beta}'.$$

Equation (5.13) can be written as

$$(5.21)\qquad P_{xs}M_{ss}P'_{xs}\hat{\beta}' - \mu\hat{\Omega}_{xx}\hat{\beta}' = 0$$

by substitution from (5.16), (5.17) and (5.19). Combining (5.20) and (5.21) we obtain

$$(5.22)\qquad (P_{xs}M_{ss}P'_{xs} - \nu W_{xx})\hat{\beta}' = 0,$$

where

$$(5.23)\qquad \nu = \mu/(1-\mu).$$

For (5.22) to have a solution, ν must be a root of

$$(4.14)\qquad |P_{xs}M_{ss}P'_{xs} - \nu W_{xx}| = 0.$$

Substituting from (5.20) into (5.18) we obtain

$$(5.24)\qquad \hat{\Omega}_{xx} = W_{xx} + \mu\left(\frac{1}{1-\mu}\right)^2 W_{xx}\hat{\beta}'\hat{\beta}W_{xx} = W_{xx} + \nu(1+\nu)W_{xx}\hat{\beta}'\hat{\beta}W_{xx}.$$

To determine which root of (4.14) to use we shall compute the value of the likelihood function when these estimates are used. It will be convenient to use the solution b of (4.13) with normalization (5.5). Thus b is proportional to $\hat{\beta}$; in fact, since

$$\hat{\beta}\hat{\Omega}_{xx}\hat{\beta}' = \frac{1}{1-\mu}\hat{\beta}W_{xx}\hat{\beta}'$$

from (5.20), we see that

$$\hat{\beta} = b\sqrt{1-\mu} = b/\sqrt{1+\nu}.$$

Let the other solutions of (4.13) be $b_2, \cdots, b_H$, with corresponding roots $\nu_2, \cdots, \nu_H$, and

$$B^* = \begin{pmatrix} b \\ b_2 \\ \cdot \\ \cdot \\ \cdot \\ b_H \end{pmatrix}.$$

Since

(5.25) $$|\hat{\Omega}_{xx}| = |W_{xx} + \nu W_{xx}b'bW_{xx}|,$$

we have

(5.26) $$|B^*||\hat{\Omega}_{xx}||B^{*\prime}| = |I + \nu B^*W_{xx}b'bW_{xx}B^{*\prime}|.$$

Since

$$bW_{xx}B^{*\prime} = (1, 0, \cdots, 0),$$

and since

$$|B^*|^2 = |W_{xx}|^{-1},$$

we deduce from (5.26)

$$|\hat{\Omega}_{xx}| = |W_{xx}|(1+\nu).$$

Multiplying (5.10) by $\hat{\Omega}_{xx}^{-1}$, taking the trace, and substituting in (5.6) we obtain

(5.27) $$\hat{L} = (2\pi e)^{-\frac{1}{2}TH}|W_{xx}|^{-\frac{1}{2}T}(1+\nu)^{-\frac{1}{2}T}.$$

This is a maximum if ν is the smallest root of (4.14).

The theorem now results. The expression for $\hat{\sigma}^2$ follows from

$$\hat{\sigma}^2 = \hat{\beta}\hat{\Omega}_{xx}\hat{\beta}' = b\hat{\Omega}_{xx}b'/b\hat{\Phi}_{xx}b'.$$

If Φ_{xx} is a known constant matrix, $\hat{\Phi}_{xx} = \Phi_{xx}$; if Φ_{xx} is a function of the parameters, $\hat{\Phi}_{xx}$ is the same function of the estimates.

If we define

$$\hat{\gamma} = -\hat{\beta}\hat{\Pi}^{*}_{xu}, \tag{5.28}$$

we have by (4.9)

$$\hat{\gamma} = -\hat{\beta}(\hat{\Pi}_{xu} - \hat{\Pi}_{xs}M_{su}M_{uu}^{-1}). \tag{5.29}$$

Since $\hat{\beta}$ annihilates $\hat{\Pi}_{xs}$, (5.3) results.

The estimate of Π_{xv} is given by (5.17) and the estimate of Ω_{xx} is

$$\hat{\Omega}_{xx} = W_{xx} + \nu W_{xx}b'bW_{xx}. \tag{5.30}$$

6. The likelihood ratio test of restrictions. It has been assumed that the selected structural equation is identified by imposing the restrictions that certain coefficients are zero. It was noted in Section 3 that at least $G - 1$ such restrictions are necessary. If D, the number of restrictions on the predetermined variables, is more than $H - 1$, we can test the hypothesis that these D coefficients are zero against the alternative that only a smaller number are zero. This is equivalent to a test that Π_{xv} is of rank $H - 1$ against the alternative that the rank is H.

It can be seen intuitively that the smallest root ν of (4.14) indicates how near P_{xs} is to being singular. This statistic can be used to test the hypothesis that Π_{xv} is of rank $H - 1$. The test is similar to the test of rank suggested by P. L. Hsu [8]. The test is stated precisely in the following theorem:

THEOREM 2. *Under assumptions A, B, C, and D the likelihood ratio criterion for testing the hypothesis that Π_{xv} is of rank $H - 1$ against the alternative that it is of rank H is*

$$(1 + \nu)^{-\frac{1}{2}T}, \tag{6.1}$$

where ν is the smallest root of (4.14).

PROOF. If there is no restriction on Π_{xs}, the maximum likelihood estimate of Π_{xs} is P_{xs}, of Π_{xu} is P_{xu}, and of Ω_{xx} is W_{xx}. Then the likelihood function is

$$(2\pi e)^{-\frac{1}{2}TH} \mid W_{xx} \mid^{-\frac{1}{2}T}. \tag{6.2}$$

The ratio between this and the likelihood function (5.27) maximized under the hypothesis that the rank of Π_{xv} is $H - 1$ is (6.1).

It is proved in the paper following the present one that under certain conditions (more general than those of Theorem 2)

$$-2 \log [(1 + \nu)^{-\frac{1}{2}T}] = T \log (1 + \nu) \tag{6.3}$$

is distributed asymptotically as χ^2 with $D - H + 1$ degrees of freedom. Thus an approximate test of significance is given by comparing (6.3) with a significance point of the χ^2-distribution with degrees of freedom equal to the excess number of coefficients required to be zero (i.e., the number beyond the minimum required for identification).

7. Computational procedure. The estimation procedure in sections 4 and 5 does not indicate the most efficient method for computing those estimates. The procedure given here is believed to be efficient for ordinary computational equipment and can easily be adapted for sequence-controlled computing machines.

Let us see what expressions occur in the estimation procedure for β and γ. We find that we must first know $P_{xs}M_{ss}P'_{xs}$, W_{xx}, and P_{xu}; these will suffice if Φ_{xx} is constant or Ω_{xx} to estimate β, γ, and σ^2. In what follows, we shall assume the normalization is $\beta^1 = 1$, as the results for other normalizations follow immediately. Examining the estimation equations, we see that we may use any matrices proportional to the moment matrices. If equation (3.11) has a constant term, it is better to use moments about the mean and estimate the constant term by setting the calculated mean of the disturbances equal to zero. One possible method of correcting for the mean is to calculate

$$m^*_{pq} = T \sum_{t=1}^{T} p_t q_t - \left(\sum_{t=1}^{T} p_t\right)\left(\sum_{t=1}^{T} q_t\right). \tag{7.1}$$

The estimation procedure for β, σ^2, and the remainder of γ is not affected by correcting for the mean. The computational procedure indicated here is unchanged except for a factor of proportionality in the equation for σ^2 if a different form of correction for the mean is used.

7.1. *Calculation of $M_{xz}M_{zz}^{-1}M_{zx}$ and W_{xx}.* It is known that

$$W_{xx} = M_{xx} - M_{xz}M_{zz}^{-1}M_{zx}. \tag{7.2}$$

We shall use (7.2) to compute W_{xx}. We shall compute $M_{xz}M_{zz}^{-1}M_{zx}$ by the method given by Dwyer [4]. Let us denote the element in the ith row and jth column of M_{zz} by a_{ij}, and the element in the ith row and jth column of M_{zx} by b_{ij}. Let us construct the following array

$$\begin{array}{llllllll}
c_{11} & c_{12} & \cdots & c_{1K} & e_{11} & e_{12} & \cdots & e_{1H} \\
d_{11} & d_{12} & \cdots & d_{1K} & f_{11} & f_{12} & \cdots & f_{1H} \\
 & c_{22} & \cdots & c_{2K} & e_{21} & e_{22} & \cdots & e_{2H} \\
 & d_{22} & \cdots & d_{2K} & f_{21} & f_{22} & \cdots & f_{2H} \\
 & & \cdots & & & & \cdots & \\
 & & & c_{KK} & e_{K1} & e_{K2} & \cdots & e_{KH} \\
 & & & d_{KK} & f_{K1} & f_{K2} & \cdots & f_{KH}
\end{array}$$

where

$$c_{ij} = a_{ij} - \sum_{k<i} d_{ki} c_{kj}, \qquad 1 \le i \le j \le k,$$

$$e_{ij} = b_{ij} - \sum_{k<i} d_{ki} e_{ki}, \qquad 1 \le i \le k, 1 \le j \le H$$

$$d_{ij} = \frac{c_{ij}}{c_{ii}}, \qquad 1 \le i \le j \le K,$$

$$f_{ij} = \frac{e_{ij}}{c_{ii}}, \qquad 1 \le i \le K, 1 \le j \le H.$$

Then the element in the ith row and jth column of the symmetric matrix $M_{xz}M_{zz}^{-1}M_{zx}$ is

$$\sum_{k=1}^{K} e_{ki} f_{kj} .$$

If we wish to estimate several equations in the system by this method, this step need only be done once, as $M_{xz}M_{zz}^{-1}M_{zx}$ and W_{xx} do not depend upon the equation (except that x would be enlarged).

7.2. *Computation of* P_{xu}. We shall compute P_{xu} by the abbreviated Doolittle method. Let us now denote the element in the ith row and jth column of M_{uu} by a_{ij}, of M_{ux} by b_{ij}. Then let us perform the previous operations, not including the last step. We may arrange the work, if only one equation is to be estimated, so that this is already done. Then define

$$g_{ij} = f_{ij} - \sum_{i<k\leq F} d_{ik} g_{kj}, \qquad 1 \leq i \leq F, 1 \leq j \leq H.$$

Then the element in the ith row and jth column of P_{xu} is g_{ji}.

7.3. *Computation of* $P_{xs}M_{ss}P'_{xs}$. We know that

$$P_{xs}M_{ss}P'_{xs} = M_{xz}M_{zz}^{-1}M_{zx} - M_{xu}M_{uu}^{-1}M_{ux}. \tag{7.3}$$

Let us compute $P_{xs}M_{ss}P'_{xs}$, using (7.3). We must first calculate $M_{xu}M_{uu}^{-1}M_{ux}$. We may do this either by the method of section 7.1, or as $P_{xu}M_{ux}$.

7.4. *Computation of* ν, $\hat{\beta}$, *and* $\hat{\gamma}$. We shall use

$$\hat{\gamma} = -\hat{\beta} P_{xu} \tag{5.3}$$

to compute $\hat{\gamma}$ after has$\hat{\beta}$ been computed.

Case 1) $H = 1$. In this case the vector $\hat{\beta} = (1)$, $\nu = P_{xs}M_{ss}P'_{xs}/W_{xx}$.

Case 2) $H = 2$, $D > 1$. Let a_{ij} denote the element in the ith row and jth column of $P_{xs}M_{ss}P'_{xs}$, w_{ij} the element in the ith row and jth column of W_{xx}. Define

$$k_0 = | P_{xs}M_{ss}P'_{xs} |,$$

$$k_1 = | W_{xx} |$$

$$k_2 = \tfrac{1}{2}(a_{11}w_{22} + a_{22}w_{11} - 2a_{12}w_{12}).$$

Then

$$\nu = \frac{k_2 - \sqrt{k_2^2 - k_0 k_1}}{k_1}.$$

Let $\hat{\Theta} = P_{xs}M_{ss}P'_{xs} - \nu W_{xx}$. Then

$$\hat{\beta}^1 = 1,$$

$$\hat{\beta}^2 = -\frac{\hat{\theta}_{11}}{\hat{\theta}_{12}} = -\frac{\hat{\theta}_{21}}{\hat{\theta}_{22}}.$$

Case 3) $H = 2, D = 1$. In this case $\nu = 0$. Then $\hat{\Theta} = P_{xs}M_{ss}P'_{xs}$, and $\hat{\beta}$ may be computed as before.

Case 4) $H > 2, D > H - 1$. Using the procedure of section 7.2, compute $A = (P_{xs}M_{ss}P)'^{-1}_{xs}W_{xx}$. Let us multiply equation (5.22) by $-\frac{1}{\nu}(P_{xs}M_{ss}P'_{xs})^{-1}$, and set $1/\nu = \lambda$. We obtain

$$(A - \lambda I)\hat{\beta}' = 0, \tag{7.4}$$

where λ is the largest characteristic root of A. Then we may employ the method of Aitken [1] to estimate λ and $\hat{\beta}$. Let q_0 be an approximation to $\hat{\beta}$. The column of A with largest absolute values is generally a satisfactory approximation. Define

$$q'_i = Aq'_{i-1},$$

$$\lambda_{ij} = \frac{q^j_i}{q^j_{i-1}}.$$

The quantities λ_{ij} approach λ as i increases, and the normalized vectors q_i approach $\hat{\beta}$. The convergence may be accelerated by the methods given by Aitken. The normalization should not be carried out until the λ_{ij} are sufficiently close for different j.

Case 5) $H > 2, D = H - 1$. Let us go through the procedure of section 7.2 with $A = P_{xs}M_{ss}P'_{xs}$, and with no matrix B. Then $c_{HH} = 0$. Set $g_H = 1$, and compute

$$g_i = -\sum_{i<k\leq H} d_{ik}\, g_k,$$

Then

$$\beta^i = \frac{g_i}{g_1}, \qquad \nu = 0.$$

7.5. *Computation of* $\hat{\sigma}^2$. We have

$$\hat{\sigma}^2 = \hat{\beta}\Omega_{xx}\hat{\beta}' = (1 + \nu)\hat{\beta}W_{xx}\hat{\beta}'. \tag{7.5}$$

If we use the m^*'s instead of the m's, we must divide by T^2, and if other factors of proportionality are used, we must divide by them. σ^2 is in general biased, but the bias depends upon the nature of the complete system, and is not easy to calculate. The bias is of the order of $1/T$.

8. Confidence regions based on small sample theory.[5] If all of the predetermined variables in the system are exogenous (i.e., "fixed"), we can obtain confidence regions for the coefficients of one equation on the basis of small sample theory. To do this we require only that the disturbance of the selected equation be normally distributed; that is, the linear form in the observations $\beta x'_t + \gamma u'_t$

[5] We are indebted to Professor A. Wald for assistance in simplifying our approach to this problem.

is normally distributed with mean zero and variance σ^2. The regression of this on fixed variates is normally distributed and certain quadratic forms in these linear forms have χ^2-distributions. On the basis of this we can set up confidence regions for the coefficients..

In addition to assumptions A and B we use the following:

ASSUMPTION E. *All of the coordinates of $z_t = (u_t\ v_t)$ are exogenous. The moment matrix M_{zz} is non-singular. The disturbances of the selected equation are distributed independently and normally with mean 0 and variance σ^2.*

Suppose we have a set of observations $(x_1, u_1, v_1), \cdots (x_T, u_T, v_T)$. If we know β and γ we can obtain T values of

$$w_t = \beta x_t' + \gamma u_t', \qquad t = 1, \cdots, T. \tag{8.1}$$

The sample regression coefficients of w_t on u_t and s_t are

$$c = \frac{1}{T}\sum_{t=1}^{T} w_t u_t M_{uu}^{-1} = \beta M_{xu} M_{uu}^{-1} + \gamma, \tag{8.1}$$

$$e = \frac{1}{T}\sum_{c=1}^{T} w_t s_t M_{ss}^{-1} = \beta M_{xs} M_{ss}^{-1}. \tag{8.3}$$

The two vectors c and e are distributed independently and normally with mean 0 and covariance matrices

$$\mathcal{E}(c'c) = \sigma^2 M_{uu}^{-1}, \tag{8.4}$$

$$\mathcal{E}(e'e) = \sigma^2 M_{ss}^{-1}, \tag{8.5}$$

Hence (by usual regression theory)

$$C = \frac{1}{\sigma^2} c M_{uu} c' = \frac{1}{\sigma^2}[\beta M_{xu} M_{uu}^{-1} M_{ux}\beta' + \beta M_{xu}\gamma' + \gamma M_{ux}\beta' + \gamma M_{uu}\gamma], \tag{8.6}$$

$$E = \frac{1}{\sigma^2} e M_{ss} e' = \frac{1}{\sigma^2}\beta M_{xs} M_{ss}^{-1} M_{sx}\beta' \tag{8.7}$$

$$= \frac{1}{\sigma^2}\beta(M_{xv} - M_{xu}M_{uu}^{-1}M_{uv})(M_{vv} - M_{vu}M_{uu}^{-1}M_{uv})^{-1}(M_{vx} - M_{vu}M_{uu}^{-1}M_{ux})\beta',$$

$$A = \frac{1}{\sigma^2}\left(\frac{1}{T}\sum_{t=1}^{T} w_t^2 - C - E\right) = \frac{1}{\sigma^2}\beta W_{xx}\beta', \tag{8.8}$$

are distributed independently as χ^2 with F, D, and $T - K$ degrees of freedom, respectively. The ratio of any two has an F-distribution.

On the basis of these considerations we can obtain the desired confidence regions.

THEOREM 3. *Suppose assumptions A, B, and E are true. If the normalization is*

$$\beta \Phi_{xx} \beta' = 1. \tag{8.9}$$

where Φ_{xx} *is a given matrix, (a) a confidence region for* β *of confidence* ϵ *consists of all* β^* *satisfying* (8.9) *and*

$$(8.10) \qquad \frac{\beta^* M_{xs} M_{ss}^{-1} M_{sx} \beta^{*\prime}}{\beta^* W_{xx} \beta^{*\prime}} \cdot \frac{T-K}{D} \leq F_{D,T-K,}(\epsilon),$$

where $F_{D,T-K}(\epsilon)$ *is chosen so the probability of* (8.10) *for* $\beta^* = \beta$ *is* ϵ. (*b*). *A confidence region for* β *and* γ *simultaneously consists of all* β^* *and* γ^* *satisfying* (8.9) *and*

$$(8.11) \qquad \frac{\beta^* M_{xu} M_{uu}^{-1} M_{ux} \beta^{*\prime} + \beta^* M_{xu} \gamma^{*\prime} + \gamma^* M_{xu} \beta^{*\prime} + \gamma^* M_{uu} \gamma^* + \beta^* M_{xs} M_{ss}^{-1} M_{sx} \beta^{*\prime}}{\beta^* W_{xx} \beta^{*\prime}} \cdot \frac{T-K}{K} \leq F_{K,T-K}(\epsilon).$$

(*c*) *If the normalization is* $\sigma^2 = 1$, *then a confidence region for* β *of confidence* $\epsilon_1\epsilon_2$ *consists of all* β^* *satisfying*

$$(8.12) \qquad \beta^* M_{xs} M_{ss}^{-1} M_{sx} \beta^{*\prime} \leq \chi_D^2(\epsilon_1),$$

$$(8.13) \qquad \underline{\chi}^2_{T-K}(\epsilon_2) \leq \beta^* W_{xx} \beta^{*\prime} \leq \bar{\chi}^2_{T-K}(\epsilon_2),$$

where $\chi_D^2(\epsilon_1)$ *is chosen so that the probability of* (8.12) *is* ϵ_1 *when* $\beta^* = \beta$ *and* $\underline{\chi}^2_{T-K}(\epsilon_2)$ *and* $\bar{\chi}^2_{T-K}(\epsilon_2)$ *are chosen so that the probability of* (8.13) *is* ϵ_2 *when* $\beta^* = \beta$ *and*

$$(8.14) \qquad \underline{\chi}^2(\epsilon_2) \leq 1 \leq \bar{\chi}^2(\epsilon_2).$$

(*d*) *A confidence region for* β *and* γ *simultaneously consists of all* β^* *and* γ^* *satisfying* (8.13) *and*

$$(8.15) \qquad \beta^* M_{xu} M_{uu}^{-1} M_{ux} \beta^{*\prime} + \beta^* M_{xu} \gamma^{*\prime} + \gamma^* M_{ux} \beta^{*\prime} + \gamma^* M_{uu} \gamma^{*\prime} + \beta^* M_{xs} M_{ss}^{-1} M_{sx} \beta^{*\prime} \leq \chi_K^2(\epsilon_1).$$

Region (c) is the interior of an ellipsoid and an ellipsoidal shell in the β^*-space; region (d) is similar in the β^*, γ^*-space. Region (a) consists of the intersection of the quadric surface (8.9) and the interior of a cone in the β^*-space; region (b) is similar in the β^*, γ^*-space.

It is clear that there are many other ways of constructing confidence regions by taking regression on other fixed variates. Of these the best seem to be those of theorem 3. It has been proved [2] that the regions of theorem 3 are consistent in the sense that for sufficiently large T the probability is arbitrarily near 1 that all of the confidence region is within a certain distance of β or β, γ. For an application of this technique to economic data see a paper by Bartlett [3] who suggested this method independently.

9. An approximate small sample test of restrictions. When $\beta^* = \beta$, the probability of (8.10) is ϵ. If β^* is replaced by $\hat{\beta}$ which minimizes the expression on the left, the probability is at least as great; it is, say, $1 - \delta$. This ratio is λ, the smallest root of

$$\left| \frac{1}{D} M_{xs} M_{ss}^{-1} M_{sx} - \lambda \frac{T}{T-K} W_{xx} \right| = 0, \tag{9.1}$$

Since

$$\lambda = \frac{T-K}{TD} \nu, \tag{9.2}$$

where ν is the smallest root of (4.14), the probability of

$$\nu \geq \frac{TD}{T-K} F_{D,T-K}(\epsilon) \tag{9.3}$$

is $\delta \leq (1 - \epsilon)$. We summarize this as follows:

THEOREM 4. *Under assumptions A, B, and E, the inequality* (9.3), *where* ν *is the smallest root of* (4.14), *constitutes a test of the hypothesis that the coefficients of* v_t *in the selected structural equation are zero of significance less than* $1 - \epsilon$.

This test is simply an approximation to the test given in section 6. The exact probability, δ, of (9.3) is unknown; in fact the distribution of ν depends on Π_{zv} and the distribution of δ_t. However, since δ lies between 0 and $1 - \epsilon$, we know that if the test is used as though the level were $1 - \epsilon$, the test will be "conservative."

Another approximate test of the restrictions can be obtained from the inequality (8.11). If the hypothesis is rejected on the basis of one of these tests, the corresponding confidence region (for β or for β and γ) is imaginary, for all β or β and γ are excluded. It should be noticed that the use of a given ratio to test the hypothesis at significance level $\delta(\leq 1 - \epsilon)$ does not affect the confidence coefficient ϵ of the confidence region when the hypothesis is true.

REFERENCES

[1] A. C. AITKEN, "Studies in practical mathematics II. The evaluation of the latent roots and latent vectors of a matrix," *Edinb. Math. Soc. Proc.*, Vol. 57 (1936–7), pp. 269–305.

[2] T. W. ANDERSON AND HERMAN RUBIN, "The asymptotic properties of estimates of the parameters of a single equation in a complete system of stochastic equations," to be published.

[3] M. S. BARTLETT, "A note on the statistical estimation of demand and supply relations from time series," *Econometrica*, Vol. 16 (1948), pp. 323–329.

[4] P. S. DWYER, "Evaluation of linear forms," *Psychometrika*, Vol. 6 (1941), pp. 355–365.

[5] R. A. FISHER, "The statistical utilization of multiple measurements," *Annals of Eugenics*, Vol. 8 (1938), pp. 376–386.

[6] M. A. GIRSHICK AND T. HAAVELMO, "Statistical analysis of the demand for food: examples of simultaneous estimation of structural equations," *Econometrica*, Vol. 15 (1947), pp. 79–110.

[7] T. HAAVELMO, "Statistical implications of a system of simultaneous equations," *Econometrica*, Vol. 11 (1943), pp. 1–12.

[8] P. L. Hsu, "On the problem of rank and the limiting distribution of Fisher's test function," *Annals of Eugenics*, Vol. 11 (1941), pp. 39–41.

[9] H. B. Mann and A. Wald, "On the statistical treatment of linear stochastic difference equations," *Econometrica*, Vol. 11 (1943), pp. 173–220.

[10] Olav Reiersøl, "Confluence analysis by means of lag moments and other methods of confluence analysis," *Econometrica*, Vol. 9 (1941), pp. 1–24.

[11] *Statistical Inference in Dynamic Economic Systems*, to be published as Cowles Commission Monograph No. 10.

THE ASYMPTOTIC PROPERTIES OF ESTIMATES OF THE PARAMETERS OF A SINGLE EQUATION IN A COMPLETE SYSTEM OF STOCHASTIC EQUATIONS[1, 2]

By T. W. Anderson and Herman Rubin

1. Summary. In a previous paper [2] the authors have given a method for estimating the coefficients of a single equation in a complete system of linear stochastic equations. In the present paper the consistency of the estimates and the asymptotic distributions of the estimates and the test criteria are studied under conditions more general than those used in the derivation of these estimates and criteria. The point estimates, which can be obtained as maximum likelihood estimates under certain assumptions including that of normality of disturbances, are consistent even if the disturbances are not normally distributed and (a) some predetermined variables are neglected (Theorem 1) or (b) the single equation is in a non-linear system with certain properties (Theorem 2).

Under certain general conditions (normality of the disturbances not being required) the estimates are asymptotically normally distributed (Theorems 3 and 4). The asymptotic covariance matrix is given for several cases. The criteria derived in [2] for testing the hypothesis of over-identification have, asymptotically, χ^2-distributions (Theorem 5). The exact confidence regions developed in [2] for the case that all predetermined variables are exogenous (that is, that the difference equations are of zero order) are shown to be consistent and to hold asymptotically even when this assumption is not true (Theorem 6).

2. Introduction. The complete system of linear stochastic equations considered by the authors in [2] was written

$$B_{yy}y_t' + \Gamma_{yz}z_t' = \epsilon_t' , \tag{2.1}$$

where y_t is a row vector of G jointly dependent variables at "time" t, z_t is a row vector of K variables predetermined at t, and ϵ_t is a row vector of "disturbances," and B_{yy} and Γ_{yz} are matrices. If B_{yy} is non-singular the distribution of ϵ_t induces the distribution of y_t given z_t.

One component equation of (2.1) was given special treatment. Let β be

---

[1] This paper will be included in Cowles Commission Papers, New Series, No. 36.

[2] The results of this paper were presented to meetings of the Institute of Mathematical Statistics at Washington, D. C., April 12, 1946 (Washington Chapter) and at Ithaca, New York, August 23, 1946. Most of the research was done at the Cowles Commission for Research in Economics; the authors are indebted to the members of the Cowles Commission staff for many helpful discussions.

composed of the coefficients of the coordinates of y_t which are not assumed zero in the specified equation, and let x_t be composed of the corresponding components of y_t; similarly let γ be composed of the coefficients of the coordinates of z_t which are not assumed zero, and u_t the corresponding components of z_t; and let ζ_t be the component of ϵ_t associated with the specified equation. Then the single equation is

$$\beta x_t' + \gamma u_t' = \zeta_t . \tag{2.2}$$

Suppose we have a set of observations $x_t, z_t, t = 1, \cdots, T$. For sets of any two vectors a_t and b_t, let the second-order moment matrix be

$$M_{ab} = \frac{1}{T}\sum_{t=1}^{T} a_t' b_t . \tag{2.3}$$

Let s_t be some linear transform of v_t, the set of coordinates of z_t not contained in u_t, chosen so $M_{su} = 0$. Defining

$$W_{xx} = M_{xx} - M_{xz}M_{zz}^{-1}M_{zx} , \tag{2.4}$$

and assuming ϵ_t normally distributed with mean 0, covariance matrix Σ, and independently of $\epsilon_{t'}(t \neq t')$, we find $\hat{\beta}$, the maximum likelihood estimate of β, to be proportional to a vector defined by

$$(M_{xs}M_{ss}^{-1}M_{sx} - \nu W_{xx})b' = 0, \tag{2.5}$$

taking ν as the smallest root of

$$| M_{xs}M_{ss}^{-1}M_{sx} - \nu W_{xx} | = 0. \tag{2.6}$$

The vector is normalized by

$$\hat{\beta}\hat{\Phi}_{xx}\hat{\beta}' = 1, \tag{2.7}$$

where $\hat{\Phi}_{xx}$ may be a function of the estimates of other parameters. The estimate of γ is $\hat{\gamma} = -\hat{\beta}M_{xu}M_{uu}^{-1}$ [2; Theorem 1]. These estimates were derived under the following explicit Assumptions A, B, C, and D:

Assumption A. *The selected structural equation* (2.2) *is one equation of a complete linear system of stochastic equations. It is identified by the fact that if H is the number of coordinates in x_t, there are at least $H - 1$ coordinates in v_t, the vector of predetermined variables in the system, but missing in* (2.2).

Assumption B. *At time t all of the coordinates of $z_t = (u_t, v_t)$ are given.*

Assumption C. *The coordinates of z_t are given functions of exogenous variables and of coordinates of $y_{t-1}, y_{t-2}, \cdots$. If coordinates of $y_0, y_{-1}, \cdots$ are involved in z_t, they will be considered as given numbers. The moment matrix M_{zz} is non-singular with probability one.*

Assumption D. *The disturbance vectors ϵ_t are distributed serially independently and normally with mean zero and covariance matrix Σ_{xx}.*

Under these assumptions it is found that $(1 + \nu)^{-\frac{1}{2}T}$ is the likelihood ratio criterion for testing the hypothesis that the number of components of z_t assumed to have zero coefficients is so great.

If there are no lagged endogenous variables in z_t, we can find confidence regions for β and for β and γ simultaneously as well as an approximate test for the above hypothesis. The assumptions used for these results are A, B, and

ASSUMPTION E. *All the coordinates of* $z_t = (u_t, v_t)$ *are exogenous. The moment matrix* M_{zz} *is non-singular. The disturbances of the selected equation are distributed independently and normally with mean zero and variance* σ^2.

Assumptions A and B are used in this paper and a number in addition, which will be lettered similarly. It is to be emphasized that the various assumptions are used alternatively, never all at once; in fact many assumptions are mutually exclusive.

3. Consistency of the estimates. The estimates $\hat{\beta}$ and $\hat{\gamma}$ are consistent not only in the case for which they are maximum likelihood estimates, but also in cases in which the disturbances are not normally or even identically distributed. Moreover, for consistency of the estimates it is not necessary that the investigator know all of the components of v_t or use them. Another direction in which the assumptions may be relaxed is to permit the other equations in the system to be non-linear.

3.1. *The linear case.* This case is characterized by Assumption A. We need also to assume:

ASSUMPTION F. M_{zz} *converges to a fixed non-singular limit* R *in probability.*

Let u_t consist of the part of z_t that enters the selected structural equation (22). The remainder of the components of z_t are divided into two groups as to whether they are known or not. Let c_t be a linear transform of the known components not entering the specified equation such that

$$\operatorname*{plim}_{t\to\infty} M_{uc} = 0, \tag{3.1}$$

and let r_t be a linear transform of the components of z_t not known such that

$$\operatorname*{plim}_{t\to\infty} M_{ur} = 0, \tag{3.2}$$

$$\operatorname*{plim}_{t\to\infty} M_{cr} = 0. \tag{3.3}$$

The relevant part of the "reduced form," obtained from (2.1) by multiplication by B_{yy}^{-1} is

$$x_t' = \bar{\Pi}_{xu}u_t' + \Pi_{xc}c_t' + \Pi_{xr}r_t' + \delta_t'. \tag{3.4}$$

The matrix $(\Pi_{xc}\Pi_{xr})$ is Π_{xs} (defined in [2]) multiplied on the right by a non-singular matrix; hence, $\beta\Pi_{xc} = 0$, and similarly $\beta\bar{\Pi}_{xu} = \gamma$. We shall find it convenient to assume

ASSUMPTION G. Π_{xc} *has rank* $H - 1$.

This means that for T sufficiently large the probability is arbitrarily near 1 that (2.2) is identified.

However, these conditions still do not insure consistency. We need the asymptotic analogue of lack of correlation:

ASSUMPTION H.

$$\operatorname*{plim}_{T\to\infty} \frac{1}{T} \sum_{t=1}^{T} \delta_t' z_t = 0.$$

We do not need to require that the covariance matrices of δ_t are the same or even that they exist. We shall make an assumption about

$$W_{xx}^* = M_{xx} - (M_{xu} M_{xc}) \begin{pmatrix} M_{uu} & M_{uc} \\ M_{cu} & M_{cc} \end{pmatrix}^{-1} \begin{pmatrix} M_{ux} \\ M_{cx} \end{pmatrix}. \tag{3.5}$$

ASSUMPTION I. *The ratio of the largest to the smallest characteristic roots of* W_{xx}^* *is bounded in probability.*

This means that for a suitable constant K

$$\lim_{T\to\infty} P\left(\frac{l(W_{xx}^*)}{s(W_{xx}^*)} > K\right) = 0, \tag{3.6}$$

where $P(E)$ denotes the probability of event E and $s(A)$ and $l(A)$ are the smallest and largest roots of the matrix A, respectively.

Assumptions F and H imply that $P_{xu} \to \bar{\Pi}_{xu}$ and $P_{xc} \to \Pi_{xc}$ in probability, where $P_{xu} = M_{xu} M_{uu}^{-1}$ and P_{xc} is the part of

$$(M_{xu} M_{xc}) \begin{pmatrix} M_{uu} & M_{uc} \\ M_{cu} & M_{cc} \end{pmatrix}^{-1} \tag{3.7}$$

corresponding to the vector[5] c_t. The first assertion follows because $M_{xu} M_{uu}^{-1} = (\Pi_{xu} M_{uu} + \Pi_{xc} M_{xc} + \Pi_{xr} M_{ru} + M_{\delta u}) M_{uu}^{-1}$ and $M_{xc} \to 0$, $M_{ru} \to 0$, and $M_{\delta u} \to 0$ in probability by (3.1), (3.3) and Assumption H; the second assertion follows similarly. Since matrix multiplication is continuous, and the characteristic roots of a matrix are continuous functions of the matrix,[6]

$$\operatorname*{plim}_{T\to\infty} s[P_{xc} M_{ss} P_{xc}'] = 0, \tag{3.8}$$

where $M_{ss} = (M_{cc} - M_{cu} M_{uu}^{-1} M_{uc})$. This follows from the well-known theorem (a proof of which is given in [4]) that if a random vector X_T converges stochastically to X, then $f(X_T)$ converges stochastically to $f(X)$ if $f(y)$ is continuous at X.

We shall find the following lemmas convenient. The proofs are simple and have been given in [1].

LEMMA 1. *Let B be positive definite, A positive semi-definite. Then the smallest root ν of* $|A - xB| = 0$ *is less than or equal to* $s(A)/s(B)$.

[5] See Section 4 of [2].

[6] Because of the assertion above and Assumptions F and G only one characteristic root of the matrix approaches zero in probability.

LEMMA 2. *Each element of a positive definite matrix is less in absolute value than the largest characteristic root.*

Let ν be the smallest root of

$$|P_{xc}M_{ss}P'_{xc} - \nu W^*_{xx}| = 0. \tag{3.9}$$

Then $\operatorname*{plim}_{T\to\infty} \nu W^*_{xx} = 0$. This statement follows from (3.8) and Lemmas 1 and 2.

Since 0 is a simple characteristic root of $\Pi_{xc} \operatorname*{plim}_{T\to\infty} M_{ss}\Pi'_{xc}$, it follows from (3.9) and the consistency of P_{xu} and P_{xc} that $\hat{\beta}$ approaches β apart from normalization. The following theorem results directly:

THEOREM 1. *Under Assumptions* A, F, G, H, *and* I, *and if* $\operatorname*{plim}_{T\to\infty} \beta\hat{\Phi}_{xx}\beta' = 1$,

$$\operatorname*{plim}_{T\to\infty} \hat{\beta} = \beta, \tag{3.10}$$

$$\operatorname*{plim}_{T\to\infty} \hat{\gamma} = \gamma, \tag{3.11}$$

where $\hat{\beta}$ *and* $\hat{\gamma}$ *are calculated as if* $r_t = 0$ *and as if the remainder of* A, B, C, *and* D *were satisfied.*[7]

3.2. *The non-linear case.* In this section we apply the estimates obtained in [2] to an equation of a complete system in which the remaining equations may be non-linear. We replace Assumption A by the following assumption:

ASSUMPTION J. *The selected structural equation* (2.2) *is one equation of a complete system of stochastic equations*:

$$F_i(y_t, z_t) = \epsilon_{ti} \qquad (i = 1, \cdots, G). \tag{3.11}$$

Let us solve the complete system (3.11) for the components of y_t. We obtain

$$y_{tj} = h_j(z_t, \epsilon_t). \tag{3.12}$$

Let u_t be the subvector of z_t occurring in the selected structural equation. Let c_t be a vector function of z_t such that $\operatorname*{plim}_{T\to\infty} M_{cu} = 0$. We may write (3.12) for those y's occurring in the selected structural equation as

$$x'_t = \bar{\Pi}_{xu}u'_t + \Pi_{xc}c'_t + \varphi'(z_t, \epsilon_t), \tag{3.13}$$

where the components of $\varphi(z_t, \epsilon_t)$ are the residuals from the formal limiting regression of x_t on u_t and c_t. The proof of Theorem 1 can be used to prove the following:

THEOREM 2. *If Assumptions* F, G, H, I, *and* J *are satisfied with* z_t *replaced by* (u_t, c_t) *and* δ_t *replaced by* $\varphi(z_t, \epsilon_t)$, *and* $r_t = 0$, *and if* $\operatorname*{plim}_{T\to\infty} \beta\hat{\Phi}_{xx}\beta' = 1$, *then*

$$\operatorname*{plim}_{T\to\infty} \hat{\beta} = \beta, \tag{3.14}$$

$$\operatorname*{plim}_{T\to\infty} \hat{\gamma} = \gamma. \tag{3.15}$$

---

[7] This follows from the above statements because $\hat{\beta}$ and $\hat{\gamma}$ are (vector-valued) rational functions of M_{zz}, P_{xs}, W^*_{xx} and Φ_{xx} which approach limits in probability.

4. The asymptotic distribution of the estimates.

4.1. *The asymptotic distribution of P_{xs} and P_{xu}.* To obtain the asymptotic distribution of the estimates we need stronger assumptions. Throughout Sections 4.1 and 4.2 we use Assumptions A, B, F, H, I, and the following:

ASSUMPTION K. *The exogenous variables are bounded; the vector of disturbances of the complete system has mean zero, and is serially independent; for some $\lambda > 0$ and some M, $\mathcal{E}(|\delta_{ti}|^{4+\lambda}) < M$; the coordinates of z_t may be linear combinations of lagged endogenous variables. If the endogenous part of a coordinate is*

$$\sum_{\tau=1}^{\infty}\sum_{i=1}^{G} g_{\tau i}y_{t-\tau,i},$$

then

$$\sum_{\tau=1}^{\infty}\sum_{i=1}^{G} |g_{\tau i}| < \infty$$

and

$$\sum_{\tau=t}^{\infty}\sum_{i=1}^{G} g_{\tau i}y_{t-\tau,i}$$

is bounded.

ASSUMPTION L. *The matrix Φ_{xx} is known and constant.*

ASSUMPTION M. *For each i, j, k, l, $1 \leq i, j \leq H$, $1 \leq k, l \leq K$,*

$$\lim_{T\to\infty}\frac{1}{T}\sum_{t=1}^{T}\mathcal{E}(\delta_{ti}\delta_{tj}z_{tk}z_{tl}) = \kappa_{ijkl}$$

exists.

Let the components of M_{yy}, M_{yz}, M_{zz} be arranged as a vector $m(T)$ with mean value $\mu(T)$. It has been shown [3] that $\sqrt{T}(m(T) - \mu(T))$ is asymptotically distributed according to $N(0, \Sigma)$, the normal distribution with mean 0 and covariance matrix Σ composed of elements

$$\sigma_{ij} = \lim_{T\to\infty}\mathcal{E}(T[m_i(T) - \mu_i(T)]\,[m_j(T) - \mu_j(T)]).$$

In conjunction with this result we make repeated use of a special case of Theorem 6 of [4]:

Suppose $\sqrt{T}(x_{jT} - \xi_{jT})$ $(j = 1, \cdots, n)$ have the joint asymptotic distribution $N(0, \Psi)$ with ξ_{jT} being functions of T such that $\lim_{T\to\infty}\xi_{jT} = \xi_j$. Let $f_{kT}(z_1, \cdots, z_n)$ be random Borel-measurable functions of n real variables such that $\frac{\partial f_{kT}}{\partial z_j} = \alpha_{kjT}(z)$ exists with probability one for T sufficiently large and z in a fixed neighborhood of ξ, and suppose that there exist numbers α_{kj} such that for any $\epsilon > 0$, and $\lambda > 0$, $P(\sup_{(z-\xi_T)(z-\xi_T)' \leq (\lambda/T)} |\alpha_{kjT}(z) - \alpha_{kj}| > \epsilon)$ approaches zero. Then if $y_{kT} = f_{kT}(x_{1T}, \cdots, x_{nT})$ and $\eta_{kT} = f_{kT}(\xi_{1T}, \cdots, \xi_{nT})$, the random variables $\sqrt{T}(y_{kT} - \eta_{kT})$ have the joint asymptotic distribution $N(0, A\Psi A')$, where $A = (\alpha_{ij})$.

To obtain the asymptotic distributions we have only to verify that the assumptions of this statement are satisfied, and compute A, since the asymptotic distribution is characterized completely by $A\Psi A'$. We shall denote the element in the k-th row and l-th column of $A\Psi A'$ by $\sigma(f_k, f_l)$. We shall find it convenient to use the notation $df = Adx$; that is, the differential df is defined in terms of the limit matrix A.

Let

(4.1) $$A = M_{\delta u},$$

(4.2) $$B = M_{\delta s},$$

(4.3) $$C = \operatorname*{plim}_{T\to\infty} M_{uu},$$

(4.4) $$E = \operatorname*{plim}_{T\to\infty} M_{ss},$$

(4.5) $$L = P_{xu},$$

(4.6) $$P = P_{xs} = M_{xs}M_{ss}^{-1},$$

(4.7) $$\Lambda = \bar{\Pi}_{xu},$$

(4.8) $$\Pi = \Pi_{xs}.$$

The matrix L is the random function $AM_{uu}^{-1} + \Pi_{xc}M_{cu}M_{uu}^{-1} + \Lambda$ of A, P is the random function $BM_{ss}^{-1} + \Pi$ of B. Then

(4.9) $$dL = (dA)C^{-1},$$

(4.10) $$dP = (dB)E^{-1}.$$

However

(4.11) $$\sigma(a_{ik}, a_{jl}) = \alpha_{ijkl},$$

(4.12) $$\sigma(a_{ik}, b_{jl}) = \beta_{ijkl},$$

(4.13) $$\sigma(b_{ik}, b_{jl}) = \gamma_{ijkl},$$

where α_{ijkl}, β_{ijkl}, γ_{ijkl} are the appropriate quantities κ_{abcd}, respectively. From these we may compute $\sigma(l_{ij}, l_{kl})$, $\sigma(l_{ij}, p_{kl})$, and $\sigma(p_{ij}, p_{kl})$, the elements of the asymptotic covariance matrix of the elements of L and P (which are asymptotically normally distributed by the above). These elements can be estimated consistently from the sample (the proof follows from Theorem 1).

4.2. *The asymptotic distribution of $\hat{\beta}$ and $\hat{\gamma}$ for constant normalization.* In this section we shall show that $\hat{\beta}$ and $\hat{\gamma}$ are asymptotically normally distributed (Theorem 3). In view of the above theorem on asymptotic distributions the intricate part of the proof is in obtaining the covariance matrix. First we shall demonstrate that the elements of νW are $o(1/\sqrt{T})$ in probability. Since Assumption I holds, it is sufficient to show that $s(P_{xs}M_{ss}P'_{xs})$ is $o(1/\sqrt{T})$ in probability. This means $d \mid P_{xs}M_{ss}P'_{xs} \mid = 0$, since each of the characteristic roots of $P_{xs}M_{ss}P'_{xs}$ except the smallest approaches a non-zero limit in probability.

For any matrix A, A_{ij} denotes the matrix obtained by deleting the i-th row and j-th column from A, and $A_{ik,jl}$ is the matrix obtained by deleting the i-th and k-th rows and the j-th and l-th columns. Let

$$A^{ij} = (-1)^{i+j} | A_{ij} |,$$
$$A^{ij,kl} = (-1)^{i+j+k+l+\epsilon} | A_{ik,jl} |,$$

where $\epsilon = 0$ if $(i - k)(j - l) > 0$, 1 otherwise when $i \neq k, j \neq l$. $A^{ij,kl} = 0$ if $i = k$ or $j = l$. In the rest of the paper we use the summation convention of tensor calculus for lower case indices; namely, that whenever a lower case letter appears as a superscript and a subscript in an expression, the corresponding terms are to be summed on that index.

In general

$$d | A | = A^{ij} da_{ij} . \tag{4.14}$$

We may consider $P_{xs}M_{ss}P'_{xs}$ as a random function of P_{xs}. Then

$$d(i,j\text{-th element of } P_{xs}M_{ss}P'_{xs}) = \pi^k_i e_{kl}\, dp^l_j + \pi^l_j e_{kl}\, dp^k_i . \tag{4.15}$$

However

$$(\Pi_{xs}E\Pi'_{xs})^{ij} = \rho^j\beta^i = \rho^i\beta^j, \tag{4.16}$$

where ρ^i is a factor of proportionality. Since $\beta\Pi_{xs} = 0$, we have $d | P_{xs}M_{ss}P'_{xs} | = 0$. Then it can be shown that $d(\hat{\Pi}_{xs}M_{ss}\hat{\Pi}'_{xs} - P_{xs}M_{ss}P'_{xs}) = 0$, where $\hat{\Pi}_{xs} = \left(I - \frac{W_{xx}\hat{\beta}'\hat{\beta}}{\hat{\beta}W_{xx}\hat{\beta}'}\right) P_{xs}$.

Let $\Theta = \Pi_{xs}E\Pi'_{xs}$ and $F = P_{xs}M_{ss}P'_{sx}$. We know that $\hat{\beta}_i = \hat{\rho}_J\hat{\Theta}^{iJ}$, where $\rho_J = 1/\rho^J$ (and the capital letter J indicates that there is not to be a sum on that index), and $\hat{\Theta} = \hat{\Pi}_{xs}M_{ss}\hat{\Pi}'_{xs}$. Hence

$$d\hat{\beta}^i = \rho_J d\hat{\Theta}^{iJ} + \Theta^{iJ} d\hat{\rho}_J . \tag{4.17}$$

However $\hat{\beta}^i\hat{\beta}^j\varphi_{ij} = 1$; therefore $\hat{\rho}_J = (\hat{\Theta}^{iJ}\hat{\Theta}^{kJ}\varphi_{ik})^{-\frac{1}{2}}$. From this it follows that

$$d\hat{\rho}_J = -(\hat{\rho}_J)^3\Theta^{iJ}\varphi_{ik}\, d\hat{\Theta}^{kJ}. \tag{4.18}$$

From (4.14) we see $d\hat{\Theta}^{kJ} = \Theta^{kJ,\alpha\beta} d\hat{\theta}_{\alpha\beta}$. Therefore

$$d\hat{\beta}^i = \rho_J[\Theta^{iJ,\alpha\beta} - \beta^i\beta^l\Theta^{kJ,\alpha\beta}\varphi_{kl}]d\hat{\theta}_{\alpha\beta} . \tag{4.19}$$

Let us define $\psi_j = \beta^i\varphi_{ij}$. Let us multiply (4.19) by $\theta_{\gamma i}$ and ψ_i. We obtain

$$\begin{aligned} \theta_{\gamma i}d\hat{\beta}^i &= \rho_J\theta_{\gamma i}\Theta^{iJ,\alpha\beta}d\hat{\theta}_{\alpha\beta} \\ &= \rho_J\delta_\gamma^{\ J}\Theta^{\alpha\beta}d\hat{\theta}_{\alpha\beta} - \rho_J\Theta^{J\beta}d\hat{\theta}_{\gamma\beta} = -\beta^\alpha d\hat{\theta}_{\gamma\alpha} , \end{aligned} \tag{4.20}$$

$$\psi_i d\beta^i = 0. \tag{4.21}$$

Let us simplify (4.20). We see that

$$\beta^\alpha d\hat{\theta}_{\gamma\alpha} = \beta^\alpha\pi^k_\gamma e_{kl} dp^l_\alpha . \tag{4.22}$$

Hence

$$\sigma(\beta^\alpha d\hat{\theta}_{\gamma\alpha}, \beta^\mu d\hat{\theta}_{\gamma\mu}) = \beta^\alpha \pi^k_\gamma e_{kl} \beta^\mu \pi^h_\gamma e_{hj} e^{lm} e^{ji} \gamma_{\alpha\mu mi} \tag{4.23}$$
$$= \beta^\alpha \beta^\mu \pi^m_\gamma \pi^i_\nu \gamma_{\alpha\mu mi} = r_{1\gamma\nu},$$

say. Let $\sigma(\hat{\beta}^i, \hat{\beta}^j) = q_1^{ij}$, and let $Q_1 = (q_1^{ij})$. Then from (4.20) and (4.23) we obtain

$$\Theta Q_1 \Theta = R_1, \tag{4.24}$$

and (4.21) is

$$\psi Q_1 = 0. \tag{4.25}$$

It may be shown (see [1], for example) that the solution is

$$Q_1 = (I - \beta'\psi)_{\cdot k}(\Theta_{kk})^{-1}(R_1)_{kk}(\Theta_{kk})^{-1}(I - \psi'\beta)_{k\cdot}, \tag{4.26}$$

where $k(1 \leq k \leq H)$ is arbitrary except that $\beta^k \neq 0$, and $A_{\cdot k}$ denotes A with the k-th column deleted, etc. If the normalization is $\beta^i = 1$, $k = i$ is a convenient choice.

Since $\hat{\gamma} = -\hat{\beta}L$,

$$d\hat{\gamma}^m = -d\hat{\beta}^i \lambda_i^m - \beta^i dl_i^m. \tag{4.27}$$

Hence

$$\sigma(\hat{\beta}^j, \hat{\gamma}^m) = -\sigma(\hat{\beta}^j, \hat{\beta}^i)\lambda_i^m - \sigma(\hat{\beta}^j, l_i^m)\beta^i, \tag{4.28}$$

$$\sigma(\hat{\gamma}^m, \hat{\gamma}^n) = \sigma(\hat{\beta}^j, \hat{\beta}^i)\lambda_i^m \lambda_j^n + \sigma(\hat{\beta}^j, l_i^m)\beta^i \lambda_j^n + \sigma(\hat{\beta}^j, l_i^n)\beta^i \lambda_j^m + \sigma(l_i^m, l_j^n)\beta^i \beta^j. \tag{4.29}$$

We, therefore, see that we must compute $\sigma(\hat{\beta}^j, l_i^m)\beta^i$ and $\sigma(l_i^m, l_j^n)\beta^i\beta^j$. We find, from (4.20), (4.21), and (4.22) that

$$\theta_{\gamma j}\beta^i \sigma(\hat{\beta}^j, l_i^m) = -\beta^i \beta^j \pi_j^k c^{mp} \beta_{ijpk} = r_{2\gamma}^m, \tag{4.30}$$

say. Let $(\sigma(\hat{\beta}^j, l_i^m)\beta^i) = Q_2$, and let $R_2 = (r_{2\gamma}^m)$. Then, from (4.30) and (4.21) we obtain

$$\Theta Q_2 = R_2, \tag{4.31}$$

$$\psi Q_2 = 0. \tag{4.32}$$

The solution is

$$Q_2 = (I - \beta'\psi)_{\cdot k}(\Theta_{kk})^{-1}(R_2)_{k\cdot}. \tag{4.33}$$

We find, readily, that

$$\beta^i \beta^j \sigma(l_i^m, l_j^n) = \beta^i \beta^j c^{mp} c^{nq} \alpha_{ijpq} = q_3^{mn}, \tag{4.34}$$

say, where $(c^{mp}) = C^{-1}$. Let $Q_3 = (q_3^{mn})$. This concludes the proof of Theorem 3.

THEOREM 3. *If Assumptions* A, B, F, H, I, K, L, *and* M *are satsfied,* $\sqrt{T}(\hat{\beta} - \beta)$ *and* $\sqrt{T}(\hat{\gamma} - \gamma)$ *are asymptotically jointly normally distributed with means zero and covariance matrix*

$$\sigma(\hat{\beta}', \hat{\beta}) = Q_1, \tag{4.35}$$

$$(4.36)\qquad \sigma(\hat{\beta}', \hat{\gamma}) = -Q_2\bar{\Pi}_{xu} - Q_2,$$

$$(4.37)\qquad \sigma(\hat{\gamma}', \hat{\gamma}) = \bar{\Pi}'_{xu}Q_1\bar{\Pi}_{xu} + \bar{\Pi}'_{xu}Q_2 + Q'_2\bar{\Pi}_{xu} + Q_3,$$

where Q_1 *is given by* (4.26), Q_2 *by* (4.33), *and* Q_3 *by* (4.34).

If there is a kind of asymptotic independence of ζ_t and z_t, then the above expressions may be simplified. Corollary 1 results from Theorem 3 and the following assumption:

ASSUMPTION N. $\lim_{T\to\infty} \frac{1}{T}\sum_{t=1}^{T} \mathcal{E}(\zeta_t^2 z'_t z_t) = \sigma^2 R$, *where* R *is defined in Assumption* F.

COROLLARY 1. *If Assumptions* A, B, F, H, I, K, L, M, *and* N *are satisfied,* $\sqrt{T}(\hat{\beta} - \beta)$ *and* $\sqrt{T}(\hat{\gamma} - \gamma)$ *are asymptotically jointly normally distributed with means zero and covariance matrix*

$$(4.38)\qquad \sigma(\hat{\beta}', \hat{\beta}) = \sigma^2(I - \beta'\psi)_{\cdot k}(\Theta_{kk})^{-1}(I - \psi'\beta)_{k\cdot},$$

$$(4.39)\qquad \sigma(\hat{\beta}', \hat{\gamma}) = -\sigma^2(I - \beta'\psi)_{\cdot k}(\Theta_{kk})^{-1}(\bar{\Pi}_{xu} + \psi'\gamma)_{k\cdot},$$

$$(4.40)\qquad \sigma(\hat{\gamma}', \hat{\gamma}) = \sigma^2[(\bar{\Pi}'_{xu} + \gamma'\psi)_{\cdot k}(\Theta_{kk})^{-1}(\bar{\Pi}_{xu} + \psi'\gamma)_{k\cdot} + C^{-1}].$$

4.3. *Asymptotic distribution of the estimates of the parameters* β *and* γ *with normalization a function of* Ω_{xx}.

If we relax Assumption L that Φ_{xx} is constant, we obtain a more general result. Since the proof, however, is more involved, we shall not give it here; the reader is referred to [1]. In the derivation of the estimates Ω_{xx} was defined as $\mathcal{E}(\delta'_t\delta_t)$. In the asymptotic theory we do not assume that this is the same for each t. We use the following assumption:

ASSUMPTION O.
$$\lim_{T\to\infty} \frac{1}{T}\sum_{t=1}^{T} \mathcal{E}(\delta_{ti}\delta_{tj}\delta_{tk}z_{tl}) = n_{ijkl} \text{ exists;}$$

$$\lim_{T\to\infty} \frac{1}{T}\sum_{t=1}^{T} \mathcal{E}(\delta_{ti}\delta_{tj}) = \bar{\omega}_{ij} \text{ exists;}$$

$$\lim_{T\to\infty} \frac{1}{T}\sum_{t=1}^{T} \mathcal{E}(\delta_{ti}\delta_{tj}\delta_{tk}\delta_{tl}) = \bar{\omega}_{ijkl} + \bar{\omega}_{ij}\bar{\omega}_{kl} \text{ exists.}$$

Let δ_{ijkl} be the quantities n_{ijkl} corresponding to the u's, ϵ_{ijkl}, the quantities corresponding to the c's. Define

$$(4.41)\qquad \chi^{ij} = \tfrac{1}{2}\beta^k\beta^l\frac{\partial\varphi_{kl}}{\partial\omega_{ij}},$$

$$(4.42)\qquad r_{4\gamma} = \beta^k\pi^l_{\gamma}\chi^{ij}\epsilon_{ijkl},$$

$$(4.43)\qquad q'_4 = (I - \beta'\psi)_{\cdot k}(\Theta_{kk})^{-1}(r'_4)_{k\cdot},$$

$$(4.44)\qquad q_5 = \chi^{ij}\chi^{kl}\bar{\omega}_{ijkl},$$

$$(4.45)\qquad q_6^k = \chi^{ij}\beta^m\delta_{ijml}c^{kl}.$$

With the aid of the matrices Q_1, Q_2, and Q_3, the vectors q_4 and q_6, and the scalar q_5, we may express the asymptotic covariance matrix of the estimates. We obtain

THEOREM 4. *If Assumptions* A, B, F, H, I, K, M, *and* O *are satisfied, and* Φ_{xx} *is a function of* Ω_{xx}, $\sqrt{T}(\hat{\beta} - \beta)$ *and* $\sqrt{T}(\hat{\gamma} - \gamma)$ *are asymptotically jointly normally distributed with means zero and covariance matrix*

$$\sigma(\hat{\beta}', \hat{\beta}) = Q_1 + q_4'\beta + \beta' q_4 + q_5 \beta'\beta, \tag{4.46}$$

$$\sigma(\hat{\beta}', \hat{\gamma}) = -Q_1\bar{\Pi}_{xu} + q_4'\gamma - \beta' q_4 \bar{\Pi}_{xu} + q_5\beta'\gamma - Q_2 - \beta' q_6, \tag{4.47}$$

$$\begin{aligned}\sigma(\hat{\gamma}', \hat{\gamma}) = {} & \bar{\Pi}_{xu}' Q_1 \bar{\Pi}_{xu} - \bar{\Pi}_{xu}' q_4'\gamma - \gamma' q_4 \bar{\Pi}_{xu} + q_5\gamma'\gamma \\ & + \bar{\Pi}_{xu}' Q_2 + Q_2'\bar{\Pi}_{xu} - \gamma' q_6 - q_6'\gamma + Q_3,\end{aligned} \tag{4.48}$$

where Q_1, Q_2, Q_3, q_4, q_5, *and* q_6 *are given by* (4.26), (4.33), (4.34), (4.43), (4.44), *and* (4.45) *respectively.*

COROLLARY 2. *If Assumptions* A, B, D, F, H *and* K *are satisfied, and* $\Phi_{xx} = \Omega_{xx}$, $\sqrt{T}(\hat{\beta} - \beta)$ *and* $\sqrt{T}(\hat{\gamma} - \gamma)$ *are asymptotically jointly normally distributed with means zero and covariance matrix*

$$\sigma(\hat{\beta}', \hat{\beta}) = (I - \beta'\psi)_{\cdot k}(\Theta_{kk})^{-1}(I - \psi'\beta)_{k\cdot} + \tfrac{1}{2}\beta'\beta, \tag{4.49}$$

$$\sigma(\hat{\beta}', \hat{\gamma}) = -(I - \beta'\psi)_{\cdot k}(\Theta_{kk})^{-1}(\bar{\Pi}_{xu} + \psi'\gamma)_{k\cdot} + \tfrac{1}{2}\beta'\gamma, \tag{4.50}$$

$$\sigma(\hat{\gamma}', \hat{\gamma}) = (\bar{\Pi}_{xu}' + \gamma'\psi)_{\cdot k}(\Theta_{kk})^{-1}(\bar{\Pi}_{xu} + \psi'\gamma)_{k\cdot} + C^{-1} + \tfrac{1}{2}\gamma'\gamma. \tag{4.51}$$

5. Asymptotic distribution of the likelihood ratio criterion and the small sample criterion for testing a certain hypothesis. The likelihood ratio criterion for testing the hypothesis that the number of coordinates of z_t with zero coefficients in the selected structural equation is as great as it is assumed to be is $(1 + \nu)^{-\frac{1}{2}T}$ [2, Theorem 2], where ν is the smallest root of

$$| P_{xs} M_{ss} P_{xs}' - \nu W_{xx} | = 0. \tag{5.1}$$

Then

$$T\nu = T\frac{\hat{\beta} P_{xs} M_{ss} P_{xs}' \hat{\beta}'}{\hat{\beta} W_{xx} \hat{\beta}'} = (\sqrt{T}\hat{\beta} P_{xs}) \frac{M_{ss}}{\hat{\beta} W_{xx} \hat{\beta}'} (\sqrt{T}\hat{\beta} P_{xs})'. \tag{5.2}$$

From Theorem 5 of [4] it follows that the asymptotic distribution of $T\nu$ is the same as that of the quadratic form $x \frac{E}{\sigma^2} x'$, where x has the limiting distribution of $\sqrt{T}\hat{\beta} P_{xs}$, use being made of $\operatorname{plim}_{T\to\infty} \hat{\beta} W_{xx} \hat{\beta}' = \sigma^2$. We have

$$dx^i = \beta^j dp_j^i + d\hat{\beta}^j \pi_j^i. \tag{5.3}$$

Let $\Upsilon = (I - \beta'\psi)_{\cdot k}(\Theta_{kk})^{-1}(I - \psi'\beta)_{k\cdot}$. Then

$$d\hat{\beta}^j = -\upsilon^{jk}\beta^l \pi_k^m e_{mn} dp_l^n. \tag{5.4}$$

Substituting in (5.3), we obtain

$$dx^i = \beta^j dp_j^i - \upsilon^{lk}\beta^j \pi_k^m e_{mn} dp_j^n \pi_l^i. \tag{5.5}$$

Then

$$\sigma(x^i, x^g) = \sigma^2(e^{ig} - \pi_k^i \pi_q^g v^{kq}) = \sigma^2 \xi^{ig} \tag{5.6}$$

say, and $(\xi^{ig}) = \Xi$.

Let F be chosen so $E = FF'$ and $F'\Xi F = \Psi$ is diagonal. Since $E\Xi E\Xi E = E\Xi E$, the diagonal elements of Ψ are 1 and 0. The number of elements that are 1 is the rank of $E\Xi E$, namely, $D - H + 1$, where D is the number of coordinates of v_t (the number of coordinates whose coefficients in the selected equation are assumed to be zero). Let $z = \frac{1}{\sigma} xF$. Then the asymptotic distribution of $T\nu$ is the distribution of zz' where z is normally distributed with mean zero and covariance matrix Ψ. It is the χ^2-distribution with $D - H + 1$ degrees of freedom. We observe that $T \log (1 + \nu)$ and $TD\lambda$ are asymptotically equal to $T\nu$, where λ is the criterion based on small sample theory [2, Theorem 4]. Finally, we note that ν is independent of the normalization of β.

THEOREM 5. *If Assumptions* A, B, F, H, I, K, M, *and* N *are satisfied*, -2 *times the logarithm of the likelihood ratio criterion*, $-T/2 \log (1 + \nu)$, *the asymptotically equivalent* $T\nu$ *and* TD *times the small sample criterion*, λ, *for testing the hypothesis that the number of coordinates with zero coefficients is* D *are asymptotically distributed as* χ^2 *with* $D - H + 1$ *degrees of freedom.*

This theorem indicates how conservative the small sample test is asymptotically, for that test asymptotically is equivalent to using $T\nu$ as having an asymptotic χ^2-distribution with D degrees of freedom.

6. Asymptotic behavior of confidence regions based on small sample theory. In [2] we deduced confidence regions for β and for β and γ when Assumption E holds. If the normalization of β is

$$\beta\Phi_{xx}\beta' = 1, \tag{6.1}$$

where Φ_{xx} is a given matrix, then a confidence region (a) for β of confidence ϵ consists of all β^* satisfying (6.1) and

$$\frac{\beta^* M_{xs} M_{ss}^{-1} M_{sx} \beta^{*\prime}}{\beta^* W_{xx} \beta^{*\prime}} \leq \frac{D}{T - K} F_{D,T-K}(\epsilon), \tag{6.2}$$

where $F_{D,T-K}(\epsilon)$ is chosen so the probability of (6.2) for $\beta^* = \beta$ is ϵ and K is the number of coordinates of z_t and D is the number of coordinates of v_t. A region (b) for β and γ simultaneously consists of β^* and γ^* satisfying (6.1) and

$$\frac{\beta^* M_{xu} M_{uu}^{-1} M_{ux} \beta^{*\prime} + \beta^* M_{xu} \gamma^{*\prime} + \gamma^* M_{ux} \beta^{*\prime} + \gamma^* M_{uu} \gamma^{*\prime} + \beta^* M_{xs} M_{ss}^{-1} M_{sx} \beta^{*\prime}}{\beta^* W_{xx} \beta^{*\prime}} \leq \frac{K}{T - K} F_{K,T-K}(\epsilon). \tag{6.3}$$

We shall now show that even if Assumption E does not hold the regions have asymptotically confidence coefficients ϵ and they are consistent under general conditions.

Let $c = \beta M_{xu} M_{uu}^{-1} + \gamma$, $e = \beta M_{xs} M_{ss}^{-1}$. We observe from Section 4 that if Assumptions A, B, F, H, K, L, M and N are satisfied, the vectors $\sqrt{T}c$ and $\sqrt{T}e$ have asymptotic independent distributions $N(0, \sigma^2 C^{-1})$ and $N(0, \sigma^2 E^{-1})$, respectively. Then $TcM_{uu}c'/\sigma^2$ and $TeM_{ss}e'/\sigma^2$ will have asymptotic independent χ^2-distributions with $F(= K - D)$ and D degrees of freedom, respectively. Also $\beta W_{xx}\beta'$ approaches σ^2 stochastically. By Theorems 5 and 6 of [4], the left-hand sides of (6.2) and (6.3) have asymptotic F-distributions with D and $T - K$ degrees of freedom and K and $T - K$ degrees of freedom, respectively.

We shall prove that (a) is consistent for β; the proof is similar for (b) as a region for β and γ. If we replace β by b in the definition of e, $eM_{ss}e' = bM_{xs}M_{ss}^{-1}M_{sx}b'$. For $b \neq \beta$ we must show that the probability that b will fall in the confidence region for β approaches zero. The above form approaches $b\Pi_{xs}E\Pi_{xs}'b'$ in probability. If $b \neq \beta$ and satisfies (6.1) then $b\Pi_{xs} \neq 0$ and $eM_{ss}e'$ has a non-zero limit in probability since E is positive definite. Thus b is not in the limiting confidence region.

THEOREM 6. *If Assumptions* A, B, F, H, I, K, M, *and* N *are satisfied, the confidence regions of Theorem* 3 *of* [2] (*including* (a) *and* (b) *above*) *are consistent, and the regions* (a) *and* (b) *have asymptotically the confidence levels* ϵ.

REFERENCES

[1] T. W. ANDERSON AND HERMAN RUBIN, "Estimation of the parameters of a single stochastic difference equation in a complete system," Cowles Commission for Research in Economics, 1947, dittoed.

[2] T. W. ANDERSON AND HERMAN RUBIN, "Estimation of the parameters of a single equation in a complete system of stochastic equations," *Annals of Math. Stat.*, Vol. 20 (1949), pp. 46–63.

[3] H. RUBIN, "Consistency and asymptotic normality in stable linear stochastic difference systems," to be published.

[4] H. RUBIN, "Topological properties of measures on topological spaces," *Duke Math. Journ.*, to be published.

DOUBLE k-CLASS ESTIMATORS OF PARAMETERS IN SIMULTANEOUS EQUATIONS AND THEIR SMALL SAMPLE PROPERTIES

BY A. L. NAGAR[1]

1. INTRODUCTION

IT IS WELL-KNOWN that there exist situations in statistics in which minor changes in an estimation procedure lead to a rather considerable computational simplification while leaving asymptotic properties intact, and also that there are situations in which minor changes lead to an improvement at the finite-sample level. An example of the first category is the two-stage-least-squares estimation procedure for systems of simultaneous linear equations, which is an improvement over the older method of limited-information-maximum-likelihood in the sense that the computational burden is lighter, and which is equivalent with the latter method as far as asymptotic properties are concerned. See [1] and [5]. These two estimation methods are members of the so-called k-class, and a third member of this class provides an example of the second category mentioned above. Most of the studies published in the field of simultaneous-equation estimation deal with large-sample properties, that is, with the limits of the expected values, with the moments of the second order to $O(1/T)$, where T is the number of observations, and with asymptotic normality. The usual estimators in this field are indeed asymptotically normal under the usual assumptions; they are asymptotically unbiased, and they have an asymptotic covariance matrix which equals the probability limit of the sample moment matrix.

In actual practice, of course, we frequently have to apply such methods when the sample is of only moderate size. It is then of considerable importance to know more about the estimators than that they behave satisfactorily for asymptotic samples. To have the complete finite-sample distribution would be the best thing that could be obtained, but unfortunately this is not available at the moment. The present author derived in [3] the bias of the k-class estimators to the order $1/T$, and it is here where the third member of this class, mentioned already in

[1] The author is grateful to Professor Theil for giving encouragement in the preparation of this article. This article was written while the author was a staff member of the Econometric Institute of the Netherlands School of Economics, Rotterdam.

the preceding paragraph, enters into the picture. The bias of this particular estimator vanishes to $O(1/T)$, so that this estimator is to be preferred if bias is indeed our criterion, and if we are willing to stay in the k-class.

But bias is only one criterion, and it may be that the price we have to pay for a smaller bias is an increase in the stochastic variability of the estimator around the true parameter. A criterion which is preferable in this respect is that of the mean-squared error, although it should be added that this measure is certainly not the only one that can be used for controlling the sampling variability of the estimator. However, it is convenient in such fields as simultaneous-equation estimation because it can be handled by means of the second-order moment matrix. Now, when we base the estimation procedure on the information which is commonly called "limited" (implying that, for each equation, only the constraints on its own coefficients are taken into account), the leading term of this moment matrix in the expansion according to powers of T is the same for all consistent members of the k-class. Therefore, if we want to gain in this respect, we should concentrate on the second term as was done by the present author in [3].

This paper is an attempt to increase our knowledge about simultaneous-equation estimators further, particularly with regard to their small-sample properties. The introduction of the k-class was a considerable addition to our stock of knowledge, since it united two-stage least-squares and limited-information-maximum-likelihood, as well as ordinary least-squares, and it led to a continuous set of consistent and asymptotically unbiased estimation methods. However, this class is somewhat restrictive in the sense that its parameter k enters in the left and right-hand side of the estimation equations (generalized normal equations) in the same manner. If we consider the h-class, also introduced in [5], instead of the k-class, this feature is no longer present. The object of this paper is to embrace both classes by proposing what will be called the double-k-class, which is a two-parameter family, and to analyze its bias to $O(1/T)$, its moment matrix to $O(1/T^2)$, and the bias of the corresponding residual-variance estimator to $O(1/T)$, thus contributing further to our knowledge of simultaneous-equation estimators "around" two-stage-least-squares and limited-information-maximum-likelihood. The results are presented in Section 2 and discussed in Section 3, while the proofs are all gathered in Section 4.

2. THE ESTIMATION PROCEDURE AND THEOREMS

Let the equation to be estimated be written as

(2.1) $$y = Y\gamma + X_1\beta + u = (Y\ X_1)\delta + u\,,$$

where $\delta = \binom{\gamma}{\beta}$ is the parameter vector to be estimated, y is a column vector of T observations on the jointly dependent variable "to be explained," Y is a $T \times m$ matrix of observations on m explanatory jointly dependent variables, X_1 is a $T \times l$ matrix of observations on l explanatory predetermined variables, and u is a column vector of T disturbances. Further, if X_2 is a $T \times (\Lambda - l)$ matrix of observations on $(\Lambda - l)$ predetermined variables which occur in the complete system but not in the equation (2.1), then we have

(2.2) $$X = [X_1\ X_2]\,,$$

which is now a $T \times \Lambda$ matrix of observations on all Λ predetermined variables.

Let us now consider only that part of the complete reduced form which corresponds to the explanatory jointly dependent variables of (2.1). We can write this as:

(2.3) $$Y = X\Pi + \bar{V} = X_1\Pi_1 + X_2\Pi_2 + \bar{V} = \bar{Y}_1 + \bar{Y}_2 + \bar{V} = \bar{Y} + \bar{V}\,,$$

where $\Pi = \binom{\Pi_1}{\Pi_2}$ is the $\Lambda \times m$ matrix of parent reduced-form coefficients, and the submatrices Π_1 and Π_2 have their proper orders; $\bar{V}$ is the $T \times m$ matrix of parent reduced-form disturbances, and $\bar{Y}_1 = X_1\Pi_1$, $\bar{Y}_2 = X_2\Pi_2$ and $\bar{Y} = X\Pi$.

As before in the earlier article [3] we use the following symbols:

(2.4) $$Z = [\bar{Y}\ X_1],\ V_z = [\bar{V}\ 0],\ M = I - M^* \text{ and } M^* = X(X'X)^{-1}X'\,.$$

The least-squares estimate of $\bar{V}$ is

(2.5) $$V = Y - X(X'X)^{-1}X'Y = MY = M\bar{V}\,,$$

because $MX = 0$.

The double k-class estimator $d = \binom{c}{b}$ of the parameter vector $\delta = \binom{\gamma}{\beta}$ of (2.1) is defined by

(2.6) $$\begin{bmatrix} Y' - k_2V' \\ X_1' \end{bmatrix} y = \begin{bmatrix} Y'Y - k_1V'V & Y'X_1 \\ X_1'Y & X_1'X_1 \end{bmatrix} d\,,$$

where k_1 and k_2 are any two arbitrary real numbers. This is a generalization of the k-class, which is the case in which the two k's are equal: $k_1 = k_2 = k$, say. Thus the k-class is given by

(2.6a) $$\begin{bmatrix} Y' - k\,V' \\ X_1' \end{bmatrix} y = \begin{bmatrix} Y'Y - k\,V'V & Y'X_1 \\ X_1'Y & X_1'X_1 \end{bmatrix} d^*\,.$$

It is also a generalization of the h-class:

$$(2.6b)\quad \begin{bmatrix} Y' - (1-h)V' \\ X_1' \end{bmatrix} y = \begin{bmatrix} Y' - (1-h)V' \\ X_1' \end{bmatrix} [Y - (1-h)V \quad X_1] d^{**}$$
$$= \begin{bmatrix} Y'Y - (1-h^2)V'V & Y'X_1 \\ X_1'Y & X_1'X_1 \end{bmatrix} d^{**} .$$

See Theil [5, (Ch. 6)].

Before presenting the theorems on small-sample properties of the double k-class estimators, it is useful to lay down the underlying assumptions.

Assumption I. Equation (2.1) is one of a complete system of M ($\geqq m+1$) linear stochastic equations in M jointly dependent and Λ predetermined variables. The reduced form of this system exists.

Assumption II. The matrix Π_2, which is of order $(\Lambda - l) \times m$, has rank m.[2]

Assumption III. The matrix X, which is of order $T \times \Lambda$, has rank Λ, and it consists of nonstochastic elements.[3]

Assumption IV. The scalars k_1 and k_2 involved in the equation (2.6) are nonstochastic and they differ from 1 to the order $1/T$. That is, we can write

$$(2.7)\qquad k_1 = 1 + \frac{\kappa_1}{T}, \quad \text{and} \quad k_2 = 1 + \frac{\kappa_2}{T},$$

neglecting the terms of higher order of smallness than $1/T$ because they are irrelevant for our purpose. Both κ_1 and κ_2 are nonstochastic real numbers, independent of T.

Assumption V.[4] The T disturbance vectors are independent random drawings from the same M-dimensional normal parent with zero means.

Under this last assumption, we can always write the reduced-form disturbances of (2.3) as

$$(2.8)\qquad \bar{V} = u\pi' + W,$$

which describes the normally distributed reduced-form disturbances as

[2] This is equivalent to the rank condition of identifiability given by W. C. Hood and T. C. Koopmans [2]. Further, this statement implies $\Lambda \geqq m + l$, which is equivalent to the order condition of identifiability of (2.1).

[3] The second part of this assumption requires that there be no lagged endogenous variables in the complete system. This is useful for the small sample analysis which we are going to present. However, for asymptotic samples the presence of lagged endogenous variables does not present any difficulty.

[4] Cf. footnote 8 of [3].

consisting of a part which is proportional to the corresponding disturbance in (2.1) (viz., $u\pi'$, π being a column vector of m components, which are simply constants) and a part (viz., W) which is also normally distributed but independently of the u-vector.

Further, we introduce the column vector

$$q = \begin{bmatrix} \mathrm{cov}(y_1, u) \\ \vdots \\ \mathrm{cov}(y_m, u) \\ \mathrm{cov}(x_1, u) \\ \vdots \\ \mathrm{cov}(x_l, u) \end{bmatrix} = \frac{1}{T}\begin{bmatrix} E(\bar{V}' u) \\ 0 \end{bmatrix} = \sigma^2\begin{pmatrix} \pi \\ 0 \end{pmatrix}, \tag{2.9}$$

σ^2 being the variance of the disturbance in (2.1), and the matrix

$$Q = \begin{bmatrix} \bar{Y}'\bar{Y} & \bar{Y}'X_1 \\ X_1'\bar{Y} & X_1'X_1 \end{bmatrix}^{-1} = \begin{bmatrix} \omega_{11} & \omega_{12} \\ \omega_{21} & \omega_{22} \end{bmatrix}, \tag{2.10}$$

where

$$\begin{aligned} \omega_{11} &= (\bar{Y}'M_1\bar{Y})^{-1}, \\ \omega_{21} &= -(X_1'X_1)^{-1}X_1'\bar{Y}(\bar{Y}'M_1\bar{Y})^{-1}, \\ \omega_{12} &= \omega_{21}', \\ M_1 &= I - X_1(X_1'X_1)^{-1}X_1'. \end{aligned} \tag{2.11}$$

It is instructive to observe that Q is the parent analogue of the matrix

$$\begin{bmatrix} Y'Y - V'V & Y'X_1 \\ X_1'Y & X_1'X_1 \end{bmatrix}^{-1}, \tag{2.12}$$

which is required for obtaining the two-stage-least-squares estimates.

From the equation (2.8), we have for the moment matrix of $\bar{V}$

$$\frac{1}{T}\mathrm{E}(\bar{V}'\bar{V}) = \sigma^2\pi\pi' + \frac{1}{T}\mathrm{E}(W'W). \tag{2.13}$$

This equation describes the covariance matrix of the explanatory dependent variables of (2.1) as the sum of two matrices, one of which is concerned with the random variation of the structural disturbance of (2.1), the other being independent of this source of randomness. It will prove useful to enlarge these matrices so that they refer not only to the explanatory dependent variables of (2.1), but also to the explanatory predetermined variables. As the latter variables are not characterized by any randomness at all, we should border these matrices with l rows and l columns of zeros. We thus obtain three square matrices of order $m + l$,

$$(2.14)\qquad C=\begin{bmatrix} C^* & 0 \\ 0 & 0 \end{bmatrix},\quad C_1=\begin{bmatrix} C_1^* & 0 \\ 0 & 0 \end{bmatrix}=\frac{1}{\sigma^2}qq',\quad C_2=\begin{bmatrix} C_2^* & 0 \\ 0 & 0 \end{bmatrix},$$

where, of course,

$$(2.15)\qquad C=C_1+C_2,\ C^*=\frac{1}{T}\mathrm{E}(\bar{V}'\bar{V}),\ C_1^*=\sigma^2\pi\pi',\ C_2^*=\frac{1}{T}\mathrm{E}(W'W)\,.$$

Now we can present the following theorems:

THEOREM 1. *Under Assumptions* I, II, III, IV *and* V *the bias, to order* $1/T$, *of the double* k*-class estimator* d *(defined in* (2.6) *above) of the parameter vector* δ *of* (2.1) *is given by*

$$(2.16)\qquad \mathrm{E}(e)=(-\kappa_2+L-1)Qq+(\kappa_1-\kappa_2)QC\delta\,,$$

where e *is the sampling error*

$$(2.17)\qquad e=d-\delta\,,$$

and L *is the number of predetermined variables in excess of the number of coefficients to be estimated, i.e.,*

$$(2.18)\qquad L=\Lambda-(m+l)\,.$$

THEOREM 2. *Under the assumptions of Theorem* 1, *the moment matrix, to order* $1/T^2$, *of the double* k*-class estimator* d *around the parameter vector* δ *is given by*

$$(2.19)\qquad \mathrm{E}(ee')=\sigma^2[(1+\beta_0)Q+\beta_1QC_1Q+\beta_2QC_2Q+\beta_3(Qqr'+rq'Q)+\beta_4rr'],$$

where

$$\beta_0=-2(\kappa_1-\kappa_2)\frac{r'q}{\sigma^2}-\left[-2\kappa_2+2L-3+2(\kappa_1-\kappa_2)\frac{\delta'q}{\sigma^2}\right]\mathrm{tr}C_1Q+\mathrm{tr}C_2Q\,,$$

$$\beta_1=2(\kappa_1+1)+\left[(\kappa_1-\kappa_2)\frac{\delta'q}{\sigma^2}-\kappa_2+L-2\right]^2,$$

$$(2.20)\qquad \beta_2=2\kappa_1-L+2\,,$$

$$\beta_3=\frac{\kappa_1-\kappa_2}{\sigma^2}\left[(\kappa_1-\kappa_2)\frac{\delta'q}{\sigma^2}-\kappa_2+L-2\right],$$

$$\beta_4=\frac{(\kappa_1-\kappa_2)^2}{\sigma^2}\,,$$

$$r=QC_2\delta.$$

Finally, we consider the residual variance estimator. The double k-class estimated vector of disturbances of equation (2.1) is

$$(2.21)\qquad u_e=y-(Y\ X_1)d=u-(Y\ X_1)e\,,$$

where e is defined above in (2.17), and the residual variance estimator is defined as $u_e'u_e/T$.

THEOREM 3. *Under the assumptions of Theorem 1, the bias, to order 1/T, of the residual variance estimator of the double k-class is given by*

$$\frac{1}{T}\mathrm{E}(u_e'u_e) - \sigma^2 = -\sigma^2\Big[2\Big\{-\kappa_2 + L - 1 + (\kappa_1 - \kappa_2)\frac{\delta' q}{\sigma^2}\Big\}\mathrm{tr}C_1Q \tag{2.22}$$
$$- \mathrm{tr}CQ + \frac{1}{T}(m + l) + 2(\kappa_1 - \kappa_2)\frac{q'r}{\sigma^2}\Big].$$

3. GENERAL DISCUSSION OF THE RESULTS

It seems interesting to make a comparison of our earlier results on the k-class estimators with the new results on the double k-class and the h-class estimators. For deriving the results on the k-class estimators from the above theorems, we write $k_1 = k_2 = k$, i.e., $\kappa_1 = \kappa_2 = \kappa$. Similarly, for deriving the results on the h-class estimators from the above theorems, we write $k_1 = 1 - h^2$ and $k_2 = 1 - h$. Further, as for k_1 and k_2 we assume that h is nonstochastic and that it differs from 0, to order $1/T$; i.e., we can write $h = \iota/T$, ι being a nonstochastic real number independent of T. Therefore, $k_1 = 1 - h^2$ gives $\kappa_1 = -\iota^2/T$, which is zero to our order of approximation, and $k_2 = 1 - h$ gives $\kappa_2 = -\iota$.

3.1. *The bias.* Considering the result of Theorem 1 we observe that the bias of the double k-class estimator consists of two parts, the first of which is a scalar times Qq and the second a scalar times $QC\delta$. If we refer to equation (2.9) we find that

$$q = \begin{bmatrix} \mathrm{cov}(y_1, u) \\ \vdots \\ \mathrm{cov}(y_m, u) \\ \mathrm{cov}(x_1, u) \\ \vdots \\ \mathrm{cov}(x_l, u) \end{bmatrix}$$

is the column vector of covariances between the explanatory variables $y_1, \cdots, y_m, x_1, \cdots, x_l$ and the structural disturbance u of (2.1). We also have

$$C\delta = \frac{1}{T}\begin{bmatrix} \mathrm{E}(\bar{V}'\bar{V})\gamma \\ 0 \end{bmatrix} = \frac{1}{T}\begin{bmatrix} \mathrm{E}(Y - \bar{Y})'(y - \bar{y}) \\ 0 \end{bmatrix} - q$$
$$= \begin{bmatrix} \mathrm{cov}(y_1, y) \\ \vdots \\ \mathrm{cov}(y_m, y) \\ \mathrm{cov}(x_1, y) \\ \vdots \\ \mathrm{cov}(x_l, y) \end{bmatrix} - q\,, \tag{3.1.1}$$

where $\bar{y} = \mathrm{E}(y)$ and $\bar{Y} = \mathrm{E}(Y)$ as before. Thus $C\delta$ is a column vector of differences between the covariances of the explanatory variables; $y_1, \cdots, y_m, x_1, \cdots, x_l$; with the jointly dependent variable (to be explained), viz., y of (2.1), and the covariances of the explanatory variables; $y_1, y_2, \cdots, y_m, x_1, \cdots, x_l$; with the structural disturbance u of (2.1). Therefore, it turns out that the bias, to order $1/T$, of the double k-class estimator is a homogeneous linear combination of covariances of the explanatory variables with the structural disturbance and jointly dependent variable, to be explained, of equation (2.1).

Now putting $\kappa_1 = \kappa_2 = \kappa$ in (2.16) we find that the bias of the k-class estimator is simply[5]

$$\mathrm{E}(e_k) = (-\kappa + L - 1)Qq \,. \tag{3.1.2}$$

This is a homogeneous linear combination of covariances between the explanatory variables and the structural disturbance of (2.1). It is free of the covariances between the explanatory variables and the dependent variable. The bias of the two-stage-least-squares estimator as derived from (3.1.2) (by putting $\kappa = 0$) is $\mathrm{E}(e_1) = (L - 1)Qq$.

The bias, to order $1/T$, of the h-class estimator

$$\mathrm{E}(e_h) = (\iota + L - 1)Qq + \iota QC\delta \,, \tag{3.1.3}$$

is obtained from (2.16) by putting $\kappa_1 = 0$ and $\kappa_2 = -\iota$. Thus $\mathrm{E}(e_h)$ is only slightly simpler than the bias of the double k-class estimator.

3.2. *The moment matrix.* The moment matrix, to order $1/T^2$, of the k-class estimator as derived from the Theorem 2 is[6]

$$\mathrm{E}(e_k e_k') = \sigma^2[(1 + \beta_0')Q + \beta_1' QC_1Q + \beta_2' QC_2Q] \,, \tag{3.2.1}$$

where

$$\begin{aligned} \beta_0' &= (2\kappa - 2L + 3)\mathrm{tr}C_1Q + \mathrm{tr}C_2Q \,, \\ \beta_1' &= 2(\kappa + 1) + (\kappa - L + 2)^2 \,, \\ \beta_2' &= 2\kappa - L + 2 \,. \end{aligned} \tag{3.2.2}$$

For two-stage-least-squares we write $\kappa = 0$ (and $k = 1$), and then from (3.2.1) and (3.2.2) we get the moment matrix:

$$\mathrm{E}(e_1 e_1') = \sigma^2[(1 + \beta_0'')Q + \beta_1'' QC_1Q + \beta_2'' QC_2Q] \,, \tag{3.2.3}$$

where

$$\begin{aligned} \beta_0'' &= -(2L - 3)\mathrm{tr}C_1Q + \mathrm{tr}C_2Q \,, \\ \beta_1'' &= 2 + (L - 2)^2 \,, \\ \beta_2'' &= -\,(L - 2) \,. \end{aligned} \tag{3.2.4}$$

[5] Cf. Theorem 1 of [3, (578)].

[6] Cf. Theorem 2 of [3, (579)].

Both for the k-class and the two-stage-least-squares estimator, the moment matrices consist of only the first three parts of the moment matrix of the double k-class estimator. The last two parts do not appear because $\beta_3 = \beta_4 = 0$ in these cases.

The moment matrix, to order $1/T^2$, of the h-class estimator is given by

$$\text{(3.2.5)} \qquad \mathrm{E}(e_h e_h') = \sigma^2[(1 + \alpha_0)Q + \alpha_1 Q C_1 Q + \alpha_2 Q C_2 Q + \alpha_3(Qqr' + rq'Q) + \alpha_4 rr'] ,$$

where

$$\text{(3.2.6)} \qquad \begin{aligned} \alpha_0 &= -2\iota\frac{q'r}{\sigma^2} - \left(2\iota + 2L - 3 + 2\iota\frac{\delta' q}{\sigma^2}\right)\mathrm{tr}C_1 Q + \mathrm{tr}C_2 Q , \\ \alpha_1 &= 2 + \left(\iota\frac{\delta' q}{\sigma^2} + \iota + L - 2\right)^2 , \\ \alpha_2 &= -(L - 2) , \\ \alpha_3 &= \frac{\iota}{\sigma^2}\left(\iota\frac{\delta' q}{\sigma^2} + \iota + L - 2\right) , \\ \alpha_4 &= \frac{\iota^2}{\sigma^2} , \\ r &= QC_2\delta_u' . \end{aligned}$$

As for the double k-class estimator, this matrix also consists of five parts, and the two moment matrices are perfectly comparable.

The quantity $\delta' q/\sigma^2$ is rather frequently observed in the α and β coefficients of the above moment matrices. Trying to interpret what it means, we write

$$\text{(3.2.7)} \qquad \begin{aligned} q &= \frac{1}{T}\begin{bmatrix} \mathrm{E}(\bar{V}'u) \\ 0 \end{bmatrix} = \frac{1}{T}\begin{bmatrix} \mathrm{E}(Y'u) \\ \mathrm{E}(X_1'u) \end{bmatrix} , \\ \delta' q &= \frac{1}{T}\mathrm{E}(Y\gamma + X_1\beta)'u = \frac{1}{T}\mathrm{E}(y - u)'u . \end{aligned}$$

Thus

$$\text{(3.2.8)} \qquad \frac{\delta' q}{\sigma^2} = \frac{\mathrm{E}(y'u)}{T\sigma^2} - 1 = \frac{\mathrm{cov}(y, u)}{\sigma^2} - 1 ,$$

which will be equal to zero if we are dealing with the classical least-squares regression situation because then $\mathrm{cov}(y, u)/\sigma^2 = 1$. Hence we may interpret $\delta' q/\sigma^2$ as an index of departure from the least-squares case or an index of interdependence in the equation system as far as this interdependence is relevant for the equation under consideration.

3.3. *The residual variance.* The bias, to order $1/T$, of the residual variance estimator $u_e'u_e/T$, where u_e has been derived according to the k-class estimation procedure, can be obtained from (2.22) by writing $\kappa_1 = \kappa_2 = \kappa$. Thus[7]

$$\text{(3.3.1)}\quad \frac{1}{T}\mathrm{E}(u_e'u_e) - \sigma^2 = \sigma^2\Big[2(\kappa - L + 1)\mathrm{tr}C_1Q + \mathrm{tr}CQ - \frac{1}{T}(m + l)\Big],$$

and for $\kappa = 0$ we get from (3.3.1) the bias of the residual variance estimator, where u is estimated according to two-stage-least-squares.

For $\kappa_1 = 0$ and $\kappa_2 = -\iota$, we get from (2.22) the bias, to $O(1/T)$, of $u_e'u_e/T$ when u is estimated according to the h-class; then

$$\text{(3.3.2)}\quad \begin{aligned}\frac{1}{T}\mathrm{E}(u_e'u_e) - \sigma^2 = -\sigma^2\Big[2\Big(\iota + L - 1 + \iota\frac{\delta'q}{\sigma^2}\Big)\mathrm{tr}C_1Q - \mathrm{tr}CQ \\ + \frac{1}{T}(m + l) + 2\iota\frac{r'q}{\sigma^2}\Big].\end{aligned}$$

4. PROOF OF THE THEOREMS[8]

4.1. *Proof of Theorem* 1. Let us write equation (2.1) as[9]

$$\text{(4.1.1)}\quad \begin{aligned} y &= \Big(Y - \frac{k_1 - k_2}{1 - k_2}V\Big)\gamma + X_1\beta + u^* \\ &= \Big(Y - \frac{k_1 - k_2}{1 - k_2}V \;\; X_1\Big)\delta + u^*,\end{aligned}$$

where

$$\text{(4.1.2)}\quad u^* = u + \frac{k_1 - k_2}{1 - k_2}V\gamma = u + \frac{k_1 - k_2}{1 - k_2}MV_z\delta\,.$$

Then combining (4.1.1) with (2.6), we get for the sampling error of the double k-class estimator

$$\text{(4.1.3)}\quad e = d - \delta = \begin{bmatrix} Y'Y - k_1V'V & Y'X_1 \\ X_1'Y & X_1'X_1\end{bmatrix}^{-1}\begin{bmatrix} Y' - k_2V' \\ X_1'\end{bmatrix}u^*,$$

which, on using (2.3) and (2.4), can be written as

[7] See also [4].

[8] In this section it is always implied that summation over t, with whatever accent, extends from 1 to T, and that over μ, with any accent, from 1 to m.

[9] Division by $1 - k_2$ is of course possible only if $k_2 \neq 1$; hence the proof is not directly applicable to the case $k_2 = 1$. But indirectly it is, since the bias and moment matrix are continuous functions of k_1 and k_2 in the neighbourhood of 1; so the case $k_2 = 1$ is treated as the limit for $k_2 \to 1$.

$$
(4.1.4)\quad
\begin{aligned}
e &= [Q^{-1} + \{Z'V_z + V_z'Z + (1-k_1)V_z'V_z + k_1 V_z'M^*V_z\}]^{-1} \\
&\quad \times [Z' + (1-k_2)V_z' + k_2 V_z'M^*]u^* \\
&= [I + Q\{Z'V_z + V_z'Z + (1-k_1)V_z'V_z + k_1 V_z'M^*V_z\}]^{-1}Q \\
&\quad \times [Z'u^* + (1-k_2)V_z'u^* + k_2 V_z'M^*u^*] .
\end{aligned}
$$

Neglecting the terms of higher order of smallness than $1/T$, remembering (2.7), we get

$$
(4.1.5)\quad e = Q\left[Z'u^* - \frac{\kappa_2}{T}V_z'u^* + V_z'M^*u^* - Z'V_zQZ'u^* - V_z'ZQZ'u^*\right],
$$

where it should be noted that $Z'u^* = Z'u$ and $V_z'M^*u^* = V_z'M^*u$. For deriving the expectation $\mathrm{E}(e)$ from (4.1.5), let us write

$$
u^* = u + \frac{\kappa_2 - \kappa_1}{\kappa_2}V_z\delta - \frac{\kappa_2 - \kappa_1}{\kappa_2}M^*V_z\delta .
$$

As Z is nonstochastic, it follows from Assumption V that

$$
(4.1.6)\quad \mathrm{E}(Z'u^*) = 0 .
$$

Further, we have

$$
(4.1.7)\quad \mathrm{E}(V_z'u^*) = \mathrm{E}(V_z'u) + \frac{\kappa_2 - \kappa_1}{\kappa_2}\mathrm{E}(V_z'V_z)\delta ,
$$

to order T. Here, $(1/T)E(V_z'u) = q$, and $(1/T)E(V_z'V_z) = C$, introduced earlier in Section 2, and we require

$$
(4.1.8)\quad
\begin{aligned}
\mathrm{E}(V_z'M^*u^*) &= \mathrm{E}(V_z'M^*u) = \Lambda q , \\
\mathrm{E}(Z'V_zQZ'u^*) &= \mathrm{E}(Z'V_zQZ'u) = q , \\
\mathrm{E}(V_z'ZQZ'u^*) &= \mathrm{E}(V_z'ZQZ'u) = (m + l)q ,
\end{aligned}
$$

which have been evaluated in equations (3.2.6), (3.2.10) and (3.2.11) of [3].

Therefore, using (4.1.6), (4.1.7) and (4.1.8), we get from (4.1.5)

$$
(4.1.9)\quad \mathrm{E}(e) = (-\kappa_2 + \Lambda - m - l - 1)Qq + (\kappa_1 - \kappa_2)QC\delta ,
$$

which is the result given in Theorem 1.

4.2. *Proof of Theorem* 2. Writing

$$
(4.2.1)\quad \nabla = Z'V_z + V_z'Z + (1-k_1)V_z'V_z + k_1 V_z'M^*V_z ,
$$

and

$$
(4.2.2)\quad
\begin{aligned}
S &= [Z'u + (1-k_2)V_z'u^* + k_2 V_z'M^*u] \\
&\quad \times [u'Z + (1-k_2)(u^*)'V_z + k_2 u'M^*V_z] ,
\end{aligned}
$$

we have from the second equality of (4.1.4)

$$
(4.2.3)\quad ee' = [I + Q\nabla]^{-1}QSQ[I + Q\nabla]'^{-1} .
$$

Expanding the right-hand side of (4.2.3), we can write

$$Q^{-1}ee'Q^{-1} = S - (SQ\nabla + \nabla QS) + (SQ\nabla Q\nabla + \nabla QSQ\nabla + \nabla Q\nabla QS) - \cdots . \tag{4.2.4}$$

Since all the terms in Q^{-1} are of order T, to derive the moment matrix $E(ee')$, to order $1/T^2$, we should retain terms only up to order 1 on the right-hand side of (4.2.4).

Further, for the sake of brevity in writing, let us introduce

$$N_1 = -\frac{1}{T}\kappa_1 I + M^* , \qquad N_2 = -\frac{1}{T}\kappa_2 I + M^* , \tag{4.2.5}$$

$$\nabla_{\frac{1}{2}} = Z'V_z + V_z'Z , \qquad \nabla_0 = V_z'N_1V_z , \tag{4.2.6}$$

and

$$\begin{aligned} S_1 &= Z'uu'Z , \\ S_{\frac{1}{2}} &= Z'u\left[u'N_2V_z + \frac{1}{T}(\kappa_1 - \kappa_2)\delta' V_z' V_z\right] \\ &\quad + \left[V_z'N_2u + \frac{1}{T}(\kappa_1 - \kappa_2)V_z'V_z\delta\right]u'Z , \\ S_0 &= \left[V_z'N_2u + \frac{1}{T}(\kappa_1 - \kappa_2)V_z'V_z\delta\right] \\ &\quad \times\left[u'N_2V_z + \frac{1}{T}(\kappa_1 - \kappa_2)\delta' V_z' V_z\right] , \end{aligned} \tag{4.2.7}$$

where the suffixes of ∇'s and S's indicate their orders. Thus, $\nabla_{\frac{1}{2}}$ means that part of ∇ which is $O(T^{\frac{1}{2}})$; ∇_0 means that of ∇ which is $O(T^0)$ or $O(1)$; $S_{\frac{1}{2}}$ means that part of S which is $O(T^{\frac{1}{2}})$; etc. Evidently, up to $O(1)$

$$\nabla = \nabla_{\frac{1}{2}} + \nabla_0 \quad \text{and} \quad S = S_1 + S_{\frac{1}{2}} + S_0 . \tag{4.2.7a}$$

For the E(S) we have

$$E(S_1) = \sigma^2 Z'Z = \sigma^2 Q^{-1} \quad \text{and} \quad E(S_{\frac{1}{2}}) = 0 , \tag{4.2.8}$$

due to Assumption V. To obtain $E(S_0)$, we require

$$\begin{aligned} E(S_0) &= E(V_z'N_2uu'N_2V_z) + \frac{1}{T}(\kappa_1 - \kappa_2)E(V_z'N_2u\delta' V_z' V_z) \\ &\quad + \frac{1}{T}(\kappa_1 - \kappa_2)E(V_z'V_z\delta u'N_2V_z) + \frac{1}{T^2}(\kappa_1 - \kappa_2)^2E(V_z'V_z\delta\delta' V_z' V_z) , \end{aligned} \tag{4.2.9}$$

where the expectations on the right-hand side are to be evaluated one by one.

First,

$$\text{(4.2.10)} \qquad \mathrm{E}(V_z' N_2 uu' N_2 V_z) = \sigma^2[\{2\Lambda + (\Lambda - \kappa_2)^2\}C_1 + \Lambda C_2] ,$$

which is derived from (3.3.13) of [3] by replacing N by N_2.

Secondly,

$$\text{(4.2.11)} \qquad \mathrm{E}(V_z' N_2 u\delta' V_z' V_z) = \begin{bmatrix} \mathrm{E}(\bar{V}' N_2 u\gamma' \bar{V}' \bar{V}) & 0 \\ 0 & 0 \end{bmatrix} ,$$

for which we can write

$$\text{(4.2.12)} \qquad \begin{aligned} \mathrm{E}(\bar{V}' N_2 u\gamma' \bar{V}' \bar{V}) &= (\gamma'\pi)\mathrm{E}(u' N_2 uu'u)\pi\pi' + \mathrm{E}(u' N_2 u)\pi\gamma' \mathrm{E}(W'W) \\ &\quad + \mathrm{E}(W' N_2 uu' W)[(\gamma'\pi)I + \gamma\pi'] , \end{aligned}$$

where use has been made of (2.8) and $\gamma' W' u = u' W\gamma$.

It is easy to see that

$$\text{(4.2.13)} \qquad \mathrm{E}(u' N_2 u) = \sigma^2 \mathrm{tr} N_2 = (\Lambda - \kappa_2)\sigma^2 ,$$

and we have $\mathrm{E}(W'W) = TC_2^*$ from (2.15). Further,

$$\text{(4.2.14)} \qquad \mathrm{E}(u' N_2 uu'u) = \sum_t \sum_{t'} \sum_{t''} n_2(t, t') \mathrm{E}[u(t)u(t')u^2(t'')] ,$$

where $n_2(t, t')$ is the term in the t-th row and t'-th column of N_2. It is easily seen that the terms under the summation sign are nonzero only if $t = t'$, due to Assumption V; therefore

$$\text{(4.2.15)} \qquad \begin{aligned} \mathrm{E}(u' N_2 uu'u) &= \sum_t \sum_{t''} n_2(t, t) \mathrm{E}[u^2(t)u^2(t'')] \\ &= \sum_t n_2(t, t)\mathrm{E}[u^4(t)] + \sum_t \sum_{\substack{t'' \\ t \neq t''}} n_2(t, t) \mathrm{E}[u^2(t)]\mathrm{E}[u^2(t'')] \\ &= (T + 2)\sigma^4 \mathrm{tr} N_2 = (T + 2)(\Lambda - \kappa_2)\sigma^4 . \end{aligned}$$

We can derive the expectation $\mathrm{E}(W' N_2 uu' W)$ involved in (4.2.12) in exactly the same way as (A.11.1) of [3]; thus

$$\text{(4.2.16)} \qquad \mathrm{E}(W' N_2 uu' W) = \sigma^2(\Lambda - \kappa_2)C_2^* .$$

Using (4.2.11), (4.2.12), (4.2.13), (4.2.15) and (4.2.16), we get

$$\text{(4.2.17)} \qquad \frac{1}{T}(\kappa_1 - \kappa_2)\mathrm{E}(V_z' N_2 u\delta' V_z' V_z) = (\kappa_1 - \kappa_2)(\Lambda - \kappa_2)[(\delta' q)C_1 + q\delta' C_2] .$$

The second and third terms on the right-hand side of (4.2.9) are transposes of each other. Therefore, we have

$$\text{(4.2.18)} \qquad \frac{1}{T}(\kappa_1 - \kappa_2)\mathrm{E}(V_z' V_z \delta u' N_2 V_z) = (\kappa_1 - \kappa_2)(\Lambda - \kappa_2)[(\delta' q)C_1 + C_2\delta q'] .$$

Coming to the fourth term on the right-hand side of (4.2.9), we write

$$\text{(4.2.19)} \qquad E(V_z'V_z\delta\delta'V_z'V_z) = \begin{bmatrix} E(\bar{V}'\bar{V}\gamma\gamma'\bar{V}'\bar{V}) & 0 \\ 0 & 0 \end{bmatrix},$$

where on using (2.8) and simplifying, we have

$$\text{(4.2.20)} \qquad \begin{aligned} E(\bar{V}'\bar{V}\gamma\gamma'\bar{V}'\bar{V}) &= (\gamma'\pi)^2\pi\pi' E(u'uu'u) \\ &+ (\gamma'\pi)[E(u'u)\pi\gamma' E(W'W) + E(W'W)\gamma\pi' E(u'u)] \\ &+ [\pi E(u'W\gamma u'W)\gamma'\pi + E(u'W\gamma\gamma'W'u)\pi\pi' + (\gamma'\pi)^2 E(W'uu'W) \\ &+ E(W'u\gamma'W'u)\gamma'\pi\pi'] + E(W'W\gamma\gamma'W'W) . \end{aligned}$$

If we write $E(u'u) = T\sigma^2$, $E(W'W) = TC_2^*$, and note that $u'W\gamma = \gamma'W'u$, we can rewrite (4.2.20) as follows:

$$\text{(4.2.21)} \qquad \begin{aligned} E(\bar{V}'\bar{V}\gamma\gamma'\bar{V}'\bar{V}) &= (\gamma'\pi)^2\pi\pi' E(u'uu'u) \\ &+ T^2\sigma^2(\gamma'\pi)[\pi\gamma'C_2^* + C_2^*\gamma\pi'] \\ &+ [\pi\gamma'\Xi(\gamma'\pi) + \gamma'\Xi\gamma\pi\pi' + (\gamma'\pi)^2\Xi + \Xi\gamma\pi'(\gamma'\pi)] \\ &+ E(W'W\gamma\gamma'W'W) , \end{aligned}$$

where to save space we have written Ξ for $E(W'uu'W)$. Using (A.1.1) and (A.11.1) of [3] (replacing N by I in both cases), we have

$$\text{(4.2.22)} \qquad E(u'uu'u) = T(T+2)\sigma^4 \quad \text{and} \quad \Xi = E(W'uu'W) = T\sigma^2 C_2^* .$$

We still require the value of $E(W'W\gamma\gamma'W'W)$, which is a matrix of order $m \times m$. The term in the μ-th row and μ'-th column of $E(W'W\gamma\gamma'W'W)$ is

$$\text{(4.2.23)} \qquad \begin{aligned} &\sum_{\mu''}\sum_{\mu'''}\sum_{t}\sum_{t'} \gamma_{\mu''}\gamma_{\mu'''} E[w_\mu(t)w_{\mu''}(t)w_{\mu'''}(t')w_{\mu'}(t')] \\ &= \sum_{\mu''}\sum_{\mu'''}\sum_{t} \gamma_{\mu''}\gamma_{\mu'''} E[w_\mu(t)w_{\mu''}(t)w_{\mu'''}(t)w_{\mu'}(t)] \\ &+ \sum_{\mu''}\sum_{\mu'''}\sum_{t}\sum_{\substack{t' \\ t\neq t'}} \gamma_{\mu''}\gamma_{\mu'''} \operatorname{cov}(w_\mu, w_{\mu''})\operatorname{cov}(w_{\mu'''}, w_{\mu'}) . \end{aligned}$$

Since the fourth order moment $E[w_\mu(t)w_{\mu''}(t)w_{\mu'''}(t)w_{\mu'}(t)]$, the covariances $\operatorname{cov}(w_\mu, w_{\mu''})$, and $\operatorname{cov}(w_{\mu'''}, w_{\mu'})$ are independent of t (cf. Assumption V.) we get

$$\text{(4.2.24)} \qquad \begin{aligned} &\sum_{\mu''}\sum_{\mu'''}\sum_{t}\sum_{t'} \gamma_{\mu''}\gamma_{\mu'''} E[w_\mu(t)w_{\mu''}(t)w_{\mu'''}(t')w_{\mu'}(t')] \\ &= T\sum_{\mu''}\sum_{\mu'''} \gamma_{\mu''}\gamma_{\mu'''} E[w_\mu(t)w_{\mu''}(t)w_{\mu'''}(t)w_{\mu'}(t)] \\ &+ T(T-1)\sum_{\mu''}\sum_{\mu'''} \gamma_{\mu''}\gamma_{\mu'''} \operatorname{cov}(w_\mu, w_{\mu''})\operatorname{cov}(w_{\mu'''}, w_{\mu'}) . \end{aligned}$$

Therefore, up to order 1 we have

$$\text{(4.2.25)} \qquad \frac{1}{T^2}(\kappa_1 - \kappa_2)^2 E(W'W\gamma\gamma'W'W) = (\kappa_1 - \kappa_2)^2 C_2^*\gamma\gamma'C_2^* .$$

Finally, combining (4.2.19), (4.2.21), (4.2.22) and (4.2.25), we get

$$\text{(4.2.26)}\quad \begin{aligned} &\frac{1}{T^2}(\kappa_1-\kappa_2)^2\mathrm{E}(V_z'V_z\delta\delta'V_z'V_z) \\ &= (\kappa_1-\kappa_2)^2\left[\left(\frac{\delta'q}{\sigma^2}\right)^2\sigma^2C_1+\frac{\delta'q}{\sigma^2}\left(q\delta'C_2+C_2\delta q'\right)+C_2\delta\delta'C_2\right]. \end{aligned}$$

Using (4.2.10), (4.2.17), (4.2.18) and (4.2.26), we get from (4.2.9)

$$\text{(4.2.27)}\quad \begin{aligned} \mathrm{E}(S_0) &= \sigma^2\left[2\Lambda+\left\{\Lambda-\kappa_2+(\kappa_1-\kappa_2)\frac{\delta'q}{\sigma^2}\right\}^2\right]C_1+\sigma^2\Lambda C_2 \\ &\quad +(\kappa_1-\kappa_2)\left\{\Lambda-\kappa_2+(\kappa_1-\kappa_2)\frac{\delta'q}{\sigma^2}\right\}(q\delta'C_2+C_2\delta q') \\ &\quad +(\kappa_1-\kappa_2)^2C_2\delta\delta'C_2\,. \end{aligned}$$

Then using (4.2.7a), (4.2.8) and (4.2.27), we have

$$\text{(4.2.28)}\quad \mathrm{E}(S)=\sigma^2Q^{-1}+\mathrm{E}(S_0)\,.$$

Next, we consider the second term on the right-hand side of (4.2.4),

$$\text{(4.2.29)}\quad SQ\nabla = S_1Q\nabla_{\frac{1}{2}}+S_1Q\nabla_0+S_{\frac{1}{2}}Q\nabla_{\frac{1}{2}}\,,$$

where use has been made of (4.2.7a) and terms of higher order of smallness than $O(1)$ have been neglected.

Using Assumption V, it is easy to see that

$$\text{(4.2.30)}\quad \mathrm{E}(S_1Q\nabla_{\frac{1}{2}})=Z'\mathrm{E}(uu'ZQZ'V_z)+Z'\mathrm{E}(uu'ZQV_z')Z=0\,,$$

and for $\mathrm{E}(S_1Q\nabla_0)$ we have

$$\text{(4.2.31)}\quad \begin{aligned} \mathrm{E}(S_1Q\nabla_0) &= Z'\mathrm{E}(uu'ZQV_z'N_1V_z) \\ &= Z'\left[\mathrm{E}(uu'A'\bar{V}'N_1\bar{V})\ \vdots\ 0\right] \\ &= Z'\left[\mathrm{E}(uu'A'\pi u'N_1u)\pi'+\sigma^2A'\mathrm{E}(W'N_1W)\ \vdots\ 0\right], \end{aligned}$$

where use has been made of Lemma 3 of [3] and of equation (2.8) above. A is the same as defined in Lemma 3 of [3], viz.,

$$A=(\bar{Y}'M_1\bar{Y})^{-1}\bar{Y}'M_1\,.$$

To evaluate the expectations on the right-hand side of the third equality of (4.2.31), we make use of (A.2.1) and (A.7.1) of [3] (replacing N by N_1). Thus

$$\text{(4.2.32)}\quad \begin{aligned} \mathrm{E}(uu'A'\pi u'N_1u) &= \sigma^4[(\Lambda-\kappa_1)I+2N_1]A'\pi\,, \\ \mathrm{E}(W'N_1W) &= (\Lambda-\kappa_1)C_2^*\,; \end{aligned}$$

therefore we get from (4.2.31)

$$\text{(4.2.33)}\quad \mathrm{E}(S_1Q\nabla_0)=\sigma^2[(\Lambda-\kappa_1+2)C_1+(\Lambda-\kappa_1)C_2]\,.$$

Let us consider the third term on the right-hand side of (4.2.29)

$$S_{\frac{1}{2}} Q \nabla_{\frac{1}{2}}$$

$$= \Big[(Z'uu'N_2V_z + V_z'N_2uu'Z) + \frac{1}{T}(\kappa_1 - \kappa_2) \times (Z'u\delta'V_z'V_z + V_z'V_z\delta u'Z)\Big]Q(Z'V_z + V_z'Z)$$

$$= [(Z'uu'N_2V_z + V_z'N_2uu'Z)Q(Z'V_z + V_z'Z)] + \frac{1}{T}(\kappa_1 - \kappa_2)[(Z'u\delta'V_z'V_z + V_z'V_z\delta u'Z)Q(Z'V_z + V_z'Z)] \tag{4.2.34}$$

$$= [Z'uu'N_2V_zQZ'V_z + Z'uu'N_2V_zQV_z'Z + V_z'N_2uu'ZQZ'V_z + V_z'N_2uu'ZQV_z'Z] + \frac{1}{T}(\kappa_1 - \kappa_2)[Z'u\delta'V_z'V_zQZ'V_z + Z'u\delta'V_z'V_zQV_z'Z + V_z'V_z\delta u'ZQZ'V_z + V_z'V_z\delta u'ZQV_z'Z]\,,$$

where it can be observed that the quantity between the first pair of square brackets on the right-hand side of the third equality of (4.2.34) is almost the same as $P_{\frac{1}{2}}Q\Delta_{\frac{1}{2}}$ (except for the replacement of N by N_2) given in the equation (3.3.19) of [3]. Therefore, we derive

$$\begin{aligned} Z'\mathrm{E}(uu'N_2V_zQZ'V_z) &= \sigma^2[(\Lambda - \kappa_2 + 2)C_1 + C_2]\,, \\ Z'\mathrm{E}(uu'N_2V_zQV_z')Z &= \sigma^2[(\Lambda - \kappa_2 + 2)\mathrm{tr}C_1Q + \mathrm{tr}C_2Q]Q^{-1}, \\ \mathrm{E}(V_z'N_2uu'ZQZ'V_z) &= \sigma^2(m + l)[(\Lambda - \kappa_2 + 2)C_1 + C_2]\,, \\ \mathrm{E}(V_z'N_2uu'ZQV_z')Z &= \sigma^2[(\Lambda - \kappa_2 + 2)C_1 + C_2] \end{aligned} \tag{4.2.35}$$

from equations (3.3.21), (3.3.25), (3.3.23) and (3.3.27), respectively, of [3]. We still require expectations of the terms between the second pair of square brackets on the right-hand side of the third equality of (4.2.34). The first of these terms is $Z'u\delta'V_z'V_zQZ'V_z$, and for this we have

$$\mathrm{E}(Z'u\delta'V_z'V_zQZ'V_z) = Z'\Big[\mathrm{E}(u\gamma'\bar{V}'\bar{V}A\bar{V}) \,\vdots\, 0\Big]\,, \tag{4.2.36}$$

where use has been made of Lemma 3 of [3]. Using (2.8), we get

$$\begin{aligned} \mathrm{E}(u\gamma'\bar{V}'\bar{V}A\bar{V}) &= \mathrm{E}(u\gamma'\pi u'u\pi'Au\pi') + \mathrm{E}(u\gamma'\pi u'WAW) \\ &\quad + \mathrm{E}(u\gamma'W'u\pi'AW) + \mathrm{E}(u\gamma'W'WAu\pi') \\ &= (\gamma'\pi)\mathrm{E}(uu'uu')A'\pi\pi' + \sigma^2(\gamma'\pi)\mathrm{E}(WAW) \\ &\quad + \sigma^2\mathrm{E}(W\gamma\pi'AW) + T\sigma^2A'C_2^*\gamma\pi'\,. \end{aligned} \tag{4.2.37}$$

We can derive $\mathrm{E}(uu'uu')$ in the same way as $\mathrm{E}(uu'Nuu')$ in (A.3.1) of [3]. Thus $\mathrm{E}(uu'uu') = (T+2)\sigma^4 I$. Further, we have $\mathrm{E}(WAW) = A'C_2^*$

from (A.5.1) of [3]. To evaluate the expectation on the left-hand side of (4.2.37) we still require $E(W\gamma\pi' AW)$, which is a $T \times m$ matrix, the term in the t-th row and μ-th column being

$$\sum_{\mu'}\sum_{\mu''}\sum_{t'} \gamma_{\mu'}\pi_{\mu''}a_{\mu'' t'} E[w_{\mu'}(t)w_{\mu}(t')] \tag{4.2.38}$$
$$= \sum_{\mu'}\sum_{\mu''} \gamma_{\mu'}\pi_{\mu''}a_{\mu'' t}\operatorname{cov}[w_{\mu}, w_{\mu'}] .$$

Therefore,

$$E(W\gamma\pi' AW) = A'\pi\gamma' C_2^* . \tag{4.2.39}$$

Using these results, we have from (4.2.36) and (4.2.37)

$$\frac{1}{T}(\kappa_1 - \kappa_2)E(Z'u\delta' V_z' V_z QZ' V_z) = (\kappa_1 - \kappa_2)[(\delta' q)C_1 + C_2\delta q'] , \tag{4.2.40}$$

where the terms of higher order of smallness than $O(1)$ have been neglected. For the second term between the second pair of square brackets on the right-hand side of the third equality of (4.2.34), we have

$$E(Z'u\delta' V_z' V_z Q V_z' Z) = Z' E(u\delta' V_z' V_z Q V_z')Z = Z' E(u\gamma' \bar{V}' \bar{V}\omega_{11} \bar{V}')Z. \tag{4.2.41}$$

On applying (2.8), we get

$$E(u\gamma' \bar{V}' \bar{V}\omega_{11} \bar{V}') = E(u\gamma'\pi u' u\pi'\omega_{11}\pi u') + E(u\gamma'\pi u' W\omega_{11} W')$$
$$+ E(u\gamma' W' u\pi'\omega_{11} W') + E(u\gamma' W' W\omega_{11}\pi u') \tag{4.2.42}$$
$$= (\gamma'\pi)(\pi'\omega_{11}\pi)E(uu'uu') + \sigma^2(\gamma'\pi)E(W\omega_{11} W')$$
$$+ \sigma^2 E(W\gamma\pi'\omega_{11} W') + T\sigma^2(\gamma' C_2^*\omega_{11}\pi)I .$$

Using Lemma 6 of [3], we have $\pi'\omega_{11}\pi = (1/\sigma^2)\operatorname{tr}C_1 Q$ and $E(uu'uu') = (T+2)\sigma^4 I$ as discussed above. From (A.6.1) of [3] we have $E(W\omega_{11} W') = (\operatorname{tr} QC_2)I$. Further, $E(W\gamma\pi'\omega_{11} W')$ is a $T \times T$ matrix, the term in the t-th row and the t'-th column being

$$\sum_{\mu}\sum_{\mu'}\sum_{\mu''} \gamma_{\mu}\pi_{\mu'}\omega_{11}(\mu', \mu'')E[w_{\mu}(t)w_{\mu''}(t')] \tag{4.2.43}$$
$$= \begin{cases} \sum_{\mu}\sum_{\mu'}\sum_{\mu''} \gamma_{\mu}\pi_{\mu'}\omega_{11}(\mu', \mu'')\operatorname{cov}(w_{\mu}, w_{\mu''}), & \text{if } t = t' , \\ 0, & \text{if } t \neq t' . \end{cases}$$

Hence,

$$E(W\gamma\pi'\omega_{11} W') = (\gamma' C_2^*\omega_{11}\pi)I , \tag{4.2.44}$$

and, simplifying, we get

$$\frac{1}{T}(\kappa_1 - \kappa_2)Z' E(u\delta' V_z' V_z Q V_z')Z \tag{4.2.45}$$
$$= (\kappa_1 - \kappa_2)[(\delta' q)\operatorname{tr}QC_1 + (\delta' C_2 Qq)]Q^{-1} ,$$

where terms of higher order smallness than $O(1)$ have been neglected. Coming to the third term between the second pair of square brackets on the right-hand side of the third equality of (4.2.34), we have

$$\text{(4.2.46)} \qquad \mathrm{E}(V_z' V_z \delta u' ZQZ' V_z) = \begin{bmatrix} \mathrm{E}(\bar{V}' \bar{V} \gamma u' B \bar{V}) & 0 \\ 0 & 0 \end{bmatrix},$$

where $B = ZQZ'$. Using (2.8), we get

$$\text{(4.2.47)} \qquad \begin{aligned} \mathrm{E}(\bar{V}' \bar{V} \gamma u' B \bar{V}) &= \mathrm{E}(\pi u' u \pi' \gamma u' B u \pi') + \mathrm{E}(\pi u' W \gamma u' B W) \\ &\quad + \mathrm{E}(W' u \pi' \gamma u' B W) = \mathrm{E}(W' W) \gamma \mathrm{E}(u' B u) \pi' \\ &= (\pi' \gamma) \mathrm{E}(u' u u' B u) \pi \pi' + \pi \gamma' \mathrm{E}(W' u u' B W) \\ &\quad + (\pi' \gamma) \mathrm{E}(W' u u' B W) + T \sigma^2 (m + l) C_2^* \gamma \pi' . \end{aligned}$$

We derive from (4.2.15) above (after replacing N_2 by B), $\mathrm{E}(u'uu'Bu) = (T + 2)(m + l)\sigma^4$, and along the same lines as in (A.11.1) of [3], we derive $\mathrm{E}(W'uu'BW) = \sigma^2(m + l)C_2^*$. Thus we get

$$\text{(4.2.48)} \quad \frac{1}{T}(\kappa_1 - \kappa_2)\mathrm{E}(V_z' V_z \delta u' ZQZ' V_z) = (\kappa_1 - \kappa_2)(m + l)[(\delta' q)C_1 + C_2 \delta q'] .$$

For the last term in the second pair of square brackets on the right-hand side of the third equality of (4.2.34), we have

$$\text{(4.2.49)} \qquad \mathrm{E}(V_z' V_z \delta u' ZQ V_z' Z) = \begin{bmatrix} \mathrm{E}(\bar{V}' \bar{V} \gamma u' A' \bar{V}') \\ 0 \end{bmatrix} [\bar{Y} \;\; X_1] ,$$

where $V_z QZ' = \bar{V} A$ (cf. Lemma 3 of [3]) and

$$\text{(4.2.50)} \qquad \begin{aligned} \mathrm{E}(\bar{V}' \bar{V} \gamma u' A' \bar{V}') &= \mathrm{E}(\pi u' u \pi' \gamma u' A' \pi u') + \mathrm{E}(\pi u' W \gamma u' A' W') \\ &\quad + \mathrm{E}(W' u \pi' \gamma u' A' W') + \mathrm{E}(W' W \gamma u' A' \pi u') \\ &= (\pi' \gamma) \pi \mathrm{E}(u' u u' A' \pi u') + \pi \gamma' \mathrm{E}(W' u u' A' W') \\ &\quad + (\pi' \gamma) \mathrm{E}(W' u u' A' W') + T C_2^* \gamma \mathrm{E}(\pi' A u u'). \end{aligned}$$

Now let us refer to (A.2.1) of [3]. We replace N by I and take the transpose of the expectation to get $\mathrm{E}(u'uu'A'\pi u') = (T + 2)\sigma^4 \pi' A$. From (A.12.1) of [3], we get (replacing N by I) $\mathrm{E}(W'uu'A'W') = \sigma^2 C_2^* A$. Hence we have from (4.2.49) and (4.2.50),

$$\text{(4.2.51)} \quad \frac{1}{T}(\kappa_1 - \kappa_2)\mathrm{E}(V_z' V_z \delta u' ZQ V_z' Z) = (\kappa_1 - \kappa_2)[(\delta' q)C_1 + C_2 \delta q'] ,$$

where the terms of higher order of smallness than $O(1)$ have been neglected.

Using (4.2.35), (4.2.40), (4.2.45), (4.2.48) and (4.2.51), we get from (4.2.34)

$$\mathrm{E}(S_{\frac{1}{2}}Q\nabla_{\frac{1}{2}}) = \sigma^2(m+l+2)\left\{\Lambda - \kappa_2 + 2 + (\kappa_1 - \kappa_2)\frac{\delta' q}{\sigma^2}\right\}C_1$$
$$+ \sigma^2(m+l+2)C_2$$
$$\text{(4.2.52)} \qquad + \sigma^2\left\{\Lambda - \kappa_2 + 2 + (\kappa_1 - \kappa_2)\frac{\delta' q}{\sigma^2}\right\}\mathrm{tr}QC_1Q^{-1}$$
$$+ \sigma^2\mathrm{tr}QC_2Q^{-1} + (\kappa_1 - \kappa_2)(m+l+2)C_2\delta q'$$
$$+ (\kappa_1 - \kappa_2)(\delta' C_2 Q q)Q^{-1}$$

and, therefore, using (4.2.30), (4.2.33) and (4.2.52), it follows from (4.2.29) that

$$\mathrm{E}(SQ\nabla) = \sigma^2\left[(m+l+2)\left\{\Lambda - \kappa_2 + 2 + (\kappa_1 - \kappa_2)\frac{\delta' q}{\sigma^2}\right\}\right.$$
$$\left. + (\Lambda - \kappa_1 + 2)\right]C_1 + \sigma^2[\Lambda - \kappa_1 + m + l + 2]C_2$$
$$\text{(4.2.53)} \qquad + \sigma^2\left\{\Lambda - \kappa_2 + 2 + (\kappa_1 - \kappa_2)\frac{\delta' q}{\sigma^2}\right\}\mathrm{tr}QC_1Q^{-1}$$
$$+ \sigma^2\mathrm{tr}QC_2Q^{-1} + (\kappa_1 - \kappa_2)(m+l+2)C_2\delta q'$$
$$+ (\kappa_1 - \kappa_2)(\delta' C_2 Q q)Q^{-1}\,.$$

As ∇, Q and S are all symmetric,

$$\text{(4.2.54)} \qquad \mathrm{E}(\nabla QS) = [\mathrm{E}(SQ\nabla)]'\,,$$

which is required for the third term on the right-hand side of (4.2.4).

Now coming to the fourth and the fifth terms on the right-hand side of (4.2.4) we find that up to $O(1)$

$$\text{(4.2.55)} \qquad \begin{aligned} \mathrm{E}(SQ\nabla Q\nabla) &= \mathrm{E}(S_1 Q\nabla_{\frac{1}{2}}Q\nabla_{\frac{1}{2}})\,, \\ \mathrm{E}(\nabla QSQ\nabla) &= \mathrm{E}(\nabla_{\frac{1}{2}}QS_1Q\nabla_{\frac{1}{2}})\,. \end{aligned}$$

From (3.3.6) and (3.3.9) of [3], we have $S_1 = Z'uu'Z = P_1$, and $\nabla_{\frac{1}{2}} = Z'V_z + V_z'Z = \Delta_{\frac{1}{2}}$. Therefore, up to $O(1)$

$$\mathrm{E}(SQ\nabla Q\nabla) = \mathrm{E}(P_1 Q\Delta_{\frac{1}{2}}Q\Delta_{\frac{1}{2}})$$
$$\text{(4.2.56)} \qquad = 2\sigma^2(m+l+3)C_1 + \sigma^2(m+l+2)C_2$$
$$+ \sigma^2(m+l+3)\mathrm{tr}QC_1Q^{-1} + \sigma^2\mathrm{tr}QC_2Q^{-1}\,,$$

and

$$\mathrm{E}(\nabla QSQ\nabla) = \mathrm{E}(\Delta_{\frac{1}{2}}QP_1Q\Delta_{\frac{1}{2}})$$
$$\text{(4.2.57)} \qquad = \sigma^2\{(m+l+2)^2 + 2\}C_1 + \sigma^2(m+l+2)C_2$$
$$+ \sigma^2\mathrm{tr}QC_1Q^{-1} + \sigma^2\mathrm{tr}QC_2Q^{-1}\,,$$

where use has been made of (3.3.40) and (3.3.46) of [3]. Regarding the sixth term on the right-hand side of (4.2.4), we find that

(4.2.58) $$E(\bar{V}Q\bar{V}QS) = [E(SQ\bar{V}Q\bar{V})]' .$$

Thus we are now completely ready to get the result stated in Theorem 2. The result is obtained by using (4.2.4) together with (4.2.27), (4.2.28), (4.2.53), (4.2.54), (4.2.56), (4.2.57) and (4.2.58).

4.3. *Proof of Theorem* 3. Using (2.21), we have defined the residual variance estimator as $(1/T)u_e'u_e$. Therefore, the bias of the residual variance estimator can be derived from

(4.3.1) $$E(u_e'u_e) = T\sigma^2 - 2E[u'(Y \quad X_1)e] + E\left[e'\begin{pmatrix} Y'Y & Y'X_1 \\ X_1'Y & X_1'X_1 \end{pmatrix}e\right].$$

To derive the expectations on the right-hand side of (4.3.1), we write[10]

(4.3.2) $$\begin{aligned} u'(Y \quad X_1)e = {} & u'V_zQZ'u + u'ZQZ'u \\ & + u'V_zQ\Big[V_z'M^*u - Z'V_zQZ'u - V_z'ZQZ'u \\ & - \frac{1}{T}\kappa_2 V_z'u + \frac{1}{T}(\kappa_1 - \kappa_2)V_z'V_z\delta\Big], \end{aligned}$$

and

(4.3.3) $$e'\begin{pmatrix} Y'Y & Y'X_1 \\ X_1'Y & X_1'X_1 \end{pmatrix}e = u'ZQZ'u + u'ZQV_z'V_zQZ'u ,$$

where the terms of higher order of smallness than $O(1)$ have been neglected, and use has been made of (2.3), (2.4) and (4.1.5).

Now it is not very difficult to derive the required expectations. It can be verified that up to $O(1)$

(4.3.4) $$\begin{aligned} E(u'V_zQZ'u) &= 0 , \\ E(u'ZQZ'u) &= \sigma^2(m + l) , \\ E(u'V_zQV_z'M^*u) &= T\Lambda\sigma^2 \mathrm{tr} C_1Q , \\ E(u'V_zQZ'V_zQZ'u) &= T\sigma^2 \mathrm{tr} C_1Q , \\ E(u'V_zQV_z'ZQZ'u) &= T\sigma^2(m + l)\mathrm{tr} C_1Q , \\ E(u'V_zQV_z'u) &= T^2\sigma^2 \mathrm{tr} C_1Q,^{11} \\ E(u'V_zQV_z'V_z) &= T^2 \mathrm{tr} C_1Q\, q' + T^2 q'QC_2,^{11} \\ E(u'ZQV_z'V_zQZ'u) &= T\sigma^2 \mathrm{tr} CQ . \end{aligned}$$

Using these results, we arrive at the result stated in Theorem 3.

Netherlands School of Economics, Netherlands

[10] Remember that by definition of u^* given in (4.1.2) we have $Z'u^* = Z'u$, and $V_z'M^*u^* = V_z'M^*u$.

[11] This expression is correct only to order $O(T)$, but this is irrelevant in this connection because the expression is to be divided by T in (4.3.2), after which it is of the required order, $O(1)$.

REFERENCES

[1] ANDERSON, T. W., AND H. RUBIN, "Estimation of the Parameters of a Single Equation in a Complete System of Stochastic Equations," *Annals of Mathematical Statistics*, XX (March, 1949), 46-63.

[2] HOOD, Wm. C., AND T. C. KOOPMANS, "The Estimation of Simultaneous Linear Economic Relationships," *Studies in Econometric Method*, Wm. C. Hood and T. C. Koopmans, ed. (New York: John Wiley & Sons, Inc., 1953).

[3] NAGAR, A. L., "The Bias and Moment Matrix of the General *k*-Class Estimators of the Parameters in Simultaneous Equations," *Econometrica*, XXVII (October, 1959), 575-95.

[4] ———, "A Note on the Residual Variance Estimation in Simultaneous Equations," *Econometrica*, XXIX (April, 1961), 238-43.

[5] THEIL, H., *Economic Forecasts and Policy* (Amsterdam: North-Holland Publishing Company, 1958).

RECURSIVE *VS.* NONRECURSIVE SYSTEMS: AN ATTEMPT AT SYNTHESIS

(PART I OF A TRIPTYCH ON CAUSAL CHAIN SYSTEMS)

BY ROBERT H. STROTZ AND H. O. A. WOLD

This paper, which in part serves as a common introduction to the two papers following in this issue, attempts to define the meaning of the "causal interpretability of a parameter" in a system of simultaneous linear relationships. It attempts, moreover, to expound a basis for interpreting the parameters of a nonrecursive or interdependent system causally. This is done in terms of an underlying causal chain system to which the interdependent system is either an approximation or a description of the equilibrium state.

OVER THE PAST fifteen years there has been an extended discussion of the meaning and applicability of nonrecursive as distinct from recursive systems in econometrics, and throughout this discussion there has been a marked divergence of views as to the merits of the two types of models. It is not the purpose of this note to extend that controversy further, but rather to attempt a constructive statement of the relationship between the two approaches and the circumstances under which each is applicable.

We assume that the reader is generally familiar with the past discussion[1] and that it will suffice here simply to recall that a recursive, or causal-chain, system has the formal property that the coefficient matrix of the non-lagged endogenous variables is triangular (upon suitable ordering of rows and columns) whereas a nonrecursive, or interdependent, system is one for which this is not the case. While the triangularity of the coefficient matrix is a formal property of recursive models, the essential property is that each relation is provided a causal interpretation in the sense of a stimulus-response relationship. The question of whether and in what sense nonrecursive systems allow a causal interpretation is the main theme of this paper.

1. FUNDAMENTAL PRINCIPLES

Much controversy can, in our opinion, be resolved once there is agreement on some initial points of principle.

(1) The first thing to consider when constructing an economic model is its purpose, that is, how it is to be applied in dealing with economic facts. We want to distinguish in this connection between descriptive and explanatory models. A descriptive model simply sets forth a set of relationships which have "bound together" different variables in situations in which they have

[1] See references appended at end. An extensive bibliography is included in [8].

previously been observed. More generally, these relationships may be described in probability terms, certain terms in these relationships representing the "disturbances" which in fact occurred. One can in this way describe given observations as a random drawing from a joint conditional probability distribution. Methodologically, the estimation of such a distribution is an exercise in n-dimensional "curve fitting." A descriptive model is thus cognate to the notion of a vector *function* such as (in the linear case)

$$\text{(1)} \qquad \mathrm{A}x' = u'$$

where A is a (not necessarily square) matrix of constants, x' is a column vector of the variables in question, and u' is a vector of zeros in the exact case or of stochastic variables in the case of a probability model. Whatever the validity of such a specification, the validity of any other model obtained by applying any linear transformation is the same. If a priori restrictions are imposed upon the sort of distribution which is to be used for this descriptive model, this may, of course, circumscribe the acceptable transformations.

Explanatory models, by contrast, are causal. This means that each relation (equation) in the model states something about "directions of influence" among the variables. (But see Section 3(b) below.) In the case of explanatory models, then, the theorist asserts more than functional relationships among the variables; he also invests those relationships with a special interpretation, that is, with a causal interpretation. But what is a "causal interpretation" to mean?

(2) No one has monopoly rights in defining "causality." The term is in common parlance and the only meaningful challenge is that of providing an explication of it. No explication need be unique, and some may prefer never to use the word at all. For us, however, the word in common scientific and statistical-inference usage has the following general meaning.[2] z is a cause of y if, by hypothesis, it is or "would be" possible by *controlling* z indirectly to control y, at least stochastically. But it may or may not be possible by controlling y indirectly to control z. A causal relation is therefore in essence asymmetric, in that in any instance of its realization it is asymmetric. Only in special cases may it be reversible and symmetric in a causal sense. These are the cases in which sometimes a controlled change in z may cause a change in y and at other times a controlled change in y may cause a change in z, but y and z cannot both be subjected to simultaneous controlled changes independently of one another without the causal relationship between them being violated.

The asymmetry of causation in any instance of its realization has the following probability counterpart. It may make sense to talk about the

[2] H. O. A. Wold has elaborated his views in [**6, 7**].

probability distribution of y as being *causally conditional* on z, but not make sense to talk about the probability distribution of z as being *causally conditional* on y. This asymmetry is classical in statistical theory. It appears in the difference between a sample statistic and a population parameter. We speak of the probability that the sample frequency of successes will be 0.5 conditional upon the population frequency being 0.4. We do not speak of the probability that the population frequency is 0.4 conditional upon the sample frequency being 0.5.[3] Thus if we wish to estimate (by the maximum likelihood method) a population parameter knowing a sample of observations, we write the likelihood function as the conditional probability distribution of the *sample*.

Suppose we were to estimate by the maximum likelihood method the nth value of a causal variable (population parameter) $z(n)$ on the basis of the nth value of a resultant variable (a sample observation) $y(n)$ by use of a regression fitted to $n - 1$ previous observations in all of which z has been causal. We should use the regression of y on z—not of z on y—over the previous observations, although this point is occasionally misunderstood.[4] Causality as used here is an essential notion in the statistical inference of population parameters by the maximum likelihood method. We must hypothesize how the sample observations are *generated* (i.e., caused) in order to proceed.

The concept of causality presented here is intended to be that of the everyday usage in the laboratory and emphasizes mainly the notion of control. Now, others may present a different explication of causality. Other versions may involve strange and seemingly unnatural notions, two of which are of particular interest to us. (a) The first involves accepting simultaneously the two statements: (1) "y has the value 100 because of (by cause of) z having the value 50" and (2) "z has the value 50 because of (by cause of) y having the value of 100." (b) The second involves accepting simultaneously the two statements: (1) "z causes y in accordance with the function $y = f(z)$" and (2) "z causes y in accordance with the function $y = g(z) \neq f(z)$." Usage (a) we shall describe as a "causal circle" and discuss in Section 3(c). Usage (b) we describe as "bicausality" and discuss in Section 3(d).

Whether such notions of causality seem weird or not, whether or not

[3] "Probability" is used here in the "relative frequency," not in the "degree of belief" sense.

[4] For what we regard as the correct treatment, see A. Mood, [**2**, Sec. 13.4]. For the contrary view see F. V. Waugh [**5**]. A qualification is needed: one must not have any constraining a priori knowledge about the possible values of z, or, if z is itself a random variable, about its probability distribution. The model we have in mind is given by $y = \alpha + \beta z + u$, with u and z statistically independent. Otherwise, the likelihood function is $f(y(1), \ldots, y(n) | z(1), \ldots z(n)) \cdot g(z(n))$, rather than the f function alone, where f and g are probability density functions.

they conform to usage in the scientific workshop, there is nothing to prevent their use in theory construction. Argument for the interpretation of causality presented by us is not an argument for "strait-jacketing" the freedom of the theorist and econometrician to use other interpretations. But we would (and will) argue that the notion of causality in economics is the one we have presented. Examples are: "Income is the cause of consumer expenditure (the consumption function)," "Price is a cause of quantity demanded," and "Price is a cause of quantity supplied." Most of the problems in assessing this claim arise in equilibrium models.

2. THE CAUSAL INTERPRETATION OF A RECURSIVE SYSTEM

It was not our purpose in the previous section to provide a precise definition of "causation." The term enters our discussion essentially as a "primitive," and what efforts we have made at definition have been ostensive: we have pointed to the familiar usage of the word in the laboratory. With reference to this primitive meaning of "causation," however, we wish to define the concept of "the causal interpretability of a parameter." This is what will occupy us next.

Suppose a recursive system is written in the form

$$
\begin{aligned}
y_1 + \beta_{11}y_2 + \dots + \beta_{1g}y_g + \beta_{1,g+1}y_{g+1} + \dots + \beta_{1G}y_G + \sum_k \gamma_{1k}z_k &= u_1\,, \\
y_2 + \dots + \beta_{2g}y_g + \beta_{2,g+1}y_{g+1} + \dots + \beta_{2G}y_G + \sum_k \gamma_{2k}z_k &= u_2\,, \\
\dots\dots\dots\dots\dots\dots\dots\dots\dots & \\
y_g + \beta_{g,g+1}y_{g+1} + \dots + \beta_{gG}y_G + \sum_k \gamma_{gk}z_k &= u_g\,, \\
\dots\dots\dots\dots\dots\dots\dots\dots\dots & \\
y_G + \sum_k \gamma_{Gk}z_k &= u_G\,,
\end{aligned}
\tag{2}
$$

where the y's are causally dependent variables, the z's predetermined variables, and the u's stochastic variables statistically independent of the z's. Each u_g is assumed, moreover, to be statistically independent of y_{g+1}, $y_{g+2}, \dots, y_G$.[5] In each equation the y variable with unit coefficient is regarded as the resultant variable and the other y variables and the z's are regarded as causal variables. We now consider the possibility that we gain direct control over y_g, that is, we can manipulate y_g by use of variables

[5] Although Wold has imposed this specification in his definition of a causal chain system, Strotz feels it may be too restrictive and would classify causal chain systems under two headings: those that are causal chains in their stochastic form (Wold's case) and those that are causal chains only in their exact part. In the latter case the covariance matrix of the u_g's need not be diagonal. For further discussion of this, see Strotz, *infra*, p. 430, fn. 6.

other than the z's appearing in the model. In this case we now need a new model. It can be obtained, however, by a single change in the old one. We merely strike out the gth equation and reclassify y_g as an exogenous (predetermined) variable rather than as a dependent variable. The coefficients of y_g in the $G - 1$ equations of the new model will be the same as they were before, namely, $\beta_{1g}, \ldots, \beta_{g-1,g}$, and zeros. It is in this sense that each non-unit coefficient in a recursive system has a causal interpretation. It describes the influence of the variable whose coefficient it is on the resultant variable, irrespective of whether the causal variable is dependent or exogenous in the system. Such a parameter has causal interpretability.

3. THE CAUSAL INTERPRETATION OF NONRECURSIVE SYSTEMS

We now turn our attention to nonrecursive systems. What is the possibility of causal interpretation in these systems?

(a) *No causal interpretation.* It may be that no causal interpretation of a nonrecursive system is intended. The relations in the system may be asserted only to define the joint probability distribution of the dependent variables conditional upon the predetermined variables. The coefficients to be estimated are then simply parameters in the joint conditional distribution of y given z. With nothing further claimed, there is no objection to such a model or to efforts to estimate the parameters of the distribution.

(b) *Vector causality.* It may be asserted for the *nonrecursive* model

$$\mathrm{B}y' + \Gamma z' = u' \tag{3}$$

that the vector z *causes* the vector y. Causality in this sense goes beyond the definition of "causality" given in Wold [**6, 7**]. It may readily be accepted, however, as an abstract terminological extension of the more usual notion of causation and may be employed in the everyday sense of the statement, "The food supply causes the fish population." An example may be useful. Suppose z is a vector whose elements are the amounts of various fish feeds (different insects, weeds, etc.) available in a given lake, and that y is a vector whose elements are the numbers of fish of various species in the lake. The reduced form $y' = -\mathrm{B}^{-1}\Gamma z' + \mathrm{B}^{-1}u'$ would tell us specifically how the number of fish of any species depends on the availabilities of different feeds. The coefficient of any z is the partial derivative of a species population with respect to a food supply. It is to be noted, however, that the reduced form tells us nothing about the interactions among the various fish populations—it does not tell us the extent to which one species of fish feeds on another species. Those are causal relations among the y's.[6]

[6] Indeed, even though $\partial y_g/\partial z_k > 0$, this does not imply that fish species g consumes food supply k. It may be that species g consumes species h which consumes food supply k.

Suppose, in another situation, we continuously restock the lake with species g, increasing y_g by any desired amount. How will this affect the values of the other y's? If the system were recursive and we had estimates of the elements of B, we would simply strike the gth equation out of the model and regard y_g, the number of fish of species g, as exogenous—as a food supply or, when appearing with a negative coefficient, as a poison. It will be the purpose of subsections (c) and (d) to determine whether if the model is not recursive the problem can be dealt with in this same way. The nonrecursive model does, in any case, enable us to predict the effects on the y's of controlled variations in the z's.

Herbert Simon in developing a sense of causality for econometric models [**3**] has used this notion of vector causality. He defines causal relations among *subsets* of dependent variables by using a model recursive in these subsets. Partition y' into three subsets, that is, into three column vectors, y_1', y_2', and y_3', so that $y' = (y_1, y_2, y_3)'$ and partition B conformally. Consider the system (3) in which B may be written as

$$\text{(4)} \qquad B = \begin{pmatrix} B_{11} & B_{12} & B_{13} \\ 0 & B_{22} & B_{23} \\ 0 & 0 & B_{33} \end{pmatrix}$$

consisting of nine submatrices. Then y_3' is caused by z'; y_2' is caused by y_3' and z'; and y_1' is caused by y_2', y_3', and z'. In the previous sentence the word "caused" is used in the sense of vector causation, and B is "block triangular." No causal relations among the variables *within* a subset are defined. Press this logic further. If each subset consists of but a single endogenous variable, and a causal sequence is established among subsets, B is triangular and the system is recursive.

If, by way of contrast with vector causality, each effect variable is given as an explicit function of only variables that are its causes, we may speak of *explicit causality*.

(c) *Causal Circles, Mutual Causation, and Equilibrium Conditions.* By a "causal circle" we shall mean a system such as

$$\text{(5a)} \qquad p(t) = \alpha_1 + \beta_1 q(t) + \gamma_1 z_1(t) + u_1(t)\,,$$

$$\text{(5b)} \qquad q(t) = \alpha_2 + \beta_2 p(t) + \gamma_2 z_2(t) + u_2(t)\,,$$

where $z_1(t)$ and $z_2(t)$ are exogenous and for which the following two statements are asserted: (1) In equation (5a) $q(t)$ is a cause of $p(t)$; (2) In equation (5b) $p(t)$ is a cause of $q(t)$. Causation is here used in a sense not allowed by the operative meaning that causation has in an experimental laboratory. To accept a causal circle is, in the laboratory meaning of the word "cause," to suppose that the value of one variable is determined by the value of another variable whose value cannot be determined until that of the first has been determined. To assume that the values of the two variables determine each other makes sense only in an equilibrium system, and such a system provides no explanation of how the equilibrium comes about (of change or of causal connections among the endogenous variables of the system).[7]

The familiar illustration of the three balls in the bowl mutually *causing* one another's location, which has been advanced as an example of mutual causation,[8] might be considered in this connection. For the steady state (equilibrium) there are certain mutual conditions which must be satisfied; but if the balls are displaced and then roll towards equilibrium they are either in mutual contact and roll (or slide) as a single mass or the position of each can depend on the positions of the others only when the latter are lagged in time. Indeed, mutual causation in a dynamic system can have meaning only as a limit form of the arrow schemes shown in Figure 1 where the time lag θ is reduced towards zero.[9]

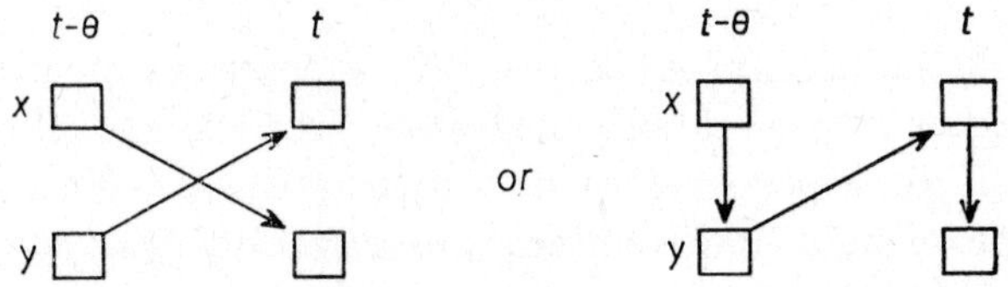

FIGURE 1

There is, however, a sense in which the coefficients of an equilibrium system may be given a causal interpretation, even though the relations in an equilibrium system may not themselves be causal relations. Let us take first an imaginary case in ecology: the balanced aquarium. Suppose there are two species of fish in an aquarium, big, b, and small, s. Their populations are y_b and y_s. The big fish feed on the small ones and on weed type a, available in quantity x_a. The small fish feed only on weed type c,

[7] If, for example, an entrepreneur wishing to produce a given amount of product at minimum cost decides simultaneously on how much of each of two factors of production, x_1 and x_2, to employ, it might be said that his decision as to x_1 causes his decision as to x_2 and his decision as to x_2 causes his decision as to x_1. We do not believe this conforms to the "laboratory" meaning of causation and we therefore reject this usage. On this, see [**1**].

[8] This illustration, due to Marshall, has been referred to recently by Stone [**4**] in this connection. Marshall spoke of mutual "determination" rather than "causation" and it is not clear whether these words are to be regarded as synonyms.

[9] In equilibrium when $x(t) = x(t-\theta)$ and $y(t) = y(t-\theta)$, these structures may be collapsed into one of apparent "mutual causation," but what are simultaneous equilibrium conditions ought not to be confused with causal relations.

available in quantity x_c. It takes time for the big fish to catch the small ones. The model is linear and stochastic, thus:

(6a) $$y_b(t) = \alpha_1 + \beta_1 y_s(t-\theta) + \gamma_1 x_a(t) + u_1(t)\,,$$

(6b) $$y_s(t) = \alpha_2 + \beta_2 y_b(t-\theta) + \delta_2 x_c(t) + u_2(t)\,.$$

Suppose now that every time we observe the aquarium it is in equilibrium. Moreover, we wish to estimate two numbers—are they β_1 and β_2?—so that we can answer these questions:

If we controlled the population of the big (small) fish, y_b (resp., y_s), by adding them to the aquarium or taking them out, and thereby held y_b (resp., y_s) at some arbitrary level, what would the expected value of the population of small (resp., big) fish, y_s (resp., y_b), be at the new equilibrium level, conditional upon the values of x_a and x_c?

Suppose we next formulated the model:

(7a) $$y_b(t) = \alpha_1 + \beta_1 y_s(t) + \gamma_1 x_a(t) + u_1(t)\,,$$

(7b) $$y_s(t) = \alpha_2 + \beta_2 y_b(t) + \delta_2 x_b(t) + u_2(t)\,.$$

To control the population of big fish is to wipe out or invalidate relation (6a) and to regard $y_b(t-\theta)$ as exogenous. To control the population of small fish is to wipe out (6b) and to regard $y_s(t-\theta)$ as exogenous. In the absence of such intervention, we certainly cannot say that $y_s(t)$ *causes* $y_b(t)$ and that $y_b(t)$ *causes* $y_s(t)$, i.e., we cannot use model (7) as a *causal* model telling us what happens through time in the uncontrolled aquarium. Nevertheless, the values of β_1 and β_2 appearing in model (7) do tell us what a second fish population will be conditional upon our specifying (controlling, manipulating) a first fish population—provided that the aquarium is then brought back to an equilibrium situation. Equilibrium models do tell us (enable us to predict) something about equilibrium values under *control*.

A comparable example in economics might well be the cobweb model. The model is:

(8a) $$p(t) = a - \beta q_h(t) + \varepsilon z_1(t) + u_1(t) \quad \text{(demand)}\,,$$

(8b) $$q_h(t) = \gamma + \delta p(t-1) + \eta z_2(t) + u_2(t) \quad \text{(supply)}\,,$$

where $p(t)$ is price at time t, q_h is quantity harvested, z_1 and z_2 are exogenous variables, and u_1 and u_2 are stochastic shocks. This system is recursive, but if observed in equilibrium may, by use of the equilibrium condition

$$p(t-1) = p(t)\,,$$

be written as

(9a) $$p(t) = a - \beta q_h(t) + \varepsilon z_1(t) + u_1(t) \quad \text{(demand)}\,,$$

(9b) $$q_h(t) = \gamma + \delta p(t) + \eta z_2(t) + u_2(t) \quad \text{(supply)}\,,$$

and will be subject to the same causal interpretation as given in the previous example. The question of how β and δ are best to be estimated is left open.

(d) *Bicausality*. Suppose we confront a demand-supply model of the following sort

$$q(t) = a_{10} + a_{11}p(t) + a_{13}z_1(t) + u_1(t) \text{ (demand)}, \tag{10a}$$

$$q(t) = a_{20} + a_{21}p(t) + a_{24}z_2(t) + u_2(t) \text{ (supply)}, \tag{10b}$$

where $q(t)$ is quantity, $p(t)$ is price, $z_1(t)$ and $z_2(t)$ are exogenous variables, and $u_1(t)$ and $u_2(t)$ are stochastic shocks.

Now suppose this system is given the following causal interpretation: $p(t)$ causes $q(t)$ in accordance with equation (10a) and $p(t)$ also causes $q(t)$ in accordance with equation (10b). This notion of causality is certainly out of accord with the usual laboratory or control notion which we find so natural. Those who write such systems do not, however, really mean what they write, but introduce an ellipsis which is familiar to economists. What is meant is that

$$q_d(t) = a_{10} + a_{11}p(t) + a_{13}z_1(t) + u_1(t), \tag{11a}$$

$$q_s(t) = a_{20} + a_{21}p(t) + a_{24}z_2(t) + u_2(t), \tag{11b}$$

$$q_d(t) = q_s(t), \tag{11c}$$

where $q_d(t)$ is quantity demanded and $q_s(t)$ is quantity supplied. This is an equilibrium model (nonrecursive), and (11c) is not an *identity*, but an *equality* which is assumed to hold in fact over the observations.[10]

A somewhat far-fetched example, but in a surer context, is the following. Suppose there are two crops, d and s, whose yield is measured in bushels, and that (over the relevant range) the yield of one, q_d, is a positive linear function of rainfall, p, while the yield of the other, q_s, is a negative linear function of rainfall, and that these functions intersect within the relevant range. An amount z_1 of fertilizer 1 is applied to crop d and an amount z_2 of fertilizer 2 is applied to s. Suppose for each of N years we conduct an experiment for each crop, applying different amounts of fertilizer. Rainfall is uncontrolled. Imagine now the amazing result that each year of the experiment Nature chooses a rainfall that makes the two yields equal. We may then represent the experiment by system (11) and reduce this to system (10) simply by dropping the subscripts on q and keeping track of which equation is for which crop.

Now, while it would be remarkable for Nature to choose rainfall so as

[10] Especially for one not familiar with the economist's ellipsis, difficulty may result from the careless use of symbols in this reduction. Strictly speaking, the q in (10a and b) should be either a q_d or a q_s, or an additional equation such as $q = \min(q_d, q_s)$ or $q = q_d$ should be added to model (11). Otherwise, identity (and not simply equality) of quantities demanded and supplied is technically implied.

to give us this strange result, it may be not so remarkable for the market to choose price so that quantity demanded equals quantity supplied, at least approximately. This is because, while rainfall is independent of past crop yields, price may well depend on past quantities demanded and supplied, and, if the system is not subject to violent change, the price adjustment relation may work with great efficiency. Whether it will or not is, of course, an empirical question: the answer may vary from market to market and time to time; but this is a matter of realism which need not concern us here. When the equality holds the theoretical system (11) may be represented by system (10), although if (11c) holds only approximately, system (10) is one with errors in the variables.

The causal system which underlies the equilibrium model (11) is then one in which (11c) is replaced by some function such as

$$\text{(11d)} \qquad p(t) = f[q_d(t-\theta), q_s(t-\theta), p(t-\theta), z_1(t), z_2(t), z_1(t-\theta), z_2(t-\theta)] + u_3(t)$$

and the causal (and, in this case, dynamic) model is recursive. If $p(t)$ were now to be subject to direct control, (11d) must be abandoned and $p(t)$ must be regarded as exogenous. Equations (11a) and (11b) would then answer questions regarding the causal effect of controlled variation in $p(t)$ on $q_d(t)$ and $q_s(t)$, and a_{11} and a_{12} would be causally interpretable coefficients. They are, moreover, the same coefficients which enter the "bicausal" system (10).

What is to be concluded from all this is that equilibrium systems may appear to entail "causal circles" or "bicausality," but that this is not what is intended. The causal interpretation of a coefficient in either of these types of equilibrium models is to be found in the underlying dynamic model which, *if the laboratory notion of causality is to be sustained*, will be recursive in character.[11]

Two major questions remain: (1) Can a stochastic shock model of the sort commonly considered—i.e., equation (1)—ever be assumed to be always in equilibrium whenever observed?[12] (2) If not, must it not be said that either there are measurement errors introduced by the assumption of equilibrium (for example, ought not (11c) be regarded as an *approximate* equality) or there is a specification error? If so, this raises questions as to appropriate estimation procedure and as to the properties of estimates that ignore these model qualifications. The subsequent paper by Strotz deals with this problem.

[11] Incidentally, differential equation systems are regarded as recursive with respect to infinitesimal time intervals. See [**8**].

[12] For (11a, b, and c) to hold exactly, (11d) would need to include $u_1(t)$ and $u_2(t)$ as arguments and exclude $u_3(t)$.

Our contribution ends with a paper by Wold, who gives a brief presentation of conditional causal chains, a new type of model which is designed as an extension of ordinary (pure) causal chains in the direction of independent systems.

REFERENCES

[1] BENTZEL, R., AND B. HANSEN: "On Recursiveness and Interdependency in Economic Models," *Review of Economic Studies*, 22, pp. 153–168.

[2] MOOD, A.: *Introduction to the Theory of Statistics*, McGraw-Hill, 1950.

[3] SIMON, HERBERT A.: "Causal Ordering and Identifiability," in Wm. C. Hood and Tjalling C. Koopmans, eds., *Studies in Econometric Method*. Wiley & Sons, 1953.

[4] STONE, RICHARD: "Discussion on Professor Wold's Paper," *Journal of the Royal Statistical Society*, Series A, 119, I, 1956, p. 51.

[5] WAUGH, FREDERICK: "Choice of the Dependent Variable in Regression," *Journal of the American Statical Association*, 38, 22 (June, 1943), pp. 210–214.

[6] WOLD, H. O. A.: "Causality and Econometrics," *Econometrica*, 22, pp. 114 ff.

[7] ———: "On the Definition and Meaning of Causal Concepts," manuscript, submitted to *Philosophy of Science*.

[8] ———: "Ends and Means in Econometric Model Building. Basic Considerations Reviewed," in U. Grenander, ed., *Probability and Statistics* (The Harald Cramer volume), Stockholm: Almqvist & Wiksell, 1959.

[9] WOLD, H. O. A., AND L. JURÉEN, *Demand Analysis*, Almqvist & Wiksell, 1952.

INTERDEPENDENCE AS A SPECIFICATION ERROR

(PART II OF A TRIPTYCH ON CAUSAL CHAIN SYSTEMS)

BY ROBERT H. STROTZ[1]

When interdependent models are regarded as approximations to recursive models, a specification error is made. What is the importance of that specification error for the maximum likelihood estimation procedure? This question is analyzed for the case where lagged endogenous variables are treated as current on the grounds that the lag is small relative to the observation period. It is argued that the appropriate estimation procedure is qualitatively different from that which ignores the specification error, however small the omitted lag may be. It is contended that as the lag approaches zero the limit form of the likelihood function is not the likelihood function of the limit form of the model. The article is, however, exploratory and the analysis lacks complete rigor.

IF A CAUSAL interpretation of an interdependent system is possible it is to be provided in terms of a recursive system. The interdependent system is then either an approximation to the recursive system or a description of its equilibrium state. This was the conclusion of the preceding paper, written jointly with Professor Wold.[2] Whether or not one agrees that this is a general rule, the economist who formulates an interdependent stochastic model for econometric estimation may often have a recursive model in the back of his mind. The recursive model is not used, but this is either because of its complexity or because of the unavailability of required data, such as hourly, daily, or weekly observations. In these cases, some form of specification error is made, the *postulated* interdependent model being only an approximation to a *latent* recursive model which is thought to provide a better theoretical explanation of the facts. Even if the recursive system is in fact in equilibrium whenever actually observed, so that the interdependent system, conceived as the equilibrium version of the recursive system, provides correct relations among the variables as observed, a specification error is introduced. This is because the probability characteristics of the recursive model do not guarantee that the system will be always in equilibrium when observed, so that equilibrium, if it obtains, is but a chance event and not a model specification.

This paper is concerned with the significance for the estimation procedure

[1] The author is grateful to several persons for their critical comments on an earlier draft of this article, and particularly to Carl Christ, Meyer Dwass, Henry Houthakker and Tjalling Koopmans. This is not to imply that any of them is in agreement with the argument that is developed.

[2] "Recursive *vs.* Nonrecursive Systems: An Attempt at Synthesis," *Econometrica*, this issue. A kindred view is to be found in R. Bentzel and B. Hansen, "On Recursiveness and Interdependency in Economic Models," *Review of Economic Studies*, xxii, 3 (1954–55). See especially their Section 7.

of these specification errors. That a given parameter in either a recursive or nonrecursive system may be ascribed a causal interpretation in the sense of the previous paper does not by that fact resolve the question of how it is to be estimated. Unfortunately, this paper is only exploratory. I propose to consider only some illustrative problems in this area, and my work has led me not so much to proofs as to what I hope are reasonable conjectures.

I find it useful to think of three apparently distinct ways in which one may approximate a recursive model with an interdependent one:

(1) One may ignore certain time lags, commonly on the grounds that they are small relative to the period of observation. Thus, in certain equations, lagged endogenous variables may be replaced by the non-lagged variables with the result that the new coefficient matrix of the jointly dependent variables is no longer triangular.[3]

(2) One may replace dynamic adjustment relations with equilibrium conditions that state equalities among variables. This is generally handled by reducing the number of equations and then, for each equation eliminated, dropping one of the variables or eliminating the distinction between two different variables, treating them in the nonrecursive model as one. For example, one might not distinguish quantity demanded and quantity supplied.

(3) One may replace "flow" variables with "stock" variables. Instead of $x(t-\frac{1}{2})$ one might use $\int_{t-1}^{t} x(\tau)d\tau$,[4] or, similarly, one might replace a "stock" variable defined over a short interval of time with one defined over a longer interval, e.g., instead of daily sales one might use annual sales.

Although I am by no means sure that these cases are either analytically distinct or exhaustive—in fact, for the purposes of this article, they may well be the same—, this classification seems to suggest three natural ways in which specification errors arise when one goes from a recursive to a nonrecursive system. In this article I shall deal mainly with case (1) and venture only some intuitive extensions to other situations.

1

Consider the recursive model

$$\text{(I)} \qquad B_0 y'(t) + B_1 y'(t-\theta) + \Gamma z'(t) = u'(t)$$

to be the theoretically satisfactory model.[5] $y'(t)$ is a vector of endogenous

[3] The same situation may result if an "expected" variable $y^*(t+\theta)$ is replaced by its currently observed value $y(t)$.

[4] With suitable redefinition of the dimension of the coefficients in the system.

[5] I do not pretend we can ever state a particular recursive model to be the "true" one. Metaphysics aside, our starting point is with a model which, apart from computational and other statistical problems, we should want to use and in terms of which we should want to provide a theoretical explanation of how observations are generated.

variables, $z'(t)$ is a vector of exogenous variables, B_0, B_1, and Γ are matrices with B_0 triangular and with one's on the principal diagonal. $u'(t)$ is a vector of stochastic variables having a joint normal distribution independent of $z'(t)$, not serially correlated, with zero means, and with the constant covariance matrix, Σ, not necessarily diagonal.[6] I shall assume, moreover, that the functions $y(t)$ are continuous over time.

Suppose θ is very small relative to the period of observation so that we are led to formulate the nonrecursive model

$$\text{(II)} \qquad \mathrm{B}y'(t) + \Gamma z'(t) = u^{*\prime}(t)$$

by dropping the lags in the second term of (I). In this case, $\mathrm{B} = \mathrm{B}_0 + \mathrm{B}_1$. The covariance matrix of $u^{*\prime}(t)$ will be designated Σ^*. Model (II) may be called the limit form of model (I) as θ approaches 0, in the sense that $\mathrm{B}_0 y'(t) + \mathrm{B}_1 y'(t-\theta) \rightarrow (\mathrm{B}_0 + \mathrm{B}_1)y'(t) = \mathrm{B}y'(t)$ as $\theta \rightarrow 0$, noting that the functions $y(t)$ are continuous. We restrict ourselves to the case where model (II) is identifiable.

In what follows I shall accept uncritically the maximum-likelihood estimation procedure as a "good" one, and all my claims are conditional upon this assumption.

If we maximize the log likelihood function of (II) with respect to Σ^{*-1}, then substitute the maximizing values of Σ^{*-1} (which are functions of $(\mathrm{B}\,\Gamma)$) for Σ^{*-1} and next drop the additive constant term (the term in the natural number π), we obtain

$$\text{(L.II)} \qquad \ln ||\mathrm{B}|| - \tfrac{1}{2}\ln |(\mathrm{B}\,\Gamma)M^*(\mathrm{B}\,\Gamma)'|$$

where $||\ ||$ means "the absolute value of the determinant," and where M^* is the moment matrix

$$\text{(1.1)} \qquad M^* = \begin{pmatrix} M_{y(t)y(t)} & M_{y(t)z(t)} \\ M_{z(t)y(t)} & M_{z(t)z(t)} \end{pmatrix}.$$

I shall henceforth call (L.II) a "likelihood function," and I note that it is the "likelihood function of the limit form of model (I) as θ approaches 0." The values of $(\mathrm{B}\,\Gamma)$ that maximize (L.II) shall be designated $(\breve{\mathrm{B}}\,\breve{\Gamma})$. These are the usual maximum-likelihood estimates of the parameters of a simultaneous linear system.

[6] Professor Wold in a strict definition of a causal chain model would require that Σ be diagonal. In my usage here I do not require this because (a) it partially defeats the role of a stochastic formulation of the economic theory to require knowledge that there are no causal links among the disturbances, and (b) it may be that a causal and hence recursive structure underlies the vector $u'(t)$, e.g., suppose $u'(t) = Kv'(t)$, where the elements of $v'(t)$ are independent and where K is triangular.

The *non*diagonality of Σ is not essential for the analysis in this article, however, and so, in what follows, diagonality can be regarded as a special case.

Had adequate data and computational facilities been available, however, we would have stayed with model (I) and, after first maximizing with respect to Σ^{-1}, reduced its likelihood function to

$$\ln ||\mathrm{B}_0|| - \tfrac{1}{2} \ln |(\mathrm{B}_0\ \mathrm{B}_1\ \Gamma)M(\mathrm{B}_0\ \mathrm{B}_1\ \Gamma)'| \tag{1.2}$$

where

$$M = \begin{pmatrix} M_{y(t)y(t)} & M_{y(t)y(t-\theta)} & M_{y(t)z(t)} \\ M_{y(t-\theta)y(t)} & M_{y(t-\theta)y(t-\theta)} & M_{y(t-\theta)z(t)} \\ M_{z(t)y(t)} & M_{z(t)y(t-\theta)} & M_{z(t)z(t)} \end{pmatrix}. \tag{1.3}$$

Noting that $|\mathrm{B}_0| = 1$, $\ln |\mathrm{B}_0| = 0$, so that this function is

$$-\tfrac{1}{2} \ln |(\mathrm{B}_0\ \mathrm{B}_1\ \Gamma)M(\mathrm{B}_0\ \mathrm{B}_1\ \Gamma)'|\,. \tag{L.I}$$

Imagine now that we are prepared (as an approximation) to suppose that θ is as small as we please. We let it approach zero and find that the limit form of (L.I) is

$$-\tfrac{1}{2} \ln |(\mathrm{B}\ \Gamma)M^*(\mathrm{B}\ \Gamma)'|\,, \tag{1.4}$$

which is the second term of (L.II). Let the values that maximize (1.4) be called $(\hat{\mathrm{B}}\ \hat{\Gamma})$.

What has become clear is that *the likelihood function of the limit form of model (I) as $\theta \to 0$ (which is (L.II)) is not the limit form, as $\theta \to 0$, of the likelihood function of the model, which is* (1.4). This is to say that it makes a difference whether we first substitute 0 for θ in the model itself and then write the likelihood function or whether we first write the likelihood function of the model and then substitute 0 for θ in it. It is the latter which we should want to do in order to estimate $(\mathrm{B}\ \Gamma)$, that is, we prefer the estimates $(\hat{\mathrm{B}}\ \hat{\Gamma})$ to $(\breve{\mathrm{B}}\ \breve{\Gamma})$. It is clear that these two sets of estimates will be different. Otherwise, of the two terms

$$\ln ||\mathrm{B}|| \quad \text{and} \quad -\tfrac{1}{2} \ln |(\mathrm{B}\ \Gamma)M^*(\mathrm{B}\ \Gamma)'| \tag{1.5}$$

the second must attain a maximum for the same values of B at which the first attains a stationary value, and this would be highly special.

To see what all this argument amounts to, we can say that if in a given equation an endogenous variable appears with a lag, it remains a *lagged* endogenous variable, however close to zero that lag may be, and by assumption is independent of $u'(t)$. To replace θ by zero, however, is to reclassify the variable from being a "statistical constant" to being a stochastic variable, and this affects fundamentally the form of the likelihood function.

We are, however, in hot water. In taking the likelihood function to the limit, as $\theta \to 0$, we nevertheless retained our assumption that the elements of $u'(t)$ were not autocorrelated. But $\mathscr{E}(u'(t)u(t-\theta))$ cannot reasonably have the zero matrix as its limit form. One could, of course, consider the very special case in which the functions $u'(t)$ are discontinuous at the observation dates, but this is inconsistent with the earlier assumption that the functions $y'(t)$ are *not* discontinuous.

Is it not possible that if there is significant serial correlation among the disturbances it is better to regard $y(t-\theta)$ as among the jointly dependent variables at time t than as predetermined? If so, the likelihood function (L.II) may be the one we want. We shall look into this further in Section 2. It is interesting at this point to cite Tjalling Koopmans who has commented on the same problem:[7]

If the time lag is reduced to zero, the variable is in general to be treated as one of the jointly dependent variables. This situation can be reduced *ad absurdum* by making the time unit of measurement smaller and smaller and at the same time reducing the time lag to zero. Then suddenly at the moment the time lag reaches zero the status of the variable x_1 in the first equation is changed, and with it the "unbiased" estimate of the coefficient in question is changed. The solution of this paradox is, of course, that such a procedure is illegitimate. The assumption of independent disturbances in successive observations can be maintained only if the size of the time unit to which these observations refer is not made too small. Therefore, the independence assumption makes the distinction between predetermined and dependent variables appear as absolute instead of a matter of degree, which it would be in a more refined model.

To avoid these problems, we might, of course, assume that $\mathscr{E}(u'(t)u(t-\theta)) = 0$ on the grounds that, although θ is small relative to the observation period, it is sufficiently large so as not to entail serial correlation among the disturbances. The statement that θ is "small" relative to the observation period is intended as tantamount to assuming that $|y(t)-y(t-\theta)|$ is always sufficiently small so that these differences can be tolerated as a sort of trivial "measurement" error. We shall proceed with these assumptions for awhile.

A next concern is with the sign of $|(\mathrm{B}_0\ \mathrm{B}_1\ \Gamma)M(\mathrm{B}_0\ \mathrm{B}_1\ \Gamma)'|$, which must be positive in order that the log likelihood function be defined. When we assume that the first and second vertical (and horizontal) partitions of M may be treated as identical (this being the assumption that the values $y(t)-y(t-\theta)$ are *approximately* zero), we are, however, taking M to be singular and this may cause some concern. Nevertheless, the reader may verify that, as $\theta \to 0$, $(\mathrm{B}_0\ \mathrm{B}_1\ \Gamma)M(\mathrm{B}_0\ \mathrm{B}_1\ \Gamma)' \to (\mathrm{B}\ \Gamma)M^*(\mathrm{B}\ \Gamma)'$, which, in the conventional treatment and here also, is assumed to be positive definite. Hence $|(\mathrm{B}_0\ \mathrm{B}_1\ \Gamma)M(\mathrm{B}_0\ \mathrm{B}_1\ \Gamma)'|$ will be positive even though M is treated as singular. The singularity of M, however, means that some exact multicollinearity is present, and this may prevent us from estimating all coefficients uniquely. We may quickly note, however, that the linear dependence (multicollinearity) arises among the endogenous variables, and that it is the elements of $(\mathrm{B}_0\ \mathrm{B}_1)$ which we may be unable to estimate from (L.I.) The

[7] Tjalling Koopmans, "Models Involving a Continuous Time Variable," in Koopmans, ed., *Statistical Inference in Dynamic Economic Models* (New York: John Wiley & Sons), p. 385.

elements of B can, however, by assumption, be estimated from (1.4). The problem then is how to decompose B into a set of coefficients of the *non-lagged* endogenous variables B_0 and a set of coefficients of the *lagged* endogenous variables B_1. Any element in B, say β_{gh}, which is the sum of two terms, can be decomposed uniquely if its value is known (e.g., to be zero) in either B_0 or in B_1.[8] Difficulty arises from this source then only if an endogenous variable appears both lagged and non-lagged in the same equation. Otherwise its coefficient could be found from B.

I have not investigated whether, in general, nonidentifiability of the limit form of the model corresponds to the absence of any locally unique maximum for the limit form of the likelihood function of the model. I have explored this matter only for a special case:

Consider the model

$$(1.6)\qquad \begin{cases} y_1(t) + \beta_{12}y_2(t-\theta) = u_1(t)\,, \\ y_2(t) + \beta_{21}y_1(t-\theta) = u_2(t)\,, \end{cases}$$

to be approximated by

$$(1.7)\qquad \begin{cases} y_1(t) + \beta_{12}y_2(t) = u_1^*(t)\,, \\ y_2(t) + \beta_{21}y_1(t) = u_2^*(t)\,, \end{cases}$$

which, by the usual criterion, is unidentified.[9] Using (L.I) we should estimate B by use of (1.4) and by minimizing with respect to β_{21} and β_{12}. We find, however, that in this case unique values for β_{21} and β_{12} do not exist: each of the first order conditions for a maximum reduces to $\beta_{21}\beta_{12} = 1$, which tells us only that both equations must be *estimated* to be the same, though it matters not what common slope they have.

2

I propose to consider next a model in which serial dependence of $u'(t)$ is explicitly assumed and which is otherwise the same as model (I). To reconcile this analysis with the assumptions underlying the usual approach, I assume that for any two stochastic variables u_g and u_h (not necessarily distinct) $\sigma_{u_g(t)u_h(t-1)} = 0$, so that from one observation point to the next, there is no serial correlation. But for a lag of θ, $\theta \leqslant H < 1$, H fixed, I suppose that $\sigma_{u_g(t)u_h(t-\theta)}$ is not necessarily zero, and is constant for all t. Our observation points shall be dated by $t = 1, 2, \ldots, T$, although for some purposes we shall want to think to t as taking on the values: $\theta, 2\theta, \ldots,$

[8] This holds only for the off-diagonal elements of B_0. That $\beta_{gg} = 1$ in B_0 is only a normalizing restriction and does not enable us to find the corresponding element in B_1.

[9] We must suppose $|\beta_{12}\beta_{21}| \leqslant 1$ or the system is explosive in its exact formulation, and our so-called "measurement" errors would tend to increase with time.

$k\theta, \ldots, H, \ldots, 1; 1+\theta, \ldots, 2; \ldots; T$; proceeding from θ to T by units of θ. I suppose, accordingly, that $1/\theta$ is an integer and that H is an integral multiple of θ.

Values for the vector $u(t)$ occur at each of these T/θ dates and are to be thought of as constituting a single drawing from a joint normal density function in these $G{\cdot}T/\theta$ variables, G being the number of elements in $u(t)$, i.e., the number of equations in the system. The unconditional expectation of each $u_g(t)$ is zero. The covariance matrix of the distribution is

$$(2.1) \qquad \Sigma = \begin{bmatrix} \Sigma_{0,0} & \Sigma_{0,\theta} & \Sigma_{0,2\theta} & \cdots & \Sigma_{0,H} & 0 & \cdots & 0 \\ \Sigma_{\theta,0} & \Sigma_{0,0} & \Sigma_{0,\theta} & \ddots & & \ddots & \ddots & \vdots \\ \Sigma_{2\theta,0} & \Sigma_{\theta,0} & \Sigma_{0,0} & \ddots & \ddots & & \ddots & 0 \\ \vdots & \ddots & \ddots & \ddots & \ddots & \ddots & & \Sigma_{0,H} \\ \Sigma_{H,0} & & \ddots & \ddots & \ddots & \ddots & \ddots & \vdots \\ 0 & \ddots & & \ddots & \ddots & \ddots & \ddots & \Sigma_{0,2\theta} \\ \vdots & \ddots & \ddots & & \ddots & \ddots & \ddots & \Sigma_{0,\theta} \\ 0 & \cdots & 0 & \Sigma_{H,0} & \cdots & \Sigma_{2\theta,0} & \Sigma_{\theta,0} & \Sigma_{0,0} \end{bmatrix}$$

whose elements are $G \times G$ submatrices, thus

$$(2.2) \qquad \Sigma_{0,k\theta} = \mathscr{E}[u'(t)u(t-k\theta)] = (\sigma_{u_g(t)u_h(t-k\theta)}) \,,$$

independently of t. To stress the independence of the elements of $\Sigma_{0,k\theta}$ from t, we shall write

$$(2.3) \qquad \sigma_{u_g(t)u_h(t-k\theta)} \equiv \sigma_{u_g u_h(-k\theta)} \,.$$

Note that $\sigma_{u_g u_h(-k\theta)}$ is not necessarily equal to $\sigma_{u_h u_g(-k\theta)}$. Nevertheless, Σ is symmetric, as required. (The element symmetric to $\sigma_{u_g u_h(-k\theta)}$ is $\sigma_{u_h(t-k\theta)u_g(t)} \equiv \sigma_{u_h u_g(+k\theta)}$.)

We have in mind, of course, a situation of this sort: Given adequate data, the model we should like to work with is

$$(\mathrm{I}) \qquad \mathrm{B}_0 y'(t) + \mathrm{B}_1 y'(t-\theta) + \Gamma z'(t) = u'(t) \,,$$

the same as (I) in the previous section, except for the specifications regarding serial correlation. Suppose now that observations are made only every December 31 for T successive years; but the lag θ is, for example, one day, so that $\theta = 1/365$. The possibility of serial correlation of the shock variables for a lag of one day, indeed of H/θ days, is allowed, but not for a lag as great as a year.

By letting θ approach 0, we obtain the limit form of (I):

$$(\mathrm{II}) \qquad \mathrm{B}y'(t) + \Gamma z'(t) = u^{*\prime}(t) \qquad (t = 1,2, \ldots, T),$$

where $\mathrm{B} = \mathrm{B}_0 + \mathrm{B}_1$, with B_0 triangular, B not.

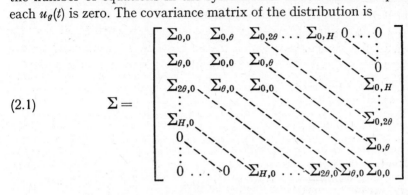

The log likelihood function of (II), associated with the developments connected with the Cowles Commission,[10] is (in "concentrated" form, as before)

$$L^* = \ln \|\mathrm{B}\| + \tfrac{1}{2} \ln |\Sigma^{*-1}| - \tfrac{1}{2} \operatorname{tr} (\Sigma^{*-1} (\mathrm{B}\ \Gamma) M^* (\mathrm{B}\ \Gamma)'), \tag{2.L.II}$$

where M^* is the moment matrix of Section 1.

It is worth noting at this point just what the role of $\ln \|\mathrm{B}\|$ is. It (in the non-log form) represents the Jacobian of the transformation of the joint distribution of the vector $u(t)$ to the vector $y(t)$—actually its reciprocal. When L^* is maximized with respect to the elements of Σ^{*-1} one obtains

$$\tilde{\Sigma}^{*-1} = [(\mathrm{B}\ \Gamma) M^* (\mathrm{B}\ \Gamma)']^{-1} \tag{2.4}$$

so that the last term becomes minus half the trace of an identity matrix, i.e., the constant $-G/2$.

The concentrated log likelihood function therefore reduces to

$$\ln \|\mathrm{B}\| + \tfrac{1}{2} \ln |\tilde{\Sigma}^{*-1}| \tag{2.5}$$

from which $(\mathrm{B}\ \Gamma)$ is to be estimated. Call the estimates $(\tilde{\mathrm{B}}\ \tilde{\Gamma})$.

Suppose, by contrast with this procedure, we were for the time being to ignore our data limitations and write the log-likelihood function of model (I). It would be

$$L = -\frac{GT}{2} \ln (2\pi) + \tfrac{1}{2} \ln |\Sigma^{-1}| - \tfrac{1}{2} u\, \Sigma^{-1} u' + \ln \left|\frac{\partial u}{\partial y}\right| \tag{2.L.I}$$

where $u = (u_1(\theta), \ldots, u_G(\theta); u_1(2\theta), \ldots, u_G(2\theta); \ldots; u_1(T), \ldots, u_G(T))$, and $y = (y_1(\theta), \ldots, y_G(\theta); y_1(2\theta), \ldots, y_G(2\theta); \ldots; y_1(T), \ldots, Y_G(T))$. This is the distribution of the jointly dependent variables conditional on given values of the predetermined variables, though for the time being it is notationally simpler to use the right- rather than the left-hand side of (I), that is, to express this density function, which is with respect to y, in terms of u. The "Jacobian" term which transforms the density function from the space of the u's to the space of the y's is the term

$$|\partial u/\partial y| = \begin{vmatrix} \mathrm{B}_0 & 0 & \cdots & \cdots & 0 \\ \mathrm{B}_1 & \mathrm{B}_0 & \ddots & & \vdots \\ 0 & \ddots & \ddots & \ddots & 0 \\ \vdots & & \ddots & \ddots & \\ 0 & \cdots & 0 & \mathrm{B}_1 & \mathrm{B}_0 \end{vmatrix}, \tag{2.6}$$

which is unity, so that $\ln |\partial u/\partial y| = 0$. We may henceforth drop it from (2.L.I). The presence of $\ln \|\mathrm{B}\|$ in (2.L.II) and the absence of any such term in (2.L.I) results from the fact that θ is *not* zero, regardless of how small

[10] See Koopmans, *op. cit.* and Wm. C. Hood and Tjalling C. Koopmans, eds., *Studies in Econometric Method*, New York: Wiley & Sons, 1953, and the references contained therein.

it may be, and seems quite fundamental for our results. (The variables $y_1(0), \ldots, y_G(0)$, dating back before the first observation period, are regarded as exogenous, and the vectors $u(\theta)$, $u(2\theta), \ldots$ are assumed to be independent of the vector $y(0)$, although this is unrealistic, because neither $y(0)$ nor $u(\theta), \ldots, u(H)$ will be independent of $u(0)$. This is the problem of initial conditions, and of a sort that also arises in the conventional approach.[11] If the system is stable, however, we should expect any bias in the estimates resulting from this source to diminish as the sample size increases.)

The model just formulated entails some mathematical difficulties which do not appear essential, but which arise, as I conjecture, because our observations are within a finite span of time. This fact and the assumption that $y_1(0), \ldots, y_G(0)$ are exogenous serve to truncate the "infinite order determinant"

$$(2.7) \qquad \begin{vmatrix} \ddots & \ddots & \ddots & & 0 \\ & \Sigma_{0,0} & \Sigma_{0,\theta} & & \\ & \Sigma_{\theta,0} & \Sigma_{0,0} & \Sigma_{0,\theta} & \\ & & \Sigma_{\theta,0} & \ddots & \ddots \\ 0 & & & \ddots & \ddots \end{vmatrix}$$

and to produce "corners" which are responsible for some troublesome asymmetry. In particular, although the submatrices of Σ are constant along any diagonal falling from left to right, i.e., a diagonal such as

$$\begin{matrix} \Sigma_{0,k\theta} & & \\ & \Sigma_{0,k\theta} & \\ & & \ddots \; \Sigma_{0,k\theta}, \end{matrix}$$

this will *not* be the case for Σ^{-1}. For example, if a determinant

$$(2.8) \qquad \Sigma = \begin{vmatrix} 1 & 1/2 & 0 \\ 1/2 & 1 & 1/2 \\ 0 & 1/2 & 1 \end{vmatrix}, \quad \Sigma^{-1} = \begin{vmatrix} 3/2 & -1 & 1/2 \\ -1 & 2 & -1 \\ 1/2 & -1 & 3/2 \end{vmatrix}.$$

This, I have found, causes difficulties in maximizing the likelihood function. I choose, for this reason, to modify the assumptions of the model just developed by assuming not that the submatrices of Σ are constant

[11] See H. B. Mann and A. Wald, "On the Statistical Treatment of Linear Stochastic Difference Equations," *Econometrica*, Vol. 11, July-October, 1943, and T. C. Koopmans, H. Rubin, and R. B. Leipnik, "Measuring the Equation Systems of Dynamic Economics," in Koopmans, *Statistical Inference . . .* (*op. cit*), Section 3.3.

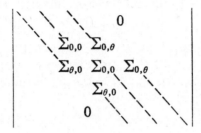

along any diagonal,[12] but that the submatrices of Σ^{-1} have this property. It is therefore the representative element of $\Sigma^{-1}, \sigma^{u_g(t)u_h(t-k\theta)}$, which can be written as $\sigma^{u_g u_h(-k\theta)}$.

This still allows for zeros in the upper right and lower left corners of Σ. An illustration of this, for the case where the submatrices are scalars, is given by

$$\text{(2.9)} \qquad \Sigma^{-1} = \begin{vmatrix} 2 & -1 & 1/2 \\ -1 & 2 & -1 \\ 1/2 & -1 & 2 \end{vmatrix}, \quad \Sigma = \begin{vmatrix} 2/3 & 1/3 & 0 \\ 1/3 & 15/18 & 1/3 \\ 0 & 1/3 & 2/3 \end{vmatrix}.$$

The assumption that it is the elements along a diagonal of Σ^{-1} that are constant, rather than the elements along a diagonal of Σ, seems unnatural because it is difficult to provide a "physical" interpretation of an element of the inverse of a covariance matrix. Nevertheless, the constant diagonality assumption on Σ^{-1} is not so much more arbitrary than the same assumption on Σ. What is needed is to reduce the number of independent parameters to be estimated, and this necessitates constraints on Σ (hence, on Σ^{-1}). In the absence of any information about how a (lagged or non-lagged) covariance changes over time, it seems natural to suppose that it does not change at all: hence, the "naturalness" of a homoscedasticity assumption on Σ, namely that $\sigma_{u_g(t)u_h(t-k\theta)} = \sigma_{u_g u_h(-k\theta)}$ for all t. But that implies that the elements in Σ^{-1} are *not* constant over time, and that implication is arbitrary and seems unnatural in its own right. On the other hand, if we assume the elements of Σ^{-1} to be constant with respect to time, that is, that $\sigma^{u_g(t)u_h(t-k\theta)} = \sigma^{u_g u_h(-k\theta)}$ for all t, we imply that the elements of Σ may change with time, which is admittedly also arbitrary. We cannot have it both ways; that is, we cannot assume the elements of *both* Σ and Σ^{-1} to be constant over time if those matrices are of finite order. I find it preferable to assume constant elements along the diagonals of Σ^{-1}. A bit of heuristics to support this choice: it is the elements of Σ^{-1} which enter more directly into the joint normal distribution; they—not the elements of Σ—are, after all, the coefficients of the quadratic forms which are the terms in the summation over time that enters as the exponent. Moreover, the constant diagonality assumption on Σ^{-1} simplifies the mathematics considerably. I find that reassuring, too, for it suggests that the constant diagonality assumption, regarded as a simplification, enters the analysis more immediately and essentially if imposed on Σ^{-1} instead of on Σ. With these heuristic arguments aside, it appears that in any case the choice between simplifying Σ or Σ^{-1} arises only because of the finiteness of

[12] Meaning always one falling from left to right.

the sample size and does not seem critical for the general conclusions we are working to derive.

(2.L.I) may therefore be written as

$$(2.10)\quad L = \tfrac{1}{2}\ln|\Sigma^{-1}| - \tfrac{1}{2}\sum_{g=1}^{G}\sum_{h=1}^{G}\sum_{\substack{t=k\theta+\theta\\ \text{by }\theta}}^{T}\sum_{k=0}^{T/\theta-1} u_g(t)u_h(t-k\theta)\sigma^{u_g u_h(-k\theta)}$$

$$-\tfrac{1}{2}\sum_{g=1}^{G}\sum_{h=1}^{G}\sum_{\substack{t=\theta\\ \text{by }\theta}}^{T+k\theta}\sum_{k=1-T/\theta}^{-1} u_g(t)u_h(t-k\theta)\sigma^{u_g u_h(-k\theta)}.$$

Differentiating partially with respect to each $\sigma^{u_g u_h(-k\theta)}$ and setting the derivatives equal to zero gives[13]

$$(2.11)\quad \left\{\begin{array}{l} \text{if } k \geqslant 0, \quad \sum\limits_{\substack{t=k\theta+\theta\\ \text{by }\theta}}^{T} \hat{\sigma}_{u_g(t)u_h(t-\theta)} = \sum\limits_{\substack{t=k\theta+\theta\\ \text{by }\theta}}^{T} u_g(t)u_h(t-k\theta), \\ \text{if } k < 0, \quad \sum\limits_{\substack{t=\theta\\ \text{by }\theta}}^{T+k\theta} \hat{\sigma}_{u_g(t)u_h(t-k\theta)} = \sum\limits_{\substack{t=\theta\\ \text{by }\theta}}^{T+k\theta} u_g(t)u_h(t-k\theta), \end{array}\right\} \text{for all } g,h.^{14}$$

These conditions plus the constant diagonality assumption on Σ^{-1} would in principle provide an estimate of Σ^{-1}, namely $\hat{\Sigma}^{-1}$.This I have not proved rigorously. I can only note that there are as many independent conditions as unknowns, taking account of the symmetry of Σ and Σ^{-1}. There are G^2T/θ independent elements in $\hat{\Sigma}^{-1}$ and $(G^2T/\theta)\ (G^2T/\theta + 1)/2$ independent elements in $\hat{\Sigma}$. These are to be determined by the $(G^2T/\theta)\ (G^2T/\theta + 1)/2$ relations $\sigma_{u_g(t)u_h(t-k\theta)} = \hat{\Sigma}^{-1}{}_{u_h(t)u_g(t-k\theta)}/|\hat{\Sigma}^{-1}|$, where the numerator is a cofactor in $\hat{\Sigma}^{-1}$, and by the G^2T/θ independent conditions in (2.11).

Substituting these elements of $\hat{\Sigma}^{-1}$ and using (2.11), (2.10) becomes

$$(2.12)\quad L(B_0, B_1, \Gamma) = \tfrac{1}{2}\ln|\hat{\Sigma}^{-1}| - \tfrac{1}{2}\sum_{g}\sum_{h}\sum_{k=0}^{T/\theta-1}\sum_{\substack{t=k\theta+\theta\\ \text{by }\theta}}^{T} \hat{\sigma}_{u_g(t)u_h(t-k\theta)}\hat{\sigma}^{u_g u_h(-k\theta)}$$

$$-\tfrac{1}{2}\sum_{g}\sum_{h}\sum_{k=1-T/\theta}^{-1}\sum_{\substack{t=\theta\\ \text{by }\theta}}^{T+k\theta} \hat{\sigma}_{u_g(t)u_h(t-k\theta)}\hat{\sigma}^{u_g u_h(-k\theta)} = \tfrac{1}{2}\ln|\hat{\Sigma}^{-1}|$$

$$-\tfrac{1}{2}\sum_{g}\sum_{\substack{t\\ \text{by }\theta}}^{T/\theta}\sum_{h}\sum_{\substack{s\\ \text{by }\theta}}^{T/\theta} \hat{\sigma}_{u_g(t)u_h(s)}\hat{\sigma}^{u_g(t)u_h(s)} = \tfrac{1}{2}\ln|\hat{\Sigma}^{-1}| - \frac{GT}{2\theta}.$$

[13] It may be noted that in maximizing with respect to the elements of Σ^{-1}, we do not *impose* the requirement that certain elements of Σ be zero. This is the usual "trust to luck" procedure. We trust that if we could later test our non-serial correlation assumption, it would be borne out, and, otherwise, we stand prepared to reject our estimates.

[14] Because of symmetry, the conditions for $k < 0$ are redundant.

The likelihood function may be "concentrated" further by dropping the final term. Hence we may write

(2.L.I′) $$L(B_0, B_1, \Gamma) = -\tfrac{1}{2} \ln | \hat{\Sigma} |,$$

and contrast it with what we obtain using the conventional approach (2.L.II), namely,

(2.L.II′) $$L^*(B, \Gamma) = -\tfrac{1}{2} \ln |\tilde{\Sigma}^*| + \ln ||B||.$$

I see no reason to expect that, even as θ approaches zero, with H (the maximum lag for which serial correlation occurs) remaining fixed, and even as T becomes infinite, the values $(\hat{B}_0, \hat{B}_1, \hat{\Gamma})$ which maximize (2.L.I′) and the values $(\tilde{B}, \tilde{\Gamma})$ which maximize (2.L.II′) will approach the equalities $\tilde{B} = \hat{B}_0 + \hat{B}_1$ and $\tilde{\Gamma} = \hat{\Gamma}$. I proceed on the basis of this conjecture.

With observations only at $t = 1, 2, \ldots, T$, what now should be done? We cannot maximize (2.L.I′) with respect to all unknown parameters. Let us deal first with the fact that submatrices along a diagonal of Σ will not be all alike. This is because the observation period has a beginning and an end. At the first observation point we do not look backwards, and at the last we do not look forwards. This accounts for the asymmetry. As a practical matter, my recommendation would be to ignore this and to admit whatever bias thereby results. Then, for $k = 0$, we should choose (from (2.11))

(2.13) $$\hat{\sigma}_{u_g(t)u_h(t)} = \frac{\theta}{T} \sum_{\substack{t=\theta \\ \text{by } \theta}}^{T} u_g(t)u_h(t), \quad \text{for each } t,$$

and, with observations only at $t = 1, 2, \ldots, T$, we should use the estimate

(2.14) $$\hat{\sigma}_{u_g(t)u_h(t)} = \frac{1}{T} \sum_{t=1}^{T} u_g(t)u_h(t), \quad \text{for each } t,$$

or, as $\theta \to 0$,

(2.15) $$\hat{\Sigma}_{0,0} = (B\ \Gamma)M^*(B\ \Gamma)',$$

where $(B\ \Gamma)$ are to be estimated. Unable to observe what a choice of $(\hat{B}\ \hat{\Gamma})$ implies for the off-diagonal submatrices of $\hat{\Sigma}$, I should think it then reasonable to minimize $|\hat{\Sigma}_{0,0}|$ rather than $|\hat{\Sigma}|$.[15] This is to minimize $|(B\ \Gamma)M^*(B\ \Gamma)'|$.

[15] This recommendation is essentially of the following sort: suppose a likelihood function of a parameter a is

$$L(a) = f(a) + g(a)$$

where the function $f(a)$ is known, while $g(a)$ and, hence, $L(a)$ is not known. Then, the recommendation is, choose a so as to maximize $f(a)$. This is to choose the value that makes what we can observe as "credible" as possible. We ought not be concerned with what our estimate implies about things we cannot at present observe. The best hypothesis or estimate is the one that fits the known facts as well as possible. That facts yet to be revealed may later discredit it is always a danger, but not a guide to the decision to accept a hypothesis or estimate for the time being.

By contrast, the conventional procedure would lead us to maximize (2.L.II′) or to minimize

$$(2.16) \qquad |(\mathrm{B}\ \Gamma)M^*(\mathrm{B}\ \Gamma)'\,|\cdot|\,\mathrm{B}^{-1}|^2 .$$

For these procedures to be equivalent it is necessary that $|\mathrm{B}^{-1}|$ should have a stationary value where $|(\mathrm{B}\ \Gamma)M^*(\mathrm{B}\ \Gamma)'|$ has a minimum. I can see no reason why this should be the case.[16]

The difference between the two procedures arises because of a difference in the Jacobian. What we need to know to transform the density function from the space of the u's to that of the y's is what the increments of the y's will be given an increment of the u's. This is an exact and not a stochastic relationship. It does not matter that as $u_g(t)$ increases, there is high *probability* that $u_g(t-\theta)$ will also have increased. Even though the correlation of $u(t-\theta)$ and $u(t)$ approaches unity as θ approaches zero,

$$(2.17) \qquad |\partial u/\partial y| = \begin{vmatrix} \mathrm{B}_0 & 0 & \cdots & 0 \\ \mathrm{B}_1 & \mathrm{B}_0 & \ddots & \vdots \\ 0 & \mathrm{B}_1 & \ddots & 0 \\ \vdots & \ddots & \ddots & \\ 0 & \cdots & 0 \quad \mathrm{B}_1 & \mathrm{B}_0 \end{vmatrix} = 1$$

and does not approach

$$(2.18) \qquad \left\| \begin{matrix} \mathrm{B}_0+\mathrm{B}_1 & & 0 & \cdots & 0 \\ 0 & \mathrm{B}_0+\mathrm{B}_1 & & & \vdots \\ \vdots & & \ddots & & 0 \\ 0 & \cdots & & 0 & \mathrm{B}_0+\mathrm{B}_1 \end{matrix} \right\| = ||\mathrm{B}||^{T/\theta} .$$

My view is that approximating $|(\mathrm{B}_0\ \mathrm{B}_1\ \Gamma)M(\mathrm{B}_0\ \mathrm{B}_1\ \Gamma)'|$ with $|(\mathrm{B}\ \Gamma)M^*(\mathrm{B}\ \Gamma)'|$ is a *measurement* error which need not be of great consequence. To ignore this kind of measurement error is therefore a specification error which, however, may be of little importance; but in replacing B_0 by B in the Jacobian term another kind of *specification* error is made, and this is one which the desire for an approximation to the latent model does not warrant.

My tentative conclusion is therefore, once again, that *the values of the parameters that maximize the limit form of the likelihood function of the*

[16] Note that also in applying the conventional procedure one ignores whatever the estimates of the structural parameters imply about the serial correlation coefficients of the u's for lags not exceeding H. These implied values can simply not be observed because of the large size of the observation period. Hence, the procedure recommended in the previous footnote is followed in both approaches.

latent model are not the same as those that maximize the likelihood function of the limit form of the model.

3

I think this analysis leads to three further propositions. Though I state them boldly, the tentative character of this paper should not be overlooked.

(1) Whenever an interdependent model is in fact proposed as an approximation to a recursive one, interdependence involves a specification error. If the conclusions of the previous paper, written jointly with Professor Wold, are accepted, however, all stochastic interdependent models purporting to explain, according to the usual notion of causation, how observed values of economic variables are generated, must be regarded as approximations to an underlying or latent recursive model. All interdependent models then *necessarily* involve a specification error. It is this latter point of view which is adopted here, but disagreement about it is important only for the question of the universality of the problem we have treated.

There is nothing improper about using an interdependent system. If it is regarded as an equilibrium system, a causal interpretation of its parameters should be sought in an implicit dynamic system, which will be recursive. If the model is stochastic, however, the specification that the system is *precisely* in equilibrium whenever observed cannot be maintained without error. If the interdependent system is not regarded as an equilibrium system but as an approximation to a recursive one, its causal structure is to be found in the recursive system it approximates. Provided the approximation is reasonable, there is no harm in replacing slightly lagged variables by their current values if they are highly correlated with them, and then treating these variables as stochastic rather than as predetermined; but the Jacobian should nevertheless be regarded as unity. *This procedure may be followed even though the latent recursive model (significantly, its lag structure) is not precisely specified.* Whatever the underlying recursive model may be, its Jacobian is always unity.

(2) Although we examined only the case in which interdependence arises from the suppression of a slight time lag, interdependence may arise for other reasons which are possibly different, e.g., those discussed as (2) and (3) on page 429. I should expect our present results to hold for those cases as well. This is to say that interdependent systems related to recursive systems in these other ways can be treated in a straightforward manner, except that the Jacobian must always be set equal to one. This assures that the use of the interdependent system as an approximation introduces only measurement errors which may, in principle, be small,

and does not introduce the specification error which a nonrecursive Jacobian entails.

(3) Although our criticism has been directed against the conventional formulation of full-information maximum-likelihood estimators, the criticism applies also to other estimators that have the same probability limits, such as the conventional limited-information maximum-likelihood estimators and the two-stage least-squares estimators. In all these methods, the specification error of interdependence, however inconsequential it may seem viewed as a measurement error, appears to introduce a bias of unforeseeable magnitude.

A GENERALIZATION OF CAUSAL CHAIN MODELS

(PART III OF A TRIPTYCH ON CAUSAL CHAIN SYSTEMS)

By H. O. A. Wold

The parting of the ways between causal chain (recursive) and interdependent (non-recursive) systems is reviewed from the point of view of explanatory relations specified in terms of conditional expectations. On the customary assumptions, a causal chain system is designed so that its relations both in the original form and in the reduced form can be specified in terms of conditional expectations, whereas the relations of interdependent systems allow such specification only in the reduced form. A third type of model is discussed, called *conditional causal chains*, which formally is similar to interdependent systems, with the important difference that the behavioural relations of the original system are specified in terms of conditional expectations.

In this triptych communication by Professor Strotz and myself, our joint paper provides a common basis for the two appended contributions, which are of more recent origin and deal with different aspects of simultaneous equation systems.

1. THREE APPROACHES IN THE CONSTRUCTION OF ECONOMETRIC MODELS

The discussion in recent years on causal chains *vs*. interdependent systems is closely linked to the debate on single-relation methods, and particularly to the choice of regression in the regression approach. From the general point of view of scientific model construction the three approaches are of general scope within a broad area: *explanatory analysis* on the basis of *nonexperimental* data.

1.1. *The regression approach*: explanatory models in the form of a single relationship, say

(1) $$y = \beta_0 + \beta_1 x_1 + \ldots + \beta_h x_h + u \,.$$

The problem about "the choice of regression" was vigorously stressed by R. Frisch (1928; 1934). Further references are [**27**, **25**, **14**, **45**, **28**, **35**, **36**, **44**, **42**].

1.2. *Causal chain systems*: explanatory models in the form of a system (S–W 2)[1] of explicit relations for the current endogenous variables.

The causal chain approach was initiated by J. Tinbergen in his macroeconomic models for the Netherlands (1937), United States (1939), and United Kingdom (1951). Some further references are [**32**, **3**, **7**, **37**, **44**, **39**, **41**].

[1] Here and in the following, S–W (for Strotz, Wold) and S refer to the first and second parts of this joint communication.

1.3. *Interdependent systems*: explanatory models in the form of a system (S–W 3) of *implicit* relations for the current endogenous variables.

The *reduced form* of the system is obtained by solving for the current endogenous variables, which thereby come out explicitly in terms of *predetermined variables*, that is, exogenous and lagged endogenous variables. Initiated by T. Haavelmo in 1943, interdependent systems were studied intensely under the auspicies of the Cowles Commission [**16**, **23**, **19**]. Some further references are [**20**, **6**, **9**, **18**, **22**, **29**].

2. BASIC PROCEDURES OF INFERENCE IN THE OPERATIVE USE OF THE MODELS

The approaches 1.1-3 have different aspiration levels. The differences manifest themselves in the operative use of the models in applied work. The following brief review brings out the distinction under 1.2-3 between explicit and implicit systems; and we further show how the operative use of single relationships provides a common denominator for the three types of models.

2.1. *The regression approach.* We shall write

$$y = b_0 + b_1 x_1 + \ldots + b_h x_h + v \tag{2}$$

for the relation (1) as estimated from the observed sample.

PROCEDURE 2.10. *Predictive inference from a single-relation model*: In this well known procedure, relation (2) is used for predicting an unknown y in terms of known $x_1, \ldots, x_h$. The procedure ignores the residual v.

REMARK 2.10: The notations in (1)–(2) emphasize the difference between theoretical and empirical concepts. To avoid a double set of notations for multiple-relations models, we shall often take (S–W 2) and (S–W 3) to cover both the theoretical and the estimated models.

2.2. *Causal chains.* Again with reference to the causal chain systems constructed by Tinbergen in the 1930's [**30**—**33**], the following two procedures are fundamental in his applied work.

PROCEDURE 2.20. *Predictive inference from a single relation in the system*: As applied to the system (S–W 2)—after estimation of the parameters—the procedure is to predict an endogenous variable, say $y_g(t)$, by using the explanatory relation that the system gives for $y_g(t)$.

REMARK 2.20: Causal chains being constructed so as to contain one, and only one, explanatory relation for each endogenous variable, Procedure 2.20 is, at least formally, the same as Procedure 2.10.

REMARK 2.21: As seen from (S–W 2), the explanatory variables in the relation for $y_g(t)$ will in general include not only the exogenous and lagged endogenous variables, $z_i(t)$, (predetermined variables, in the terminology of interdependent systems) but also the current endogenous variables $y_{g+1}(t), \ldots, y_G(t)$.

PROCEDURE 2.21. *Substitutive elimination of variables from a relation in the system*: As applied to the relation for a specified endogenous variable $y_g(t)$, the procedure is to eliminate one or more endogenous variables from the relation by means of the corresponding relations of the system.

Procedure 2.21 in general involves iterated substitutions. A typical application is to deduce a difference equation for $y_g(t)$, that is, a relation that involves current and lagged values of y_g and current and lagged values of the exogenous variables, but no endogenous variables y_i with $i \neq g$. The difference relation is taken as a basis for further inference, notably about the intrinsic oscillations of the system.

2.3. *Interdependent systems.* The applied work here involves two basic procedures that are similar to Procedures 2.20–21, except that they are now applied to the reduced form of the system.

PROCEDURE 2.30. *Predictive inference from a single relation in the reduced form*: For typical applications, see [**20, 18, 4, 22, 29**].

REMARK 2.30: By construction of the reduced form, the variables exploited in the predictive inference involve no current endogenous variables, only exogenous and lagged endogenous variables. With reference to Remark 2.21, this distinguishes them in character from causal chain systems.

PROCEDURE 2.31. *Substitutive elimination of variables from a relation in the reduced form*: For typical applications, see [**20, 22, 29**].

3. THE APPLIED PROCEDURES AS OPERATIONS WITH CONDITIONAL EXPECTATIONS

The procedures under 2.1–3 have their rationale in the design of the various types of models. Several features of the design being of relevance in this context, we shall in this section review the situation from the point of view of conditional expectations.[2]

3.1. *The regression approach*: *On Procedure* 2.10. The simplest device for establishing the rationale of Procedure 2.10 is perhaps provided by the following argument:

ASSUMPTION 3.10. Relation (1) gives the conditional expectation of y for known $x_1, \ldots, x_h$. In symbols,

$$\mathscr{E}(y|x_1, \ldots, x_h) = \beta_0 + \beta_1 x_1 + \ldots + \beta_h x_h. \tag{3}$$

We note three theorems that are almost direct implications of (3).

[2] Theorems 3.10–12 are, in essence, restatements from Wold (1959b).

THEOREM 3.10. *On assumption* (3) *the residual u in* (1) *has zero conditional expectation,*

$$\mathscr{E}(u|x_1, \ldots, x_h) = 0\,. \tag{4}$$

THEOREM 3.11. *On assumption* (3) *the residual u in* (1) *has zero product moment with any function* $f(x_1, \ldots, x_h)$ *of the explanatory variables. Making* $f \equiv 1$ *and* $f \equiv x_i$ *it follows, in particular, that* u *has zero expectation and zero correlation with any* x_i:

$$\mathscr{E}(u \cdot f(x_1, \ldots, x_h)) = 0\,; \quad \mathscr{E}(u) = 0\,; \quad r(u, x_i) = 0 \qquad (i = 1, \ldots, h)\,. \tag{5a–c}$$

THEOREM 3.12. *Let* (2) *denote the observed least-squares regression of y on* $x_1, \ldots, x_h$. *Then on assumption* (3) *the observed regression coefficients* $b_0, b_1, \ldots, b_h$ *will under very general conditions have the true parameters* $\beta_0, \beta_1, \ldots, \beta_h$ *for limiting values, in the sense of weak stochastic convergence, as the sample size increases indefinitely. In symbols*

$$\text{prob lim } b_i = \beta_i \qquad (i = 1, \ldots, h)\,. \tag{6}$$

Theorem 3.12 rests on the simple facts that the observed regression coefficients b_i are rational functions of the sample moments of first and second order and that the observed residual v has zero correlation with $x_1, \ldots, x_h$. Hence the unspecified conditions of the theorem require merely that the joint distribution of $x_1, \ldots, x_h$ should be nonsingular, and that the observed second order moments of $y, x_1, \ldots, x_h$ should tend to the corresponding theoretical moments as the sample size increases.

REMARK 3.10: In one stroke, assumption (3) has thus established the rationale of the Procedure 2.10 and of the least-squares estimation (2). The residual noncorrelation properties (5c) come out as a byproduct. The customary device is to start from a linear relation (1), adopting the noncorrelation hypotheses (5c), and assuming that the residual u is normally distributed.[3]

3.2. *Causal chain systems.* Since the requisite assumptions are not the same, we shall take up Procedures 2.20–21 one by one.

3.20. *On Procedure* 2.20. The argument in Theorems 3.10–12 is of general scope and can be adapted to establish the rationale of Procedure 2.20.

ASSUMPTION 3.20. For any endogenous variable, say y_g, the relation for $y_g(t)$ in system (S–W 2) gives the conditional expectation of $y_g(t)$ for known values of the explanatory variables. In symbols,

$$\mathscr{E}(y_g|y_{g+1}, \ldots, y_G, z_1, z_2, \ldots) = -\beta_{g,g+1}y_{g+1} - \ldots - \beta_{gG}y_G - \sum_k \gamma_{gk}z_k\,. \tag{7}$$

[3] For approaches of this type, see, e.g., the review in Wold-Juréen (1952), Chs. 12–13.

Adopting assumption (7), Theorems 3.10–11 can be directly extended to the relations of system (S–W 2). The analogous extension of Theorem 3.12 lies somewhat deeper when it comes to the supplementary requirement that the observed moments of second order should tend to the corresponding theoretical moments. A sufficient condition for this requirement to be fulfilled is that the stochastic process defined by system (S–W 2) is stationary and ergodic.[4]

Prodecure 2.20 is thus valid under fairly general conditions. On the same conditions, we have established the rationale of estimating systems (S–W 2) by the method of least-squares regression.

3.21. *On Procedure* 2.21. To establish this procedure, Assumption 3.20 must be supplemented by additional requirements. A simple device for this purpose is to make the following assumption:

ASSUMPTION 3.21. Considering the substitutive procedure as applied to the relation for $y_g(t)$, the residual $u_g(t)$ is independent of all variables—endogenous and exogenous, current and lagged—that occur in the auxiliary relation or relations that are used in the substitution.

In fact, if we form the conditional expectation of $y_g(t)$ after the substitution, Assumption 3.21 implies that the result will be the same as if we had performed the substitution in (7) with disregard of the residuals involved. Thus established, Procedure 2.21 is at the same time interpreted as an operation with conditional expectations.

REMARK 3.20: An alternative device to establish Procedure 2.21 is to assume that the causal chain defines a stochastic process that is stationary and Gaussian and that all residuals are mutually uncorrelated. This device makes for easy comparison with the situation in interdependent systems and emphasizes that the requisite noncorrelation between current residuals is not a necessary implication of Assumption 3.20.

REMARK 3.21: At first sight it may seem that the field of potential applications is much narrower for Procedure 2.21 than for 2.20, in view of the additional assumption about zero intercorrelation between current residuals. However, the requisite noncorrelation is in accordance, at least approximately, with the resolving power of causal chain systems. In fact,[5] it is a general property of causal chains that the lags and the coefficients β_{gi}, γ_{gk} can be specified in such manner that all intercorrelations between the residuals, lagged or nonlagged will be numerically smaller that any prescribed $\varepsilon > 0$.

3.3. *Interdependent systems.* The situation is here analogous to causal chains except that the requisite assumptions will have reference to the re-

[4] See Wold (1959b), also for further references.

[5] See Wold-Juréen (1952), Theorem 12.7.1.

duced form of the system. We shall not enter upon a detailed treatment, for it is not our purpose to explore what are the most general assumptions under which Procedures 2.20–21 and 2.30–31 are valid. It will suffice to restate the typical assumptions used in the theory of interdependent systems, assumptions which provide a clearcut rationale for Procedures 2.30–31.[6]

ASSUMPTIONS 3.30–31. The interdependent system defines a stochastic process with the following properties:

(i) The process is stationary and Gaussian;

(ii) All residuals referring to different time periods are mutually uncorrelated;

(iii) The current residuals are uncorrelated with the predetermined variables, that is, with the relevant exogenous and lagged endogenous variables.

REMARK 3.30: While Assumptions 3.30–31 establish the rationale of Procedures 2.30–31, they also establish the *limited-information method* of estimation; that is, the method of least-squares regression provides consistent estimates for the interdependent system in its reduced form.

When the reduced form has been estimated, the interdependent system itself is estimated by transforming back to the system in its original, unreduced form. The reverse transformation involves the *identification problem* of interdependent systems. Thus in the case of *just-identified* systems the reverse transformation leads to unique and consistent estimates for the parameters. Otherwise, the system is either *under-* or *over-identified.*

4. A PROVISIONAL SUMMARY

The review in sections 1–3 brings into relief that causal chains and interdependent systems are distinctly different approaches, each with its attractive features. Interdependent systems have the advantage of being more general than causal chains in their formal design. First, with regard to the coefficient matrix of the current endogenous variables, the matrix of causal chains has mere units in the main diagonal and mere zeros below the diagonal, while the matrix of interdependent systems is not subject to these restrictions. This is so because a causal chain is constructed as a purely dynamic system of behaviour relations (sometimes with identities interpreted as behaviour relations), while the interdependent approach is more flexible. Secondly, the assumptions about residuals are more restrictive for causal chains, and in the two respects that correspond to Procedures 2.20–21 compared to 2.30–31. As a consequence, if the triangular system (S–W 2) were specified as an interdependent system, then (i) the

[6] See the references in Section 1.3.

residual $u_g(t)$ would be uncorrelated with the $z_k(t)$'s but not necessarily with $y_{g,g+i}(t)$, and (ii) any two current residuals $u_g(t)$, $u_h(t)$ would not necessarily have to be uncorrelated.

On the other hand, causal chains have the advantage of providing the formal framework for a stimulus-response interpretation of the behaviour relations that constitute the system. At bottom, this is the key argument for putting the behaviour relations to direct operative use in this approach. In interdependent systems the behaviour relations do not lend themselves to the same direct stimulus-response interpretation, and in accordance herewith the operative use of the model is based on the reduced form. A relaxed causal interpretation of interdependent systems is, however, perfectly admissible (see S–W, Section 3).

In view of the different merits of the two types of models it is a natural question whether their merits can be combined by some sort of synthesis. An attempt in this direction is commented upon in the remaining Sections 5–6. To distinguish between models of Tinbergen's type and the new approach we shall use the terms *pure* vs. *conditional* causal chains.

5. CONDITIONAL CAUSAL CHAINS

Generally speaking, the design of this type of simultaneous equation system involves (i) constructing a model on the basis of behaviour relations; (ii) accepting relations other than behaviour relations, and particularly equilibrium relations and other approximations that may break the triangular pattern of the coefficient matrix of current endogenous variables; and (iii) maintaining a stimulus-response interpretation of the behaviour relations by specifying them in accordance with Assumption 3.10. These construction principles ensure that Procedure 2.20 for predictive inference applies to any behaviour relation of a conditional causal chain system. Hence Procedure 2.20 provides a minimum program for the operative use of such models. Problems referring to the extension of the operation program fall outside the scope of this paper. In Section 6.5, however, we shall briefly consider whether and under what further assumptions it is legitimate to use the reduced form of a conditional causal chain. A more detailed account of the approach, including applications to empirical data, is given elsewhere.[7]

ILLUSTRATION 5.10: We illustrate the close similarities as well as the sharp contrast between interdependent and conditional causal chain systems

[7] See [**42**]. There the new approach is introduced under the name of *implicit* causal chains, whereas Tinbergen's systems are referred to as *explicit* causal chains.

with two simple demand-supply models. A specific feature of the illustration is that the two models define one and the same stochastic process.

We form a stochastic process as a sequence of two-dimensional random variables,

$$(8) \qquad \ldots, (p_{t-1}, q_{t-1}), (p_t, q_t), (p_{t+1}, q_{t+1}), (p_{t+2}, q_{t+2}), \ldots$$

letting the sequence be specified as follows:

(i) The sequence is a stationary, Gaussian and Markovian process;

(ii) The variables are measured from their means in standard deviation units:

$$(9) \qquad \mathscr{E}(p_t) = \mathscr{E}(q_t) = 0\,; \quad \sigma(p_t) = \sigma(q_t) = 1 \qquad (t = 0, \pm 1, \pm 2, \ldots)\,;$$

(iii) Five basic covariances are specified as follows,

$$(10a\text{–}c) \qquad \mathscr{E}(p_t\, q_t) = -\frac{4}{5}, \; \mathscr{E}(p_{t-1}\, q_t) = \frac{3}{5}, \; \mathscr{E}(p_{t-1}\, p_t) = \varrho\,,$$

$$(10d\text{–}e) \qquad \mathscr{E}(q_{t-1}\, q_t) = -\frac{12}{25}, \; \mathscr{E}(q_{t-1}\, p_t) = -\frac{4}{5}\varrho\,,$$

where ϱ is an arbitrarily fixed number in the interval

$$(11) \qquad -\frac{24}{25} \leq \varrho \leq 0\,.$$

By assumption (i) and the nine parameters (9)–(10) the sequence (8) is completely specified as a two-dimensional vector process. Condition (11) ensures that the three-dimensional distribution (p_{t-t}, p_t, q_t) is well defined, and thereby the whole process. Artificial time series can be constructed as realizations of the process by using the relations

$$(12a\text{–}b) \qquad q_t = \frac{3}{5} p_{t-1} + u_t'\,; \quad p_t = \varrho\, p_{t-1} + u_t''$$

for recursive calculation of the sequence (p_t, q_t), taking

$$(13) \qquad \ldots, u_{t-1}', u_t', u_{t+1}', \ldots \quad \text{and} \quad \ldots, u_{t-1}'', u_t'', u_{t+1}'', \ldots$$

to be two independent sequences of independent and normally distributed variables with means and standard deviations given by

$$(14a\text{–}d) \qquad \mathscr{E}(u_t') = \mathscr{E}(u_t'') = 0, \; \sigma(u_t') = \frac{4}{5}; \; \sigma(u_t'') = \sqrt{(1-\varrho^2)}$$

REMARK 5.10: For a Gauss-Markov process (8) the construction of artificial time series should in general be based on the multiple regressions of q_t on p_{t-1} and q_{t-1} and of p_t on p_{t-1} and q_{t-1}. For simplicity, the covariances (10) have been chosen so that these multiple regressions reduce to the simple regressions (12a–b).

Model IS. This is an interdependent system with two behaviour relations and one equilibrium relation,

$$\text{(15a–c)}\qquad \begin{cases} d_t = \dfrac{3}{5\varrho} p_t + u_t & \text{(demand relation)}, \\ s_t = \dfrac{3}{5} p_{t-1} + u_t' & \text{(supply relation)}, \\ d_t = s_t = q_t, & \text{(assumption of instantaneous equilibrium)} \end{cases}$$

and with noncorrelation properties in accordance with Assumptions 3.30–31 (ii), that is

$$\text{(16a–b)}\qquad r(u_t, p_{t-1}) = 0\,; \quad r(u_t', p_{t-1}) = 0\,.$$

The reduced form of Model IS is given by (12a–b) with

$$\text{(17)}\qquad u_t'' = \frac{5\varrho}{3}(u_t' - u_t)\,.$$

As is readily verified, the residuals satisfy Assumptions 3.30–31 (iii).

If we interpret Model IS as a stochastic process (8) with properties (i)-(ii), again letting ϱ be arbitrarily fixed in the interval (11), an elementary calculation shows that relations (10a–e) are fulfilled, which implies that the process is well defined and completely specified. Hence, if artificial time series are constructed in accordance with (12)–(14), the series can be regarded as generated from Model IS. In particular, the series will satisfy the noncorrelation assumptions (16) in the large sample sense. It follows that the reduced form (12) can be estimated from the artificial time series by the method of least-squares regression. System (15) happens to be *just-identified*, and so we obtain consistent estimates of the system if the estimated reduced form (12) is transformed back to the original, "structural" form (15).

Model BC. This is a conditional causal chain,

$$\text{(18a–c)}\qquad \begin{cases} d_t = -\dfrac{4}{5} p_t + v_t & \text{(demand relation)}, \\ s_t = \dfrac{3}{5} p_{t-1} + v_t' & \text{(supply relation)}, \\ d_t = s_t = q_t & \text{(assumption of instantaneous equilibrium)}, \end{cases}$$

with noncorrelation properties in accordance with Assumption 3.20, that is

$$\text{(19a–b)}\qquad r(v_t, p_t) = 0\,, \quad r(v_t', p_{t-1}) = 0\,.$$

If we interpret Model BC as a stochastic process (8) with properties (i)-(ii) and (11), it is readily verified that relations (10a–e) are fulfilled. Hence the process is well defined, and coincides with the process defined by Model IS. It follows that (12a-b) remain valid as regression relations, but not as a reduced form. Thus, if artificial time series are constructed in accordance with (12)–(14), these can be regarded as generated from either model IS or BC. Furthermore, it follows that the demand and supply relations (18a–b) of Model BC can be estimated from the constructed time series by applying the method of least-squares regression to each relation separately.

We note that the construction gives us the series (8), so if we regard the series as belonging to Model BC, the residuals will be given by

$$v_t = q_t + \frac{4}{5} p_t ; \quad v_t' = u_t' . \tag{20a–b}$$

REMARK 5.11: To conform with Assumption 3.21 of ordinary (pure) causal chains, so as to pave the way for inference under Procedure 2.21, the residuals v_t, v_t' that refer to different time periods should be independent. It is not immediately seen from (20a) that they actually are, but it is a direct matter to verify the independence.

6. COMPARATIVE COMMENTS ON CONDITIONAL CAUSAL CHAINS AND INTERDEPENDENT SYSTEMS

We have seen that the parting of the ways between causal chains and interdependent systems lies at the level of explicit *vs.* implicit inference from the behaviour relations of the model: explicit inference in causal chains (whether they are defined as pure or conditional), and implicit inference in the case of interdependent systems. The parting of the ways being at a basic level, the ensuing differences in approach show up in many features of the construction of the model. In the following comparative comments, 6.1 gives some further details on Illustration 5.10, and 6.2–8 takes up general questions that have been much discussed in the literature on interdependent systems *vs.* causal chains.[8] Emphasis is placed on the need for further research, both theoretical and empirical.

6.1. *Two special cases of Illustration* 5.10. If the parameter is taken to be $\varrho = -3/4$ we see that models BC and IS will coincide. In particular, the four noncorrelation assumptions (16a–b) and (19a–b) will be fulfilled simultaneously. For any other value of ϱ in the interval (11), models BC and IS will be different.

The difference between the two models is brought into relief if we consider small values of ϱ. Letting ϱ tend to zero, the three-dimensional distribution (p_{t-1}, p_t, q_t) will degenerate into a single distribution, and in the

[8] See the references in Section 2.3. For comparative reviews of the two approaches, see [**3**, **37**, **2**, **1**, **21**, **39**, **41**, **42**].

limit, $\varrho = 0$, the three variables will satisfy the exact relationship

$$(21) \qquad q_t = -\frac{4}{5} p_t + \frac{3}{5} p_{t-1},$$

that is, the entire distribution will be situated in the plane (21).

For any ϱ, the demand relation (18a) of model BC can be interpreted as the conditional expectation of q_t for given p_t, with a residual which has a conditional expectation of zero, and this interpretation remains valid as $\varrho \to 0$. In the demand relation (15a) of model IS, on the other hand, the residual u_t is correlated with p_t (except when $\varrho = -3/4$), and therefore (15a) cannot be interpreted as a conditional expectation that is unbiased in the same sense as (18a). In the limit, $\varrho = 0$, the difference between the models is carried to the extreme, inasmuch as the coefficient $3/5\varrho$ in (15a) will tend to infinity and the residual u_t will have an infinite standard deviation.

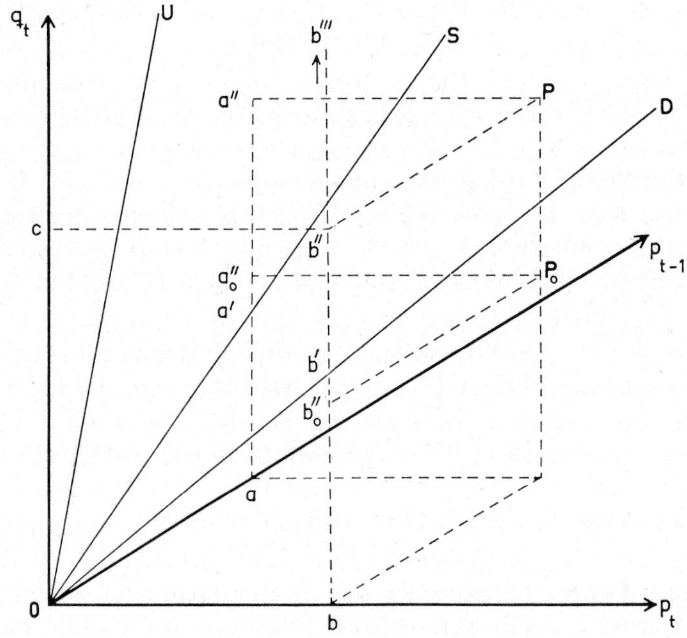

FIGURE 1

The situation is illustrated in the graph. In the sample space (p_{t-1}, p_t, q_t) the point P is arbitrary with coordinates (a, b, c). In the coordinate plane q_tOp_t, line OD is the demand relation (18a) and the segment $b'b''$ is the residual v_t. In the plane q_tOp_{t-1}, line OS is the supply relation (18b) and $a'a''$ is the residual v'_t. In the plane q_tOp_t, line OU is the demand relation (15a), and the residual u_t is $b''b'''$, where b''' is the intersection between the lines OU and $bb'b''$. As $\varrho \to 0$ the probability tends to 1 that the sample point P will lie in the plane DOS, i.e. plane (21). Letting the sample point now be P_0 in plane (21), the residuals v_t, v_t' will be given by $b_0'' b'$ and $a_0'' a'$. Line OU will in the limit coincide with the axis Oq_t, the point b''' will be at infinite distance, and the residual $u_t = b_0'' b'''$ will be infinite.

6.2. *Different types of explanatory relations.* As is clear from Illustration 5.10, the behaviour relations of causal chains and interdependent systems are not explanatory in the same sense. In fact, Models IS and BC generate the same time series, and yet their demand relations differ. Or, to put it otherwise, if the variables p_t, q_t are given as logarithms, the coefficient $3/5\varrho$ in (15a) cannot be a price elasticity of consumer demand in the same sense as the coefficient —4/5 in (18a).

The difference between the demand relations can be illustrated by sample series constructed in accordance with (12)–(14), and by regarding the constructed series alternatively to belong to Models BC and IS. In any case (10a) implies that if we plot q_t against p_t and consider two p_t-levels with unit difference, the average values of q_t at these two levels will differ by —4/5. Now with regard to Model BC this sampling experiment is in accordance with a stimulus-response interpretation of the demand relation (18a). This is so under two different assumptions:

Assumption 6.20. The behavioural relation is applied in a situation where one explanatory variable changes, the other explanatory variables remain constant, and the disturbance factors that are summed up in the residual follow the same distribution pattern as in the observed sample.

Assumption 6.21. The behavioural relation is applied in a situation where one explanatory variable changes, the other explanatory variables remain constant, and the disturbance factors that are summed up in the residual cease to occur when we enter the time period to which the application refers.

As applied to the demand relation (18a) of Model BC, Assumption 6.20 implies that the residual v_t can be ignored, for its expected, or average, value is zero. Hence the expected change in demand for a unit change in the price level is given by —4/5. On Assumption 6.21 the residual v_t ceases to occur and can again be ignored. Hence the change in demand for a unit change in the price level can be predicted exactly (without residual error) and is given by —4/5.

Considering Model IS, on the other hand, only the second of these interpretations applies to the demand relation (15a). Thus on Assumption 6.20, the expected change in q_t is not given by $3/5\varrho$, for q_t changes not only because of the change in p_t but also because of the correlation between p_t and u_t. As regards Assumption 6.21, we shall come back to this situation in Section 6.5.

Applied to the case where the variables in the demand relation (18a) are given as logarithms, the above argument shows that the coefficient —4/5 (or rather 4/5) is a price elasticity in the sense of Marshall (1890); that is, if price drops by 1% while other factors remain constant, the demand will increase by 4/5%. The coefficient $3/5\varrho$ in the demand relation (15a), on the other hand, is not a price elasticity in the same sense.

Being of general scope, the above argument applies to any causal chain (pure or conditional) and any interdependent system. The argument links up this paper with my earlier studies into the rationale of simultaneous equations systems, studies which have stressed the difference in the causal inference from interdependent systems and (pure) causal chains.[9] Confirming that there is a difference at the level of causal inference, the new approach of conditional causal chains—and in particular Illustration 5.10—shows that the difference goes deeper, inasmuch as the behaviour relations of causal chains and interdependent systems differ with regard to the specification in terms of conditional expectations, and deeper still, the parting of the ways being at the level of explicit *vs.* implicit inference from the behaviour relations of the system.

To sum up, the difference between the models is a matter of the hypothetical mechanism that is assumed to generate the empirical data, and hence of the operative use of the models in applied work. It is not a matter of statistical estimation, for the parameters of each model can be consistently estimated by an estimation procedure that is appropriate for that model. Nor is the difference a matter of realism, of goodness of fit between the model and the empirical data, for in the case of models IS and BC the models are different, and yet they define the same stochastic process, with the result that they yield precisely the same goodness of fit to a given set of data.

6.3. *Exact vs. approximate models.* There are interesting parallels between interdependent systems and the cobweb models of the early 1930's.[10] For one thing, the hypothesis of instantaneous equilibrium enters as a key device in both approaches; and in the pioneering works on interdependent systems the first illustrations are ordinary cobweb models, except for the fact that the exact demand and supply relations of cobweb theory have been generalized by introducing stochastic residuals to allow for unspecified disturbance factors.[11] The connection with cobweb theory sheds light on the pedigree of the interdependent approach, but the reference is made here for another reason. In generalizing the cobweb models so as to allow

[9] See [**37**], [**39–42**] and [**44**].

[10] On the cobweb theory, and also for further references, see Ezekiel (1938).

[11] For a case in point, see Girschick-Haavelmo (1947, formulas (1.2) and (1.3b)).

for disturbed relationships, two lines of approach open up, a dualism that illustrates the parting of the ways between interdependent systems and conditional causal chains.

For illustration we shall consider the following simple model of the cobweb type

(22a–c) $$d_t = \alpha_1 - \beta_1 p_t\,; \quad s_t = \alpha_2 + \beta_2 p_{t-1}\,; \quad d_t = s_t = q_t\,.$$

Its reduced form is

(23a–b) $$q_t = \alpha_2 + \beta_2 p_{t-1}\,; \quad p_t = \frac{\alpha_1 - \alpha_2}{\beta_1} - \frac{\beta_2}{\beta_1}\, p_{t-1}\,.$$

For purposes of predictive inference from the model, it does not matter whether the inference is based on the original system (22) or its reduced form (23). For example, if we know p_{t-1} and wish to predict q_t ($= d_t = s_t$) we get the same result if we use (22b) directly, or if we first use (23b) to predict p_t and then substitute in (22a) to obtain q_t. The equivalence of the two modes of inference breaks down if the relations are approximate. Covering the approximation by residual disturbances, the model will yield predictive inference in the form of conditional expectations. At this point there is a parting of the ways.[12] When specifying the relations in terms of conditional expectations, this can be done *either* with the model in reduced form *or* with the model in original form, but in general *not* with both forms simultaneously. Interdependent systems adopt the first line of approach, conditional causal chains the second. Pure causal chains, it may be added, have the advantage that both forms can be specified simultaneously in terms of conditional expectations.

6.4. *What is the numerical relevance?* When it comes to the numerical results, the difference in approach may be quite consequential.

With reference to the coefficients in Models BC and IS as elasticities, we see that the conditional causal chain (18) gives 0.8 for the price elasticity of consumer demand, whereas the interdependent system (15) gives the elasticity as 2.0 if the parameter ϱ is assumed to be —0.3, say, and for numerically smaller values of ϱ the elasticity will be still higher.

Evidence in the same direction is given by the following empirical findings, which refer to three models that have been estimated from one and the same set of statistical data. For details and further results, reference is made to the original papers.

ILLUSTRATION 6.40: *The demand relations in three simultaneous equation models for the watermelon market in the United States,* 1930–51.
Notation: X is demand, P is price, Y is income, N is population, F is

[12] See Wold (1959b) for details and further comments.

freight rate, L is the cost-of-living index. All variables are given as logarithms, and the ratios are logarithms of nonlogarithmic ratios.

Interdependent system (Suits, 1955):

$$(24) \qquad \frac{X}{N} = -0.901P + 1.378\frac{Y}{N} - 0.614F - 0.126\,.$$

Pure causal chain (Wold, 1959a):

$$(25) \qquad \frac{X}{N} = -0.206\frac{P}{L} + 0.430\frac{Y}{NL} - 1.088\,.$$

Conditional causal chain, first variant (Wold, 1959b):

$$(26) \qquad \frac{X}{N} = -0.417P + 0.776\frac{Y}{N} - 0.563F - 0.882\,.$$

Conditional causal chain, second variant (Wold, 1959b):

$$(27) \qquad \frac{X}{N} = -0.315\frac{P}{L} + 0.509\frac{Y}{NL} - 1.077\,.$$

Since the transformation to the reduced form involves the inversion of the demand relation, it is hardly surprising that the coefficients turn out to be greater in absolute value in interdependent systems than in causal chains. Without being quite the same, this situation is related to the well known fact that the reverse of the regression of x on y has a steeper slope than the regression of y on x.

The above numerical findings are in line with some earlier applied work with interdependent systems, where elasticities have been reported to be somewhat higher than the values obtained for comparable markets by traditional methods.[13] The situation is not very clear, however, and in other investigations it has been claimed that interdependent systems give much the same empirical results as other approaches.[14] Thus far, reports on applied work with simultaneous equation systems are relatively scarce. It is plain that much more empirical research is needed to explore and assess the practical value of the various types of models. This is particularly so for pure *vs.* conditional causal chain systems.

6.5. *Identifiability*. We have seen that the identification problem—a cumbersome feature of interdependent systems—does not arise for causal chain systems, whether they are pure or conditional. This is so because causal chains are estimated in their original form, whereas interdependent systems are first transformed to the reduced form before the estimation procedure is applied.

[13] See [**18**, **4**, **5**].

[14] See [**9**].

Identification problems of another order arise in situations where (as illustrated by Models IS and BC) two models of different types generate one and the same stochastic process. Model IS has been constructed so as to be just identifiable, in the sense of the theory of interdependent systems, that is, when the parameters of the reduced form (12) have been estimated, the ensuing transformation back to the original system (15) will provide a unique set of estimates for its parameters. With regard to Illustration 5.10 we may say that Model IS is just identifiable *within the class of interdependent systems*. In the combined class of interdependent systems and conditional causal chains, however, both models IS and BC are unidentifiable, since they define one and the same stochastic process.

The identification problem that arises when two models are equivalent in the sense of Models IS and BC has not been explored. Generally speaking, when two models define the same process the observed sample provides no criterion for discriminating and choosing between the models. Hence the discrimination must be based on ancillary information, either in the form of *a priori* arguments, or of empirical evidence outside the observed sample, or of both. A related situation occurs when an interdependent system and a conditional causal chain have the same zero elements in the coefficient matrix and coincide with regard to some but not all first and second order moments. In such a case one can, in principle, discriminate between the models on the basis of the observed sample, but to strengthen the inference it may be desirable here, also, to use ancillary information.

The difference between interdependent systems and conditional causal chains shows up in the reduced form, and in principle this provides a clue to the discrimination problem. Again with reference to Illustration 5.10, while Model IS has the reduced form (12a–b), that of model BC is given by

$$\text{(28a–c)} \quad q_t = \frac{3}{5} p_{t-1} + v_t' ; \quad p_t = -\frac{3}{4} p_{t-1} + v_t'' \text{ with } v_t'' = \frac{5}{4}(v_t - v_t') .$$

Relation (28a) is the same as (12a) and has the same interpretation as a behaviour relation. To interpret (28b) we shall distinguish between the two situations in Assumptions 6.20 and 6.21.

On Assumption 6.20 the expected value (conditional expectation) of p_t for known p_{t-1} is given by (12b), for both models IS and BC. In BC (but not in IS) relation (28b) shows, again for known p_{t-1}, what value the current price p_t must have in order that the expected demand d_t should equal the expected supply $3p_{t-1}/5$. Thus (12b) in the specification of Model IS is a predictive relation, while (28b) in the specification of Model BC is not predictive (let alone a behavioural relation). Hence on Assumption 6.20 the relations (12b) and (28b) are not comparable, and so they do not provide a basis for discriminating between the models IS and BC.

On the *ceteris paribus* clause of Assumption 6.21 on the other hand, both models reduce to the cobweb model (22) with its exact relationships. Relation (28b) then becomes a predictive relation for p_t, the interpretation being that when p_{t-1} is known and the residuals v_t, v'_t are zero, current demand d_t as given by (18a) will equal the available supply as given by (18b). This makes relations (12b) and (28b) comparable on the logic of the two models, and since the relations differ they provide a basis for discriminating between the models. There is the snag, however, that Assumption 6.21 refers to the situation when p_{t-1} and the residual factors that influence p_t and q_t cease to occur from a certain time point on, a hypothetical situation that differs from the conditions of the observed sample. Hence in practice this solution to the discrimination problem is not very satisfactory. The problem is solved on the basis of potential empirical observations outside the sample, but the argument gives no clue to the question of how to provide such ancillary information.

An *a priori* argument that speaks in favour of causal chain systems is that their behaviour relations are specified in terms of conditional expectations and thereby allow a simple stimulus-response interpretation of economic behaviour.[15] This argument is forceful, and may be decisive. However, the ultimate test on the various types of models is how well they work in practice, and in this respect nothing definite can be said at present. The applied work with simultaneous equation systems is still, I repeat, in its beginnings.

6.6. *Autonomous behaviour.* Both in causal chains, pure or conditional, and in interdependent systems, behavioural relations are the basic material for building the models.[16] We have seen that in causal chain systems the behavioural relations are specified just as in a single-relation model, allowing a simple stimulus-response interpretation of each relation separately. In other words, the individual or collective actors (behaving units), whose economic behaviour it is the system's purpose to explain, are assumed to be *autonomous* in the sense that the behaviour of each actor is completely specified by the corresponding relation in the system.[17] Thus if one actor changes his pattern of behaviour, this will call for a respecification of his behaviour relation, but not necessarily of the other relations of the model. Or, in yet another formulation, the behaviour relations are autonomous in the sense that they can be broken out of the system and used just as a single-relation model.

This last comment can be phrased as follows: While interdependent

[15] See above, Section 3.2.

[16] Regarding pure causal chains, see Tinbergen (1939; 1940).

[17] This usage of the term "autonomy" follows Tinbergen (1939).

systems draw a line of demarcation between results obtained by single- and multiple-relation models, the results obtained by causal chain systems merge perfectly well with the empirical findings of single-relation approaches. For a demand relation (18a), for example, it does not matter whether it constitutes a single-relation model or enters in a pure or conditional causal chain. This is a great advantage in the construction of causal chain models, for single-relation methods are extensively used, and experience shows that they come off fairly well in several fields of application. In the interdependent approach, on the other hand, the logic of the construction of the model is in potential conflict with single-relation methods.[18] As illustrated by (24)–(27), the conflict may be quite acute.

REMARK 6.60: The autonomy of behaviour relations in causal chain systems is closely linked up with the argument in Strotz's part of this triptych that there is a lack of continuity in the specification of interdependent systems with regard to small lags in the endogenous variables. The discontinuity arises as the lag is ignored and taken to be zero. As is clear from Strotz's argument, the discontinuity is a consequence of the transformation to the reduced form in the estimation of the system and in its operative use. It is also clear that this type of difficulty is absent in the approach of causal chains, pure or conditional, the system here being estimated and used in its original form.

6.7. *Completely dynamic vs. mixed static-dynamic approaches.* In the natural sciences it is customary to speak of *kinematics* as the purely mathematical deduction of motion patterns from a theoretical model, while the model belongs to *dynamics* if it gives a subject-matter interpretation in terms of force fields. Thus in Newtonian theory with its differential equation systems for planetary orbits the kinematic theorems give the mathematical form of the movements, while the dynamic propositions explain the movements in terms of a field of gravitational forces. Reference is further made to statics as the special case of dynamics when the forces are in equilibrium and the movement comes to a state of rest.

The same general notions apply in the social sciences and are particularly relevant in economics.[19] Behavioural relations are here a main vehicle for dynamic analysis, inasmuch as they enable us to specify the economic changes caused by human actions and by the postulated motives behind these actions. The economic motives of the various behaving units, as specified, e.g., in terms of maximal profit in production theory and optimal preference levels in the theory of consumer demand, have the nature of

[18] All through the literature on interdependent systems this has been emphasized as a characteristic feature of the approach; see the references in Section 1.3.

[19] Frisch (1929). See also Wold-Jureén (1952), p. 65.

driving forces in model construction. We shall add two comments from this general point of view.

Causal chains and interdependent systems are an innovation in the broad area of scientific model construction, and especially so relative to the approach of differential equation systems.[20] The point I wish to make refers to the analogy between differential equation systems and the reduced form of an econometric model. A differential equation system can always be written as a linear system, where current endogenous variables are explained by a relation that involves (infinitesimal) lags in all explanatory endogenous variables. In the reduced form the situation is the same, except that the lags run in years or other finite periods. In the structural forms of causal chains and interdependent systems, on the other hand, a relation may involve nonlagged values for two or more endogenous variables, and it is in this respect that the econometric models make an innovation.[21] This comment serves to stress that, in the treatment of the models at issue, problems come up for which the natural sciences give no guidance, an unusual situation in the social sciences. This is in particular so with regard to the causal interpretation of econometric models. Hence it is no wonder that this area has been subject to a long debate.

Pure causal chains are completely dynamic, all relations of the system being behavioural relations, the propositions on equilibrium tendencies being implications of the model, and no equilibrium assumptions entering in the construction of the model. The residuals enter as unspecified forces that interact with the specified driving forces of the model and prevent the system from ever reaching a state of complete rest.

Interdependent systems and conditional causal chains mark a drastic cut in the aspiration level of a completely dynamic approach. The introduction of equilibrium assumptions is a key device, a shortcut that refrains from obtaining the equilibrium as a deductive implication of the model. There is no objection against the shortcut as such, for it is a good thing to have models that work at different aspiration levels. It is rather that owing to their mixed static-dynamic nature the approaches are of limited scope for purposes of dynamic inference. What in particular is a serious limitation is that every equilibrium assumption is an approximation that ignores a potential driving force of the model. To assume instantaneous

[20] This comment follows up an earlier argument; see [**40**, p. 60] and [**42**, section 6].

[21] Involving a shortcut where small time lags in the causal dependencies are taken to be zero, the innovation may be regarded as a device for approximate aggregation of causal relations. Pure and conditional causal chains and interdependent systems are three different devices for carrying out the approximation. On the disregard of time lags, see also Bentzel-Hansen (1954), who discuss the approximation from the point of view of the Stockholm school, especially the disequilibrium analysis of Lindahl (1939).

equilibrium between demand and supply is to ignore changes in stocks; to equilibrate savings and investments is to ignore the unplanned changes in money holdings and inventories, and so on. In reality, according to observed facts, such disequilibrium gaps are often quite considerable and to disregard them in model construction is in conflict with basic arguments in dynamic economic theory. This comment goes some way to explain why it is that the applied work with interdependent systems has given meagre results when it comes to actual forecasting.[22] The same critical argument applies to conditional causal chains. Indeed, it is an open question whether and under what circumstances the adoption of equilibrium assumptions in a causal chain system will retain sufficient explanatory power in the system for it to be useful in practice for dynamic inference.[23]

REFERENCES

[**1**] Baumol, W. J. (1951): *Economic dynamics.* New York: Macmillan. 2nd ed. 1959.

[**2**] Bentzel, R., and B. Hansen (1954): *Review of Economic Studies,* 22, pp. 153–168.

[**3**] Bentzel, R., and H. Wold (1946): *Skandinavisk Aktuarietidskrift,* 29, pp. 95–114.

[**4**] Bergstrom, A. R. (1955): *Econometrica,* 23, pp. 259–276.

[**5**] Briggs, F. E. A. (1957): *Econometrica,* 25, pp. 444–455.

[**6**] Christ, C. (1951): Paper in *Conference on Business Cycles,* pp. 35–107. New York: National Bureau of Economic Research.

[**7**] Clark, C. (1949): *Econometrica,* 17, pp. 93–123.

[**8**] Ezekiel, M. (1938): *Quarterly Journal of Economics,* 52, pp. 255–280.

[**9**] Fox, K. (1953): *The Analysis of Demand for Agricultural Products.* Washington, D.C.: U.S. Dept. of Agriculture, Techn. Bull. no. 1081.

[**10**] Frisch, R. (1928): *Nordisk Statistisk Tidskrift,* 8, pp. 36–102.

[**11**] ——— (1929): *Nationaloekonomisk Tidsskrift,* 41, pp. 321–379.

[**12**] ——— (1933): Paper in *Economic Essays in Honour of Gustav Cassel,* pp. 171–205. London: Allen & Unwin.

[**13**] ——— (1934): *Statistical Confluence Analysis by Means of Complete Regression Systems.* Oslo Univ. Inst. of Economics, Publ. no. 5.

[**14**] Gini, C. (1921): *Metron,* 1, no. 3, pp. 63–82.

[**15**] Girschick, M. A., and T. Haavelmo (1947): *Econometrica,* 15, pp. 79–110. Revised ed. in Ref. 19.

[**16**] Haavelmo, T. (1943): *Econometrica,* 11, pp. 1–12.

[**17**] ——— (1958): *Econometrica,* 26, pp. 351–357.

[**18**] Hildreth, C., and F. G. Jarrett (1955): *A Statistical Study of Livestock Production and Marketing.* New York: Wiley and Sons.

[**19**] Hood, W. C., and T. C. Koopmans, eds. (1953): *Studies in Econometric Method.* New York: Wiley and Sons.

[**20**] Klein, L. R. (1950): *Economic Fluctuations in the United States, 1921–1941.* New York: Wiley and Sons.

[22] See the sweeping negative appraisal recently given by Haavelmo (1958).

[23] For a partial answer to the question, see [**44**, Section 6].

[21] ——— (1953): *A Textbook of Econometrics*. Evanston: Row, Peterson.
[22] ——— AND A. GOLDBERGER (1955): *An Econometric Model of the United States 1929–1952*. Amsterdam: North-Holland Publ. Co.
[23] KOOPMANS, T. C., ed. (1950): *Statistical Inference in Dynamic Economic Models*. New York: Wiley and Sons.
[24] LINDAHL, E. (1939): *Studies in the Theory of Money and Capital*. London: King.
[25] MACKEPRANG, E. P. (1906): *Price Theories*. (Danish) Copenhagen: Bagge.
[26] MARSHALL, A. (1890): *Principles of Economics*. London: Macmillan. 8th ed., 1946.
[27] PEARSON, K. (1901): *Philosophical Magazine* (6), 2, pp. 559–572.
[28] SCHULTZ, H. (1938): *The Theory and Measurement of Demand*. Chicago: Univ. of Chicago Press.
[29] SUITS, D. (1955): *Journal of Farm Economics*, 37, pp. 237–251.
[30] TINBERGEN, J. (1937): *An Econometric Approach to Business Cycle Problems*. Paris: Hermann.
[31] ———(1939): *Statistical Testing of Business Cycle Theories, II*. Geneva: League of Nations.
[32] ——— (1940): *Review of Economic Studies*, 7, pp. 73–90.
[33] ——— (1951): *Business Cycles in the United Kingdom, 1870–1914*. Amsterdam: North-Holland Publ. Co. 2nd ed. 1956.
[34] TINTNER, G. (1952): *Econometrics*. New York: Wiley and Sons.
[35] WOLD, H. (1940): *The Demand for Agricultural Products and Its Sensitivity to Price and Income Changes*. (Swedish) Stockholm: Statens Offentliga Utredningar, 1940:16.
[36] ——— (1945): *Skandinavisk Aktuarietidskrift*, 28, pp. 181–200.
[37] ——— (1949): *Econometrica*, 17, Suppl., pp. 1–22.
[38] ——— (1950): Paper in *Travaux présentés à la 26e Session de l'Institut International de Statistique*, pp. 277–289. Berne: Stämpfli.
[39] ——— (1955): *Cahiers du séminaire d'économétrie de R. Roy*, 3, pp. 81–101. Paris: C.N.R.S.
[40] ——— (1956): *Journal of the Royal Statistical Society*, A, 119, pp. 28–61.
[41] ——— (1959a): *Revue de l'Institut International de Statistique*, 26 (1958), pp. 1–15.
[42] ——— (1959b): Paper in *Recent Advances in Probability and Statistics*, pp. 355–434. Stockholm: Almqvist & Wiksell.
[43] ——— (1960): Paper forthcoming in *Bulletin de l'Institut International de Statistique*.
[44] WOLD, H., in association with L. Juréen (1952): *Demand Analysis. Å Study in Econometrics*. Stockholm: Almqvist & Wiksell. NewYork: Wiley and Sons, 1953.
[45] WORKING, E. J. (1927): *Quarterly Journal of Economics*, 41, pp. 212–235.

SMALL SAMPLE PROPERTIES

A NOTE ON THE EXACT FINITE SAMPLE FREQUENCY FUNCTIONS OF GENERALIZED CLASSICAL LINEAR ESTIMATORS IN TWO LEADING OVER-IDENTIFIED CASES*

R. L. BASMANN†

The asymptotic unbiasedness and normality of alternative statistical estimators θ, $\theta_{,}^{1}$ · · · of a given parameter θ^* are generally proved without reference to any explicit knowledge of the exact finite sample distribution functions, $F_n(x)$, $G_n(x)$ · · ·. (Here n denotes sample size.) Within the class of asymptotically unbiased and normally distributed estimators of a given parameter it is sometimes possible to demonstrate that one estimator possesses a smaller asymptotic variance than another, or that one estimator possesses the smallest asymptotic variance within a particular subclass. Asymptotic theory obviously does not predict anything about finite sample distribution functions $F_n(x)$, $G_n(x)$ · · ·. In particular we cannot deduce from asymptotic theorems that the estimator with the smallest asymptotic variance will continue to exhibit the smallest *dispersion* in finite samples. Consequently it remains an essential task in positive estimation theory to derive the exact finite sample distribution functions of the alternative estimators that appear to be promising on the basis of asymptotic considerations.

In econometric statistics the alternative estimators of structural coefficients in systems of simultaneous equations appear to possess rather complicated finite sample distribution functions. Monte Carlo experiments are resorted to for the purpose of providing useful leads in mathematical research into the nature of these distributions. In this article are presented some leading results of a mathematical investigation of the exact finite sample distribution functions of generalized classical linear estimators. The results presented here exhibit some particularly important implications for the conduct and evaluation of Monte Carlo experiments in econometric statistics.

1. INTRODUCTION

SAMPLING experiments that utilize Monte Carlo techniques have been widely applied in the study of the finite sample distributions of several alternative structural coefficient estimators employed in econometric statistics, namely, the so-called *full information* estimators (FI), [17, 19], the limited information or *least variance ratio* estimators (LVR), [1, 2, 17], the *generalized classical linear* estimators (GCL) and *Theil's k-Class* estimators, [3, 4, 5, 23, 24, pp. 334ff], and the *direct least squares* estimators (DLS). The use of Monte Carlo techniques has been motivated by the understandable desire to avoid the difficult task of working out the *exact* finite sample distributions and frequency functions of these alternative estimators.

---

* Work performed partly in connection with Project Numbers 1300086 and 1300071, Technical Military Planning Operation, General Electric Company, Santa Barbara, California. This topic was first presented in a seminar held in the Department of Economics, Purdue University, April 25, 1960. It was also presented in a Special Statistical Seminar, Statistical Laboratory, Iowa State University, April 29, 1960.

† I am indebted to the following persons for valuable criticisms of the original draft of this paper: Professors Gerhard Tintner, Arnold Zellner, Stanley Reiter, Mitchell Harwitz, Sudish Ghurye, Martin Shubik and Dr. Ernest J. Mosbaek. All errors and omissions remain my own responsibility.

In most of the sampling experiments published so far the authors have sought to provide experimental support to normative comparisons between two or more types of estimator in respect of finite sample *bias* and *mean-square deviations.* [21, 22; 25, p. 88; 27]. It is generally conceded that a rational criterion of choice between two alternative estimators of a given population parameter should be formulated in terms of the relative degrees of concentration of their distributions about the true parameter point. If the finite sample distributions of the GCL, LVR, FI and DLS estimators are at the least approximately normally distributed and possess finite variances, then it is clear that any rational measures of concentration will depend predominantly on the second moments. We must be prepared to find, however, that not any, or, at least, not all of these alternative estimators are approximately normally distributed in finite samples, nor even possess finite variances. In respect of the FI, LVR, GCL and Theil's k-Class estimators, and in respect of the DLS estimators, the existence of mathematical expectations defining means and variances has been widely accorded uncritical acceptance.[1]

Yet, if it is proposed to use the *mean-square deviation* as a criterion of choice, and if it is proposed to employ a Monte Carlo experiment to measure the supposed means and variances of alternative estimators, then it is essential to verify in advance, by mathematical analysis, whether the parameters, e.g., means and variances, of the *exact* distribution functions actually exist and do thereby allow the application of the *Law of Large Numbers* [12, p. 228] to go validly through. Suppose u, with range $-\infty < u < +\infty$, is one kind of estimator of some population parameter θ, and suppose that $f(u)$ is the unknown frequency function of u. Suppose we construct a Monte Carlo experiment to generate a sequence $\{u_k\}$ of mutually independent estimates, u_k. *If the integral*

$$\mu_1 = \int_{-\infty}^{+\infty} uf(u)du \tag{1.1}$$

exists, i.e., *is finite, then, according to the Law of Large Numbers, for every* $\epsilon > 0$,

$$Pr\left\{\left|\frac{u_1 + u_2 + \cdots + u_n}{n} - \mu_1\right| > \epsilon\right\} \to 0 \tag{1.2}$$

as $n \to \infty$. If, however, this integral does not exist, then the average of estimates u_k does not converge in probability to any finite value; in such a case, it is, of course, meaningless to speak of the Monte Carlo experiment providing information about the *bias* of u, and *a fortiori* it is meaningless to speak of the Monte Carlo experiment providing information about the *mean-square deviation* of u, if *bias* and *mean-square deviation* are understood in the usual sense of mathematical expectations. Fortunately, however, regardless of the non-existence of moments, it is possible to test hypotheses about the *exact* finite sample *distribution function* by means of its sampling experimental counterpart

$$F_n(x) = \frac{n(x)}{n} \tag{1.3}$$

[1] See especially the paper by C. F. Christ [10, p. 840]. Professor Christ evaluates the results of some Monte Carlo experiments [7, 22, 27] solely by comparing *mean-square deviations* of the alternative estimators studied.

where x is continuous and $n(x)$ denotes the number of estimates u_k that do not exceed x, [16; 8] since

$$\lim_{n\to\infty} F_n(x) = F(x) = \int_{-\infty}^{x} f(u)du. \tag{1.4}$$

The result expressed by equation (1.4) does not require that the distribution function $F(x)$ possess any finite moment whatsoever. [6; 7, Sec. 4 pp. 73–88].

In order to demonstrate the cogency of the moment existence problem in respect to GCL estimation, I shall present here the *exact* finite sample frequency function of a GCL coefficient estimator in each of two leading over-identified cases. In the first of these cases, the *mean* of the GCL estimator exists but the variance does not. In the second case the variance exists, but the higher moments do not.[2]

It is appropriate to mention that even though the *exact* distribution function $F(x)$ of some estimator fails to possess moments of lower order (say) a variance, it is still possible in many cases to *approximate* $F(x)$ by a distribution function $G(x)$ that does possess (say) a variance and even possesses moments of still higher order. Thus A. L. Nagar has made an important contribution to econometric statistics by working out formulas for the bias and moment matrices of *approximate* distributions for Theil's k-Class estimators, [20]. The reader will easily satisfy himself that Nagar's approximations do not depend on the *exact* distributions possessing a finite variance. Examine the *exact* frequency function exhibited in Figure 1 below. This frequency function does not possess a finite variance. Consider the approximation obtained by truncating the *exact* frequency function at the points $v_1 = -3$, $v_1 = 3$. The approximate frequency function obtained in this way possesses finite moments of all orders. The approximate distribution function will be an excellent one, indeed.

As has been mentioned already, the use of Monte Carlo techniques for the examination of the finite sample distribution functions of GCL, LVR, FI and DLS structural coefficient estimators has been prompted by the opinion that these distributions are very complicated. The opinion is, I believe, essentially sound. For all that, derivation of the GCL frequency function given in Sec. 3 provides some much needed perspective on the matter and constitutes a central topic of this article.

2. ASSUMPTIONS AND SPECIFICATIONS

Equations (2.1) and (2.2) afford the simplest typical example of a system of simultaneous structural equations that can be estimated by GCL, LVR and FI methods with different results.

---

[2] In an article published in 1932 E. C. Fieller [13] worked out the exact finite sample distribution and frequency function of the quotient of two non-singular correlated random normal variates with non zero means. [13, eqn. (24), p. 432]. The essential feature of the Fieller distribution is that, like the Cauchy distribution to which it is closely related, all of its moments are infinite. The Fieller distribution should be of practical interest to econometricians, for in the leading two-equation, just-identifiable case of structural estimation [26, Ch. 7] where no lagged endogenous variables are present, and structural disturbances are normally distributed, the maximum-likelihood (ML) estimates of structural coefficients are distributed according to Fieller's law. Consequently, it is not possible meaningfully to compare this (ML) estimator with (say) the so-called "direct least squares" (DLS) estimator of the same coefficient in respect of the criterion of mean-square deviation. A meaningful comparison has to be made in terms of distribution function properties more fundamental than moments.

$$- y_{t1} + \beta_{12}y_{t2} + \gamma_{11}x_{t1} + \gamma_{12}x_{t2} + \gamma_{13}x_{t3} + \gamma_{14}x_{t4} + \gamma_{10} + e_{t1} = 0 \qquad (2.1)$$
$$- y_{t1} + \beta_{22}y_{t2} + \gamma_{21}x_{t1} + \gamma_{22}x_{t2} + \gamma_{23}x_{t3} + \gamma_{24}x_{t4} + \gamma_{20} + e_{t2} = 0 \qquad (2.2)$$
$$\beta_{22} - \beta_{12} \neq 0.$$

The variables y_{t1}, y_{t2} are called endogenous variables and are determined within the system of equations (2.1) and (2.2) are supposed to represent. The variables $x_{t1}, \cdots, x_{t4}$ are called pre-determined and represent lagged values of endogenous variables, and variables that are otherwise determined outside of the system represented by (2.1) and (2.2).

The vectors (e_{t1}, e_{t2}), $t=1, 2, \cdots, n$ are identically and independently distributed, and the joint distribution function of (e_{t1}, e_{t2}) possesses the following finite moments:

$$E(e_{ti}) = 0$$
$$E(e_{ti}e_{tj}) = \omega_{i,j} \qquad i, j = 1, 2.$$

The random variables e_{ti} and the pre-determined variables $x_{t1}, \cdots, x_{t4}$ are independently distributed. Moreover, if no x_{tk} is a lagged endogenous variable, then the random variables e_{ti}, $i=1, 2$, are distributed independently of x_{sk} where $s \neq t$.

Estimation is accomplished under the identifiability *hypotheses*, which are like

$$H_1: \gamma_{11} = 0, \quad \gamma_{12} = 0; \qquad \gamma_{13} \neq 0, \quad \gamma_{14} \neq 0; \qquad (2.3)$$
$$H_2: \gamma_{23} = 0, \quad \gamma_{24} = 0; \qquad \gamma_{21} \neq 0, \quad \gamma_{22} \neq 0. \qquad (2.4)$$

The system (2.1) and (2.2) is represented in its reduced form by

$$y_{t1} = \pi_{11}x_{t1} + \pi_{12}x_{t2} + \pi_{13}x_{t3} + \pi_{14}x_{t4} + \pi_{10} + \eta_{t1} \qquad (2.5)$$
$$y_{t2} = \pi_{21}x_{t1} + \pi_{22}x_{t2} + \pi_{23}x_{t3} + \pi_{24}x_{t4} + \pi_{20} + \eta_{t2} \qquad (2.6)$$

where, under (2.3) and (2.4)

$$\eta_{t1} = - \frac{\beta_{22}e_{t1} + \beta_{12}e_{t2}}{\beta_{12} - \beta_{22}}$$
$$\eta_{t2} = - \frac{e_{t1} + e_{t2}}{\beta_{12} - \beta_{22}} \cdot$$

The vectors (η_{t1}, η_{t2}), $t=1, 2, \cdots, n$ consequently are identically and independently distributed with the finite moments

$$E(\eta_{ti}) = 0$$
$$E(\eta_{ti}\eta_{tj}) = \sigma_{ij} \qquad i, j = 1, 2.$$

The random variables η_{ti}, $i=1, 2$, and the pre-determined variables $x_{t1}, \cdots, x_{t4}$ are independently distributed. Moreover, if no x_{tk} is a lagged endogenous variable, then the random variables η_{ti} are distributed independently of x_{sk} where $s \neq t$.

As the reduced-form coefficients π_{ik}, $i=1, 2$; $k=1, 2, 3, 4, 0$ in (2.5) and (2.6)

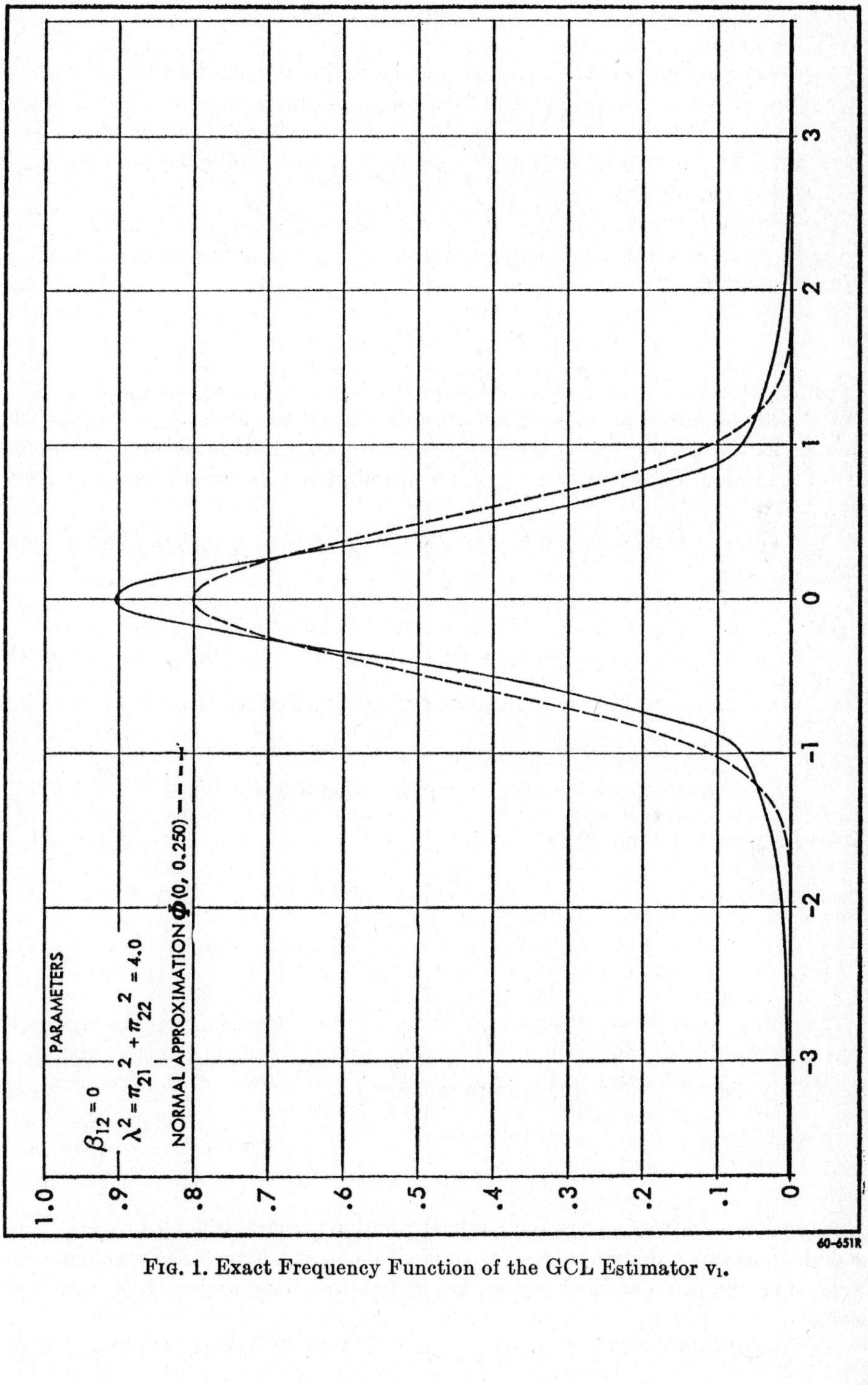

FIG. 1. Exact Frequency Function of the GCL Estimator v_1.

are well-defined functions of the structural coefficients in (2.1) and (2.2), the following restrictions on the former are implied by the identifiability hypotheses (2.3) and (2.4);

H_1 implies, but is not implied by,

$$\text{matrix} \begin{bmatrix} \pi_{11}\pi_{12} \\ \pi_{21}\pi_{22} \end{bmatrix} \text{ is of rank } \rho_1 \leq 1; \tag{2.7a}$$

$$\text{not both } \pi_{21} = 0 \text{ and } \pi_{22} = 0. \tag{2.7b}$$

H_2 implies, but is not implied by,

$$\text{matrix} \begin{bmatrix} \pi_{13}\pi_{14} \\ \pi_{23}\pi_{24} \end{bmatrix} \text{ is of rank } \rho_2 \leq 1; \tag{2.8a}$$

$$\text{not both } \pi_{23} = 0 \text{ and } \pi_{24} = 0. \tag{2.8b}$$

In the sequel we shall assume (because it will ease the reader's task in following the argument) that

$$\begin{aligned} \sigma_{11} &= 1, \\ \sigma_{12} &= 0, \\ \sigma_{22} &= 1; \end{aligned} \tag{2.9}$$

moreover, that

$$\begin{aligned} \pi_{10} &= 0, \\ \pi_{20} &= 0; \end{aligned} \tag{2.10}$$

that

$$\begin{aligned} \sum_{t=1}^{N} y_{ti} &= 0, \qquad i = 1, 2; \\ \sum_{t=1}^{N} x_{tk} &= 0 \qquad k = 1, 2, 3, 4; \end{aligned} \tag{2.11}$$

and that

$$\sum_{t=1}^{N} x_{tk}x_{tm} \begin{aligned} &= 0\, m \neq k \\ &= 1\, m = k. \end{aligned} \tag{2.12}$$

We assume that none of the x_k, $k=1, 2, 3, 4$ is a lagged endogenous variable.

The specialization (2.12) is equivalent to the statement that the sample of exogenous variables has been *orthogonalized*. The x_{tk} are the orthogonalized forms. The π_{ik} are supposed to have been adjusted conformably with such an orthogonal transformation. We assume that the disturbances e_{t1}, e_{t2} are normally distributed. We denote by $p_{11}, \cdots, p_{14}, p_{21}, \cdots, p_{24}$ the unrestricted maximum likelihood estimates of $\pi_{11}, \cdots, \pi_{14}, \pi_{21}, \cdots, \pi_{24}$. Under the conditions assumed, the p_{ik} are distributed according to

$$f(p_{11}, \cdots, p_{24})dp_{11} \cdots dp_{24}$$

$$= \frac{1}{(2\pi)^4} \exp\left[-\tfrac{1}{2}\{(p_{11} - \pi_{11})^2 + \cdots + (p_{24} - \pi_{24})^2\}\right]dp_{11} \cdots dp_{24}. \tag{2.13}$$

From (2.13) and the transformations (3.5)–(3.12) and (4.3)–(4.10) that follow, we shall derive the joint frequency functions of the GCL estimates of equation (2.1) in the following cases:

Case I. $\gamma_{11}=0$, $\gamma_{12}=0$. Of the $K(=4)$ exogenous variables appearing in both structural equations. $K_2(=2)$ are excluded from the equation (2.1) to be estimated. There are $G(=2)$ endogenous variables appearing in equation (2.1). Therefore, $K_2-G+1=1$. Necessary conditions for over-identifiability are met, [26, pp. 156–7]. In this case the GCL estimates of β_{12}, γ_{13}, γ_{14} possess finite means but do not possess finite variances.

Case II. $\gamma_{11}=0$, $\gamma_{12}=0$, $\gamma_{13}=0$. Here $K_2=3$, $G=2$, so that $K_2-G+1=2$. In this case the GCL estimates possess finite variances but no higher moments.

These results can be demonstrated by means of the *exact* marginal frequency functions of GCL estimates of β_{12} alone. The results are independent of the sample size, N. For *Case I* we shall also present the sub-case in which $\beta_{12}=0$, as well as the general sub-case in which $\beta_{12}\neq 0$. For *Case II* we shall present only the sub-case in which $\beta_{12}=0$, as this will be sufficient to demonstrate the existence of a finite variance.

In following the derivations in Sec. 3 and Sec. 4 below the reader will note that the assumptions (2.9) about the variances and covariance of the disturbances η_{t1}, η_{t2}, and the assumptions (2.11) and (2.12) about the moments of exogenous variables are of no consequence except for minor parameter changes in the *exact* distributions arrived at. For instance, generalization of the frequency functions (3.48) and (4.14) to the case in which $\sigma_{12}\neq 0$ is straightforward. Moreover, an important implication of the orthogonalization of exogenous variables is that

$$\pi_{21}^{2}+\pi_{22}^{2}\rightarrow\infty, \qquad N\rightarrow\infty, \tag{2.14}$$

provided that at least one of the original, unadjusted reduced-form coefficients π_{21}^{*}, π_{22}^{*} is not equal to zero. (See fn. 3 below.)

3. DERIVATION OF FREQUENCY FUNCTION. CASE I

In the application of GCL theory to equation (2.1) the statistics of chief interest are the estimates of coefficients β_{12}, γ_{13}, γ_{14} and the identifiability test statistic, [4, Sec. 5; 6]. The GCL method resolves the sample information contained in the estimates $p_{11}, \cdots, p_{14}, p_{21}, \cdots, p_{24}$, into two parts: that which is to be used in the estimation of β_{12}, γ_{13}, γ_{14}, and that which is contained in the numerator of the identifiability test statistic. We therefore express these GCL statistics as functions of the reduced-form estimates $p_{11}, \cdots, p_{14}; p_{21}, \cdots, p_{24}$.

We have

$$v_1=\frac{p_{11}p_{21}+p_{12}p_{22}}{p_{21}^{2}+p_{22}^{2}}; \tag{3.1}$$

$$v_2^{2}=(p_{11}-v_1p_{21})^{2}+(p_{12}-v_1p_{22})^{2}; \tag{3.2}$$

$$v_3=p_{13}-v_1p_{23}; \tag{3.3}$$

$$v_4=p_{14}-v_1p_{24}; \tag{3.4}$$

where v_1 is the GCL estimate of β_{12}; v_2^2 is essentially the numerator of the identifiability test statistic; v_3 is the GCL estimate of γ_{13}; v_4 is the GCL estimate of γ_{14}. The essential feature of the GCL method is the minimization of the quadratic form (3.2) with respect to v_1 [3; 4, Sec. 3; 5; 6]. We thus obtain the form (3.1) by setting equal to zero the partial derivative of v_2^2 with respect to v_1 and solving for v_1. We obtain the GCL estimates v_3, v_4 by making the appropriate substitution in equations (3.3) and (3.4).

Formulas (3.1)–(3.4) suggest the following transformation:

$$p_{11} = rv_1 \cos\theta - v_2 \sin\theta \tag{3.5}$$

$$p_{12} = rv_1 \sin\theta + v_2 \cos\theta \tag{3.6}$$

$$p_{21} = r \cos\theta \tag{3.7}$$

$$p_{22} = r \sin\theta \tag{3.8}$$

$$p_{13} = v_3 + v_1 v_5 \tag{3.9}$$

$$p_{14} = v_4 + v_1 v_6 \tag{3.10}$$

$$p_{23} = v_5 \tag{3.11}$$

$$p_{24} = v_6. \tag{3.12}$$

We note that

$$v_1 = \frac{p_{11}\cos\theta + p_{12}\sin\theta}{r}$$

by means of which (3.1) can be deduced from (3.7)–(3.8).

We also note that

$$p_{11} - v_1 p_{21} = -v_2 \sin\theta$$

$$p_{12} - v_1 p_{22} = v_2 \cos\theta,$$

from which (2.2) can be deduced. It is also not difficult to show that v_2 can be expressed by

$$v_2 = p_{11}p_{22} - p_{12}p_{21},$$

or

$$v_2 = -p_{11}p_{22} + p_{12}p_{21},$$

under the special assumption (2.12).

The new variables are defined over the domains

$$0 \leq r \leq \infty,$$

$$0 \leq \theta \leq 2\pi,$$

$$-\infty \leq v_1 \leq +\infty,$$

$$-\infty \leq v_2 \leq +\infty,$$

$$-\infty \leq v_3 \leq +\infty,$$

$$-\infty \leq v_4 \leq +\infty,$$

$$-\infty \leq v_5 \leq +\infty,$$

$$-\infty \leq v_6 \leq +\infty.$$

The Jacobian of the transformation defined by (3.5)–(3.12) is

$$J = \frac{\delta(p_{11}, \cdots, p_{24})}{\delta(v_1, v_2, r, \theta, \cdots, v_6)} = r^2. \tag{3.13}$$

Since the new variables v_2, r, θ do not appear in connection with p_{13}, p_{14}, p_{23} and p_{24} in (3.9)–(3.12), and since the new variables v_3, v_4, v_5, v_6 do not appear in connection with p_{11}, p_{12}, p_{21}, p_{22} in (3.5)–(3.9) it is natural and convenient to express the probability density function (2.13) as the product of the two independent factors as in (3.14).

$$\begin{aligned} f(p_{11}, \cdots ; p_{24})dp_{11} \cdots dp_{24} &= \frac{1}{(2\pi)^2} \exp\left[-\tfrac{1}{2}Q_1\right] dp_{11}dp_{12}dp_{21}dp_{22} \\ &\quad \times \frac{1}{(2\pi)^2} \exp\left[-\tfrac{1}{2}Q_2\right] dp_{13}dp_{14}dp_{23}dp_{24} \end{aligned} \tag{3.14}$$

where

$$Q_1 = (p_{11} - \pi_{11})^2 + (p_{12} - \pi_{12})^2 + (p_{21} - \pi_{21})^2 + (p_{22} - \pi_{22})^2 \tag{3.15}$$

and

$$Q_2 = (p_{13} - \pi_{13})^2 + (p_{14} - \pi_{14})^2 + (p_{23} - \pi_{23})^2 + (p_{24} - \pi_{24})^2, \tag{3.16}$$

before making the substitutions (3.5) through (3.12).

Upon making the substitutions (3.5) through (3.8) in (3.15) we obtain

$$\begin{aligned} Q_1 &= (1 + v_1)^2 r^2 - 2\left[r(\pi_{11}v_1 + \pi_{21}) + v_2\pi_{12}\right] \cos\theta \\ &\quad - 2\left[r(\pi_{12}v_1 + \pi_{22}) - v_2\pi_{11}\right] \sin\theta + v_2^2 \\ &\quad + \pi_{11}^2 + \pi_{12}^2 + \pi_{21}^2 + \pi_{22}^2. \end{aligned}$$

We suppose that $\beta_{12} = \beta$. Since $\pi_{11} = \beta\pi_{21}$, $\pi_{12} = \beta\pi_{22}$, we let

$$\lambda^2 = (1 + \beta^2)(\pi_{21}^2 + \pi_{22}^2), \tag{3.18}$$

$$Z_1 = r\pi_{21}(\beta v_1 + 1) + \pi_{22}\beta v_2, \tag{3.19}$$

$$Z_2 = -\, r\pi_{22}(\beta v_1 + 1) + \pi_{21}\beta v_2. \tag{3.20}$$

Making the substitutions (3.18) and (3.19) in (3.15) and using

$$\sin\theta = \cos\left(\theta - \frac{\pi}{2}\right), \tag{3.21}$$

we obtain

$$Q_1 = (1 + v_1^2)r^2 + v_2^2 - 2Z_1 \cos\theta + 2Z_2 \cos\left(\theta - \frac{\pi}{2}\right). \tag{3.22}$$

The transformation of Q_2 is somewhat more tedious: we first make the substitutions (3.9) through (3.12) into (3.16); then we complete squares on v_5 and v_6. Furthermore, we find it convenient to make the following additional transformation:

$$v_5 = \frac{X_5}{\sqrt{(1+v_1^2)}} - \frac{v_1v_3 - \pi_{13}v_1 - \pi_{23}}{(1+v_1^2)} \tag{3.23}$$

$$v_6 = \frac{X_6}{\sqrt{(1+v_1^2)}} - \frac{v_1v_4 - \pi_{14}v_1 - \pi_{24}}{1+v_1^2} \tag{3.24}$$

in Q_2, and, consequently

$$dv_5 = \frac{dX_5}{\sqrt{(1+v_1^2)}} \tag{3.25}$$

$$dv_6 = \frac{dX_6}{\sqrt{(1+v_1^2)}} \cdot \tag{3.26}$$

Finally we have

$$Q_2 = \frac{(v_3 - \pi_{13} + v_1\pi_{23})^2 + (v_4 - \pi_{14} + v_1\pi_{24})^2}{1+v_1^2} + X_5^2 + X_6^2. \tag{3.27}$$

Using (2.14), (3.8) and (3.27) in (3.14) we obtain

$$g(v_1, v_2, r, \theta, v_3, v_4, X_5, X_6)dX_6dX_5dv_4dv_3d\theta dv_2drdv_1$$

$$= \frac{1}{(2\pi)^2}\exp\left[-\frac{\lambda^2}{2} - \frac{1+v_1^2}{2}r^2 - \frac{v_2^2}{2}\right]$$

$$\cdot\exp\left[Z_1\cos\theta - Z_2\cos\left(\theta - \frac{\pi}{2}\right)\right]r^2d\theta dv_2drdv_1$$

$$\times\frac{1}{2\pi(1+v_1^2)}\exp\left[-\frac{1}{2}\left\{\frac{(v_3 - \pi_{13} + v_1\pi_{23})^2 + (v_4 - \pi_{14} + v_1\pi_{24})^2}{1+v_1^2}\right\}\right]dv_3dv_4$$

$$\times\frac{1}{2\pi}\exp\left[-\tfrac{1}{2}\{X_5^2 + X_6^2\}\right]dX_5dX_6. \tag{3.28}$$

The exact joint frequency function $h(v_1, v_3, v_4)$ we are seeking is the coefficient of $dv_1dv_3dv_4$ in the expression that we obtain by integrating the right-hand member of (3.28) with respect to dX_6, dX_5, $d\theta$, dv_2 and dr over the corresponding ranges of integration. The form of (3.28) indicates, however, that the joint probability density function of v_1, v_3, v_4 is of the form

$$\begin{aligned} h(v_1, v_3, v_4)dv_1dv_3dv_4 &= h_1(v_1)h_2(v_1, v_2, v_3)dv_1dv_3dv_4 \\ &= h_1(v_1)dv_1f(X_3, X_4)dX_3dX_4, \end{aligned} \tag{3.29}$$

where

$$v_3 = X_3\sqrt{1+v_1^2} - v_1\pi_{23} + \pi_{13}, \tag{3.30}$$

$$v_4 = X_4\sqrt{1+v_1^2} - v_1\pi_{24} + \pi_{14}. \tag{3.31}$$

and

$$\frac{\partial(v_3, v_4)}{\partial(X_3, X_4)} = 1 + v_1^2, \tag{3.32}$$

$$h_2(v_1, v_2, v_3) = \frac{1}{2\pi(1 + v_1^2)} \cdot \exp\left[-\frac{1}{2}\frac{(v_3 - \pi_{13} + v_1\pi_{23})^2 + (v_4 - \pi_{14} + v_1 + \pi_{24}^2)}{1 + v_1^2}\right] \tag{3.33}$$

and

$$f(X_3, X_4) = \frac{1}{2\pi}\exp\left[-\tfrac{1}{2}\{X_3^2 + X_4^2\}\right]. \tag{3.34}$$

Thus we see at once that the statistics

$$X_3 = \frac{v_3 - (\pi_{13} - v_1\pi_{23})}{\sqrt{(1 + v_1^2)}} \tag{3.35}$$

$$X_4 = \frac{v_4 - (\pi_{14} - v_1\pi_{24})}{\sqrt{(1 + v_1^2)}} \tag{3.36}$$

are mutually independent standard normal variates and are not dependent on v_1. This result, however, is easily deduced directly from equations (3.3)–(3.4). Consequently it is apparent that we require only to find the function $h_1(v_1)$ in (3.29).

Making the substitutions (3.30) through (3.32) in (3.28) and integrating the latter with respect to dX_6, dX_5, dX_4, dX_3 over $-\infty < X_k < +\infty$, we obtain

$$g_1(v_1, v_2, r, \theta)d\theta dv_2 dr dv_1 = \frac{e^{-\lambda^2/2}}{2\pi}\exp\left[-\frac{(1 + v_1^2)}{2}r^2 - \frac{v_2^2}{2}\right] \times \frac{\exp\left[Z_1\cos\theta - Z_2\cos(\theta - \pi/2)\right]}{2\pi} r^2 d\theta dv_2 dr dv_1. \tag{3.37}$$

Integrating (3.37) with respect to $d\theta$ over $0 \leqq \theta \leqq 2\pi$, we obtain

$$g_2(v_1, v_2, r)dv_2 dr dv_1 = \frac{e^{-\lambda^2/2}}{2\pi}\cdot\exp\left[-\frac{(1 + v_1^2)}{2}r^2 - \frac{v_2^2}{2}\right]r^2 \cdot I_0\{\sqrt{Z_1^2 + Z_2^2}\}dv_2 dr dv_1, \tag{3.38}$$

where $I_0(Z)$ denotes the modified Bessel function of the first kind of zero order, and Z_1, Z_2 are defined as in (3.19) and (3.20).

Recall from (3.19) and (3.20) that Z_1 and Z_2 are functions of both v_2 and r. Three considerations, namely, the algebraic forms of the estimated sampling variance of v_1 [cf also 4 formula (3.15), p. 102], the necessity for integrating

(3.38) over v_2 and r independently, and the form of the *Generalized Addition Formula* for $I_0(Z)$, [13, pp. 128–9, p. 95] lead us to make the following transformation:

$$b_1 = \sqrt{\pi_{21}^2 + \pi_{22}^2}\,(\beta v_1 + 1) \tag{3.39}$$

$$b_2 = \sqrt{\pi_{21}^2 + \pi_{22}^2}\,\beta. \tag{3.40}$$

from which it follows that

$$Z_1^2 + Z_2^2 = b_1^2 r^2 + b_2^2 v_2^2 \tag{3.41}$$

consequently

$$\begin{aligned} I_0(\sqrt{Z_1^2 + Z_2^2}) &= I_0(\sqrt{b_1^2 r^2 + b_2^2 v_2^2}) \\ &= I_0(b_1 r) I_0(b_2 v_2) + 2 \sum_{n=1}^{\infty} (-1)^n I_{2n}(b_1 r) I_{2n}(b_2 v_2) \end{aligned} \tag{3.42}$$

by the *Generalized Addition Formula* for $I_0(Z)$.

Substituting (3.42) into (3.38) we obtain

$$\begin{aligned} &\frac{e^{-\lambda^2/2}}{2\pi} \left\{ \exp\left[-\frac{(1+v_1^2)r^2}{2} \right] I_0(b_1 r) r^2 e^{-v_2^2/2} I_0(b_2 v_2) \right. \\ &\left. + 2 \sum_{n=1}^{\infty} (-1)^n \exp\left[-\frac{(1+v_1^2)r^2}{2} \right] I_{2n}(b_1 r) r^2 \cdot e^{-v_2^2/2} I_{2n}(b_2 v_2) \right\} dv_2 dr dv_1. \end{aligned} \tag{3.43}$$

We have now to integrate (3.43) with respect to dr over $0 < r < \infty$, and with respect to dv_2 over $-\infty < v_2 < +\infty$.

Since the *Bessel* functions $I_{2n}(b_2 v_2)$, $n = 0, 1, 2, \cdots$, contain even powers of v_2 only, we have

$$\int_{-\infty}^{+\infty} e^{-v_2^2/2} I_{2n}(b_2 v_2) dv_2 = \sqrt{2\pi}\, e^{b_2^2/4} I_n\left(\frac{b_2^2}{4}\right). \tag{3.44}$$

Letting

$$X_1 = \frac{b_1}{\sqrt{1 + v_1^2}},$$

we obtain

$$\begin{aligned} &\int_0^{\infty} \exp\left[-\frac{(1+v_1^2)r^2}{2} \right] I_{2n}(b_1 r) r^2 dr \\ &= \frac{\sqrt{2}\,\Gamma(n + \frac{3}{2})(\frac{1}{2} X_1^2)^n}{(1+v_1^2)\ (2n+1)}\ {}_1F_1\left(n + \frac{3}{2};\ 2n+1;\ \frac{X_1^2}{2}\right) \end{aligned} \tag{3.45}$$

by Hankel's generalization of Weber's first exponential integral, [28, pp. 393–394], where ${}_1F_1(\alpha; \rho; z)$ denotes the confluent hypergeometric function, [29, pp. 337–51]. Upon integrating (3.43) over $-\infty < v_2 < +\infty$, $0 < r < +\infty$, we obtain by using (3.44) and (3.45), the *exact* finite sample frequency function, $h_1(v_1)$ or v_1:

$$h_1(v_1) = \frac{e^{-\lambda^2/2+b_2^2/4}}{\sqrt{\pi}(1+v_1^2)^{3/2}}\left\{\Gamma\left(\frac{3}{2}\right)I_0\left(\frac{b_2^2}{4}\right){}_1F_1\left(\frac{3}{2};1;\frac{X_1^2}{2}\right)\right.$$

$$\left. + 2\sum_{n=1}^{\infty}(-1)^n \frac{\Gamma\left(n+\frac{3}{2}\right)\left(\frac{X_1^2}{2}\right)^n}{\Gamma(2n+1)} I_n\left(\frac{b_2^2}{4}\right){}_1F_1\left(n+\frac{3}{2};2n+1;\frac{X_1^2}{2}\right)\right\}; \quad (3.46)$$

$$-\infty < v_1 < +\infty.$$

Consequently, the exact joint frequency function is

$$h(v_1, v_3, v_4) = h_1(v_1)h_2(v_1, v_3, v_4) = h_1(v_1)\frac{1}{2\pi(1+v_1^2)}$$

$$\cdot \exp\left\{-\frac{1}{2}\left[\frac{(v_3-\pi_{13}+v_1\pi_{23})^2+(v_4-\pi_{14}+v_1\pi_{24})^2}{1+v_1^2}\right]\right\}. \quad (3.47)$$

The function $h_2(v_1, v_3, v_4)$ is the conditional frequency function for v_3, v_4, given v_1. When it has been shown that v_1, the GCL estimator of β_{12} in (2.1), does not possess a finite variance, it will follow that v_3, and v_4, the GCL estimators of γ_{13} and γ_{14} in (2.1), also do not possess finite variances.

To show that the frequency function (3.46) possesses a finite first moment, but not a finite second moment, we require only to examine the first term in the following series expansion:

$$h_1(v_1) = \frac{e^{-\lambda^2/2+b_2^2/4}}{\sqrt{\pi}(1+v_1^2)^{3/2}}\left\{\sum_{m=0}^{\infty} A_m\left(\frac{X_1^2}{2}\right)^m\right\} \quad (3.48)$$

where

$$A_m = \Gamma\left(m+\frac{3}{2}\right)\left[\frac{I_0\left(\frac{b_2^2}{4}\right)}{m!m!} + \sum_{s=1}^{m}(-1)^s \frac{2I_s\left(\frac{b_2^2}{4}\right)}{(m+s)!(m-s)!}\right]. \quad (3.49)$$

It will be convenient, however, to introduce here the special sub-case in which $\beta_{12}=0$. If $\beta_{12}=0$, then $b_2=0$, $\lambda^2=b_1^2=\pi_{21}^2+\pi_{22}^2$, and the frequency function (3.46) reduces directly to

$$\overset{*}{h}_1(v_1) = \frac{e^{-\lambda^2/2}}{2(1+v_1^2)^{3/2}}\,{}_1F_1\left(\frac{3}{2};1;\frac{X_1^2}{2}\right)$$

$$= \frac{e^{-\lambda^2/2}}{2(1+v_1^2)^{3/2}}\left\{1+\sum_{s=1}^{\infty}\frac{\Gamma(\frac{3}{2}+s)}{\Gamma(\frac{3}{2})s!s!}\left[\frac{b_1^2}{2(1+v_1^2)}\right]^s\right\} \quad (3.50)$$

$$-\infty < v_1 < +\infty.$$

Using

$$\int_{-\infty}^{+\infty} \frac{dv_1}{(1+v_1^2)^{s+3/2}} = \frac{\sqrt{\pi}s!}{\Gamma(3/2+s)} \qquad s = 0, 1, 2, \cdots, \tag{3.51}$$

we find, upon integrating $h_1^*(v_1)$ in formula (3.50) that

$$\int_{-\infty}^{+\infty} h_1^*(v_1)dv_1 = 1. \tag{3.52}$$

We are thereby satisfied that $h_1^*(v_1)$ is indeed a frequency function. Now using

$$\int_{-\infty}^{+\infty} \frac{v_1 dv_1}{(1+v_1{}^2)^{s+3/2}} = 0 \qquad s = 0, 1, 2, \cdots, \tag{3.53}$$

we obtain

$$\int_{-\infty}^{+\infty} v_1 h_1^*(v_1)dv_1 = 0. \tag{3.54}$$

We see that the frequency function $h_1^*(v_1)$ possesses a finite mean. Finally, using

$$\int_{-\infty}^{+\infty} \frac{v_1^2 dv_1}{(1+v_1^2)^{3/2}} = \int_{\pi/2}^{\pi/2} (\sec\alpha - \cos\alpha)d\alpha = +\infty, \tag{3.55}$$

we obtain

$$\int_{-\infty}^{+\infty} v_1^2 h_1^*(v_1)dv_1 = +\infty.$$

Thus we see that the frequency function $h_1^*(v_1)$ of the GCL estimator v_1 possesses a finite mean, but not a finite variance. It is a simple matter to show that the mode, m, of the frequency function $h_1^*(v_1)$ is located at the origin $v_1=0$.

The frequency function $h_1^*(v_1)$ with $\lambda^2=4.0$, $\beta_{12}=0$, is illustrated graphically in Figure 1, where it is also compared with the normal frequency function $\phi(0, 1/\lambda^2)$; this comparison illustrates very clearly the inadequacy of the *mean square deviation* as a measure of efficiency.[3]

---

[3] We can, of course, try to approximate the frequency function $h_1^*(v_1)$ by a frequency function that does possess a finite variance, e.g., *Pearson's Type VII* in this case. Dr. Ernest J. Mosbaek has tabulated the more general form of frequency function (3.48) for $\beta_{12}\neq 0$, [7, pp. 42–3]. The latter is skew, with the property that the mode lies between the origin, $v_1=0$, and the exact parameter point, $v_1=\beta_{12}$. *Pearson's Type IV* is a plausible approximation to the frequency function (3.48). In the more general case involving three equations treated in the sampling experiment [7, Sec. 3, 4], *Pearson's Type IV* emerges as a suitable approximation to each of the GCL estimator distribution functions examined.

Recall formula (2.14). Note that as the sample size increases indefinitely, i.e., as $N\to\infty$, we have

$$\lambda^2 - \frac{b_2}{2} \to \infty,$$

and $\sqrt{N}(v_1-\beta)$ asymptotically unbiased and normally distributed, [4, pp. 103–5]. Moreover, for any fixed N, the distribution of v_1 will tend to be approximately normal and unbiased whenever $\lambda^2-(b_2^2/2)$ is large, for whatever reason, [7, pp. 50–7].

4. DERIVATION OF FREQUENCY FUNCTION. CASE II

We shall now consider the exact finite sample frequency function of v_1, the GCL estimator of β_{12}, when the identifiability hypothesis is

$$H_0: \gamma_{11} = 0, \quad \gamma_{12} = 0, \quad \gamma_{13} = 0. \tag{4.1}$$

This example is of importance, for it provides the first case in which the GCL estimator possesses a finite variance. Moreover, when we consider the special form in which $\beta_{12}=0$, *and in which sufficient conditions for identifiability are not* met, namely, where

$$\pi_{21} = \pi_{22} = \pi_{23} = 0 \tag{4.2}$$

in (2.6), we encounter the first case in which the sampling variance of a GCL estimate does not tend to infinity when sufficient conditions for identifiability are not met, [cf. 17 p. 175]. The existence of finite moments of the GCL coefficient estimators is not connected with the *sufficiency* of identifying restrictions.

It will serve our immediate purpose, which is to forestall premature generalization of the propositions about the non-existence of finite variances of GCL estimators, to consider only the special case just mentioned; namely, where the equations (4.2) hold and $\beta_{12}=0$. Of course we do not assume that the statistician has this information.

The GCL coefficients v_1, v_4, and statistics v_2, v_3 are related to the unrestricted reduced-form estimates $p_{11}, \cdots, p_{24}$ by the transformation:

$$p_{11} = v_1 r \sin\theta \cos\phi + v_2 \cos\theta \cos\phi - v_3 \sin\phi \tag{4.3}$$

$$p_{12} = v_1 r \sin\theta \sin\phi + v_2 \cos\theta \sin\phi - v_3 \cos\phi \tag{4.4}$$

$$p_{13} = v_1 r \cos\theta \qquad - v_2 \sin\theta \tag{4.5}$$

$$p_{14} = v_4 + v_1 v_5 \tag{4.6}$$

$$p_{21} = r \sin\theta \cos\phi \tag{4.7}$$

$$p_{22} = r \sin\theta \sin\phi \tag{4.8}$$

$$p_{23} = r \cos\theta \tag{4.9}$$

$$p_{24} = v_5 \tag{4.10}$$

$$\begin{aligned} &0 \le r < +\infty, \\ &0 \le \phi \le 2\pi, \\ &0 \le \theta \le \pi; \end{aligned} \tag{4.11}$$

where v_1 is the GCL estimator of β_{12} in (2.1) and v_4 is the GCL estimator of γ_{14} in (2.1); and

$$v_2^2 + v_3^2 = (p_{11} - v_1 p_{21})^2 + (p_{12} - v_1 p_{22})^2 + (p_{13} - v_1 p_{23})^2 \tag{4.12}$$

is essentially the numerator of the GCL identifiability test statistic. The Jacobian of (4.3) is

$$J = r^3 \sin\theta. \tag{4.13}$$

Using $\beta_{12}=0$, and (4.2), we transform the probability density function (2.13) according to (4.3) and (4.13); integrating with respect to v_5, v_4, v_3, v_2, ϕ, r, θ, we obtain the *exact* finite sample marginal frequency function of v_1:

$$h_1(v_1) = \frac{2}{\pi(1+v_1^2)^2}, \qquad -\infty < v_1 < +\infty. \tag{4.14}$$

The frequency function (4.14) possesses a finite *mean*

$$\mu_1 = \int_{-\infty}^{+\infty} \frac{2v_1 dv_1}{\pi(1+v_1^2)^2} = 0; \tag{4.15}$$

and a finite *variance*

$$\mu_2 = \int_{-\infty}^{+\infty} \frac{2v_1^2 dv_1}{\pi(1+v_1^2)^2} = 1.$$

The frequency function (4.14) possesses no finite moments of higher order than two.

The results (4.16) taken together with the results (3.49) and its consequences suggest the conjecture that the exact finite sample distribution functions of GCL coefficient estimators possess finite moments of order $\nu=K_2-G+1$. The proof of this conjecture is beyond the scope of the present study.

The results of Sections 3 and 4 continue to hold if the normally distributed disturbances e_{t1} and e_{t2} in equations (2.1)–(2.2) are serially correlated, provided, of course, that no lagged endogenous variables appear in the structural equations, and that the sample of exogenous variables $x_1, \cdots, x_4$ remains fixed. In this case, the estimates $p_{11}, \cdots, p_{14}$ are normally distributed and unbiased; their variances, however, depend upon the *correlograms* of η_{t1}, η_{t2}, $t=1, 2, \cdots, N$, and upon the sample serial covariances of exogenous variables. The precision with which the exact distribution functions of GCL estimates can be approximated by the normal form, or by some other convenient distribution functions, is, of course, affected by the *correlograms* and the sample serial covariances of exogenous variables.

5. CONCLUSION

While it is true that the forms of the exact frequency functions (3.46) and (4.14) depend on the normality assumptions made in respect of the disturbances e_{t1} and e_{t2} in the structural equations (2.1)–(2.2), and on the assumption that no x_{tk} is a lagged endogenous variable, still it is plausible that the GCL estimator v_1 in Section 3 does not possess a finite variance even when the foregoing assumptions are relaxed.

The results derived in Section 3 and Section 4 provide a cogent argument against the uncritical practice of casting away the so-called "outliers," i.e., the extreme deviations encountered in Monte Carlo studies of estimator distributions, especially in those cases in which the number K_2 of predetermined variables excluded from a structural equation is exactly equal to the number, G, of endogenous variables present, i.e., $K_2-G+1=1$, [22], and *a fortiori* in those cases for which $K_2-G+1=0$ [7, p. 15].

It is clearly not possible to make any meaningful comparison between the GCL estimator v_1 in Section 3 and the corresponding LVR, DLS, and FI estimators of β_{12} in respect of putative *mean-square deviations.* The same is true in respect of the three-equation case ($G=3$) corresponding to case I in Section 3, i.e., in which K_2, the number of exogenous variables hypothetically excluded from the structural equation is $K_2=3$, so that $K_2-G+1=1$.[4] When the exact finite sample frequency functions of the corresponding LVR, DLS, and FI estimators have been worked out and are available, and when some appropriate measure of dispersion has been invented, it will then be possible to undertake some sort of meaningful normative comparisons among these estimator types.

REFERENCES

[1] Anderson, T. W. and Rubin, H., "Estimation of the parameters of a single equation in a complete system of stochastic equations," *Annals of Mathematical Statistics*, 20. (1949), 570–82.

[2] Anderson, T. W. and Rubin, H., "The asymptotic properties of estimates of the parameters of a single equation in a complete system of stochastic equations," *Annals of Mathematical Statistics*, 21 (1950), 570–82.

[3] Basmann, R. L. "A generalized classical method of linear estimation of coefficients in a structural equation," *Econometrica*, 25 (1957), 77–83.

[4] Basmann, R. L. "On the asymptotic distribution of generalized linear estimators," *Econometrica*, 28 (1960), 97–107.

[5] Basmann, R. L. "An expository note on the estimation of simultaneous structural equations," *Biometrics*, 15 (1960), (forthcoming).

[6] Basmann, R. L. "On finite sample distributions of GCL identifiability test statistics," *Journal of the American Statistical Association*, 55 (1960) 650–9.

[7] Basmann, R. L. *On the Exact Finite Sample Distributions of Generalized Classical Linear Structural Estimators.* (SP-91) Santa Barbara: Technical Military Planning Operation, General Electric Company. July 1, 1960.

[8] Birnbaum, Z. W. "Numerical tabulation of the distribution of Kolmogorov's statistic for finite sample size," *Journal of the American Statistical Association*, 47 (1962) 425–41.

[9] Bowman, Frank. *Introduction to Bessel Functions.* New York: Dover Publications, Inc., 1958.

[10] Christ, Carl F., "Simultaneous equation estimation: any verdict yet?" *Econometrica*, 28 (1960), 835–45.

[11] Craig, C. C. "The frequency function of y/x," *Annals of Mathematics*, Second Series, 30 (1929), 471–86.

[12] Feller, William. *An Introduction to Probability Theory and its Applications. Vol. 1, Second Edition.* New York: John Wiley and Sons, Inc., 1957.

[13] Fieller, E. C. "The distribution of the index in a normal bivariate population," *Biometrika*, 24 (1932), 428–40.

[14] Hood, Wm. C. and Koopmans, Tjalling C., Editors. *Studies in Econometric Method.* New York: John Wiley and Sons, Inc., 1953.

[15] Kendall, Maurice G. *The Advanced Theory of Statistics* (Three-Volume Edition) London: Griffin, 1958.

[16] Kolmogorov, A. N. "Confidence limits for an unknown distribution function," *Annals of Mathematical Statistics*, 12 (1941), 461–3.

[17] Koopmans, Tjalling C. and Hood, Wm. C., "The estimation of simultaneous linear economic relationships," Chapter VI in [14], pp. 112–99.

---

[4] I have worked out the exact joint frequency functions of GCL estimators for this three-equation case. The results, however, are preliminary, the derivations are tedious, and being analogous to the derivations in Section 3, can contribute very little to the immediate purpose of this article.

[18] Koopmans, Tjalling C., Editor. *Statistical Inference in Dynamic Economic Models.* New York: John Wiley, 1950.

[19] Koopmans, T. C., Rubin, H., and Leipnik, R. B., "Measuring the equation systems of dynamic economics," in [18], pp. 53–237.

[20] Nagar, A. L., "The bias and moment matrix of the general k-class estimators of the parameters in structural equations," *Econometrica,* 27 (1959), 575–95.

[21] Neiswanger, W. A. and Yancey, T. A., "Parameter estimates and autonomous growth," *Journal of the American Statistical Association,* 54 (1959), 389–402.

[22] Summers, Robert, "A capital-intensive approach to the small-sample properties of various simultaneous equations estimators," (Abstract), *Econometrica,* 27 (1959), 302–3.

[23] Theil, H., *Estimation and Simultaneous Correlation in Complete Equation Systems.* The Hague: Centraal Planbureau, 1953. (mimeo.)

[24] Theil, H., *Economic Forecasts and Policy.* Amsterdam: North-Holland Publishing Company, 1958.

[25] Theil, H. and Kloek, T., "The statistics of systems in simultaneous economic relationships," *Statistica Neerlandica,* 13 (1959), 65–89.

[26] Tintner, Gerhard. *Econometrics.* New York: John Wiley and Sons, Inc., 1952.

[27] Wagner, Harvey M., "A Monte Carlo study of estimates of simultaneous linear structural equations," *Econometrica,* 26 (1958), 117–33.

[28] Watson, G. N., *A Treatise on the Theory of Bessel Functions,* (Second Edition), Cambridge: University Press, 1952.

[29] Whittaker, E. T. and Watson, G. N., *A Course of Modern Analysis,* (Fourth Edition). Cambridge: University Press, 1952.

A NOTE ON THE EXACT FINITE SAMPLE FREQUENCY FUNCTIONS OF GENERALIZED CLASSICAL LINEAR ESTIMATORS IN A LEADING THREE-EQUATION CASE*

R. L. BASMANN

In this article some leading results of a mathematical investigation of exact finite sample distributions of GCL estimators are given. These results pertain to the distributions of estimators of coefficients appearing in econometric systems of three structural equations. The results show that the general forms of exact distributions derived for coefficient estimators in two-equation systems re-appear in the corresponding cases of three equations systems.

1. BACKGROUND

IN A recent paper [3] I presented the exact finite sample frequency functions of some *generalized classical linear* (GCL) estimators in two leading over-identified cases. The purpose of that paper was chiefly to indicate some arguments against the employment of Monte Carlo experimental *mean squared deviations* for the making of normative comparisons of alternative estimators of structural coefficients in certain cases, namely, those for which the number K_2 of predetermined variables excluded from the supposedly identifiable structural equation is less than or exactly equal to the number, G, of endogenous variables contained therein. Illustrations of exact frequency functions for the case $K_2=G=2$ were provided, [3, pp. 625–34], and the non-existence of finite variances was demonstrated for this case. The *main* theoretical argument against second-moment comparisons was shown, by demonstration of the existence of a finite variance in the case $K_2=3$, $G=2$, [2, pp. 633–4], to be limited to the cases $K_2=G$.

Several readers have inquired about the possible generality of the results given in that early paper, [3]. The question whether the *forms* of frequency functions derived for coefficient estimates in two-equations systems will re-appear in the corresponding cases of three or more equations appears to hinge on the generality of the transformation that carries the joint probability density function of *reduced-form estimates* (Section 2) into the joint probability density function of structural coefficient estimators and the extraneous random variables which have to be integrated out. The transformation employed in the two-equation cases [3, pp. 626, 633] appears to be general in its applicability to any number G of structural equations and number K_2 of exclusions of exogenous variables, but its generality is not obvious, especially in the rather compact two-equation applications shown in the paper [3]. The full generality of the transformation is more clearly revealed, however, in the case $G=3$ equations and $K_2=3$ exclusions. Therefore, it seems desirable to publish a concise but

* Work performed partly in connection with Projects Nos. 1300086 and 1300071, Technical Military Planning Operation, General Electric Company, Santa Barbara, California. I am indebted to Dr. Harold Asher and Dr. E. J. Mosbaek for criticism and encouragement. All errors and omissions remain my own responsibility.

moderately detailed exposition of the transformation involved in the case $G=3$, $K_2=3$, (*cf.* 3, p. 635n].

To keep this note tolerably brief I shall illustrate the complete derivation of marginal frequency functions of structural coefficient estimates only for one of the leading special cases in which sufficient conditions for identifiability are not met.[1]

The mathematical investigations reported here in part have been undertaken in connection with a *Monte Carlo* experiment, [4]. Like the results of the Monte Carlo experiment, the mathematical investigations undertaken thus far must be regarded as only exploratory in nature; the ultimate goal, a definitive exact finite sample theory of GCL estimators, remains, of course, to be achieved.

2. ASSUMPTIONS AND SPECIFICATIONS

Let a system of structural equations be denoted by

$$B'y'_{t.} + \Gamma' x'_{t.} + \zeta'_{t.} = 0 \tag{2.1–2.3}$$

where B' is 3×3, $|B| \neq 0$, $\beta_{11} = -1$; Γ' is $3\times K$. In matrix notation $y_{t.}$ denotes a row-vector of elements y_{th}, $t=1, 2, \cdots, N$ and constitutes a single observation of $G=3$ *endogenous* variables. The row-vector $x_{t.}$ of elements x_{tk} denotes a single observation of K *exogenous* variables. Finally $\zeta_{t.}$ denotes a row vector of random disturbances ζ_{th}, $h=1, 2, 3$ in the structural equations (2.1)–(2.3). The vectors $\zeta_{t.}$, $t=1, 2, \cdots, N$ are independently and identically distributed according to the normal law $\Phi(0, \Omega)$, and Ω^{-1} is assumed to exist.

In its reduced form, the system (2.1)–(2.3) is represented by the equations

$$y'_{t.} = \Pi' x'_{t.} + \eta'_{t.} \tag{2.4-2.6}$$

$$\Pi' = -(B')^{-1}\Gamma' \tag{2.7}$$

$$\eta'_{t.} = -(B')^{-1}\zeta'_{t.}. \tag{2.8}$$

The disturbance vectors $\eta_{t.}$, $t=1, 2, \cdots, N$ are thus independently and identically normally distributed, $\Phi(0, \sum)$.

As in the earlier paper, [3, p. 624] we shall assume

$$\sum = I_3; \tag{2.9}$$

$$\sum_{t=1}^{n} y_{th} = \sum_{t=1}^{n} x_{tk} = 0, \qquad h = 1, 2, 3; \quad k = 1, 2, \cdots, K \tag{2.10}$$

and

$$\sum_{t=1}^{n} x_{tk}x_{tm} = \begin{cases} 0, & m \neq k \\ 1, & m = k \end{cases} \tag{2.11}$$

---

[1] As the transformation of reduced form estimators is unaffected by this specialization, we lose no generality from the point of view of present purposes. After the transformation is applied, the process of removing the extraneous variables by integration is much less complicated and far shorter than in the most general case involving $K_2=G=3$. I have carried the latter derivation through; but in its present form its length would be intolerable in a journal article; nor, it must be admitted, have I been able thus far to verify to my complete satisfaction the correctness of the expression arrived at. It suffices to say that the putative marginal frequency function for the general case of $K_2=G=3$ is of the same form *in the variable* as in the case $K_2=G=2$, [3, p. 631] and that this is in agreement with the Monte Carlo investigation of the most general case involving $K_2=G=3$, [4].

These assumptions have no consequence for the general *form* of the exact distributions finally arrived at. We can regard assumptions (2.9)–(2.11) as "standardizing" the distribution functions of estimates of β_{12} and β_{13} in equation (2.1). This remark is clarified in the Appendix. Let it be required to estimate the structural equation (2.1)—*in extenso*

$$-y_{t1} + \beta_{12}y_{t2} + \beta_{13}y_{t3} + \gamma_{11}x_{t1} + \gamma_{12}x_{t2} + \cdots + \gamma_{1K}x_{tK} + \zeta_{t1} = 0 \quad (2.12)$$

under the identifiability hypothesis, $\gamma_{11}=\gamma_{12}=\gamma_{13}=0$. Let the GCL-LVD estimates of β_{12}, β_{13} be denoted by v_2, v_3, respectively; v_1^2 will denote the variance-difference, [1, p. 101], i.e., the numerator of the *identifiability test statistic* [cf. 1, p. 105; 2, p. 651; 3, p. 625]; $v_4, \cdots, v_K$ will denote the GCL-LVD estimates of $\gamma_{14}, \cdots, \gamma_{1K}$, respectively. Finally, let p_{ik}, $i=1, 2, 3$; $k=1, 2, \cdots, K$ denote unrestricted maximum likelihood estimates of Π_{ik} in the equations (2.4)–(2.6). Under the assumptions (2.9–(2.11), the p_{ik} are independently and normally distributed with means Π_{ik}, and variances$=1.0$.

The *variance difference*

$$v_1^2 = \sum_{i=1}^{3} (p_{1i} - v_2p_{2i} - v_3p_{3i})^2 \quad (2.13)$$

is minimized with respect to v_2, v_3, [2, p. 651; 3 p. 626]. Consequently v_1, and the coefficient estimates v_2, v_3 depend only on the reduced-form estimates p_{hj}, $h=1, 2, 3, j=1, 2, 3$. Moreover, since

$$v_k = p_{1k} - v_2p_{2k} - v_3p_{3k}$$
$$k = 4, \cdots, K; \quad (2.14)$$

it is clear that the *conditional* joint distribution function of the estimates $v_4, \cdots, v_K$, given v_2, v_3, is normal, [cf. 3, p. 629]. Therefore, we shall consider only the transformation by means of which the joint frequency function of p_{hj}, $h=1, 2, 3$; $j=1, 2, 3$ is carried into the joint frequency function of the structural estimates v_2, v_3.

3. THE TRANSFORMATION

A geometrical approach to the case $K_2=G=3$ will help to exhibit the generality of the transformation to be employed. Let us regard the 3-tuple (p_{11}, p_{12}, p_{13}) of reduced-form coefficient estimates as a vector $\overrightarrow{OP}_1$; (p_{21}, p_{22}, p_{23}) as a vector $\overrightarrow{OP}_2$; and (p_{31}, p_{32}, p_{33}) as a vector $\overrightarrow{OP}_3$ in a three-dimensional Euclidean space with coordinate axes $OX_1X_2X_3$, the vectors having O as a common origin. p_{11} is the component of $\overrightarrow{OP}_1$ along OX_1, p_{12} the component of $\overrightarrow{OP}_1$ along OX_2, etc. Since the GCL-LVD estimates v_2, v_3 minimize the variance difference v_1^2, (2.13), we note directly that v_2^2 is the squared distance from the point P, (p_{11}, p_{12}, p_{13}), to the plane OP_2P_3 determined by the vectors $\overrightarrow{OP}_2$ and $\overrightarrow{OP}_3$. Since v_2^2 is one of the new variables whose joint frequency function we are required to find [2], it is natural to consider a *rotation* of the coordinate system such that one of the new reference planes coincides with the plane OP_2P_3 determined by $\overrightarrow{OP_2}$ and $\overrightarrow{OP_3}$, i.e., so that the new variable v_2 has its component orthogonal to the plane OP_2P_3, [cf. 3, p. 626; 633].

For this purpose we introduce a form of the well-known *Euler* transformation [8, pp. 37–9] to relate the new coordinate system $OX_1'X_2'X_3'$ to the original $OX_1X_2X_3$:

	X_1'	X_2'	X_3'	
X_1	l_1	l_2	l_3	(3.1)
X_2	m_1	m_2	m_3	(3.2)
X_3	n_1	n_2	n_3	(3.3)

where

$$\begin{cases} l_1 = \sin\theta\cos\phi \\ m_1 = \sin\theta\sin\phi \\ n_1 = \cos\theta \end{cases} \tag{3.4}$$

$$\begin{cases} l_2 = \sin\phi \\ m_2 = -\cos\phi \\ n_2 = 0 \end{cases} \tag{3.5}$$

$$\begin{cases} l_3 = \cos\theta\cos\phi \\ m_3 = \cos\theta\sin\phi \\ n_3 = -\sin\theta. \end{cases} \tag{3.6}$$

$$0 < \theta < \pi$$

$$0 < \phi < 2\pi$$

The new axis OX_1' is perpendicular to the plane OP_2P_3; the new axis OX_2' coincides with the intersection of the planes OP_2P_3 and OX_1X_2, with positive direction chosen to conform to OX_1' according to the right-hand rule.

We note that θ is the angle between OX_3 and OX_1'; and ϕ is the angle between the planes OX_3X_1 and OX_3X_1.

Using the Euler transformation we express the old variables in terms of the new:

$$p_{11} = v_1l_1 + v_2(l_2\bar{p}_{22} + l_3\bar{p}_{23}) + v_3(l_2\bar{p}_{32} + l_3\bar{p}_{33}) \tag{3.7}$$

$$p_{12} = v_1m_1 + v_2(m_2\bar{p}_{22} + m_3\bar{p}_{23}) + v_3(m_2\bar{p}_{32} + m_3\bar{p}_{33}) \tag{3.8}$$

$$p_{13} = v_1n_1 + v_2(n_2\bar{p}_{22} + n_3\bar{p}_{23}) + v_3(n_2\bar{p}_{32} + n_3\bar{p}_{33}) \tag{3.9}$$

$$p_{21} = l_2\bar{p}_{22} + l_3\bar{p}_{23} \tag{3.10}$$

$$p_{22} = m_2\bar{p}_{22} + m_3\bar{p}_{23} \tag{3.11}$$

$$p_{23} = p_2\bar{p}_{22} + n_3\bar{p}_{23} \tag{3.12}$$
$$p_{31} = l_2\bar{p}_{32} + l_3\bar{p}_{33} \tag{3.13}$$
$$p_{32} = m_2\bar{p}_{32} + m_3\bar{p}_{33} \tag{3.14}$$
$$p_{33} = n_2\bar{p}_{32} + n_3\bar{p}_{33}. \tag{3.15}$$

It is convenient to replace the new variables $\bar{p}_{22}, \cdots, \bar{p}_{33}$ by

$$\bar{p}_{22} = r_2 \cos \psi_2 \qquad 0 \leq \psi_2 \leq 2\pi \quad r_2 > 0 \tag{3.16}$$
$$\bar{p}_{23} = r_2 \sin \psi_2 \tag{3.17}$$
$$\bar{p}_{32} = r_3 \cos \psi_3 \qquad 0 \leq \psi_3 \leq 2\pi \quad r_3 > 0; \tag{3.18}$$
$$\bar{p}_{33} = r_3 \sin \psi_3 \tag{3.19}$$

where r_2, r_3 are the lengths of vectors $\overrightarrow{OP_2}$ and $\overrightarrow{OP_3}$, respectively; ψ_2 is the angle between OX_2' and $\overrightarrow{OP_2}$; ψ_3 is the angle between OX_2' and $\overrightarrow{OP_3}$.

Upon making the substitutions (3.16)–(3.19) in the transformation (3.7)–(3.15) we evaluate the Jacobian

$$J = \frac{\delta(p_{11}, \cdots, p_{33})}{\delta(v_1 \cdots, v_3; \theta, \phi, r_2, r_3; \psi_2, \psi_3)} = r_2^3 r_3^3 \sin\theta \sin^2(\psi_3 - \psi_2). \tag{3.20}$$

Finally it is convenient to replace $|\psi_3 - \psi_2|$ by ω_2, where[2] $0 \leq \omega_2 \leq \pi$, and ψ_3 by ω_3 so that

$$J = r_2^3 r_3^3 \sin\theta \sin^2 \omega_2. \tag{3.21}$$

We note that $J \geq 0$.

4. THE EXACT MARGINAL FREQUENCY FUNCTION $h_2(v_2)$ IN THE SECOND LEADING CASE: $K_2 = G = 3$

We shall derive the joint frequency function of the GCL-LVD estimates v_2, v_3 of β_{12} and β_{13}, respectively, for the case in which

$$\beta_{12} = \beta_{13} = 0 \tag{4.1}$$
$$\Pi_{ij} = 0 \qquad i = 1, 2, 3; \quad j = 1, 2, 3; \quad \text{not both } i = 3, \quad j = 3; \tag{4.2}$$

i.e., $\Pi_{33} \neq 0$. In this case the transformation described in Section 3 carries

$$f(p_{11}, \cdots, p_{33})dp_{11} \cdots dp_{33}$$
$$= \left(\frac{1}{2\pi}\right)^{9/2} \exp\left\{-\tfrac{1}{2}[(p_{11} - \Pi_{11})^2 + \cdots + (p_{33} - \Pi_{33})^2]\right\} dp_{11} \cdots dp_{33} \tag{4.3}$$

---

[2] In order to avoid integrating twice over the same region, ω_2 is defined as the positive angle between OP_2 and OP_3, i.e., measured counter clockwise from the smaller of ψ_2, ψ_3.

into the probability density function

$$g_1(v_1, v_2, v_3, r_2, r_3, \omega_2, \omega_3, \theta, \phi)dv_1 \cdots d\phi$$

$$= \exp \frac{\left(\dfrac{-\Pi_{33}^2}{2}\right)}{(2\pi)^{9/2}} \exp\left\{-\tfrac{1}{2}[v_1^2 + (1 + v_2^2)r_2^2 + (1 + v_3^2)r_3^2]\right.$$

$$\times \exp\left\{-Z_1 \cos \omega_2 - Z_2 \sin\theta \sin\omega_3\right\} \times r_2^3 r_3^3 \sin^2 \omega_2 \sin\theta \, dv_1 \cdots d\phi, \quad (4.4)$$

where

$$Z_1 = v_2 v_3 r_2 r_3 \quad (4.5)$$

$$Z_2 = r_3 \Pi_{33}. \quad (4.6)$$

To find the joint frequency function of the coefficient estimators v_2, v_3 we have to integrate the expression (4.4) with respect to $d\phi$, $d\omega_3$, $d\theta$, $d\omega_2$, dr_2, dr_3, dv_1. In the present case, with $\beta_{12}=\beta_{13}=0$, it is convenient to begin by integrating with respect to dv_1, $d\phi$. Thus our first step is

$$\int_0^{2\pi}\int_{-\infty}^{\infty} g_1 dv_1 d\phi = \exp \frac{(-\frac{1}{2}\Pi_{33}^2)}{(2\pi)^{1/2}} \exp\left\{\tfrac{1}{2}[(1 + v_2^2)r_2^2 + (1 + v_3^2)r_3]\right\} r_2^3 r_3^3$$

$$\times \frac{1}{2\pi} \exp\left\{-Z_1 \cos\omega_2\right\} \sin^2 \omega_2$$

$$\times \frac{1}{(2\pi)^{3/2}} \exp\left\{-Z_2 \sin\theta \sin\omega_3\right\} \sin\theta. \quad (4.7)$$

We employ Poisson's integral, [6, p. 25, see 337.15b, p. 145]:

$$\frac{1}{2\pi}\int_0^{\pi} \exp\{-Z_1 \cos\omega_2\} \sin^2 \omega_2 d\omega_2 = \frac{I_1(v_2 v_3 r_2 r_3)}{2(v_2 v_3 r_2 r_3)}; \quad (4.8)$$

and an adaptation of *Gegenbauer's* double integral, [10, p. 51]:

$$\frac{1}{(2\pi)^{3/2}}\int_0^{2\pi}\int_0^{\pi} \exp\{-Z_2 \sin\theta \sin\omega_3\} \sin\theta d\theta \, d\omega_3 = \frac{I_{1/2}(\Pi_{33} r_3)}{(\Pi_{33} r_3)^{1/2}}, \quad (4.9)$$

where $I_\nu(Z)$ denotes the modified *Bessel function* of the first kind of order ν. Upon integrating the expression (4.7) with respect to $d\omega_3 d\theta d\omega_2$ we obtain

$$g_2(v_2, v_3, r_2, r_3) = \frac{\exp(-\frac{1}{2}\Pi_{33}^2)}{2(2\pi)^{1/2}} \exp\left\{-\tfrac{1}{2}[(1 + v_2^2)r_2^2 + (1 + v_3^2)r_3^2]\right\}$$

$$\times \frac{r_2^2 r_3^2}{v_2 v_3} \frac{I_1(v_2 v_3 r_2 r_3) I_{1/2}(\Pi_{33} r_3)}{(\Pi_{33} r_3)^{1/2}}. \quad (4.10)$$

For removing r_2 and r_3 from the expression (4.10) repeated integration in the order dr_2, dr_3 is clearly indicated. By means of the *Weber-Hankel* exponential integral, [10, p. 394] we integrate the expression (4.10) with respect to dr_2 and obtain

$$g_3(v_2, v_3, r_3) = \frac{\exp(-\frac{1}{2}\Pi_{33}^2)}{2(2\pi)^{1/2}(1+v_2^2)^2} \exp\left\{-\frac{1}{2}\left[\frac{(1+v_2^2+v_3^2)r_3^2}{1+v_2^2}\right]\right.$$

$$\times \frac{r_3^{5/2}}{(\Pi_{33})^{1/2}} I_{1/2}(\Pi_{33}r_3). \tag{4.11}$$

Using the *Weber-Hankel* exponential integral once more, [10, p. 393], we integrate the expression (4.11) with respect to dr_3 and thus obtain the joint frequency function of the GCL-LVD coefficient estimators v_2, v_3:

$$g(v_2, v_3) = \frac{\exp(-\frac{1}{2}\Pi_{33}^2)}{\pi(1+v_2^2+v_3^2)^2}\, {}_1F_1\left\{2; 3/2; \frac{\Pi_{33}^2(1+v_2^2)}{2(1+v_2^2+v_3^2)}\right\}, \quad \begin{array}{c} -\infty < v_2 < \infty \\ -\infty < v_3 < \infty \end{array} \tag{4.12}$$

where ${}_1F_1(\alpha; \rho; Z)$ denotes the confluent hypergeometric function, [7, p. 2].[3]

Finally, integrating the expression (4.12) with respect to v_3 we obtain the marginal frequency function of v_2:

$$h_2(v_2) = \frac{1}{2(1+v_2^2)^{3/2}}, \qquad -\infty < v_2 < \infty. \tag{4.13}$$

To find the marginal frequency function of v_3 we integrate the expression (4.12) with respect to v_2. It is convenient first to replace v_2 in the expression (4.12) by

$$\sqrt{Z}\tan\omega, \qquad \frac{-\pi}{2} < \omega < \frac{\pi}{2}, \qquad Z = (1+v_3^2)$$

and interchange the order of integration and summation. Under this transformation we have

$$\begin{aligned} \frac{(1+v_2^2)^m dv_2}{(1+v_2+v_3^2)^{m+2}} &= \frac{1}{Z^{m+3/2}} \frac{(1+Z\tan^2\omega)^m d\omega}{(\sec^2\omega)^{m+1}} \\ &= \frac{1}{Z^{3/2}} \sum_{n=0}^{m} \binom{m}{n} \frac{1}{Z^n} (\sin^2\omega)^{m-n}(\cos^2\omega)^{n+1} d\omega. \end{aligned} \tag{4.14}$$

Upon expanding the confluent hypergeometric function in expression (4.12)

[3] It should be noted that the confluent hypergeometric function is absolutely convergent. Moreover, if we regard the right-hand member of expression (4.12) as an infinite series of functions (say) (1) $\phi_n(v_2)$, v_3 fixed, and alternatively, (2) $\bar{\phi}_n(v_3)$, v_2 fixed, then the series is readily seen to be uniformly convergent in the interval $(-\infty, \infty)$ by Weierstrass' M-test, [5, p. 124]. Moreover, $\phi_n(v_2)$ and $\bar{\phi}_n(v_3)$ are continuous in $(-\infty, \infty)$. Consequently, the term-by-term integration of infinite series as employed subsequently in this note is permissible, [5, p. 130]. The same remarks apply to the integration of expression (4.18) below.

and substituting the finite series (4.14) we obtain

$$g(v_2, v_3)\, dv_2 = \frac{\exp(-\tfrac{1}{2}\Pi_{33}^2)\cdot\Gamma(3/2)}{\pi Z^{3/2}} \times \sum_{m=0}^{\infty} \frac{(m+1)!}{\Gamma(m+3/2)m!}\left(\frac{\Pi_{33}^2}{2}\right)^m \left\{\sum_{n=0}^{m}\binom{m}{n}\frac{(\sin^2\omega)^{m-n}(\cos^2\omega)^{n+1}\,d\omega}{Z^n}\right\}. \tag{4.15}$$

Upon integrating the expression (4.15) with respect to $d\omega$ and rearranging the resulting double series we obtain

$$\begin{aligned} h_3(v_3) &= \frac{\exp(-\tfrac{1}{2}\Pi_{33}^2)\Gamma(3/2)}{\pi Z^{3/2}} \times \sum_{n=0}^{\infty}\frac{\Gamma(n+3/2)}{n!}\left(\frac{\Pi_{33}^2}{2Z}\right)^n \\ &\quad \times \sum_{s=0}^{\infty}\frac{\Gamma(s+1/2)}{\Gamma(n+s+3/2)s!}\left(\frac{\Pi_{33}^2}{2}\right)^s \\ &= \frac{\exp(-\tfrac{1}{2}\Pi_{33}^2)}{2(1+v_3^2)^{3/2}}\cdot\sum_{n=0}^{\infty}\frac{A_n}{n!}\left(\frac{\Pi_{33}^2}{2(1+v_3^2)}\right)^n \end{aligned} \tag{4.16}$$

where

$$\begin{aligned} A_n &= \frac{1}{n!}\,{}_1F_1\left\{\frac{1}{2}, n+3/2; \frac{\Pi_{33}^2}{2}\right\}, \\ &= \frac{1}{n!}\exp(\tfrac{1}{2}\Pi_{33}^2)\,{}_1F_1\left\{n+1; n+3/2; \frac{-\Pi_{33}^2}{2}\right\} \end{aligned} \tag{4.17}$$

by *Kummer's* relation, [7, p. 6]. Consequently the marginal frequency function of the coefficient estimator v_3 is

$$h_3(v_3) = \frac{1}{2(1+v_3^2)^{3/2}}\sum_{n=0}^{\infty}\frac{B_n}{n!}\left\{\frac{\Pi_{33}^2}{2(1+v_3^2)}\right\}^n \tag{4.18}$$

where B_n is the confluent hypergeometric function

$${}_1F_1\left\{n+1; n+3/2; \frac{-\Pi_{33}^2}{2}\right\}.$$

It is not transparent that the expression (4.18) satisfies the essential requirement

$$\int_{-\infty}^{+\infty} h_3(v_3)dv_3 = 1. \tag{4.19}$$

Upon integrating the series (4.18) term-by-term[4] we obtain the double series

$$\int_{-\infty}^{+\infty} h_3(v_3)dv_3 = \frac{1}{2}\sum_{n=0}^{\infty}\sum_{s=0}^{\infty} a_{n,s} \tag{4.20}$$

[4] See footnote 3. Note also that the rows and columns of the double series (4.20) are absolutely convergent; hence that the double series has a definite limit.

where

$$a_{n,s} = \frac{(-)^s(n+s)!\Gamma(\frac{1}{2})}{\Gamma(n+s+3/2)n!s!}\left(\frac{\Pi_{33}^2}{2}\right)^{n+s} \tag{4.21}$$

Summing series (4.20) by diagonals we find that

$$\sum_{n=0}^{\infty}\sum_{s=0}^{\infty} a_{n,s} = 2, \tag{4.22}$$

thus verifying the requirement (4.19).

We note that the frequency function $h_2(v_2)$, (4.13), is identical in form to the frequency function obtained in the corresponding case for $K_2=G=2$, [cf. 3, pp. 630–1]. Moreover, the frequency function (4.13) is clearly a special case of the form (4.18).

5. CONCLUSION

The modest leading results presented in this note serve well to strengthen the conjecture that the *exact* finite sample frequency functions of the GCL-LVD estimators in systems of any number of equations will continue to exhibit the same general form as found in the corresponding two-equation cases reported in the earlier note, [3]. Of course, these leading results are not to be considered definitive in that connection. Possibly the chief merit in making them known at this time is that they strongly support the view that the mathematical problem of working out the *exact* finite sample distributions of alternative simultaneous equations estimators [9] is not intractable.

APPENDIX[5]

The following considerations are put forward to clarify the remark that the assumptions (2.9), (2.10), and (2.11) have no consequence for the general form of GCL distribution functions:

1. The assumption (2.10) probably needs no comment.
2. We can regard the variables x_{tk}, $k=1, 2, \cdots, K$, $t=1, 2, \cdots, N$ and the coefficients γ_{hk} in the matrix Γ as having been arrived at by an orthogonal transformation of original variables x_{tk}^* and of γ_{hk}^* conformably such that
   (i) if $\gamma_{ij}^*=0$, then $\gamma_{ij}=0$ and, generally, if $\gamma_{ik}^*\neq 0$ then $\gamma_{ik}\neq 0$.
   (ii) the estimators v_2, v_3 of coefficients of endogenous variables y_{t2} and y_{t3} in equation (2.1) are invariant against the orthogonalization, hence their frequency functions remain invariant against this transformation.

---

[5] The Appendix has been added in response to a suggestion made by one of the referees, a good suggestion I believe, because the generality of form I have referred to in the text is not likely to be readily transparent. The paper could have been written without putting the variables and frequency functions into "standardized" form as I have preferred to do, but then the derivations would have been intolerably long for the reader. My own approach has been to carry derivations through in "standardized" form and then return to the derivations of more general forms with the previous results to guide me.

The original coefficients γ_{hk}^* are constants but the new coefficients γ_{hk} depend on the sample of exogenous variables. The *conditional frequency functions* of $v_4, \cdots, v_k$, given v_2, v_3, do not remain invariant against the orthogonalization. The marginal frequency functions of $v_4^*, \cdots, v_k^*$—the estimators of the original $\gamma_{14}^*, \cdots, \gamma_{1k}^*$—have to be recovered.]

3. The assumption (2.9) does not result in loss of generality for it is equivalent to the replacement of the matrix B^* in an original system of equations

$$B^{*\prime} y_{t.}^{*\prime} + \Gamma^{*\prime} x_{t.}^{*\prime} + \zeta_{t.}^{*\prime} = 0$$

by the matrix $(B^{*1}O_1\Lambda_1)$ and the vector $y_t^{*\prime}$. by $(\Lambda_1 O_1)^{-1}y_t^{*\prime}$. where $O_1'O_1 = I_3$, $\Lambda_1 = \Lambda_1$ is diagonal and $O_1^* \sum O_1 = \Lambda_1^2$. In particular the hypothetical exclusions of exogenous variables are not affected by this transformation.

It is worthwhile to illustrate this point in a little more detail by a sketch of the derivation of the marginal frequency functions of v_2 and v_3 when the assumption (2.9) is relaxed. To keep the sketch tolerably brief we shall assume that $\Pi_{33} = 0$, this assumption being made in addition to the assumptions (4.1) and (4.2).[6] Let σ_{ij}, $i, j = 1, 2, 3$ denote the (i, j)th element of the inverse variance covariance matrix $\sum^{-1}$.

$$\begin{aligned} g_1(v_1, v_2, v_3, r_2, r_3, \omega_2, \omega_3, \theta, \phi)dv_1 \cdots d\phi \\ = \left(\frac{1}{2\pi}\right)^{9/2} |\sigma^{ij}|^{3/2} \exp\{-\tfrac{1}{2}\sigma^{11}v_1^2\} \\ \cdot \exp\{-\tfrac{1}{2}(\sigma^{22} + 2\sigma^{12}v_2 + \sigma^{11}v_2^2)r_2^2\} \qquad \text{(A—4.4)} \\ \cdot \exp\{-\tfrac{1}{2}(\sigma^{33} + 2\sigma^{13}v_3 + \sigma^{11}v_3^2)r_3^2\} \\ \cdot \exp\{-Z_1 \cos \omega_2\} r_2^3 r_3^3 \sin^2 \omega_2 \sin \theta \, dv_1 \cdots d\phi, \end{aligned}$$

where

$$Z_1 = (\sigma^{23} + \sigma^{13}v_2 + \sigma^{12}v_3 + \sigma^{11}v_2v_3)r_2r_3. \qquad \text{(A—4.5)}$$

[Note that the numbering of formulas repeats that of the text.]

Upon integrating the function (A—4.4) with respect to dv_1, $d\theta$, $d\phi$, $d\omega_3$, $d\omega_2$, dr_2, dr_3 we obtain the joint frequency function

$$\begin{aligned} g(v_2, v_3) = \frac{|\sigma_{ij}|^{1/2}}{\pi\sqrt{\sigma^{11}}(\sigma_{11} - 2\sigma_{12}v_2 + \sigma_{22}v_2^2 - 2\sigma_{13}v_3 + 2\sigma_{23}v_2v_3 + \sigma_{33}v_3^2)^2} \\ -\infty < v_2 < \infty, \qquad \text{(A—4.12)} \\ -\infty < v_3 < \infty, \end{aligned}$$

Upon integrating (A—4.12) with respect to dv_3 we obtain the marginal frequency function of v_2:

$$h_2(v_2) = \frac{|\sigma^{ij}|\,\sigma_{33}}{2\sqrt{\sigma^{11}}(\sigma^{22} + 2\sigma^{12}v_2 + \sigma^{11}v_2)^{3/2}} \qquad -\infty < v_2 < \infty; \quad \text{(A—4.13)}$$

---

[6] Without this assumption the derivation is extremely long and difficult. My results for the case $\pi_{33} \neq 0$ and $\sigma_{ij} \neq 0$, $i \neq j$ and $\sigma_{ii} \neq 1$, have not been checked thoroughly enough to warrant their publication.

and upon integrating (A—4.12) with respect to dv_2 we obtain the marginal frequency function of v_3:

$$h_3(v_3) = \frac{|\sigma^{ij}|\,\sigma_{22}}{2\sqrt{\sigma^{11}}(\sigma^{33} + 2\sigma^{13}v_3 + \sigma^{33}v_3)^{3/2}} \qquad -\infty < v_3 < \infty. \quad \text{(A—4.18)}$$

We note that the frequency functions (A—4.13) and (4.13) are of the same general form; also that the frequency functions (A—4.18) and (4.18) are the same general form, account being taken of the assumption that $\Pi_{33} = 0$.

It is worthwhile noting that the frequency functions (4.13) and (4.18) are unbiased, their means being zero whereas the frequency functions (A—4.13) and (A—4.18) have biases equal to $-\sigma^{12}/\sigma^{11}$ and $-\sigma^{13}/\sigma^{11}$, respectively.[7]

REFERENCES

[1] Basmann, R. L., "On the asymptotic distribution of generalized linear estimators," *Econometrica*, 28, (1960), 97–107.

[2] ———, "On finite sample distributions of GCL identifiability test statistics," *Journal of the American Statistical Association*, 55 (1960), 650–9.

[3] ———, "A note on the exact finite sample frequency functions of generalized classical linear estimators in two leading overidentified cases," *Journal of the American Statistical Association*, 56 (1961), 619–36.

[4] Basmann, R. L., and Mosbaek, E. J., "An experimental investigation of finite sample distribution functions of LVD, LVR and OLS coefficient estimators," 1961 (unpublished manuscript).

[5] Bromwich, T. J. I'a., *An Introduction to the Theory of Infinite Series*, Second Edition. London: Macmillan, 1959.

[6] Gröbner, W., and Hofreiter, N., *Integraltafel*, 2te Teil. Vienna: Springer, 1958.

[7] Slater, L. J., *Confluent Hypergeometric Functions*. Cambridge: University Press, 1960.

[8] Sommerville, D. M. Y., *Analytical Geometry of Three Dimensions*. Cambridge: University Press, 1959.

[9] Theil, H., *Economic Forecasts and Policy*. Amsterdam: North-Holland Publishing Company, 1958.

[10] Watson, G. N., *A Treatise on the Theory of Bessel Functions*, Second Edition. Cambridge: University Press, 1952.

---

[7] The means of GCL distributions turn out to be "nuisance parameters." This is no paradox and is not really surprising when the logical structure of simultaneous equations models is considered in detail. The exact distributions of GCL estimators can be used for hypothesis testing in practice but it must be kept in mind that the *set of* hypotheses linked up in a simultaneous equations model is a rather complicated affair in comparison with the kind of hypothesis to which the normal distribution or Student's *t* are usually applied.

THE BIAS AND MOMENT MATRIX OF THE GENERAL k-CLASS ESTIMATORS OF THE PARAMETERS IN SIMULTANEOUS EQUATIONS[1]

BY A. L. NAGAR

In this article we study the small sample properties of the so called general k-class estimators of simultaneous equations. Two members of the family of k-class estimators are found, one of which is unbiased to the degree of our approximation and the other possesses a minimum second moment around the true parameter value, again to the order of our approximation.

1. INTRODUCTION

LITTLE IS KNOWN about the small-sample properties of simultaneous-equations estimators; as far as the author is aware, the only results in this field are those of the multidimensional confidence regions obtained by Anderson and Rubin [**1**] and by Theil [**6**] for the coefficients of a structural equation. The object of this note is to analyse the bias (to the order of T^{-1}, T being the number of observations) and the moment matrix (to the order of T^{-2}) of the general k-class estimators of the coefficients of a single (just- or over-identified) equation which is part of a system of simultaneous equations. Section 2 of the present article gives the two resulting theorems on bias and moment matrix, and also the necessary assumptions involved. As a corollary to the theorem on bias we obtain the bias of the Two-Stage Least-Squares estimator and also an unbiased estimator, to the order of T^{-1}. Further, the two corollaries of the theorem on the moment matrix give the moment matrix of the two-stage least-squares estimator and the "best" value of k, in a certain sense. The proofs of Theorems I and II are presented in Section 3; and Section 4 gives an example illustrating the selection of the best k value.

2. GENERAL ASSUMPTIONS, THEOREMS I AND II

Let the equation to be estimated be written as

$$y = Y\gamma + X_1\beta + u, \tag{2.1}$$

where y is the column vector of T observations on the jointly dependent variable "to be explained," Y is a $T \times m$ matrix of values taken by the m

[1] I am indebted to Professor H. Theil for the suggestion of the problem and for valuable discussions from time to time.

This study was done under the tenure of a scholarship from the Hoogeschool-Fonds 1920 in cooperation with the Netherlands Universities Foundation for International Co-operation while the author was a member of the Econometric Institute, Netherlands School of Economics.

explanatory jointly dependent variables, X_1 is a $T \times l$ matrix of values taken by the l explanatory predetermined variables, u is the disturbance vector, and γ and β are unknown parameter vectors. We write X_2 for a $T \times (\Lambda - l)$ matrix of observations on $\Lambda - l$ predetermined variables which do not occur in (2.1), and X for the matrix of values taken by all Λ predetermined variables; thus

$$X = [X_1 \quad X_2]. \tag{2.2}$$

The reduced form corresponding to the explanatory jointly dependent variables of (2.1) can be written as

$$Y = X\Pi + \bar{V} = X_1\Pi_1 + X_2\Pi_2 + \bar{V} = \bar{Y}_1 + \bar{Y}_2 + \bar{V} = \bar{Y} + \bar{V}, \tag{2.3}$$

where $\Pi = [\Pi_1 \quad \Pi_2]'$, Π_1 and Π_2 being the matrices of parent reduced form coefficients, $\bar{V}$ the matrix of parent reduced form disturbances, and $\bar{Y}_1 = X_1\Pi_1$, $\bar{Y}_2 = X_2\Pi_2$, $\bar{Y} = \bar{Y}_1 + \bar{Y}_2 = X\Pi$.

It would have been a simple matter to estimate the parameters of equation (2.1) if all the explanatory variables were nonstochastic, because in that case we could apply the classical least squares method. However, as it appears from the usual assumptions, given below, the explanatory jointly dependent variables Y are stochastic and explanatory predetermined variables X_1 are nonstochastic.[2] In this case classical least squares does not lead to consistent estimates.

On the other hand, if we consider the reduced form (2.3) we find that the right-hand variables (except for the disturbances) are all nonstochastic and, therefore, classical least squares can validly be applied. Further, it is observed from (2.3) that although Y is stochastic, $Y - \bar{V} = X\Pi$ is nonstochastic. Hence, if we write the equation (2.1) as

$$y = (Y - \bar{V})\gamma + X_1\beta + (u + \bar{V}\gamma), \tag{2.1$'$}$$

we can apply classical least squares to obtain the estimates of the coefficients.

However, $\bar{V}$ is not known; but it can be estimated by classical least squares as follows:

$$V = Y - X(X'X)^{-1}X'Y. \tag{2.4}$$

Now, the first stage of two-stage least-squares consists in estimating parent reduced form disturbances by applying classical least squares to (2.3), thus obtaining V. In the second stage we apply classical least squares to (2.1) after Y has been replaced by $Y - V$.

[2] It should be noted that this assumption of X_1 being nonstochastic does not permit the presence of lagged endogenous variables (which are stochastic) in the group of predetermined variables. For asymptotic samples, however, the consistency of estimates obtained by applying any of the well-known estimation procedures is not affected by such variables.

Two-stage least-squares estimates are, therefore, given by

$$\begin{bmatrix} (Y-V)' \\ X_1' \end{bmatrix} y = \begin{bmatrix} Y'Y - V'V & Y'X_1 \\ X_1'Y & X_1'X_1 \end{bmatrix} \begin{pmatrix} c \\ b \end{pmatrix}.$$

The k-class estimation procedure, as proposed by Theil [**5**], is a generalisation of two-stage least squares and is

$$\begin{bmatrix} (Y-kV)' \\ X_1' \end{bmatrix} y = \begin{bmatrix} Y'Y - kV'V & Y'X_1 \\ X_1'Y & X_1'X_1 \end{bmatrix} \begin{pmatrix} c \\ b \end{pmatrix}_k, \tag{2.5}$$

where k is an arbitrary scalar, stochastic or nonstochastic. For $k = 1$, we get two-stage least squares.

The following assumptions are made:

ASSUMPTION I. *Equation* (2.1) *is one of a complete system of* M ($\geqslant m + 1$) *linear stochastic equations in* M *jointly dependent variables and* Λ *predetermined variables. The reduced form of this system exists.*

ASSUMPTION II. *The matrix* Π_2, *which is of order* $(\Lambda - l) \times m$, *has rank* m.[3]

ASSUMPTION III. *The matrix* X, *which is of order* $T \times \Lambda$ *has rank* Λ *and consists of nonstochastic elements. Also the "k" of* (2.5) *is nonstochastic.*

As to the T vectors of M disturbances corresponding to each of the M structural equations, we assume:

ASSUMPTION IV.[4] *The* T *disturbance vectors are independent random drawings from the same* M*-dimensional normal parent with zero means.*

We can then write

$$\bar{V} = u\pi' + W, \tag{2.6}$$

which describes the (normally distributed) reduced form disturbances as consisting of a part which is proportional to the corresponding disturbance of (2.1) (viz., $u\pi'$, π being a column vector of m components) and a part (viz., W) which is also normally distributed but independently of the u vector. Consider then the vector of covariances of the disturbances of (2.1) and the right-hand variables of that equation:

[3] Note that $\Lambda \geqslant m + l$ is the order condition of identifiability, and that the rank condition implies that the rank of Π_2 should be m. The latter statement can easily be derived from the equation (4.22), p. 138, of T. C. Koopmans and W. C. Hood [**4**].

[4] Cf. footnote 8.

$$q = \begin{bmatrix} \text{cov}\,(y_1\,,\,u) \\ \vdots \\ \text{cov}\,(y_m,\,u) \\ \text{cov}\,(x_1\,,\,u) \\ \vdots \\ \text{cov}\,(x_l\,,\,u) \end{bmatrix} = \frac{1}{T}\begin{bmatrix} E(\bar{V}'u) \\ 0 \end{bmatrix} = \sigma^2 \begin{bmatrix} \pi \\ 0 \end{bmatrix}, \tag{2.7}$$

σ^2 being the variance of the disturbances of (2.1).

Further, we write

$$Q = \begin{bmatrix} \bar{Y}'\bar{Y} & \bar{Y}'X_1 \\ X_1'\bar{Y} & X_1'X_1 \end{bmatrix}^{-1} = \begin{bmatrix} \omega_{11} & \omega_{12} \\ \omega_{21} & \omega_{22} \end{bmatrix}, \tag{2.8}$$

where it can easily be verified that

$$\omega_{11} = (\bar{Y}'M_1\bar{Y})^{-1}, \qquad \omega_{12} = \omega_{21}', \tag{2.9}$$

$$\omega_{21} = -(X_1'X_1)^{-1}X_1'\bar{Y}(\bar{Y}'M_1\bar{Y})^{-1},$$

where

$$M_1 = I - X_1(X_1'X_1)^{-1}X_1'.$$

Finally, we consider an arbitrary member of the k-class, subject to the restrictions that k is nonstochastic (cf. Assumption III) and that $1 - k$ is of the order of T^{-1}.[5] Thus we can write k as:

$$k = 1 + \frac{\varkappa}{T}, \tag{2.10}$$

neglecting the terms of higher powers of T^{-1} (because they are irrelevant for our purpose); $\varkappa$ is a real number independent of T.

THEOREM 1. *Under the Assumptions I, II, III and IV, the bias (to the order of T^{-1}) of the estimator $\binom{c}{b}_k$ [defined in (2.5)] of the parameter vector $\binom{\gamma}{\beta}$ of (2.1) is given by:*

$$E(e_k) = [-\varkappa + L - 1]Qq, \tag{2.11}$$

where e_k is the sampling error:

$$e_k = \binom{c}{b}_k - \binom{\gamma}{\beta}, \tag{2.12}$$

and L is the number of predetermined variables in excess of the number of coefficients to be estimated, i.e.,

$$L = \Lambda - (m + l). \tag{2.13}$$

[5] The second restriction implies that the estimators to be considered are asymptotically unbiased and have the same asymptotic covariance matrix as two-stage least-squares estimators.

COROLLARY 1. *The bias of the two-stage least-squares estimator, to the order of T^{-1}, is*

$$E(e_1) = (L - 1)Qq. \tag{2.14}$$

COROLLARY 2. *The bias vanishes for*

$$k = 1 + \frac{L-1}{T}, \tag{2.15}$$

which provides, to the order of T^{-1}, an unbiased estimator of $\binom{\gamma}{\beta}$.

Using (2.6), we can write for the moment matrix of $\bar{V}$:

$$\frac{1}{T} E(\bar{V}'\bar{V}) = \sigma^2 \pi\pi' + \frac{1}{T} E(W'W), \tag{2.16}$$

and bordering these matrices with l rows and l columns of zeros, we obtain three square matrices of order $m + l$:

$$C = \begin{bmatrix} C^* & 0 \\ 0 & 0 \end{bmatrix}; \quad C_1 = \begin{bmatrix} C_1^* & 0 \\ 0 & 0 \end{bmatrix} = \frac{1}{\sigma^2} qq'; \quad C_2 = \begin{bmatrix} C_2^* & 0 \\ 0 & 0 \end{bmatrix}; \tag{2.17}$$

where, of course,

$$C = C_1 + C_2; \quad \text{and } C^* = \frac{1}{T} E(\bar{V}'\bar{V}), \; C_1^* = \sigma^2 \pi\pi', \; C_2^* = \frac{1}{T} E(W'W). \tag{2.18}$$

THEOREM 2. *Under the assumptions of Theorem 1, the moment matrix, to the order of T^{-2}, of the estimator $\binom{c}{b}_k$ around the parameter vector $\binom{\gamma}{\beta}$ is given by:*

$$E(e_k e_k') = \sigma^2 Q(I + A^*), \tag{2.19}$$

where A^* is a matrix of order T^{-1}:

$$\begin{aligned} A^* = {} & [(2\varkappa - 2L + 3) \operatorname{tr}(C_1Q) + \operatorname{tr}(C_2Q)] \cdot I \\ & + \{(\varkappa - L + 2)^2 + 2(\varkappa + 1)\} C_1Q + (2\varkappa - L + 2)C_2Q, \end{aligned} \tag{2.20}$$

and σ^2 is the variance of the disturbances of (2.1).

COROLLARY 1. *The moment matrix, to the order of T^{-2}, of the two-stage least-squares estimator, around the parameter vector $\binom{\gamma}{\beta}$, is given by* (2.19) *where*

$$\begin{aligned} A^* = {} & [-(2L - 3) \operatorname{tr}(C_1Q) + \operatorname{tr}(C_2Q)] \cdot I \\ & + \{(L-2)^2 + 2\} C_1Q - (L-2)C_2Q. \end{aligned} \tag{2.21}$$

For the choice of the "best" k we consider the criterion of the minimum determinant value of the moment matrix,[6] i.e., we minimise

[6] This determinant might be called the "generalised second moment" by analogy with the generalised variance (the determinant of a covariance matrix).

$$(2.22)\qquad |E(e_k e_k')| = \sigma^2|Q| \cdot |I + A^*| = \sigma^2|Q| \cdot (1 + \text{tr } A^*),$$

to the order of T^{-2}, for variations in k or $\varkappa$.

COROLLARY 2. *The $\varkappa$-value which minimises the determinant value of the moment matrix* (2.19) *is*

$$(2.23)\qquad \varkappa = \Lambda - 2(m + l) - 3 - \frac{\text{tr }(C_2Q)}{\text{tr }(C_1Q)}.$$

3. PROOF OF THEOREMS[7]

3.1. *Preliminary*

We start by presenting the symbols which will be used repeatedly in what follows.

Let us write

$$(3.1.1)\qquad M^* = X(X'X)^{-1}X',$$

$$(3.1.2)\qquad N = -\frac{1}{T} \cdot \varkappa I + M^*,$$

$$(3.1.3)\qquad Z = [\bar{Y} \quad X_1],$$

and

$$(3.1.4)\qquad V_z = [\bar{V} \quad 0],$$

where the zero matrix is of order $T \times l$. It is easily verified that

$$(3.1.5)\qquad Q = (Z'Z)^{-1} \qquad \text{[cf. (2.8)]}.$$

Further, we write

$$(3.1.6)\qquad A = \omega_{11}\bar{Y}' + \omega_{12}X_1',$$

$$(3.1.7)\qquad B = ZQZ'.$$

The following lemmas can then be proved.

LEMMA 1. *If $m^*_{tt'}$ and $n_{tt'}$ are the elements in the t-th row and t'-th column of the matrices M^* and N respectively, then*

$$(3.1.8)\qquad \text{tr } M^* = \sum_t m^*_{tt} = \text{tr }(X'X)^{-1}X'X = \Lambda;$$

$$(3.1.9)\qquad \text{tr } M^{*2} = \sum_t \sum_{t'} m^*_{tt'}m^*_{t't} = \sum_t \sum_{t'} m^{*2}_{tt'} = \text{tr } M^* = \Lambda,$$

because $M^{*2} = M^*$; and hence

$$(3.1.10)\qquad \text{tr } N = \sum_t n_{tt} = \Lambda - \varkappa;$$

[7] In this section, and also in the Appendix, it is always implied that the summation over t, with whatever accent, extends from 1 to T, and that over μ, with any accent, extends from 1 to m.

(3.1.11) $$\text{tr } N^2 = \sum_t \sum_{t'} n_{tt'} n'_{t't} = \sum_t \sum_{t'} n^2_{tt'} = \Lambda - \frac{1}{T} \cdot \varkappa (2\Lambda - \varkappa).$$

LEMMA 2. *If $b_{tt'}$ is the element in the t-th row and t'-th column of the matrix B, defined in* (3.1.7), *then*

(3.1.12) $$\text{tr } M^*B = \sum_t \sum_{t'} m^*_{tt'} b_{t't} = \sum_t \sum_{t'} m^*_{tt'} b_{tt'} = \text{tr } M^*ZQZ'$$
$$= \text{tr } B = \text{tr } ZQZ' = \text{tr } QZ'Z = m + l,$$

because

(3.1.13) $$M^*ZQZ' = X(X'X)^{-1}X'[\bar{Y}\ \ X_1]QZ' = X(X'X)^{-1}X'\left[X\Pi\ \ X\begin{pmatrix} I \\ \hdashline 0 \end{pmatrix}\right]QZ',$$

where the unit matrix I on the right-hand side is of order l, the 0 *matrix is* $(\Lambda - l) \times l$, *and use has been made of* (2.3). *Thus*

(3.1.14) $$M^*ZQZ' = X\left[\Pi\ \ \begin{matrix} I \\ \hdashline 0 \end{matrix}\right]QZ' = [\bar{Y}\ \ X_1]QZ' = ZQZ'.$$

Using (3.1.2) and (3.1.12) it follows that

(3.1.15) $$\text{tr } NB = \sum_t \sum_{t'} n_{tt'} b_{tt'} = \left(1 - \frac{\varkappa}{T}\right)(m + l).$$

LEMMA 3. *Using* (2.8) *it can be verified that*

(3.1.16) $$V_z QZ' = \bar{V}A, \qquad \text{[cf. (3.1.6)]}$$

and further using (2.9) *we have*

(3.1.17) $$A = (\bar{Y}'M_1\bar{Y})^{-1}\bar{Y}'M_1.$$

LEMMA 4. *Writing* $\bar{Y} = X\Pi$, *we find that*

(3.1.18) $$\bar{Y}'M^*M_1\bar{Y} = \bar{Y}'M_1\bar{Y};\ \bar{Y}'NM_1\bar{Y} = \left(1 - \frac{\varkappa}{T}\right)\bar{Y}'M_1\bar{Y},$$

and further, writing $X_1 = X\begin{pmatrix} I \\ \hdashline 0 \end{pmatrix}$, *we have*

(3.1.19) $$X_1'M^*M_1\bar{Y} = X_1'M_1\bar{Y} = 0;\ X_1'NM_1\bar{Y} = \left(1 - \frac{\varkappa}{T}\right)X_1'M_1\bar{Y} = 0,$$

where I and 0 *are the same as used in* (3.1.13) *and* M_1 *has been defined in* (2.9).

LEMMA 5. *Just as in Lemma* 4, *it can be proved that*

(3.1.20) $$Z'M^*Z = Z'Z = Q^{-1}, \quad \text{and} \quad Z'NZ = \left(1 - \frac{\varkappa}{T}\right)Q^{-1}.$$

LEMMA 6. *Using* (2.7) *and* (2.8) *we observe that*

(3.1.21) $$\pi'\omega_{11}\pi = (\pi'\ \ 0)\begin{bmatrix} \omega_{11} & \omega_{12} \\ \omega_{21} & \omega_{22} \end{bmatrix}\begin{pmatrix} \pi \\ 0 \end{pmatrix}$$

$$= \frac{1}{\sigma^4} q'Qq = \frac{1}{\sigma^2} \operatorname{tr} \left\{ Q \cdot \frac{1}{\sigma^2} qq' \right\} = \frac{1}{\sigma^2} \operatorname{tr} QC_1 \qquad \text{[cf. (2.17)].}$$

3.2. *Proof of Theorem 1*

The estimation procedure being as given in (2.5), we have

$$\text{(3.2.1)} \qquad e_k = \begin{bmatrix} Y'Y - kV'V & Y'X_1 \\ X_1'Y & X_1'X_1 \end{bmatrix}^{-1} \begin{bmatrix} (Y - kV)' \\ X_1' \end{bmatrix} u,$$

where e_k has been defined in (2.12). Using (2.3), (3.1.1), (3.1.3) and (3.1.4), we have[8]

$$\text{(3.2.2)} \quad e_k = [Q^{-1} + Z'V_z + V_z'Z + (1-k)V_z'V_z + kV_z'M^*V_z]^{-1}$$
$$\times [Z' + (1-k)V_z' + kV_z'M^*]u$$
$$= [I + Q\{Z'V_z + V_z'Z + (1-k)V_z'V_z + kV_z'M^*V_z\}]^{-1}Q$$
$$\times [Z'u + (1-k)V_z'u + kV_z'M^*u]$$
$$= Q[Z'u + (1-k)V_z'u + kV_z'M^*u]$$
$$- Q[Z'V_z + V_z'Z + (1-k)V_z'V_z + kV_z'M^*V_z]Q$$
$$\times [Z'u + (1-k)V_z'u + kV_z'M^*u] + \ldots$$

Using (2.10) and neglecting terms of higher order of smallness than T^{-1} we get

$$\text{(3.2.3)} \qquad e_k = Q[Z'u - \frac{1}{T}\varkappa \cdot V_z'u + V_z'M^*u] - QZ'V_zQZ'u - QV_z'ZQZ'u.$$

[8] The derivation given below presupposes the validity of the expansion of $(I + Q\Delta)^{-1}$, where

$$\Delta = Z'V_z + V_z'Z + (1-k)V_z'V_z + kV_z'M^*V_z.$$

As $Q\Delta$ is of order $T^{-\frac{1}{2}}$ in probability, we find that the successive terms of the expansion are of decreasing order in T. It is to be realized, however, that this as such does not ensure the validity of the expansion. For, if the random variation is normal, Δ may even be such that the matrix $I + Q\Delta$ is singular, in which case the expansion is out of the question. The assumption of normality must therefore be amended such that all variates are "near-normal" in the sense that the first four moments are identical with those of the normal distribution (symmetry and mesokurticity), but that the range is finite in such a way that the expansion does hold. This aspect deserves further investigation, which is beyond the scope of the present paper, but it is useful to note that it is relevant not only for our small-sample analysis, but even for asymptotic samples, a point not generally realized. This is easily illustrated for the simple just-identification case $l = 0$, $m = \Lambda = 1$, for which the two-stage least-squares sampling error is a scalar and equal to the ratio of two normal variates. The variance is then of course infinite. We can make it finite, as Geary [2] did, by postulating that the possibility of a negative denominator can be neglected, i.e., that the denominator is a near-normal variate.

As Z is nonstochastic and $E(u) = 0$, according to Assumption IV, we have

(3.2.4) $$E(Z'u) = 0,$$

and

(3.2.5) $$E(V_z'u) = Tq \qquad \text{[cf. (2.6) and (2.7)]}.$$

Further, using (3.1.4) and (2.6), we have

(3.2.6) $$E[V_z'M^*u] = E[\begin{pmatrix}\bar{V}'\\0\end{pmatrix}M^*u] = \begin{pmatrix}\pi E(u'M^*u)\\0\end{pmatrix} = \sigma^2 \operatorname{tr} M^* \cdot \begin{pmatrix}\pi\\0\end{pmatrix} = \Lambda q.$$

[cf. (3.1.8)].

Now we consider

(3.2.7) $$E(QZ'V_zQZ'u) = QZ'E(\bar{V}Au) = QZ'E(u\pi'Au),$$

where use has been made of (3.1.16) of Lemma 3, and of (2.6). It is to be observed that the expectation on the right-hand side of the second equality of (3.2.7) is a column vector of T components, the tth of which is

(3.2.8) $$\sum_{\mu}\sum_{t'} \pi_\mu a_{\mu t'} E[u(t) \cdot u(t')],$$

where $a_{\mu t'}$ is the element in the μth row and t'th column of the matrix A and π_μ is the μth element in the column vector π of m components, [cf. (2.6)]. Hence using Assumption IV, we find that (3.2.8) is non-zero only if $t = t'$ and in that case its value is $\sigma^2 \sum_\mu \pi_\mu a_{\mu t}$. Thus

(3.2.9) $$E(u\pi'Au) = \sigma^2 A'\pi = \sigma^2 M_1\bar{Y}(\bar{Y}'M_1\bar{Y})^{-1}\pi \qquad \text{[cf. Lemma 3]},$$

which gives,

(3.2.10) $$E(QZ'V_zQZ'u) = \sigma^2 Q\begin{pmatrix}\bar{Y}'\\X_1'\end{pmatrix} M_1\bar{Y}(\bar{Y}'M_1\bar{Y})^{-1}\pi = \sigma^2 Q\begin{pmatrix}\pi\\0\end{pmatrix} = Qq.$$

Finally,

(3.2.11) $$E(QV_z'ZQZ'u) = QE\left[\begin{pmatrix}\bar{V}'\\0\end{pmatrix}Bu\right] = Q\begin{bmatrix}\pi E(u'Bu)\\0\end{bmatrix} = Q\begin{bmatrix}\sigma^2 \operatorname{tr} B\cdot\pi\\0\end{bmatrix}$$
$$= (m + l) \cdot Qq \quad \text{[cf. (3.1.12)]}.$$

Now using (3.2.3), (3.2.4), (3.2.5), (3.2.6), (3.2.10) and (3.2.11),

(3.2.12) $$E(e_k) = (-\varkappa + L - 1)Qq,$$

where L has been defined in (2.13).

3.3. Proof of Theorem 2

Writing

(3.3.1) $$\Delta = Z'V_z + V_z'Z + (1 - k)V_z'V_z + kV_z'M^*V_z,$$

and using the second equality of (3.2.2) we have

(3.3.2) $$e_k e'_k = [I + Q\Delta]^{-1} QPQ [I + Q\Delta]'^{-1},$$

where Δ is symmetric and P, which is also symmetric, is

(3.3.3) $$P = [Z'u + (1-k)V_z'u + kV_z'M^*u]\,[Z'u + (1-k)\,V_z'u + kV_z'M^*u]'.$$

For deriving the moment matrix, to the order of T^{-2}, we must consider the first three terms in the expansion between brackets, on the right-hand side of (3.3.2); and hence, retaining terms to the order of T^{-2} only, we have

(3.3.4) $$Q^{-1} e_k e'_k Q^{-1} = P - \{PQ\Delta + \Delta QP\} + \{PQ\Delta Q\Delta + \Delta QPQ\Delta + \Delta Q\Delta QP\}.$$

Now, for the sake of brevity in writing, we introduce the following:

(3.3.5) $$P = P_1 + P_{\frac{1}{2}} + P_0 \quad \text{and} \quad \Delta = \Delta_{\frac{1}{2}} + \Delta_0,$$

where the suffixes indicate the order of the terms; thus, P_1 means that part of P which is $O(T^1)$, $\Delta_{\frac{1}{2}}$ means that part of Δ which is $O(T^{\frac{1}{2}})$ and Δ_0 means that part of Δ which is $O(T^0)$ or $O(1)$, and so on. Hence:

(3.3.6) $$P_1 = Z'uu'Z,$$

(3.3.7) $$P_{\frac{1}{2}} = Z'uu'NV_z + V_z'Nuu'Z,$$

(3.3.8) $$P_0 = V_z'Nuu'NV_z\,;$$

and

(3.3.9) $$\Delta_{\frac{1}{2}} = Z'V_z + V_z'Z,$$

(3.3.10) $$\Delta_0 = V_z'NV_z\,,$$

where N has been defined in (3.1.2).

To derive the expectation of the right-hand side of (3.3.4) we can neglect the terms which are of a higher order of smallness than $O(1)$, because on the left-hand side $e_k e_k'$ has already been pre- and post-multiplied by Q^{-1}. Further, we observe that

(3.3.11) $$E(P_1) = \sigma^2 Z'Z = \sigma^2 Q^{-1},$$

(3.3.12) $$E(P_{\frac{1}{2}}) = 0,$$

where use has been made of (2.6) and Assumption IV. To obtain $E(P_0)$ we require

(3.3.13) $$E(P_0) = E[V_z'Nuu'NV_z] = E\left[\begin{pmatrix}\bar{V}'\\ 0\end{pmatrix} Nuu'N(\bar{V}\quad 0)\right]$$

$$= \begin{bmatrix}\pi E(u'Nuu'Nu)\pi' + E(W'Nuu'NW) & 0\\ 0 & 0\end{bmatrix} = \sigma^2[\{(\Lambda - \varkappa)^2 + 2\Lambda\}C_1 + \Lambda C_2],$$

where we have used (2.18), (A.1.1) and (A.11.1) (see the Appendix). Therefore, it follows from (3.3.5), (3.3.11), (3.3.12) and (3.3.13) that

(3.3.14) $$E(P) = \sigma^2 Q^{-1} + \sigma^2[\{(\Lambda - \varkappa)^2 + 2\Lambda\}C_1 + \Lambda C_2].$$

For the expectation of the second term on the right-hand side of (3.3.4) we write

(3.3.15) $$PQ\Delta = P_1 Q\Delta_{\frac{1}{2}} + P_1 Q\Delta_0 + P_{\frac{1}{2}} Q\Delta_{\frac{1}{2}},$$

to the order of our approximation.

Using (2.6) and Assumption IV it is easy to see that

(3.3.16) $$E(P_1 Q\Delta_{\frac{1}{2}}) = 0.$$

We can write

(3.3.17) $$E[P_1 Q\Delta_0] = Z'E[uu'ZQV_z'NV_z] = Z'E[uu'A'\bar{V}'N(\bar{V} \quad 0)]$$
$$= Z'[E\{uu'A'\pi u'Nu\}\pi' + E\{uu'A'W'NW\} \mid 0].$$

Now using (3.1.17), (A.2.1) and (A.7.1) we get

(3.3.18) $$E[P_1 Q\Delta_0] = \sigma^2 Z'[\{(\Lambda - \varkappa) \cdot I + 2N\}A'C_1^* + (\Lambda - \varkappa)A'C_2^* \mid 0]$$
$$= \sigma^2[(\Lambda - \varkappa + 2)C_1 + (\Lambda - \varkappa)C_2]$$

to the order of our approximation.[9]

Considering the expected value of the third term on the right-hand side of (3.3.15) we write

(3.3.19) $$P_{\frac{1}{2}} Q\Delta_{\frac{1}{2}} = Z'uu'NV_z QZ'V_z + V_z'Nuu'ZQZ'V_z$$
$$+ Z'uu'NV_z QV_z'Z + V_z'Nuu'ZQV_z'Z,$$

and take up the terms on the right-hand side one by one.

First, we have (using Lemma 3)

(3.3.20) $$Z'E[uu'NV_z QZ'V_z] = Z'[E\{uu'N\bar{V}A\bar{V}\} \mid 0]$$
$$= Z'[E\{uu'Nu\pi'Au\}\pi' + E\{uu'NWAW\} \mid 0];$$

and, using (A.2.1)[10] and (A.5.1) along with (2.18), this is

(3.3.21)[9] $$(3.3.20) = \sigma^2 Z'[\{(\Lambda - \varkappa) \cdot I + 2N\}A'C_1^* + NA'C_2^* \mid 0]$$
$$= \sigma^2[(\Lambda - \varkappa + 2)C_1 + C_2].$$

Secondly, we consider

(3.3.22) $$E[V_z'Nuu'ZQZ'V_z] = E\left[\begin{pmatrix}\bar{V}'\\ 0\end{pmatrix} Nuu'B(\bar{V} \quad 0)\right]$$
$$= \begin{bmatrix}\pi E\{u'Nuu'Bu\}\pi' + E\{W'Nuu'BW\} & 0\\ 0 & 0\end{bmatrix},$$

and find that the two expectations involved here, on the right-hand side

[9] It should be observed that $Z'A' = Z'NA' = \begin{pmatrix}I\\ 0\end{pmatrix}$ to the order of our approximation.

[10] It should be noted that the first expectation on the right-hand side of the second equality of (3.3.20) is exactly the same as (A.2.1), except for the arrangement of the scalar quantities, viz., $u'Nu$ and $\pi'Au$, occurring in the two.

of the second equality of (3.3.22), can be derived in exactly the same way as (A.1.1) and (A.11.1), respectively. Thus we have

$$(3.3.23)\qquad (3.3.22) = \sigma^2(m + l)\,[(\Lambda - \varkappa + 2)C_1 + C_2],$$

where the terms of higher order of smallness than $O(1)$ have been neglected.

Thirdly,

$$(3.3.24)\quad Z'E[uu'NV_{\mathfrak{z}}QV'_{\mathfrak{z}}]Z = Z'E\left[uu'N(\bar{V}\quad 0)\begin{pmatrix}\omega_{11} & \omega_{12}\\ \omega_{21} & \omega_{22}\end{pmatrix}\begin{pmatrix}\bar{V}'\\ 0\end{pmatrix}\right]Z$$
$$= Z'E[uu'N\bar{V}\omega_{11}\bar{V}']Z = Z'[E\{uu'Nu\pi'\omega_{11}\pi u'\} + E\{uu'NW\omega_{11}W'\}]Z.$$

Using (A.3.1) and (A.6.1) we get

$$(3.3.25)\quad (3.3.24) = \sigma^2Z'[\operatorname{tr} QC_1\cdot\{(\Lambda - \varkappa)\cdot I + 2\,N\} + \operatorname{tr} QC_2\cdot N]Z$$
$$= \sigma^2[(\Lambda - \varkappa + 2)\operatorname{tr} QC_1 + \operatorname{tr} QC_2]Q^{-1},$$

where the terms of higher order of smallness have been neglected and use has been made of Lemma 5.

Finally, for the fourth term on the right-hand side of (3.3.19) we have

$$(3.3.26)\quad E[V'_{\mathfrak{z}}Nuu'ZQV'_{\mathfrak{z}}]Z = E\left[\begin{pmatrix}\bar{V}'\\ 0\end{pmatrix}Nuu'A'\bar{V}'\right]Z$$
$$= \begin{bmatrix}\pi E\{u'Nuu'A'\pi u'\} + E\{W'Nuu'A'W'\}\\ \hdashline 0\end{bmatrix}Z.$$

Using (A.2.1)[11] and (A.12.1) we get, to the order of our approximation,

$$(3.3.27)\quad (3.3.26) = \begin{bmatrix}\sigma^4\pi\pi'A\{(\Lambda - \varkappa)\cdot I + 2\,N\} + \sigma^2C^*_2AN\\ \hdashline 0\end{bmatrix}(\bar{Y}\quad X_1)$$
$$= \sigma^2[(\Lambda - \varkappa + 2)C_1 + C_2].$$

Now using (3.3.19), (3.3.21), (3.3.23), (3.3.25), and (3.3.27) we get

$$(3.3.28)\quad E(P_{\frac{1}{2}}Q\Delta_{\frac{1}{2}}) = \sigma^2(m + l + 2)\,[(\Lambda - \varkappa + 2)C_1 + C_2]$$
$$+ \sigma^2[(\Lambda - \varkappa + 2)\operatorname{tr} QC_1 + \operatorname{tr} QC_2]\cdot Q^{-1},$$

and combining (3.3.16), (3.3.18), (3.3.28) with the expected value of the left-hand side of (3.3.15) we get

$$(3.3.29)\quad E(PQ\Delta) = \sigma^2[(m + l + 3)\,(\Lambda - \varkappa + 2)C_1$$
$$+ (\Lambda - \varkappa + m + l + 2)C_2] + \sigma^2[(\Lambda - \varkappa + 2)\operatorname{tr} QC_1 + \operatorname{tr} QC_2]\cdot Q^{-1}.$$

As we find (3.3.29) to be symmetric, we have[12]

$$(3.3.30)\qquad E(PQ\Delta) = E(\Delta QP),$$

which is required for the third term on the right-hand side of (3.3.4).

[11] It should be observed that the only difference between the first expectation on the right-hand side of the second equality of (3.3.26) and (A.2.1) is that the former is a row vector and the latter is a column vector.

[12] P and Δ being already symmetric.

For the fourth term on the right-hand side of (3.3.4) we write

$$(3.3.31)\quad PQ\Delta Q\Delta = P_1 Q\Delta_{\frac{1}{2}} Q\Delta_{\frac{1}{2}} = Z'uu'ZQZ'V_z QZ'V_z + Z'uu'ZQZ'V_z QV_z'Z$$
$$+ Z'uu'ZQV_z'ZQZ'V_z + Z'uu'ZQV_z'ZQV_z'Z = Z'uu'B\bar{V}A(\bar{V} \quad 0)$$
$$+ Z'uu'BV\omega_{11}\bar{V}'Z + Z'uu'A'\bar{V}'B(\bar{V} \quad 0) + Z'uu'A'\bar{V}'A'\bar{V}'Z.$$

Now, to obtain the expected value of (3.3.31), we find the expected values of the terms on the right-hand side of (3.3.31), one by one. First of all we consider

$$(3.3.32)\quad Z'E[uu'B\bar{V}A(\bar{V} \quad 0)] = Z'[E\{uu'Bu\pi'Au\}\pi' + E\{uu'BWAW\} \mid 0]$$
$$= \sigma^2 Z'[\{(\text{tr } B)\cdot I + 2\,B\}A'C_1^* + BA'C_2^* \mid 0],^{13}$$

where use has been made of (A.2.1) (the expectation required here can be derived simply by replacing N in (A.2.1) by B) and (A.5.1). Hence it is easy to verify that

$$(3.3.33)\qquad (3.3.32) = \sigma^2[(m + l + 2)C_1 + C_2].$$

Next we have

$$(3.3.34)\quad Z'E[uu'B\bar{V}\omega_{11}\bar{V}']Z = Z'[E\{uu'Bu\pi'\omega_{11}\pi u'\} + E\{uu'BW\omega_{11}W'\}]Z$$
$$= Z'[(\pi'\omega_{11}\pi)\cdot E\{uu'Buu'\} + \sigma^2 BE\{W\omega_{11}W'\}]Z$$

and using (A.3.1) (again replacing N by B in (A.3.1)) and (A.6.1) we obtain

$$(3.3.35)\quad (3.3.34) = \sigma^2 Z'[\text{tr } QC_1\cdot\{\text{tr } B\cdot I + 2\,B\} + \text{tr } QC_2\cdot B]Z$$
$$= \sigma^2[(m + l + 2)\text{ tr } QC_1 + \text{tr } QC_2]\cdot Q^{-1}.$$

Thirdly, let us consider

$$(3.3.36)\quad Z'E[uu'A'\bar{V}'B(\bar{V} \quad 0)] = Z'[E\{uu'A'\pi u'Bu\}\pi' + E\{uu'A'W'BW\} \mid 0],$$

and using (A.2.1) and (A.7.1) (replacing in both cases N by B) we get

$$(3.3.37)\quad (3.3.36) = \sigma^2 Z'[\{\text{tr } B\cdot I + 2\,B\}A'C_1^* + (\text{tr } B)\cdot A'C_2^* \mid 0].$$
$$= \sigma^2[(m + l + 2)C_1 + (m + l)C_2].$$

Lastly, we have

$$(3.3.38)\quad Z'E[uu'A'\bar{V}'A'\bar{V}']Z = Z'[E\{uu'A'\pi u'A'\pi u'\} + E\{uu'A'W'A'W'\}]Z,$$

and using (A.4.1) and (A.8.1) we get

$$(3.3.39)\quad (3.3.38) = \sigma^2 Z'[\sigma^2\{\text{tr } A'\pi\pi'A\cdot I + 2\,A'\pi\pi'A\} + A'C_2^*A]Z$$
$$= \sigma^2[(\text{tr } QC_1)\cdot Q^{-1} + 2\,C_1 + C_2].$$

Now using (3.3.31), (3.3.33), (3.3.35), (3.3.37) and (3.3.39) we get

$$(3.3.40)\quad E(PQ\Delta Q\Delta) = \sigma^2[2(m + l + 3)C_1 + (m + l + 2)C_2]$$
$$+ \sigma^2[(m + l + 3)\text{ tr } QC_1 + \text{tr } QC_2]Q^{-1},$$

[13] Note that $Z'A' = Z'BA' = \begin{pmatrix} I \\ 0 \end{pmatrix}$.

and which is symmetric. Therefore,

$$E(PQ\Delta Q\Delta) = E(\Delta Q\Delta QP), \tag{3.3.41}$$

as required for the sixth term on the right-hand side of (3.3.4).

Now we come to the fifth term on the right-hand side of (3.3.4). We can write

$$\begin{aligned}\Delta QPQ\Delta &= \Delta_{\frac{1}{2}} QP_1Q\Delta_{\frac{1}{2}} = Z'V_z QZ'uu'ZQZ'V_z + Z'V_z QZ'uu'ZQV_z'Z \\ &+ V_z'ZQZ'uu'ZQZ'V_z + V_z'ZQZ'uu'ZQV_z'Z = Z'\bar{V}Auu'B(\bar{V} \quad 0) \\ &+ Z'\bar{V}Auu'A'\bar{V}'Z + \begin{pmatrix}\bar{V}'\\0\end{pmatrix} Buu'B(\bar{V} \quad 0) + \begin{pmatrix}\bar{V}'\\0\end{pmatrix} Buu'A'\bar{V}'Z,\end{aligned} \tag{3.3.42}$$

to the order of our approximation.

As regards the expected value of the first term on the right-hand side of the third equality of (3.3.42) we have:

$$\begin{aligned}Z'E[\bar{V}Auu'B(\bar{V} \quad 0)] &= Z'[E\{u\pi'Auu'Bu\}\pi' + E\{WAuu'BW\} \mid 0] \\ &= \sigma^2 \cdot Z'[\{(\mathrm{tr}\ B)\cdot I + 2\,B\}A'C_1^* + BA'C_2^* \mid 0] = \sigma^2[(m+l+2)C_1 + C_2],\end{aligned} \tag{3.3.43}$$

where use has been made of (A.2.1) (replacing N by B), (A.9.1) and footnote 13.

Secondly, we consider

$$\begin{aligned}Z'E[\bar{V}Auu'A'\bar{V}']Z &= Z'[E\{u\pi'Auu'A'\pi u'\} + E\{WAuu'A'W'\}]Z \\ &= \sigma^2 Z'[\sigma^2\{\mathrm{tr}\ (A'\pi\pi'A)\cdot I + 2\,A'\pi\pi'A\} + \mathrm{tr}\ QC_2 \cdot I]Z \\ &= 2\,\sigma^2 C_1 + \sigma^2\{\mathrm{tr}\ QC_1 + \mathrm{tr}\ QC_2\}\cdot Q^{-1},\end{aligned} \tag{3.3.44}$$

where use has been made of (A.4.1) and (A.10.1).

Thirdly, for the third term on the right-hand side of the third equality of (3.3.42) we have

$$\begin{aligned}E\left[\begin{pmatrix}\bar{V}'\\0\end{pmatrix} Buu'B(\bar{V} \quad 0)\right] &= \begin{bmatrix}E\{\bar{V}'Buu'B\bar{V}\} & 0\\ 0 & 0\end{bmatrix} \\ &= \begin{bmatrix}\pi E\{u'Buu'Bu\}\pi' + E\{W'Buu'BW\} & 0\\ 0 & 0\end{bmatrix} \\ &= \sigma^2[\{(\mathrm{tr}\ B)^2 + 2\ \mathrm{tr}\ B^2\}\cdot C_1 + (\mathrm{tr}\ B^2)\cdot C_2] = \sigma^2(m+l)\ [(m+l+2)C_1 + C_2],\end{aligned} \tag{3.3.45}$$

where we have used (A.1.1) and (A.11.1), replacing N by B in both the cases.

In the end it should be noted that the fourth term, on the right-hand side of the third equality of (3.3.42), is the transpose of the first term therein and, as it appears from (3.3.43), its expected value is symmetric. Hence using (3.3.42), (3.3.43), (3.3.44) and (3.3.45) we get

$$\begin{aligned}E[\Delta QPQ\Delta] &= \sigma^2[\{(m+l+2)^2 + 2\}C_1 + (m+l+2)C_2] \\ &+ \sigma^2[\mathrm{tr}\ QC_1 + \mathrm{tr}\ QC_2]\cdot Q^{-1}.\end{aligned} \tag{3.3.46}$$

Hence combining (3.3.14), (3.3.29), (3.3.30), (3.3.40), (3.3.41) and (3.3.46) with the expected value of the left-hand side of (3.3.4) we get the result stated in Theorem 2.

4. AN EXAMPLE: ILLUSTRATING THE SELECTION OF THE BEST k-VALUE

Accepting the determinant value criterion (2.22) for determining the optimum value of k we find that the $\varkappa$ value (cf. (2.23)) will usually be negative,[14] and hence a k value above unity (as, for example, in limited-information maximum-likelihood) is less plausible. To estimate the trace ratio involved in the formula (2.23) we use the following:

$$\text{(4.1)} \qquad \text{estimate of } Q = \begin{bmatrix} Y'Y - V'V & Y'X_1 \\ X_1'Y & X_1'X_1 \end{bmatrix}^{-1};$$

$$\text{(4.2)} \qquad \text{estimate of } C = \begin{bmatrix} \frac{1}{T}V'V & 0 \\ 0 & 0 \end{bmatrix}, \qquad \text{[cf. (2.17)]};$$

$$\text{(4.3)} \qquad \text{estimate of } q = \begin{bmatrix} \frac{1}{T}Y'(y - Yc - X_1b) \\ 0 \end{bmatrix}, \qquad \text{[cf. (2.7)]};$$

where c and b are two-stage least-squares estimates of γ and β of equation (2.1), and

$$\text{(4.4)} \qquad \text{estimate of } \sigma^2 = \frac{1}{T}(y - Yc - X_1b)'(y - Yc - X_1b).$$

In the accompanying table we obtain the optimum values of k (and $\varkappa$) and the corresponding point estimates of the coefficients for Klein's Model I.[15] We have also given the alternative point estimates according to two-stage least-squares ($k = 1$), classical least squares ($k = 0$), and unbiased estimates to $O(T^{-1})$ ($k = 1 + (L-1)/T, L = \Lambda - (m + l) = 4$ for all three equations). The limited-information and full-information maximum-likelihood estimates (the latter with a diagonal variance-covariance matrix of the structural disturbances) are as given by Klein [**3**] on pages 68 and 73. Furthermore, in each case (except for limited-information and full-information maximum-likelihood estimates) we obtain the bias and standard error, both to $O(T^{-1})$, of these estimates accoring to (2.11) and (2.19), respectively.

It appears from the table that the optimal k is below 1 for all three equations and the point estimates according to the optimum value of k are nearly always between two-stage least-squares and classical least-squares estimates. The unbiased estimates have larger standard errors than the estimates corresponding to optimal k.

[14] This $\varkappa$ value may be positive only if Λ is very large, but the sample size will usually make it necessary to work with a moderate number of predetermined variables, and thus a positive $\varkappa$ value will seldom occur.

[15] Cf. Klein [**3**, Ch. 3].

ALTERNATIVE POINT ESTIMATES OF THE COEFFICIENTS IN KLEIN'S MODEL I AND THEIR ESTIMATED FINITE SAMPLE BIAS AND STANDARD ERRORS*

Equation	Optimal value of $\varkappa$	Optimal value of k		Point estimates according to: $k = 1$ two-stage least-squares**	k optimal	$k = 0$ classical lst-sqs.	$k = 1 + (L - 1)/T$ unbiased to (O) (T^{-1})	$k = 1 + \nu$ limited-information	full-information max. lik. (diag. var.-cov. matrix)
Consumption	—3.389	0.8386	α_1:	0.0173	0.0611	0.0899	—0.0311	—0.22	0.02
			bias:	0.0433	0.0923	0.3466	0		
			s.e.:	0.1179 (.1181)	0.1203	0.3075	0.1318	0.19	
			α_2:	0.2162	0.1840	0.1929	0.2522	0.40	0.23
			bias:	—0.0320	—0.0682	—0.2562	0		
			s.e.:	0.1059 (.1073)	0.1049	0.2280	0.1167	0.17	
			α_3:	0.8102	0.8074	0.7962	0.8130	0.82	0.80
			bias:	—0.0027	—0.0056	—0.0212	0		
			s.e.:	0.0392 (.0402)	0.0370	0.0286	0.0411	0.05	
Investment	—2.421	0.8847	β_1:	0.1502	0.2273	0.4796	0.0137	0.08	0.23
			bias:	0.1103	0.1993	0.8825	0		
			s.e.:	0.1755 (.1732)	0.1896	0.7766	0.2153	0.23	
			β_2:	0.6159	0.5498	0.3330	0.7332	0.68	0.55
			bias:	—0.0947	—0.1712	—0.7579	0		
			s.e.:	0.1618 (.1628)	0.1704	0.6634	0.1971	0.21	
			β_3:	—0.1578	—0.1470	—0.1118	—0.1768	—0.17	—0.15
			bias:	0.0154	0.0278	0.1232	0		
			s.e.:	0.0342 (.0361)	0.0334	0.1047	0.0409	0.04	
Demand for labour	—8.139	0.6125	γ_1:	0.4389	0.4392	0.4395	0.4387	0.43	0.42
			bias:	0.0061	0.0228	0.0491	0		
			s.e.:	0.0353 (.0356)	0.0333	0.0449	0.0379	0.03	
			γ_2:	0.1467	0.1464	0.1461	0.1468	0.15	0.16
			bias:	—0.0015	—0.0055	—0.0119	0		
			s.e.:	0.0292 (.0291)	0.0283	0.0281	0.0296	0.03	
			γ_3:	0.1304	0.1303	0.1302	0.1304	0.13	0.13
			bias:	—0.0058	—0.0215	—0.0464	0		
			s.e.:	0.0386 (.0388)	0.0367	0.0461	0.0409	0.02	

* Here standard error is meant to stand for the square root of the estimated second moment around the true parameter value.

** The figures within brackets corresponding to "s.e." are the asymptotic standard errors.

APPENDIX

A.1. Having defined N, in (3.1.2), we have

(A.1.1) $$E[u'Nuu'Nu] = \sigma^4[(\Lambda - \varkappa)^2 + 2\,\Lambda],$$

to the order of our approximation.

PROOF. We can write

(A.1.2) $$E[u'Nuu'Nu] = \sum_t \sum_{t'} \sum_{t''} \sum_{t'''} n_{tt'} n_{t''t'''} E[u(t)u(t')u(t'')u(t''')],$$

the $n_{tt'}$ being defined in Lemma 1. The expectation of such a product of four u's is nonzero only if the t's are pair-wise equal (including the case in which they are all equal). The following cases can then be specified:

Cases	*Contribution to* (A.1.2.)
$t = t',\ t'' = t'''$ but $t \neq t''$	$\sigma^4[(\mathrm{tr}\ N^2) - \sum_t n_{tt}^2]$;
$t = t'',\ t' = t'''$ but $t \neq t'$	$\sigma^4[(\mathrm{tr}\ N^2) - \sum_t n_{tt}^2]$;
$t = t''',\ t' = t''$ but $t \neq t'$	$\sigma^4[(\mathrm{tr}\ N^2) - \sum_t n_{tt}^2]$;
$t = t' = t'' = t'''$	$3\,\sigma^4 \sum n_{tt}^2$;

where use has been made of Assumption IV. Adding these results and using (3.1.10) and (3.1.11) we get (A.1.1).

A.2. Defining A as in (3.1.6), we have

(A.2.1) $$E[uu'A'\pi u'Nu] = \sigma^4[(\Lambda - \varkappa) \cdot I + 2\,N]A'\pi.$$

PROOF. We notice that the expectation on the left-hand side of (A.2.1) is a column vector of T components, the tth of which is

(A.2.2) $$\sum_\mu \sum_{t'} \sum_{t''} \sum_{t'''} a_{\mu t'} \pi_\mu n_{t''t'''} E[u(t)u(t')u(t'')u(t''')],$$

where $a_{\mu t'}$ is the term in the t'th row and μth column of A', and π_μ is the μth element of the column vector π, defined in (2.6). To get the value of (A.2.2) we specify the following cases in which it is nonzero:

Cases	*Contribution to* (A.2.2)
$t' = t,\ t'' = t'''$ but $t'' \neq t$	$\sigma^4[(\mathrm{tr}\ N) \cdot \sum_\mu a_{\mu t}\pi_\mu - \sum_\mu a_{\mu t}\pi_\mu n_{tt}]$,
$t'' = t,\ t' = t'''$ but $t' \neq t$	$\sigma^4[\sum_{t'} \sum_\mu a_{\mu t'}\pi_\mu n_{tt'} - \sum_\mu a_{\mu t}\pi_\mu n_{tt}]$,
$t''' = t,\ t' = t''$ but $t' \neq t$	$\sigma^4[\sum_{t'} \sum_\mu a_{\mu t'}\pi_\mu n_{t't} - \sum_\mu a_{\mu t}\pi_\mu n_{tt}]$,
$t = t' = t'' = t'''$	$3\,\sigma^4 \sum_\mu a_{\mu t}\pi_\mu n_{tt}$.

Thus, adding these results we find that (A.2.2) is equal to

(A.2.3) $$\sigma^4[(\Lambda - \varkappa) \sum_\mu a_{\mu t}\pi_\mu + 2 \sum_{t'} \sum_\mu a_{\mu t'}\pi_\mu n_{t't}],$$

and using this we get (A.2.1).

A.3. We have

(A.3.1) $E[uu'Nu\pi'\omega_{11}\pi u'] = (\pi'\omega_{11}\pi) \cdot E[uu'Nuu'] = \sigma^2(\text{tr } QC_1)\ [(\Lambda - \varkappa) \cdot I + 2\, N]$,

where ω_{11} and C_1 have been defined in (2.8) and (2.17), repsectively.

PROOF. Here we require the value of $E[uu'Nuu']$ which is a $T \times T$ matrix, the term in the tth row and t'th column being:

(A.3.2) $$\sum_{t''} \sum_{t'''} n_{t''t'''} E[u(t)u(t')u(t'')u(t''')],$$

and we observe that (A.3.2) is nonzero only in the cases specified below:

Cases	*Contribution to* (A.3.2)
$t = t'',\ t' = t'''$ but $t \neq t'$	$\sigma^4 n_{tt'}$,
$t = t''',\ t' = t''$ but $t \neq t'$	$\sigma^4 n_{t't}$,
$t = t',\ t'' = t'''$ but $t \neq t''$	$\sigma^4[\text{tr } N - n_{tt}]$,
$t = t' = t'' = t'''$	$3\,\sigma^4 n_{tt}$.

Thus we have

(A.3.3) $$(\text{A.3.2}) = \begin{cases} \sigma^4[\Lambda - \varkappa + 2\, n_{tt}], & \text{if } t = t', \\ 2\,\sigma^4 n_{tt'}, & \text{if } t \neq t', \end{cases}$$

and hence using Lemma 6 we get the result of (A.3.1).

A.4. We prove below that:

(A.4.1) $$E[uu'A'\pi u'A'\pi u'] = \sigma^4[\text{tr } (A'\pi\pi'A) \cdot I + 2\, A'\pi\pi'A].$$

PROOF. We find that (A.4.1) is a $T \times T$ matrix, the term in the tth row and t'th column being

(A.4.2) $$\sum_{\mu} \sum_{\mu'} \sum_{t''} \sum_{t'''} a_{\mu t''}\pi_\mu a_{\mu' t'''}\pi_{\mu'} E[u(t)u(t')u(t'')u(t''')],$$

which is nonzero only in the following cases:

Cases	*Contribution to* (A.4.2)
$t = t'',\ t' = t'''$ but $t \neq t'$	$\sigma^4 \sum_{\mu} \sum_{\mu'} a_{\mu t} a_{\mu' t'} \pi_\mu \pi_{\mu'}$;
$t = t''',\ t' = t''$ but $t \neq t'$	$\sigma^4 \sum_{\mu} \sum_{\mu'} a_{\mu' t} a_{\mu t'} \pi_\mu \pi_{\mu'}$;
$t = t',\ t'' = t'''$ but $t \neq t''$	$\sigma^4[\sum_{\mu} \sum_{\mu'} \sum_{t''} a_{\mu t''} a_{\mu' t''} \pi_\mu \pi_{\mu'} - \sum_{\mu} \sum_{\mu'} a_{\mu t} a_{\mu' t} \pi_\mu \pi_{\mu'}]$;
$t = t' = t'' = t'''$	$3\,\sigma^4 \sum_{\mu} \sum_{\mu'} a_{\mu t} a_{\mu' t} \pi_\mu \pi_{\mu'}$.

Therefore, we have

(A.4.3) $$(\text{A.4.2}) = \begin{cases} \sigma^4[\sum_{\mu} \sum_{\mu'} \sum_{t''} a_{\mu t''} a_{\mu' t''} \pi_\mu \pi_{\mu'} + 2 \sum_{\mu} \sum_{\mu'} a_{\mu t} a_{\mu' t'} \pi_\mu \pi_{\mu'}], & \text{if } t = t'; \\ \sigma^4[\sum_{\mu} \sum_{\mu'} a_{\mu t} a_{\mu' t'} \pi_\mu \pi_{\mu'} + \sum_{\mu} \sum_{\mu'} a_{\mu' t} a_{\mu t'} \pi_\mu \pi_{\mu'}], & \text{if } t \neq t'; \end{cases}$$

which leads to (A.4.1).

A.5. We have

(A.5.1) $$E[WAW] = A'C_2^*$$

where C_2^* has been defined in (2.18).

PROOF. Here the expectation on the left-hand side is a $T \times m$ matrix, the term in the tth row and μth column being:

(A.5.2) $$\sum_{\mu'} \sum_{t'} a_{\mu' t'} E[w_{\mu'}(t) w_{\mu}(t')],$$

which is nonzero only if $t = t'$ and in that case its value is $\Sigma_{\mu'} a_{\mu' t} \operatorname{cov}(w_{\mu}, w_{\mu'})$, which yields the result given in (A.5.1).

A.6. Further we prove that

(A.6.1) $$E[W\omega_{11}W'] = (\operatorname{tr} QC_2) \cdot I.$$

PROOF. The term on the left-hand side of (A.6.1) is a $T \times T$ matrix, the element in the tth row and t'th column being

(A.6.2) $$\sum_{\mu} \sum_{\mu'} \omega_{11}(\mu, \mu') \cdot E[w_{\mu}(t) w_{\mu'}(t')],$$

where $\omega_{11}(\mu, \mu')$ is the term in the μth row and μ'th column of ω_{11} defined in (2.9). It should be noted that (A.6.2) is nonzero only if $t = t'$ and then it is equal to

(A.6.3) $$\sum_{\mu} \sum_{\mu'} [\omega_{11}(\mu, \mu') \cdot \operatorname{cov}(w_{\mu}, w_{\mu'})] = \operatorname{tr} C_2^* \omega_{11} = \operatorname{tr} QC_2,$$

which is independent of t and t'. Thus we obtain (A.6.1).

A.7. Now we have

(A.7.1) $$E[W'NW] = (\Lambda - \varkappa) \cdot C_2^*.$$

PROOF. Here (A.7.1) is an $m \times m$ matrix of which the term in the μth row and μ'th column is

(A.7.2) $$\sum_{t} \sum_{t'} n_{tt'} E[w_{\mu}(t) w_{\mu'}(t')],$$

which is nonzero only if $t = t'$ and then it is equal to

(A.7.3) $$\sum_{t} n_{tt} \cdot \operatorname{cov}(w_{\mu}, w_{\mu'}) = \operatorname{tr} N \cdot \operatorname{cov}(w_{\mu}, w_{\mu'}) = (\Lambda - \varkappa) \cdot \operatorname{cov}(w_{\mu}, w_{\mu'}),$$

giving the result (A.7.1).

A. 8. Let us prove that

(A.8.1) $$E[W'A'W'] = C_2^* A.$$

PROOF. This is a $m \times T$ matrix, the term in the μth row and tth column being

(A.8.2) $$\sum_{t'} \sum_{\mu'} a_{\mu' t'} E[w_{\mu}(t') w_{\mu'}(t)],$$

which is nonzero only if $t = t'$, and then (A.8.2) is equal to

(A.8.3) $$\sum_{\mu'} a_{\mu' t} \operatorname{cov}(w_{\mu}, w_{\mu'}),$$

and this gives (A.8.1).

A.9. We have

(A.9.1) $$E[WAuu'BW] = \sigma^2 BA'C_2^*.$$

PROOF. Here we observe that $E[WAuu'BW]$ is a $T \times m$ matrix of which the term in the tth row and μth column is

(A.9.2) $$\sum_{\mu'} \sum_{t'} \sum_{t''} \sum_{t'''} a_{\mu' t'} b_{t'' t'''} E[w_{\mu'}(t) u(t') u(t'') w_{\mu}(t''')],$$

which is nonzero only if $t = t'''$ and $t' = t''$. Then its value is

$$\sigma^2 \sum_{\mu'} \sum_{t'} a_{\mu' t'} b_{t' t} \operatorname{cov}(w_\mu, w_{\mu'}), \tag{A.9.3}$$

and this leads to (A.9.1).

A.10. Here we prove that

$$E[WAuu'A'W'] = \sigma^2(\operatorname{tr} QC_2) \cdot I. \tag{A.10.1}$$

PROOF. We see that (A.10.1) is a $T \times T$ matrix, the term in the tth row and t'th column being

$$\sum_{\mu} \sum_{\mu'} \sum_{t''} \sum_{t'''} a_{\mu t''} a_{\mu' t'''} E[w_\mu(t) u(t'') u(t''') w_{\mu'}(t')], \tag{A.10.2}$$

which is nonzero only if $t = t'$ and $t'' = t'''$; and in that case it is equal to:

$$\sigma^2 \sum_{\mu} \sum_{\mu'} \sum_{t''} a_{\mu t''} a_{\mu' t''} \operatorname{cov}(w_\mu, w_{\mu'}) = \sigma^2 \operatorname{tr} A'C_2^* A, \tag{A.10.3}$$

and using (3.1.17) and (2.9) this gives (A.10.1).

A.11. Further, we have

$$E[W'Nuu'NW] = \sigma^2 AC_2^*. \tag{A.11.1}$$

PROOF. (A.11.1) is an $m \times m$ matrix, the term in the μth row and μ'th column being

$$\sum_{t} \sum_{t'} \sum_{t''} \sum_{t'''} n_{tt'} n_{t''t'''} E[w_\mu(t) u(t') u(t'') w_{\mu'}(t''')], \tag{A.11.2}$$

which is nonzero only if $t = t'''$ and $t' = t''$; and then it is equal to

$$\sigma^2 \sum_{t} \sum_{t'} n_{tt'} n_{t't} \operatorname{cov}(w_\mu, w_{\mu'}) = \sigma^2(\operatorname{tr} N^2) \cdot \operatorname{cov}(w_\mu, w_{\mu'}); \tag{A.11.3}$$

and using (3.1.11) this gives (A.11.1), to the order of our approximation.

A. 12. Finally, we have

$$E[W'Nuu'A'W'] = \sigma^2 C_2^* AN. \tag{A.12.1}$$

PROOF. We notice that the left-hand side of (A.12.1) is an $m \times T$ matrix, the term in the μth row and tth column being

$$\sum_{t'} \sum_{t''} \sum_{t'''} \sum_{\mu'} n_{t't''} a_{\mu' t'''} E[w_\mu(t') u(t'') u(t''') w_{\mu'}(t)], \tag{A.12.2}$$

which is nonzero only if $t = t'$ and $t'' = t'''$. Then it is equal to

$$\sigma^2 \sum_{t''} \sum_{\mu'} n_{tt''} a_{\mu' t''} \operatorname{cov}(w_\mu, w_{\mu'}), \tag{A.12.3}$$

and this gives (A.12.1).

REFERENCES

[1] ANDERSON, T. W., AND H. RUBIN: "Estimation of the Parameters of a Single Equation in a Complete System of Stochastic Equations," *Annals of Mathematical Statistics*, Vol. 20, No. 1 (1949).

[2] GEARY, R. C.: "The Frequency Distribution of the Quotient of Two Normal Variables," *Journal of Royal Statistical Society*, Vol. 93, 1930, p. 442.

[3] KLEIN, L. R.: *Economic Fluctuations in the United States*, 1921-1941. New York-London: John Wiley & Sons, Inc. (1950).

[4] Koopmans, T. C., and W. C. Hood: "The Estimation of Simultaneous Linear Economic Relationships," Chapter VI of *Studies in Econometric Method*, Cowles Commission Monograph No. 14, W. C. Hood and T. C. Koopmans, ed., New York: John Wiley & Sons, Inc. (1953).

[5] Theil, H.: *Economic Forecasts and Policy*. Amsterdam: North-Holland Publishing Company (1958), Chapter VI.

[6] Theil, H.: "A Rank-Invariant Method of Linear and Polynomial Regression Analysis, Part III," *Proceedings of the Koninklijke Akademie van Wetenschappen*, Vol. 53 (1950), pp. 1397-1412.

A SYMPOSIUM ON SIMULTANEOUS EQUATION ESTIMATION*

SIMULTANEOUS EQUATION ESTIMATION: ANY VERDICT YET?[1]

By Carl F. Christ

This paper discusses the relative merits of ordinary least squares estimation and several simultaneous-equations methods for econometric purposes. Most of the evidence appealed to is in the form of Monte Carlo experiments, because there is as yet little small sample theory of the properties of the different estimators.

In this paper I will assess what we know today about the merits of simultaneous equations methods of estimation of economic parameters, as opposed to single-equation methods.

I am going to argue that the *idea* of a system of simultaneous structural economic equations is very important, and indispensable to good work in econometrics. I am going to argue further that the available evidence suggests that, although the ordinary old-fashioned economical least squares method sometimes gives estimates that are at least as good as if not better than the simultaneous equations methods, even for structural equations where the least squares estimates are admittedly biased, there are some situations in which simultaneous equations estimation methods are called for. The main problem, of course, is to know when they are and when they aren't.

As the lead-off man, I will first set forth some standard definitions and concepts that I trust will be useful to the other authors and their audience too.

Let us discuss a linear stochastic model that is *overidentified*. Models that are not identified do not lend themselves to estimation. Just-identified models are not very interesting for the current topic, because for them the instrumental variables method, the limited and full information maximum likelihood methods, and the two stage least squares method all give identical estimates.

* Editor's Note: This symposium originated with the papers presented in the panel discussion on "Simultaneous Equation Estimation: Any Verdict Yet?" presented at the December, 1958 meetings of the Econometric Society, held in Chicago.

[1] This paper is a revised version of the first of four papers by four authors on this topic, presented at the meeting of the Econometric Society in Chicago in December, 1958. The position taken here is somewhat more favorable to simultaneous equations methods than that taken in the paper presented in 1958.

Let the model be given by

$$\text{(1)} \qquad \mathrm{B}y_t + \Gamma z_t = u_t$$

where the following assumptions are made:

y_t is a column vector of observed values of jointly dependent variables, G in number, for the tth period or individual in the sample. The elements of y_t are $y_{1t}, y_{2t}, \ldots, y_{Gt}$. The index t runs from 1 to T, i.e., there are T observations in the sample.

z_t is a column vector of observed values of predetermined variables, K in number, for the tth observation in the sample: $z_{1t}, z_{2t}, \ldots, z_{Kt}$. Again $t = 1, \ldots, T$.

u_t is a column vector of unobservable random variables, G in number, for the tth observation in the sample: $u_{1t}, u_{2t}, \ldots, u_{Gt}$. Again $t = 1, \ldots, T$. The population means of the elements of u_t are zero, i.e., Eu_t is the zero vector, and their population variance-covariance matrix is a nonsingular matrix Σ whose elements are finite and constant, i.e., $Eu_t u'_t = \Sigma$. It is assumed that the u's are independent between different observations in the sample, i.e., that $Eu_s u'_t$ is the zero matrix as long as s is not equal to t.

B is a square nonsingular matrix of order $G \times G$, whose elements are constant but unobservable coefficients of the y's in the model.

Γ is a rectangular matrix of order $G \times K$, whose elements are constant but unobservable coefficients of the z's in the model.

It may be noted that these assumptions mean that u_t is statistically independent of z_t, z_{t-1}, z_{t-2}, etc., but not necessarily independent of z_{t+1}, z_{t+2}, etc. Any variable z that meets this condition is by definition a predetermined variable. Any variable z that meets this condition, and also the condition that u_t is independent of z_{t+1}, z_{t+2}, etc., is by definition exogenous. Thus all exogenous variables are predetermined, but not vice versa, the exceptions including lagged values of jointly dependent variables.

It may also be noted that the disturbance u_{it}, in the ith equation of the model for the tth sample observation, is assumed independent of *all* disturbances in *other* sample observations, but is *not* assumed independent of disturbances u_{jt}, u_{kt}, etc. in *other* equations for the *same* sample observation.

The equations of the model (1) are called *structural equations*; each is supposed to represent some homogeneous sector or some regular feature of the economy. It is often desirable to estimate their parameters, called structural parameters.

The *reduced form* of the model (1) is obtained by solving it for the jointly dependent variables, thus:

$$\text{(2)} \qquad y_t = -\mathrm{B}^{-1}\Gamma z_t + \mathrm{B}^{-1}u_t\,.$$

If $-B^{-1}\Gamma$ and $B^{-1}u_t$, respectively, are rechristened Π and v_t, the reduced form becomes

$$y_t = \Pi z_t + v_t \,. \tag{3}$$

For predicting the y's given the z's, one wants estimates of the reduced form parameters.

The estimation methods that I propose to discuss for a *structural equation* are as follows, with the abbreviations I shall use:

OLS: ordinary least squares, with some arbitrarily chosen dependent variable.

2SLS: two stage least squares, with some arbitrarily chosen dependent variable.

LI: limited information single equation maximum likelihood.

FI: full information maximum likelihood.

The estimation methods I propose to discuss for a *reduced form equation* are as follows, with the abbreviations I shall use:

OLSRF: ordinary least squares, with the equation's single jointly dependent variable y_{it} used as the dependent variable.

Solved OLS structure: first compute OLS estimates of the structure, and then solve for the reduced form as was done in passing from equations (1) to (3).

Solved 2SLS structure: compute 2SLS estimates of the structure, and solve for the reduced form.

Solved LI structure: compute LI estimates of the structure and solve for the reduced form.

Solved FI structure: compute FI estimates of the structure, and solve for the reduced form.

The literature contains theorems that imply the following properties (among others) of these various estimates, under certain stability assumptions. First, for structural equations: OLS estimates are in general biased, even asymptotically, but have the minimum variance among those discussed here. The 2SLS, LI, and FI estimates are consistent.

Second, for reduced form equations: the OLS estimates are unbiased, and consistent. The solved OLS structure gives biased estimates, even asymptotically. The solved 2SLS, LI, and FI structures give consistent estimates.

It should be noted that if a model is overidentified, then the overidentifying restrictions on the model imply certain restrictions on the reduced form parameters. The OLSRF estimates of the reduced form ignore these restrictions, but any reduced form estimates obtained by solving an estimated structure will take some account of them. If the overidentifying restrictions are correct, the OLSRF estimates can be expected to have larger errors than could be obtained by using the overidentifying restrictions. If the overidentifying restrictions are not correct (and in practice we usually are not really sure about all of them), then the OLSRF estimates may be as good as any.

Except for the ordinary least squares method the desirable properties that have been proved for the foregoing estimation methods are generally *asymptotic* properties. This means they are properties that appear only in the limit as the sample size becomes infinite. We do not know, from the mathematical theorems about these asymptotic properties, much about how the estimates will behave when the sample size is 20 or 30, or 100, or even several thousand. But of course this is what we want to know. So far, theoretical attacks on this problem using mathematical statistics have not been very successful.[2]

We have two other kinds of evidence about the relative merits of different estimation methods when sample sizes are small. One kind is given by econometric studies of real-world data in which two or more estimation methods have been used for the same structural equation or equations. In most cases, it is the OLS and LI methods that have been used. Comparisons of this kind cannot be conclusive, because the true values of the parameters are not known; hence all one has is two or more estimates of each structural equation, made by different methods. I have not seen all the studies which provide such comparisons. My subjective impression from what I have seen is that in many cases the OLS and LI estimates do not differ grossly from each other—say by the order of the sum of their estimated standard deviations or less—but that in cases where they differ strikingly, particularly where they have opposite signs or very different magnitudes, it is more often the LI estimates that are unreasonable in sign and magnitude, and the LS estimates that are reasonable, in the light of economic theory and other empirical evidence. This may be due to the tendency for a certain matrix, whose inverse plays an important role in the LI method, to be almost singular in some cases, thus giving a fairly high probability that LI estimates in those cases will have the wrong sign or at least have large estimated standard errors.[3]

[2] But see A. L. Nagar, *Statistical Estimation of Simultaneous Economic Relationships* (paperbound processed unpublished dissertation at Netherlands School of Economics, Rotterdam, 1959), pp. 21-65.

[3] H. Theil on pp. 233-5 of his book *Economic Forecasts and Policy* (Amsterdam, North-Holland Publishing Co., 1958), gives evidence suggesting why the LI estimates may sometimes be very far wrong.

So-called Monte Carlo experiments provide the second kind of evidence about the relative merits of different estimation methods when sample sizes are small. A Monte Carlo experiment is essentially an empirical method of learning about the probability distribution of a statistic that one is interested in. It consists in drawing a large number of samples from the population in question, computing the value of the interesting statistic for each sample, and recording the empirically observed sampling distribution of that statistic. This method is sometimes used when mathematical attacks have not succeeded, and it has become more practical with the advent of electronic computers.

In the case of a comparison between estimation methods for structural parameters, it works as follows. First, an artificial structure is set up, consisting of a model like equation (1), with *known* parameters B and Γ, and with a *known* distribution function of the disturbance vector u_t including its parameters Σ (and any other parameters it may have). Second, a set of values of exogenous variables (i.e., those z's that are not lagged values of the y's)for $t = 1, \ldots, T$ is chosen, and a set of initial values of the y's for $t = 0, -1, -2, \ldots,$ is chosen. Then a large number of samples of size T are chosen and observed from the known distribution of u_t. For each of these samples, the reduced form equations (2) are used to generate a set of values of the jointly dependent variables y_t and the predetermined variables for $t = 1, \ldots T$, in terms of the known parameters B and Γ, the known exogenous variables and initial values of predetermined variables, and the observed values of the random disturbances u_t. This yields a large number of artificial samples of data for y_t and z_t for $t = 1, \ldots T$ that have been generated by the artificial structure that was set up to begin with.

Then the known values of B, Γ, and Σ and the values of u_t are, so to speak, locked up in a drawer, and one pretends they are not known. One then uses the artificial sample data for y_t and z_t to estimate the parameters B, Γ, and Σ by each method that is in question. This can be done using the correct model, i.e., using a priori restrictions that correctly describe the artificial structure that was used, or it can be done with an incorrect model. The latter is useful for studying the consequences of using a wrong model to estimate parameters one wants. Most studies so far have used the correct model.

When the estimated values of the parameters have been computed by each method for each sample, one can then, so to speak, unlock the drawer, and compare each estimation method's sampling distribution of estimates of any parameter with the true value of that parameter, and hence arrive at a judgment as to which estimation method one prefers for that parameter with a sample of size T.

Of course it is to be emphasized that the Monte Carlo method does not give the *true* probability distribution of the estimates, but rather an empirical estimate of that distribution. It is analogous to determining the probability of heads with a coin by tossing it a large number of times and recording the proportion of heads that occurs. The Monte Carlo method is subject to sampling error itself. But if the number of samples used is large, the error is likely to be small.

When one compares a *distribution* of estimates with a single number, i.e., the true value of the parameter, it is necessary to have some measure of how good or how bad the correspondence is. Let the parameter be denoted by α, and the estimate by a. Then the expected value of the estimate is $\mathscr{E}a$, the bias of the estimate is $\mathscr{E}a - \alpha$, and the variance of the estimate is $\mathscr{E}(a - \mathscr{E}a)^2$. The variance is a poor measure, because it can be small (or even zero, in the case of an estimate that is a constant independent of the data!) and yet the bias can be very large, as shown by curve A in Figure 1. The bias is a poor measure, because it can be small or even zero and yet the variance can be very large, as shown by curve B in Figure 1. I shall adopt the expected squared error of the estimate as my criterion, namely $\mathscr{E}(a - \alpha)^2$. It is easy to show that it is the sum of the variance and the squared bias,

$$\mathscr{E}(a - \alpha)^2 = \mathscr{E}(a - \mathscr{E}a)^2 + (\mathscr{E}a - \alpha)^2 \, . \tag{4}$$

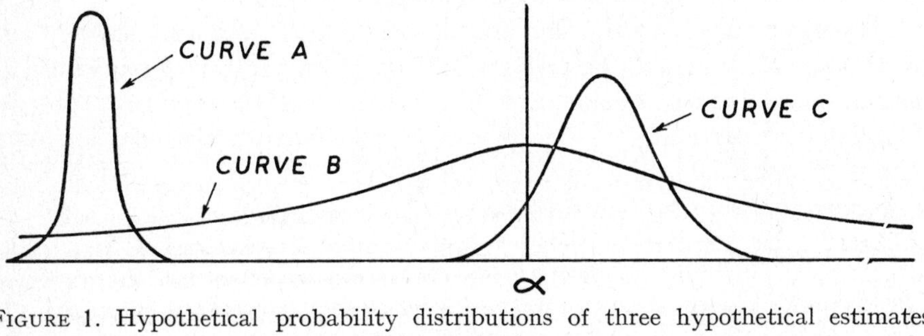

FIGURE 1. Hypothetical probability distributions of three hypothetical estimates of a parameter α.

The estimate whose distribution is shown in Curve C in Figure 1 would be preferred to the other two by the expected squared error criterion. This criterion has an intuitive appeal to many statisticians, and has often been used as the loss function in statistical decision theory. It has the advantage of taking account of both variance and bias, and of weighting large errors more heavily than small ones. Of course, it is not always appropriate: In situations where there is a certain threshhold level of error, below which there is no loss but above which everything is lost, then the obvious cirterion to use is the probability of making an error less than the threshhold level. I believe that in most real situations the costs of error are a fairly smooth increasing function of the size of the error, so I prefer the expected squared error criterion. The comparisons made below will be based on the root mean square error, which is the square root of the mean square error and is hence a monotonic increasing function of it, unless otherwise stated.

A comparison of OLS and simultaneous equations methods of estimating individual *structural* parameters is clearly what is wanted when the problem at hand depends on knowledge of individual structural equations or parameters. Sometimes one wants a comparison of the forecasting ability of reduced form equations like (3) estimated by different methods, because an important use of structural parameters is to obtain the reduced form and make forecasts. Most of the few Monte Carlo studies that have been done are confined to the estimation of structural parameters. While there is a relationship between the quality of structural estimates and the quality of reduced form estimates obtained by solving the estimated structure, it is difficult to make very simple statements about this that are useful for the case of small samples and biased estimators in which economists usually find themselves. If structural parameters are known exactly then of course reduced form parameters can be computed exactly, as in equation (2). If structural estimators are consistent then reduced form estimators obtained by solving the estimated structure are also consistent. Beyond this, relatively little theoretical progress has been made on this point.[4]

I report on three Monte Carlo studies of the kind described above, those by Harvey M. Wagner,[5] Robert L. Basmann,[6] and Robert Summers.[7] Let me take them in that order.

[4] When I presented this paper in December, 1958, I conjectured that if structural estimation method A gives smaller expected squared errors for structural parameters than method B, then the reduced form estimators obtained by solving method A's estimate of the structure are likely to have smaller expected squared errors than reduced form estimators obtained by solving method B's estimate of the structure. I have been persuaded, by an unsuccessful attempt to prove this and by an exchange of conjectures with H. Theil, that this is not necessarily so, and in particular that if OLS structural estimators have smaller expected squared errors than other structural estimators there is no general presumption that reduced form estimators obtained from the solved OLS structure will have smaller expected squared errors than other reduced form estimators. The difficulty with the solved OLS structure method is that it has no necessary connection with maximizing the likelihood function of the reduced form or minimizing some increasing function of the reduced form's errors.

[5] Harvey M. Wagner, "A Monte Carlo Study of Estimates of Simultaneous Linear Structural Equations," *Econometrica*, Vol. 26 (1958), pp. 117-133.

[6] Robert L. Basmann, "An Experimental Investigation of Some Small Sample Properties of Generalized Classical Linear Estimators of Structural Equations: Some Preliminary Results," presented at the December, 1958 meetings of the Econometric Society in Chicago.

[7] Robert Summers, "A Capital-Intensive Approach to the Small Sample Properties of Various Simultaneous Equation Estimators," presented at the December, 1958 meetings of the Econometric Society in Chicago.

Wagner used two models, differing only in the variance-covariance matrix Σ. The equations in the models were as follows:

$$C = 0.5Y + 0.25 + u_1 , \tag{5}$$

$$I = 0.1Y + 0.3Y_{-1} + 0.15 + u_2 , \tag{6}$$

$$Y = C + I + Z , \tag{7}$$

where C is consumption, Y is income, I is induced investment, Y_{-1} is lagged income, and Z is a linear trend variable. Endogenous variables are C, Y, and I. Wagner took 100 samples of size 20 from each of his two models, and in each case estimated the parameters of the overidentified equation (5) by OLS and LI. He also used the instrumental variables methods, once using Y_{-1} as the instrumental variable and once using Z. The root mean square errors for all 16 cases are shown in Table I. It will be seen that the LS and LI estimates in this experiment are almost equally good as judged by the mean square error. The only difference worth mentioning is in the estimation of the intercept in Model II, where the OLS estimate has a root mean square error about 10 per cent less than the LI estimate. The instrumental variables estimates are about as good as the others, better than both OLS and LI in 2 of the 8 relevant cases and worse than both in 6. As might be expected, the OLS estimates have relatively large biases and relatively small variances (this is not shown in Table I).[8]

TABLE I

ROOT MEAN SQUARE ERRORS OF WAGNER'S ESTIMATES OF PARAMETERS OF A CONSUMPTION FUNCTION IN A MONTE CARLO EXPERIMENT

(Source: see text, especially equation (5) and footnote 5.)

Parameter	Marginal Propensity to Consume				Consumption Function's Income Intercept			
True Value of Parameter	0.5				0.25			
Estimation Method[1]	OLS	LI	IV(Y_{-1})	IV(Z)	LS	LI	IV(Y_{-1})	IV(Z)
Model I	0.0174	0.0179	0.0191	0.0163	0.433	0.476	0.509	0.446
Model II	0.0462	0.0463	0.0456	0.0464	1.2677	1.2676	1.277	1.275

[1] IV (Y_{-1}) and IV(Z) refer respectively to instrumental variables estimates using Y_{-1} and Z as the instrumental variable.

[8] Since this paper was presented in 1958 A. L. Nagar (*op. cit.*, pp. 70-88) has done further experiments with Wagner's models, using newly generated synthetic data. He repeated the OLS but not the LI estimation of equation (1), and applied 2SLS to equation (1), and applied both OLS and 2SLS to equation (2) (here LI and 2SLS are identical), and also applied two other simultaneous-equations methods (not considered here) to both equations. The differences among methods for equation (2) are considerably greater than for equation (1) because the matrix inverse required

Basmann's results pertain to the following model (which he calls variant A):

$$(8)\quad -y_1 - 2y_2 + 1.5y_3 + 3x_1 \qquad\qquad\qquad\qquad - 0.6x_5 + 10 = u_1,$$

$$(9)\quad 1.5y_1 - y_2 \qquad - 0.5x_1 + 1.5x_2 + 2x_3 - 2.5x_4 \qquad + 12 = u_2,$$

$$(10)\quad 0.1y_1 - 4y_2 - y_3 \quad + 1.6x_1 - 3.5x_2 \qquad + 1.2x_4 + 0.4x_5 - 5 = u_3.$$

The endogenous variables are y_1, y_2, and y_3. The exogenous variables $x_1, \ldots, x_5$ are random. The disturbances u_i are jointly normally distributed. Equation (10) is not identified. Basmann took 200 samples of size 16, and in each case estimated the parameters of the overidentified equation (8) by the OLS, LI, and 2SLS methods. The root mean square errors are shown for all 15 cases in Table II. It will be seen that for every one of the five parameters, the OLS estimates have substantially smaller root mean square errors than the LI estimates. Also, for 4 of the 5 parameters the OLS estimates have smaller root mean square errors than the 2SLS estimates, though the differences between these two methods are not very great, less than 15 per cent for every parameter. In this experiment the OLS estimates again had the largest biases in most cases, but relatively small variances (this is not shown in Table II.)

TABLE II

ROOT MEAN SQUARE ERRORS OF BASMANN'S ESTIMATES OF A STRUCTURAL EQUATION IN A MONTE CARLO EXPERIMENT

(Source: see text, especially equation (8) and footnote 6.)

Parameter of	y_2	y_3	x_1	x_5	1
True value of Parameter	–2.0	1.5	3.0	–0.6	10.0
OLS	1.50	0.43	1.24	0.68	152
2SLS	1.56	0.37	1.45	0.79	174
LI	4.23	1.05	3.90	1.32	318

turns out to be more sensitive to the choice of method for equation (2). Nagar found that 2SLS was about the same as OLS for equation (1) in both models and for equation (2) in Model II (in these cases the root mean square error for 2SLS varied from 0.98 to 1.05 times that for OLS), but for equation (2) in Model I 2SLS was much better (there the root mean square errors for 2SLS were about 0.68 times those for OLS). His other methods usually but not always did a little better than OLS and 2SLS. It is interesting that for his samples the OLS root mean square error for the slope in equation (1) was only about 0.68 times Wagner's.

Summers conducted 6 experiments. For his experiments 1 and 2 he used the following equations, changing only the sample size.

$$(11)\quad y_1 - 0.7y_2 + 0.8z_1 + 0.7z_2 \qquad\qquad\qquad - 149.5 = u_1 ,$$

$$(12)\quad y_1 + 0.4y_2 \qquad\qquad\qquad + 0.6z_3 - 0.4z_4 - 149.6 = u_2 .$$

Here the endogenous variables are y_1 and y_2. The exogenous (and *a fortiori* predetermined) variables are based on per capita index numbers made from some real U.S. economic time series for about 1922–1941 compiled by L. R. Klein for one of his early models. The equations used by Summers for experiments 3 and 4 differed from (11) and (12) above in that the coefficient of y_2 in (11) was changed from —0.7 to 0.1 and to —1.3 in experiments 3 and 4 respectively. The equations he used for experiments 5 and 6 were like (11) and (12) expect that the variable z_1 was inserted in equation (12) with coefficients +0.5 and —0.5, respectively (though in estimation z_1 was omitted from (12); thus experiments 5 and 6 are a small step in the direction of investigating the effects of using an incorrect model.) Summers used 50 samples in each experiment and a sample size of 20 (except that 40 was used in experiment 2.) He estimated all the structural parameters in each experiment by the OLS, 2SLS, LI, and FI methods. In addition he did each experiment twice, using two different sets of exogenous variables, the main difference being that one set had higher intercorrelations than the other. He then obtained five sets of estimates of the reduced form for each experiment, by five methods: OLSRF, and the solved structures as estimated by OLS, LI, 2SLS, and FI. He then computed conditional forecasts of his endogenous variables y_1 and y_2 for a given set of values of the exogenous variables, and repeated this five times using the five different sets of reduced form estimates. He gives the root mean square errors for structural and reduced form parameters, and also some tests based on the mean absolute errors of the forecasts. Results for root mean square errors and mean absolute errors would be similar, but the former would penalize large errors more heavily.

It is expected that Summers's work will soon be published, so a brief qualitative summary of some of his results will suffice here. (1) For structural parameters: The OLS method was usually poorer than the other three methods, but it was the best of all in some of those experiments where an incorrect model was used, and it usually ranked better when the exogenous variables were highly intercorrelated than when they were not. The FI method was usually best except when the wrong model was used, in which case it was sometimes poorest. (2) For reduced form parameters: The solved OLS structure was usually poorest of the 5 methods and the solved FI structure was usually the best, but when an incorrect model was used this ranking was sometimes reversed! The OLSRF method was usually relatively bad, but when an incorrect model was used, it was sometimes relatively good. (3) For predictions: The solved OLS structure was consistently the worst. There was little to choose among the other four methods, except that when the incorrect model was used the OLSRF method did a bit better than the others.

These Monte Carlo studies[9] do not cover much ground. They suggest, however, that while there will be cases in which the simultaneous equations methods of structural estimation do not give sufficient (if any) improvement over OLS to make their extra cost worth while, either for the purpose of getting the structural parameters per se or for the purpose of solving the structure to get reduced form parameters, there will also be cases in which the 2SLS and LI methods are worth while, and in which the FI method gives still better results. It might be noted that as the services of high-speed computers become available to more economists, the cost advantage of ordinary least squares will dwindle.

In summary, it is not yet clear that the least squares method for structural estimation is dead and should be discarded. It is now clear, however, that even for small samples least squares sometimes will not do as well as simultaneous equations methods. The important task ahead is to learn more about how to decide which estimation method is likely to be best for any given actual econometric problem. For the present, the situation appears to be as follows: For structural parameters, least squares sometimes is preferable to simultaneous equations methods and sometimes is not. For reduced form parameters and forecasts in *just-identified* models, ordinary least squares estimation of the reduced form is good; in this case it is equivalent to solving the structure as estimated by two stage least squares, limited information, or full information methods. For reduced form parameters and forecasts in *overidentified* models, it seems well to begin by estimating structural parameters by simultaneous equations methods, and then to solve the estimated structure to get estimates of the reduced form. This appears to be true even in some cases where least squares estimates of the structure are better than simultaneous equations estimates of the structure, as suggested in footnote 4 above.

[9] See also W. A. Neiswanger and T. A. Yancey, "Parameter Estimates and Autonomous Growth," *Journal of the American Statistical Association* Vol. 54 (June, 1959), pp. 389-402 for another recent Monte Carlo study. They compare OLS and LI estimates of structural parameters in a two-equation model, under several sets of conditions. They find that LI does slightly better than OLS when a correct model is used, and that both do very poorly under certain types of mis-specification of the model.

A CAPITAL INTENSIVE APPROACH TO THE SMALL SAMPLE PROPERTIES OF VARIOUS SIMULTANEOUS EQUATION ESTIMATORS[1]

BY ROBERT SUMMERS

The small sample properties of five standard simultaneous equation estimating methods are examined by means of the distribution sampling technique. The methods are appraised on the basis of the sampling properties of three different kinds of estimates generated by them: (1) conditional predictions, (2) structural coefficient estimates, and (3) Studentized estimates of structural coefficients. Though one basic model is employed in the investigation, variants used in particular sampling experiments make it possible to compare the methods with respect to bias and efficiency in estimation in the presence of substantial multicollinearity in the predetermined variables and under certain conditions of misspecification. Careful attention is paid to the stochastic variation which necessarily is present in distribution sampling applications.

I. INTRODUCTION

1. A GREAT DEAL of work has been done since Haavelmo's pioneering work on estimating the parameters of a system of simultaneous stochastic equations [**15**]. A number of estimating methods have been devised, but little is known about their sampling properties when they are applied to small samples (except [**27**]). In this paper a report will be given on a series of sampling experiments performed to display the small sample properties of five of the most commonly used methods.

2. The estimators to be considered are: (1) Full Information Maximum Likelihood (FIML),[2] (2) Limited Information, Single Equation (LISE),[3] (3) Ordinary Least Squares (OLS),[4] (4) Two-Stage Least Squares (TSLS),[5] and (5) Least

[1] The author acknowledges with appreciation the material assistance he received for this research from the National Science Foundation and the Massachusetts Institute of Technology Computation Center. Kazuo Sato provided invaluable assistance that could be a model for graduate students everywhere; his work is convincing proof that constructing a large special purpose computer program is not best done by a professional programmer who lacks a deep understanding of the applied program. The research was carried on while the author was a member of the staff of the Cowles Foundation for Research in Economics at Yale University, and was first reported on at the December, 1958, meetings of the Econometric Society. The manuscript was first submitted to *Econometrica* on March 18, 1960; the final revised version was submitted on Nov. 21, 1963.

[2] [**23**, pp. 152–230; **10**, pp. 252–259].

[3] [**2**; **3**; **22**, pp. 162–176].

[4] OLS estimators are obtained by applying the Method of Least Squares individually to each equation of the system as if each equation contained only one jointly determined variable. The designation of the single jointly determined variable to be regarded as dependent is arbitrary.

[5] [**32**, pp. 223–229; **6**].

Squares, No Restrictions (LSNR).[6] It may be worthwhile to sketch very briefly what is known about these estimators. The Method of Maximum Likelihood is, of course, a standard estimating technique of statisticians. Both FIML and LISE are maximum likelihood methods and so they have the usual optimal asymptotic properties of maximum likelihood estimators. In FIML all parameters of the simultaneous equation system are estimated at the same time, and the likelihood maximization process takes into account all of the a priori information available. LISE is applied one equation at a time and in estimating the parameters of a particular equation, only the a priori information relating to that equation is utilized. Therefore, for large samples FIML is to be preferred to LISE. Both estimators are biased for small samples but have the important property of consistency. FIML is extremely difficult to apply computationally, and in fact it has not yet been used successfully for a large system. Of the four methods here considered, LISE is the second most difficult to apply. OLS is the most straightforward procedure, but in most sophisticated econometric circles it is in disrepute because it produces biased estimates even for large samples.[7] The essential point of Haavelmo's article was a demonstration of just this.

TSLS is the newest of the methods considered. The rationale behind it is as follows: The bias of OLS is a consequence of the fact that, quite arbitrarily, one or more jointly determined variables is treated in each of the individual equations as predetermined. The lack of independence between these variables and the structural disturbances leads to the OLS bias. In the first stage of TSLS, the "contamination" of these improperly specified predetermined variables is eliminated, at least partially, by estimating (using least squares) the reduced form disturbances of the equations containing the variables and then subtracting the disturbances from the corresponding variables. In the second stage, these new "purified" jointly dependent variables are used in the OLS manner as if they really were predetermined variables. It has been shown that TSLS yields consistent estimates and that asymptotically the estimates are indeed as efficient as LISE estimates. As in the use of OLS, an element of arbitrariness is present in the application of TSLS. All but one jointly determined variable is decontaminated in each equation; the basis for selecting optimally which variable is to remain as a dependent variable for the second stage has not been worked out.

For special simultaneous equation models (e.g., just-identifiable systems or subsystems) two or more methods may provide identical estimates. In general this would not be true, so a nondegenerate model has been considered in this investigation.

The four methods, FIML, LISE, OLS, and TSLS, are all used to estimate

[6] LSNR estimators are produced by a straightforward application of the Method of Least Squares to the reduced form.

[7] See, however, [11] as modified by [12], p. 400; and also [14, pp. 130–132; 32, p. 239; and 37].

structural coefficients. In this study, the methods are appraised primarily on the basis of their predictive qualities. For this purpose reduced form coefficients derived from structural coefficients must be estimated. A fifth method is available, however, for estimating reduced form coefficients directly: Least Squares, No Restrictions (LSNR). This method gives consistent estimates of reduced form coefficients, but the estimates are not efficient because the method ignores any a priori information specified in the model. Apart from computational simplicity, LSNR's principal appeal derives from its relative insensitivity to structural specification error. LSNR will be compared with FIML, LISE, TSLS, and OLS.

3. Now that computer improvements and increased availability of machine time can lighten the computation burden, it might be conjectured on the basis of its large sample properties that FIML should be the sole estimating procedure. If the large sample optimality of FIML carries over for small samples, in the case of investigations where firmly held convictions leave no doubt about the a priori restrictions, perhaps FIML will at some future date automatically be the procedure of choice. Ordinarily, however, though economic theory serves as a guide in selecting variables to consider in a simultaneous equation model, rarely is the guidance so specific that it can be translated directly into a priori restrictions without empirical testing. This search is better carried on by means of single equation methods because they allow a very weak specification of the model as a whole while individual equations are being examined.

It must also be recognized that rounding errors in the course of calculation build up more rapidly in FIML than in the single equation methods, so the limited accuracy of economic data may impose a restraint on how large a system can be handled with FIML. Furthermore, the easing of the computation burden of FIML does not mean that we ever can expect to dismiss lightly the task of using FIML to try many possible formulations of a large system.

For each of these reasons then—the problem of finding a priori restrictions and the limitation on how large a system can be handled with FIML—an interest in LISE, TSLS, and OLS is not merely academic.

4. An analytical derivation of the sampling properties of a statistic is usually preferred to a derivation synthesized in a sampling experiment. In part, this is because an analytical derivation has a generality about it that is almost impossible to attain with a sampling experiment. Fully as important, however, is a non-rational reason. We are always attracted by the aesthetic appeal of the triumph of the unaided intellect. From a pragmatic point of view, however, this latter reason should be given no weight in deciding how to attack a sampling distribution problem. Should a computer be used? Without doubt, the small sample problem could be solved if unaided labor of sufficient quantity and quality were applied to it (for example, the Koopmans' team of the late forties, most of whom were represented

as authors in [21] or [17]). Nagar [27] has already worked out some aspects of the small sample properties of TSLS (and of the more general k-class estimators). But elementary production theory in economics tells us that the relative prices of factors of production are critical in determining the least cost method of production. Since computer services are less scarce than the services of persons able to carry out the very difficult task of analytically working out the small sample properties, there is a strong case for using a capital-intensive form of attack.

II. THE MODEL

5. The basic model to be considered here is given by Equations

$$\text{(1a)} \quad y_{1t}+\beta_{12}y_{2t}+\gamma_{11}Z_{1t}+\gamma_{12}Z_{2t} \qquad\qquad +\gamma_{10}=u_{1t},$$

$$\text{(1b)} \quad y_{1t}+\beta_{22}y_{2t} \qquad\qquad +\gamma_{23}Z_{3t}+\gamma_{24}Z_{4t}+\gamma_{20}=u_{2t}.$$

The y's are jointly determined variables while the Z's are predetermined. The u's are bivariate normal variables with zero mean and a variance-covariance matrix denoted by Σ_u. This particular model was selected because it was the simplest one conceivable embodying the essential character of a simultaneous system for which the differences between the estimating procedures were interesting. It is easy to confirm that each of the equations is overidentified. The reduced form of the model is given by

$$\text{(2a)} \quad y_{1t}=\pi_{11}Z_{1t}+\pi_{12}Z_{2t}+\pi_{13}Z_{3t}+\pi_{14}Z_{4t}+\pi_{10}+v_{1t},$$

$$\text{(2b)} \quad y_{2t}=\pi_{21}Z_{1t}+\pi_{22}Z_{2t}+\pi_{23}Z_{3t}+\pi_{24}Z_{4t}+\pi_{20}+v_{2t}.$$

The π's are functions of the β's and γ's, and the v's are linear combinations of the u's. Of crucial importance is the fact that the absence of Z_3 and Z_4 from Equation (1a) and the absence of Z_1 and Z_2 from (1b) imply certain interdependencies among the π's in (2a) and (2b).

6. The model described in the last section was deliberately made economically anonymous, with no direct real-life counterpart. This was so that an appraisal of the estimating methods of Section 2 would have general applicability. The price of generality, however, is that the criterion for comparing the various estimating methods is not clear cut. Ordinarily one estimating method is deemed superior to another if the estimates of a population parameter produced by it are "closer" to the true value of the parameter than those produced by the other. If estimates of more than one population parameter are of interest, however, an unequivocal ranking of a number of methods is possible only if the relative standings of the different methods are uniform for each of the parameters. Since such uniformity is likely to be unusual, it is necessary to attempt to reduce the number of dimensions entering into the comparisons from the number of parameters of the model to some smaller number, preferably unity. For a model reflecting some real aspect of economic life, a unique basis of comparison natural to the economic circumstances

is likely to present itself. For example, in a demand and supply sector model different estimating methods could be compared on the basis of how well they estimated the parameter of greatest interest, say, the price elasticity or income elasticity of demand. Or perhaps they could be compared by seeing how well they provided a basis for conditionally predicting the value of the most interesting of the jointly determined variables, say, price. This last example could be generalized to the conditional prediction of some interesting function of the entire set of jointly determined variables, like price-times-quantity, the volume of transactions.

The artificial model described above provides no clue to a single parameter which could be used as a basis for appraising the methods. The primary criterion finally adopted as an uneasy compromise was the accuracy of conditional predictions of each of the jointly determined variables. Thus the number of parameters of concern was reduced from eight, the structural coefficients of Equations (1a) and (2b), to two.[8] The structural and reduced form coefficients are intermediate products in obtaining the conditional predictions, so they were also examined, if not analyzed in detail. Readers who consider structural estimation of greater interest than conditional prediction will have in Section 20 and Appendix Tables IA–VIA and IB–VIB a partial basis for judging the estimating methods from this other point of view.

The criterion problem is further complicated by the fact that even though a distinct ranking of the methods can be achieved for every particular specification of the values of the parameters, it is quite possible, and even likely, that the rankings will not be the same for all specifications. It is to be hoped that something systematic can be learned about how the different methods compare for different parameter combinations, i.e., for different regions in the parameter space.

7. The model defined by equations (1a) and (1b) was used for most of the sampling experiments to be reported on here. The model was modified, however, for one group of experiments. These experiments were designed to explore the conse-

[8] The remaining two dimensions could be reduced to one by using some measure of joint dispersion of the two conditional predictions around their true values. One possible measure is the mean Euclidean distance; this measure, however, is not invariant under a change of units of the original variables of the model. Another is the generalized variance around the true values. For a bivariate normal population this measure is approximately proportional to the area within a particular confidence contour (and exactly proportional if the predictions are unbiased). If the generalized variance were used as a criterion, the method producing pairs of predictions nestling within the elliptical contour with the smallest area would be judged best. A quite reasonable application of the minimax principle would suggest that it is not desirable, however, to compare a method generating a circular contour with another generating an extremely attenuated ellipse of the same area. These remarks point up the impossibility of defining a general loss function.

Since the predictions are conditional upon values of the predetermined variables, which necessarily are selected arbitrarily, any criterion based upon a one dimensional combination of the predictions is still not unidimensional. This is discussed in Section 18 below.

quences for the different estimating methods of one kind of specification error. In all experiments, in carrying out the calculations required by each of the estimating methods, it was assumed that the model was as specified in (1a) and (1b). In the misspecification experiments, however, the data on y_1 and y_2 actually were generated by the model defined by (1a) and (1b′):

$$\text{(1b')} \quad y_{1t}+\beta_{22}y_{2t}+\gamma_{21}Z_1+\gamma_{23}Z_3+\gamma_{24}Z_4+\gamma_{20}=u_{2t}\,.$$

In this misspecification model, the second equation is just-identifiable instead of being over-identified.

The actual values used for the parameters in the sampling experiments are given in Section 9, and then discussed in greater detail in Section 15.

III. THE SAMPLING EXPERIMENT

8. Only since the advent of the high speed computer has it been feasible to investigate numerically and in detail the small sample properties of simultaneous equation estimators by performing sampling experiments. A number of such investigations have now been reported ([**35**, **24**, **28**, **29**, **27**, **7**, **26**]). The sampling experiment approach, known as distribution sampling, is a variation of the so-called Monte Carlo technique.[9]

The sampling procedure used in obtaining the empirical results reported in Sections 15 to 21 consisted of the following steps:

(a) Equations (1a) and (1b) (or (1b′)) were used as the basic model of a hypothetical economy. In any particular experiment the values of all of the parameters of the model, both the structural coefficients and the variance-covariance matrix of structural disturbances, were specified. In addition, the values taken on by all of the predetermined variables were specified for each of the T observation periods considered.

(b) Using a random sampling method,[10] T observations were generated on both y_1 and y_2, conditioned by the set of values of the predetermined variables. The T sets of observations on y_1, y_2, Z_1, Z_2, Z_3, and Z_4 constituted a sample.

(c) LISE, TSLS, OLS, and FIML were each applied to the sample to estimate the following parameters:[11]

[9] An eminent practitioner of the art of Monte Carlo suggests, however, that straight distribution sampling without sampling tricks should not be dignified by that name [**34**, p. 64].

[10] A random normal deviate generator [**31**, Chapters 3 and 5] was used to produce structural disturbances which were then transformed into reduced-form disturbances. (In the actual computing, these two processes were combined into one step.)

[11] As stated in Section 2, in TSLS the selection of a jointly determined variable as dependent in the second stage is arbitrary. The same is true in OLS. In Step (c) for each equation TSLS and OLS were computed two ways: first with y_1 dependent and then with y_2 dependent. Since y_1 was always treated as the normalized variable in LISE and FIML, the TSLS and OLS structural coefficient estimates based upon y_1 dependent were directly comparable with the FIML and LISE ones.

(1) the structural coefficients of the model, the β's and γ's, and their asymptotic standard errors in the case of LISE, TSLS, and OLS;

(2) the reduced form coefficients, the π's; and

(3) conditional predictions of y_1 and y_2 for a prescribed set of Z's. These predictions were based upon the estimates of the π's.

(d) LSNR was applied to the sample to obtain:

(1) estimates of the reduced form coefficients, the π's; and

(2) conditional predictions of y_1 and y_2 for the same prescribed set of Z's as in (c) (3). These predictions were based upon the estimates of the π's.

(e) Steps (b), (c) and (d) were then repeated N times to get N different estimates of each of the parameters by each estimating method.

(f) The N different estimates of each parameter obtained for each estimating method were organized into a relative frequency distribution and summary measures were computed for each distribution.

(g) Then a new specification of the values of the parameters was made and Steps (b), (c), (d), (e), and (f) were repeated. A variety of specifications was made in order to observe the sensitivity of the relative frequency distributions to the specification of the characteristics of the model.

9. In Section 6 it was pointed out that in judging the estimating methods under consideration it was necessary to compare the methods for a variety of specifications of the parameters of the model. Step (g) of the preceding section indicates that for this reason the sampling experiment design provided for multiple experiments. Table I gives the parameter constellations used in the twelve sampling experiments which were performed. Five different sets of parameters were used; four were used with a single sample size, $T=20$, but the fifth was used with two sample sizes, $T=20$ and $T=40$. If T is thought of as a parameter, there were six distinct parameter constellations. Each was used twice, once in an A experiment and once in a B one. The A experiments differ from the B ones in the extent to which the predetermined variables were specified to be intercorrelated. Table II gives the correlation matrices for the two alternative specifications.

The ones based upon y_2 dependent were not directly comparable. To make them so required multiplying each estimated coefficient by the reciprocal of the estimate of the coefficient of y_1. As would be expected, this transformation of the coefficients made the observed variances of the TSLS and OLS estimates with y_2 dependent considerably larger than those of the others. Whether the observed variances were larger because the estimators were intrinsically worse or because the transformation had to be performed is unknown, of course. Since the transformation would have put an undue handicap on the y_2 dependent estimates in any comparisons of variances, they were ignored in reporting on how the estimating methods compared with respect to structural coefficient estimation.

TABLE I

PARAMETER COMBINATIONS USED IN SAMPLING EXPERIMENTS

	β_{12}	γ_{11}	γ_{12}	γ_{10}	β_{22}	γ_{23}	γ_{24}	γ_{20}	σ_{11}	σ_{12}	σ_{22}	T	N
Experiments 1A and 1B	−.7	.8	.7	−149.5	.4	.6	−.4	−149.6	400	200	400	20	50
Experiments 2A and 2B	−.7	.8	.7	−149.5	.4	.6	−.4	−149.6	400	200	400	40	50
Experiments 3A and 3B	−.1	.8	.7	−149.5	.4	.6	−.4	−149.6	400	200	400	20	50
Experiments 4A and 4B	−1.3	.8	.7	−149.5	.4	.6	−.4	−149.6	400	200	400	20	50
Experiments 5A and 5B*	−.7	.8	.7	−149.5	.4	.6	−.4	−149.6	400	200	400	20	50
Experiments 6A and 6B**	−.7	.8	.7	−149.5	.4	.6	−.4	−149.6	400	200	400	20	50

T: Number of observations in each sample in the experiment.
N: Number of observations in the sampling experiment.

* In Experiments 5A and 5B, $\gamma_{21} = +.5$ instead of zero as assumed in all other experiments except Experiments 6A and 6B.

** In Experiments 6A and 6B, $\gamma_{21} = -.5$ instead of zero as assumed in all other experiments except Experiments 5A and 5B.

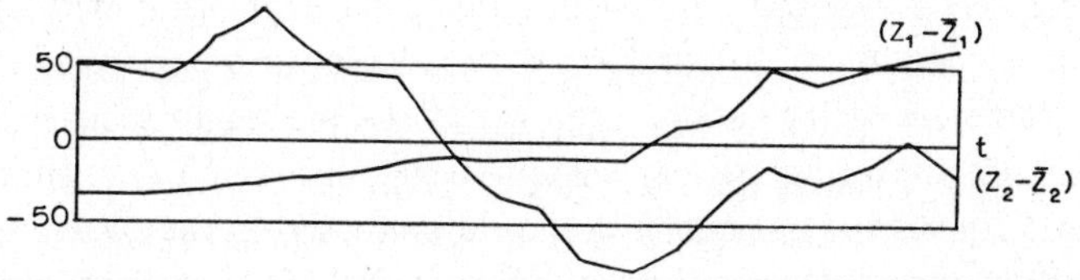

Fig. 1. Timepath of the variables $(Z_1 - \bar{Z}_1)$ and $(Z_2 - \bar{Z}_2)$ in B experiments.

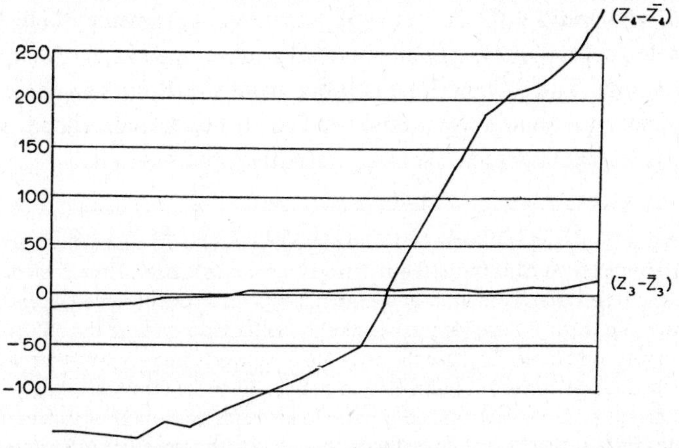

Fig. 2. Timepath of the variables $(Z_3 - \bar{Z}_3)$ and $(Z_4 - \bar{Z}_4)$ in B experiments.

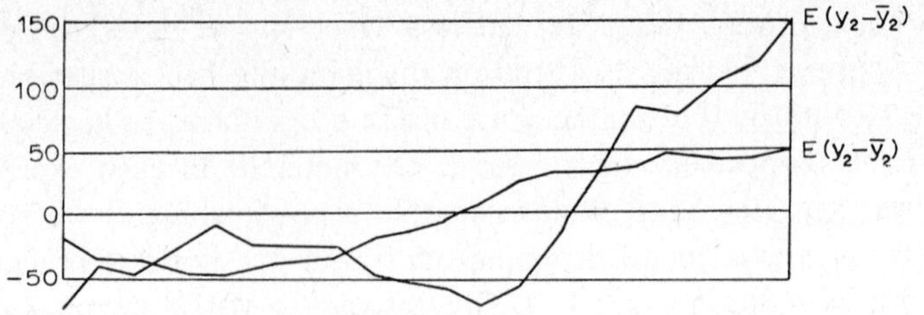

Fig. 3. Timepath of the expected values of the variables $(y_1 - \bar{y}_1)$ and $(y_2 - \bar{y}_2)$ in experiments 1B.

TABLE II

INTERCORRELATIONS OF THE Z VARIABLES

CORRELATION MATRICES

	A Experiments				B Experiments			
	Z_1	Z_2	Z_3	Z_4	Z_1	Z_2	Z_3	Z_4
Z_1	1	.078	.16	.38	1	−.37	.86	.98
Z_2		1	.017	−.057		1	−.52	−.43
Z_3			1	.31			1	.83
Z_4				1				1

The data on the Z's for the B experiments were selected to resemble real economic data. Figures 1 and 2 depict the values of $(Z_{it} - \bar{Z}_i)$ that were used. The values are index numbers, deflated by population size, selected from the data presented in [**18**, pp. 143–145]. The variables were: Z_1, labor income originating in government; Z_2, residential construction (non-farm); Z_3, stock of non-farm housing, and Z_4, excise taxes. Selection of these variables may seem to destroy some of the anonymity of the model, but any set of highly correlated variables would have done as well. Figure 3 shows the influence of the exogenous variables on the endogenous variables for the parameter constellation of Experiment 1B. The data on the Z's for the A experiments were obtained by scrambling each of the four time series above so that, though the means and variances of the four variables remained the same, the covariances differed from zero only because of sampling fluctuations in the scrambling.

10. Table II shows how highly intercorrelated the realistic Z's were. It was distressing to discover that such a high intercorrelation, and the resulting near-singularity of the variance-covariance matrix of the Z's, led to significant computational difficulties in the B experiments. Despite the small size of the simultaneous equation system, it was found that round-off errors built up to substantial levels during certain matrix inversion operations. In the course of computing LISE and TSLS estimates this occasionally resulted in negative elements along the principal diagonals of matrices purported to be the asymptotic variance-covariance matrices

of estimators; and, more often, to matrices which should have been positive definite, but were not. During its operation the computer kept a sharp lookout for such cases. Arbitrarily (but on the order of the programmer rather than as an act of free-will) it dropped all such cases it encountered. In each experiment, the sampling was repeated until fifty acceptable sets of estimates were computed. Whether this is equivalent to dropping outliers, a questionable practice, will be discussed briefly in Section 22 below. That discussion will be anticipated here only to the extent of remarking that the evidence suggests that this censoring procedure did not invalidate the generalizations based upon the included cases.

The flavor of the difficulties encountered may best be conveyed by describing an outrageously pathological case that was encountered. Detailed investigation revealed that in this case a structural coefficient estimate produced by one estimating method varied from -5 to -10 to -19, depending upon whether the variance-covariance matrix of observations of the Z's was inverted by means of a standard IBM 704 library routine, a special homemade IBM 704 routine which took account of the symmetry of a moment matrix, or an IBM 650 library routine.[12] When tested on matrices which were not close to singular, the three inversion routines produced virtually identical inverses. Note that the order of the matrix being inverted was only five. This result does not augur well for persons seeking estimates of structural coefficients of large aggregate models where multicollinearity of predetermined variables is likely to be common.[13]

IV. PROCEDURE FOR ANALYZING THE RESULTS OF THE SAMPLING EXPERIMENTS

11. The twelve sampling experiments generated a very substantial amount of computer output, but, as extensive as the data were, they still represent only a series of twelve samples from as many populations. The possibility of making useful inferences about these population is greatly enhanced by the fact that the different estimating methods are applied to the *same* sets of pseudo-economic data. The number of hours of computing would have had to be increased twentyfold to yield output with the same information content if the same sets of data were not used. But using the same sets leads to samples of estimates which are not independent between estimating methods. This lack of independence unfortunately eliminates the possibility of using simple standard statistical tests. The statistical difficulties are a consequence of a natural greed for statistical "power." The power is not achieved cheaply for it has necessitated falling back on nonparametric tests.

[12] The true value of the parameter estimated was $-.7$!

[13] E. Ames and S. Reiter [1], using a quite different methodological approach, have found the same intercorrelations among time series. K. J. Arrow and M. Hoffenberg [5] ran into difficulties in coping with a set of nineteen highly intercorrelated exogenous variables in their analysis of inter-industry demands. L. R. Klein and M. Nakamura [20] through analytical techniques have illuminated the consequences of multicollinearity for OLS, LISE, and TSLS.

Fortunately the efficiency of the tests is fairly high, so the gain from using the same sets of data is substantial.

Applying the rules of statistical inference is essential in interpreting the summary numbers which describe the different estimating methods. This is because though differences may appear to be negligible considering the measures of precision of the individual numbers, they may in fact point to substantial differences between the relevant populations. Intuition is a poor guide in judging whether observed differences are statistically significant when the data are from correlated samples, as is the case here.

12. The sampling procedure outlined in Section 8 is in detail as follows. For each set of pseudo-economic data generated in Step (b), the structural coefficients, the β's and γ's of equations (1a) and (1b) were estimated by each of the estimating methods. Let these be designated $\tilde{\beta}_{ij}^k$ and $\tilde{\gamma}_{ij}^k$, where the superscript indicates the estimating method. Estimates of the π's of equations (2a) and (2b), designated $\tilde{\pi}_{ij}^k$, were computed as functions of the $\tilde{\beta}_{ij}^k$'s and $\tilde{\gamma}_{ij}^k$'s (in matrix notation: $\tilde{\Pi}^k = (\tilde{B}^k)^{-1}, \tilde{\Gamma}^k$, where $\tilde{B}^k$, $\tilde{\Gamma}^k$, and $\tilde{\Pi}^k$ are the matrices of estimates by the kth method of the coefficients of (1a), (1b), (2a), and (2b)). Then conditional predictions of y_1 and y_2, designated $\tilde{y}_1^k|Z^*$ and $\tilde{y}_2^k|Z^*$ for a particular set of Z^* values, were made on the basis of the reduced form coefficients, the $\tilde{\pi}_{ij}^k$'s, for each of the methods. The $\tilde{y}_1^k|Z^*$ and $\tilde{y}_2^k|Z^*$ obtained were then compared with the population values of y_1 and y_2 as determined by the structural parameters specified in the experiment, conditional upon the same Z^* values, to appraise the various methods. (In matrix notation: $\tilde{y}^k|Z^* = \tilde{\Pi}^k \cdot Z^*$ and $y|Z^* = \Pi Z^*$, where $\tilde{y}^k|Z^*$ is the vector of estimates of the jointly determined variables, here y_1 and y_2, as obtained from the kth method; $y|Z^*$ is the vector of values taken on by the jointly determined variables when the disturbances of the v's of equations (2a) and (2b) are suppressed; and Z^* is an arbitrary vector of values of the predetermined variables.) A comparison of the absolute differences $|\tilde{y}_i^k|Z^* - y_i|Z^*|$ was then made for each of the different estimating methods. Within each sampling experiment this was repeated fifty times, the number of sets of pseudo-economic data generated per experiment.

In the next two sections the statistical inference procedures used in this investigation are described. Because they have been applied to the β's and γ's in a few cases in addition to the $\tilde{y}_i^k|Z^*$'s, the procedures will be discussed in general terms.

13. Until now reference has been made to comparing the performances of different estimating methods, but the exact nature of the comparison has not been made explicit. Suppose the parameter being estimated is α (standing for $y_i|Z^*$, β_{ij}, or γ_{ij}) and an estimate of α produced by the kth estimating method is $\tilde{\alpha}^k$. Associated with each method is a frequency function, $f_k(\tilde{\alpha}^k|\alpha)$. Some measure of the dispersion of $f_k(\tilde{\alpha}^k|\alpha)$ around α is called for; clearly the estimating method with the frequency function with the smallest dispersion is best. The measure most commonly used for

this purpose is the Root Mean Square Error (RMSE). Alternatives are the Mean Absolute Error (MAE) and $P = \text{Prob}\ \{|\tilde{\alpha} - \alpha| < \delta\}$. The RMSE is to be preferred in the event that the "loss" associated with an estimate which differs from the value of the parameter being estimated is proportional to the square of the size of the deviation; the MAE is to be preferred if the loss is proportional to the absolute size of the deviation; and P is to be preferred if all absolute deviations less than δ are considered harmless and all absolute deviations greater than δ are considered equally harmful. On a priori grounds, it is hard to choose between RMSE and MAE. The virtue of RMSE is that it is a simple function of the bias and variance of the frequency function, and therefore its sampling distribution is relatively simple. Whether or not the assumption that a quadratic loss function is reasonable is a moot point. The MAE figures importantly below only because it was extremely easy to make certain statistical tests based indirectly upon the MAE. The measure P seems to depend too much upon an arbitrary selection of δ. In general the results of using P will be highly sensitive to the choice of δ; admittedly, however, in a particular applied situation an appropriate δ may suggest itself.

14. In Section 19, below, and the Appendix, the bias, standard deviation, and RMSE are presented for the $f_k(\tilde{\alpha}^k|\alpha)$'s of many different $\tilde{\alpha}$'s ($\tilde{\beta}_{ij}^k$'s, $\tilde{\gamma}_{ij}^k$'s, $\tilde{\pi}_{ij}^k$'s, $\tilde{y}_1^k|Z^*$'s, and $\tilde{y}_2^k|Z^*$'s) of the twelve sampling experiments. The bias and variance measures are not very interesting in themselves, but they give an idea of the relative sizes of the two components of the RMSE. Unfortunately it is not easy to compare RMSE's for two different methods, say the kth and the lth, within a sampling experiment because of the correlation between $\tilde{\alpha}^k$ and $\tilde{\alpha}^l$. Without a detailed knowledge of the correlations it is impossible to judge which observed differences are in fact significant. Even knowing the correlations, it is difficult computationally to test for significant differences in a statistically efficient manner. (Comparisons of the relative sizes of the RMSE's for different experiments may be made, though, because the $\tilde{\alpha}$'s of one sampling experiment are independent of the $\tilde{\alpha}$'s of all other experiments.)

In principle it would be desirable to examine the RMSE's for all estimating methods at the same time. While it is not hard to devise a test of the hypothesis that there is no difference between the methods (e.g., the Friedman matched sample test of ranks[14]), finding a test which provides an ordering of the methods is another matter. As a consequence, the procedure adopted in this study was to make pairwise comparisons of the methods.

Even making pairwise comparisons is awkward. Testing for the equality of variances would be easy enough; the Pitman test **[30]** is designed for just this purpose when the two underlying populations are correlated (and normal). But the presence of bias, known theoretically to be present in all cases and even demonstrable in a fair number, makes the Pitman test inappropriate for analyzing the

[14] **[36**, pp. 601–602].

RMSE's.[15] Perhaps the most efficient test statistically would be a Likelihood Ratio Test in which the asymptotic properties of the λ statistic were used. The computation for the numerator of this statistic would be extremely burdensome, however.

The test finally settled upon was a nonparametric one of the equality of the MAE's. The null hypothesis, H_0: $MAE_{\tilde{\alpha}^k} = MAE_{\tilde{\alpha}^l}$, is equivalent to the null hypothesis, $H_0' : P_{kl} = \frac{1}{2}$, where $P_{kl} = \text{Prob}\ \{|\tilde{\alpha}^k - \alpha| > |\tilde{\alpha}^l - \alpha|\}$. Since $\tilde{\alpha}^k$ and $\tilde{\alpha}^l$ were highly correlated in virtually every case and therefore were nearly always on the same side of α, p_{kl}, the proportion of cases in which $|\tilde{\alpha}^k - \alpha|$ exceeded $|\tilde{\alpha}^l - \alpha|$ was extremely easy to obtain by visual inspection. The power-efficiency of this "sign" test is about two-thirds, a small price to pay for the freedom to leave unspecified the exact functional form of $f_k(\tilde{\alpha}^k|\alpha)$ and the saving in computation. Since $\tilde{\alpha}^k$ is in every case the ratio of sums of random variables, it has been argued that for finite samples $f_k(\tilde{\alpha}^k|\alpha)$ does not have well-behaved moments. The use of p_{kl} as a test statistic circumvents the difficulty of measuring the dispersion $f_k(\tilde{\alpha}^k|\alpha)$ with moments which may not be well behaved.[16]

Two alternatives to the null hypothesis were used: $H_1' : P_{kl} > \frac{1}{2}$ and $H_2' : P_{kl} < \frac{1}{2}$ which are equivalent to $H_1 : MAE_{\tilde{\alpha}^k} > MAE_{\tilde{\alpha}^l}$ and $H_2 : MAE_{\tilde{\alpha}^k} < MAE_{\tilde{\alpha}^l}$. The extra exposure to the risk of making a wrong decision in the three-alternative test over the risk in the standard two-alternative one is trivial, and it is highly desirable to have a definite ranking of two methods indicated when the null hypothesis is rejected.

An additional comment on the problem of computation is in order. Justifying the use of the simple nonparametric test on the grounds of computational simplicity must appear ludicrous to the reader in view of the author's willingness to shoulder the extremely heavy burden of computing the parameter estimates. As a minimum, it shows a substantial imbalance in computing effort. The explanation lies in the fluctuation in the relative prices of capital and labor during the course of the investigation. After the parameter estimates were computed, machine time became scarce. As a consequence, a more labor-intensive procedure was followed. Not every possible test was performed. In some cases only sampling was done, not necessarily randomly. Scarce resources and an indefinitely large number of avenues of research imposed their constraints.

15 It was thought at an early stage that since the observed biases of different methods were of approximately the same size, perhaps the Pitman test could be utilized after all. If it really were true that the biases were equal, equality of the variances would imply equality of the RMSE's. This line of argument led to the computation involved in a host of Pitman tests. Unfortunately the results seemed to be quite sensitive to the assumption of the equality of the biases. A byproduct of the Pitman test was a statistic which revealed that the biases were actually significantly different in most cases. Incidentally, the results of these tests correlated poorly with the results of the tests described below.

16 Basmann [8] argues that since in fact the distributions of the various estimators do not possess finite first and second moments, bias and RMSE are not meaningful parameters. The nonparametric test treatment of MAE is a way of meeting his objection.

15. The particular parameter constellations of the twelve experiments were selected to illuminate a particular part of the parameter space. When the value of β_{12} is varied from $-.1$ to $-.7$ to -1.3 in Experiments 3, 1, and 4, the determinant of the matrix of coefficients of the jointly determined variables varies from .5 to 1.1 to 1.7. Thus the effect of near singularity of the B matrix can be explored.[17] Experiments 1 and 2 were designed to throw light on the difference between estimates based upon twenty observations and ones based upon forty. In Experiments 6, 1, and 5 the parameter γ_{21} varies from $-.5$ to 0 to $+.5$. The estimates of the β's and γ's for each method were obtained on the assumption that $\gamma_{21}=0$. By generating the pseudo-economic data with reduced forms which reflected the non-zero γ_{21}'s, it was possible to get from Experiments 6, 1, and 5 some idea of the consequences of misspecification.

It is not so easy to characterize the essential difference between the time series of the Z's of the A and B experiments in quantitative terms. Certainly, the strength of the overidentification in the B experiments is less than in the A experiments. To the extent that Z_1 and Z_4 are practically the same variables, the only variable in (1a) which does not appear in (1b) is Z_2; similarly, only Z_3 is present in (1b) but absent in (1a). Then both equations would be practically just-identifiable; and FIML, LISE, and TSLS would all be practically equivalent. But to go further, since Z_3 is highly correlated with Z_1 and Z_4, the over-identification of equation (1a) would be much weaker than that of (1b).

Recall that the estimates of a parameter obtained by different estimating methods are correlated within an experiment. Estimates of different parameters obtained by a particular method from any particular sample are also correlated. Estimates from any one experiment, however, are independent of estimates from all of the other experiments. This is because different sets of random numbers were used in the six experiments. It is possible, therefore, to aggregate across similar experiments. For the purpose of aggregation the experiments were divided into two groups: Experiments 1, 2, 3, and 4 constituted one group, and 5 and 6 the other. The groupings were based upon the similarity of parameter constellations within the groupings.

[17] It seems reasonable to conjecture that the interesting range of variation of the parameters is the one which covers a wide variety of angles of intersection of the planes represented by the two equations of the model. More specifically, the projections of the planes in the (y_1, y_2) space form two straight lines, and it is the angle of intersection of the lines which is of interest rather than the orientation of the lines. If this is so, the important contrast between the Marshallian "Cross" (i.e., supply and demand curves) and the simple-minded Keynesian "Cross" (the $C+I$ curve and the 45-degree line) is not that the one involves lines with slopes of opposite sign and the other involves lines with slopes of the same sign, but rather that the acute angle between the intersecting lines is much smaller in the Keynesian case. The variation in the sizes of the angles defined by the range of variation of β_{12} is from 27° to 74°. A marginal propensity to consume of about .672, the value found by Haavelmo in his well-known investigation of the bias in least squares estimation of a simple Keynesian model [16], implies an angle of 11°; a larger marginal propensity to consume would lead to an even smaller angle. Thus, the range of variation of β_{12} undertaken in this study does not cover the entire interesting range.

V. SUBSTANTIVE RESULTS: STUDENTIZED ESTIMATES OF STRUCTURAL COEFFICIENTS

16. Before looking at the results of the tests described in Section 14, it is of considerable interest to know whether a method, optimal or not, is serviceable. For all but trivial purposes, it is essential that an estimate $\tilde{\alpha}^k$ of a parameter α be accompanied by a measure of its precision. Each of the estimating methods prescribes a formula for computing an estimate of the standard error of $\tilde{\alpha}^k$, $\tilde{\sigma}_{\tilde{\alpha}^k}$. For all estimating methods except OLS, $\tilde{\sigma}_{\tilde{\alpha}^k}$ will be a consistent estimate of $\text{RMSE}_{\tilde{\alpha}^k}$ for the distribution which the actual distribution of $\tilde{\alpha}^k$ approaches as T approaches infinity. The question is, how good is $\tilde{\sigma}_{\tilde{\alpha}^k}$ as an estimate of $\text{RMSE}_{\tilde{\alpha}^k}$ for small samples? If it is reasonably good, can judgments about α be made on the basis of $\tilde{\alpha}^k$ and $\tilde{\sigma}_{\tilde{\alpha}^k}$ in the usual way, namely through the use of the Studentized ratio, $\mathscr{T}_{\tilde{\alpha}^k}=(\tilde{\alpha}^k-\alpha^*)/\tilde{\sigma}_{\tilde{\alpha}^k}$, where α^* is a hypothesized value of α? The second question

TABLE III

RESULTS OF APPLYING THE KOLMOGOROFF-SMIRNOV TEST TO THE SAMPLE DISTRIBUTIONS OF STUDENTIZED STRUCTURAL COEFFICIENT ESTIMATES TO TEST FOR NORMALITY

$$H_0 : f_k\left(\frac{\tilde{\alpha}-\alpha}{\tilde{\sigma}_{\tilde{\alpha}}}\right) : N(0, 1) \qquad .95 \text{ Significance Level}$$

Table entries are frequency of acceptances of H_0 for the tests associated with the four parameters of each equation

	LISE		TSLS		OLS	
Experiment	Eq. I	Eq. II	Eq. I	Eq. II	Eq. I	Eq. II
1A	4	4	4	4	2	1
2A	4	4	4	4	1	2
3A	4	4	4	4	1	2
4A	4	4	4	4	1	2
5A	4	1	4	2	2	2
6A	4	2	4	2	2	2
Percentage of Acceptances of H_0 in A Experiments	100.0	79.2	100.0	83.3	37.5	45.8
1B	4	4	2	4	0	1
2B	4	4	4	4	0	1
3B	0	2	0	2	0	1
4B	4	4	4	4	0	0
5B	4	3	4	3	0	1
6B	4	2	4	2	0	3
Percentage of Acceptances of H_0 in B Experiments	83.3	79.2	75.0	79.2	0	29.2
Percentage of Acceptances of H_0 in A and B Experiments	91.7	79.2	87.5	81.2	18.7	37.5

essentially encompasses the first, and so a series of Kolmogoroff-Smirnov tests [9] was performed to see if the $\mathcal{T}_{\tilde{\alpha}^k}$'s were approximately normally distributed with a zero mean and unit variance. This was done for structural coefficients only.

Table III presents the results of these tests. LISE, TSLS, and OLS were the estimating methods examined. (The asymptotic variances for FIML were not estimated.) All of the structural parameters were considered. Except for Experiment 3B, in the experiments where there was no specification error the null hypothesis was accepted in almost every case for LISE and TSLS. In the experiments containing a specification error, the results for LISE and TSLS were only slightly less favorable. OLS did not fare so well, however. In almost no case could one have made a sensible judgment about β_{ij} or γ_{ij} on the basis of an OLS estimate.

VI. SUBSTANTIVE RESULTS: CONDITIONAL PREDICTIONS

17. The results of a series of pairwise comparisons of the different estimating methods appear in Table IV. The nonparametric test described in Section 14 above was applied to the conditional predictions $\tilde{y}_1^k|Z^*$, and $\tilde{y}_2^k|Z^*$ for the six A experiments and the six B experiments. Each of the values of the Z^*'s upon which the $y_i^k|Z^*$'s were conditional was set at the mean of the Z variable in the sample plus one standard deviation of the Z variables observed in the sample (i.e., $Z_i^* = \bar{Z}_i + \sigma_{Z_i}$).

The decision was made to move away from the sample mean in order to give errors in estimating slope coefficients an opportunity to do mischief; the deviation was selected above the mean, in the absence of any reasonable guidance, because in real-life models, where there is trend in the predetermined variables, predictions will usually be made for values of the predetermined variables in excess of their means in the observed sample. The sensitivity of the test to this selection of Z^* will be commented upon in the next section.

The test for each experiment was a binomial one which was carried out by means of the normal distribution approximation. Each test statistic was expressed as a standardized normal deviate, $N(0, 1)$ and classified as being either inside or outside the critical region. After that, the test statistics of each group of experiments were added together; the sums were then divided by their standard errors (the square root of the number of experiments in the group). Thus the numbers in the twelve columns are standardized normal variables under the hypothesis that the MAE's of each method in a two way comparison are equal. The numbers always appear in the row of the method observed to be superior. A method will be described as "revealed superior" to another method if its superiority is statistically significant. The parenthetical number within a cell indicates the number of individual experiments contained within the aggregate in which significant differences were observed (e.g., of the four experiments, 1A to 4A, LISE was revealed superior to OLS in all four comparisons of $\tilde{y}_1^k|Z^*$; in only two cases, however, was TSLS revealed superior to LSNR). An asterisk beside a number indicates that at the .95 level of significance

TABLE IV

RESULTS OF PAIRWISE COMPARISONS OF LISE, TSLS, OLS, FIML, AND LSNR IN PREDICTING $y_1|Z^*$ AND $y_2|Z^*$

$H_0 : \mathrm{MAE}\tilde{y}_i^k|z^* = \mathrm{MAE}\tilde{y}_i^l|z^*$

Estimating Methods	$\tilde{y}_1\|Z^*$ Exp. 1A–4A	Exp. 1B–4B	Exp. 5A, 6A	Exp. 5B, 6B	Exp. 5A, 5B	Exp. 6A, 6B	$\tilde{y}_2\|Z^*$ Exp. 1A–4A	Exp. 1B–4B	Exp. 5A, 6A	Exp. 5B, 6B	Exp. 5A, 5B	Exp. 6A, 6B
LISE		+1.27	+4.20(2)*		+2.20(1)*	+1.00(1)	+ .71	+ 1.27	+1.80	+ .40	+ .80	+1.4
TSLS	− .14			−1.00								
LISE	+8.20(4)*	+5.66(3)*	+8.80(2)*	+3.60(1)*	+6.80(2)*	+5.60(1)*	+7.21(4)*	+10.89(4)*	+6.00(2)*	+7.40(2)*	+6.40(2)*	+7.00(2)*
OLS												
LISE		+1.41					+ .28(1)			+ .40(1)	+1.20(1)	
FIML	− .28		−2.40(1)*	− .20	− .60	−2.00(1)*		− .57	− .60			−1.40
LISE	+ .85	+ .99(1)	+ .60	+ .20	+ .40	+ .40	+ .14(1)	+ .42		+ .20		0
LSNR									− .80		− .60	
TSLS	+8.49(4)*	+5.66(3)*	+9.20(2)*	+5.80(2)*	+7.60(2)*	+7.40(2)*	+8.34(4)*	+11.74(4)*	+7.40(2)*	8.20(2)*	+7.40(2)*	+8.20(2)*
OLS												
TSLS	+ .42	+ .57		0						0	+ .40	
FIML			−5.40(2)*		+3.00(1)*	−2.40(1)*	−1.13(1)	− 1.98(2)*	−1.80(1)			−2.20(1)*
TSLS	+2.83(2)*	+1.56(1)		+ .60				+ .14		+ .60		
LSNR			−4.60(2)*		−2.20(1)*	−1.80(1)	− .14		−2.00*		− .60	− .80
OLS												
FIML	−7.92(3)*	−5.37(3)*	−8.80(2)*	−4.80(2)*	−7.00(2)*	−6.60(2)*	−7.21(4)*	−11.74(4)*	−6.00(2)*	−7.20(2)*	−5.20(2)*	−8.00(2)*
OLS												
LSNR	−7.35(3)*	−6.08(3)*	−8.80(2)*	−3.40(2)*	−6.00(2)*	−6.20(2)*	−6.36(3)*	−10.61(4)*	−6.60(2)*	−8.00(2)*	−6.20(2)*	−8.40(2)*
FIML	+ .99	+1.13	+1.00	+ .80	+1.00	+ .80	+ .28			+ .80	+1.40	+1.00
LSNR								− 1.27	−1.20			

A table entry represents the proportion of times one method gave estimates closer to the true value than the other, expressed in standardized normal units (i.e., $(p_{kl} - P_{kl})/\sigma_{p_{kl}}|P_{kl}$ where $P_{kl} = 1/2$). Thus each entry is a test statistic for the null hypothesis.

Asterisks indicate cases where proportions are significantly different from one-half at the .95 confidence level. Numbers in parentheses indicate the number of significant cases that have been aggregated.

the method whose label shares the line with the number is revealed superior to its opponent in that comparison for the group of experiments. If the method appearing on the upper line of a comparison gave estimates of y_i which were closer to the true value than the method on the lower line, the corresponding $(p_{kl}-P_{kl})/\sigma_{p_{kl}}$ entry would be positive; otherwise it would be negative.

The results of the tests are presented by A and B groupings: Experiments 1A–4A, Experiments 1B–4B, Experiments 5A and 6A, and Experiments 5B and 6B. Two additional groupings, Experiments 5A and 5B and Experiments 6A and 6B were formed.[18]

One pattern of significant differences in Table IV stands out. In almost every individual contest OLS was revealed inferior to its opponent. The aggregate statistics for the various groups in every case reveal FIML, LISE, TSLS, and LSNR to be superior to OLS. The significant differences for the other pairwise comparisons are not as striking, however.

The pattern of parenthetical numbers indicates that combining the experiments into groups did not cover up important differences between experiments within groups. Within a group for any two-way comparison, a revealed superiority appeared in almost all of the experiments or in none. In Experiments 3A and 3B, however, OLS fared significantly less badly than in the other experiments of the first group. The fact that these were the two experiments where the value of the determinant of the matrix of coefficients of the y's was smallest suggests that perhaps the differences between the methods become smaller as that matrix approaches singularity. With only this qualification, it appears that in each of the regions of the parameter space represented by the two groups the ranking of the methods is fairly uniform.

In addition, there is fairly good agreement between the results of the A experiments and the B's. It is excellent between the first four A's and B's. It is quite good between the A and B misspecification experiments, for estimates of $y_2|Z^*$, but less so for estimates of $y_1|Z^*$. Because of the difference in the degree of intercorrelation of the predetermined variables between the A and B experiments, one would expect that the power to discriminate between methods would be greater for the A experi-

[18] Though Experiments 5A and 5B appear to differ from Experiments 6A and 6B in a symmetrical way, $\gamma_{21} = +.5$ and $\gamma_{21} = -.5$, it was expected that the effects of the two deviations of γ_{21} from zero would not be equivalent, at least for FIML. The estimates of the β's and γ's produced by FIML are derived from estimates of the π's. These have been obtained through a likelihood maximization process where the π's have been constrained by the a priori specification of the model. The constraining relationships were $\pi_{12}/\pi_{11} = \pi_{22}/\pi_{21}$ and $\pi_{14}/\pi_{13} = \pi_{24}/\pi_{23}$. The populations which generated the pseudo-economic data for the Experiments 5A, 5B, 6A, and 6B complied with the second constraint but not the first. The values of the parameters specified in Experiments 5A and 5B where $\gamma_{21} = +.5$ yield for the first constraint a left side equal to .42 and a right side equal to 2.33; in Experiments 6A and 6B where $\gamma_{21} = -.5$ the corresponding values are 9.33 and .54; if γ_{21} had been equal to zero each side would have been equal to .875. This would lead one to conjecture that FIML would perform better in Experiments 5A and 5B than in Experiments 6A and 6B.

ments than for the B. This expectation was not borne out in the first four experiments. While the A's seem to have greater power than the B's in tests involving $y_1|Z^*$, the opposite appears to be the case in those involving $y_2|Z^*$. In the misspecification experiments, however, the A's do seem to exhibit the greater power. In fact, the disagreements between the results of the A and B experiments can be accounted for by the greater power manifested by the A experiments. The grouping of the misspecification experiments by number instead of letter was unrewarding. It appears that the consequences of the difference in the degree of misspecification between Experiments 5A and 5B, and 6A and 6B are less important than the consequences of the difference in intercorrelation of the predetermined variables. As far as conditional predictions are concerned, the conjecture of footnote 18 seems not to be borne out.

Given, then, that experiments can be combined into groups and that the results of the A experiments are reasonably consistent with those of the B's, what can be said about the relative standings of FIML, LISE, TSLS, and LSNR? Making pairwise comparisons was an expedient which had to be resorted to for technical statistical reasons. A five-way ranking of all the methods is desired. Can the ten pairwise comparisons of the five estimating methods for each group of experiments be combined to form a five-way ranking of the methods? Is it possible that the pairwise comparisons might give an inconsistent ranking? More specifically, might the pairwise comparisons display intransitivity so that a consistent five-way ranking cannot be achieved?[19] The answer is that for "large" samples the pairwise comparisons *must* display transitivity; for "small" samples (like $N=50$?), they need not.

Figure 4 is a schematic representation of the five-way rankings built up out of the pairwise comparisons of Table IV. In the upper half of the chart, eight lists of the five methods appear, one list per grouping for each conditional prediction. Within each list the methods appear in order of decreasing merit in the sequence implied by the two-way comparisons indicated in Table IV. Statistically significant differences are indicated by arrows pointing from the revealed superior method to the revealed inferior one. The presence of intransitivities would indicate that the experiments did not provide a satisfactory basis for discriminating between the methods. The fact that no intransitivities were actually observed is therefore encouraging (but see footnote 20).

In the lower half of Figure 4 are four lists of methods based upon a consolidation of the A and B experiments. The rankings were obtained by making pairwise comparisons between methods after adding together the matching A and B entries in Table IV.[20] The dissimilarity of the A and B lists in Figure 4 appears to contra-

[19] Shades of welfare economics [4], homo stochasticus [13], and measurement theory [25].

[20] A partial check on the adequacy of this way of combining the A and B experiments was carried out. A score was assigned to each method in each list in the upper half of Figure 4 by comparing it with all methods in the same list to which it was superior. The points awarded to a method in a particular comparison depended upon the size of the entry in Table IV corresponding to the comparison. As in the case of the Olympic games, any scoring system must be considered

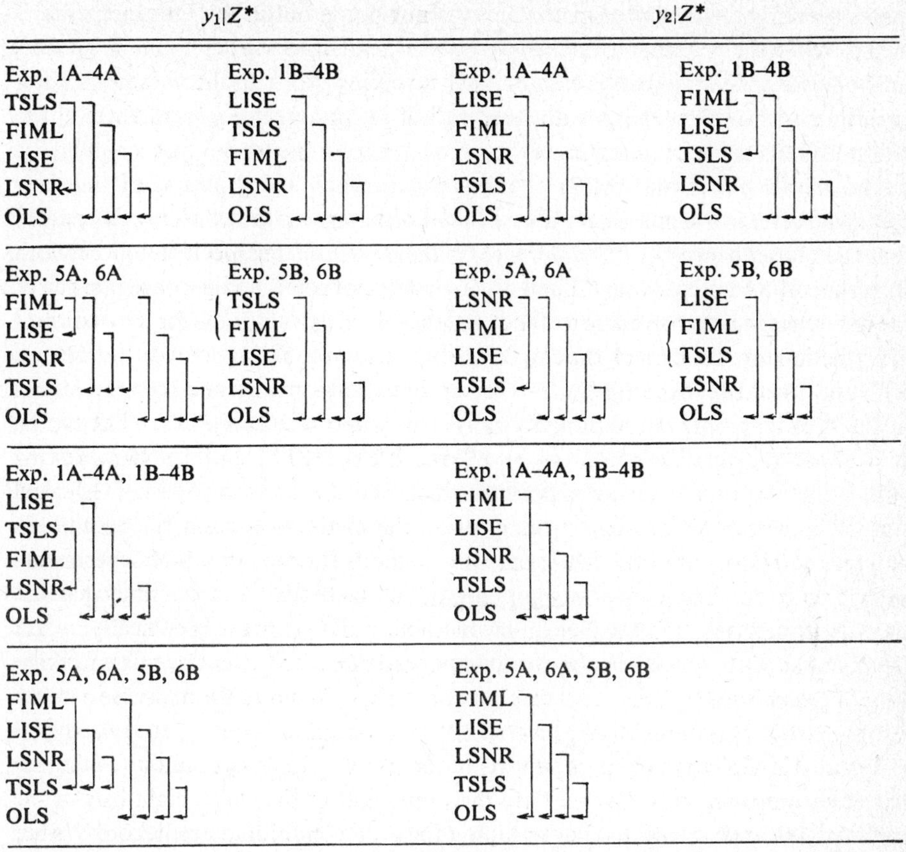

Arrows joining two methods indicate that the method higher in the list is revealed superior to the method lower in the list.

Figure 4.—A schematic representation of the five-way rankings of conditional predictions of FIML, LISE, TSLS, OLS, and LSNR

quite unofficial. Since the size of the entry is monotonically related to the probability that the method is really superior, the points were awarded according to the size of the entry (specifically, 1 point for entries between 0 and .49, 2 points for entries between .50 and .99, 3 points for entries between 1.00 and 1.49, 4 points for entries between 1.50 and 1.96, and 6 points for entries over 1.96—i.e., significant at the .95 level). Within each group and for each y variable an average score was computed for each method. These average scores were then compared with the scores of the methods computed for the list based upon the consolidation of the A and B experiments. In two of the four lists the rankings were identical; in the other two, the differences were slight. In one case the scores assigned to the methods in the consolidated list implied a ranking of the methods which was slightly different from that of the consolidated list. This indicates a second order "comparative-score" intransitivity. It is chains of such comparative score intransitivities which make it possible every fall for sports writers to "demonstrate" the superiority of an unimposing, relatively weak football team over a team of national rank.

dict the assertion above that there is fairly good agreement between the results of the A and B experiments. The explanation is that rankings in the chart reflect trivial differences between methods in some comparisons and non-trivial differences in others. In arriving at the conclusion that the agreement was good, trivial differences were ignored.

Of the four consolidated lists in the lower half of Figure 4, one contains three revealed superiorities among FIML, LISE, TSLS, and LSNR, but the other three among them contain only one. As a consequence, any ranking of these four methods must be extremely tentative.[21] The least ambiguous case will be examined first. In the misspecification experiments, TSLS is distinctly inferior to the other three methods when the predetermined variables are not highly intercorrelated; it performs much better, relatively, when they are. This may only be a consequence of an inability to perceive the inferiority of TSLS because of lack of power. On balance, it seems appropriate to rank TSLS low. Surprisingly, FIML appears somewhat better than the others. It was expected that FIML would be thrown off the scent more than the others by the misspecification. Surely for large enough values of γ_{21} this would happen. Also surprisingly, LSNR did not distinguish itself in these experiments. It appears that when dealing with a small sample, exploiting the a priori information about the model through the use of FIML or LISE will more than compensate for slight errors in specifying the model. LSNR is not misled by the incorrect constraint on the π's, but at the same time it does not make use of the correct one (see footnote 18); on balance, in competing with LISE and FIML, LSNR is the loser for the compromise when the degree of inaccuracy of the constraint is not too great.

The differences between the methods in the first four experiments were quite small. One would be rash here to conclude more than that LSNR is relatively weak. FIML's performance is again surprising. On the basis of its optimum large sample properties, one would have expected it to stand out much more in comparison with the other methods. In the region of the parameter space covered by the first four experiments, it appears that, as far as conditional predictions are concerned, economy in computation can safely supplant statistical efficiency as a basis for choosing among FIML, LISE, TSLS, and LSNR.

18. In the twelve sampling experiments upon which the conclusions of the last section were based, a particular set of values of the predetermined variables was used. The choice of Z_i^* values at one standard deviation above their means was a reasonable one, but it was by no means unique. The appraisal given above of the estimating methods would be of limited usefulness if it held only for this choice of the Z_i^*'s. To see if the appraisal had general applicability (as far as the choice of Z_i^*'s was concerned) Experiment 1A was repeated with $Z_i^* = \bar{Z}_i - 2\sigma_{Z_i}$. Admittedly, this

[21] In what immediately follows, judgments will be made, at least partially, on the basis of the scores developed for checking purposes, and described in footnote 20.

TABLE V

COMPARISON OF THE EFFECTS OF USING $Z^* = Z + \sigma_Z$ AND $Z^* = Z - 2\sigma_Z$ IN EXPERIMENT 1A

	$\tilde{y}_1 \mid Z^*$			$\tilde{y}_2 \mid Z^*$		
	Experiment 1A		Exp. 1A–4A	Experiment 1A		Exp. 1A–4A
Estimating Methods	$Z+\sigma_Z$	$Z-2\sigma_Z$	$Z+\sigma_Z$	$Z+\sigma_Z$	$Z-2\sigma_Z$	$Z+\sigma_Z$
LISE TSLS	−1.414	+ .566	− .141	+ .566	− .283	+ .707
LISE OLS	+3.677*	+3.960*	+8.202(3)*	+2.263*	+6.789*	+7.212(4)*
LISE FIML	− .849	− .283	− .282	+ 2.83	− .283	+ .283
LISE LSNR	+1.697	+1.697	+ .849	0	+1.414	+ .141(1)
TSLS OLS	+3.677*	+5.092*	+8.485(4)*	+3.112*	+6.789*	+8.344(4)*
TSLS FIML	− .283	− .283	+ .424	0	− .566	−1.132(1)
TSLS LSNR	+2.546*	+2.263*	+2.828(2)*	+ .566	+ .849	− .141
OLS FIML	−3.677*	−4.243*	−7.920(3)*	−2.546*	−6.789*	−7.212(3)*
OLS LSNR	−3.395*	−3.677*	−7.354(3)*	−2.546*	−6.789*	−6.364(3)*
FIML LSNR	+1.697	+1.697	+ .990	+ .283	+1.132	+ .282

A table entry represents the proportion of times one method gave estimates closer to the true value than the other, expressed in standardized normal units (i.e., $(p_{kl} - P_{kl})/\sigma_{p_{kl}} | P_{kl}$ where $P_{kl} = 1/2$). Thus each entry is a test statistic for the null hypothesis.

Asterisks indicate cases where proportions are significantly different from one-half at the .95 significance level. Numbers in parentheses indicate the number of significant cases that have been aggregated.

second choice was only one more point in the vast (k_1, k_2, k_3, k_4) space where $Z_i^* = Z_i + k_i \sigma_{Z_i}$ but $(-2, -2, -2, -2)$ is far enough removed from $(1, 1, 1, 1)$ to provide valuable information about the sensitivity of the comparisons of the various methods to differences in the k_i's.

Table V contains the results of pairwise comparisons of the estimating methods for Experiment 1A when $Z_i^* = Z_i - 2\sigma_{Z_i}$. The format of the table is the same as that of Table IV, and in fact two columns of Table IV are repeated in Table V to make it easy to see the consequences of changing the Z_i^*'s. The test statistics based upon $Z_i^* = Z_i - 2\sigma_{Z_i}$ are very close to those based upon $Z_i^* = Z_i + \sigma_{Z_i}$. No formal test of hypothesis is necessary to conclude that the appraisal in the previous section holds for sets of values of the predetermined variables other than $Z_i^* = Z_i + \sigma_{Z_i}$.

19. The last two sections have dealt only with the question of the statistical significance of observed differences between the conditional predictions produced by different estimating methods. Tables VI and VII describe the magnitudes of the conditional predictions of the twelve experiments. The meaning of the labels on the tables is self evident. Corresponding to each estimating method and each $y_i|Z^*$, there is a cell containing three entries. The upper one is the observed mean of $(\tilde{y}_i^k|Z^* - y_i|Z^*)$, an estimate of the bias of $\tilde{y}_i^k|Z^*$; the entry in italics in the lower right is the RMSE of $\tilde{y}_i^k|Z^*$; and the entry in the lower left is the standard deviation of $\tilde{y}_i^k|Z^*$. If a dagger (†) appears next to an observed mean, then that mean is more then 1.96 standard errors (as estimated from the empirical sampling distribution) from zero. This means that the estimates of the procedure associated with the cell have been *revealed* to be biased. Of course, all of the methods in fact produce biased estimates, so the daggers should be interpreted only as signals that the associated estimating methods may be particularly bad.

In these tables the distinct inferiority of OLS again stands out. There is only barely an indication that one can carry over to conditional predictions in the small asymptotic standard errors than those of the other estimating methods [**33**, pp. 204–05]. In seven of twenty-four possible comparisons OLS estimates had the smallest standard deviation instead of the twenty per cent expected because of change alone. But in eight of the twenty-four comparisons the OLS standard deviations were largest, again instead of the expected twenty per cent. In any case, the biases of OLS are so large that the RMSE's of OLS substantially overshadow the RMSE's of the other methods, sometimes by between 100 and 400 per cent. It should be noted, though, that in Experiment 3B OLS performs quite creditably. This supports the remark made in Section 17—but not on the basis of independent evidence—that the closeness to singularity of the matrix of coefficients of the jointly determined variables may be an important conditioning variable in appraising the methods.

The nonparametric tests on the MAE's were compared in an informal way with ordinal rankings of the RMSE's as obtained from Tables VI and VII to see whether the choice of dispersion measure used made a difference. It appears that the appraisal of the estimating methods given in Section 17 would have been essentially the same if RMSE had been used as a criterion instead of MAE. In the four cases where LISE performed worse, Experiments 1B ($y_2|Z^*$), 3B ($y_1|Z^*$ and $y_2|Z^*$), 4B ($y_2|Z^*$), and 6B ($y_2|Z^*$), it was, however, always only one or two outlying ob-

TABLE VI

THE MEAN BIASES, STANDARD DEVIATIONS, AND ROOT-MEAN-SQUARE-ERRORS OF THE CONDITIONAL PREDICTIONS OF THE A EXPERIMENTS

	Exp. 1A		Exp. 2A		Exp. 3A		Exp. 4A		Exp. 5A		Exp. 6A	
Parameters	$y_1\|Z^*$	$y_2\|Z^*$	$y_1\|Z^*$	$y_2\|Z^*$	$y_1\|Z^*$	$y_2\|Z^*$	$y_1\|Z^*$	$y_2\|Z^*$	$y_1\|Z^*$	$y_2\|Z^*$	$y_1\|Z^*$	$y_2\|Z^*$
True values	113.588	298.191	113.588	298.191	−29.586	656.215	155.691	193.008	61.169	223.407	166.006	373.157
LISE	1.88 7.23 *7.47*	† 2.354 7.38 *7.74*	1.07 5.35 *5.45*	.320 5.79 *5.80*	−.59 7.20 *7.23*	−1.11 14.98 *15.02*	−.70 6.97 *7.00*	.03 5.63 *5.63*	−1.48 6.69 *6.85*	.38 8.11 *8.12*	1.44 6.66 *6.82*	† 3.61 8.79 *9.50*
TSLS	.90 6.83 *6.89*	1.16 7.38 *7.47*	.67 5.31 *5.35*	−.17 5.76 *5.76*	−.76 7.20 *7.24*	−1.86 14.97 *15.08*	† −3.17 7.84 *8.45*	† −1.92 6.66 *6.93*	† −5.53 6.35 *8.42*	† −5.27 8.82 *10.27*	† −6.88 6.62 *9.55*	† −8.32 10.98 *13.77*
OLS	† −8.76 5.08 *10.13*	† −11.21 9.34 *14.58*	† −10.40 4.36 *11.27*	† −14.24 6.11 *15.49*	† −3.01 7.23 *7.84*	† −8.98 16.10 *58.31*	† −20.31 8.16 *21.89*	† −14.95 7.99 *16.95*	† −11.13 5.73 *12.51*	† 11.56 8.63 *14.42*	† −19.00 5.56 *19.79*	† −24.82 12.10 *27.63*
FIML	1.56 7.02 *7.19*	1.82 7.51 *7.73*	1.17 5.44 *5.56*	.39 5.77 *5.78*	−.48 7.27 *7.29*	−.74 15.22 *15.24*	−.84 6.79 *6.84*	.13 5.30 *5.30*	−1.37 6.53 *6.67*	−.98 9.35 *9.41*	1.72 6.46 *6.68*	.58 8.71 *8.72*
LSNR	† 2.15 7.55 *7.85*	1.43 7.88 *8.01*	.96 5.34 *5.44*	.47 5.89 *5.91*	−.95 7.46 *7.52*	−.19 15.95 *15.95*	−.56 7.14 *7.17*	−.24 5.17 *5.17*	−1.14 6.72 *6.82*	.42 8.52 *8.53*	−.68 6.66 *6.70*	.76 8.29 *8.33*

The upper entry in each cell is the mean bias; the lower left entry is the standard deviation (s.d.); the lower right entry, in italics, is the root-mean-square-error (RMSE).

† indicates that the bias exceeds 1.96 s.d./$\sqrt{50}$.

TABLE VII

THE MEAN BIASES, STANDARD DEVIATIONS, AND ROOT-MEAN-SQUARE-ERRORS OF THE CONDITIONAL PREDICTIONS OF THE B EXPERIMENTS

	Exp. 1B		Exp. 2B		Exp. 3B		Exp. 4B		Exp. 5B		Exp. 6B	
Parameters	$y_1 \mid Z^*$	$y_2 \mid Z^*$	$y_1 \mid Z^*$	$y_2 \mid Z^*$	$y_1 \mid Z^*$	$y_2 \mid Z^*$	$y_1 \mid Z^*$	$y_2 \mid Z^*$	$y_1 \mid Z^*$	$y_2 \mid Z^*$	$y_1 \mid Z^*$	$y_2 \mid Z^*$
True values	113.588	298.191	113.588	298.191	−29.586	656.215	155.691	193.008	61.169	223.407	166.006	373.157
LISE	+1.30 10.10 *10.18*	+4.14 17.20 *17.69*	+.52 5.22 *5.25*	+1.60 6.98 *7.16*	−.96 14.04 *14.07*	−.42 39.30 *39.30*	−1.46 10.40 *10.50*	+.68 14.83 *14.84*	−.39 8.19 *8.20*	+.76 12.16 *12.19*	+1.99 10.03 *10.23*	† +4.23 12.53 *13.22*
TSLS	+.20 9.70 *9.70*	−1.84 12.65 *12.78*	−.60 4.95 *6.99*	+.21 6.99 *6.99*	−.32 10.46 *10.46*	−3.91 25.72 *26.01*	† −4.50 9.71 *10.70*	† −3.81 8.39 *9.22*	† −2.24 7.70 *8.02*	−1.91 11.72 *11.87*	−.57 8.35 *8.37*	−.67 9.90 *9.92*
OLS	† −7.45 9.16 *12.16*	† −26.36 12.87 *29.33*	† −10.10 5.40 *11.45*	† −24.97 8.29 *26.31*	+.03 9.45 *9.45*	† −25.46 21.78 *33.50*	† −18.86 11.23 *21.95*	† −23.19 8.08 *24.56*	† −9.53 8.62 *12.85*	† −25.47 10.13 *27.41*	† −10.47 9.68 *14.26*	† −26.42 13.35 *29.60*
FIML	+2.09 9.92 *10.14*	+.96 9.99 *10.04*	+.47 5.19 *5.21*	+.73 5.87 *5.91*	+.69 9.71 *9.73*	−4.77 20.47 *21.01*	−1.04 10.63 *10.68*	−.85 5.81 *5.87*	−1.03 8.02 *8.09*	−3.01 15.98 *16.26*	+2.31 9.39 *9.67*	+1.93 9.18 *9.38*
LSNR	+1.02 10.27 *10.32*	+.98 11.06 *11.11*	+1.10 6.15 *6.24*	+.45 6.64 *6.65*	+.64 11.00 *11.02*	−5.26 22.63 *23.23*	−.40 11.66 *11.67*	−1.17 6.13 *6.24*	+1.93 8.71 *8.92*	† +3.31 11.48 *11.95*	−.55 9.66 *9.68*	+.34 10.63 *10.64*

The upper entry in each cell is the mean bias; the lower left entry is the standard deviation (s.d.); the lower right entry, in italics, is the root-mean-square-error (RMSE).

† Indicates that the bias exceeds 1.96 s.d./$\sqrt{50}$.

servations which made all the difference.[22] Thus the choice of dispersion measure did make a difference in these cases, but in the other cases the rankings obtained by the two criteria were approximately equivalent.

The biases that appear in Tables VI and VII are all of quite moderate size. While they run as high as 18 per cent of the value predicted for OLS, the largest one for the other methods is only 9 per cent. Among LISE, TSLS, FIML, and LSNR, ratios of the largest RMSE of a column to the smallest, however, run as high as 2.53, with 17 out of 24 greater than 1.10, and 7 out of 24 greater than 1.40. It is clear that the penalty one pays for selecting the worst method of FIML, LISE, TSLS, and LSNR is not inconsequential.[23]

VII. SUBSTANTIVE RESULTS: STRUCTURAL COEFFICIENTS

20. In the previous sections the various estimating methods were appraised with respect to how well they provide a basis for prediction. A less thorough comparison of the methods with respect to structural coefficient estimation will now be given. The methodology of the analysis is the same as that used above, so a description of it will not be repeated.

The nonparametric test described in Section 14 was applied to estimates of structural coefficients of both equations in Experiment 1A and the first equation of Experiment 3A. Table VIII, constructed just like Table IV but on a less aggregative basis, summarizes the results of these tests. The entries in the table are again standardized normal variables under the null hypothesis that the MAE's of each of the two methods being compared are equal. As before, significant deviations leading to rejection of the null hypothesis are asterisked. The evidence here points in the same direction as that of the conditional prediction tests. OLS is revealed inferior to LISE, TSLS, and FIML in almost three-fourths of the thirty-six possible comparisons. In the ten comparisons where it is not revealed inferior, it is observed inferior with only three exceptions. No such uniform domination is displayed among LISE, TSLS, and FIML, however. In Experiment 1A, FIML is distinctly best, but there is little difference between LISE and TSLS. In Experiment 3A, no significant

[22] This last remark was not meant as a general defense of the eliminating of outliers. For some purposes it may be worthwhile to discriminate between different degrees of kurtosis as well as dispersion. If, for example, the kurtosis is so very great that outliers are manifestly ridiculous and can be ruled out on a priori grounds (e.g., an estimate of the marginal propensity to consume equal to more than, say, two) then excess kurtosis may help to mitigate excess variance. The question is simply how heavy a weight should occasional large errors be given? Even if the weight increases with the size of the error, there may be a threshold beyond which the error should be given zero weight.

[23] The penalty can be interpreted as a data cost. Suppose one estimator of a population parameter has a standard error k times as great as another one. Then the precision of an estimate obtained by using the first estimator will be the same as that by using the second only if the sample size of the first is k^2 times as great as that of the second.

TABLE VIII

RESULTS OF PAIRWISE COMPARISONS OF LISE, TSLS, OLS, AND FIML

$H_0 : \text{MAE}\tilde{a}_k = \text{MAE}\tilde{a}_l$

	Experiment 1A										Experiment 3A					
	β_{11}	γ_{11}	γ_{12}	γ_{10}	β_{22}	γ_{23}	γ_{24}	γ_{20}	$y_1\|Z^*$	$y_2\|Z^*$	β_{12}	γ_{11}	γ_{12}	γ_{10}	$y_1\|Z^*$	$y_2\|Z^*$
LISE	+1.56	+2.12*	+1.56	+1.70			+1.41	+ .57		+ .28	+ .99	+ .57	+.99	0	+1.13	
TSLS					− .57	− .85			−1.41							− .85
LISE	+3.11*	+3.11*	+2.26*	+2.12*	+1.98*		+1.98*	+ .57	+3.68*	+2.26*	+3.68*	+2.26*	+2.55*	+.57	+1.98*	+1.98*
OLS						− .85										
LISE			0		+2.55*					+ .28			+ .28	+ .57		+1.70
FIML	− .28	− .85		−1.41		−1.98*	−2.55*	−2.83*	− .57		− .57	− .28			− .28	
TSLS	+3.11*	+3.11*	+2.26*	+2.55*	+2.26*		+2.26*	+ .57	+3.68*	+3.11*	+3.68*	+2.26*	+2.55*	+ .57	+2.26*	+2.83*
OLS						−1.13										
TSLS			+ .28		+1.70					0			+ .57	+ .57	+ .57	+1.13
FIML	−1.13	−1.70		−1.41		−1.98*	−2.83*	−3.11*	− .28		− .57	− .28				
OLS														0		
FIML	−3.39*	−2.55*	− .57	−1.13	−1.98*	−2.55*	−1.98*	−2.55*	−3.96*	−2.26*	−2.83*	−1.98*	− .57		−1.98*	−1.70

A table entry represents the proportion of times one method gave estimates closer to the true value than the other, expressed in standardized normal units[i.e., $(p_{kl} - P_{kl})/\sigma_{p_{kl}}|P_{kl}]$, where $P_{kl} = 1/2$. Thus each entry is a test statistic for the null hypothesis.

Asterisks indicate cases where proportions are significantly different from one-half at the .95 significance level.

difference between the methods appears.[24] No intransitivities were observed.

It should be emphasized that these tests are not independent of the tests on conditional predictions. One would expect that the two tests would agree, but they need not. For example, one very bad set of structural coefficient estimates gave rise to quite respectable conditional predictions.[25] The $y_1|Z^*$ and $y_2|Z^*$ columns of Table VIII show that the agreement is close but by no means perfect.

Appendix Tables IA–VIA and IB–VIB describe the generated frequency distributions of the estimates of the structural coefficients obtained by using the various estimating methods. The cell entries are to be interpreted analogously to those of Tables VI and VII: the upper cell entry is the observed mean of $\tilde{\alpha}_i^k - \alpha_i$, an estimate of the bias of the kth method in estimating the ith structural coefficient; the entry in italics in each cell is the observed RMSE of $\tilde{\alpha}_i^k$; the entry in the lower left corner of each cell is the observed standard deviation of $\tilde{\alpha}_i^k$; and the asterisk indicates a bias which is significant at the 95 per cent level.

An outstanding characteristic of the tables is that the ranking of a method relative to that of its competitors is rarely uniform from one structural coefficient to another. One of the reasons for concentrating on conditional predictions was that in making an overall appraisal it provided a basis for weighting these diverse results for individual structural coefficients. In the absence of any satisfactory procedures for coping with the stochastic character of the data of the tables, simple ranking methods were resorted to. Out of an examination embracing a number of methods of comparison (no one of which could be justified over the others) the following judgments about structural coefficient estimation emerge:

(1) The minimum variance property of large sample OLS structural coefficient estimates certainly is preserved for small samples (but compare this conclusion with the analogous one for conditional prediction in Section 19).

(2) The structural coefficient bias of OLS was by far the greatest of the four methods examined. The bias swamped the smaller standard deviation in all but one of the A experiments and in the first two B experiments. In Experiments 3B and

[24] The data of one-and-a-half experiments are too scanty to provide any definitive ranking. Initially, when it was expected that more resources would be available, a sequential sampling strategy was devised. Out of the "population" of 96 sets of parameter estimates (eight per experiment, twelve experiments) and six possible pairwise comparisons, successive comparisons were to be made for parameters selected on a randomized basis until a definite conclusion about which of the two methods being compared was superior was reached. Unfortunately, it was necessary to cut back to the number of tests reported in Table VIII.

[25] This remarkable "rescue" was a happy consequence of the substantial covariance among estimates of the different structural coefficients. Despite this, one should not derive too much consolation from the fact that such covariance is to be expected. An important reason for seeking structural coefficients rather than just the reduced form is that new a priori information can be combined with old empirical results only through alterations in the structural coefficients. Unfortunately there is very little assurance that the conditional predictions based upon altered structural coefficients will be good simply because the original conditional predictions were good.

6B, though the biases were large, the standard deviations were small enough relatively to make the RMSE's the smallest of the four methods. In the remaining B experiments, the OLS bias was just large enough to leave its RMSE's intermediate between the other methods. It is noteworthy that Experiment 3B was the one for which none of the Studentized statistics was reliable.

(3) For large samples, the standard errors of estimates produced by each method are inversely proportional to the square root of the sample size. The simplest reasonable conjecture for small samples is that the RMSE's of the consistent methods are approximately inversely proportional to the square root of the sample size. A comparison of the results of Experiments 1A and 1B with those of Experiments 2A and 2B are consistent with that conjecture.

(4) The difference between the best estimating method and the worst was substantial in virtually every experiment. In Experiment 3A, for example, of eight structural coefficients estimated, the ratio of the largest RMSE of the four estimating methods to that of the smallest ranged up to 1.29. In the other experiments they ranged higher, reaching 6.95 in Experiment 5B. In Experiments 1A to 4A, the differences between the RMSE's of LISE, TSLS, and FIML were trivial, the main differences being between OLS and the others; in Experiments 1B to 4B, however, where the extreme LISE observations were encountered, the differences between the first three methods were substantial. In the misspecification experiments large differences again showed up, with LISE and FIML both performing poorly.

(5) In Experiments 1A to 4A, FIML was clearly best with TSLS second, LISE third, and OLS last. In Experiments 1B to 4B, TSLS passed up FIML and OLS passed up LISE. FIML performed badly in the four misspecification experiments. Looking only at estimates of parameters of the first structural equation, the one specified correctly, FIML seemed to be a little better in Experiments 5A and 5B than in Experiments 6A and 6B, as originally conjectured.[26] In these experiments, TSLS was distinctly best; LISE was second in the A experiments but third in the B ones.

(6) In Section 15 it was conjectured that the effect of the covariances among the Z's in the B experiments would be to make equation (1b) more heavily identified than (1a). The Appendix tables confirm this. The increase in RMSE of corresponding structural coefficient estimates between the A and B experiments is much greater for coefficients of the first equation than for the second.

Summarizing the results of examining the Appendix tables describing structural coefficient estimates, we may say: OLS appears somewhat less unattractive than the work on conditional prediction and Studentized estimates would have suggested.

[26] See footnote 18 above. Note though that this is contrary to the finding for conditional predictions (see page 19 above).

TABLE IX

BIASES AND STANDARD DEVIATIONS OF ESTIMATES OF STRUCTURAL COEFFICIENTS AND CONDITIONAL PREDICTIONS IN THE SET OF OBSERVATIONS WHERE COMPUTATIONAL DIFFICULTIES WERE ENCOUNTERED

	N	β_{12}		γ_{11}		γ_{12}		γ_{10}		β_{22}	
		$B_{\tilde\beta_{12}}$	$S_{\tilde\beta_{12}}$	$B_{\tilde\gamma_{11}}$	$S_{\tilde\gamma_{11}}$	$B_{\tilde\gamma_{12}}$	$S_{\tilde\gamma_{12}}$	$B_{\tilde\gamma_{10}}$	$S_{\tilde\gamma_{10}}$	$B_{\tilde\beta_{22}}$	$S_{\tilde\beta_{22}}$
Exp. 1B	18										
LISE		−.64	1.86	+1.56	4.37	.36	1.19	−120.44	346.30	.04	.15
TSLS		−.26	.51	.65	1.10	.10	.27	−44.46	77.33	.03	.15
OLS		.29	.23	−.60	.57	−.18	.14	43.85	47.10	−.13	.11
FIML		−.26	.34	.64	.81	.11	.21	−46.10	65.62	.04	.15
LSNR											
Exp. 2B	1										
LISE		−.16		−1.06		−.23		82.62		.10	
TSLS		−.16		−1.06		−.23		82.63		.10	
OLS		−.14		−1.11		−.24		86.05		−.17	
FIML		−.19		−.99		−.22		76.77		.11	
LSNR											
Exp. 3B	16										
LISE		.104	.35	−.41	1.86	−.12	.46	26.53	152.20	.03	.08
TSLS		−.05	.43	.33	2.19	.09	.62	32.72	182.50	.03	.08
OLS		.17	.06	−.81	.31	−.21	.10	58.82	26.98	.05	.05
FIML		−.03	.27	.25	1.39	.56	.67	25.74	113.98	.02	.08
LSNR											
Exp. 4B	15										
LISE		−.49	1.74	.67	2.41	.18	.62	−47.12	167.59	.08	.20
TSLS		.06	.53	−.09	.74	−.02	.18	6.28	56.54	.08	.20
OLS		.91	.40	−.88	.60	−.21	.14	63.46	49.49	−.15	.16
FIML		−.32	.74	.44	1.02	.12	.27	−31.82	74.03	.95	.20
LSNR											
Exp. 5B	10										
LISE		−5.10	18.27	8.84	33.12	1.415	6.08	−668.26	2680.52	−.35	.54
TSLS		−.36	1.04	.66	1.78	.211	.71	−64.29	179.46	.12	.16
OLS		.48	.22	−.90	.49	−.29	.15	87.96	161.80	−.05	.08
FIML		−.38	.54	.68	.94	.15	.39	−58.85	93.80	.53	1.33
LSNR											
Exp. 6B	12										
LISE		−.29	.57	.82	1.51	.11	.23	−52.05	265.96	−.01	.19
TSLS		−.15	.36	.44	.97	.05	.17	−29.52	58.52	−.01	.19
OLS		.24	.11	−.63	.29	−.15	.12	37.54	29.74	−.16	.12
FIML		−.18	.41	.51	1.07	.05	.20	−31.21	65.27	.11	.48
LSNR											

γ_{23}		γ_{24}		γ_{20}		$y_1 \mid Z^*$		$y_2 \mid Z^*$	
$B_{\tilde{\gamma}_{23}}$	$S_{\tilde{\gamma}_{23}}$	$B_{\tilde{\gamma}_{24}}$	$S_{\tilde{\gamma}_{24}}$	$B_{\tilde{\gamma}_{20}}$	$S_{\tilde{\gamma}_{20}}$	$B_{\tilde{y}_1 \mid Z^*}$	$S_{\tilde{y}_1 \mid Z^*}$	$B_{\tilde{y}_2 \mid Z^*}$	$S_{\tilde{y}_2 \mid Z^*}$
−.19	1.30	.01	.08	8.79	135.11	−.25	6.57	.98	6.93
−.20	1.29	.01	.08	10.49	134.64	−.53	6.57	.14	7.81
−.44	1.22	.08	.06	51.96	127.10	−11.65	9.61	−22.08	7.08
−.24	1.24	.01	.06	13.60	129.83	−.26	6.98	.70	6.14
						−.26	7.73	.98	5.08
−.36		−.05		33.69		−1.09		−.69	
−.36		−.05		33.47		−1.09		−.69	
−1.09		.09		136.00		−6.09		−26.41	
−.11		−.07		6.50		−1.09		−.69	
						−1.09		−.69	
.62	.83	−.04	.11	−71.24	96.70	−2.60	7.99	−8.41	20.27
.60	.83	−.04	.10	−69.91	96.63	−3.85	6.17	−4.66	18.73
.21	.71	.04	.07	−12.31	79.35	−3.54	5.23	−23.41	22.39
.37	1.00	−.03	.11	−44.36	108.64	−3.54	7.02	−2.16	18.27
						−6.35	9.13	−.28	20.89
.11	1.13	−.02	.09	−20.08	120.10	−1.52	8.44	−.84	4.50
.11	1.13	−.01	.10	−19.95	120.28	−1.52	8.44	−.51	4.83
−.28	1.05	.06	.08	36.45	110.34	−17.52	10.58	−20.51	7.30
.74	.55	−.02	.09	−45.00	119.74	−1.86	8.90	−1.84	5.19
						−1.86	8.90	−2.18	7.31
.63	1.01	.78	.06	−28.39	100.63	−1.17	7.50	−4.91	7.68
.63	1.02	.02	.06	−28.51	100.60	−2.17	7.09	−4.41	5.94
.31	1.05	.10	.06	15.36	108.05	−6.67	8.43	−22.91	7.14
−.07	2.60	−.08	.34	23.72	206.44	−2.17	7.09	−5.91	11.62
						−.17	7.43	−3.41	8.14
.12	1.35	−.10	.14	−55.22	151.36	3.16	8.91	−3.58	7.92
.12	1.35	−.10	.14	−55.32	151.44	3.16	8.91	−3.16	7.50
−.16	1.23	−.02	.10	−7.17	134.36	−10.18	8.06	−26.49	12.79
.29	1.86	−.17	.33	−87.37	243.92	2.74	9.38	−4.41	10.83
						2.32	8.68	−2.33	6.75

FIML performs admirably under favorable conditions, but it loses ground when complications such as high interdependence of the jointly determined variables or structural misspecification arise. The steadiest method appears to be TSLS. LISE is so erratic in the presence of interdependence of the predetermined variables that its use seems risky.

21. Since the essence of a reduced form is contained in a conditional prediction based upon it, a detailed comparison of the reduced form estimates produced by the various methods seems superfluous. Tables analogous to Appendix Tables IA–VIA and IB–VIB describing reduced form estimates may be obtained by writing directly to the author.

22. For the sake of completeness, Table IX is presented to allow the reader to judge the consequences of excluding from the analysis of the previous sections the set of observations where computational difficulties were encountered. In the bulk of these excluded cases, the $B^{-1}W$ matrix[27] from which characteristic roots were calculated for LISE was so close to singular that the buildup of rounding errors in computing the matrix's elements made it no longer positive definite. (The computer signaled the occurrence of a negative characteristic root but went on to complete the calculations as if the root were positive.) LISE estimates based upon the resulting negative root were not meaningful, so such cases were not considered in the comparisons of the different estimating methods. Much less frequently, negative estimates of asymptotic variances of LISE structural coefficient estimates were encountered; such cases were also excluded. By the same token, near-singular W matrices turned out to be negative difinite for some sets of observations because of rounding errors and this led to TSLS estimates which were not meaningful.[28] These cases too were calculated in detail even though they were excluded from the analysis. As would be expected, the computational difficulties arose in connection with the B experiments where the π's were highly intercorrelated. The fact that only one negative characteristic root occurred in Experiment 2B, where $N=40$, suggests that the problem here is primarily a small-sample one.

It is not necessarily true that LISE or TSLS estimates tainted as described above are bad. It is at least possible that compensating errors might leave such estimates as good as untainted ones. Of more interest, however, is whether the population from which the excluded cases were drawn was different from the population analyzed in detail. If there were a significant difference, doubt would be cast upon the conclusions of the preceding sections. The entries of Table IX may be compared with those of Table VII and Appendix Tables IB, IIIB, IVB, VB, and VIB to resolve this problem. Standard t and F tests were applied to average biases and standard deviations for "included" and "excluded" observations in Experiments 1B, 3B, 4B,

[27] [**19**, pp. 128–130].

[28] [**32**, pp. 228–231]. Theil does not use the symbol W; in his notation, W is $V'V$.

5B, and 6B, both for conditional predictions and structural coefficients. Only a simple impressionistic overview of the results of a series of tests of "included" *versus* "excluded" observations is worth giving.

The OLS, FIML, and LSNR estimates of conditional predictions seem to exhibit approximately equal amounts of bias in the two populations. The same is true of OLS and FIML estimates of structural coefficients. However, almost uniformly, the variance of the "excluded case" population was smaller for conditional predictions. To a much lesser extent, the tests suggested a similar tendency in the estimates of structural coefficients. The finding about bias was encouraging. The discovery that the excluded cases had a smaller variance was surprising and somewhat disappointing, but not as much as it would have been if the excluded-case variance were the larger one. It would appear that the computational problems (the $B^{-1}W$ and W matrices turning negative definite because of rounding errors) arose mostly for sets of observations giving rise to relatively good estimates of the conditional predictions and structural coefficients. Why this should be the case is not at all apparent.[29] In any case, it was reassuring that there was no evidence of the variance being differentially smaller for any particular method.

The tainted LISE and OLS estimates themselves were distributed rather like those that had been accepted for analysis. Estimates for the second equation of the system were distributed very similarly; estimates for the first equation were somewhat less so. Here, however, in some experiments the variances of the excluded cases were larger.

It surely would have been inappropriate to include in the analysis of the estimating methods the tainted estimates. By excluding them, however, the relevant populations were sampled with a special kind of censorship which itself could introduce a bias in favor of one or more particular methods. Fortunately, the results of the crude comparisons described above suggest that this is probably not the case.[30]

[29] It might be conjectured that the OLS, FIML, and LSNR estimates in the excluded cases might also have been tainted. For example, in OLS the moment matrices of the Z's and the y treated as predetermined might have been so sufficiently close to singular in the excluded cases that their computed inverses were negative definite. In fact, however, that particular outcome would have been revealed by an estimated variance being negative. The few negative variance estimates that appeared were for LISE, however.

[30] An important lesson to be derived from the discussion of this section is that even a small two-equation model can give rise to substantial computational problems in as many as one-fourth of all cases when the Z's are highly intercorrelated. There is reason to believe, however, that greater precision in carrying on the arithmetic, i.e., carrying more than just eight significant digits, might have eliminated most of these difficulties **[20]**.

APPENDIX

TABLE IA

Experiment 1A

Structural Coefficients

Parameters	β_{12}	γ_{11}	γ_{12}	γ_{10}	β_{22}	γ_{23}	γ_{24}	γ_{20}
True values	−.7	.8	.7	−149.5	.4	.6	−.4	−149.6
LISE	.01295	−.03515	−.01656	4.14148	−.01953	† −.25920	† .01496	† 28.81921
	.089 *.089*	.177 *.180*	.104 *.105*	22.1 *22.5*	.106 *.107*	.582 *.638*	.052 *.054*	68.6 *74.4*
TSLS	.01724	−.04111	−.01895	4.37490	−.02509	† −.25962	† .01725	† 29.41459
	.089 *.091*	.177 *.181*	.103 *.105*	22.0 *22.4*	.106 *.109*	.582 *.638*	.052 *.053*	68.6 *74.6*
OLS	† .07303	† −.11956	† −.04916	† 7.39781	† −.08545	† −.27049	† .04190	† 36.60219
	.085 *.112*	.175 *.212*	.101 *.112*	21.8 *23.0*	.098 *.130*	.579 *.639*	.049 *.064*	66.3 *75.7*
FIML	.01129	−.02807	−.01872	3.76882	−.02090	† −.15688	.00168	† 17.57064
	.090 *.091*	.159 *.161*	.103 *.105*	20.8 *21.2*	.106 *.108*	.477 *.502*	.051 *.051*	55.7 *58.4*

$T = 20$; $N = 50$. † indicates that bias > 1.96 s.d.$/\sqrt{50}$; standard deviation (s.d.) appears on the left; the root mean square error appears in italics on the right.

TABLE IB

Experiment 1B

Structural Coefficients

Parameters	β_{12}	γ_{11}	γ_{12}	γ_{10}	β_{22}	γ_{23}	γ_{24}	γ_{20}
True values	−.7	+.8	+.7	−149.5	.4	.6	−.4	−149.6
LISE	.0307	−.1204	−.0340	12.90	−.0208	.0161	.0078	−.5799
	.696 *.697*	1.59 *1.60*	.404 *.405*	124. *124.*	.162 *.163*	1.27 *1.27*	.104 *.104*	139. *139.*
TSLS	.0990	−.2569	−.0719	† 22.47	−.0360	−.0236	.0157	5.000
	.423 *.434*	.923 *1.23*	.254 *.264*	72.2 *75.6*	.150 *.154*	1.21 *1.21*	.094 *.095*	131. *131.*
OLS	† .4244	† −.9925	† −.2548	† 77.99	† −.1571	−.2966	† .0750	† 45.49
	.205 *.471*	.480 *1.10*	.147 *.294*	43.2 *89.2*	.134 *.207*	1.13 *1.17*	.081 *.110*	121. *129.*
FIML	−.0532	.1002	.0095	−5.113	−.0231	−.0029	.0094	1.646
	.406 *.410*	.892 *.898*	.236 *.236*	69.8 *70.0*	.161 *.163*	1.13 *1.13*	.098 *.098*	124. *124.*

$T = 20$; $N = 50$. † indicates that bias > 1.96 s.d.$/\sqrt{50}$; standard deviation (s.d.) appears on the left; the root mean square error appears in italics on the right.

TABLE IIA

EXPERIMENT 2A

STRUCTURAL COEFFICIENTS

Parameters	β_{12}		γ_{11}		γ_{12}		γ_{10}		β_{22}		γ_{23}		γ_{24}		γ_{20}	
True values	−.7		.8		.7		−149.5		.4		.6		−.4		−149.6	
LISE		−.0050		−.0056		−.0023		1.769		−.0174		.0618		.0025		−4.283
	.070	*.070*	.140	*.140*	.076	*.076*	14.9	*15.0*	.084	*.084*	.402	*.407*	.037	*.037*	49.2	*49.*
TSLS		−.0035		−.0078		−.0032		1.862		−.0201		.0612		.0036		−3.954
	.069	*.069*	.140	*.140*	.076	*.076*	14.8	*15.0*	.084	*.084*	.401	*.406*	.037	*.037*	49.2	*49.*
OLS		† .0591		† −.0964		† −.0366		† 5.333		† −.1074		.0348		† .0393		7.451
	.065	*.088*	.135	*.166*	.074	*.083*	14.8	*15.7*	.075	*.130*	.376	*.378*	.033	*.052*	44.8	*45.*
FIML		−.0076		.0066		−.0054		.9888		−.0172		.0345		.0028		−1.292
	.071	*.072*	.136	*.136*	.074	*.074*	14.3	*14.4*	.084	*.086*	.382	*.384*	.037	*.037*	46.9	*47.*

$T = 40$; $N = 50$. † indicates that bias > 1.96 s.d./$\sqrt{50}$; standard deviation (s.d.) appears on the left; the roo mean square error appears in italics on the right.

TABLE IIB

EXPERIMENT 2B

STRUCTURAL COEFFICIENTS

Parameters	β_{12}		γ_{11}		γ_{12}		γ_{10}		β_{22}		γ_{21}		γ_{22}		γ_{20}	
True values	−.7		+.8		+.7		−149.5		+.4		+.6		−.4		−149.6	
LISE		−.0460		.0979		.0308		−7.804		.0052		−.0175		−.0080		2.908
	.341	*.344*	.835	*.841*	.212	*.214*	70.6	*71.1*	.110	*.110*	.855	*.855*	.070	*.071*	92.1	*92*
TSLS		−.0209		.0409		.0169		−3.497		−.0014		−.0296		−.0049		4.808
	.333	*.334*	.821	*.822*	.209	*.210*	69.9	*70.0*	.111	*.111*	.852	*.853*	.070	*.072*	91.9	*92.*
OLS		† .3655		† −.8521		† −.1992		† 65.19		† −.1453		† −.3302		† .0653		† 50.27
	.146	*.394*	.356	*.923*	.108	*.226*	32.4	*72.8*	.083	*.168*	.792	*.858*	.059	*.088*	84.6	*98*
FIML		−.0748		.1649		.0454		−12.79		.0085		.0519		−.0120		−4.708
	.323	*.331*	.796	*.813*	.198	*.203*	67.6	*68.8*	.105	*.106*	.807	*.809*	.063	*.064*	86.0	*86*

$T = 40$; $N = 50$. † indicates that bias > 1.96 s.d./$\sqrt{50}$; standard deviation (s.d.) appears on the left; the ro mean square error appears in italics on the right.

TABLE IIIA

EXPERIMENT 3A

STRUCTURAL COEFFICIENTS

Parameters	β_{12}	γ_{11}	γ_{12}	γ_{10}	β_{22}	γ_{23}	γ_{24}	γ_{20}
True values	−.1	+.8	+.7	−149.5	.4	+.6	−.4	−149.6
LISE	.0074	−.0091	−.0142	−.6529	.0018	.0955	−.0007	−11.07
	.046 *.046*	.208 *.208*	.111 *.112*	21.2 *21.2*	.053 *.053*	.597 *.605*	.056 *.056*	68.4 *69.3*
TSLS	.0085	−.0126	−.0156	−.5179	−.0021	.0943	.0028	−10.13
	.046 *.046*	.208 *.208*	.111 *.112*	21.1 *21.1*	.051 *.051*	.596 *.603*	.054 *.054*	68.4 *69.1*
OLS	† .0334	† −.0885	† −.0452	2.353	† −.0353	.0764	† .0329	−1.202
	.041 *.053*	.198 *.217*	.104 *.113*	20.6 *20.7*	.046 *.066*	.577 *.582*	.050 *.060*	66.3 *66.3*
FIML	.0075	−.0108	−.0152	−.3724	.0019	.0392	.0002	−4.894
	.046 *.046*	.200 *.200*	.111 *.112*	20.6 *20.7*	.052 *.052*	.602 *.603*	.055 *.055*	69.4 *70.3*

$T = 20$; $N = 50$. † indicates that bias > 1.96 s.d./$\sqrt{50}$; standard deviation (s.d.) appears on the left; the root mean square error appears in italics on the right.

TABLE IIIB

EXPERIMENT 3B

STRUCTURAL COEFFICIENTS

Parameters	β_{12}	γ_{11}	γ_{12}	γ_{10}	β_{22}	γ_{23}	γ_{24}	γ_{20}
True values	−.1	.8	.7	−149.5	.4	.6	−.4	−149.6
LISE	† −.2103	† 1.045	† .2131	† −74.92	.0198	† .3900	† −.0333	† −45.25
	.720 *.750*	3.59 *3.74*	.707 *.738*	251. *260.*	.074 *.076*	1.18 *1.25*	.094 *.100*	131. *138.*
TSLS	−.0406	.2002	.0353	−14.65	.0093	† .3382	.0220	−37.55
	.225 *.228*	1.08 *1.10*	.288 *.290*	82.4 *83.7*	.067 *.067*	1.16 *1.21*	.088 *.091*	127. *133.*
OLS	† .1442	† −.7204	† −.1863	† 54.77	† −.0658	−.0261	† .0596	16.44
	.100 *.182*	.541 *.901*	.142 *.234*	44.0 *70.3*	.068 *.095*	1.05 *1.05*	.071 *.092*	112. *113.*
FIML	† −.1000	† .5010	† .1003	† −36.72	.0156	† .3823	† −.0288	−43.64
	.255 *.274*	1.25 *1.34*	.323 *.338*	94.8 *102.*	.067 *.068*	1.24 *1.30*	.092 *.096*	135. *142.*

$T = 20$; $N = 50$. † indicates that bias > 1.96 s.d./$\sqrt{50}$; standard deviation (s.d.) appears on the left; the root mean square error appears in italics on the right.

TABLE IVA

EXPERIMENT 4A

STRUCTURAL COEFFICIENTS

Parameters	β_{12}	γ_{11}	γ_{12}	γ_{10}	β_{22}	γ_{23}	γ_{24}	γ_{20}
True values	−1.3	.8	.7	−149.5	.4	.6	−.4	−149.6
LISE	.0276	−.0279	−.0022	.2019	.0118	.0084	.0043	−4.032
	.129 *.132*	.170 *.173*	.105 *.105*	22.3 *22.3*	.182 *.182*	.669 *.669*	.062 *.062*	74.9 *75.*
TSLS	.0326	−.0322	−.0040	.3508	−.0005	.0079	.0075	−3.190
	.129 *.133*	.170 *.173*	.105 *.105*	22.3 *22.3*	.175 *.175*	.668 *.668*	.061 *.061*	75.0 *75.*
OLS	† .1051	† −.0958	−.0290	2.565	† −.1294	−.0174	† .0410	7.876
	.134 *.170*	.173 *.197*	.106 *.110*	22.0 *22.2*	.175 *.218*	.640 *.640*	.060 *.072*	72.3 *72.*
FIML	.0280	−.0279	−.0038	.3471	.0099	.0488	.0045	−8.484
	.128 *.131*	.162 *.164*	.103 *.103*	22.0 *22.0*	.181 *.181*	.626 *.628*	.062 *.062*	71.3 *71.*

$T = 20$; $N = 50$. † indicates that bias > 1.96 s.d./$\sqrt{50}$; standard deviation (s.d.) appears on the left; the roo mean square error appears in italics on the right.

TABLE IVB

EXPERIMENT 4B

STRUCTURAL COEFFICIENTS

Parameters	β_{12}	γ_{11}	γ_{12}	γ_{10}	β_{22}	γ_{23}	γ_{24}	γ_{20}
True values	−1.3	+.8	+.7	−149.5	+.4	+.6	−.4	−149.6
LISE	−.3577	.5505	.1364	−44.38	.0285	−.0732	.0001	5.235
	1.71 *1.75*	2.54 *2.60*	.701 *.714*	203. *208.*	.265 *.268*	1.29 *1.29*	.108 *.108*	141. *141*
TSLS	−.0566	.1059	.0149	−8.893	.0040	−.1096	.0078	10.62
	.873 *.875*	1.29 *1.29*	.311 *.311*	99.1 *103.*	.242 *.242*	1.27 *1.27*	.102 *.102*	138. *139*
OLS	† .6136	† −.8873	† −.2205	† 66.34	† −.1848	† −.3834	† .0681	† 51.13
	.324 *.694*	.467 *1.00*	.156 *.271*	40.4 *77.7*	.200 *.271*	1.23 *1.28*	.091 *.114*	133. *143*
FIML	† −.2891	† .4514	† .0897	† −34.42	.0335	−.0149	.0038	−1.045
	.920 *.965*	1.34 *1.42*	.312 *.326*	101. *107.*	.273 *.275*	1.20 *1.20*	.105 *.105*	133. *13*

$T = 20$; $N = 50$. † indicates that bias > 1.96 s.d./$\sqrt{50}$; standard deviation (s.d.) appears on the left; the roo mean square error appears in italics on the right.

TABLE VA

Experiment 5A
Structural Coefficients

Parameters	β_{12}	γ_{11}	γ_{12}	γ_{10}	β_{22}	γ_{23}	γ_{24}	γ_{20}
True values	−.7	.8	.7	−149.5	.4	.6	−.4	−149.6
LISE	.0081	−.0164	.0116	.5413	† .2871	.1154	† −.0632	31.01
	.078 *.078*	.175 *.176*	.081 *.082*	23.2 *23.2*	.223 *.364*	.649 *.659*	.088 *.108*	70.7 *77.2*
TSLS	.0126	−.0204	.0092	.7452	† .1669	.0643	−.0188	† 42.22
	.077 *.078*	.175 *.176*	.081 *.082*	23.2 *23.2*	.174 *.241*	.605 *.609*	.068 *.071*	65.2 *77.7*
OLS	† .0704	† −.0742	−.0217	3.680	.0325	.0099	† .0307	† 54.58
	.069 *.099*	.167 *.183*	.080 *.083*	22.6 *22.9*	.140 *.144*	.582 *.582*	.056 *.064*	63.2 *83.5*
FIML	† .0363	† −.1443	.0186	† 13.09	† .3396	.1027	† −.0823	† 30.11
	.094 *.101*	.245 *.284*	.098 *.100*	28.1 *31.0*	.355 *.491*	.777 *.783*	.142 *.164*	87.6 *92.7*

$\gamma_{21} = +0.5$; $T = 20$; $N = 50$; † indicates that bias > 1.96 s.d./$\sqrt{50}$; standard deviation (s.d.) appears on the left; the root mean square error appears in italics on the right.

TABLE VB

Experiment 5B
Structural Coefficients

Parameters	β_{12}	γ_{11}	γ_{12}	γ_{10}	β_{22}	γ_{23}	γ_{24}	γ_{20}
True values	−.7	.8	.7	−149.5	.4	.6	−.4	−149.6
LISE	−.1365	.2298	.0907	−23.66	.0360	† .3987	† .0713	−1.262
	.612 *.627*	1.15 *1.17*	.389 *.400*	118. *120.*	.159 *.163*	1.24 *1.30*	.078 *.106*	134. *134.*
TSLS	−.0367	.0447	.0324	−5.432	.0194	† .3555	† .0782	4.264
	.403 *.405*	.753 *.754*	.256 *.258*	76.1 *77.3*	.149 *.150*	1.22 *1.28*	.075 *.109*	132. *132.*
OLS	† .3645	† −.6856	† −.2039	† 65.38	† −.1252	.0132	† .1360	† 48.92
	.220 *.426*	.436 *.813*	.167 *.264*	48.5 *81.4*	.118 *.172*	1.16 *1.16*	.068 *.153*	123. *133.*
FIML	−.0558	.0514	−.0136	−1.800	† .4366	† 1.226	† −.1004	−106.9
	.425 *.428*	.765 *.767*	.280 *.281*	78.1 *78.1*	1.47 *1.54*	4.35 *4.52*	.688 *.695*	509. *520.*

$\gamma_{21} = +0.5$; $T = 20$; $N = 50$; † indicates that bias > 1.96 s.d./$\sqrt{50}$; standard deviation (s.d.) appears on the left; the root mean square error appears in italics on the right.

TABLE VIA

Experiment 6A

Structural Coefficients

Parameters	β_{12}	γ_{11}	γ_{12}	γ_{10}	β_{22}	γ_{23}	γ_{24}	γ_{20}
True values	−.7	.8	.7	−149.5	.4	.6	−.4	−149.6
LISE	−.0059 .077 *.077*	.0271 .173 *.175*	.0063 .096 *.096*	−2.390 17.9 *18.1*	† −.2080 .102 *.231*	−.1726 .626 *.649*	† .0511 .057 *.076*	−5.623 68.9 *69.1*
TSLS	−.0025 .077 *.077*	.0204 .171 *.172*	.0045 .096 *.096*	−2.151 17.8 *17.9*	† −.2211 .086 *.237*	−.1719 .617 *.640*	† .0570 .051 .076	−3.746 68.3 *68.4*
OLS	† .0526 .072 *.090*	† −.0832 .168 *.188*	−.0257 .094 *.098*	−1.092 17.4 *17.4*	† −.2526 .077 *.264*	† −.1728 .606 *.631*	† .0709 .048 *.086*	1.068 67.6 *67.6*
FIML	† −.0463 .080 *.092*	† .2326 .209 *.313*	† −.0771 .128 *.150*	† −10.10 19.2 *21.7*	† −.2089 .101 *.232*	† −.1417 .472 *.493*	† .0512 .057 *.076*	−8.959 52.9 *53.7*

$\gamma_{21} = -.5$; $T = 20$; $N = 50$; † indicates that bias > 1.96 s.d./$\sqrt{50}$; standard deviation (s.d.) appears on the left; the root mean square error appears in italics on the right.

TABLE VIB

Experiment 6B

Structural Coefficients

Parameters	β_{12}	γ_{11}	γ_{12}	γ_{10}	β_{22}	γ_{23}	γ_{24}	γ_{20}
True values	−.7	.8	.7	−149.5	.4	.6	−.4	−149.6
LISE	−.1094 .686 *.694*	.3430 1.84 *1.87*	.0700 .383 *.390*	−26.57 117. *120.*	† −.0773 .177 *.193*	−.0822 1.11 *1.12*	† −.0560 .111 *.124*	−24.32 124. *126.*
TSLS	−.0504 .446 *.449*	.1647 1.22 *1.23*	.0258 .268 *.269*	−12.82 80.8 *81.8*	† −.0867 .167 *.188*	−.1019 1.09 *1.09*	† −.0505 .104 *.116*	−21.00 120. *122.*
OLS	† .3555 .222 *.419*	† −.9623 .625 *1.15*	† −.2056 1.73 *.268*	† 60.42 47.9 *77.1*	† −.1833 .129 *.224*	−.2771 .998 *1.04*	.0040 .082 *.082*	10.49 107. *107.*
FIML	† −.3134 .486 *.578*	† .8947 1.33 *1.60*	† .1717 .274 *.324*	† −59.87 86.7 *105.*	−.0713 .173 *.188*	−.0797 1.15 *1.16*	† −.0590 .108 *.123*	−25.42 126. *128.*

$\gamma_{21} = -.5$; $T = 20$; $N = 50$; † indicates that bias > 1.96 s.d./$\sqrt{50}$; standard deviation (s.d.) appears on the left; the root mean square error appears in italics on the right.

REFERENCES

[1] AMES, E. AND S. REITER: "Distributions of Correlation Coefficients in Economic Time Series." *Journal of the American Statistical Association*, Vol. 56, September, 1961.

[2] ANDERSON, T. W. AND H. RUBIN: "Estimation of Parameters in a Complete System of Stochastic Equations," *Annals of Mathematical Statistics*, Vol. 20, March, 1949.

[3] ———: "The Asymptotic Properties of Estimates of the Parameters in a Complete System of Stochastic Equations," *Annals of Mathematical Statistics*, Vol. 21, December, 1950.

[4] ARROW, K. J.: "A Difficulty in the Concept of Social Welfare," *Journal of Political Economy*, Vol. LVIII, August, 1950.

[5] ARROW, K. J. AND M. HOFFENBERG: *A Time Series Analysis of Interindustry Demands* (Amsterdam: North Holland Publishing Co., 1959).

[6] BASMANN, R. L.: "A Generalized Classical Method of Linear Estimation of Coefficients in a Structural Equation," *Econometrica*, Vol. 25, January, 1957.

[7] ———: "An Experimental Investigation of Some Small Properties of GCL Estimators of Structural Equations: Some Preliminary Results," November 21, 1958 (Mimeographed).

[8] ———: "A Note on the Exact Finite Sample Frequency Functions of Generalized Classical Linear Estimators in Two Leading Over-Identified Cases," *Journal of the American Statistical Association*, Vol. 56, September, 1961.

[9] BIRNBAUM, Z. W.: "Numerical Tabulation of the Distribution of Kolmogorov's Statistic for Finite Sample Size," *Journal of the American Statistical Association*, Vol. 47, September, 1952.

[10] CHERNOFF, H. AND N. DIVINSKY: "The Computation of Maximum-Likelihood Estimates of Linear Structural Equations," Chapter X, *Studies in Econometric Method*, Cowles Commission Monograph No. 14, W.C. Hood and T. C. Koopmans, ed. (New York: John Wiley, 1953).

[11] CHRIST, C.: "Aggregate Econometric Models," *American Economic Review*, Vol. 46, June, 1956.

[12] ———: "Simultaneous Equation Estimation: Any Verdict Yet?" *Econometrica*, Vol. 28, October, 1960.

[13] DAVIDSON, D. AND J. MARSCHAK: "Experimental Tests of a Stochastic Decision Theory," Chapter 13, *MEASUREMENT: Definitions and Theories*, C. W. Churchman and P. Ratoosh, ed. (New York: John Wiley, 1959).

[14] FOX, K. A.: "Econometric Models of the United States," *Journal of Political Economy*, Vol. 64, April, 1956.

[15] HAAVELMO, T.: "The Statistical Implications of a System of Simultaneous Equations," *Econometrica*, Vol. 11, January, 1943.

[16] ———: "Methods of Measuring the Marginal Propensity to Consume," *Journal of the American Statistical Association*, Vol. 42, March, 1947.

[17] *Studies in Econometric Method*, Cowles Commission Monograph No. 14, W. C. Hood and T. C. Koopmans, ed. (New York: John Wiley, 1953).

[18] KLEIN, L. R.: *Economic Fluctuations in the United States 1921–1941*, Cowles Commission Monograph No. 11 (New York: John Wiley, 1950).

[19] ———: *Textbook of Econometrics* (Evanston: Row-Peterson, 1953).

[20] KLEIN, L. R. AND M. NAKAMURA: "Singularity in the Equation System of Econometrics: Some Aspects of the Problem of Multicollinearity," *International Economic Review*, Vol. 3, September, 1962.

[21] *Statistical Inference in Dynamic Economic Models*, Cowles Commission Monograph No. 10, T. C. Koopmans, ed. (New York: John Wiley, 1950).

[22] Koopmans, T. C. and W. C. Hood: "The Estimation of Simultaneous Linear Economic Relationships," Chapter VI, *Studies in Econometric Method*, Cowles Commission Monograph No. 14, W. C. Hood and T. C. Koopmans, ed. (New York: John Wiley, 1953).

[23] Koopmans, T. C., H. Rubin and R. B. Leipnik: "Measuring the Equation Systems of Dynamic Economics," Chapter II, *Statistical Inference in Dynamic Economic Models*, Cowles Commission Monograph No. 10, T. C. Koopmans, ed. (New York: John Wiley, 1950).

[24] Ladd, G. W.: "Effects of Shocks and Errors in Estimation: An Empirical Comparison," *Journal of Farm Economics*, Vol. 38, May, 1956.

[25] Menger, K.: "Statistical Metrics," *Proceedings of the National Academy of Science*, Vol. 28 (1942).

[26] Mosbaek, E.: "Experimental Investigation of Studentized Estimates of Coefficients in Structural Equations" (Abstract) *Econometrica*, Vol. 30, July, 1962.

[27] Nagar, A. L.: "Statistical Estimation of Simultaneous Economic Relationships," (Unpublished Ph. D. Dissertation, Netherlands School of Economics, 1959).

[28] Neiswanger, W. A. and T. A. Yancey: "Parameter Estimates and Autonomous Growth," *Journal of the American Statistical Association*, Vol. 54, June, 1959.

[29] ———: "Specification Errors and Estimates of Parameters in Economic Models" (Abstract) *Econometrica*, Vol. 28, July, 1960.

[30] Pitman, E. J. G.: "A Note on Normal Correlation," *Biometrika*, Vol. 31, July, 1939.

[31] Teichroew, D.: "Distribution Sampling with High Speed Computers," (Unpublished Ph. D. dissertation, North Carolina State College, 1953).

[32] Theil, H.: *Economic Forecasts and Policy* (Amsterdam: North-Holland Publishing Co., 1961) Second Revised Edition.

[33] ———: Discussion of "Structural Models," by T. Haavelmo, *Econometrica*, Vol. 23, April, 1955.

[34] Trotter, H. F. and J. W. Tukey: "Conditional Monte Carlo for Normal Samples," in *Symposium on Monte Carlo Methods*, H. A. Meyer, ed. (New York: John Wiley, 1956).

[35] Wagner, H. M.: "A Monte Carlo Study of Estimates of Simultaneous Linear Structural Equations," *Econometrica*, Vol. 26, January, 1958.

[36] Wallis, A. W. and H. Roberts: *Statistics: A New Approach* (Glencoe: The Free Press, 1956).

[37] Waugh, F. V.: "The Place of Least Squares in Econometrics," *Econometrica*, Vol. 29, July, 1961.